Collins

French
School
Dictionary

HarperCollins Publishers
Westerhill Road
Bishopbriggs
Glasgow
G64 2QT
Great Britain

Third Edition 2010

Reprint 10 9 8 7 6 5 4 3 2 1 0

© HarperCollins Publishers 2005,
2006, 2010

ISBN 978-0-00-732546-7

Collins Gem® is a registered
trademark of HarperCollins
Publishers Limited

www.collinslanguage.com

A catalogue record for this book is
available from the British Library

Typeset by Davidson Publishing
Solutions, Glasgow

When you buy a Collins dictionary
or thesaurus and register on
www.collinslanguage.com for the
free online and digital services, you
will not be charged by HarperCollins
for access to Collins free Online
Dictionary content or Collins free
Online Thesaurus content on that
website. However, your operator's
charges for using the internet on
your computer will apply. Costs
vary from operator to operator.
HarperCollins is not responsible
for any charges levied by online
service providers for accessing
Collins free Online Dictionary or
Collins free Online Thesaurus on
www.collinslanguage.com using
these services.

HarperCollins does not warrant
that the functions contained in
www.collinslanguage.com content
will be uninterrupted or error free,
that defects will be corrected, or that
www.collinslanguage.com or the
server that makes it available are
free of viruses or bugs. HarperCollins
is not responsible for any access
... ...enced
... web,
... ...ations

William Collins' dream of knowledge for all began with the publication of his first book in 1819. A self-educated mill worker, he not only enriched millions of lives, but also founded a flourishing publishing house. Today, staying true to this spirit, Collins books are packed with inspiration, innovation, and practical expertise. They place you at the centre of a world of possibility and give you exactly what you need to explore it.

Language is the key to this exploration, and at the heart of Collins Dictionaries is language as it is really used. New words, phrases, and meanings spring up every day, and all of them are captured and analysed by the Collins Word Web. Constantly updated, and with over 2.5 billion entries, this living language resource is unique to our dictionaries.

Words are tools for life. And a Collins Dictionary makes them work for you.

Collins. Do more

CONTENTS

Acknowledgements

We are grateful to all those teachers and students who have contributed to the development of the *Collins French School Dictionary* by advising us on how to tailor it to their needs. We also gratefully acknowledge the help of the examining boards, whom we have consulted throughout this project, and whose word lists and exam papers we carefully studied when compiling this dictionary in order to ensure appropriate coverage and support for GCSE and other exams of a similar level.

USING THIS DICTIONARY

The *Collins French School Dictionary* is designed specifically for anyone starting to learn French, and has been carefully researched with teachers and students. It is very straightforward, with an accessible layout that is easy on the eye, guiding students quickly to the right translation. It also offers essential help on French culture.

This section gives useful tips on how to use the *Collins French School Dictionary* effectively.

▷ Make sure you look in the right side of the dictionary

There are two sides in a bilingual dictionary. Here, the French–English side comes first, and the second part is English–French. At the top of each page there is a reminder of which side of the dictionary you have open. The middle pages of the book have a blue border so you can see where one side finishes and the other one starts.

▷ Finding the word you want

To help you find a word more quickly, use the **alphabet tabs** down the side of the page, then look at the words in **blue** at the top of pages. They show the first and last words on the two pages where the dictionary is open.

▷ Make sure you use the right part of speech

Some entries are split into several parts of speech. For example '**glue**' can either be a noun ("Can I borrow your **glue**?") or a verb ("**Glue** this into your exercise book"). Parts of speech within an entry are separated by a black triangle ▶ and are given on a new line. They are given in their abbreviated form (*n* for noun, *adj* for adjective, etc). For the full list of abbreviations, look at page x.

> **glue** ▶ *n* <u>colle</u> *f*
>   ▶ *vb* <u>coller</u>

> Choosing the right translation

The main translation of a word is underlined and is shown after the part of speech. If there is more than one main translation for a word, each one is numbered. You may also sometimes find bracketed words in *italics* which give you some context. They help you to choose the translation you want.

> **pool** *n* ① (puddle) <u>flaque</u> *f* ② (pond)
> <u>étang</u> *m* ③ (for swimming) <u>piscine</u> *f*
> ③ (game) <u>billard</u> *m* <u>américain</u>

Often you will see phrases in *italics*, preceded by a white triangle ▷. These are examples of the word being used in context.

> **numérique** *adj* <u>digital</u> ▷ *un appareil
> photo numérique* a digital camera

Phrases in **bold type** are phrases which are particularly common and important. Sometimes these phrases have a completely different translation.

> **chausson** *nm* <u>slipper</u>; **un
> chausson aux pommes** an apple
> turnover

Once you have found the right translation, remember that you may need to adapt the French word you have found. You may need to make a **noun** plural, or make an **adjective** feminine or plural. Remember that the feminine form is given for nouns and adjectives, and that irregular plural forms are given also.

> **dancer** *n* <u>danseur</u> *m*, <u>danseuse</u> *f*
> **horse** *n* <u>cheval</u> *m* (*pl* chevaux)
> **salty** *adj* <u>salé(e)</u>

You may also need to adapt the **verb**. Verbs are given in the infinitive form, but you may want to use them in the present, past or future tense. To do this, use the **verb tables** in the last section of the dictionary. All the verbs on the French–English side are followed by a number in square brackets. This number corresponds to a page number in the Verb Tables at the back of the dictionary.

In the following example, **imprimer** follows the same pattern as **donner**, shown on page **29** in the Verb Tables.

> **imprimer** [**29**] *vb* <u>to print</u>

▷ Find out more

In the *Collins French School Dictionary*, you will find lots of extra information about the French language. These **usage notes** help you understand how the language works, draw your attention to false friends (words which look similar but have a different meaning), and give you some word-for-word translations.

> **te** *pron* ❶ <u>you</u> ▷ *Je te vois.* I can
> see you.
>
> | **te** changes to **t'** before a vowel
> | and most words beginning
> | with "h".

> **librairie** *nf* <u>bookshop</u>
>
> | Be careful! **librairie** does not
> | mean **library**.

> **chauve-souris** (*pl* **chauves-souris**) *nf (animal)* <u>bat</u>
>
> | Word for word, the French
> | means "bald mouse".

You can also find out more about life in France and French-speaking countries by reading the **cultural notes**.

> **half-term** *n* <u>vacances</u> *fpl*
>
> | There are two half-term holidays
> | in France: **les vacances de la**
> | **Toussaint** (in October/
> | November) and **les vacances de**
> | **février** (in February).

Remember!

Never take the first translation you see without looking at the others. Always look to see if there is more than one translation, or more than one part of speech.

ABBREVIATIONS USED IN THIS DICTIONARY

abbr	abbreviation
adj	adjective
adv	adverb
art	article
conj	conjunction
excl	exclamation
f	feminine
n	noun
nf	feminine noun
nm	masculine noun
nmf	masculine or feminine noun
nm/f	masculine or feminine noun
npl	plural noun
num	number
prep	preposition
pron	pronoun
vb	verb

SYMBOLS

▷	example
▶	new part of speech
⊙	new meaning
[29]	verb table number (see Verb Tables section at the back of the dictionary)
accident	Key words which you need for your GCSE or other exams of a similar level are highlighted in light blue throughout both sides of the dictionary to help you find them more easily.

Note that to help you decide whether to use **le, la** or **l'** in front of a word starting with 'h', the article is given for all the nouns in letter H on the **French–English** side of the dictionary.

TIME

Quelle heure est-il? What time is it?
Il est... It's...

À quelle heure? At what time?

une heure

une heure dix

une heure et quart

une heure et demie

deux heures moins vingt

deux heures moins le quart

à minuit

à midi

à une heure (de l'après-midi)

à huit heures (du soir)

In French times are often given using the 24-hour clock.

à onze heures quinze (11h15)

à vingt heures quarante-cinq (20h45)

DATES

▷ Days of the Week

lundi	Monday
mardi	Tuesday
mercredi	Wednesday
jeudi	Thursday
vendredi	Friday
samedi	Saturday
dimanche	Sunday

▷ Months of the Year

janvier	January	**juillet**	July
février	February	**août**	August
mars	March	**septembre**	September
avril	April	**octobre**	October
mai	May	**novembre**	November
juin	June	**décembre**	December

▷ Quand?

en février
le 1er décembre
le premier décembre
en 2006
en deux mille six

▷ When?

in February
on 1 December
on the first of December
in 2006
in two thousand and six

▷ Quel jour sommes nous?

Nous sommes le...
dimanche 1er octobre *or*
dimanche premier octobre
lundi 10 février *or*
lundi dix février

▷ What day is it?

It's...
Sunday 1 October *or*
Sunday, the first of October
Monday, 10 February *or*
Monday, the tenth of February

NUMBERS

▷ Cardinal numbers

1	un (une)	21	vingt et un (une)
2	deux	22	vingt-deux
3	trois	30	trente
4	quatre	40	quarante
5	cinq	50	cinquante
6	six	60	soixante
7	sept	70	soixante-dix
8	huit	71	soixante et onze
9	neuf	72	soixante-douze
10	dix	80	quatre-vingts
11	onze	81	quatre-vingt-un (-une)
12	douze	90	quatre-vingt-dix
13	treize	91	quatre-vingt-onze
14	quatorze	100	cent
15	quinze	101	cent un (une)
16	seize	200	deux cents
17	dix-sept	201	deux cent un (une)
18	dix-huit	300	trois cents
19	dix-neuf	1000	mille
20	vingt	1,000,000	un million

▷ Fractions

1/2	un demi, une demie	1/5	un cinquième
1/3	un tiers	0.5	zéro virgule cinq (0,5)
2/3	deux tiers	10%	dix pour cent
1/4	un quart	100%	cent pour cent
3/4	trois quarts		

NUMBERS

▷ Ordinal numbers

1st	premier (1er), première (1re)
2nd	deuxième (2e or 2ème)
3rd	troisième (3e or 3ème)
4th	quatrième (4e or 4ème)
5th	cinquième (5e or 5ème)
6th	sixième (6e or 6ème)
7th	septième (7e or 7ème)
8th	huitième (8e or 8ème)
9th	neuvième (9e or 9ème)
10th	dixième (10e or 10ème)
11th	onzième (11e or 11ème)
12th	douzième (12e or 12ème)
13th	treizième (13e or 13ème)
14th	quatorzième (14e or 14ème)
15th	quinzième (15e or 15ème)
16th	seizième (16e or 16ème)
17th	dix-septième (17e or 17ème)
18th	dix-huitième (18e or 18ème)
19th	dix-neuvième (19e or 19ème)
20th	vingtième (20e or 20ème)
21st	vingt-et-unième (21e or 21ème)
22nd	vingt-deuxième (22e or 22ème)
30th	trentième (30e or 30ème)
100th	centième (100e or 100ème)
101st	cent-unième (101e or 101ème)
1000th	millième (1000e or 1000ème)

a

a *vb see* **avoir**

  a should not be confused with the preposition **à**.

Il a beaucoup d'amis. He has a lot of friends.; **Il a mangé des frites.** He had some chips.; **Il a neigé pendant la nuit.** It snowed during the night.; **il y a (1)** there is ▷ *Il y a un bon film à la télé.* There's a good film on TV. **(2)** there are ▷ *Il y a beaucoup de monde.* There are lots of people.

à *prep*

  a should not be confused with the preposition **à**. See also **au** (=**à**+**le**) and **aux** (=**à**+**les**).

① at ▷ *être à la maison* to be at home ▷ *à trois heures* at 3 o'clock **②** in ▷ *être à Paris* to be in Paris ▷ *habiter au Portugal* to live in Portugal ▷ *habiter à la campagne* to live in the country ▷ *au printemps* in the spring ▷ *au mois de juin* in June **③** to ▷ *aller à Paris* to go to Paris ▷ *aller au Portugal* to go to Portugal ▷ *aller à la campagne* to go to the country ▷ *donner quelque chose à quelqu'un* to give something to somebody ▷ *Cette veste appartient à Marie.* This jacket belongs to Marie. ▷ *Je n'ai rien à faire.* I've got nothing to do.; **Ce livre est à Paul.** This book is Paul's.; **Cette voiture est à nous.** This car is ours. **④** by ▷ *à bicyclette* by bicycle ▷ *être payé à l'heure* to be paid by the hour; **à pied** on foot; **C'est à côté de chez moi.** It's near my house.; **C'est à dix kilomètres d'ici.** It's 10 kilometres from here.; **C'est à dix minutes d'ici.** It's 10 minutes from here.; **cent kilomètres à l'heure** 100 kilometres an hour; **À bientôt!** See you soon! ▷ *À demain!* See you tomorrow! ▷ *À samedi!* See you on Saturday! ▷ *À tout à l'heure!* See you later!

abandonner [29] *vb* **①** to abandon **②** to give up ▷ *J'ai décidé d'abandonner la natation.* I've decided to give up swimming.

abeille *nf* bee

abîmer [29] *vb* to damage; **s'abîmer** to get damaged

abonnement *nm* **①** season ticket **②** (to magazine) subscription

s'abonner [29] *vb* **s'abonner à une revue** to take out a subscription to a magazine

abord nm **d'abord** first

aboyer [54] vb to bark

abri nm shelter; **être à l'abri** to be under cover; **se mettre à l'abri** to shelter

abricot nm apricot

s' **abriter** [29] vb to shelter

absence nf absence; **Il est passé pendant ton absence.** He came while you were away.

absent, e adj absent

absolument adv absolutely

accélérateur nm accelerator

accélérer [35] vb to accelerate

accent nm accent ▷ Il a l'accent de Marseille. He has a Marseilles accent.; **un accent aigu** an acute accent; **un accent grave** a grave accent; **un accent circonflexe** a circumflex

accentuer [29] vb to stress

accepter [29] vb to accept; **accepter de faire quelque chose** to agree to do something

accès nm access ▷ avoir accès à quelque chose to have access to something; **"Accès aux quais"** "To the trains"

accessoire nm ❶ accessory ❷ prop

accident nm accident; **par accident** by chance

accompagner [29] vb to accompany

accomplir [39] vb to carry out ▷ Il n'a pas réussi à accomplir cette tâche. He didn't manage to carry out this task.

accord nm agreement; **être**

d'accord to agree ▷ Tu es d'accord avec moi? Do you agree with me?; **se mettre d'accord** to come to an agreement; **D'accord!** OK!

accordéon nm accordion

accoudoir nm armrest

accrochage nm collision

accrocher [29] vb **accrocher quelque chose à** (1) to hang something on ▷ Il a accroché sa veste au portemanteau. He hung his jacket on the coat rack. (2) to hitch something up to ▷ Ils ont accroché la remorque à leur voiture. They hitched the trailer up to their car.; **s'accrocher à quelque chose** to catch on something ▷ Sa jupe s'est accrochée aux ronces. Her skirt got caught on the brambles.

s' **accroupir** [39] vb to squat down

accueil nm welcome; **Elle s'occupe de l'accueil des visiteurs.** She's in charge of looking after visitors.; **"Accueil"** "Reception"

accueillant, e adj welcoming

accueillir [23] vb to welcome

accumuler [29] vb to accumulate; **s'accumuler** to pile up

accusation nf accusation

accusé (f accusée) nm/f accused ▶ nm **un accusé de réception** an acknowledgement of receipt

accuser [29] vb to accuse ▷ accuser quelqu'un de quelque chose to accuse somebody of something

achat nm purchase; **faire des achats** to do some shopping

acheter [2] vb to buy ▷ J'ai

acheté des gâteaux à la pâtisserie. I bought some cakes at the cake shop.; **acheter quelque chose à quelqu'un (1)** to buy something for somebody ▷ Qu'est-ce que tu lui as acheté pour son anniversaire? What did you buy him for his birthday? **(2)** to buy something from somebody ▷ J'ai acheté des œufs au fermier. I bought some eggs from the farmer.

acide adj acid
▶ nm acid

acier nm steel

acné nf acne

acquérir [3] vb to acquire

acquis vb see **acquérir**

acquitter [29] vb to acquit
▷ L'accusé a été acquitté. The accused was acquitted.

acte nm act; **un acte de naissance** a birth certificate

acteur nm actor

actif (f active) adj active; **la population active** the working population

action nf action; **une bonne action** a good deed

s'**activer** [29] vb ❶ to bustle about ▷ Elle s'activait à préparer le repas. She bustled about preparing the meal. ❷ to move oneself ▷ Allez! Active-toi! Come on! Get moving!

activité nf activity

actrice nf actress

actualité nf current events; **un problème d'actualité** a topical issue; **les actualités** the news

actuel (f actuelle) adj present; **à l'heure actuelle** at the present time

▌Be careful! **actuel** does not mean **actual**.

actuellement adv at present

▌Be careful! **actuellement** does not mean **actually**.

adaptateur nm adaptor

addition nf ❶ addition ❷ bill
▷ L'addition, s'il vous plaît! Can we have the bill, please?

additionner [29] vb to add up

adhérent (f adhérente) nm/f member

adhésif (f adhésive) adj **le ruban adhésif** sticky tape

adieu excl farewell!

adjectif nm adjective

admettre [48] vb ❶ to admit ▷ Il refuse d'admettre qu'il s'est trompé. He won't admit that he made a mistake. ❷ to allow ▷ Les chiens ne sont pas admis dans le restaurant. Dogs are not allowed in the restaurant.

administration nf administration; **l'Administration** the Civil Service

admirable adj wonderful

admirateur (f admiratrice) nm/f admirer

admirer [29] vb to admire

admis vb see **admettre**

adolescence nf adolescence

adolescent (f adolescente) nm/f teenager

adopter [29] vb to adopt

adorable adj lovely

adorer [29] vb to love ▷ Elle adore le chocolat. She loves chocolate. ▷ J'adore jouer au tennis. I love playing tennis.

adresse nf address; **mon adresse électronique** my email address; **une adresse Web** a web address

adresser [29] vb **adresser la parole à quelqu'un** to speak to somebody; **s'adresser à quelqu'un** **(1)** to speak to somebody ▷ C'est à toi que je m'adresse. It's you I'm speaking to. **(2)** to go and see somebody ▷ Adressez-vous au patron. Go and see the boss. **(3)** to be aimed at somebody ▷ Ce film s'adresse surtout aux enfants. This film is aimed mainly at children.

adulte nmf adult

adverbe nm adverb

adversaire nmf opponent

aérien (f **aérienne**) adj **une compagnie aérienne** an airline

aérobic nm aerobics

aérogare nf terminal

aéroglisseur nm hovercraft

aéroport nm airport

affaire nf ❶ case ▷ une affaire de drogue a drugs case ❷ business ▷ Son affaire marche bien. His business is doing well.; **une bonne affaire** a real bargain; **Ça fera l'affaire.** This will do nicely.; **avoir affaire à quelqu'un** to deal with somebody

affaires nfpl ❶ things ▷ Va chercher tes affaires! Go and get your things! ❷ business; **un homme d'affaires** a businessman; **le ministre des**

Affaires étrangères the Foreign Secretary

affection nf affection

affectueusement adv affectionately

affectueux (f **affectueuse**) adj affectionate

affiche nf poster

afficher [29] vb to put up ▷ Ils ont affiché les résultats dehors. They've put the results up outside.; **"Défense d'afficher"** "Stick no bills"

affilée: **d'affilée** adv at a stretch

affirmation nf assertion

affirmer [29] vb to claim ▷ Il a affirmé que c'était la vérité. He claimed it was the truth.; **s'affirmer** to assert yourself ▷ Il est trop timide, il faut qu'il s'affirme. He's too shy, he should assert himself.

affluence nf **les heures d'affluence** the rush hour

s' **affoler** [29] vb to panic ▷ Ne t'affole pas! Don't panic!

affranchir [39] vb to stamp

affreux (f **affreuse**) adj awful

affronter [29] vb to face ▷ L'Allemagne affronte l'Italie en finale. Germany will face Italy in the final.

afin de conj **afin de faire quelque chose** so as to do something ▷ Je me suis levé très tôt afin d'être prêt à temps. I got up very early so as to be ready on time.

afin que conj so that

afin que is followed by a verb in the subjunctive.

▷ Il m'a téléphoné afin que je sois prêt à temps. He phoned me so that I'd be ready on time.

africain, e adj African
▶ nm/f un Africain (man) an African; une Africaine (woman) an African

Afrique nf Africa; en Afrique (1) in Africa (2) to Africa; l'Afrique du Sud South Africa

agacer [13] vb to get on somebody's nerves ▷ Tu m'agaces avec tes questions! You're getting on my nerves with all your questions!

âge nm age; Quel âge as-tu? How old are you?

âgé, e adj old; les personnes âgées the elderly

agence nf ❶ agency; une agence de voyages a travel agency ❷ office; une agence immobilière an estate agent's

agenda nm diary; un agenda électronique a PDA (personal digital assistant)

> Be careful! The French word **agenda** does not mean agenda.

s' **agenouiller** [29] vb to kneel down

agent nm un agent de police a policeman; un agent d'entretien a cleaner

agglomération nf town; l'agglomération parisienne Greater Paris

aggraver [29] vb to make worse; s'aggraver to worsen

agir [39] vb to act ▷ Il a agi par

vengeance. He acted out of vengeance.; Il s'agit de... It's about ... ▷ Il s'agit du club de sport. It's about the sports club. ▷ De quoi s'agit-il? What is it about?; Il s'agit de faire attention. We must be careful.

agité, e adj ❶ restless ❷ rough; un sommeil agité broken sleep

agiter [29] vb to shake ▷ Agitez la bouteille. Shake the bottle.

agneau (pl agneaux) nm lamb

agrafe nf (for papers) staple

agrafeuse nf stapler

agrandir [39] vb ❶ to enlarge ▷ J'ai fait agrandir mes photos. I've had my photos enlarged. ❷ to extend ▷ Ils ont agrandi leur jardin. They've extended their garden.; s'agrandir to expand ▷ Leur magasin s'est agrandi. Their shop has expanded.

agréable adj nice

agréer [19] vb Veuillez agréer, Monsieur, l'expression de mes sentiments les meilleurs. Jean Ormal. Yours sincerely, Jean Ormal.

agressif (f agressive) adj aggressive

agressivité nf aggression; faire preuve d'agressivité envers de quelqu'un to be aggressive to somebody; l'agressivité au volant road rage

agricole adj agricultural; une exploitation agricole a farm

agriculteur nm farmer; Il est agriculteur. He's a farmer.

agriculture nf farming

a
b
c
d
e
f
g
h
i
j
k
l
m
n
o
p
q
r
s
t
u
v
w
x
y
z

ai vb see **avoir**; **J'ai deux chats.** I have two cats.; **J'ai bien dormi.** I slept well.

aide nf ❶ help; **À l'aide!** Help! ❷ aid; **à l'aide de** using

aider [29] vb to help

aide-soignant (f **aide-soignante**) nm/f auxiliary nurse

aie vb see **avoir**

aïe excl ouch!

aigre adj sour

aigu (f **aiguë**) adj (pain) sharp; **e accent aigu** e acute

aiguille nf needle; **les aiguilles d'une montre** the hands of a watch

ail nm garlic

aile nf wing

aille vb see **aller**

ailleurs adv somewhere else; **partout ailleurs** everywhere else; **nulle part ailleurs** nowhere else; **d'ailleurs** besides

aimable adj kind

aimant nm magnet

aimer [29] vb ❶ to love ▷ **Elle aime ses enfants.** She loves her children. ❷ to like ▷ **Tu aimes le chocolat?** Do you like chocolate? ▷ **J'aime bien ce garçon.** I like this boy. ▷ **J'aime bien jouer au tennis.** I like playing tennis. ▷ **J'aimerais aller en Grèce.** I'd like to go to Greece.; **J'aimerais mieux ne pas y aller.** I'd rather not go.

aîné, e adj elder ▷ **mon frère aîné** my big brother
▶ nm/f eldest child ▷ **Elle est l'aînée.** She's the oldest child.

ainsi adv in this way; **C'est ainsi qu'il a réussi.** That's how he succeeded.; **ainsi que** as well as; **et ainsi de suite** and so on

air nm ❶ air; **prendre l'air** to get some fresh air ❷ tune ▷ **Elle a joué un air au piano.** She played a tune on the piano.; **Elle a l'air fatiguée.** She looks tired.; **Il a l'air d'un clown.** He looks like a clown.

aire de jeux nf playground

aire de repos nf (on motorway) rest area

aise nf **être à l'aise** to be at ease; **être mal à l'aise** to be ill at ease; **se mettre à l'aise** to make oneself comfortable

ait vb see **avoir**

ajouter [29] vb to add

alarme nf alarm

Albanie nf Albania

album nm album

alcool nm alcohol; **les alcools forts** spirits

alcoolisé, e adj alcoholic; **une boisson non alcoolisée** a soft drink

alentours nmpl dans les alentours in the area; **aux alentours de Paris** in the Paris area; **aux alentours de cinq heures** around 5 o'clock

algèbre nf algebra

Alger n Algiers

Algérie nf Algeria

algérien (f **algérienne**) adj Algerian
▶ nm/f **un Algérien** (man) an Algerian; **une Algérienne** (woman) an Algerian

algue nf seaweed

aliment nm food

alimentation nf ❶ groceries ▷ le rayon alimentation du supermarché the grocery department in the supermarket ❷ diet ▷ Elle a une alimentation saine. She has a healthy diet.

allée nf ❶ path ❷ (in street names) drive; **les allées et venues** comings and goings

allégé, e adj low-fat

Allemagne nf Germany; **en Allemagne (1)** in Germany **(2)** to Germany

allemand, e adj German
▶ nm German ▷ Elle parle allemand. She speaks German.
▶ nm/f **un Allemand** (man) a German; **une Allemande** (woman) a German; **les Allemands** the Germans

aller [4] vb to go ▷ Je suis allé à Londres. I went to London. ▷ Je vais me fâcher. I'm going to get angry.; **s'en aller** to go away ▷ Je m'en vais demain. I'm going tomorrow.; **aller bien à quelqu'un** to suit somebody ▷ Cette robe te va bien. This dress suits you.; **Allez! Dépêche-toi!** Come on! Hurry up!; **Comment allez-vous? — Je vais bien.** How are you? — I'm fine.; **Comment ça va? — Ça va bien.** How are you? — I'm fine.; **aller mieux** to be better
▶ nm ❶ outward journey
❷ (ticket) single; **un aller simple** a single; **un aller retour (1)** a return

ticket **(2)** a round trip

allergique adj **allergique à** allergic to

allô excl Hello! ▷ Allô! Je voudrais parler à Monsieur Simon. Hello! I'd like to speak to Mr Simon.

⎸ **allô** is only used when talking to someone on the phone.

allocation nf allowance; **les allocations chômage** unemployment benefit

s'**allonger** [46] vb to lie down ▷ Il s'est allongé sur son lit. He lay down on his bed.

allumer [29] vb ❶ (light) to put on ▷ Tu peux allumer la lumière? Can you put the light on? ❷ to switch on ▷ Allume la radio. Switch on the radio. ❸ to light ▷ Elle a allumé une cigarette. She lit a cigarette.; **s'allumer** (light) to come on ▷ La lumière s'est allumée. The light came on.

allumette nf match ▷ une boîte d'allumettes a box of matches

allure nf ❶ speed ❷ look ▷ avoir une drôle d'allure to look odd

allusion nf reference

alors adv ❶ then ▷ Tu as fini? Alors je m'en vais. Have you finished? I'm going then. ❷ so ▷ Alors je lui ai dit de partir. So I told him to leave.; **Et alors?** So what? ❸ at that time; **alors que (1)** ▷ Il est arrivé alors que je partais. He arrived just as I was leaving. **(2)** while ▷ Alors que je travaillais dur, lui se reposait. While I was working hard, he was resting.

Alpes nfpl Alps

alphabet nm alphabet

alphabétique adj alphabetical

alpinisme nm mountaineering

alpiniste nmf mountaineer

Alsace nf Alsace

altermondialisation nf antiglobalization

amande nf almond; **la pâte d'amandes** marzipan

amant nm lover

amateur adj inv amateur
▸ nm amateur; **en amateur** as a hobby; **C'est un amateur de musique.** He's a music lover.

ambassade nf embassy

ambassadeur nm ambassador

ambiance nf atmosphere; **la musique d'ambiance** background music

ambitieux (f **ambitieuse**) adj ambitious

ambition nf ambition; **Il a beaucoup d'ambition.** He's very ambitious.

ambulance nf ambulance

âme nf soul

amélioration nf improvement

améliorer [29] vb to improve; **s'améliorer** to improve ▸ Le temps s'améliore. The weather's improving.

amende nf fine

amener [44] vb to bring ▸ Qu'est-ce qui t'amène? What brings you here? ▸ Est-ce que je peux amener un ami? Can I bring a friend?

amer (f **amère**) adj bitter

américain, e adj American
▸ nm/f **un Américain** (man) an

American; **une Américaine** (woman) an American

Amérique nf America; **en Amérique** (1) in America (2) to America; **l'Amérique du Nord** North America; **l'Amérique du Sud** South America

ami (f **amie**) nm/f friend; **un petit ami** a boyfriend; **C'est sa petite amie.** She's his girlfriend.

amical, e (mpl **amicaux**) adj friendly

amicalement adv in a friendly way; **amicalement, Pierre** best wishes, Pierre

amitié nf friendship; **Fais mes amitiés à Paul.** Give my regards to Paul.; **Amitiés, Christèle.** (in letter) Best wishes, Christèle.

amour nm love; **faire l'amour** to make love

amoureux (f **amoureuse**) adj in love ▷ être amoureux de quelqu'un to be in love with somebody

amour-propre nm self-esteem

amphithéâtre nm lecture theatre

amplement adv **Nous avons amplement le temps.** We have plenty of time.

ampoule nf ① light bulb ② blister

amusant, e adj amusing

amuse-gueule nmpl party nibbles

amuser [29] vb to amuse; **s'amuser** (1) to play ▷ Les enfants s'amusent dehors. The children are playing outside. (2) to enjoy oneself ▷ On s'est bien amusés à cette soirée. We really enjoyed ourselves at that party.

an nm year; **le premier de l'an** New Year's Day; **le nouvel an** New Year

analyse nf ① analysis ② (medical) test

ananas nm pineapple

ancêtre nmf ancestor

anchois nm anchovy

ancien (f **ancienne**) adj ① former ▷ C'est une ancienne élève. She's a former pupil. ② ▷ notre ancienne voiture our old car ③ antique

ancre nf anchor

Andorre nf Andorra

âne nm donkey

ange nm angel; **être aux anges** to be over the moon

angine nf throat infection

anglais, e adj English
▶ nm English ▷ Est-ce que vous parlez anglais? Do you speak English?
▶ nm/f **un Anglais** an Englishman; **une Anglaise** an Englishwoman; **les Anglais** the English

angle nm ① angle ② corner

Angleterre nf England; **en Angleterre** (1) in England ▷ J'habite en Angleterre. I live in England. (2) to England ▷ Je suis allée en Angleterre le mois dernier. I went to England last month.

anglo- prefix anglo-; **les îles Anglo-Normandes** the Channel Islands

anglophone adj English-speaking

angoissé, e adj stressed

animal (pl **animaux**) nm animal

animateur (f **animatrice**) nm/f ① host ② youth leader

animé, e adj lively; **un dessin animé** a cartoon

anis nm aniseed

anneau (pl **anneaux**) nm ring

année nf year

anniversaire nm ① birthday ② anniversary

annonce nf advert; **les petites annonces** the small ads

annoncer [13] vb to announce ▷ Ils ont annoncé leurs fiançailles. They've announced their engagement.

annuaire nm phone book

annuel (f **annuelle**) adj annual

annuler [29] vb to cancel

anonyme adj anonymous

anorak nm anorak

ANPE nf (= Agence nationale pour l'emploi) job centre

Antarctique nm Antarctic

antenne nf ① aerial; **antenne parabolique** satellite dish; **être à l'antenne** to be on the air ② antenna

antibiotique nm antibiotic

antidépresseur nm antidepressant

antigel nm antifreeze

Antilles nfpl West Indies; **aux Antilles** (1) in the West Indies (2) to the West Indies

antipathique adj unpleasant

antipelliculaire adj anti-dandruff

antiquaire nmf antique dealer

antiquité nf antique; **pendant l'antiquité** in classical times

antiseptique adj antiseptic
▶ nm antiseptic

antivirus nm antivirus (program)

antivol nm ❶ (on bike) lock ❷ (on car) steering lock

anxieux (f **anxieuse**) adj anxious

août nm August; **en août** in August

apercevoir [68] vb to see ▷ J'aperçois la côte. I can see the shore.; **s'apercevoir de quelque chose** to notice something; **s'apercevoir que ...** to notice that ...

apéritif nm aperitif

apparaître [57] vb to appear

appareil nm device; **un appareil dentaire** (for teeth) a brace; **les appareils ménagers** domestic appliances; **un appareil photo** a camera; **Qui est à l'appareil?** (on phone) Who's speaking?

apparemment adv apparently

apparence nf appearance

apparition nf appearance

appartement nm flat

appartenir [84] vb **appartenir à quelqu'un** to belong to somebody

apparu vb see **apparaître**

appel nm ❶ cry ▷ un appel au secours a cry for help ❷ phone call; **faire appel à quelqu'un** to appeal to somebody; **faire l'appel** (in school) to call the register; **faire un appel de phares** to flash one's headlights

appeler [5] vb to call; **s'appeler** to be called ▷ Elle s'appelle Muriel. Her name's Muriel. ▷ Comment tu t'appelles? What's your name?

appendicite nf appendicitis

appétissant, e adj appetizing

appétit nm appetite; **Bon appétit!** Enjoy your meal!

applaudir [39] vb (applaud) to clap

applaudissements nmpl applause

appliquer [29] vb ❶ to apply ❷ to enforce ▷ appliquer la loi to enforce the law; **s'appliquer** to apply oneself

apporter [29] vb to bring

apprécier [20] vb to appreciate

appréhender [29] vb to dread ▷ J'appréhende cette réunion. I'm dreading this meeting.

apprendre [66] vb ❶ to learn ▷ apprendre quelque chose par cœur to learn something by heart; **apprendre à faire quelque chose** to learn to do something ▷ J'apprends à faire la cuisine. I'm learning to cook. ❷ to hear ▷ J'ai appris son départ. I heard that she had left.; **apprendre quelque chose à quelqu'un (1)** to teach somebody something ▷ Ma mère m'a appris l'anglais. My mother taught me English. **(2)** to tell somebody something ▷ Jean-Pierre m'a appris la nouvelle. Jean-Pierre told me the news.

apprentissage nm learning

appris vb see **apprendre**

approbation nf approval

approcher [29] vb **approcher de** to approach ▷ Nous approchons de Paris. We are approaching Paris.; **s'approcher de** to come closer to ▷ Ne t'approche pas, j'ai la grippe! Don't get too close to me,

I've got flu!

approprié, e adj suitable

approuver [29] vb to approve of
▷ Je n'approuve pas ses méthodes. I don't approve of his methods.

approximatif (f approximative) adj ❶ approximate ❷ rough

appui nm support

appuyer [54] vb ❶ to press
▷ appuyer sur un bouton to press a button ❷ to lean ▷ Elle a appuyé son vélo contre la porte. She leaned her bike against the door.; **s'appuyer** to lean ▷ Elle s'est appuyée contre le mur. She leaned against the wall.

après prep, adv ❶ after ▷ après le déjeuner after lunch ▷ après son départ after he had left
❷ afterwards ▷ aussitôt après immediately afterwards; **après coup** afterwards ▷ J'y ai repensé après coup. I thought about it again afterwards.; **d'après** according to ▷ D'après lui, c'est une erreur. According to him, that's a mistake.; **après tout** after all

après-demain adv the day after tomorrow

après-midi nm or nf afternoon

après-rasage nm aftershave

aquarium nm aquarium

arabe adj ❶ Arab ❷ Arabic
▶ nm Arabic ▷ Il parle arabe. He speaks Arabic.
▶ nm/f **un Arabe** (man) an Arab; **une Arabe** (woman) an Arab

Arabie Saoudite nf Saudi Arabia

araignée nf spider

arbitre nm ❶ referee ❷ umpire

arbre nm tree; **un arbre généalogique** a family tree

arbuste nm shrub

arc nm bow

arc-en-ciel (pl arcs-en-ciel) nm rainbow

archéologie nf archaeology

archéologue nmf archaeologist

archipel nm archipelago

architecte nm architect

architecture nf architecture

Arctique nm Arctic

ardoise nf slate

arène nf bullring; **des arènes romaines** a Roman amphitheatre; **l'arène politique** the political arena

arête nf fish bone

argent nm ❶ silver ❷ money
▷ Je n'ai plus d'argent. I haven't got any more money.; **l'argent de poche** pocket money; **l'argent liquide** cash

argentin, e adj Argentinian
▶ nm/f **un Argentin** (man) an Argentinian; **une Argentine** (woman) an Argentinian

Argentine nf Argentina

argile nf clay

argot nm slang

arme nf weapon; **une arme à feu** a firearm

armée nf army; **l'armée de l'air** the Air Force

armistice nm armistice

armoire nf wardrobe

armure nf armour

arnaquer [29] vb (informal) to con

arobase nf at sign (@)

a
b
c
d
e
f
g
h
i
j
k
l
m
n
o
p
q
r
s
t
u
v
w
x
y
z

aromatisé, e adj flavoured

arôme nm ❶ aroma ❷ (added to food) flavouring

arpenter [29] vb ❶ to pace up and down ▷ Il arpentait le couloir. He was pacing up and down the corridor.

arrache-pied: d'arrache-pied adv furiously

arracher [29] vb ❶ to take out ▷ Le dentiste m'a arraché une dent. The dentist took one of my teeth out. ❷ to tear out ▷ Arrachez la page. Tear the page out. ❸ to pull up ▷ Elle a arraché les mauvaises herbes. She pulled up the weeds.; **arracher quelque chose à quelqu'un** to snatch something from somebody

arranger [46] vb ❶ to arrange ▷ arranger des fleurs dans un vase to arrange flowers in a vase ❷ to suit ▷ Ça m'arrange de partir plus tôt. It suits me to leave earlier.; **s'arranger** to come to an agreement; **Je vais m'arranger pour venir.** I'll organize things so that I can come.; **Ça va s'arranger.** Things will work themselves out.

arrestation nf arrest

arrêt nm stop; **sans arrêt (1)** non-stop **(2)** continually

arrêter [29] vb ❶ to stop; **Arrête!** Stop it!; **arrêter de faire quelque chose** to stop doing something ❷ to switch off ▷ Il a arrêté le moteur. He switched the engine off. ❸ to arrest ▷ Mon voisin a été arrêté. My neighbour's been arrested.;

s'arrêter to stop ▷ Elle s'est arrêtée devant une vitrine. She stopped in front of a shop window.; **s'arrêter de faire quelque chose** to stop doing something ▷ s'arrêter de fumer to stop smoking

arrhes nfpl deposit ▷ verser des arrhes to pay a deposit

arrière nm back; **à l'arrière** at the back; **en arrière** behind ▶ adj inv back ▷ le siège arrière the back seat

arrière-grand-mère (pl **arrière-grands-mères**) nf great-grandmother

arrière-grand-père (pl **arrière-grands-pères**) nm great-grandfather

arrivée nf arrival

arriver [6] vb ❶ to arrive ▷ J'arrive à l'école à huit heures. I arrive at school at 8 o'clock. ❷ to happen ▷ Qu'est-ce qui est arrivé à Christian? What happened to Christian?; **arriver à faire quelque chose** to manage to do something ▷ J'espère que je vais y arriver. I hope I'll manage it.; **Il m'arrive de dormir jusqu'à midi.** I sometimes sleep till midday.

arrogant, e adj arrogant

arrondissement nm district
- Paris, Lyons and Marseilles are
- divided into numbered districts
- called **arrondissements**.

arroser [29] vb ❶ to water ▷ Daphne arrose ses tomates. Daphne is watering her tomatoes.; **Ils ont arrosé leur victoire.** They had a drink to celebrate their victory.

arrosoir nm watering can

art nm art

artère nf ❶ artery
❷ thoroughfare

artichaut nm artichoke

article nm ❶ article ❷ item

articulation nf joint

articuler [29] vb to pronounce
clearly

artificiel (f **artificielle**) adj
artificial

artisan nm self-employed
craftsman

artiste nmf ❶ artist ❷ performer

artistique adj artistic

as vb see **avoir**; **Tu as de beaux
cheveux.** You've got nice hair.
▶ nm ace

ascenseur nm lift

Ascension nf Ascension

asiatique adj Asiatic

Asie nf Asia; **en Asie (1)** in Asia
(2) to Asia

aspect nm appearance

asperge nf asparagus

aspirateur nm vacuum cleaner;
passer l'aspirateur to vacuum

aspirine nf aspirin

assaisonner [29] vb to season

assassin nm murderer

assassiner [29] vb to murder

assembler [29] vb to assemble;
s'assembler to gather ▷ Une foule
énorme s'était assemblée. A huge
crowd had gathered.

s'asseoir [7] vb to sit down
▷ Asseyez-vous! Sit down! ▷ Assieds-
toi! Sit down!

assez adv ❶ enough; **J'en ai assez!**

I've had enough! ❷ quite ▷ Il
faisait assez beau. The weather was
quite nice.

assiette nf plate; **une assiette
anglaise** assorted cold meats

assis, e adj sitting
▶ vb see **asseoir**

assistance nf ❶ audience
❷ aid ▷ l'assistance humanitaire
humanitarian aid ❸ assistance

assistant (f **assistante**) nm/f
assistant; **une assistante sociale**
a social worker

assister [29] vb **assister à un
accident** to witness an accident;
assister à un cours to attend a
class; **assister à un concert** to be
at a concert

association nf association

associé (f **associée**) nm/f (in
business) partner

s' associer [20] vb to go into
partnership

assommer [29] vb to knock out
▷ Il l'a assommé avec une bouteille. He
knocked him out with a bottle.

Assomption nf Assumption

assorti, e adj ❶ matching
❷ assorted; **être assorti
à quelque chose** to match
something

assortiment nm assortment

assurance nf ❶ insurance
❷ confidence

assurer [29] vb ❶ to insure ▷ La
maison est assurée. The house
is insured. ▷ être assuré contre
quelque chose to be insured against
something ❷ to assure ▷ Je t'assure

que c'est vrai! I assure you it's true!;
s'assurer de quelque chose to
make sure of something ▷ *Il s'est
assuré que la porte était fermée.* He
made sure the door was shut.

asthme *nm* asthma

astronaute *nmf* astronaut

astronomie *nf* astronomy

astucieux (fastucieuse) *adj*
clever

atelier *nm* ❶ workshop ❷ (artist's)
studio

Athènes *n* Athens

athlète *nmf* athlete

athlétisme *nm* athletics

Atlantique *nm* Atlantic

atlas *nm* atlas

atmosphère *nf* atmosphere

atomique *adj* atomic

atout *nm* ❶ asset ❷ trump card

atroce *adj* terrible

attachant, e *adj* lovable

attacher [29] *vb* to tie up ▷ *Elle a
attaché ses cheveux avec un élastique.*
She tied her hair up with an elastic
band.; **s'attacher à quelqu'un** to
become attached to somebody;
une poêle qui n'attache pas a
non-stick frying pan

attaquer [29] *vb* to attack

atteindre [61] *vb* to reach

attendant: en attendant *adv* in
the meantime

attendre [8] *vb* to wait ▷ *attendre
quelqu'un* to wait for someone;
attendre un enfant to be
expecting a baby; **s'attendre à** to
expect ▷ *Je m'attends à ce qu'il soit en
retard.* I expect he'll be late.

Be careful! **attendre** does not
mean **to attend**.

attentat *nm* **un attentat à la
bombe** a terrorist bombing

attente *nf* wait; **la salle d'attente**
the waiting room

attentif (fattentive) *adj*
attentive

attention *nf* attention; **faire
attention** to be careful;
Attention! Watch out!

attentionné, e *adj* thoughtful

atterrir [39] *vb* to land

atterrissage *nm* (of plane) landing

attirant, e *adj* attractive

attirer [29] *vb* to attract ▷ *attirer
l'attention de quelqu'un* to attract
somebody's attention; **s'attirer
des ennuis** to get into trouble
▷ *Si tu continues, tu vas t'attirer des
ennuis.* If you keep on like that,
you'll get yourself into trouble.

attitude *nf* attitude

attraction *nf* **un parc
d'attractions** an amusement park

attraper [29] *vb* to catch

attrayant, e *adj* attractive

attrister [29] *vb* to sadden

au *prep* see **à**

au is the contracted form
of **à + le**.

au printemps in the spring

aube *nf* dawn ▷ *à l'aube* at dawn

auberge *nf* inn; **une auberge de
jeunesse** a youth hostel

aubergine *nf* aubergine

aucun, e *adj, pron* ❶ no ▷ *Il n'a
aucun ami.* He's got no friends.
❷ none ▷ *Aucun d'entre eux n'est*

venu. None of them came.; **sans aucun doute** without any doubt

au-delà *adv* **au-delà de** beyond

au-dessous *adv* ❶ downstairs
▷ *Ils habitent au-dessous.* They live downstairs. ❷ underneath;
au-dessous de under

au-dessus *adv* ❶ upstairs
▷ *J'habite au-dessus.* I live upstairs.
❷ above; **au-dessus de** above

audiovisuel (*f* audiovisuelle) *adj* audiovisual

auditeur (*f* auditrice) *nm/f* (to radio) listener

augmentation *nf* rise

augmenter [29] *vb* to increase

aujourd'hui *adv* today

auparavant *adv* first

auquel (*mpl* auxquels, *fpl* auxquelles) *pron*

auquel is the contracted form of **à** + **lequel**.

▷ *l'homme auquel j'ai parlé* the man I spoke to

aura, aurai, auras, aurez, aurons, auront *vb see* **avoir**

aurore *nf* daybreak

ausculter [29] *vb* **Le médecin l'a ausculté.** The doctor listened to his chest.

aussi *adv* ❶ too ▷ *Dors bien.* — *Toi aussi.* Sleep well. — You too. ❷ also ▷ *Je parle anglais et aussi allemand.* I speak English and also German.;
aussi ... que as ... as ▷ *aussi grand que moi* as big as me

aussitôt *adv* straight away;
aussitôt que as soon as

Australie *nf* Australia; **en**

Australie (1) in Australia (2) to Australia

australien (*f* australienne) *adj* Australian
▶ *nm/f* **un Australien** (man) an Australian; **une Australienne** (woman) an Australian

autant *adv* **autant de** (1) so much (2) so many; **autant ... que** (1) as much ... as (2) as many ... as;
d'autant plus que all the more since; **d'autant moins que** even less since

auteur *nm* author

auto *nf* car

autobus *nm* bus

autocar *nm* coach

autocollant, e *adj* self-adhesive;
une enveloppe autocollante a self-seal envelope
▶ *nm* sticker

auto-école *nf* driving school

automatique *adj* automatic

automne *nm* autumn; **en automne** in autumn

automobile *adj* **une course automobile** a motor race
▶ *nf* car

automobiliste *nmf* motorist

autoradio *nm* car radio

autorisation *nf* ❶ permission
❷ permit

autoriser [29] *vb* to give permission for ▷ *Il m'a autorisé à en parler.* He's given me permission to talk about it.

autoritaire *adj* authoritarian

autorité *nf* authority

autoroute *nf* motorway

a
b
c
d
e
f
g
h
i
j
k
l
m
n
o
p
q
r
s
t
u
v
w
x
y
z

auto-stop nm **faire de l'auto-stop**
to hitchhike

auto-stoppeur (f **auto-
stoppeuse**) nm/f hitchhiker

autour adv around

autre adj, pron other ▷ **J'ai d'autres
projets.** I've got other plans.; **autre
chose** something else; **autre
part** somewhere else; **un autre**
another ▷ **Tu veux un autre morceau
de gâteau?** Would you like another
piece of cake?; **l'autre** the other;
d'autres others; **les autres** the
others; **ni l'un ni l'autre** neither
of them; **entre autres** among
other things

autrefois adv in the old days

autrement adv ❶ differently
❷ otherwise; **autrement dit** in
other words

Autriche nf Austria; **en Autriche**
(1) in Austria **(2)** to Austria

autrichien (f **autrichienne**) adj
Austrian
▶ nm/f **un Autrichien** (man) an
Austrian; **une Autrichienne**
(woman) an Austrian

autruche nf ostrich

aux prep see **à**
　aux is the contracted form
　of **à** + **les**.
　▷ **J'ai dit aux enfants d'aller jouer.** I
　told the children to go and play.

auxquelles pron
　auxquelles is the contracted
　form of **à** + **lesquelles**.
　▷ **les revues auxquelles il est abonné**
　the magazines to which he
　subscribes

auxquels pron
　auxquels is the contracted
　form of **à** + **lesquels**.
　▷ **les enfants auxquels il a parlé** the
　children he spoke to

avaient, avais, avait vb see
avoir; **Il y avait beaucoup de
monde.** There were lots of people.

avalanche nf avalanche

avaler [29] vb to swallow

avance nf **être en avance** to be
early; **à l'avance** beforehand;
d'avance in advance

avancé, e adj advanced; **bien
avancé** well under way

avancer [13] vb ❶ to move forward
❷ to bring forward ▷ **La date de
l'examen a été avancée.** The date of the
exam has been brought forward.
❸ to put forward ▷ **Il a avancé
sa montre d'une heure.** He put his
watch forward an hour. ❹ (watch)
to be fast ▷ **Ma montre avance d'une
heure.** My watch is an hour fast.
❺ to lend ▷ **Peux-tu m'avancer dix
euros?** Can you lend me 10 euros?

avant prep, adj ❶ before ▷ **avant
qu'il ne pleuve** before it rains ▷ **avant
de partir** before leaving ❷ front ▷ **le
siège avant** the front seat; **avant
tout** above all
▶ nm front; **à l'avant** in front; **en
avant** forward

avantage nm advantage

avant-bras (pl **avant-bras**) nm
forearm

avant-dernier (f **avant-dernière**,
mpl **avant-derniers**) adj last
but one

a
b
c
d
e
f
g
h
i
j
k
l
m
n
o
p
q
r
s
t
u
v
w
x
y
z

avant-hier *adv* the day before yesterday

avare *adj* miserly
▶ *nmf* miser

avec *prep* with ▷ *avec mon père* with my father; **Et avec ça?** (*in shop*) Anything else?

avenir *nm* future; **à l'avenir** in future; **dans un proche avenir** in the near future

aventure *nf* adventure

avenue *nf* avenue

averse *nf* (*of rain*) shower

avertir [**39**] *vb* to warn; **avertir quelqu'un de quelque chose** to warn somebody about something

avertissement *nm* warning

aveugle *adj* blind

avion *nm* plane; **aller en avion** to go by plane; **par avion** by airmail

aviron *nm* rowing

avis *nm* ❶ opinion; **à mon avis** in my opinion ❷ notice; **changer d'avis** to change one's mind

avocat *nm* ❶ lawyer ❷ avocado

avocate *nf* lawyer

avoine *nf* oats

avoir [**9**] *vb* ❶ to have ▷ *Ils ont deux enfants.* They have two children. ▷ *Il a les yeux bleus.* He's got blue eyes. ▷ *J'ai déjà mangé.* I've already eaten.; **On t'a bien eu!** (*informal*) You've been had! ❷ to be ▷ *Il a trois ans.* He's three.; **il y a (1)** there is ▷ *Il y a quelqu'un à la porte.* There's somebody at the door. **(2)** there are ▷ *Il y a des chocolats sur la table.* There are some chocolates on the table. **(3)** ago ▷ *Je l'ai rencontré il y a*

deux ans. I met him two years ago.; **Qu'est-ce qu'il y a?** What's the matter?; **Il n'y a qu'à partir plus tôt.** We'll just have to leave earlier.

avortement *nm* abortion

avouer [**29**] *vb* to admit

avril *nm* April; **en avril** in April

ayez, ayons *vb* see **avoir**

b

baby-foot nm table football

baby-sitting nm faire du baby-sitting to babysit

bac nm = **baccalauréat**

baccalauréat nm A levels

- The French **baccalauréat**, or
- **bac** for short, is taken at the age
- of 17 or 18. Students have to sit
- one of a variety of set subject
- combinations, rather than being
- able to choose any combination
- of subjects they want. If you
- pass you have the right to a
- place at university.

bâcler [**29**] vb to botch up

bagage nm luggage; faire ses bagages to pack; les bagages à main hand luggage

bagarre nf fight

se **bagarrer** [**29**] vb to fight

bagnole nf (informal) car

bague nf ring

baguette nf ❶ stick of French bread ❷ chopstick; une baguette magique a magic wand

baie nf bay

baignade nf "baignade interdite" "no swimming"

se **baigner** [**29**] vb to go swimming ▷ Si on allait se baigner? Shall we go swimming?

baignoire nf (bathtub) bath

bâiller [**29**] vb to yawn

bain nm bath ▷ prendre un bain to take a bath ▷ prendre un bain de soleil to sunbathe

baiser nm kiss

baisse nf fall; être en baisse to be falling; revoir les chiffres à la baisse to revise figures downwards

baisser [**29**] vb ❶ to turn down ▷ Il fait moins froid, tu peux baisser le chauffage. It's not so cold, you can turn down the heating. ❷ to fall ▷ Le prix des CD a baissé. The price of CDs has fallen.; se baisser to bend down

bal nm dance

balade nf (informal) walk

se **balader** [**29**] vb (informal) to wander around

baladeur nm personal stereo

balai nm broom

balance nf (for weighing) scales; la Balance Libra

se **balancer** [**13**] vb to swing

balançoire nf swing

balayer [60] *vb* ❶ to sweep ❷ to sweep up

balayeur *nm* roadsweeper

balbutier [20] *vb* to stammer

balcon *nm* balcony

baleine *nf* whale

balle *nf* ❶ ball ▷ *une balle de tennis* a tennis ball ❷ bullet

ballerine *nf* ❶ ballet dancer ❷ ballet shoe

ballet *nm* ballet

ballon *nm* ❶ ball; **un ballon de football** a football ❷ balloon

balnéaire *adj* **une station balnéaire** a seaside resort

banal, e *adj (mpl* banaux*) adj* ❶ commonplace ❷ hackneyed

banane *nf* ❶ banana ❷ bumbag

banc *nm* bench

bancaire *adj* **une carte bancaire** a bank card

bandage *nm* bandage

bande *nf* ❶ gang ▷ *une bande de voyous* a gang of louts ❷ bunch ▷ *C'est une bande d'idiots!* They are a bunch of idiots! ❸ bandage; **une bande dessinée** a comic strip

○ Comic strips are very popular in France with people of all ages.

une bande magnétique a tape; **la bande sonore** the sound track; **Elle fait toujours bande à part.** She always keeps to herself.

bandeau *(pl* bandeaux*) nm* headband

bander [29] *vb* to bandage ▷ *L'infirmière lui a bandé la jambe.* The nurse bandaged his leg.

bandit *nm* bandit

banlieue *nf* suburbs; **les lignes de banlieue** suburban lines; **les trains de banlieue** commuter trains

banque *nf* bank

banquet *nm* dinner

banquette *nf* seat

banquier *nm* banker

baptême *nm* christening; **C'était mon baptême de l'air.** It was the first time I had flown.

baquet *nm* tub

bar *nm* bar

baraque *nf (informal)* house

barbant, e *adj (informal)* boring

barbare *adj* barbaric

barbe *nf* beard ▷ *Il porte la barbe.* He's got a beard.; **Quelle barbe!** *(informal)* What a drag!; **la barbe à papa** candyfloss

barbecue *nm* barbecue

barbouiller [29] *vb* to daub ▷ *Les murs étaient barbouillés de graffitis.* The walls were daubed with graffiti.; **J'ai l'estomac barbouillé.** *(informal)* I'm feeling queasy.

barbu, e *adj* bearded

barder [29] *vb (informal)*: **Ça va barder!** There's going to be trouble!

baromètre *nm* barometer

barque *nf* rowing boat

barrage *nm* dam; **un barrage de police** a police roadblock

barre *nf (metal)* bar

barreau *(pl* barreaux*) nm* (on window) bar

barrer [29] *vb* to block ▷ *Il y a un tronc d'arbre qui barre la route.* There's a tree trunk blocking the

road.; **se barrer** (informal) to clear
off ▷ Barre-toi! Clear off!

barrette nf hair slide

barrière nf fence

bar-tabac (pl **bars-tabacs**) nm
 - A **bar-tabac** is a bar which also
 - sells cigarettes and stamps; you
 - can tell a **bar-tabac** by the red
 - diamond-shaped sign outside it.

bas nm ❶ bottom ▷ en bas de la
page at the bottom of the page
❷ stocking
 ▶ adj (f **basse**) low ▷ parler à voix
basse to speak in a low voice
 ▶ adv **en bas** (1) down ▷ Ça me
donne le vertige de regarder en bas. I
get dizzy if I look down. (2) (down)
at the bottom ▷ Son nom est tout
en bas. His name is down at the
bottom. (3) downstairs ▷ Elle
habite en bas. She lives downstairs.

bas-côté nm verge

bascule nf **un fauteuil à bascule** a
rocking chair

base nf base; **de base** basic; **à
base de** made from; **une base de
données** a database

basilic nm basil

basket nm basketball

baskets nfpl trainers ▷ une paire de
baskets a pair of trainers

Basque nmf (person, language)
 Basque

basque adj Basque

basse adj see **bas**

basse-cour (pl **basses-cours**) nf
farmyard

bassin nm ❶ pond ❷ pelvis

bassine nf (for washing) bowl

bas-ventre nm stomach

bataille nf battle

bateau (pl **bateaux**) nm boat

bateau-mouche (pl **bateaux-
mouches**) nm pleasure boat

bâti, e adj **bien bâti** well-built

bâtiment nm building

bâtir [39] vb to build

bâton nm stick

battement nm **J'ai dix minutes de
battement.** I've got ten minutes
free.

batterie nf ❶ battery ❷ drums;
 la batterie de cuisine the pots
and pans

batteur nm drummer

battre [10] vb to beat ▷ Quand
je le vois, mon cœur bat plus vite.
When I see him, my heart beats
faster.; **se battre** to fight ▷ Je me
bats souvent avec mon frère. I fight
a lot with my brother.; **battre
les cartes** to shuffle the cards; **battre
les blancs en neige** beat the egg
whites until stiff; **battre son plein**
to be in full swing

bavard, e adj talkative

bavarder [29] vb to chat

baver [29] vb to dribble

baveux (f **baveuse**) adj runny

bavure nf blunder

bazar nm general store; **Quel
bazar!** (informal) What a mess!

BCBG adj (= bon chic bon genre)
posh

BD nf (= bande dessinée) comic strip

béant, e adj gaping

beau (msg also **bel**, f **belle**, mpl
beaux) adj, adv

beau changes to **bel** before a vowel and most words beginning with "h".

① lovely ② beautiful ③ good-looking ④ handsome; Il fait beau aujourd'hui. It's a nice day today.; **J'ai beau essayer, je n'y arrive pas.** However hard I try, I just can't do it.

beaucoup adv **①** a lot ▷ **Il boit beaucoup.** He drinks a lot. **②** much ▷ **Elle n'a pas beaucoup d'argent.** She hasn't got much money.; **beaucoup de** a lot of; **J'ai eu beaucoup de chance.** I was very lucky.

beau-fils (pl **beaux-fils**) nm **①** son-in-law **②** stepson

beau-frère (pl **beaux-frères**) nm brother-in-law

beau-père (pl **beaux-pères**) nm **①** father-in-law **②** stepfather

beauté nf beauty

beaux-arts nmpl fine arts

beaux-parents nmpl in-laws

bébé nm baby

bec nm beak

bécane nf (informal) bike

bêche nf spade

bêcher [29] vb to dig ▷ **Il bêchait son jardin.** He was digging the garden.

bégayer [60] vb to stammer

beige adj beige

beignet nm fritter

bel adj see **beau**

Belge nmf Belgian

belge adj Belgian

Belgique nf Belgium; **en Belgique** (1) in Belgium (2) to Belgium

bélier nm ram; **le Bélier** Aries

belle adj see **beau**

belle-famille (pl **belles-familles**) nf in-laws

belle-fille (pl **belles-filles**) nf **①** daughter-in-law **②** stepdaughter

belle-mère (pl **belles-mères**) nf **①** mother-in-law **②** stepmother

belle-sœur (pl **belles-sœurs**) nf sister-in-law

bénédiction nf blessing

bénéfice nm profit

bénévole adj voluntary ▷ **du travail bénévole** voluntary work

bénir [39] vb to bless

bénit, e adj consecrated ▷ **l'eau bénite** holy water

béquille nf crutch

berceau (pl **berceaux**) nm cradle

bercer [13] vb to rock

berceuse nf lullaby

béret nm beret

berge nf (of river) bank

berger nm shepherd

bergère nf shepherdess

besoin nm need; **avoir besoin de quelque chose** to need something ▷ **J'ai besoin d'argent.** I need some money.; **une famille dans le besoin** a needy family

bétail nm livestock

bête nf animal

▶ adj stupid

bêtise nf **faire une bêtise** to do something stupid; **dire des bêtises** to talk nonsense

béton nm concrete; **un alibi en béton** a cast-iron alibi

a
b
c
d
e
f
g
h
i
j
k
l
m
n
o
p
q
r
s
t
u
v
w
x
y
z

betterave nf beetroot

beur nmf (informal)
- A **beur** is a young person of
- North African origin born in
- France.

beurre nm butter

beurrer [**29**] vb to butter

Beyrouth n Beirut

bibelot nm ornament

biberon nm baby's bottle

Bible nf Bible

bibliothécaire nmf librarian

bibliothèque nf ❶ library
- ❷ bookcase

bic® nm Biro®

biche nf doe

bicyclette nf bicycle

bidet nm bidet

bidon nm can
- ▶ adj (informal) phoney

bidonville nm shanty town

Biélorussie nf Belarus

bien adj, adv ❶ well ▷ Daphne
travaille bien. Daphne works well.
▷ Je ne me sens pas bien. I don't feel
well. ❷ good ▷ Ce restaurant est
vraiment bien. This restaurant is
really good. ❸ quite; **Je veux bien
le faire.** I'm quite willing to do it.;
bien mieux much better; **J'espère
bien y aller.** I very much hope to
go. ❹ right; **C'est bien fait pour
lui!** It serves him right!
- ▶ nm ❶ good; **faire du bien à
quelqu'un** to do somebody good
❷ possession

bien-être nm well-being

bienfaisance nf charity; **une
œuvre de bienfaisance** a charity

bien que conj although
- ▌ **bien que** is followed by a verb
  in the subjunctive.
- ▷ Il fait assez chaud bien qu'il n'y
  ait pas de soleil. It's quite warm
  although there's no sun.

bien sûr adv of course

bientôt adv soon

bienvenu nm **Vous êtes le
bienvenu!** You're welcome!

bienvenue nf welcome
- ▷ Bienvenue à Paris! Welcome to
  Paris!

bière nf beer; **la bière blonde**
lager; **la bière brune** brown ale;
la bière pression draught beer

bifteck nm steak

bigoudi nm (in hair) roller

bijou (pl bijoux) nm jewel

bijouterie nf jeweller's

bijoutier (f bijoutière) nm/f
jeweller

bilan nm **faire le bilan de quelque
chose** to assess something

bilingue adj bilingual

billard nm billiards; **le billard
américain** pool

bille nf (toy) marble

billet nm ❶ ticket ▷ un billet
d'avion a plane ticket
❷ banknote ▷ un billet de dix euros
a 10 euro note

billion nm billion

biographie nf biography

biologie nf biology

biologique adj ❶ organic
❷ biological

Birmanie nf Burma

bis adv **Il habite au douze bis rue**

des Fleurs. He lives at 12A rue des Fleurs.
▶ *nm* encore

biscotte *nf* (sold in packets) toasted bread

biscuit *nm* biscuit; **un biscuit de Savoie** a sponge cake

bise *nf* kiss ▷ *Grosses bises de Bretagne.* Love and kisses from Brittany.; **faire la bise à quelqu'un** (informal) to give somebody a peck on the cheek
- Between girls and boys, and
- between girls, the normal
- French way of saying hello and
- goodbye is with kisses, usually
- one on each cheek. Boys shake
- hands with each other instead.

bisou *nm* (informal) kiss

bissextile *adj* **une année bissextile** a leap year

bistrot *nm* (informal) café
- Cafés in France sell both
- alcoholic and non-alcoholic
- drinks.

bizarre *adj* strange

blague *nf* ❶ (informal) joke ▷ *raconter une blague* to tell a joke; **Sans blague!** No kidding! ❷ trick

blaguer [29] *vb* (informal) to joke

blaireau (*pl* blaireaux) *nm* shaving brush

blâmer [29] *vb* to blame

blanc (*f* blanche) *adj* ❶ white ▷ *un chemisier blanc* a white blouse ❷ blank ▷ *une page blanche* a blank page
▶ *nm* ❶ white ❷ white wine; **un**

blanc d'œuf an egg white; **un blanc de poulet** a chicken breast

Blanc *nm* white man

Blanche *nf* white woman

blanche *adj see* blanc

blanchisserie *nf* laundry

blé *nm* wheat

blessé, e *adj* injured
▶ *nm/f* injured person

blesser [29] *vb* ❶ to injure ▷ *Il a été blessé dans un accident de voiture.* He was injured in a car accident. ❷ to hurt ▷ *Il a fait exprès de le blesser.* He hurt him on purpose.; **se blesser** to hurt oneself

blessure *nf* injury

bleu, e *adj* ❶ blue; **bleu marine** navy blue ❷ (steak) very rare
▶ *nm* ❶ blue ❷ bruise

bleuet *nm* cornflower

bloc *nm* pad; **le bloc opératoire** the operating theatre

bloc-notes (*pl* blocs-notes) *nm* note pad

blond, e *adj* blond; **blond cendré** ash blond

bloquer [29] *vb* to block ▷ *bloquer le passage* to block the way; **être bloqué dans un embouteillage** to be stuck in a traffic jam

se blottir [39] *vb* to huddle

blouse *nf* overall

blouson *nm* jacket

bob *nm* cotton sunhat

bobine *nf* reel

bocal (*pl* bocaux) *nm* jar

bœuf *nm* ❶ ox ❷ beef

bof *excl* (informal): **Le film t'a plu? — Bof!** C'était pas terrible! Did you like the film? — Well ... it wasn't that great!; **Comment ça va? — Bof! Pas terrible.** How is it going? — Oh ... not too well actually.

bohémien (f **bohémienne**) nm/f gipsy

boire [11] vb to drink; **boire un coup** (informal) to have a drink

bois nm wood; **en bois** wooden; **avoir la gueule de bois** (informal) to have a hangover

boisson nf drink

boîte nf ① box ▷ *une boîte d'allumettes* a box of matches; **une boîte aux lettres** a letter box; **une boîte postale** a PO Box ② tin; **une boîte de conserve** a tin; **en boîte** tinned; **une boîte de nuit** a night club; **sortir en boîte** to go clubbing

boiter [29] vb to limp

bol nm bowl; **en avoir ras le bol** (informal) to be fed up

bombarder [29] vb to bomb

bombe nf ① bomb ② aerosol

bon (f **bonne**) adj, adv ① good; **être bon en maths** to be good at maths; **sentir bon** to smell nice; **Bon courage!** Good luck!; **Bon voyage!** Have a good trip!; **Bon week-end!** Have a nice weekend!; **Bonne chance!** Good luck!; **Bonne journée!** Have a nice day!; **Bonne nuit!** Good night!; **Bon anniversaire!** Happy birthday!; **Bonne année!** Happy New Year! ② right ▷ *Ce n'est pas la bonne réponse.* That's not the right answer.; **Il fait bon aujourd'hui.**

It's nice today.; **de bonne heure** early; **bon marché** cheap; **Ah bon?** Really?; **J'aimerais vraiment que tu viennes! — Bon, d'accord.** I'd really like you to come! — OK then, I will.; **Est-ce que ce yaourt est encore bon?** Is this yoghurt still OK?

▶ nm voucher ▷ *un bon d'achat* a voucher; **pour de bon** for good

bonbon nm sweet

bondé, e adj crowded

bondir [39] vb to leap

bonheur nm happiness; **porter bonheur** to bring luck

bonhomme (pl **bonshommes**) nm **un bonhomme de neige** a snowman

bonjour excl ① Hello! ▷ *Donne le bonjour à tes parents de ma part.* Say hello to your parents for me. ② Good morning! ③ Good afternoon!

> bonjour is used in the morning and afternoon; in the evening bonsoir is used instead.

C'est simple comme bonjour! It's easy as pie!

bonne adj see **bon**

bonnet nm hat; **un bonnet de bain** a bathing cap

bonsoir excl Good evening!

bonté nf kindness

bord nm ① edge ② side; **au bord de la mer** at the seaside; **au bord de l'eau** by the water; **monter à bord** to go on board; **être au bord des larmes** to be on the verge of tears

bordeaux nm Bordeaux wine; **du bordeaux rouge** claret
▸ adj maroon

bordel nm (rude) brothel; **Quel bordel!** (informal) What a bloody mess!

border [**29**] vb ❶ to line ▸ une route bordée d'arbres a tree-lined street ❷ to trim ▸ un col bordé de dentelle a collar trimmed with lace ▸ Sa mère vient la border tous les soirs. Her mother comes and tucks her up every night.

bordure nf border; **une villa en bordure de mer** a villa right by the sea

borne nf (of computer) terminal

Bosnie nf Bosnia; **la Bosnie-Herzégovine** Bosnia-Herzegovina

bosse nf bump

bosser [**29**] vb (informal) to work; **bosser un examen** to study for an exam

bossu (f **bossue**) nm/f hunchback

botanique adj botanic
▸ nf botany

botte nf ❶ boot; **les bottes de caoutchouc** wellington boots ❷ bunch ▸ une botte de radis a bunch of radishes

bottin® nm phone book

bouc nm ❶ goatee beard ❷ billy goat; **un bouc émissaire** a scapegoat

bouche nf mouth; **le bouche à bouche** the kiss of life; **une bouche d'égout** a manhole; **une bouche de métro** an entrance to the underground

bouchée nf mouthful; **une bouchée à la reine** a chicken vol-au-vent

boucher [**29**] vb ❶ to fill ▸ boucher un trou to fill a hole ❷ to block ▸ L'évier est bouché. The sink is blocked. ▸ J'ai le nez bouché. My nose is blocked.
▸ nm butcher

bouchère nf butcher

boucherie nf butcher's

bouchon nm ❶ (of plastic bottle) top ❷ (of wine bottle) cork ❸ hold-up

boucle nf (of hair) curl; **une boucle d'oreille** an earring

bouclé, e adj curly

bouclier nm shield

bouddhiste nmf Buddhist

bouder [**29**] vb to sulk

boudin nm **le boudin noir** black pudding; **le boudin blanc** white pudding

boue nf mud

bouée nf buoy; **une bouée de sauvetage** a life buoy

boueux (f **boueuse**) adj muddy

bouffe nf (informal) food

bouffée nf **une bouffée d'air frais** a breath of fresh air

bouffer [**29**] vb (informal) to eat

bougeoir nm candlestick

bouger [**46**] vb to move

bougie nf candle

bouillabaisse nf fish soup

bouillant, e adj ❶ boiling ❷ piping hot

bouillir [**12**] vb to boil ▸ L'eau bout. The water's boiling.; **Je bous**

d'impatience. I'm bursting with impatience.

bouilloire nf kettle

bouillon nm stock

bouillotte nf hot-water bottle

boulanger (f **boulangère**) nm/f baker

boulangerie nf baker's

boule nf ball; **une boule de neige** a snowball; **jouer aux boules** to play bowls

boulevard nm boulevard

bouleverser [29] vb ❶ to move deeply ❷ to shatter ▷ *La mort de son ami l'a bouleversé.* He was shattered by the death of his friend. ❸ to turn upside down ▷ *Cette rencontre a bouleversé sa vie.* This meeting turned his life upside down.

boulot nm ❶ (informal) job ❷ work

boum nf (informal) party

bouquet nm bunch of flowers

bouquin nm (informal) book

bouquiner [29] vb (informal) to read

bourdonner [29] vb to buzz

bourg nm small market town

bourgeois, e adj middle-class

bourgeon nm bud

Bourgogne nf Burgundy

bourré, e adj **bourré de** stuffed with; **être bourré** (informal) to be plastered

bourreau (pl **bourreaux**) nm executioner; **C'est un véritable bourreau de travail.** He's a real workaholic.

bourrer [29] vb to stuff

bourse nf grant; **la Bourse** the Stock Exchange

bous vb see **bouillir**

bousculade nf crush

bousculer [29] vb ❶ to jostle ▷ *être bousculé par la foule* to be jostled by the crowd ❷ to rush ▷ *Je n'aime pas qu'on me bouscule.* I don't like to be rushed.

boussole nf compass

bout nm ❶ end ▷ *Elle habite au bout de la rue.* She lives at the end of the street. ❷ tip ▷ *le bout du nez* the tip of the nose ❸ bit; **un bout de papier** a scrap of paper; **au bout de** after; **Elle est à bout.** She's at the end of her tether.

    ▶ vb see **bouillir**

bouteille nf bottle; **une bouteille de gaz** a gas cylinder

boutique nf shop

bouton nm ❶ button ❷ (on skin) spot ❸ bud; **un bouton d'or** a buttercup

bowling nm ❶ tenpin bowling ❷ bowling alley

boxe nf boxing

boxeur nm boxer

bracelet nm bracelet

bracelet-montre (pl **bracelets-montres**) nm wristwatch

brancard nm stretcher

brancardier nm stretcher-bearer

branche nf branch

branché, e adj (informal) trendy

brancher [29] vb ❶ to connect ▷ *Le téléphone est branché?* Is the phone connected? ❷ to plug in

▷ *L'aspirateur n'est pas branché.* The hoover isn't plugged in.

bras nm arm

brasse nf breaststroke

brasserie nf café-restaurant

brave adj nice

bravo excl Bravo!

break nm estate car

brebis nf ewe; **le fromage de brebis** sheep's cheese

bref (f **brève**) adj, adv short; **en bref** in brief; ... **bref, ça s'est bien terminé.** ... to cut a long story short, it turned out all right in the end.

Brésil nm Brazil

Bretagne nf Brittany

bretelle nf strap; **les bretelles** braces

breton (f **bretonne**) adj Breton

▶ nm **Ils parlent breton.** They speak Breton.

▶ nm/f **un Breton** (man) a Breton; **une Bretonne** (woman) a Breton; **les Bretons** the Bretons

brève adj see **bref**

brevet nm certificate

brevet des collèges nm

● The **brevet des collèges** is an
● exam you take at the end of
● **collège**, at the age of 15.

bricolage nm do-it-yourself

bricole nf (informal): **J'ai acheté une bricole pour le bébé de Sabine.** I've bought a little something for Sabine's baby.; **J'ai encore quelques bricoles à faire avant de partir.** I've still got a few things to do before I go.

bricoler [29] vb to do DIY ▷ *Pascal aime bricoler.* Pascal loves doing DIY.

bricoleur (f **bricoleuse**) nm/f DIY enthusiast

bridge nm (game) bridge

brièvement adv briefly

brigade nf (of police) squad

brillamment adv brilliantly

brillant, e adj ① brilliant ② shiny

briller [29] vb to shine

brin nm **un brin d'herbe** a blade of grass; **un brin de muguet** a sprig of lily of the valley

brindille nf twig

brioche nf brioche bun

brique nf brick

briquet nm cigarette lighter

brise nf breeze

se **briser** [29] vb to break ▷ *Le vase s'est brisé en mille morceaux.* The vase broke into a thousand pieces.

Britannique nmf Briton; **les Britanniques** the British

britannique adj British

brocante nf junk

brocanteur (f **brocanteuse**) nm/f dealer in second-hand goods

broche nf brooch; **à la broche** spit-roasted

brochette nf skewer; **les brochettes d'agneau** lamb kebabs

brochure nf brochure

broder [29] vb to embroider

broderie nf embroidery

bronchite nf bronchitis

bronze nm bronze

bronzer [29] vb to get a tan ▷ *Il est*

bien bronzé. He's got a good tan.; **se bronzer** to sunbathe

brosse *nf* brush; **une brosse à cheveux** a hairbrush; **une brosse à dents** a toothbrush; **Il est coiffé en brosse.** He's got a crew cut.

brosser [29] *vb* to brush; **se brosser les dents** to brush one's teeth ▷ *Je me brosse les dents tous les soirs.* I brush my teeth every night.

brouette *nf* wheelbarrow

brouillard *nm* fog

brouillon *nm* first draft

broussailles *nfpl* undergrowth

brouter [29] *vb* (animals) to graze

broyer [54] *vb* to crush; **broyer du noir** to be down in the dumps

brugnon *nm* nectarine

bruit *nm* ❶ noise ▷ *faire du bruit* to make a noise; **sans bruit** without a sound ❷ rumour

brûlant, e *adj* ❶ blazing ❷ boiling hot

brûlé *nm* smell of burning

brûler [29] *vb* to burn; **se brûler** to burn oneself

brûlure *nf* burn; **des brûlures d'estomac** heartburn

brume *nf* mist

brumeux (f **brumeuse**) *adj* misty

brun, e *adj* brown; **Elle est brune.** She's got dark hair.

brushing *nm* blow-dry

brusque *adj* abrupt; **d'un ton brusque** brusquely

brusquer [29] *vb* to rush

brut, e *adj* **le champagne brut** dry champagne; **le pétrole brut**

crude oil; **son salaire brut** his gross salary

brutal, e (*mpl* **brutaux**) *adj* brutal

brutaliser [29] *vb* to knock about ▷ *Il a été brutalisé par la police.* He was treated roughly by the police.

Bruxelles *n* Brussels

bruyamment *adv* noisily

bruyant, e *adj* noisy

bruyère *nf* heather

bu *vb* see **boire**

bûche *nf* log; **la bûche de Noël** the Yule log
   ● This is what is usually eaten in
   ● France instead of Christmas
   ● pudding.

bûcheron *nm* woodcutter

budget *nm* budget

buffet *nm* ❶ sideboard ❷ buffet ▷ *un buffet de gare* a station buffet

buisson *nm* bush

Bulgarie *nf* Bulgaria

bulle *nf* bubble

bulletin *nm* ❶ bulletin; **le bulletin d'informations** the news bulletin ❷ report; **le bulletin météorologique** the weather report; **le bulletin de salaire** pay slip; **le bulletin de vote** the ballot paper

bureau (*pl* **bureaux**) *nm* ❶ desk ❷ office; **un bureau de change** a bureau de change; **le bureau de poste** the post office; **le bureau de tabac** the tobacconist's; **le bureau de vote** the polling station

bus *nm* bus
   ▶ *vb* see **boire**

buste *nm* bust

but nm ❶ aim; **Quel est le but de votre visite?** What's the reason for your visit?; **dans le but de** with the intention of ❷ goal ▷ *marquer un but* to score a goal
▶ vb see **boire**

butane nm Calor gas®

butin nm loot

buvais, buvait vb see **boire**

buvard nm blotter

C

c' pron see **ce**

ça pron ❶ this ▷ *Est-ce que vous pouvez me donner un peu de ça?* Can you give me a bit of this? ❷ that ▷ *Est-ce que tu peux prendre ça, là-bas dans le coin?* Can you bring that from over there in the corner? ❸ it ▷ *Ça ne fait rien.* It doesn't matter.; **Comment ça va?** How are you?; **Ça alors!** Well, welll; **C'est ça.** That's right.; **Ça y est!** That's it!

çà adv **çà et là** here and there

cabane nf hut

cabillaud nm cod

cabine nf (on a ship) cabin; **une cabine d'essayage** a fitting room; **une cabine téléphonique** a phone box

cabinet nm (of doctor, of dentist) surgery; **une chambre avec**

cabinet de toilette a room with washing facilities

cabinets *nmpl* <u>toilet</u>

câble *nm* <u>cable</u>; **la télévision par câble** (*television*) cable

cabosser [**29**] *vb* to <u>dent</u>

cacahuète *nf* <u>peanut</u>; **le beurre de cacahuète** peanut butter

cacao *nm* <u>cocoa</u>; **le beurre de cacao** cocoa butter

cache-cache *nm* jouer à cache-cache to play hide-and-seek

cachemire *nm* <u>cashmere</u>

cache-nez (*pl* cache-nez) *nm* <u>long woollen scarf</u>

cacher [**29**] *vb* to <u>hide</u> ▷ *J'ai caché les cadeaux sous le lit.* I hid the presents under the bed.; **se cacher** to hide

cachet *nm* ❶ <u>tablet</u>; **un cachet d'aspirine** an aspirin ❷ (*for performer*) <u>fee</u>; **le cachet de la poste** the postmark

cachette *nf* <u>hiding place</u>; **en cachette** on the sly

cachot *nm* <u>dungeon</u>

cactus *nm* <u>cactus</u>

cadavre *nm* <u>corpse</u>

Caddie® *nm* <u>supermarket trolley</u>

cadeau (*pl* cadeaux) *nm* <u>present</u> ▷ *un cadeau d'anniversaire* a birthday present ▷ *un cadeau de Noël* a Christmas present; **faire un cadeau à quelqu'un** to give somebody a present

cadenas *nm* <u>padlock</u>

cadet (*f* cadette) *adj* ❶ (*brother, sister*) <u>younger</u> ❷ (*son, daughter*) <u>youngest</u>
  ▶ *nm/f* <u>youngest</u> ▷ *C'est le cadet*

de la famille. He's the youngest of the family.

cadre *nm* ❶ <u>frame</u> ❷ <u>surroundings</u> ❸ <u>executive</u> ▷ *un cadre supérieur* a senior executive

cafard *nm* <u>cockroach</u>; **avoir le cafard** (*informal*) to be feeling down

café *nm* ❶ <u>coffee</u> ▷ *un café au lait* a white coffee ▷ *un café crème* a strong white coffee ❷ <u>café</u>
  ● Cafés in France sell both alcoholic and non-alcoholic drinks.

café-tabac (*pl* cafés-tabacs) *nm*
  ● A **café-tabac** is a bar which also sells cigarettes and stamps; you can tell a **café-tabac** by the red diamond-shaped sign outside it.

cafétéria *nf* <u>cafeteria</u>

cafetière *nf* ❶ <u>coffee maker</u> ❷ <u>coffee pot</u>

cage *nf* <u>cage</u>; **la cage d'escalier** the stairwell

cagoule *nf* <u>balaclava</u>

cahier *nm* <u>exercise book</u>

caille *nf* <u>quail</u>

caillou (*pl* cailloux) *nm* <u>pebble</u>

caisse *nf* ❶ <u>box</u> ❷ <u>till</u> ▷ *le ticket de caisse* the till receipt ❸ <u>checkout</u>

caissier (*f* caissière) *nm/f* <u>cashier</u>

cake *nm* <u>fruit cake</u>

calcul *nm* ❶ <u>calculation</u> ❷ <u>arithmetic</u>

calculatrice *nf* <u>calculator</u>

calculer [**29**] *vb* to <u>work out</u> ▷ *J'ai calculé combien ça allait coûter.* I worked out how much it was going to cost.

calculette nf pocket calculator

cale nf wedge

calé, e adj (informal): **Elle est calée en histoire.** She's really good at history.

caleçon nm ❶ boxer shorts ❷ leggings

calendrier nm calendar

calepin nm notebook

caler [29] vb to stall

câlin, e adj cuddly
▶ nm cuddle

calmant nm tranquillizer

calme adj ❶ quiet ❷ calm
▶ nm peace and quiet

calmer [29] vb to soothe; **se calmer** to calm down ▷ Calme-toi! Calm down!

calorie nf calorie

camarade nmf friend; **un camarade de classe** a school friend

cambriolage nm burglary

cambrioler [29] vb to burgle

cambrioleur (f **cambrioleuse**) nm/f burglar

camelote nf (informal) junk

caméra nf (cinema, TV) camera; **une caméra numérique** a digital camera

caméscope® nm camcorder

camion nm lorry

camionnette nf van

camionneur nm lorry driver

camomille nf camomile tea

camp nm camp

campagne nf ❶ country; **à la campagne** in the country ❷ campaign

camper [29] vb to camp

campeur (f **campeuse**) nm/f camper

camping nm camping ▷ **faire du camping** to go camping; **un terrain de camping** a campsite

Canada nm Canada; **au Canada (1)** in Canada **(2)** to Canada

canadien (f **canadienne**) adj Canadian
▶ nm/f **un Canadien** (man) a Canadian; **une Canadienne** (woman) a Canadian

canal (pl **canaux**) nm canal

canapé nm ❶ sofa ❷ open sandwich

canard nm duck

canari nm canary

cancer nm cancer; **le Cancer** Cancer

candidat (f **candidate**) nm/f ❶ (in exam, election) candidate ❷ (for job) applicant

candidature nf **poser sa candidature à un poste** to apply for a job

caneton nm duckling

canette nf **une canette de bière** a small bottle of beer

caniche nm poodle

canicule nf scorching heat

canif nm penknife

caniveau (pl **caniveaux**) nm gutter

canne nf walking stick; **une canne à pêche** a fishing rod

cannelle nf cinnamon

canoë nm ❶ canoe ❷ canoeing

canon nm ❶ gun ❷ cannon

canot nm dinghy; **un canot de sauvetage** a lifeboat

cantatrice nf opera singer

cantine nf canteen

caoutchouc nm rubber; **des bottes en caoutchouc** Wellington boots

cap nm cape

capable adj **Elle est capable de marcher pendant des heures.** She can walk for hours.; **Il est capable de changer d'avis au dernier moment.** He's capable of changing his mind at the last minute.

cape nf cape

capitaine nm captain

capitale nf capital

capot nm (of car) bonnet

capote nf (informal) condom

câpre nf (food) caper

caprice nm **faire des caprices** to make a fuss

capricieux (f **capricieuse**) adj **un enfant capricieux** an awkward child

Capricorne nm Capricorn

captivant, e adj fascinating

captivité nf captivity

capturer [29] vb to capture

capuche nf hood

capuchon nm (of pen) cap

capucine nf nasturtium

car nm coach ⊳ **un car scolaire** a school bus
  ▸ conj because ⊳ **Nous sommes inquiets car il n'est pas encore rentré.** We're worried because he isn't back yet.

carabine nf rifle

caractère nm personality; **Il a bon caractère.** He's good-natured.; **Elle a mauvais caractère.** She's bad-tempered.; **Il n'a pas un caractère facile.** He isn't easy to get on with.

caractéristique adj characteristic
  ▸ nf characteristic

carafe nf jug

Caraïbes nfpl Caribbean Islands

caramel nm ❶ caramel ❷ toffee

caravane nf caravan

carbonique adj **le gaz carbonique** carbon dioxide

carburant nm fuel

cardiaque adj **une crise cardiaque** a heart attack; **Ma tante est cardiaque.** My aunt has heart trouble.

cardigan nm cardigan

cardiologue nmf heart specialist

carême nm Lent

caresse nf stroke

caresser [29] vb to stroke

carie nf tooth decay

caritatif (f **caritative**) adj **une organisation caritative** a charity

carnaval nm carnival

carnet nm ❶ notebook ❷ book ⊳ **un carnet d'adresses** an address book ⊳ **un carnet de chèques** a cheque book ⊳ **un carnet de timbres** a book of stamps ⊳ **un carnet de tickets** a book of tickets
  ● In the Paris metro it is cheaper
  ● to buy tickets in a book of ten,
  ● known as a **carnet**.

mon carnet de notes my school report

carotte nf carrot

carré, e adj square; **un mètre carré** a square metre
▶ nm square

carreau (pl carreaux) nm ① check ② (on floor, wall) tile ③ pane ④ (cards) diamonds

carrefour nm junction

carrelage nm tiled floor

carrément adv ① completely ② straight out

carrière nf career; **un militaire de carrière** a professional soldier

carrure nf build

cartable nm satchel

carte nf ① card; **une carte d'anniversaire** a birthday card; **une carte postale** a postcard; **une carte de vœux** a Christmas card
■ The French send greetings cards (les cartes de vœux) in January rather than at Christmas, with best wishes for the New Year.
une carte bancaire a cash card; **une carte bleue®** a debit card; **une carte de crédit** a credit card; **une carte de fidélité** a loyalty card; **une carte d'embarquement** a boarding card; **une carte d'identité** an identity card; **une carte de séjour** a residence permit; **une carte SIM** a SIM card; **une carte téléphonique** a phonecard; **un jeu de cartes** (1) a pack of cards (2) a card game ② map ▷ une carte routière a road map ③ menu ▷ la carte des vins the

wine list; **manger à la carte** to eat à la carte ▷ Nous allons manger à la carte. We'll choose from the à la carte menu.

carton nm ① cardboard ② cardboard box

cartouche nf cartridge; **une cartouche de cigarettes** a carton of cigarettes

cas (pl cas) nm case; **ne faire aucun cas de** to take no notice of; **en aucun cas** on no account; **en tout cas** at any rate; **au cas où** in case; **en cas de** in case of

cascade nf waterfall

cascadeur nm stuntman

case nf ① (in board game) square ② (on form) box

caserne nf barracks

cash adv **payer cash** to pay cash

casier nm locker

casque nm ① helmet ② headphones

casquette nf cap

cassant, e adj (informal): **Il m'a parlé d'un ton cassant.** He spoke to me curtly.

casse-croûte (pl casse-croûte) nm snack

casse-noix (pl casse-noix) nm nutcrackers

casse-pieds adj inv (informal): **Il est vraiment casse-pieds!** He's a real pain in the neck!

casser [29] vb to break ▷ J'ai cassé un verre. I've broken a glass.; **se casser** to break ▷ Il s'est cassé la jambe au ski. He broke his leg when he was skiing.; **se casser la tête** (informal) to go to a lot of trouble

casserole nf saucepan

casse-tête (pl casse-tête) nm
C'est un vrai casse-tête! It's a real
headache!

cassette nf cassette

cassis nm blackcurrant

castor nm beaver

catalogue nm catalogue

catastrophe nf disaster

catch nm wrestling

catéchisme nm catechism

catégorie nf category

catégorique adj firm

cathédrale nf cathedral

catholique adj Catholic
  ▶ nmf Catholic

cauchemar nm nightmare

cause nf cause; **à cause de**
because of

causer [29] vb ❶ to cause ▷ La
tempête a causé beaucoup de dégâts.
The storm caused a lot of damage.
❷ to chat

caution nf ❶ bail ❷ deposit

cavalier nm ❶ rider ❷ (at dance)
partner

cavalière nf rider

cave nf cellar
  ● Be careful! The French word **cave**
    does not mean **cave**.

caverne nf cave

CD (pl CD) nm CD

CD-ROM (pl CD-ROM) nm
CD-ROM

ce (msg also **cet**, f **cette**, pl **ces**) adj
  ce changes to **cet** before
  a vowel and most words
  beginning with "h".

❶ this ▷ Tu peux prendre ce livre. You

can take this book. ▷ cet après-midi
this afternoon; **ce livre-ci** this
book; **cette voiture-ci** this car
❷ that; **ce livre-là** that book;
cette voiture-là that car
  ▶ pron
  ce changes to **c'** before
  the vowel in **est**, **était** and
  étaient.

it ▷ Ce n'est pas facile. It's not easy.;
c'est (1) it is ▷ C'est vraiment trop
cher. It's really too expensive. **(2)** he
is ▷ C'est un peintre du début du siècle.
He's a painter from the turn of the
century. **(3)** she is ▷ C'est une actrice
très célèbre. She's a very famous
actress.; **ce sont** they are ▷ Ce
sont des amis à mes parents. They're
friends of my parents.; **Qui est-ce?**
Who is it?; **Qu'est-ce que c'est?**
What is it?; **ce qui** what ▷ C'est ce
qui compte. That's what matters.;
tout ce qui everything that ▷ J'ai
rangé tout ce qui traînait par terre.
I've tidied up everything that was
on the floor.; **ce que** what ▷ Je vais
lui dire ce que je pense. I'm going
to tell him what I think.; **tout
ce que** everything ▷ Tu peux avoir
tout ce que tu veux. You can have
everything you want.

ceci pron this ▷ Prends ceci, tu
en auras besoin. Take this, you'll
need it.

céder [35] vb to give in ▷ Elle a
tellement insisté qu'il a fini par céder.
She went on so much that she
eventually gave in.; **céder à** to
give in to

cédérom nm CD-ROM

cédille nf cedilla

ceinture nf belt; **une ceinture de sauvetage** a lifebelt; **votre ceinture de sécurité** your seatbelt

cela pron ❶ it ▷ *Cela dépend.* It depends. ❷ that ▷ *Je n'aime pas cela.* I don't like that.; **C'est cela.** That's right.; **à part cela** apart from that

célèbre adj famous

célébrer [35] vb to celebrate

céleri nm **le céleri-rave** celeriac; **le céleri en branche** celery

célibataire adj single
▶ nm/f **un célibataire** a bachelor; **une célibataire** a single woman

celle pron see **celui**

celles pron see **ceux**

cellule nf cell

celui (f **celle**, mpl **ceux**, fpl **celles**) pron the one ▷ *Prends celui que tu préfères.* Take the one you like best. ▷ *Je n'ai pas d'appareil photo mais je peux emprunter celui de ma sœur.* I haven't got a camera but I can borrow my sister's. ▷ *Je n'ai pas de platine laser mais je peux emprunter celle de mon frère.* I haven't got a CD player but I can borrow my brother's.; **celui-ci** this one; **celle-ci** this one; **celui-là** that one; **celle-là** that one

cendre nf ash

cendrier nm ashtray

censé, e adj **être censé(e) faire quelque chose** to be supposed to do something

cent num a hundred ▷ *cent euros* a hundred euros

> **cent** is spelt with an **-s** when there are two or more hundreds, but not when it is followed by another number, as in "a hundred and two".

▷ *trois cents ans* three hundred years ▷ *trois cent cinquante kilomètres* three hundred and fifty kilometres
▶ nm (currency) cent
○ The euro is divided into 100 centimes or cents.

centaine nf about a hundred; **des centaines de** hundreds of

centenaire nm centenary

centième adj hundredth

centilitre nm centilitre

centime nm ❶ (of a euro) cent
○ The euro is divided into 100 centimes or cents.
❷ (of a Swiss franc) centime

centimètre nm centimetre

central, e (mpl **centraux**) adj central

centrale nf power station

centre nm centre; **un centre commercial** a shopping centre; **un centre d'appels** a call centre

centre-ville (pl **centres-villes**) nm town centre

cependant adv however

cercle nm circle; **un cercle vicieux** a vicious circle

cercueil nm coffin

céréale nf cereal; **un pain aux cinq céréales** a multigrain loaf

cérémonie nf ceremony

cerf nm stag

cerf-volant (pl **cerfs-volants**) nm kite

cerise nf cherry

cerisier nm cherry tree

cerné, e adj **avoir les yeux cernés** to have shadows under one's eyes

cerner [29] vb **J'ai du mal à le cerner.** I can't figure him out.

certain, e adj ❶ certain ❷ some; **un certain temps** quite some time

certainement adv ❶ definitely ❷ of course

certains pron ❶ some ▷ **certains de ses amis** some of his friends ❷ some people ▷ **Certains pensent que le film est meilleur que le roman.** Some people think that the film is better than the novel.

certes adv certainly

certificat nm certificate

cerveau (pl **cerveaux**) nm brain

cervelle nf brain; **se creuser la cervelle** (informal) to rack one's brains

CES nm (= Collège d'enseignement secondaire) secondary school
  ● In France pupils go to a **CES** between the ages of 11 and 15, and then to a **lycée** until the age of 18.

ces adj ❶ these; **ces photos-ci** these photos ❷ those; **ces livres-là** those books

cesse **sans cesse** adv continually; **Elle me dérange sans cesse.** She keeps interrupting me.

cesser [29] vb to stop ▷ **cesser de faire quelque chose** to stop doing something

cessez-le-feu (pl **cessez-le-feu**) nm ceasefire

c'est-à-dire adv that is

cet (f **cette**) adj
  ● **ce** changes to **cet** before a vowel and most words beginning with "h".
  ❶ this ▷ **cet hiver** this winter; **cette semaine-ci** this week ❷ that; **cet homme-là** that man; **cette nuit** (1) tonight (2) last night ▷ **J'ai très mal dormi cette nuit.** I slept very badly last night.

cette pron see **ce**

ceux (fpl **celles**) pron the ones ▷ **Prends ceux que tu préfères.** Take the ones you like best.; **ceux-ci** these ones; **celles-ci** these ones; **ceux-là** those ones; **celles-là** those ones

chacun pron ❶ each ▷ **Nous avons chacun donné dix euros.** We each gave 10 euros. ❷ everyone ▷ **Chacun fait ce qu'il veut.** Everyone does what they like.

chagrin nm **avoir du chagrin** to be very upset

chahut nm bedlam

chaîne nf ❶ chain ❷ (on TV) channel; **une chaîne hi-fi** a hi-fi system; **une chaîne laser** a CD player; **une chaîne stéréo** a music centre; **travailler à la chaîne** to work on an assembly line

chair nf flesh; **en chair et en os** in the flesh; **avoir la chair de poule** to have goose pimples
  ▌ The French actually means "to have hen's flesh"!

chaise nf chair; **une chaise longue** a deckchair

châle nm shawl

chaleur nf ❶ heat ❷ warmth

chaleureux (f **chaleureuse**) adj warm

se chamailler [29] vb (informal) to squabble ▷ Elle se chamaille sans cesse avec son frère. She's always squabbling with her brother.

chambre nf room; **une chambre à coucher** a bedroom; **une chambre d'amis** a spare room; **une chambre à un lit** a single room; **une chambre pour une personne** a single room; **une chambre pour deux personnes** a double room; **"Chambres d'hôte"** "Bed and Breakfast"

chameau (pl **chameaux**) nm camel

champ nm field

champagne nm champagne

champignon nm mushroom; **un champignon de Paris** a button mushroom

champion (f **championne**) nm/f champion

championnat nm championship

chance nf ❶ luck; **Bonne chance!** Good luck!; **par chance** luckily; **avoir de la chance** to be lucky ❷ chance

change nm exchange

changement nm change

changer [46] vb to change ▷ Il n'a pas beaucoup changé. He hasn't changed much.; **se changer** to get changed; **changer de** to change

▷ Je change de chaussures et j'arrive! I'll change my shoes and then I'll be ready!; **changer d'avis** to change one's mind ▷ Appelle-moi si tu changes d'avis. Give me a ring if you change your mind.; **changer de chaîne** to change the channel

chanson nf song

chant nm singing; **un chant de Noël** a Christmas carol

chantage nm blackmail

chanter [29] vb to sing

chanteur (f **chanteuse**) nm/f singer

chantier nm building site

Chantilly nf whipped cream

chantonner [29] vb to hum

chapeau (pl **chapeaux**) nm hat

chapelle nf chapel

chapitre nm chapter

chaque adj ❶ every ❷ each

char nm (military) tank

charabia nm (informal) gibberish

charade nf ❶ riddle ❷ charade

charbon nm coal; **le charbon de bois** charcoal

charcuterie nf ❶ pork butcher's ❷ cold meats
- A **charcuterie** sells cuts of pork
- and pork products such as
- sausages, salami and pâté, as
- well as various cooked dishes
- and salads; **charcuterie** served
- at a meal is an assortment of
- ham, sausage and pâtés.

charcutier (f **charcutière**) nm/f pork butcher

chardon nm thistle

charger [46] vb to load; **charger**

quelqu'un de faire quelque chose
to tell somebody to do something

chariot nm (at supermarket) trolley

charmant, e adj charming

charme nm charm

charmer [29] vb to charm

charrue nf plough

chasse nf ❶ hunting ❷ shooting;
tirer la chasse d'eau to flush
the toilet

chasse-neige (pl chasse-neige)
nm snowplough

chasser [29] vb ❶ to hunt ▷ Mon
père chasse le lapin. My father hunts
rabbits. ❷ to chase away ▷ Ils ont
chassé les cambrioleurs. They chased
away the robbers. ❸ to get rid of

chasseur nm hunter

chat nm cat

châtaigne nf chestnut

châtaignier nm chestnut tree

châtain adj inv brown

château (pl châteaux) nm
❶ castle; **un château fort** a castle
❷ palace

chaton nm kitten

chatouiller [29] vb to tickle

chatouilleux (f chatouilleuse)
adj ticklish

chatte nf (female) cat

chaud, e adj ❶ warm; **avoir
chaud** to be warm ❷ hot ▷ Il fait
chaud aujourd'hui. It's hot today.

chauffage nm heating; **le
chauffage central** central heating

chauffe-eau (pl chauffe-eau) nm
water heater

chauffer [29] vb to warm ▷ Je vais
mettre de l'eau à chauffer pour faire du

thé. I'm going to put some water
on to make tea.

chauffeur nm driver

chaume nm **un toit de chaume** a
thatched roof

chaussée nf road surface

chausser [29] vb **Vous chaussez
du combien?** What size shoe do
you take?

chaussette nf sock

chausson nm slipper; **un
chausson aux pommes** an apple
turnover

chaussure nf shoe; **les
chaussures de ski** ski boots

chauve adj bald

chauve-souris (pl chauves-
souris) nf (animal) bat

> The French actually means
> "bald mouse"!

chef nm ❶ head; **le chef de l'État**
the Head of State ❷ boss; **un chef
d'entreprise** a company director
❸ chef; **un chef d'orchestre** a
conductor

chef-d'œuvre (pl chefs-d'œuvre)
nm masterpiece

chemin nm ❶ path ❷ way; **en
chemin** on the way; **le chemin de
fer** the railway

cheminée nf ❶ chimney
❷ fireplace

chemise nf ❶ shirt; **une
chemise de nuit** a nightdress
❷ folder

chemisier nm blouse

chêne nm oak

chenil nm kennels

chenille nf caterpillar

chèque nm cheque; **les chèques de voyage** traveller's cheques

chéquier nm cheque book

cher (f **chère**) adj, adv ❶ dear
▷ *Chère Léa ...* Dear Léa ...
❷ expensive; **coûter cher** to be expensive

chercher [**29**] vb ❶ to look for
▷ *Je cherche mes clés.* I'm looking for my keys. ❷ to look up ▷ *chercher un mot dans le dictionnaire* to look up a word in the dictionary; **aller chercher** (1) to go to get ▷ *Elle est allée chercher du pain pour ce midi.* She's gone to get some bread for lunch. (2) to pick up ▷ *J'irai te chercher à la gare.* I'll pick you up at the station.

chercheur (f **chercheuse**) nm/f scientist

chère adj see **cher**

chéri, e adj darling
▸nm/f darling; **mon chéri** darling; **ma chérie** darling

cheval (pl **chevaux**) nm horse
▷ *un cheval de course* a racehorse; **à cheval** on horseback; **faire du cheval** to go riding

chevalier nm knight

chevalière nf signet ring

chevalin, e adj **une boucherie chevaline** a horsemeat butcher's

chevaux nmpl see **cheval**

chevet nm **une table de chevet** a bedside table; **une lampe de chevet** a bedside lamp

cheveux nmpl hair ▷ *Elle a les cheveux courts.* She's got short hair.

cheville nf ankle

chèvre nf goat; **le fromage de chèvre** goat's cheese

chevreau (pl **chevreaux**) nm (animal, leather) kid

chèvrefeuille nm honeysuckle

chevreuil nm ❶ roe deer
❷ venison

chewing-gum nm chewing gum

chez prep **chez Pierre** (1) at Pierre's house (2) to Pierre's house; **chez moi** (1) at my house ▷ *Je suis resté chez moi ce week-end.* I stayed at home this weekend. (2) to my house ▷ *Je vais rentrer chez moi.* I'm going home.; **chez le dentiste** (1) at the dentist's (2) to the dentist's

chic adj inv ❶ smart ❷ nice

chicorée nf endive

chien nm dog; **"Attention, chien méchant"** "Beware of the dog"

chienne nf (dog) bitch

chiffon nm cloth

chiffonner [**29**] vb to crease

chiffre nm figure; **les chiffres romains** Roman numerals

chignon nm (in hair) bun

Chili nm Chile

chimie nf chemistry

chimique adj chemical; **les produits chimiques** chemicals

Chine nf China

chinois, e adj Chinese
▸nm Chinese ▷ *Il apprend le chinois.* He's learning Chinese.
▸nm/f **un Chinois** (man) a Chinese; **une Chinoise** (woman) a Chinese; **les Chinois** the Chinese

chiot nm puppy

chips *nfpl* crisps

> Be careful! The French word **chips** does not mean the same as **chips** in English.

chirurgical, e (*mpl* **chirurgicaux**) *adj* **une intervention chirurgicale** an operation

chirurgie *nf* surgery; **la chirurgie esthétique** plastic surgery

chirurgien *nm* surgeon

choc *nm* shock; **Elle est encore sous le choc.** She's still in shock.

chocolat *nm* chocolate; **un chocolat chaud** a hot chocolate; **le chocolat à croquer** dark chocolate

chœur *nm* choir

choisir [39] *vb* to choose

choix *nm* ❶ choice; **avoir le choix** to have the choice ❷ selection

chômage *nm* unemployment; **être au chômage** to be unemployed

chômeur *nm* unemployed person

chômeuse *nf* unemployed woman

choquer [29] *vb* to shock

chorale *nf* choir

chose *nf* thing; **C'est peu de chose.** It's nothing really.

chou (*pl* **choux**) *nm* cabbage; **les choux de Bruxelles** Brussels sprouts; **un chou à la crème** a choux bun

chouchou (*f* **chouchoute**) *nm/f* (*informal*) teacher's pet

choucroute *nf* (*with sausages and ham*) sauerkraut

chouette *nf* owl
> ▶ *adj* (*informal*) brilliant

chou-fleur (*pl* **choux-fleurs**) *nm* cauliflower

chrétien (*f* **chrétienne**) *adj* Christian

Christ *nm* Christ

chronologique *adj* chronological

chronomètre *nm* stopwatch

chronométrer [35] *vb* to time

chrysanthème *nm* chrysanthemum
> ● Chrysanthemums are strongly associated with funerals in France.

chuchoter [29] *vb* to whisper

chut *excl* Shh!

chute *nf* fall; **faire une chute** to fall; **une chute d'eau** a waterfall; **la chute des cheveux** hair loss; **les chutes de neige** snowfalls

Chypre *n* Cyprus

-ci *adv* **ce livre-ci** this book; **ces bottes-ci** these boots

cible *nf* target

ciboulette *nf* chives

cicatrice *nf* scar

se cicatriser [29] *vb* to heal up
> ▷ *Cette plaie s'est vite cicatrisée.* This wound has healed up quickly.

ci-contre *adv* opposite

ci-dessous *adv* below

ci-dessus *adv* above

cidre *nm* cider

ciel *nm* ❶ sky ❷ heaven

cierge *nm* (*in church*) candle

cigale *nf* cicada

cigare *nm* cigar

cigarette *nf* cigarette

cigogne *nf* stork

ci-joint adv enclosed ▷ Veuillez trouver ci-joint mon curriculum vitae. Please find enclosed my CV.

cil nm eyelash

ciment nm cement

cimetière nm cemetery

cinéaste nmf film-maker

cinéma nm cinema

cinq num five ▷ Il a cinq ans. He's five.; **le cinq février** the fifth of February

cinquantaine nf about fifty; **Il a la cinquantaine.** He's in his fifties.

cinquante num fifty ▷ Il a cinquante ans. He's fifty.; **cinquante et un** fifty-one; **cinquante-deux** fifty-two

cinquième adj fifth
▶ nf year 8
In French secondary schools, years are counted from the **sixième** (youngest) to **première** and **terminale** (oldest).

cintre nm coat hanger

cirage nm shoe polish

circonflexe adj **un accent circonflexe** a circumflex

circonstance nf circumstance

circulation nf ❶ traffic ❷ circulation

circuler [29] vb to run ▷ Il n'y a qu'un bus sur trois qui circule. Only one bus in three is running.

cire nf wax

ciré nm oilskin jacket

cirer [29] vb (shoes, floor) to polish

cirque nm circus

ciseaux nmpl **une paire de ciseaux** a pair of scissors

citadin nm city dweller

citation nf quotation

cité nf estate ▷ J'habite dans une cité. I live on an estate.; **une cité universitaire** halls of residence; **une cité-dortoir** a dormitory town

citer [29] vb to quote

citoyen (f **citoyenne**) nm/f citizen

citoyenneté nf citizenship

citron nm lemon; **un citron vert** a lime; **un citron pressé** a fresh lemon juice

citronnade nf still lemonade

citrouille nf pumpkin

civet nm stew

civil, e adj civilian; **en civil** in civilian clothes

civilisation nf civilization

civique adj **l'instruction civique** PSHE

clair, e adj, adv ❶ light ❷ (water) clear; **voir clair** to see clearly; **le clair de lune** moonlight

clairement adv clearly

clairière nf clearing

clandestin, e adj **un passager clandestin** a stowaway

claque nf slap

claquer [29] vb ❶ to bang ▷ On entend des volets qui claquent. You can hear shutters banging. ❷ to slam ▷ Elle est partie en claquant la porte. She left, slamming the door behind her.

claquettes nfpl **faire des claquettes** to tap-dance

clarinette nf clarinet

classe nf ❶ class ❷ classroom

classer [29] vb to arrange
▷ *Les livres sont classés par ordre alphabétique.* The books are arranged in alphabetical order.

classeur nm ring binder

classique adj ❶ classical ❷ classic

clavier nm (of computer, typewriter) keyboard

clé nf ❶ key ❷ clef

clef nf = **clé**

client (f cliente) nm/f customer

clientèle nf customers

cligner [29] vb **cligner des yeux** to blink

clignotant nm indicator

climat nm climate

climatisation nf air conditioning

climatisé, e adj air-conditioned

clin d'œil (pl clins d'œil) nm wink; **en un clin d'œil** in a flash

clinique nf private hospital

cliquer [29] vb to click ▷ **cliquer sur une icône** to click on an icon

clochard nm tramp

cloche nf bell

clocher nm ❶ church tower ❷ steeple

clone nm clone

cloner [29] vb to clone

clou nm nail; **un clou de girofle** a clove

clown nm clown

club nm club

cobaye nm guinea pig

coca nm Coke®

cocaïne nf cocaine

coccinelle nf ladybird

cocher [29] vb to tick ▷ *Cochez la bonne réponse.* Tick the right answer.

cochon nm pig; **un cochon d'Inde** a guinea pig
▶ adj (f cochonne) (informal) dirty

cocktail nm ❶ cocktail ❷ cocktail party

coco nm **une noix de coco** a coconut

cocorico excl ❶ Cock-a-doodle-doo! ❷ Three cheers for France!
- The symbol of France is the
- cockerel and so **cocorico!**
- is sometimes used as an
- expression of French national
- pride.

cocotte nf (pan) casserole; **une cocotte-minute®** a pressure cooker

code nm code; **le code de la route** the highway code; **le code postal** the postcode

cœur nm heart; **avoir bon cœur** to be kind-hearted; **la dame de cœur** the queen of hearts; **avoir mal au cœur** to feel sick; **par cœur** by heart ▷ **apprendre quelque chose par cœur** to learn something by heart

coffre nm ❶ (of car) boot ❷ (furniture) chest

coffre-fort (pl coffres-forts) nm safe

coffret nm **un coffret à bijoux** a jewellery box

cognac nm brandy

se cogner [29] vb **se cogner à quelque chose** to bang into something

coiffé, e adj **Tu es bien coiffée.** Your hair looks nice.

coiffer [29] vb **se coiffer** to do

one's hair

coiffeur (f **coiffeuse**) nm/f hairdresser

coiffure nf hairstyle; **un salon de coiffure** a hairdresser's

coin nm corner; **au coin de la rue** on the corner of the street; **Tu habites dans le coin?** Do you live near here?; **Je ne suis pas du coin.** I'm not from here.; **le bistrot du coin** the local pub

coincé, e adj ① stuck ② stuffy

coincer [13] vb to jam ▷ **La porte est coincée.** The door's jammed.

coïncidence nf coincidence

col nm ① collar ② (of mountain) pass

colère nf anger; **Je suis en colère.** I'm angry.; **se mettre en colère** to get angry

colin nm hake

colique nf diarrhoea

colis nm parcel

collaborer [29] vb to collaborate

collant, e adj ① sticky ② clingy ▶ nm tights

colle nf ① glue ② detention; **Je n'en sais rien: tu me poses une colle.** (informal) I really don't know: you've got me there.

collecte nf (of money) collection

collection nf collection

collectionner [29] vb to collect

collège nm secondary school
- In France pupils go to a **collège** between the ages of 11 and 15, and then to a **lycée** until the age of 18.

collégien nm schoolboy

collégienne nf schoolgirl

collègue nmf colleague

coller [29] vb ① to stick ▷ **Il y a un chewing-gum collé sous la chaise.** There's a bit of chewing gum stuck under the chair. ② to be sticky ▷ **Ce timbre ne colle plus.** This stamp won't stick on. ③ to press ▷ **J'ai collé mon oreille au mur.** I pressed my ear against the wall.

collier nm ① necklace ② (of dog, cat) collar

colline nf hill

collision nf crash

colombe nf dove

colonie nf **aller en colonie de vacances** to go to summer camp

colonne nf column; **la colonne vertébrale** the spine

colorant nm colouring

coloris nm colour

coma nm coma ▷ **être dans le coma** to be in a coma

combat nm fighting; **un combat de boxe** a boxing match

combattant nm **un ancien combattant** a war veteran

combattre [10] vb to fight

combien adv ① how much; **C'est combien?** How much is that? ▷ **Combien est-ce que ça coûte?** How much does it cost? ② how many; **combien de** (1) how much (2) how many; **combien de temps** how long; **Il y a combien de temps?** How long ago?; **On est le combien aujourd'hui? — On est le vingt.** What's the date today? — It's the 20th.

combinaison nf ❶ combination ❷ (petticoat) slip; **une combinaison de plongée** a wetsuit; **une combinaison de ski** a ski suit

comble nm **Alors ça, c'est le comble!** That's the last straw!

comédie nf comedy; **une comédie musicale** a musical

comédien nm actor

Be careful! The French word **comédien** does not mean comedian.

comédienne nf actress

comestible adj edible

comique adj comical
▶ nm comedian

comité nm committee

commandant nm (of ship, plane) captain

commande nf order; **être aux commandes** to be at the controls

commander [29] vb ❶ to order ▷ J'ai commandé une robe par catalogue. I've ordered a dress from a catalogue. ❷ to give orders ▷ C'est moi qui commande ici, pas vous! I give the orders here, not you!

comme conj, adv ❶ like ▷ Il est comme son père. He's like his father. ❷ for ▷ Qu'est-ce que tu veux comme dessert? What would you like for pudding? ❸ as ▷ J'ai travaillé comme serveuse cet été. I worked as a waitress this summer. Do as you like.; **comme ça** like this ▷ Ça se plie comme ça. You fold it like this.;

comme il faut properly ▷ Mets le couvert comme il faut! Set the table properly!; **Comme tu as grandi!** How you've grown!; **Regarde comme c'est beau!** Look, isn't it lovely!; **comme ci comme ça** so-so

commencement nm beginning

commencer [13] vb to start ▷ Les cours commencent à huit heures. Lessons start at 8 o'clock.

comment adv how; **Comment allez-vous?** How are you?; **Comment dit-on "pomme" en anglais?** How do you say "pomme" in English?; **Comment s'appelle-t-il?** What's his name?; **Comment?** What did you say?

commentaire nm comment

commérages nmpl gossip

commerçant nm shopkeeper

commerce nm ❶ trade; **le commerce électronique** e-commerce; **le commerce équitable** fair trade ❷ business ❸ shop; **On trouve ça dans le commerce.** You can find it in the shops.

commercial, e (mpl commerciaux) adj **un centre commercial** a shopping centre

commettre [48] vb to commit

commissaire nm police superintendent

commissariat nm police station

commissions nfpl shopping

commode nf chest of drawers ▶ adj handy; **Son père n'est pas commode.** His father is a difficult character.

commun, e adj shared; **en commun** in common; **les transports en commun** public transport; **mettre quelque chose en commun** to share something

communauté nf community

communication nf communication; **une communication téléphonique** a telephone call

communion nf communion

communiquer [29] vb to communicate

communiste adj communist

compact, e adj compact; **un disque compact** a compact disc

compagne nf ❶ companion ❷ (living together) partner

compagnie nf company; **une compagnie d'assurances** an insurance company; **une compagnie aérienne** an airline

compagnon nm ❶ companion ❷ (living together) partner

comparaison nf comparison

comparer [29] vb to compare

compartiment nm (on train) compartment

compas nm (for drawing circles) pair of compasses

compatible adj compatible

compétence nf competence

compétent, e adj competent

compétitif (f **compétitive**) adj competitive

compétition nf competition; **avoir l'esprit de compétition** to be competitive

complet (f **complète**) adj ❶ complete ❷ full; "complet" "no vacancies"; **le pain complet** wholemeal bread
▶ nm (for man) suit

complètement adv completely

compléter [35] vb to complete
▷ Complétez les phrases suivantes. Complete the following phrases.

complexe adj complex

complexé, e adj screwed-up

complication nf complication

complice nmf accomplice

compliments nmpl compliment; **faire des compliments** to compliment

compliqué, e adj complicated

complot nm plot

comportement nm behaviour

comporter [29] vb ❶ to consist of
▷ Le château comporte trois parties. The castle consists of three parts.
❷ to have ▷ Ce modèle comporte un écran couleur. This model has a colour screen.; **se comporter** to behave

composer [29] vb (music, text) to compose; **composer un numéro** to dial a number; **se composer de** to consist of

compositeur (f **compositrice**) nm/f composer

composition nf test

compostage nm date stamping

composter [29] vb to punch
▷ N'oublie pas de composter ton billet avant de monter dans le train. Remember to punch your ticket before you get on the train.

- In France you have to punch
- your ticket on the platform to
- validate it before getting onto
- the train.

compote nf stewed fruit; **la compote de prunes** stewed plums

compréhensible adj understandable

compréhensif (f **compréhensive**) adj understanding

> Be careful! **compréhensif** does not mean **comprehensive**.

compréhension nf ❶ comprehension ❷ sympathy; **Elle a fait preuve de beaucoup de compréhension à mon égard.** She was very sympathetic towards me.

comprendre [66] vb ❶ to understand ▷ Je ne comprends pas ce que vous dites. I don't understand what you're saying. ❷ to include ▷ Le forfait ne comprend pas la location des skis. The price doesn't include ski hire.

comprimé nm tablet

compris, e adj included ▷ Le service n'est pas compris. Service is not included.; **y compris** including; **non compris** excluding; **cent euros tout compris** 100 euros all-inclusive

compromettre [48] vb to compromise

compromis nm compromise

comptabilité nf accounting

comptable nmf accountant

comptant adv **payer comptant** to pay cash

compte nm account; **Le compte est bon.** That's the right amount.; **tenir compte de (1)** to take into account **(2)** to take notice of; **travailler à son compte** to be self-employed; **en fin de compte** all things considered

compter [29] vb to count

compte rendu (pl **comptes rendus**) nm report

compteur nm meter

comptoir nm bar

con (f **conne**) adj (rude) bloody stupid

se concentrer [29] vb to concentrate

conception nf design

concernant prep regarding

concerner [29] vb to concern ▷ en ce qui me concerne as far as I'm concerned; **Je ne me sens pas concerné.** I don't feel it's anything to do with me.

concert nm concert

concierge nmf caretaker

conclure [14] vb to conclude

conclusion nf conclusion

concombre nm cucumber

concorder [29] vb to tally ▷ Les dates concordent. The dates tally.

concours nm ❶ competition ❷ competitive exam

concret (f **concrète**) adj concrete

conçu vb designed ▷ Ces appartements sont très mal conçus. These flats are very badly designed.

concurrence nf competition

concurrent (f **concurrente**) nm/f competitor

condamner [29] vb ❶ to sentence ▷ *condamner à mort* to sentence to death ❷ to condemn ▷ *Le gouvernement a condamné cette décision.* The government condemned this decision.

condition nf condition; **à condition que** provided that; **les conditions de travail** working conditions

conditionnel nm conditional tense

conducteur (f **conductrice**) nm/f driver

conduire [24] vb to drive ▷ *Est-ce que tu sais conduire?* Can you drive?; **se conduire** to behave ▷ *Il s'est mal conduit.* He behaved badly.

conduite nf behaviour

conférence nf ❶ lecture ❷ conference

se confesser [29] vb to go to confession

confettis nmpl confetti

confiance nf ❶ trust; **avoir confiance en quelqu'un** to trust somebody ❷ confidence; **Tu peux avoir confiance. Il sera à l'heure.** You don't need to worry. He'll be on time.; **confiance en soi** self-confidence

confiant, e adj confident

confidences nfpl **faire des confidences à quelqu'un** to confide in someone

confidentiel (f **confidentielle**) adj confidential

confier [20] vb **se confier à quelqu'un** to confide in somebody

▷ *Elle s'est confiée à sa meilleure amie.* She confided in her best friend.

confirmer [29] vb to confirm

confiserie nf sweet shop

confisquer [29] vb to confiscate

confit, e adj **des fruits confits** crystallized fruits

confiture nf jam; **la confiture d'oranges** marmalade

conflit nm conflict

confondre [70] vb to mix up ▷ *On le confond souvent avec son frère.* People often mix him up with his brother.

confort nm comfort; **tout confort** with all mod cons

confortable adj comfortable

confus, e adj ❶ unclear ❷ embarrassed

confusion nf ❶ confusion ❷ embarrassment

congé nm holiday; **en congé** on holiday; **un congé de maladie** sick leave

congélateur nm freezer

congeler [2] vb to freeze

conjonction nf conjunction

conjonctivite nf conjunctivitis

conjugaison nf conjugation

connaissance nf ❶ knowledge ❷ acquaintance; **perdre connaissance** to lose consciousness; **faire la connaissance de quelqu'un** to meet somebody

connaître [15] vb to know ▷ *Je ne connais pas du tout cette région.* I don't know this area at all.; **Ils se sont connus à Nantes.** They first met in Nantes.; **s'y connaître en quelque chose** to know about something ▷ *Je ne m'y connais pas beaucoup en musique classique.* I don't know much about classical music.

se connecter *vb* to log on

connerie *nf* (rude) bloody stupid thing

connu, e *adj* well-known

conquérir [3] *vb* to conquer

consacrer [29] *vb* to devote ▷ *Il consacre beaucoup de temps à ses enfants.* He devotes a lot of time to his children.

conscience *nf* conscience; **prendre conscience de** to become aware of

consciencieux (f **consciencieuse**) *adj* conscientious

conscient, e *adj* conscious

consécutif (f **consécutive**) *adj* consecutive

conseil *nm* advice; **un conseil** a piece of advice

conseiller [29] *vb* ❶ to advise ▷ *Il a été mal conseillé.* He has been badly advised. ❷ to recommend ▷ *Il m'a conseillé ce livre.* He recommended this book to me.
▶ *nm* ❶ (political) councillor ❷ adviser; **le conseiller d'orientation** the careers adviser

consentement *nm* consent

consentir [78] *vb* to agree ▷ *consentir à quelque chose* to agree to something

conséquence *nf* consequence; **en conséquence** consequently

conséquent *adj* **par conséquent** consequently

conservatoire *nm* school of music

conserve *nf* tin; **une boîte de conserve** a tin; **les conserves** tinned food; **en conserve** tinned

conserver [29] *vb* to keep ▷ *J'ai conservé toutes ses lettres.* I've kept all her letters.; **se conserver** to keep ▷ *Ce pain se conserve plus d'une semaine.* This bread will keep for more than a week.

considérable *adj* considerable

considération *nf* **prendre quelque chose en considération** to take something into consideration

considérer [35] *vb* **considérer que** to believe that ▷ *Je considère que le gouvernement devrait investir davantage dans l'éducation.* I believe that the government should invest more money in education.

consigne *nf* left-luggage office; **une consigne automatique** a left-luggage locker

consistant, e *adj* substantial

consister [29] *vb* **consister à** to consist ▷ *En quoi consiste votre travail?* What does your job involve?

console de jeu *nf* games console

consoler [29] *vb* to console

consommateur (f **consommatrice**) *nm/f* ❶ consumer ❷ (in café) customer

consommation *nf* ❶ consumption ❷ drink

consommer [29] vb ① to use
▷ Ces grosses voitures consomment beaucoup d'essence. These big cars use a lot of petrol. ② to have a drink ▷ Est-ce qu'on peut consommer à la terrasse? Can we have drinks outside?

consonne nf consonant

constamment adv constantly

constant, e adj constant

constater [29] vb to notice

constipé, e adj constipated

constitué, e adj être constitué(e) de to consist of

constituer [29] vb to make up ▷ les États qui constituent la Fédération russe the states which make up the Russian Federation

construction nf building; une maison en construction a house being built

construire [24] vb to build ▷ Ils font construire une maison neuve. They're having a new house built.

consulat nm consulate

consultation nf les heures de consultation surgery hours

consulter [29] vb ① to consult ▷ Tu devrais consulter un médecin. You should see a doctor. ② to see patients ▷ Le docteur ne consulte pas le samedi. The doctor doesn't see patients on Saturdays.

contact nm contact; Il a le contact facile. He's very approachable.; garder le contact avec quelqu'un to keep in touch with somebody

contacter [29] vb to get in touch with ▷ Je te contacterai dès que j'aurai

des nouvelles. I'll get in touch with you as soon as I have some news.

contagieux (f contagieuse) adj infectious

contaminer [29] vb to contaminate

conte de fées (pl contes de fées) nm fairy tale

contempler [29] vb to gaze at

contemporain, e adj contemporary; un auteur contemporain a modern writer

contenir [84] vb to contain ▷ un portefeuille contenant de l'argent a wallet containing money

content, e adj glad ▷ Je suis content que tu sois venu. I'm glad you've come.; content de pleased with

contenter [29] vb to please ▷ Il est difficile à contenter. He's hard to please.; Je me contente de peu. I can make do with very little.

contesté, e adj controversial

continent nm continent

continu, e adj continuous; faire la journée continue to work without taking a full lunch break

continuellement adv constantly

continuer [29] vb to carry on ▷ Continuez sans moi! Carry on without me! ▷ Il ne veut pas continuer ses études. He doesn't want to go on studying.; continuer à faire quelque chose to go on doing something ▷ Ils ont continué à regarder la télé sans me dire bonjour. They went on watching TV without saying hello to me.; continuer de faire quelque chose to go on

a
b
c
d
e
f
g
h
i
j
k
l
m
n
o
p
q
r
s
t
u
v
w
x
y
z

doing something ▷ *Il continue de fumer malgré son asthme.* He keeps on smoking, despite his asthma.

contourner [28] vb to go round
▷ *La route contourne la ville.* The road goes round the town.

contraceptif nm contraceptive

contraception nf contraception

contractuel (f **contractuelle**) nm/f traffic warden

contradiction nf contradiction; **par esprit de contradiction** just to be awkward

contraire nm opposite; **au contraire** on the contrary

contrarier [20] vb ❶ to annoy
▷ *Il avait l'air contrarié.* He looked annoyed. ❷ to upset ▷ *Est-ce que tu serais contrarié si je ne venais pas?* Would you be upset if I didn't come?

contraste nm contrast

contrat nm contract

contravention nf parking ticket

contre prep ❶ against ▷ *Ne mets pas ton vélo contre le mur.* Don't put your bike against the wall. ▷ *Tu es pour ou contre ce projet?* Are you for or against this plan? ❷ for
▷ *échanger quelque chose contre quelque chose* to swap something for something; **par contre** on the other hand

contrebande nf smuggling; **des produits de contrebande** smuggled goods

contrebasse nf double bass

contrecœur: **à contrecœur** adv reluctantly

contredire [28] vb to contradict
▷ *Il ne supporte pas d'être contredit.* He can't stand being contradicted.

contre-indication nf "Contre-indication en cas d'eczéma" "Should not be used by people with eczema"

contresens nm mistranslation

contretemps nm *Désolé d'être en retard: j'ai eu un contretemps.* Sorry I'm late: I was held up.

contribuer [29] vb **contribuer à** to contribute to ▷ *Est-ce que tu vas contribuer au cadeau pour Marie?* Do you want to contribute to Marie's present?

contrôle nm ❶ control ▷ *le contrôle des passeports* passport control ❷ check; **un contrôle d'identité** an identity check; **le contrôle des billets** ticket inspection
❸ test ▷ *un contrôle antidopage* a drugs test; **le contrôle continu** continuous assessment

contrôler [29] vb to check
▷ *Personne n'a contrôlé mon billet.* Nobody checked my ticket.

contrôleur (f **contrôleuse**) nm/f ticket inspector

controversé, e adj controversial

convaincre [87] vb ❶ to persuade
▷ *Il a essayé de me convaincre de rester.* He tried to persuade me to stay. ❷ to convince ▷ *Tu n'as pas l'air convaincu.* You don't look convinced.

convalescence nf convalescence

convenable adj decent; **Ce n'est pas convenable.** It's bad manners.

convenir [**90**] vb **convenir à**
to suit ▷ *Est-ce que cette date te
convient?* Does this date suit you?;
convenir de to agree on ▷ *Nous
avons convenu d'une date.* We've
agreed on a date.

conventionné, e adj **un médecin
conventionné** a Health Service
doctor

- All doctors in France charge
- for treatment, but patients
- of Health Service doctors get
- their money refunded by the
- government.

convenu, e adj agreed
conversation nf conversation
convocation nf notification
convoquer [**29**] vb **convoquer
quelqu'un à une réunion** to invite
somebody to a meeting
cool adj (informal) cool
coopération nf co-operation
coopérer [**35**] vb to co-operate
coordonnées nfpl contact details
copain nm ❶ (informal) friend
❷ boyfriend
copie nf ❶ copy ❷ paper ▷ *Il a des
copies à corriger ce week-end.* He's
got some papers to mark this
weekend.
copier [**20**] vb to copy; **copier-
coller** to copy and paste
copieux (f **copieuse**) adj hearty
copine nf ❶ (informal) friend
❷ girlfriend
coq nm cockerel
coque nf (of boat) hull; **un œuf à la
coque** a soft-boiled egg
coquelicot nm poppy

coqueluche nf whooping cough
coquillage nm ❶ shellfish ❷ shell
coquille nf shell; **une coquille
d'œuf** an eggshell; **une coquille
Saint-Jacques** a scallop
coquin, e adj cheeky
cor nm horn
corbeau (pl **corbeaux**) nm crow
corbeille nf ❶ basket; **une
corbeille à papier** a wastepaper
basket ❷ (computer) recycle bin
corde nf ❶ rope ❷ (of violin, tennis
racket) string; **une corde à linge** a
clothes line
cordonnerie nf shoe repair shop
cordonnier nm cobbler
coriace adj tough
corne nf horn
cornemuse nf bagpipes
cornet nm **un cornet de frites** a
bag of chips; **un cornet de glace**
an ice cream cone
cornichon nm gherkin
Cornouailles nfpl Cornwall
corps nm body
correct, e adj ❶ correct
❷ reasonable ▷ *un salaire correct* a
reasonable salary
correction nf correction
correspondance nf
❶ correspondence; **un
cours par correspondance** a
correspondence course ❷ (train,
plane) connection
correspondant (f
correspondante) nm/f
penfriend
correspondre [**70**] vb to
correspond; **Faites correspondre**

les phrases. Match the sentences together.

corridor nm corridor

corriger [46] vb to mark ▷ *Vous pouvez corriger mon test?* Can you mark my test?

corsage nm blouse

corse adj Corsican
  ▶ nm/f **un Corse** (man) a Corsican; **une Corse** (woman) a Corsican
  ▶ nf **la Corse** Corsica

corvée nf chore

costaud, e adj brawny

costume nm ❶ (man's) suit ❷ (theatre) costume

côte nf ❶ coastline; **la Côte d'Azur** the French Riviera ❷ hill ❸ rib ❹ chop; **une côte de bœuf** a rib of beef; **côte à côte** side by side

côté nm side; **à côté de (1)** next to ▷ *Le café est à côté du sucre.* The coffee's next to the sugar. **(2)** next door to ▷ *Il habite à côté de chez moi.* He lives next door to me.; **de l'autre côté** on the other side; **De quel côté est-il parti?** Which way did he go?; **mettre quelque chose de côté** to save something

côtelette nf chop

cotisation nf ❶ (to club, union) subscription ❷ (to pension, national insurance) contributions; **cotisations sociales** social security contributions

coton nm cotton; **le coton hydrophile** cotton wool

Coton-tige® (pl **Cotons-tiges**) nm cotton bud

cou nm neck

couchant adj **le soleil couchant** the setting sun

couche nf ❶ layer ▷ *la couche d'ozone* the ozone layer ❷ (of paint, varnish) coat ❸ nappy

couché, e adj ❶ lying down ▷ *Il était couché sur le tapis.* He was lying on the carpet. ❷ in bed ▷ *Il est déjà couché.* He's already in bed.

coucher nm **un coucher de soleil** a sunset

se coucher [29] vb ❶ to go to bed ▷ *Je me suis couché tard hier soir.* I went to bed late last night. ❷ (sun) to set

couchette nf ❶ (on train) couchette ❷ (on boat) bunk

coude nm elbow

coudre [16] vb ❶ to sew ▷ *J'aime coudre.* I like sewing. ❷ to sew on ▷ *Il ne sait même pas coudre un bouton.* He can't even sew a button on.

couette nf duvet

couettes nfpl bunches

couler [29] vb ❶ to run ▷ *Ne laissez pas couler les robinets.* Don't leave the taps running. ❷ to flow ▷ *La rivière coulait lentement.* The river was flowing slowly. ❸ to leak ▷ *Mon stylo coule.* My pen's leaking. ❹ to sink ▷ *Le bateau a coulé.* The boat sank.

couleur nf colour; **Tu as pris des couleurs.** You've got a tan.

couleuvre nf grass snake

coulisses nfpl (in theatre) wings; **dans les coulisses** behind the scenes

couloir nm corridor

coup nm ❶ knock ▷ donner un coup à quelque chose to give something a knock ❷ blow ▷ Il m'a donné un coup! He hit me!; **un coup de pied** a kick; **un coup de poing** a punch ❸ shock; **un coup de feu** a shot; **un coup de fil** (informal) a ring; **donner un coup de main à quelqu'un** to give somebody a hand; **un coup d'œil** a quick look; **attraper un coup de soleil** to get sunburnt; **un coup de téléphone** a phone call; **un coup de tonnerre** a clap of thunder; **boire un coup** (informal) to have a drink; **après coup** afterwards; **à tous les coups** (informal) every time; **du premier coup** first time; **sur le coup** at first

coupable adj guilty
▶ nmf culprit

coupe nf (sport) cup; **une coupe de cheveux** a haircut; **une coupe de champagne** a glass of champagne

coupe-ongle nm nail-clippers

couper [29] vb ❶ to cut ❷ to turn off ▷ couper le courant to turn off the electricity ❸ to take a short-cut ▷ On peut couper par la forêt. There's a short-cut through the woods.; **couper l'appétit** to spoil one's appetite; **se couper** to cut oneself ▷ Je me suis coupé le doigt avec une boîte de conserve. I cut my finger on a tin.; **couper la parole à quelqu'un** to interrupt somebody

couple nm couple

couplet nm verse

coupure nf cut; **une coupure de courant** a power cut

cour nf ❶ yard ▷ la cour de l'école the school yard ❷ court

courage nm courage

courageux (f **courageuse**) adj brave

couramment adv ❶ fluently ❷ commonly

courant, e adj ❶ common ❷ standard
▶ nm ❶ (of river) current; **un courant d'air** a draught ❷ power ▷ une panne de courant a power cut; **Je le ferai dans le courant de la semaine.** I'll do it some time during the week.; **être au courant de quelque chose** to know about something; **mettre quelqu'un au courant de quelque chose** to tell somebody about something; **Tu es au courant?** Have you heard about it?; **se tenir au courant de quelque chose** to keep up with something

coureur nm runner; **un coureur à pied** a runner; **un coureur cycliste** a racing cyclist; **un coureur automobile** a racing driver

coureuse nf runner

courgette nf courgette

courir [17] vb to run ▷ Elle a traversé la rue en courant. She ran across the street.; **courir un risque** to run a risk

couronne nf crown

courons, courez vb see courir

courriel nm email

a
b
c
d
e
f
g
h
i
j
k
l
m
n
o
p
q
r
s
t
u
v
w
x
y
z

courrier nm mail; **N'oublie pas de poster le courrier.** Don't forget to post the letters.; **le courrier électronique** email

> Be careful! The French word **courrier** does not mean **courier**.

courroie nf **la courroie du ventilateur** fan belt

cours nm ❶ lesson ▷ un cours d'espagnol a Spanish lesson ❷ course ▷ un cours intensif a crash course ❸ rate; **au cours de** during

course nf ❶ running ▷ la course de fond long-distance running ❷ race ▷ une course hippique a horse race ❸ shopping ▷ J'ai juste une course à faire. I've just got a bit of shopping to do.; **faire les courses** to go shopping

court, e adj short
> ▶ nm **un court de tennis** a tennis court

couru vb see **courir**

couscous nm couscous
- couscous is a spicy North
- African dish made with meat,
- vegetables and steamed
- semolina.

cousin (f cousine) nm/f cousin

coussin nm cushion

coût nm cost

couteau (pl couteaux) nm knife

coûter [29] vb to cost ▷ Est-ce que ça coûte cher? Does it cost a lot?; **Combien ça coûte?** How much is it?

coûteux (f coûteuse) adj expensive

coutume nf custom

couture nf ❶ sewing; **faire de la couture** to sew ❷ seam

couturier nm fashion designer

couturière nf dressmaker

couvercle nm ❶ (of pan) lid ❷ (of tube, jar, spray can) top

couvert, e adj (sky) overcast; **couvert de** covered with
> ▶ nm **mettre le couvert** to lay the table
> ▶ vb see **couvrir**

couverts nmpl cutlery

couverture nf blanket

couvre-lit nm bedspread

couvrir [56] vb to cover ▷ Le chien est revenu couvert de boue. The dog came back covered with mud.; **se couvrir (1)** to wrap up ▷ Couvre-toi bien: il fait très froid dehors. Wrap up well: it's very cold outside. **(2)** to cloud over ▷ Le ciel se couvre. The sky's clouding over.

crabe nm crab

cracher [29] vb to spit

crachin nm drizzle

craie nf chalk

craindre [18] vb to fear ▷ Tu n'as rien à craindre. You've got nothing to fear.

crainte nf fear; **de crainte de** for fear of

craintif (f craintive) adj timid

crampe nf cramp

cran nm (in belt) hole; **avoir du cran** (informal) to have guts

crâne nm skull

crâner [29] vb (informal) to show off

crapaud nm toad

craquer [29] vb ❶ to creak ▷ Le plancher craque. The floor creaks. ❷ to burst ▷ Ma fermeture éclair a craqué. My zip's burst. ❸ to crack up ▷ Je vais finir par craquer! (informal) I'm going to crack up at this rate!; **Quand j'ai vu cette robe, j'ai craqué!** (informal) When I saw that dress, I couldn't resist it!

crasse nf filth

cravate nf tie

crawl nm crawl

crayon nm pencil ▷ un crayon de couleur a coloured pencil; **un crayon feutre** a felt-tip pen

création nf creation

crèche nf ❶ nursery ❷ nativity scene

crédit nm credit

créer [19] vb to create

crémaillère nf **pendre la crémaillère** to have a house-warming party

crème nf cream; **la crème anglaise** custard; **la crème Chantilly** whipped cream; **la crème fouettée** whipped cream; **une crème caramel** a crème caramel; **une crème au chocolat** a chocolate dessert
  ▶ nm white coffee

crémerie nf cheese shop

crémeux (f **crémeuse**) adj creamy

crêpe nf pancake

crêperie nf pancake restaurant

crépuscule nm dusk

cresson nm watercress

Crète nf Crete

creuser [29] vb (a hole) to dig; **Ça creuse!** That gives you a real appetite!; **se creuser la cervelle** (informal) to rack one's brains

creux (f **creuse**) adj hollow

crevaison nf puncture

crevé, e adj ❶ punctured ▷ un pneu crevé a puncture ❷ (informal) knackered

crever [44] vb ❶ (balloon) to burst ❷ (motorist) to have a puncture ▷ J'ai crevé sur l'autoroute. I had a puncture on the motorway.; **Je crève de faim!** (informal) I'm starving!; **Je crève de froid!** (informal) I'm freezing!

crevette nf prawn; **une crevette rose** a prawn; **une crevette grise** a shrimp

cri nm ❶ scream ❷ call; **C'est le dernier cri.** It's the latest fashion.

criard, e adj (colours) garish

cric nm (for car) jack

crier [20] vb to shout; **crier de douleur** to scream with pain

crime nm ❶ crime ❷ murder

criminel (f **criminelle**) nm/f ❶ criminal ❷ murderer

crin nm horsehair

crinière nf mane

criquet nm grasshopper

crise nf ❶ crisis; **la crise économique** the recession ❷ attack ▷ une crise d'asthme an asthma attack ▷ une crise cardiaque a heart attack; **une crise de foie** an upset stomach; **piquer une crise de nerfs** to go hysterical;

avoir une crise de fou rire to have a fit of the giggles

cristal (pl **cristaux**) nm crystal

critère nm criterion

critique adj critical
- ▶ nm critic
- ▶ nf ❶ criticism ❷ review

critiquer [29] vb to criticize

Croatie nf Croatia

crochet nm ❶ hook ❷ detour
- ▷ **faire un crochet** to make a detour
- ❸ crochet

crocodile nm crocodile

croire [21] vb to believe; **croire que** to think that ▷ *Tu crois qu'il fera meilleur demain?* Do you think the weather will be better tomorrow?; **croire à quelque chose** to believe in something; **croire en Dieu** to believe in God

crois vb see **croire**

croîs vb see **croître**

croisement nm crossroads

croiser [29] vb J'ai croisé Anne-Laure dans la rue. I bumped into Anne-Laure in the street.; **croiser les bras** to fold one's arms; **croiser les jambes** to cross one's legs; **se croiser** to pass each other

croisière nf cruise

croissance nf growth

croissant nm croissant

croit vb see **croire**

croître [22] vb to grow

croix nf cross; **la Croix-Rouge** the Red Cross

croque-madame (pl **croque-madame**) nm toasted ham and cheese sandwich with fried egg on top

croque-monsieur (pl **croque-monsieur**) nm toasted ham and cheese sandwich

croquer [29] vb to munch; **le chocolat à croquer** plain chocolate

croquis nm sketch

crotte nf **une crotte de chien** dog dirt

crottin nm ❶ manure ❷ small goat's cheese

croustillant, e adj crusty

croûte nf ❶ (of bread) crust; **en croûte** in pastry ❷ (of cheese) rind ❸ (on skin) scab

croûton nm ❶ (end of loaf) crust ❷ crouton

croyons, croyez vb see **croire**

CRS nmpl French riot police

cru, e adj raw; **le jambon cru** Parma ham
- ▶ vb see **croire**

crû vb see **croître**

cruauté nf cruelty

cruche nf jug

crudités nfpl assorted raw vegetables

cruel (f **cruelle**) adj cruel

crustacés nmpl shellfish

cube nm cube; **un mètre cube** a cubic metre

cueillette nf picking

cueillir [23] vb (flowers, fruit) to pick

cuiller, cuillère nf spoon; **une cuiller à café** a teaspoon; **une cuiller à soupe** a soup spoon

cuillerée nf spoonful

cuir *nm* leather; **le cuir chevelu** the scalp

cuire [**24**] *vb* to cook ▷ *cuire quelque chose à feu vif* to cook something on a high heat; **cuire quelque chose au four** to bake something; **cuire quelque chose à la vapeur** to steam something; **faire cuire** to cook ▷ *"Faire cuire pendant une heure"* "Cook for one hour"; **bien cuit** well done; **trop cuit** overdone

cuisine *nf* ① kitchen ② cooking; **faire la cuisine** to cook

cuisiné, e *adj* **un plat cuisiné** a ready-made meal

cuisiner [**29**] *vb* to cook ▷ *J'aime beaucoup cuisiner.* I love cooking.

cuisinier *nm* cook

cuisinière *nf* ① cook ② cooker

cuisse *nf* thigh; **une cuisse de poulet** a chicken leg

cuisson *nf* cooking ▷ *"une heure de cuisson"* "cooking time: one hour"

cuit *vb* see **cuire**

cuivre *nm* copper

cul *nm* (rude) bum

culot *nm* (informal) cheek

culotte *nf* knickers

culpabilité *nf* guilt

cultivateur (f **cultivatrice**) *nm/f* farmer

cultivé, e *adj* cultured

cultiver [**29**] *vb* to grow ▷ *Il cultive la vigne.* He grows grapes.; **cultiver la terre** to farm the land

culture *nf* ① farming ② education; **la culture physique** physical education

culturisme *nm* body-building

curé *nm* parish priest

cure-dent *nm* toothpick

curieux (f **curieuse**) *adj* curious

curiosité *nf* curiosity

curriculum vitae *nm* CV

curseur *nm* cursor

cuvette *nf* bowl

CV *nm* (= *curriculum vitae*) CV

cybercafé *nm* internet café

cyclable *adj* **une piste cyclable** a cycle track

cycle *nm* cycle

cyclisme *nm* cycling

cycliste *nmf* cyclist

cyclomoteur *nm* moped

cyclone *nm* hurricane

cygne *nm* swan

a
b
c
d
e
f
g
h
i
j
k
l
m
n
o
p
q
r
s
t
u
v
w
x
y
z

d

d' prep, art see **de**

dactylo nf **1** typist ▷ *Elle est dactylo.* She's a typist. **2** typing

daim nm suede

dame nf **1** lady **2** (in cards, chess) queen

dames nfpl draughts

Danemark nm Denmark

danger nm danger; **être en danger** to be in danger; **"Danger de mort"** "Extremely dangerous"

dangereux (f **dangereuse**) adj dangerous

danois (f **danoise**) adj Danish
▶ nm Danish ▷ *Il parle danois.* He speaks Danish.
▶ nm/f **un Danois** (man) a Dane; **une Danoise** (woman) a Dane; **les Danois** the Danish

dans prep **1** in ▷ *Il est dans sa chambre.* He's in his bedroom. ▷ *dans deux mois* in two months' time **2** into ▷ *Il est entré dans mon bureau.* He came into my office. **3** out of ▷ *On a bu dans des verres en plastique.* We drank out of plastic glasses.

danse nf **1** dance; **la danse classique** ballet **2** dancing

danser [**29**] vb to dance

danseur (f **danseuse**) nm/f dancer

date nf date; **un ami de longue date** an old friend

dater [**29**] vb **dater de** to date from

datte nf (fruit) date

dauphin nm dolphin

davantage adv **davantage de** more

de prep, art

> See also **du** (=de+le) and **des** (=de+les). **de** changes to **d'** before a vowel and most words beginning with "h".

1 of ▷ *le toit de la maison* the roof of the house ▷ *la voiture de Paul* Paul's car ▷ *la voiture d'Hélène* Hélène's car ▷ *deux bouteilles de vin* two bottles of wine ▷ *un litre d'essence* a litre of petrol; **un bébé d'un an** a one-year-old baby; **un billet de cinquante euros** a 50-euro note **2** from ▷ *de Londres à Paris* from London to Paris ▷ *Il vient de Londres.* He comes from London. ▷ *une lettre de Victor* a letter from Victor **3** by ▷ *augmenter de dix euros* to increase by ten euros

> You use **de** to form expressions with the meaning of **some** and **any**.

Je voudrais de l'eau. I'd like some water. ▷ *du pain et de la confiture* bread and jam; **Il n'a pas de famille.** He hasn't got any family.; **Il n'y a plus de biscuits.** There aren't any more biscuits.

dé nm ❶ dice ❷ thimble

dealer nm (informal) drug-pusher

déballer [29] vb to unpack

débardeur nm tank top

débarquer [29] vb to disembark ▷ *Nous avons dû débarquer à Marseille.* We had to disembark at Marseilles.; **débarquer chez quelqu'un** (informal) to descend on somebody

débarras nm junk room; **Bon débarras!** Good riddance!

débarrasser [29] vb to clear ▷ *Tu peux débarrasser la table, s'il te plaît?* Can you clear the table please?; **se débarrasser de quelque chose** to get rid of something ▷ *Je me suis débarrassé de mon vieux frigo.* I got rid of my old fridge.

débat nm debate

se débattre [10] vb to struggle

débile adj crazy

débordé, e adj **être débordé(e)** to be snowed under

déborder [29] vb (river) to overflow; **déborder d'énergie** to be full of energy

débouché nm job prospect

déboucher [29] vb ❶ (sink, pipe) to unblock ❷ (bottle) to open; **déboucher sur** to lead into ▷ *La rue débouche sur une place.* The street leads into a square.

debout adv ❶ standing up ▷ *Il a mangé ses céréales debout.* He ate his cereal standing up. ❷ upright ▷ *Mets les livres debout sur l'étagère.* Put the books upright on the shelf. ❸ up ▷ *Tu es déjà debout?* Are you up already?; **Debout!** Get up!

déboutonner [29] vb to unbutton

débraillé, e adj sloppily dressed

débrancher [29] vb to unplug

débris nm **des débris de verre** bits of glass

débrouillard, e adj streetwise

se débrouiller [29] vb to manage ▷ *C'était difficile, mais je ne me suis pas trop mal débrouillé.* It was difficult, but I managed OK.; **Débrouille-toi tout seul.** Sort things out for yourself.

début nm beginning ▷ *au début* at the beginning; **début mai** in early May

débutant(f débutante) nm/f beginner

débuter [29] vb to start

décaféiné, e adj decaffeinated

décalage horaire nm (between time zones) time difference

décalquer [29] vb to trace

décapiter [29] vb to behead

décapotable adj convertible

décapsuler [29] vb **décapsuler une bouteille** to take the top off a bottle

décapsuleur nm bottle-opener

décéder [35] vb to die ▷ *Son père est décédé il y a trois ans.* His father died three years ago.

décembre nm December; **en décembre** in December

décemment adv decently

décent, e adj decent

déception nf disappointment

décerner [29] vb to award

décès nm death

décevant, e adj disappointing

décevoir [68] vb to disappoint

décharger [46] vb to unload

se déchausser [29] vb to take off one's shoes

déchets nmpl waste

déchiffrer [29] vb to decipher

déchirant, e adj heart-rending

déchirer [29] vb ❶ (clothes) to tear ❷ to tear up ▷ déchirer une lettre to tear up a letter ❸ to tear out ▷ déchirer une page d'un livre to tear a page out of a book; **se déchirer** to tear ▷ se déchirer un muscle to tear a muscle

déchirure nf (rip) tear; **une déchirure musculaire** a torn muscle

décidé, e adj determined; **C'est décidé.** It's decided.

décidément adv certainly

décider [29] vb to decide; **décider de faire quelque chose** to decide to do something; **se décider** to make up one's mind ▷ Elle n'arrive pas à se décider. She can't make up her mind.

décisif (f **décisive**) adj decisive

décision nf decision

déclaration nf statement; **faire une déclaration de vol** to report something as stolen

déclarer [29] vb to declare ▷ déclarer la guerre à un pays to declare war on a country; **se**

déclarer to break out ▷ Le feu s'est déclaré dans la cantine. The fire broke out in the canteen.

déclencher [29] vb (alarm, explosion) to set off; **se déclencher** to go off

déclic nm click

décoiffé, e adj Elle était toute décoiffée. Her hair was in a real mess.

décollage nm (of plane) takeoff

décollé, e adj avoir les oreilles décollées to have sticking-out ears

décoller [29] vb ❶ to unstick ▷ décoller une étiquette to unstick a label; **se décoller** to come unstuck ❷ to take off ▷ L'avion a décollé avec dix minutes de retard. The plane took off ten minutes late.

décolleté, e adj low-cut ▶ nm un décolleté plongeant a plunging neckline

se décolorer [29] vb to fade ▷ Ce T-shirt s'est décoloré au lavage. This T-shirt has faded in the wash.; **se faire décolorer les cheveux** to have one's hair bleached

décombres nmpl rubble

se décommander [29] vb to cry off ▷ Elle devait venir mais elle s'est décommandée à la dernière minute. She was supposed to be coming, but she cried off at the last minute.

déconcerté, e adj disconcerted

décongeler [2] vb to thaw

se déconnecter [29] vb to log out

déconner [29] vb (rude) to talk rubbish ▷ Non mais, sans déconner, c'est vrai? No kidding, is that true?

déconseiller [29] *vb* déconseiller à quelqu'un de faire quelque chose to advise somebody not to do something ▷ *Je lui ai déconseillé d'y aller.* I advised him not to go.; **C'est déconseillé.** It's not recommended.

décontenancé, e *adj* disconcerted

décontracté, e *adj* relaxed; **s'habiller décontracté** to dress casually

se **décontracter** [29] *vb* to relax ▷ *Il est allé faire du footing pour se décontracter.* He went jogging to relax.

décor *nm* décor

décorateur (*f* **décoratrice**) *nm* interior decorator

décoration *nf* decoration

décorer [29] *vb* to decorate

décors *nmpl* ❶ (*in play*) scenery ❷ (*in film*) set

décortiquer [29] *vb* to shell; **des crevettes décortiquées** peeled prawns

découdre [16] *vb* to unpick; **se découdre** to come unstitched

découper [29] *vb* ❶ to cut out ▷ *J'ai découpé cet article dans le journal.* I cut this article out of the paper. ❷ (*meat*) to carve

décourageant, e *adj* discouraging

décourager [46] *vb* to discourage; **se décourager** to get discouraged ▷ *Ne te décourage pas!* Don't give up!

décousu, e *adj* unstitched

découvert *nm* overdraft

découverte *nf* discovery

découvrir [56] *vb* to discover

décrire [31] *vb* to describe

décrocher [29] *vb* ❶ to take down ▷ *Tu peux m'aider à décrocher les rideaux?* Can you help me take down the curtains? ❷ to pick up the phone ▷ *Il a décroché et a composé le numéro.* He picked up the phone and dialled the number.; **décrocher le téléphone** to take the phone off the hook

déçu *vb* disappointed

dédaigneux (*f* **dédaigneuse**) *adj* disdainful

dédain *nm* disdain

dedans *adv* inside; **là-dedans** (1) in there ▷ *J'ai trouvé les clés là-dedans.* I found the keys in there. (2) in that ▷ *Il y a du vrai là-dedans.* There's some truth in that.

dédicacé, e *adj* **un exemplaire dédicacé** a signed copy

dédier [20] *vb* to dedicate

déduire [24] *vb* to take off ▷ *Tu as déduit les vingt euros que je te devais?* Did you take off the twenty euros I owed you?; **déduire que** to deduce that ▷ *J'en déduis qu'il m'a menti.* That means he must have been lying.

défaire [37] *vb* to undo; **défaire sa valise** to unpack; **se défaire** to come undone

défaite *nf* defeat

défaut *nm* fault

défavorable *adj* unfavourable

défavorisé, e *adj* underprivileged

défectueux (f **défectueuse**) adj faulty

défendre [89] vb ❶ to forbid; **défendre à quelqu'un de faire quelque chose** to forbid somebody to do something ▷ *Sa mère lui a défendu de le revoir.* Her mother forbade her to see him again. ❷ to defend ▷ *défendre quelqu'un* to defend somebody

défendu, e adj forbidden ▷ *C'est défendu.* It's not allowed.

défense nf ❶ defence; "**défense de fumer**" "no smoking" ❷ (of elephant) tusk

défi nm challenge; **d'un air de défi** defiantly; **sur un ton de défi** defiantly

défier [20] vb ❶ to challenge ▷ *Je te défie de trouver un meilleur exemple.* I challenge you to find a better example. ❷ to dare ▷ *Il m'a défié d'aller à l'école en pyjama.* He dared me to go to school in my pyjamas.

défigurer [29] vb to disfigure

défilé nm ❶ parade; **un défilé de mode** a fashion show ❷ march

défiler [29] vb to march

définir [39] vb to define

définitif (f **définitive**) adj final; **en définitive** in the end

définitivement adv for good

déformer [29] vb ❶ to stretch ▷ *Ne tire pas sur ton pull, tu vas le déformer.* Don't pull at your sweater, you'll stretch it.; **se déformer** to stretch ▷ *Ce T-shirt s'est déformé au lavage.* This T-shirt has stretched in the wash.

se défouler [29] vb to unwind

dégagé, e adj **d'un air dégagé** casually; **sur un ton dégagé** casually

dégager [46] vb ❶ to free ▷ *Ils ont mis une heure à dégager les victimes.* They took an hour to free the victims. ❷ to clear ▷ *des gouttes qui dégagent le nez* drops to clear your nose; **Ça se dégage.** (weather) It's clearing up.

se dégarnir [39] vb to go bald

dégâts nmpl damage

dégel nm thaw

dégeler [2] vb to thaw

dégivrer [29] vb ❶ to defrost ❷ to de-ice

dégonfler [29] vb to let down ▷ *Quelqu'un a dégonflé mes pneus.* Somebody let down my tyres.; **se dégonfler** (informal) to chicken out

dégouliner [29] vb to trickle

dégourdi, e adj smart

dégourdir [39] vb **se dégourdir les jambes** to stretch one's legs

dégoût nm disgust; **avec dégoût** disgustedly

dégoûtant, e adj disgusting

dégoûté, e adj disgusted; **être dégoûté de tout** to be sick of everything

dégoûter [29] vb to disgust; **dégoûter quelqu'un de quelque chose** to put somebody off something ▷ *Ça m'a dégoûté de la viande.* That put me off meat.

se dégrader [29] vb to deteriorate

degré nm degree; **de l'alcool à 90 degrés** surgical spirit

dégringoler [29] vb ❶ to rush down ▷ *Il a dégringolé l'escalier.* He rushed down the stairs. ❷ to collapse ▷ *Elle a fait dégringoler la pile de livres.* She knocked over the stack of books.

dégueulasse adj (rude) disgusting

déguisement nm disguise

déguiser [29] vb **se déguiser en quelque chose** to dress up as something ▷ *Elle s'était déguisée en vampire.* She was dressed up as a vampire.

dégustation nf tasting

déguster [29] vb ❶ (food, wine) to taste ❷ to enjoy

dehors adv outside ▷ *Je t'attends dehors.* I'll wait for you outside.; **jeter quelqu'un dehors** to throw somebody out; **en dehors de** apart from

déjà adv ❶ already ▷ *J'ai déjà fini.* I've already finished. ❷ before ▷ *Tu es déjà venu en France?* Have you been to France before?

déjeuner [29] vb to have lunch ▶ nm lunch

délai nm ❶ extension ❷ time limit
Be careful! **délai** does not mean **delay**.

délasser [29] vb to relax ▷ *La lecture délasse.* Reading's relaxing.; **se délasser** to relax ▷ *J'ai pris un bain pour me délasser.* I had a bath to relax.

délavé, e adj faded

délégué (f **déléguée**) nm/f representative ▷ *les délégués de classe* the class representatives

In French schools, each class elects two representatives or **délégués de classe**, one boy and one girl.

déléguer [35] vb to delegate

délibéré, e adj deliberate

délicat, e adj ❶ delicate ❷ tricky ❸ tactful ❹ thoughtful

délicatement adv ❶ gently ❷ tactfully

délice nm delight ▷ *Ce gâteau est un vrai délice.* This cake's a real treat.

délicieux (f **délicieuse**) adj delicious

délinquance nf crime

délinquant (f **délinquante**) nm/f criminal

délirer [29] vb **Mais tu délires!** (informal) You're crazy!

délit nm criminal offence

délivrer [29] vb (prisoner) to set free

deltaplane nm hang-glider; **faire du deltaplane** to go hang-gliding

demain adv tomorrow; **À demain!** See you tomorrow!

demande nf request; **une demande en mariage** an offer of marriage; **"demandes d'emploi"** "situations wanted"

demandé, e adj très demandé very much in demand

demander [29] vb ❶ to ask for ▷ *J'ai demandé la permission.* I've asked for permission. ❷ to require ▷ *un travail qui demande beaucoup de temps* a job that requires a lot of time; **se demander** to wonder ▷ *Je me demande à quelle heure il va* *venir.* I wonder what time he'll come.

▌Be careful! **demander** does not mean **to demand**.

demandeur d'asile (f **demandeuse d'asile**) nm/f asylum seeker

demandeur d'emploi (f **demandeuse d'emploi**) nm/f job-seeker

démangeaison nf itching

démanger [46] vb to itch ▷ *Ça me démange.* It itches.

démaquillant nm make-up remover

démaquiller [29] vb se **démaquiller** to remove one's make-up

démarche nf ❶ walk ❷ step ▷ *faire les démarches nécessaires pour obtenir quelque chose* to take the necessary steps to obtain something

démarrer [29] vb (car) to start

démêler [29] vb to untangle

déménagement nm move; un camion de déménagement a removal van

déménager [46] vb to move house

déménageur nm removal man

dément, e adj crazy

démentiel (f **démentielle**) adj insane

se **démerder** [29] vb (rude) to get by ▷ *Ne t'inquiète pas, il saura se démerder.* Don't worry, he'll get by.; **Démerde-toi tout seul.** Sort things out for yourself.

demeurer [29] vb to live

demi, e adj, adv half ▷ *Il a trois ans et demi.* He's three and a half.; **Il est trois heures et demie.** It's half past three.; **Il est midi et demi.** It's half past twelve.; **à demi endormi** half-asleep

▶ nm half pint of beer; **Un demi, s'il vous plaît!** A beer please!

demi-baguette nf half a baguette

demi-cercle nm semicircle

demi-douzaine nf half-dozen

demie nf half-hour ▷ *Le bus passe à la demie.* The bus comes by on the half-hour.

demi-écrémé, e adj semi-skimmed

demi-finale nf semifinal

demi-frère nm half-brother

demi-heure nf half an hour ▷ *dans une demi-heure* in half an hour

demi-journée nf half-day

demi-litre nm half litre

demi-livre nf half-pound

demi-pension nf half board; **Cet hôtel propose des tarifs raisonnables en demi-pension.** This hotel has reasonable rates for half board.

demi-pensionnaire nmf être demi-pensionnaire to take school lunches

demi-sel adj du beurre demi-sel slightly salted butter

demi-sœur nf half-sister

démission nf resignation; **donner sa démission** to resign

démissionner [29] vb to resign

demi-tarif nm ❶ half-price ❷ half-fare

demi-tour nm **faire demi-tour** to turn back

démocratie nf democracy

démocratique adj democratic

démodé, e adj old-fashioned

demoiselle nf young lady; **une demoiselle d'honneur** a bridesmaid

démolir [39] vb to demolish

démon nm devil

démonter [29] vb ❶ (tent) to take down ❷ (machine) to take apart

démontrer [29] vb to show

dénoncer [13] vb to denounce; **se dénoncer** to give oneself up

dénouement nm outcome

densité nf density

dent nf tooth ▷ une dent de lait a milk tooth ▷ une dent de sagesse a wisdom tooth

dentaire adj dental

dentelle nf lace

dentier nm denture

dentifrice nm toothpaste

dentiste nmf dentist

déodorant nm deodorant

dépannage nm **un service de dépannage** a breakdown service

dépanner [29] vb ❶ to fix ▷ Il a dépanné la voiture en cinq minutes. He fixed the car in five minutes. ❷ to help out ▷ Il m'a prêté dix euros pour me dépanner. (informal) He lent me 10 euros to help me out.

dépanneuse nf breakdown lorry

départ nm departure; **Je lui téléphonerai la veille de son départ.** I'll phone him the day before he leaves.

département nm ❶ department ❷ administrative area
  ● France is divided into 96 **départements**, administrative areas rather like counties.

dépasser [59] vb ❶ to overtake ❷ to pass ▷ Nous avons dépassé Dijon. We've passed Dijon. ❸ (sum, limit) to exceed

dépaysé, e adj **se sentir un peu dépaysé** to feel a bit lost

se dépêcher [29] vb to hurry ▷ Dépêche-toi! Hurry up!

dépendre [89] vb **dépendre de** to depend on ▷ Ça dépend du temps. It depends on the weather.; **dépendre de quelqu'un** to be dependent on somebody; **Ça dépend.** It depends.

dépenser [29] vb (money) to spend

dépensier (f dépensière) adj **Il est dépensier.** He's a big spender.; **Elle n'est pas dépensière.** She's not exactly extravagant.

dépilatoire adj **une crème dépilatoire** a hair-removing cream

dépit nm **en dépit de** in spite of

déplacé, e adj uncalled-for

déplacement nm trip

déplacer [13] vb ❶ to move ▷ Tu peux m'aider à déplacer la table? Can you help me move the table? ❷ to put off ▷ déplacer un rendez-vous to put off an appointment; **se déplacer (1)** to travel around ▷ Il se déplace beaucoup pour son travail. He travels around a lot for his work. **(2)** to get around ▷ Il a du mal à se déplacer. He has difficulty

a
b
c
d
e
f
g
h
i
j
k
l
m
n
o
p
q
r
s
t
u
v
w
x
y
z

getting around.; **se déplacer une vertèbre** to slip a disc

déplaire [63] vb **Cela me déplaît.** I dislike this.

déplaisant, e adj unpleasant

dépliant nm leaflet

déplier [20] vb to unfold

déposer [29] vb ❶ to leave ▷ *J'ai déposé mon sac à la consigne.* I left my bag at the left luggage office. ❷ to put down ▷ *Déposez le paquet sur la table.* Put the parcel down on the table.; **déposer quelqu'un** to drop somebody off

dépourvu, e adj **prendre quelqu'un au dépourvu** to take somebody by surprise

dépression nf depression; **faire de la dépression** to be suffering from depression; **faire une dépression** to have a breakdown

déprimant, e adj depressing

déprimer [29] vb to get depressed; *Ce genre de temps me déprime.* This kind of weather makes me depressed.

depuis prep, adv ❶ since ▷ *Il habite Paris depuis 1983.* He's been living in Paris since 1983.; **depuis que** since ❷ for ▷ *Il habite Paris depuis cinq ans.* He's been living in Paris for five years.; **Depuis combien de temps?** How long? ▷ *Depuis combien de temps est-ce que vous le connaissez?* How long have you known him?; **Depuis quand?** How long? ▷ *Depuis quand est-ce que vous le connaissez?* How long have you known him?

député (f **députée**) nm/f Member of Parliament

déraciner [29] vb to uproot

dérangement nm **en dérangement** out of order

déranger [46] vb ❶ to bother ▷ *Excusez-moi de vous déranger.* I'm sorry to bother you.; **Ne vous dérangez pas, je vais répondre au téléphone.** You stay there, I'll answer the phone. ❷ to disorganize ▷ *Ne dérange pas mes livres, s'il te plaît.* Don't disorganize my books, please.

déraper [29] vb to skid

dermatologue nmf dermatologist

dernier (f **dernière**) adj ❶ last ▷ *la dernière fois* the last time ❷ latest ▷ *le dernier film de Spielberg* Spielberg's latest film; **en dernier** last

dernièrement adv recently

dérouler [29] vb ❶ to unroll ❷ to unwind; **se dérouler** to take place; **Tout s'est déroulé comme prévu.** Everything went as planned.

derrière adv, prep behind
▶ nm ❶ back ▷ *la porte de derrière* the back door ❷ backside

des art

     des is the contracted form of de + les.

❶ some ▷ *Tu veux des chips?* Would you like some crisps?

     des is sometimes not translated.

▷ *J'ai des cousins en France.* I have cousins in France. ❷ any ▷ *Tu* as des frères? Have you got any brothers? ❸ **of the** ▷ *la fin des vacances* the end of the holidays ▷ *la voiture des Durand* the Durands' car ❹ **from the** ▷ *Il arrive des États-Unis.* He's arriving from the United States.

dès *prep* as early as ▷ *dès le mois de novembre* from November; **dès le début** right from the start; **Il vous appellera dès son retour.** He'll call you as soon as he gets back.; **dès que** as soon as ▷ *Il m'a reconnu dès qu'il m'a vu.* He recognized me as soon as he saw me.

désabusé, e *adj* disillusioned

désaccord *nm* disagreement

désagréable *adj* unpleasant

désaltérer [35] *vb* **L'eau gazeuse désaltère bien.** Sparkling water is very thirst-quenching.; **se désaltérer** to quench one's thirst

désapprobateur (*f* **désapprobatrice**) *adj* disapproving

désastre *nm* disaster

désavantage *nm* disadvantage

désavantager [46] *vb* **désavantager quelqu'un** to put somebody at a disadvantage

descendre [25] *vb* ❶ to go down ▷ *Je suis tombé en descendant l'escalier.* I fell as I was going down the stairs. ❷ to come down ▷ *Attends en bas; je descends!* Wait downstairs; I'm coming down! ❸ to get down ▷ *Vous pouvez descendre ma valise, s'il vous plaît?* Can you get my suitcase down,

please? ❹ to get off ▷ *Nous descendons à la prochaine station.* We're getting off at the next station. ❺ to get off ▷ *Je t'attendrai au bas de la descente.* I'll wait for you at the bottom of the hill.; **une descente de police** a police raid

description *nf* description

déséquilibré, e *adj* unbalanced

déséquilibrer [29] *vb* **déséquilibrer quelqu'un** to throw somebody off balance

désert, e *adj* deserted; **une île déserte** a desert island
  ▶ *nm* desert

déserter [29] *vb* to desert

désertique *adj* desert ▷ *une région désertique* a desert region

désespéré, e *adj* desperate

désespérer [35] *vb* to despair ▷ *Il ne faut pas désespérer.* Don't despair.

désespoir *nm* despair

déshabiller [29] *vb* to undress; **se déshabiller** to get undressed

déshériter [29] *vb* to disinherit; **les déshérités** the underprivileged

déshydraté, e *adj* dehydrated

désigner [29] *vb* to choose ▷ *On l'a désignée pour remettre le prix.* She was chosen to present the prize.; **désigner quelque chose du doigt** to point at something

désinfectant *nm* disinfectant

désinfecter [29] *vb* to disinfect

désintéressé, e *adj* ❶ unselfish ▷ *un acte désintéressé* an unselfish action ❷ impartial ▷ *un conseil désintéressé* impartial advice

désintéresser [29] vb se
désintéresser de quelque chose
to lose interest in something

désir nm ❶ wish ▷ Vos désirs
sont des ordres. Your wish is my
command. ❷ will ▷ le désir de
réussir the will to succeed ❸ desire

désirer [29] vb to want ▷ Vous
désirez? (in shop) What would you like?

désobéir [39] vb désobéir à
quelqu'un to disobey somebody

désobéissant, e adj disobedient

désobligeant, e adj unpleasant

désodorisant nm air freshener

désolé, e adj sorry; **Désolé!** Sorry!

désopilant, e adj hilarious

désordonné, e adj untidy

désordre nm untidiness; **Quel
désordre!** What a mess!; **en
désordre** untidy

désormais adv from now on

desquelles pron
⎜ desquelles is the contracted
⎜ form of de + lesquelles.
▷ des négociations au cours desquelles
les patrons ont fait des concessions
negotiations durlng which the
employers made concessions

desquels pron
⎜ desquels is the contracted
⎜ form of de + lesquels.
▷ les lacs au bord desquels nous avons
campé the lakes on the banks of
which we camped

dessécher [35] vb to dry out ▷ Le
soleil dessèche la peau. The sun dries
your skin out.

desserrer [29] vb to loosen

dessert nm pudding

dessin nm drawing; **un dessin
animé** (film) a cartoon; **un dessin
humoristique** (drawing) a cartoon

dessinateur nm un dessinateur
industriel a draughtsman

dessiner [29] vb to draw

dessous adv underneath; **en
dessous** underneath; **par-
dessous** underneath; **là-dessous**
under there; **ci-dessous** below
▷ Complétez les phrases ci-dessous.
Complete the sentences below.;
au-dessous de below
▶ nm underneath; **les voisins
du dessous** the downstairs
neighbours; **les dessous**
underwear

dessous-de-plat (pl dessous-de-
plat) nm tablemat

dessus adv on top; **par-dessus**
over; **au-dessus** above ▷ la
taille au-dessus the size above
▷ au-dessus du lit above the bed; **là-
dessus (1)** on there ▷ Tu peux écrire
là-dessus. You can write on there.
(2) with that ▷ "Je démissionne!"
Là-dessus, il est parti. "I resign!" With
that, he left.; **ci-dessus** above
▷ l'exemple ci-dessus the example
above
▶ nm top; **les voisins du dessus**
the upstairs neighbours; **avoir le
dessus** to have the upper hand

destinataire nmf addressee

destination nf destination; **les
passagers à destination de Paris**
passengers travelling to Paris

destiné, e adj intended for; **Elle
était destinée à faire ce métier.**

She was destined to go into that job.

destruction nf destruction

détachant nm stain remover

détacher [29] vb to undo; **se détacher de quelque chose (1)** to come off something ▷ La poignée de la porte s'est détachée. The door-handle came off. **(2)** to break away from something

détail nm detail; **en détail** in detail

détective nm detective

déteindre [61] vb (in wash) to fade

détendre [89] vb to relax ▷ La lecture, ça me détend. I find reading relaxing.; **se détendre** to relax ▷ Il est allé prendre un bain pour se détendre. He's gone to have a bath to relax.

détente nf relaxation

détenu nm prisoner

détenue nf prisoner

se détériorer [29] vb to deteriorate

déterminé, e adj ① determined ② specific ▷ un but déterminé a specific aim

détestable adj horrible

détester [29] vb to hate

détonation nf bang

détour nm detour; **Ça vaut le détour.** It's worth the trip.

détournement nm **un détournement d'avion** a hijacking

détrempé, e adj waterlogged

détritus nmpl litter

détruire [24] vb to destroy

dette nf debt

deuil nm **être en deuil** to be in mourning

deux num two ▷ Elle a deux ans. She's two.; **deux fois** twice; **deux points** colon; **tous les deux** both; **le deux février** the second of February

deuxième adj second ▷ au deuxième étage on the second floor

deuxièmement adv secondly

devais, devait, devaient vb see devoir

dévaliser [29] vb to rob

devant adv, prep ① in front ② in front of; **passer devant** to go past ▶ nm front ▷ le devant de la maison the front of the house; **les pattes de devant** the front legs

développement nm development; **les pays en voie de développement** developing countries

développer [29] vb to develop ▷ donner une pellicule à développer to take a film to be developed; **se développer** to develop

devenir [26] vb to become

devez vb see devoir

déviation nf diversion

deviez vb see devoir

deviner [29] vb to guess

devinette nf riddle

devions vb see devoir

dévisager [46] vb **dévisager quelqu'un** to stare at somebody

devise nf currency

dévisser [29] vb to unscrew

dévoiler [29] vb to unveil

devoir [27] vb ① to have to ▷ Je dois partir. I've got to go. ② must ▷ Tu dois être fatigué. You must be tired. ❸ **to be due to** ▷ *Le nouveau centre commercial doit ouvrir en mai.* The new shopping centre is due to open in May.; **devoir quelque chose à quelqu'un** to owe somebody something ▷ *Combien est-ce que je vous dois?* How much do I owe you?

▶ *nm* ❶ exercise; **les devoirs** homework; **un devoir sur table** a written test ❷ duty

devons *vb see* **devoir**

dévorer [29] *vb* to devour

dévoué, e *adj* devoted

devra, devrai, devras, devrez, devrons, devront *vb see* **devoir**

diabète *nm* diabetes

diabétique *adj* diabetic

diable *nm* devil

diabolo *nm* fruit cordial and lemonade; **un diabolo menthe** a mint cordial and lemonade

diagonal, e (*mpl* **diagonaux**) *adj* diagonal

diagonale *nf* diagonal; **en diagonale** diagonally

diagramme *nm* diagram

dialecte *nm* dialect

dialogue *nm* dialogue

diamant *nm* diamond

diamètre *nm* diameter

diapo *nf* (*informal*) slide; **une pellicule diapo** a slide film

diapositive *nf* slide

diarrhée *nf* diarrhoea

dictateur *nm* dictator

dictature *nf* dictatorship

dictée *nf* dictation

dicter [29] *vb* to dictate

dictionnaire *nm* dictionary

diététique *adj* **un magasin diététique** a health food shop

dieu (*pl* **dieux**) *nm* ❶ Dieu God ▷ *Mon Dieu!* Oh my God!

différé *nm* **une émission en différé** a recording

différence *nf* difference; **la différence d'âge** the age difference; **à la différence de** unlike

différent, e *adj* ❶ different ❷ various; **différent de** different to

difficile *adj* difficult

difficilement *adv* **faire quelque chose difficilement** to have trouble doing something; **Je pouvais difficilement refuser.** It was difficult for me to refuse.

difficulté *nf* difficulty; **être en difficulté** to be in difficulties

digérer [35] *vb* to digest

digestif *nm* after-dinner liqueur

digne *adj* **digne de** worthy of ▷ *digne de confiance* trustworthy

dignité *nf* dignity

dilemme *nm* dilemma

diluer [29] *vb* to dilute

dimanche *nm* ❶ Sunday ▷ *Aujourd'hui, on est dimanche.* It's Sunday today. ❷ on Sunday; **le dimanche** on Sundays; **tous les dimanches** every Sunday; **dimanche dernier** last Sunday; **dimanche prochain** next Sunday

diminuer [29] *vb* to decrease

diminutif *nm* pet name

diminution *nf* ❶ reduction ❷ decrease

dinde nf turkey

dindon nm turkey

> le dindon refers to a live turkey, whereas la dinde refers to the meat.

dîner [29] vb to have dinner (evening meal)
> ▶ nm (evening meal) dinner

dingue adj (informal) crazy

diplomate adj diplomatic
> ▶ nm diplomat

diplomatie nf diplomacy

diplôme nm qualification

diplômé, e adj qualified

dire [28] vb ❶ to say ▷ Il a dit qu'il ne viendrait pas. He said he wouldn't come.; **on dit que ...** they say that ... ❷ to tell; **dire quelque chose à quelqu'un** to tell somebody something ▷ Elle m'a dit la vérité. She told me the truth.; **On dirait qu'il va pleuvoir.** It looks as if it's going to rain.; **se dire quelque chose** ▷ Quand je l'ai vu, je me suis dit qu'il avait vieilli. When I saw him, I thought to myself that he'd aged.; **Est-ce que ça se dit?** Can you say that?; **Ça ne me dit rien.** That doesn't appeal to me.

direct, e adj direct; **en direct** live

directement adv straight

directeur (f **directrice**) nm/f ❶ headteacher ❷ manager

direction nf ❶ management ❷ direction

dirent vb see dire

dirigeant (f **dirigeante**) nm/f leader

diriger [46] vb to manage ▷ Il dirige une petite entreprise. He manages a small company.; **se diriger vers** to head for ▷ Il se dirigeait vers la gare. He was heading for the station.

dis vb see dire; **Dis-moi la vérité!** Tell me the truth!; **dis donc** hey ▷ Dis donc, tu te souviens de Sam? Hey, do you remember Sam?

disaient, disais, disait vb see dire

discothèque nf (club) disco

discours nm speech

discret (f **discrète**) adj discreet

discrimination nf discrimination

discussion nf discussion

discutable adj debatable

discuter [29] vb ❶ to talk ▷ Nous avons discuté pendant des heures. We talked for hours. ❷ to argue ▷ C'est ce que j'ai décidé, alors ne discutez pas! That's what I've decided, so don't argue!

disent, disiez, disions vb see dire

disons vb see dire let's say ▷ C'est à, disons, une demi-heure à pied. It's half an hour's walk, say.

disparaître [57] vb to disappear; **faire disparaître quelque chose** (1) to make something disappear (2) to get rid of something

disparition nf disappearance; **une espèce en voie de disparition** an endangered species

disparu, e adj être porté(e) **disparu(e)** to be reported missing

dispensaire nm community clinic

dispensé, e adj être dispensé(e) **de quelque chose** to be excused something

disperser [29] *vb* to break up ▷ *La police a dispersé les manifestants.* The police broke up the demonstrators.; **se disperser** to break up ▷ *Une fois l'ambulance partie, la foule s'est dispersée.* Once the ambulance had left, the crowd broke up.

disponible *adj* available

disposé, e *adj* **être disposé(e) à faire quelque chose** to be willing to do something

disposer [29] *vb* **disposer de quelque chose** to have access to something ▷ *Je dispose d'un ordinateur.* I have access to a computer.

disposition *nf* **prendre ses dispositions** to make arrangements; **avoir quelque chose à sa disposition** to have something at one's disposal; **Je suis à votre disposition.** I am at your service.; **Je tiens ces livres à votre disposition.** The books are at your disposal.

dispute *nf* argument

se disputer [29] *vb* to argue

disquaire *nm* record dealer

disque *nm* record; **un disque compact** a compact disc; **le disque dur** hard disk

disquette *nf* floppy disk

disséminé, e *adj* scattered

disséquer [35] *vb* to dissect

dissertation *nf* essay

dissimuler [29] *vb* to conceal

se dissiper [29] *vb* to clear ▷ *Le brouillard va se dissiper dans l'après-*

midi. The fog will clear during the afternoon.

dissolvant *nm* nail polish remover

dissoudre [71] *vb* to dissolve; **se dissoudre** to dissolve

dissuader [29] *vb* **dissuader quelqu'un de faire quelque chose** to dissuade somebody from doing something

distance *nf* distance

distillerie *nf* distillery

distingué, e *adj* distinguished

distinguer [29] *vb* to distinguish

distraction *nf* entertainment

distraire [86] *vb* **Va voir un film, ça te distraira.** Go and see a film, it'll take your mind off things.

distrait, e *adj* absent-minded

distribuer [29] *vb* **①** to give out ▷ *Distribue les livres, s'il te plaît.* Give out the books, please. **②** (*cards*) to deal

distributeur *nm* **un distributeur automatique** a vending machine; **un distributeur de billets** a cash dispenser

dit, e *adj* known as ▷ *Pierre, dit Pierrot* Pierre, known as Pierrot ▶ *vb* see **dire**

dites *vb* see **dire**; **Dites-moi ce que vous pensez.** Tell me what you think.; **dites donc** hey ▷ *Dites donc, vous, là-bas!* Hey, you there!

divers, e *adj* diverse; **pour diverses raisons** for various reasons

divertir [39] *vb* to enjoy oneself

divin, e *adj* divine

diviser [29] *vb* to divide ▷ *Quatre*

divisé par deux égalent deux. **4** divided by 2 equals 2.

divorcé (f**divorcée**) nm divorce

divorcer [13] vb to get divorced

dix num ten ▷ Elle a dix ans. She's ten.; **le dix février** the tenth of February

dix-huit num eighteen ▷ Elle a dix-huit ans. She's eighteen. ▷ à dix-huit heures at 6 p.m.

dixième adj tenth

dix-neuf num nineteen ▷ Elle a dix-neuf ans. She's nineteen. ▷ à dix-neuf heures at 7 p.m.

dix-sept num seventeen ▷ Elle a dix-sept ans. She's seventeen. ▷ à dix-sept heures at 5 p.m.

dizaine nf about ten

do nm (in music) ① C ② do

docteur nm doctor

document nm document

documentaire nm documentary

documentaliste nmf librarian

documentation nf documentation

documenter [29] vb se documenter sur quelque chose to gather information on something

dodu, e adj plump

doigt nm finger; **les doigts de pied** the toes

dois, doit, doivent vb see **devoir**

domaine nm ① estate ▷ Il possède un immense domaine en Normandie. He owns a huge estate in Normandy. ② field ▷ La chimie n'est pas mon domaine. Chemistry's not my field.

domestique adj domestic; **les animaux domestiques** pets
▶ nmf servant

domicile nm place of residence; **à domicile** at home ▷ Il travaille à domicile. He works at home.

domicilié, e adj "domicilié à: ..." "address: ..."

dominer [29] vb to dominate; se dominer to control oneself

dominos nmpl dominoes

dommage nm damage; **C'est dommage.** It's a shame.

dompter [29] vb to tame

dompteur (f**dompteuse**) nm animal tamer

don nm ① donation ② gift; **Elle a le don de m'énerver.** She's got a knack of getting on my nerves.

donc conj so

donjon nm (of castle) keep

données nfpl data

donner [29] vb ① to give; donner quelque chose à quelqu'un to give somebody something ▷ Elle m'a donné son adresse. She gave me her address.; **Ça m'a donné faim.** That made me feel hungry. ② to give away; donner sur quelque chose to overlook something ▷ une fenêtre qui donne sur la mer a window overlooking the sea

dont pron ① of which ▷ deux livres, dont l'un est en anglais two books, one of which is in English ② of whom ▷ dix blessés, dont deux grièvement ten people injured, two of them seriously

doré, e adj golden

dorénavant adv from now on

dorloter [29] vb to pamper

dormir [30] vb ❶ to sleep ▷ *Tu as bien dormi?* Did you sleep well? ❷ to be asleep ▷ *Ne faites pas de bruit, il dort.* Don't make any noise, he's asleep.

dortoir nm dormitory

dos nm back; **faire quelque chose dans le dos de quelqu'un** to do something behind somebody's back; **de dos** from behind; **nager le dos crawlé** to swim backstroke; **"voir au dos"** "see over"

dose nf dose

dossier nm ❶ file ▷ *une pile de dossiers* a stack of files ❷ report ▷ *un bon dossier scolaire* a good school report ❸ (in magazine) feature ❹ (of chair) back

douane nf customs

douanier nm customs officer

double nm le **double** twice as much; **en double** in duplicate; **le double messieurs** (tennis) the men's doubles

double-cliquer [29] vb to double-click ▷ *double-cliquer sur une icône* to double-click on an icon

doubler [29] vb ❶ to double ▷ *Le prix a doublé en dix ans.* The price has doubled in 10 years. ❷ to overtake ▷ *Il est dangereux de doubler sur cette route.* It's dangerous to overtake on this road.; **un film doublé** a dubbed film

douce adj see **doux**

doucement adv ❶ gently ❷ slowly ▷ *Je ne comprends pas, parle*

plus doucement. I don't understand, speak more slowly.

douceur nf ❶ softness ❷ gentleness; **L'avion a atterri en douceur.** The plane made a smooth landing.

douche nf shower; **les douches** the shower room; **prendre une douche** to have a shower

se doucher [29] vb to have a shower

doué, e adj talented; **être doué en quelque chose** to be good at something

douillet (f douillette) adj ❶ cosy ❷ soft

douleur nf pain

douloureux (f douloureuse) adj painful

doute nm doubt; **sans doute** probably

douter [29] vb to doubt; **douter de quelque chose** to doubt something ▷ *Je doute de sa sincérité.* I have my doubts about his sincerity.; **se douter de quelque chose** to suspect something; **Je m'en doutais.** I suspected as much.

douteux (f douteuse) adj ❶ dubious ❷ suspicious-looking

Douvres n Dover

doux (f douce, mpl doux) adj ❶ soft ▷ *un tissu doux* soft material ❷ sweet ▷ *du cidre doux* sweet cider ❸ mild ▷ *Il fait doux aujourd'hui.* It's mild today. ❹ gentle ▷ *C'est quelqu'un de très doux.* He's a very gentle person.; **en douce** on the quiet

douzaine nf dozen; **une douzaine de personnes** about twelve people

douze num twelve ⊳ Il a douze ans. He's twelve.; **le douze février** the twelfth of February

douzième adj twelfth ⊳ au douzième étage on the twelfth floor

dragée nf sugared almond

draguer [29] vb (informal): **draguer quelqu'un** to chat somebody up; **se faire draguer** to get chatted up

dragueur (fdragueuse) nm/f (informal: person) flirt

dramatique adj tragic; **l'art dramatique** drama

drame nm (incident) drama; **Ça n'est pas un drame si tu ne viens pas.** It's not the end of the world if you don't come.

drap nm (for bed) sheet

drapeau (pl drapeaux) nm flag

dressé, e adj trained

dresser [29] vb ① to draw up ⊳ dresser une liste to draw up a list ② to train ⊳ dresser un chien to train a dog; **dresser l'oreille** to prick up one's ears

drogue nf drug; **les drogues douces** soft drugs; **les drogues dures** hard drugs

drogué (fdroguée) nm/f drug addict

droguer [29] vb droguer **quelqu'un** to drug somebody; **se droguer** to take drugs

droguerie nf hardware shop

droit, e adj, adv ① right ⊳ le côté droit the right-hand side

② straight ⊳ Tiens-toi droite! Stand up straight!; **tout droit** straight on

▶ nm ① right ⊳ les droits de l'homme human rights; **avoir le droit de faire quelque chose** to be allowed to do something ② law ⊳ un étudiant en droit a law student

droite nf right ⊳ sur votre droite on your right; **à droite (1)** on the right ⊳ la troisième rue à droite the third street on the right **(2)** to the right ⊳ à droite de la fenêtre to the right of the window ⊳ Tournez à droite. Turn right.; **la voie de droite** the right-hand lane; **la droite** (in politics) the right

droitier (fdroitière) adj right-handed

drôle adj funny; **un drôle de temps** funny weather

drôlement adv (informal) really

du art

du is the contracted form of de + le.

① some ⊳ Tu veux du fromage? Would you like some cheese? ② any ⊳ Tu as du chocolat? Have you got any chocolate? ③ of the ⊳ la porte du garage the door of the garage ⊳ la femme du directeur the headmaster's wife ④ from the ⊳ Elle arrive du Japon. She's arriving from Japan.

dû (fdue, mpl dus) adj dû à due to

▶ vb see devoir; **Nous avons dû nous arrêter.** We had to stop.

duc nm duke

duchesse nf duchess

dupe adj Elle me ment mais je ne suis pas dupe. She lies to me but I'm not taken in by that.

duquel (mpl **desquels**, fpl **desquelles**) pron
duquel is the contracted form of **de** + **lequel**.
▷ l'homme duquel il parle the man he is talking about

dur, e adj, adv hard

durant prep ❶ during ▷ durant la nuit during the night ❷ for ▷ durant des années for years

durée nf length; **pour une durée de quinze jours** for a period of two weeks; **de courte durée** short; **de longue durée** long

durement adv harshly

durer [29] vb to last

dureté nf harshness

DVD nm DVD

dynamique adj dynamic

dyslexique adj dyslexic

e

eau (pl **eaux**) nf water; **l'eau minérale** mineral water; **l'eau plate** still water; **tomber à l'eau** to fall through

ébahi, e adj amazed

éblouir [39] vb to dazzle

éboueur nm dustman

ébouillanter [29] vb to scald

écaille nf (of fish) scale

s' **écailler** [29] vb to flake

écart nm gap; **à l'écart de** away from

écarté, e adj remote; **les bras écartés** arms outstretched; **les jambes écartées** legs apart

écarter [29] vb (arms, legs) to open wide; **s'écarter** to move ▷ Ils se sont écartés pour le laisser passer. They moved to let him pass.

échafaudage nm scaffolding

échalote nf shallot

échange nm exchange

échanger [46] vb to swap ▷ Je t'échange ce timbre contre celui-là. I'll swap you this stamp for that one.

échantillon nm sample

échapper [29] vb **échapper à** to escape from ▷ Le prisonnier a réussi à échapper à la police. The prisoner managed to escape from the police.; **s'échapper** to escape ▷ Il s'est échappé de prison. He escaped from prison.; **l'échapper belle** to have a narrow escape ▷ Nous l'avons échappé belle. We had a narrow escape.

écharde nf splinter of wood

écharpe nf scarf

s' **échauffer** [29] vb (before exercise) to warm up

échec nm failure

échecs nmpl chess

échelle nf ❶ ladder ❷ (of map) scale

échevelé, e adj dishevelled

écho nm echo

échouer [29] vb **échouer à un examen** to fail an exam

éclabousser [29] vb to splash

éclair nm flash of lightning; **un éclair au chocolat** a chocolate éclair

éclairage nm lighting

éclaircie nf bright interval

éclairer [29] vb **Cette lampe éclaire bien.** This lamp gives a good light.

éclat nm ❶ (of glass) fragment ❷ (of sun, colour) brightness; **des éclats de rire** roars of laughter

éclatant, e adj brilliant

éclater [29] vb ❶ (tyre, balloon) to burst; **éclater de rire** to burst out laughing; **éclater en sanglots** to burst into tears ❷ to break out ▷ La Seconde Guerre mondiale a éclaté en 1939. The Second World War broke out in 1939.

écœurant, e adj sickly

écœurer [29] vb **Tous ces mensonges m'écœurent.** All these lies make me sick.

école nf school ❶ aller à l'école to go to school ▷ une école publique a state school ▷ une école maternelle a nursery school

　　● The **école maternelle** is a state
　　　school for 2–6 year-olds.

écolier nm schoolboy

écolière nf schoolgirl

écologie nf ecology

écologique adj ecological

économie nf ❶ economy ❷ economics ▷ un cours d'économie an economics class

économies nfpl savings; **faire des économies** to save up

économique adj ❶ economic ❷ economical

économiser [29] vb to save

économiseur d'écran nm screen saver

écorce nf ❶ (of tree) bark ❷ (of orange, lemon) peel

s' **écorcher** [29] vb **Je me suis écorché le genou.** I've grazed my knee.

écossais, e adj ❶ Scottish ❷ tartan

a
b
c
d
e
f
g
h
i
j
k
l
m
n
o
p
q
r
s
t
u
v
w
x
y
z

▶ nm/f un **Écossais** (man) a Scot; une **Écossaise** (woman) a Scot; les **Écossais** the Scots

Écosse nf Scotland; **en Écosse** (1) in Scotland (2) to Scotland

s' **écouler** [29] vb ① (water) to flow out ② to pass ▷ Le temps s'écoule trop vite. Time passes too quickly.

écouter [29] vb to listen to ▷ J'aime écouter de la musique. I like listening to music.; **Écoute-moi!** Listen!

écouteur nm (of phone) earpiece

écran nm screen; **le petit écran** television; **l'écran total** sunblock

écraser [29] vb ① to crush ▷ Écrasez une gousse d'ail. Crush a clove of garlic. ② to run over ▷ Regarde bien avant de traverser, sinon tu vas te faire écraser. Look carefully before you cross or you'll get run over.; **s'écraser** to crash ▷ L'avion s'est écrasé dans le désert. The plane crashed in the desert.

écrémé, e adj skimmed

écrevisse nf crayfish

écrire [31] vb to write ▷ Nous nous écrivons régulièrement. We write to each other regularly.; **Ça s'écrit comment?** How do you spell that?

écrit nm written paper; **par écrit** in writing

écriteau (pl **écriteaux**) nm notice

écriture nf writing

écrivain nm writer

écrou nm (metal) nut

s' **écrouler** [29] vb to collapse

écru, e adj off-white

écureuil nm squirrel

écurie nf stable

EDF nf (= Électricité de France) French electricity company

Édimbourg n Edinburgh

éditer [29] vb to publish

éditeur nm publisher

édition nf ① edition ② publishing

édredon nm eiderdown

éducateur nm (of people with special needs) teacher

éducatif (f **éducative**) adj educational

éducation nf ① education ② upbringing

éducatrice nf (of people with special needs) teacher

éduquer [29] vb to educate

effacer [13] vb to rub out

effarant, e adj amazing

effectivement adv indeed

> Be careful! **effectivement** does not mean **effectively**.

effectuer [29] vb ① to make ② to do

effervescent, e adj effervescent

effet nm effect; **faire de l'effet** to take effect; **Ça m'a fait un drôle d'effet de le revoir.** It gave me a strange feeling to see him again.; **en effet** yes indeed

efficace adj ① efficient ② effective ▷ un médicament efficace an effective medicine

s' **effondrer** [29] vb to collapse

s' **efforcer** [13] vb **s'efforcer de faire quelque chose** to try hard to do something

effort nm effort

effrayant, e adj frightening

effrayer [60] vb to frighten

effronté, e *adj* cheeky

effroyable *adj* horrifying

égal, e (*mpl* **égaux**) *adj* equal; **Ça m'est égal.** (1) I don't mind. (2) I don't care.

également *adv* also

égaler [29] *vb* to equal

égalité *nf* equality; **être à égalité** to be level

égard *nm* **à cet égard** in this respect

égarer [29] *vb* to mislay ▷ *J'ai égaré mes clés.* I've mislaid my keys.; **s'égarer** to get lost ▷ *Ils se sont égarés dans la forêt.* They got lost in the forest.

église *nf* church

égoïsme *nm* selfishness

égoïste *adj* selfish

égout *nm* sewer

égratignure *nf* scratch

Égypte *nf* Egypt

égyptien (**f égyptienne**) *adj* Egyptian

eh *excl* hey!; **eh bien** well

élan *nm* **prendre de l'élan** to gather speed

s'élancer [13] *vb* to hurl oneself

élargir [39] *vb* to widen

élastique *nm* rubber band

électeur *nm* (man) voter

élection *nf* election

électrice *nf* (woman) voter

électricien *nm* electrician

électricité *nf* electricity; **allumer l'électricité** to turn on the light; **éteindre l'électricité** to turn off the light

électrique *adj* electric

électronique *nf* electronics

élégant, e *adj* smart

élémentaire *adj* elementary

éléphant *nm* elephant

élevage *nm* cattle rearing; **un élevage de porcs** a pig farm; **un élevage de poulets** a chicken farm; **les truites d'élevage** farmed trout

élevé, e *adj* high; **être bien élevé** to have good manners; **être mal élevé** to have bad manners

élève *nmf* pupil

élever [44] *vb* ❶ to bring up ▷ *Il a été élevé par sa grand-mère.* He was brought up by his grandmother. ❷ to breed ▷ *Son oncle élève des chevaux.* His uncle breeds horses.; **élever la voix** to raise one's voice; **s'élever à** to come to

éleveur *nm* breeder

éliminatoire *adj* **une note éliminatoire** a fail mark; **une épreuve éliminatoire** (*sport*) a qualifying round

éliminer [29] *vb* to eliminate

élire [45] *vb* to elect

elle *pron* ❶ she ▷ *Elle est institutrice.* She is a primary school teacher. ❷ her ▷ *Vous pouvez avoir confiance en elle.* You can trust her. ❸ it ▷ *Prends cette chaise: elle est plus confortable.* Take this chair: it's more comfortable.

■ **elle** is also used for emphasis. ▷ *Elle, elle est toujours en retard!* Oh, SHE'S always late!; **elle-même** herself ▷ *Elle l'a choisi elle-même.* She chose it herself.

elles pron they ▷ *Où sont Anne et Rachel? — Elles sont allées au cinéma.* Where are Anne and Rachel? — They've gone to the cinema.; **elles-mêmes** themselves

élogieux (élogieuse) adj complimentary

éloigné, e adj distant

s' **éloigner** [29] vb to go far away ▷ *Ne vous éloignez pas: le dîner est bientôt prêt!* Don't go far away: dinner will soon be ready!; **Vous vous éloignez du sujet.** You are getting off the point.

Élysée nm Élysée Palace
- The **Élysée** is the residence of the French president.

e-mail nm email

emballage nm le papier d'emballage wrapping paper

emballer [29] vb to wrap; **s'emballer** (informal) to get excited ▷ *Il s'est emballé pour ce projet.* He got really excited about this plan.

embarquement nm boarding

embarras nm embarrassment; **Vous n'avez que l'embarras du choix.** The only problem is choosing.

embarrassant, e adj embarrassing

embarrasser [29] vb to embarrass ▷ *Cela m'embarrasse de vous demander encore un service.* I feel embarrassed to ask you to do something more for me.

embaucher [29] vb to take on ▷ *L'entreprise vient d'embaucher*

cinquante ouvriers. The firm has just taken on fifty workers.

embêtant, e adj annoying

embêtements nmpl trouble

embêter [29] vb to bother; **s'embêter** to be bored ▷ *Qu'est-ce qu'on s'embête ici!* Isn't it boring here!

embouteillage nm traffic jam

embrasser [29] vb to kiss ▷ *Ils se sont embrassés.* They kissed each other.

s' **embrouiller** [29] vb to get confused ▷ *Il s'embrouille dans ses explications.* He gets confused when he explains things.

émerveiller [29] vb to dazzle

émeute nf riot

émigrer [29] vb to emigrate

émission nf programme ▷ *une émission de télévision* a TV programme

s' **emmêler** [29] vb to get tangled

emménager [46] vb to move in ▷ *Nous venons d'emménager dans une nouvelle maison.* We've just moved into a new house.

emmener [44] vb to take ▷ *Ils m'ont emmené au cinéma pour mon anniversaire.* They took me to the cinema for my birthday.

emmerder [29] vb (rude): **Ça m'emmerde!** It pisses me off!; **Je t'emmerde!** Piss off!; **s'emmerder** to be bored stiff

émoticon nm (computing) smiley

émotif (émotive) adj emotional

émotion nf emotion

émouvoir [32] vb to move ▷ *Sa*

lettre l'a beaucoup émue. She was deeply moved by his letter.

emparer [29] *vb* **s'emparer de** to grab ▷ *Il s'est emparé de ma valise.* He grabbed my case.

empêchement *nm* **Nous avons eu un empêchement de dernière minute.** We were held up at the last minute.

empêcher [29] *vb* to prevent ▷ *Le café le soir m'empêche de dormir.* Coffee at night keeps me awake.; **Il n'a pas pu s'empêcher de rire.** He couldn't help laughing.

empereur *nm* emperor

s'empiffrer [29] *vb* (informal) to stuff one's face

empiler [29] *vb* to pile up

empirer [29] *vb* to worsen ▷ *La situation a encore empiré.* The situation got even worse.

emplacement *nm* site

emploi *nm* ❶ use; **le mode d'emploi** directions for use ❷ job; **un emploi du temps** a timetable

employé (f**employée**) *nm/f* employee; **un employé de bureau** an office worker; **une employée de banque** a bank clerk

employer [54] *vb* ❶ to use ▷ *Quelle méthode employez-vous?* What method do you use? ❷ to employ ▷ *L'entreprise emploie dix ingénieurs.* The firm employs ten engineers.

employeur *nm* employer

empoisonner [29] *vb* to poison

emporter [29] *vb* to take ▷ *N'emportez que le strict nécessaire.*

Only take the bare minimum.; **plats à emporter** take-away meals; **s'emporter** to lose one's temper ▷ *Je m'emporte facilement.* I'm quick to lose my temper.

empreinte *nf* **une empreinte digitale** a fingerprint; **mon empreinte écologique** my carbon footprint

s'empresser [29] *vb* **s'empresser de faire quelque chose** to be quick to do something

emprisonner [29] *vb* to imprison

emprunt *nm* loan

emprunter [29] *vb* to borrow; **emprunter quelque chose à quelqu'un** to borrow something from somebody ▷ *Je peux t'emprunter dix euros?* Can I borrow ten euros from you?

EMT *nf* (= *éducation manuelle et technique*) design and technology

ému, e *adj* touched

en *prep, pron* ❶ in ▷ *Il habite en France.* He lives in France. ▷ *Je le verrai en mai.* I'll see him in May. ❷ to ▷ *Je vais en France cet été.* I'm going to France this summer. ❸ by ▷ *C'est plus rapide en voiture.* It's quicker by car. ❹ made of ▷ *C'est en verre.* It's made of glass. ❺ while ▷ *Il s'est coupé le doigt en ouvrant une boîte de conserve.* He cut his finger while opening a tin.; **Elle est sortie en courant.** She ran out.

When en is used with **avoir** and **il y a**, it is not translated in English. ▷ *Est-ce que tu as un dictionnaire?*

— Oui, j'en ai un. Have you got a dictionary? —Yes, I've got one.

> en is also used with verbs and expressions normally followed by **de** to avoid repeating the same word.

▷ *Si tu as un problème, tu peux m'en parler.* If you've got a problem, you can talk about it with me.; **J'en ai assez.** I've had enough.

encaisser [29] vb *(money)* to cash

enceinte adj pregnant

enchanté, e adj delighted; **Enchanté!** Pleased to meet you!

encombrant, e adj bulky

encombrer [29] vb to clutter

encore adv ❶ still ▷ *Il est encore au travail.* He's still at work. ❷ even ❸ again ▷ *Il m'a encore demandé de l'argent.* He asked me for money again.; **encore une fois** once again; **pas encore** not yet

encourager [46] vb to encourage

encre nf ink

encyclopédie nf encyclopaedia

endive nf chicory

endommager [46] vb to damage

endormi, e adj asleep

endormir [30] vb to deaden ▷ *Cette piqûre sert à endormir le nerf.* This injection is to deaden the nerve.; **s'endormir** to go to sleep

endroit nm place; **à l'endroit** (1) the right way out (2) the right way up

endurant, e adj *(person)* tough

endurcir [39] vb to toughen up; **s'endurcir** to become hardened

endurer [29] vb to endure

énergie nf ❶ energy ❷ power; **avec énergie** vigorously

énergique adj energetic; **des mesures énergiques** strong measures

énerver [29] vb **Il m'énerve!** He gets on my nerves!; **Ce bruit m'énerve.** This noise gets on my nerves.; **s'énerver** to get worked up; **Ne t'énerve pas!** Take it easy!

enfance nf childhood; **Je le connais depuis l'enfance.** I've known him since I was a child.

enfant nmf child

enfer nm hell

s' **enfermer** [29] vb **Il s'est enfermé dans sa chambre.** He shut himself up in his bedroom.

enfiler [29] vb ❶ to put on ▷ *J'ai rapidement enfilé un pull avant de sortir.* I quickly put on a sweater before going out. ❷ to thread ▷ *J'ai du mal à enfiler cette aiguille.* I am having difficulty threading this needle.

enfin adv at last

enflé, e adj swollen

enfler [29] vb to swell

enfoncer [13] vb **Il marchait, les mains enfoncées dans les poches.** He was walking with his hands thrust into his pockets.; **s'enfoncer** to sink

s' **enfuir** [40] vb to run off

engagement nm commitment

engager [46] vb *(person)* to take on ▷ *engager quelqu'un* to take somebody on s'**engager** [46] vb to commit oneself ▷ *Le Premier ministre s'est engagé à combattre le chômage.* The Prime minister has committed himself to fighting unemployment.; **Il s'est engagé dans l'armée à dix-huit ans.** He joined the army when he was 18.

engelures nfpl chilblains

engin nm device

Be careful! The French word **engin** does not mean **engine**.

s'**engourdir** [39] vb to go numb

engueuler [29] vb (informal): **engueuler quelqu'un** to tell somebody off

énigme nf riddle

s'**enivrer** [29] vb to get drunk

enjamber [29] vb to stride over ▷ *enjamber une barrière* to stride over a fence

enlèvement nm kidnapping

enlever [44] vb ❶ to take off ▷ *Enlève donc ton manteau!* Take off your coat! ❷ to kidnap

enneigé, e adj snowed up

ennemi (ennemie) nm/f enemy

ennui nm ❶ boredom ❷ problem ▷ *avoir des ennuis* to have problems

ennuyer [54] vb ❶ to bother ▷ *J'espère que cela ne vous ennuie pas trop.* I hope it doesn't bother you too much.; **s'ennuyer** to be bored

ennuyeux (ennuyeuse) adj ❶ boring ❷ awkward

énorme adj huge

énormément adv **Il a énormément grossi.** He's got terribly fat.; **Il y a énormément**

de neige. There's an enormous amount of snow.

enquête nf ❶ investigation ❷ survey

enquêter [29] vb to investigate ▷ *La police enquête actuellement sur le crime.* The police are currently investigating the crime.

enrageant, e adj infuriating

enrager [46] vb to be furious

enregistrement nm recording; **l'enregistrement des bagages** baggage check-in

enregistrer [29] vb ❶ to record ▷ *Ils viennent d'enregistrer un nouvel album.* They've just recorded a new album. ❷ to check in ▷ *Vous pouvez enregistrer plusieurs valises.* You can check in several cases.

s'**enrhumer** [29] vb to catch a cold ▷ *Je suis enrhumé.* I've got a cold.

s'**enrichir** [39] vb to get rich

enrouler [29] vb to wind ▷ *Enroulez le fil autour de la bobine.* Wind the thread round the bobbin.

enseignant (enseignante) nm/f teacher

enseignement nm ❶ education ▷ *les réformes de l'enseignement* education reforms ❷ teaching ▷ *l'enseignement des langues étrangères* the teaching of foreign languages

enseigner [29] vb to teach

ensemble adv together ▷ *tous ensemble* all together

▶ nm outfit; **l'ensemble de** the whole of; **dans l'ensemble** on the whole

ensoleillé, e *adj* sunny

ensuite *adv* then

entamer [29] *vb* to start ▷ *Qui a entamé le gâteau?* Who's started the cake?

s' **entasser** [29] *vb* to cram ▷ *Ils se sont tous entassés dans ma voiture.* They all crammed into my car.

entendre [89] *vb* ❶ to hear ▷ *Je ne t'entends pas.* I can't hear you.; **J'ai entendu dire qu'il est dangereux de nager ici.** I've heard that it's dangerous to swim here. ❷ to mean ▷ *Qu'est-ce que tu entends par là?* What do you mean by that?; **s'entendre** to get on ▷ *Il s'entend bien avec sa sœur.* He gets on well with his sister.

entendu, e *adj* **C'est entendu!** Agreed!; **bien entendu** of course

enterrement *nm* (burial) funeral

enterrer [29] *vb* to bury

entêté, e *adj* stubborn

s' **entêter** [29] *vb* to persist ▷ *Il s'entête à refuser de voir le médecin.* He persists in refusing to go to the doctor.

enthousiasme *nm* enthusiasm

s' **enthousiasmer** [29] *vb* to get enthusiastic ▷ *Il s'enthousiasme facilement.* He gets very enthusiastic about things.

entier (*f* **entière**) *adj* whole ▷ *Il a mangé une quiche entière.* He ate a whole quiche.; **le lait entier** full fat milk

entièrement *adv* completely

entorse *nf* sprain ▷ *Il s'est fait une entorse à la cheville.* He's sprained his ankle.

entourer [29] *vb* to surround

entracte *nm* interval

entraînement *nm* training

entraîner [29] *vb* ❶ to lead ▷ *Il se laisse facilement entraîner par les autres.* He's easily led. ❷ to train ▷ *Il entraîne l'équipe de France depuis cinq ans.* He's been training the French team for five years. ❸ to involve ▷ *Un mariage entraîne beaucoup de dépenses.* A wedding involves a lot of expense.; **s'entraîner** to train ▷ *Il s'entraîne au foot tous les samedis matins.* He does football training every Saturday morning.

entraîneur *nm* trainer

entre *prep* between ▷ *Il est assis entre son père et son oncle.* He's sitting between his father and his uncle.; **entre eux** among themselves; **l'un d'entre eux** one of them

entrecôte *nf* rib steak

entrée *nf* ❶ entrance ❷ (of meal) starter ▷ *Qu'est ce que vous prenez comme entrée?* What would you like for the starter?

entreprendre [66] *vb* to start on ▷ *Elle a entrepris des démarches pour adopter un enfant.* She's started on the procedures for adopting a child.

entrepreneur *nm* contractor

entreprise *nf* firm

entrer [33] *vb* ❶ to come in ▷ *Entrez donc!* Come on in! ❷ to go in ▷ Ils sont tous entrés dans la maison. They all went into the house.; **entrer à l'hôpital** to go into hospital; **entrer des données** to enter data

entre-temps adv meanwhile

entretien nm ❶ maintenance ❷ interview

entrevue nf interview

entrouvert, e adj half-open

envahir [39] vb to invade

enveloppe nf envelope

envelopper [29] vb to wrap

envers prep towards ▷ Il est bien disposé envers elle. He's well disposed towards her.
  ▶ nm **à l'envers** inside out

envie nf **avoir envie de faire quelque chose** to feel like doing something ▷ J'avais envie de pleurer. I felt like crying. ▷ J'ai envie d'aller aux toilettes. I want to go to the toilet.; **Cette glace me fait envie.** I fancy some of that ice cream.

envier [20] vb to envy

environ adv about ▷ C'est à soixante kilomètres environ. It's about 60 kilometres.

environnement nm environment

environs nmpl area ▷ Il y a beaucoup de choses intéressantes à voir dans les environs. There are a lot of interesting things to see in the area.; **aux environs de dix-neuf heures** around 7 p.m.

envisager [46] vb to consider

s' **envoler** [29] vb ❶ to fly away ▷ Le papillon s'est envolé. The butterfly flew away. ❷ to blow away ▷ Toutes mes feuilles de cours se sont envolées. All my lecture notes blew away.

envoyer [34] vb to send ▷ Ma tante m'a envoyé une carte pour mon anniversaire. My aunt sent me a card for my birthday.; **envoyer quelqu'un chercher quelque chose** to send somebody to get something ▷ Sa mère l'a envoyé chercher du pain. His mother sent him to get some bread.; **envoyer un e-mail à quelqu'un** to send sb an email

épais (f épaisse) adj thick

épaisseur nf thickness

épatant, e adj (informal) great

épaule nf shoulder

épée nf sword

épeler [5] vb to spell ▷ Est-ce que vous pouvez épeler votre nom s'il vous plaît? Can you spell your name please?

épice nf spice

épicé, e adj spicy

épicerie nf grocer's shop

épicier (f épicière) nm/f grocer

épidémie nf epidemic

épiler [29] vb **s'épiler les jambes** to wax one's legs; **s'épiler les sourcils** to pluck one's eyebrows

épinards nmpl spinach

épine nf thorn

épingle nf pin; **une épingle de sûreté** a safety pin

épisode nm episode

éplucher [29] vb to peel

éponge nf sponge

époque nf time ▷ à cette époque

de l'année at this time of year; **à l'époque** at that time

épouse nf wife

épouser [29] vb to marry

épouvantable adj awful

épouvante nf terror; **un film d'épouvante** a horror film

épouvanter [29] vb to terrify

époux nm husband; **les nouveaux époux** the newly-weds

épreuve nf ❶ test ▷ *une épreuve écrite* a written test ❷ (sport) event

éprouver [29] vb to feel ▷ *Qu'est-ce que vous avez éprouvé à ce moment-là?* What did you feel at that moment?

EPS nf (= éducation physique et sportive) PE (physical education)

épuisé, e adj exhausted

épuiser [29] vb to wear out ▷ *Ce travail m'a complètement épuisé.* This job has completely worn me out.; **s'épuiser** to wear oneself out ▷ *Il s'épuise à garder un jardin impeccable.* He wears himself out keeping his garden immaculate.

Équateur nm Ecuador

équateur nm equator

équation nf equation

équerre nf set square

équilibre nm balance ▷ *J'ai failli perdre l'équilibre. I* nearly lost my balance.

équilibré, e adj well-balanced

équipage nm crew

équipe nf team

équipé, e adj **bien équipé** well-equipped

équipement nm equipment

équipements nmpl facilities ▷ *les équipements sportifs* sports facilities

équitation nf riding

équivalent nm equivalent

erreur nf mistake; **faire erreur** to be mistaken

es vb see **être**; **Tu es très gentille.** You're very kind.

ESB nf (= encéphalite spongiforme bovine) BSE

escabeau (pl **escabeaux**) nm stepladder

escalade nf climbing

escalader [29] vb to climb

escale nf **faire escale** to stop off

escalier nm stairs

escargot nm snail

esclavage nm slavery

esclave nmf slave

escrime nf fencing

escroc nm crook

espace nm space; **espace de travail** workspace

s'espacer [13] vb to become less frequent ▷ *Ses visites se sont peu à peu espacées.* His visits became less and less frequent.

espadrille nf rope-soled sandal

Espagne nf Spain; **en Espagne (1)** in Spain **(2)** to Spain

espagnol, e adj Spanish
  ▶ nm Spanish ▷ *J'apprends l'espagnol.* I'm learning Spanish.
  ▶ nm/f **un Espagnol** (man) a Spaniard; **une Espagnole** (woman) a Spaniard

espèce nf ❶ sort ❷ species ▷ *une espèce en voie de disparition* an endangered species; **Espèce d'idiot!** You idiot!

espèces nfpl cash

espérer [35] vb to hope; **J'espère bien.** I hope so. ▷ *Tu penses avoir réussi? — Oui, j'espère bien.* Do you think you've passed? —Yes, I hope so.

espiègle adj mischievous

espion (**f**espionne) nm/f spy

espionnage nm spying; **un roman d'espionnage** a spy novel

espoir nm hope

esprit nm mind ▷ *Ça ne m'est pas venu à l'esprit.* It didn't cross my mind.; **avoir de l'esprit** to be witty

esquimau (**f** pl esquimaux®) nm ice lolly

Esquimau (**f**Esquimaude, pl Esquimaux) nm/f Eskimo

essai nm attempt; **prendre quelqu'un à l'essai** to take somebody on for a trial period

essayer [60] vb ❶ to try ▷ *Essaie de rentrer de bonne heure.* Try to come home early. ❷ to try on ▷ *Essaie ce pull: il devrait bien t'aller.* Try this sweater on: it ought to look good on you.

essence nf petrol

essentiel (**f**essentielle) adj essential; **Tu es là: c'est l'essentiel.** You're here: that's the main thing.

s' **essouffler** [29] vb to get out of breath

essuie-glace nm windscreen wiper

essuyer [54] vb to wipe; **essuyer la vaisselle** to dry the dishes;

s'**essuyer** to dry oneself ▷ *Vous pouvez vous essuyer les mains avec cette serviette.* You can dry your hands on this towel.

est vb see **être**; **Elle est merveilleuse.** She's marvellous.

▶ adj ❶ east ❷ eastern

▶ nm east; **vers l'est** eastwards; **à l'est de Paris** east of Paris; **l'Europe de l'Est** Eastern Europe; **le vent d'est** the east wind

est-ce que adv **Est-ce que c'est cher?** Is it expensive?; **Quand est-ce qu'il part?** When is he leaving?

esthéticienne nf beautician

estime nf **J'ai beaucoup d'estime pour elle.** I think a lot of her.

estimer [29] vb estimer quelqu'un to have great respect for somebody; **estimer que** to consider that ▷ *J'estime que c'est de sa faute.* I consider that it's his fault.

estivant (**f**estivante) nm/f holiday-maker

estomac nm stomach

Estonie nf Estonia

estrade nf platform

et conj and

établir [39] vb to establish; **s'établir à son compte** to set up in business

établissement nm establishment; **un établissement scolaire** a school

étage nm floor ▷ *au premier étage* on the first floor; **à l'étage** upstairs

étagère nf shelf

étaient vb see **être**

étain nm tin

a
b
c
d
e
f
g
h
i
j
k
l
m
n
o
p
q
r
s
t
u
v
w
x
y
z

étais, était vb see **être**; Il était très jeune. He was very young.

étalage nm display

étaler [29] vb to spread

étanche adj ❶ watertight ❷ (watch) waterproof

étang nm pond

étant vb see **être**; Mes revenus étant limités ... My income being limited ...

étape nf stage; faire étape to stop off

État nm (nation) state

état nm ❶ (country) state ❷ condition ▷ en mauvais état in poor condition; remettre quelque chose en état to repair something; le bureau d'état civil the registry office

États-Unis nmpl United States; aux États-Unis (1) in the United States (2) to the United States

été vb see **être**; Il a été licencié. He's been made redundant.
▶ nm summer; en été in the summer

éteindre [61] vb ❶ to switch off ▷ N'oubliez pas d'éteindre la lumière en sortant. Don't forget to switch off the light when you leave. ❷ (cigarette) to put out

étendre [89] vb to spread ▷ Elle a étendu une nappe propre sur la table. She spread a clean cloth on the table.; étendre le linge to hang out the washing; s'étendre to lie down ▷ Je vais m'étendre cinq minutes. I'm going to lie down for five minutes.

éternité nf J'ai attendu une éternité chez le médecin. I waited for ages at the doctor's.

éternuer [29] vb to sneeze

êtes vb see **être**; Vous êtes en retard. You're late.

étiez vb see **être**

étinceler [5] vb to sparkle

étions vb see **être**

étiquette nf label

s' **étirer** [29] vb to stretch ▷ Elle s'est étirée paresseusement. She stretched lazily.

étoile nf star; une étoile de mer a starfish; une étoile filante a shooting star; dormir à la belle étoile to sleep under the stars

étonnant, e adj amazing

étonner [29] vb to surprise ▷ Cela m'étonnerait que le colis soit déjà arrivé. I'd be surprised if the parcel had arrived yet.

étouffer [29] vb On étouffe ici: ouvre donc les fenêtres. It's stifling in here: open the windows.; s'étouffer to choke ▷ Ne mange pas si vite: tu vas t'étouffer! Don't eat so fast: you'll choke!

étourderie nf absent-mindedness; une erreur d'étourderie a slip

étourdi, e adj scatterbrained

étourdissement nm avoir des étourdissements to feel dizzy

étrange adj strange

étranger (f étrangère) adj foreign; une personne étrangère a stranger

▶ nm/f ❶ foreigner ❷ stranger; **à l'étranger** abroad

étrangler [29] vb to strangle; **s'étrangler** to choke ▷ *s'étrangler avec quelque chose* to choke on something

être [36] vb ❶ to be ▷ *Je suis heureux.* I'm happy. ▷ *Il est dix heures.* It's 10 o'clock. ❷ to have ▷ *Il n'est pas encore arrivé.* He hasn't arrived yet.

▶ nm **un être humain** a human being

étrennes nfpl **Nous avons donné des étrennes à la gardienne.** We gave the caretaker a New Year gift.

étroit, e adj narrow; **être à l'étroit** to be cramped

étude nf study; **faire des études** to be studying ▷ *Il fait des études de droit.* He's studying law.

étudiant (f **étudiante**) nm/f student

étudier [20] vb to study

étui nm case ▷ *un étui à lunettes* a glasses case

eu vb see **avoir**; **J'ai eu une bonne note.** I got a good mark.

euh excl er ▷ *Euh ... je ne m'en souviens pas.* Er ... I can't remember.

euro nm (currency) euro

Europe nf Europe; **en Europe (1)** in Europe **(2)** to Europe

européen (f **européenne**) adj European

eurozone nf eurozone

eux pron them ▷ *Je pense souvent à eux.* I often think of them.

> ▌ **eux** is also used for emphasis.

▷ *Elle a accepté l'invitation, mais eux ont refusé.* She accepted the invitation, but THEY refused.

évacuer [29] vb to evacuate

s' **évader** [29] vb to escape

évangile nm gospel

s' **évanouir** [39] vb to faint

s' **évaporer** [29] vb to evaporate

évasif (f **évasive**) adj evasive

évasion nf escape

éveillé, e adj ❶ awake ▷ *Il est resté éveillé toute la nuit.* He stayed awake all night. ❷ bright ▷ *C'est un enfant très éveillé pour son âge.* He's very bright for his age.

s' **éveiller** [29] vb to awaken

événement nm event

éventail nm (hand-held) fan; **un large éventail de prix** a wide range of prices

éventualité nf **dans l'éventualité d'un retard** in the event of a delay

éventuel (f **éventuelle**) adj possible

> ▌ Be careful! **éventuel** does not mean **eventual**.

éventuellement adj possibly

> ▌ Be careful! **éventuellement** does not mean **eventually**.

évêque nm bishop

évidemment adv ❶ obviously ❷ of course

évidence nf **C'est une évidence.** It's quite obvious.; **de toute évidence** obviously; **être en évidence** to be clearly visible; **mettre en évidence** to reveal

évident, e adj obvious

évier nm sink

éviter [29] vb to avoid

évolué, e adj advanced

évoluer [29] vb to progress ▷ La chirurgie esthétique a beaucoup évolué. Plastic surgery has progressed a great deal.; **Il a beaucoup évolué.** He has come on a great deal.

évolution nf ❶ development ❷ evolution

évoquer [29] vb to mention ▷ Il a évoqué divers problèmes dans son discours. He mentioned various problems in his speech.

exact, e adj ❶ right ❷ exact

exactement adv exactly

ex aequo adj Ils sont arrivés ex aequo. They finished neck and neck.

    ■ **ex aequo** is said like "ex-echo".

exagérer [35] vb ❶ to exaggerate ▷ Vous exagérez! You're exaggerating! ❷ to go too far ▷ Ça fait trois fois que tu arrives en retard: tu exagères! That's three times you've been late: you really go too far sometimes!

examen nm exam; **un examen médical** a medical

examiner [29] vb to examine

exaspérant, e adj infuriating

exaspérer [35] vb to infuriate

excédent nm l'excédent de bagages excess baggage

excéder [35] vb to exceed ▷ un contrat dont la durée n'excède pas deux ans a contract for a period not exceeding two years; **excéder quelqu'un** to drive somebody mad

▷ Les cris des enfants l'excédaient. The noise of the children was driving her mad.

excellent, e adj excellent

excentrique adj eccentric

excepté prep except ▷ Toutes les chaussures excepté les sandales sont en solde. All the shoes except sandals are reduced.

exception nf exception; **à l'exception de** except

exceptionnel (fexceptionnelle) adj exceptional

excès nm faire des excès to overindulge; **les excès de vitesse** speeding

excessif (fexcessive) adj excessive

excitant, e adj exciting ▶ nm stimulant

excitation nf excitement

exciter [29] vb to excite ▷ Il était tout excité à l'idée de revoir ses cousins. He was all excited about seeing his cousins again.; **s'exciter** (informal) to get excited ▷ Ne t'excite pas trop vite: ça ne va peut-être pas marcher! Don't get excited too soon: it may not work!

exclamation nf exclamation

exclu, e adj Il n'est pas exclu que ... It's not impossible that ...

exclusif (fexclusive) adj exclusive

excursion nf ❶ trip ❷ walk ▷ une excursion dans la montagne a walk in the hills

excuse nf ❶ excuse ❷ apology ▷ présenter ses excuses to offer one's apologies; **un mot d'excuse** a note

▷ *Vous devez apporter un mot d'excuse signé par vos parents.* You have to bring a note signed by your parents.

excuser [29] vb to excuse; **Excusez-moi.** (1) Sorry! ▷ *Excusez-moi, je ne vous avais pas vu.* Sorry, I didn't see you. (2) Excuse me. ▷ *Excusez-moi, est-ce que vous avez l'heure?* Excuse me, have you got the time?; **s'excuser** to apologize

exécuter [29] vb ❶ to execute ▷ *Le prisonnier a été exécuté à l'aube.* The prisoner was executed at dawn. ❷ to perform ▷ *Le pianiste va maintenant exécuter une valse de Chopin.* The pianist is now going to perform a waltz by Chopin.

exemplaire nm copy

exemple nm example ▷ *donner l'exemple* to set an example; **par exemple** for example

s'**exercer** [13] vb to practise

exercice nm exercise

exhiber [29] vb to show off ▷ *Il aime bien exhiber ses décorations.* He likes showing off his medals.; **s'exhiber** to expose oneself

exhibitionniste nm flasher

exigeant, e adj hard to please

exiger [46] vb ❶ to demand ▷ *Le propriétaire exige d'être payé immédiatement.* The landlord is demanding to be paid immediately. ❷ to require ▷ *Ce travail exige beaucoup de patience.* This job requires a lot of patience.

exil nm exile

exister [29] vb to exist ▷ *Ça n'existe pas.* It doesn't exist.

exotique adj exotic ▷ *un yaourt aux fruits exotiques* a tropical fruit yoghurt

expédier [20] vb to send ▷ *expédier un colis* to send a parcel

expéditeur (f**expéditrice**) nm/f sender

expédition nf expedition; **l'expédition du courrier** the dispatch of the mail

expérience nf ❶ experience ❷ experiment

expérimenter [29] vb to test ▷ *Ces produits de beauté n'ont pas été expérimentés sur des animaux.* These cosmetics have not been tested on animals.

expert nm expert

expirer [29] vb ❶ (document, passport) to expire ❷ (time allowed) to run out ❸ (person) to breathe out

explication nf explanation; **une explication de texte** (of a text) a critical analysis

expliquer [29] vb to explain ▷ *Il m'a expliqué comment faire.* He explained to me how to do it.; **ça s'explique** it's understandable

exploit nm achievement

exploitation nf exploitation; **une exploitation agricole** a farm

exploiter [29] vb to exploit

explorer [29] vb to explore

exploser [29] vb to explode

explosif nm explosive

explosion nf explosion

exportateur (f**exportatrice**) nm/f exporter

exportation nf export
exporter [29] vb to export
exposé nm talk ▷ *On nous a demandé de faire un exposé sur l'environnement.* We were asked to give a talk on the environment.
exposer [29] vb ❶ to show ▷ *Il expose ses peintures dans une galerie d'art.* He shows his paintings in a private art gallery. ❷ to expose ▷ *N'exposez pas la pellicule à la lumière.* Do not expose the film to light. ❸ to set out ▷ *Il nous a exposé les raisons de son départ.* He set out the reasons for his departure.; **s'exposer au soleil** to stay out in the sun
exposition nf exhibition
exprès adv ❶ on purpose ❷ specially
express nm ❶ (*coffee*) espresso ❷ fast train
expression nf ❶ expression ❷ phrase
exprimer [29] vb to express; **s'exprimer** to express oneself
exquis, e adj exquisite
extérieur, e adj outside
▶ nm outside; **à l'extérieur** outside ▷ *Les toilettes sont à l'extérieur.* The toilet is outside.
externat nm day school
externe nmf day pupil
extincteur nm fire extinguisher
extra adj inv excellent
extraire [86] vb to extract
extrait nm extract
extraordinaire adj extraordinary
extravagant, e adj extravagant

extrême adj extreme
▶ nm extreme
extrêmement adv extremely
Extrême-Orient nm the Far East
extrémité nf end ▷ *La gare est à l'autre extrémité de la ville.* The station is at the other end of the town.

f

F *abbr* franc

fa *nm* F

fabrication *nf* manufacture

fabriquer [29] *vb* to make
▷ *fabriqué en France* made in France;
Qu'est-ce qu'il fabrique?
(*informal*) What's he up to?

fac *nf* (*informal*) university; **à la fac**
at university

face *nf* face à face face to face; **en
face de** opposite ▷ *Le bus s'arrête en
face de chez moi.* The bus stops
opposite my house.; **faire face à
quelque chose** to face something;
Pile ou face? — Face. Heads or
tails? — Heads.

fâché, e *adj* angry; **être fâché
contre quelqu'un** to be angry
with somebody; **être fâché
avec quelqu'un** to be on bad
terms with somebody

se fâcher [29] *vb* **se fâcher contre
quelqu'un** to lose one's temper
with somebody; **se fâcher
avec quelqu'un** to fall out with
somebody

facile *adj* easy; **facile à faire** easy
to do

facilement *adv* easily

facilité *nf* un logiciel d'une
grande facilité d'utilisation a very
user-friendly piece of software; **Il a
des facilités en langues.** He has a
gift for languages.

> Be careful! **facilité** does not
> mean **facility**.

façon *nf* way ▷ *De quelle façon?*
In what way?; **de toute façon**
anyway

facteur *nm* postman

facture *nf* bill ▷ *une facture de gaz*
a gas bill

facultatif (*f* **facultative**) *adj*
optional

faculté *nf* faculty; **avoir une
grande faculté de concentration**
to have great powers of
concentration

fade *adj* tasteless

faible *adj* weak; **Il est faible en
maths.** He's not very good at maths.

faiblesse *nf* weakness

faïence *nf* pottery

faillir [13] *vb* J'ai failli tomber.
I nearly fell down.

faillite *nf* bankruptcy; **une
entreprise en faillite** a bankrupt
business; **faire faillite** to go
bankrupt

faim nf hunger; **avoir faim** to be hungry

fainéant, e adj lazy

faire [37] vb ① to make ▷ Je vais faire un gâteau pour ce soir. I'm going to make a cake for tonight. ▷ Ils font trop de bruit. They're making too much noise. ② to do ▷ Qu'est-ce que tu fais? What are you doing? ▷ Il fait de l'italien. He's doing Italian. ③ to play ▷ Il fait du piano. He plays the piano. ④ to be ▷ Qu'est-ce qu'il fait chaud! Isn't it hot! ▷ Espérons qu'il fera beau demain. Let's hope it'll be nice weather tomorrow.; **Ça ne fait rien.** It doesn't matter.; **Ça fait cinquante-trois euros en tout.** That makes fifty-three euros in all.; **Ça fait trois ans qu'il habite à Paris.** He's lived in Paris for three years.; **faire tomber** to knock over ▷ Le chat a fait tomber le vase. The cat knocked over the vase.; **faire faire quelque chose** to get something done ▷ Je dois faire réparer ma voiture. I've got to get my car repaired.; **Je vais me faire couper les cheveux.** I'm going to get my hair cut.; **Ne t'en fais pas!** Don't worry!

fais, faisaient, faisais, faisait vb see **faire**

faisan nm pheasant

faisiez, faisions, faisons, fait vb see **faire**

fait nm fact; **un fait divers** a news item; **au fait** by the way; **en fait** actually

faites vb see **faire**

falaise nf cliff

falloir [38] vb see **faut, faudra, faudrait**

famé, e adj **un quartier mal famé** a rough area

fameux (f **fameuse**) adj Ce n'est pas fameux. It's not great.

familial, e (mpl **familiaux**) adj family; **les allocations familiales** child benefit

familier (f **familière**) adj familiar

famille nf ① family ▷ une famille nombreuse a big family ② relatives ▷ Il a de la famille à Paris. He's got relatives in Paris.

famine nf famine

fanatique adj fanatical
▸ nf fanatic

fanfare nf brass band

fantaisie adj des bijoux fantaisie costume jewellery

fantastique adj fantastic

fantôme nm ghost

farce nf ① (for chicken, turkey) stuffing ② practical joke

farci, e adj stuffed ▷ des tomates farcies stuffed tomatoes

farine nf flour

fascinant, e adj fascinating

fasciner [29] vb to fascinate

fascisme nm fascism

fasse, fassent, fasses, fassiez, fassions vb see **faire**; Pourvu qu'il fasse beau demain! Let's hope it'll be fine tomorrow!

fatal, e adj fatal; C'était fatal. It was bound to happen.

fatalité nf fate

fatigant, e adj tiring

fatigue nf tiredness

fatigué, e adj tired

se fatiguer [29] vb to get tired

fauché, e adj (informal) hard up

faudra vb

> faudra is the future tense of *falloir*.

Il faudra qu'on soit plus rapide. We'll have to be quicker.

faudrait vb

> faudrait is the conditional tense of *falloir*.

Il faudrait qu'on fasse attention. We ought to be careful.

se faufiler [29] vb ▷ Il s'est faufilé à travers la foule. He made his way through the crowd.

faune nf wildlife

fausse adj see **faux**

faut vb

> faut is the present tense of *falloir*.

Il faut faire attention. You've got to be careful.; Nous n'avons pas le choix, il faut y aller. We've no choice, we've got to go.; Il faut que je parte. I've got to go.; Il faut du courage pour faire ce métier. It takes courage to do that job.; Il me faut de l'argent. I need money.

faute nf ① mistake ▷ faire une faute to make a mistake ② fault ▷ Ce n'est pas de ma faute. It's not my fault.; sans faute without fail

fauteuil nm armchair; un fauteuil roulant a wheelchair

faux (fausse) adj, adv untrue; faire un faux pas to trip; Il chante faux. He sings out of tune.
> nm fake ▷ Ce tableau est un faux. This painting is a fake.

faveur nf favour

favori (ffavorite) adj favourite

favoriser [29] vb to favour

fax nm fax

faxer [29] vb to fax; faxer un document à quelqu'un to fax somebody a document

fée nf fairy

feignant, e adj (informal) lazy

félicitations nfpl congratulations

féliciter [29] vb to congratulate

femelle nf (animal) female

féminin, e adj ① female ▷ les personnages féminins du roman the female characters in the novel ② feminine ▷ Elle est très féminine. She's very feminine. ③ women's ▷ Elle joue dans l'équipe féminine de France. She plays in the French women's team.

féministe adj feminist

femme nf ① woman ② wife; une femme au foyer a housewife; une femme de ménage a cleaning woman; une femme de chambre a chambermaid

se fendre [89] vb to crack

fenêtre nf window

fenouil nm fennel

fente nf slot

fer nm iron; un fer à cheval a horseshoe; un fer à repasser an iron

fera, ferai, feras, ferez vb see **faire**

férié, e adj **un jour férié** a public holiday

feriez, ferions vb see **faire**

ferme adj firm
▶ nf farm

fermé, e adj ❶ closed ▷ La pharmacie est fermée. The chemist's is closed. ❷ off ▷ Est-ce que le gaz est fermé? Is the gas off?

fermer [29] vb ❶ to close ▷ N'oublie pas de fermer la fenêtre. Don't forget to close the window. ❷ to turn off ▷ As-tu bien fermé le robinet? Have you turned the tap off?; **fermer à clef** to lock

fermeture nf **les heures de fermeture** closing times; **une fermeture éclair®** a zip

fermier nm farmer

fermière nf ❶ woman farmer ❷ farmer's wife

féroce adj fierce

ferons, feront vb see **faire**

fesses nfpl buttocks

festival nm festival

festivités nfpl festivities

fête nf ❶ party; **faire la fête** to party ❷ name day ▷ C'est sa fête aujourd'hui. It's his name day today.; **une fête foraine** a funfair; **la Fête Nationale** Bastille Day; **les fêtes de fin d'année** the festive season

fêter [29] vb to celebrate

feu (pl **feux**) nm ❶ fire ▷ prendre feu to catch fire ▷ faire du feu to make a fire; **Au feu!** Fire!; **un feu de joie** a bonfire ❷ traffic light ▷ un feu rouge a red light ▷ Tournez à gauche aux feux. Turn left at the lights.; **Avez-vous du feu?** Have you got a light? ❶ heat ▷ ... mijoter à feu doux ... simmer over a gentle heat; **un feu d'artifice** a firework display

feuillage nm leaves

feuille nf ❶ leaf ▷ des feuilles mortes fallen leaves ❷ sheet ▷ une feuille de papier a sheet of paper; **une feuille de maladie** a claim form for medical expenses

feuilleté, e adj **de la pâte feuilletée** flaky pastry

feuilleter [42] vb to leaf through

feuilleton nm serial

feutre nm felt; **un stylo-feutre** a felt-tip pen

fève nf broad bean

février nm February; **en février** in February

fiable adj reliable

fiançailles nfpl engagement

fiancé, e adj **être fiancé(e) à quelqu'un** to be engaged to somebody

se fiancer [13] vb to get engaged

ficelle nf ❶ string ❷ (bread) thin baguette

fiche nf form

se ficher [29] vb (informal): **Je m'en fiche!** I don't care!; **Fiche-moi la paix!** Leave me alone!; **Quoi, tu n'as fait que ça? Tu te fiches de moi?** You've only done that much? You can't be serious!

fichier nm file

fichu, e adj (informal): **Ce parapluie est fichu.** This umbrella's knackered.

97 | flacon

fidèle adj faithful

fier (f **fière**) adj proud

fierté nf pride

fièvre nf fever ▷ *J'ai de la fièvre. I've got a temperature.*

fiévreux (f **fiévreuse**) adj feverish

figue nf fig

figure nf ❶ face ▷ *Il a reçu le ballon en pleine figure.* The ball hit him smack in the face. ❷ (illustration) figure ▷ *Voir figure 2.1, page 32.* See figure 2.1, page 32.

fil nm thread; **le fil de fer** wire; **un coup de fil** a phone call

file nf (of people, objects) line; **une file d'attente** a queue; **à la file** one after the other; **en file indienne** in single file

filer [29] vb to speed along; **File dans ta chambre!** Off to your room with you!

filet nm net

fille nf ❶ girl ▷ *C'est une école de filles.* It's a girls' school. ❷ daughter ▷ *C'est leur fille aînée.* She's their oldest daughter.

fillette nf little girl

filleul nm godson

filleule nf goddaughter

film nm film; **un film policier** a thriller; **un film d'aventures** an adventure film; **un film d'épouvante** a horror film; **le film alimentaire** Clingfilm®

fils nm son

fin nf end; "Fin" "The End"; **À la fin, il a réussi à se décider.** In the end he managed to make up his mind.; **Il sera en vacances fin juin.** He'll

be on holiday at the end of June.; **en fin de journée** at the end of the day; **en fin de compte** when all's said and done; **sans fin** endless
▶ adj fine; **des fines herbes** mixed herbs

finale nf final

finalement adv ❶ at last ▷ *Nous sommes finalement arrivés.* At last we arrived. ❷ after all ▷ *Finalement, tu avais raison.* You were right after all.

fini, e adj finished

finir [39] vb to finish ▷ *Le cours finit à onze heures.* The lesson finishes at 11 o'clock.; **Il a fini par se décider.** He made up his mind in the end.

finlandais, e adj Finnish
▶ nm Finnish ▷ *Ils parlent finlandais.* They speak Finnish.
▶ nm/f **un Finlandais** (man) a Finn; **une Finlandaise** (woman) a Finn; **les Finlandais** the Finns

Finlande nf Finland

firme nf firm

fis vb see **faire**

fissure nf crack

fit vb see **faire**

fixe adj ❶ steady ▷ *Il n'a pas d'emploi fixe.* He hasn't got a steady job. ❷ set ▷ *Il mange toujours à heures fixes.* He always eats at set times.; **un menu à prix fixe** a set menu

fixer [29] vb ❶ to fix ▷ *Nous avons fixé une heure pour nous retrouver.* We fixed a time to meet. ❷ to stare at ▷ *Ne fixe pas les gens comme ça!* Don't stare at people like that!

flacon nm bottle

flageolet nm small haricot bean

flamand, e adj Flemish
▶ nm Flemish ▷ Il parle flamand chez lui. He speaks Flemish at home.
▶ nm/f **les Flamands** the Dutch-speaking Belgians

flambé, e adj des bananes flambées flambéed bananas

flamme nf flame; **en flammes** on fire

flan nm baked custard

flâner [29] vb to stroll

flaque nf (of water) puddle

flash (pl flashes) nm (of camera) flash; **un flash d'information** a newsflash

flatter [29] vb to flatter

flèche nf arrow

fléchettes nfpl darts

fleur nf flower

fleuri, e adj ❶ full of flowers ❷ flowery

fleurir [39] vb to flower ▷ Cette plante fleurit en automne. This plant flowers in autumn.

fleuriste nmf florist

fleuve nm river

flic nm (informal) cop

flipper nm pinball machine

flirter [29] vb to flirt

flocon nm flake

flotter [29] vb to float

flou, e adj blurred

fluor nm le dentifrice au fluor fluoride toothpaste

flûte nf flute; **une flûte à bec** a recorder; **Flûte!** (informal) Heck!

foi nf faith

foie nm liver; **une crise de foie** a stomach upset

foin nm hay; **un rhume des foins** hay fever

foire nf fair; **la foire aux questions** (internet) FAQs

fois nf time ▷ la première fois the first time ▷ à chaque fois each time ▷ deux fois deux font quatre 2 times 2 is 4; **une fois** once; **deux fois** twice ▷ deux fois plus de gens twice as many people; **une fois que** once; **à la fois** at once ▷ Je ne peux pas faire deux choses à la fois. I can't do two things at once.

folie nf madness; **faire une folie** to be extravagant

folklorique adj folk

folle adj see **fou**

foncé, e adj dark

foncer [13] vb (informal): Je vais foncer à la boulangerie. I'm just going to dash to the baker's.

fonction nf function; **une voiture de fonction** a company car

fonctionnaire nmf civil servant

fonctionner [29] vb to work

fond nm ❶ bottom ▷ Mon porte-monnaie est au fond de mon sac. My purse is at the bottom of my bag. ❷ end ▷ Les toilettes sont au fond du couloir. The toilets are at the end of the corridor.; **dans le fond** all things considered

fonder [29] vb to found

fondre [70] vb to melt; **fondre en larmes** to burst into tears

fondu, e adj du beurre fondu melted butter

font vb see **faire**

fontaine nf fountain

foot nm (informal) football

football nm football

footballeur nm footballer

footing nm jogging

forain, e adj **une fête foraine** a funfair
> ▸ nm fairground worker

force nf strength; **à force de** by
> ▸ Il a grossi à force de manger autant. He got fat by eating so much.; **de force** by force

forcé, e adj forced; **C'est forcé.** (informal) It's inevitable.

forcément adv **Ça devait forcément arriver.** That was bound to happen.; **pas forcément** not necessarily

forêt nf forest

forfait nm all-in price; **C'est compris dans le forfait.** It's included in the price.

forgeron nm blacksmith

formalité nf formality

format nm size

formation nf training; **la formation continue** in-house training; **Il a une formation d'ingénieur.** He is a trained engineer.

forme nf shape; **être en forme** to be in good shape; **Je ne suis as en forme aujourd'hui.** I'm not feeling too good today.; **Tu as l'air en forme.** You're looking well.

formellement adv strictly

former [29] vb to form

formidable adj great

formulaire nm form

fort, e adj, adv ❶ strong ▷ Le café est trop fort. The coffee's too strong. ❷ good ▷ Il est fort en espagnol. He's good at Spanish. ❸ loud ▷ Est-ce vous pouvez parler plus fort? Can you speak louder?; **frapper fort** to hit hard

fortifiant nm (medicine) tonic

fortune nf fortune; **de fortune** makeshift

forum de discussion nm chatroom

fossé nm ditch

fou (ffolle) adj mad; **Il y a un monde fou sur la plage!** (informal) There are loads of people on the beach!; **attraper le fou rire** to get the giggles

foudre nf lightning

foudroyant, e adj instant

fouet nm whisk

fougère nf fern

fouiller [29] vb to rummage

fouillis nm mess ▷ Il y a du fouillis dans sa chambre. His bedroom is a mess.

foulard nm scarf

foule nf crowd; **une foule de** masses of

se fouler [29] vb **se fouler la cheville** to sprain one's ankle

four nm oven ▷ un four à micro-ondes a microwave oven

fourchette nf fork

fourmi nf ant; **avoir des fourmis dans les jambes** to have pins and needles

> Word for word, the French means "to have ants in one's legs".

fourneau(pl **fourneaux**) nm stove

fourni, e adj (beard, hair) thick

fournir [39] vb to supply

fournisseur nm supplier; **un fournisseur d'accès à Internet** an internet service provider

fournitures nfpl **les fournitures scolaires** school stationery

fourré, e adj filled

fourrer [29] vb (informal) to put ▷ Où as-tu fourré mon sac? Where have you put my bag?

fourre-tout(pl **fourre-tout**) nm holdall

fourrure nf fur

foutre vb (rude) to do ▷ Qu'est-ce qu'il fout? What the hell is he doing?; **Je n'en ai rien à foutre!** I don't give a damn!

foutu, e adj ❶ (rude) knackered ❷ bloody

foyer nm home; **un foyer de jeunes** a youth club

fracture nf fracture

fragile adj fragile

fragilité nf fragility

fraîche adj see **frais**

fraîcheur nf ❶ cool ❸ freshness

frais(f **fraîche**) adj ❶ fresh ▷ des œufs frais fresh eggs ❸ chilly ▷ Il fait un peu frais ce soir. It's a bit chilly this evening. ❸ cool ▷ des boissons fraîches cool drinks; **"servir frais"** "serve chilled"; **mettre au frais** to put in a cool place
▶ nmpl expenses

fraise nf strawberry

framboise nf raspberry

franc(f **franche**) adj frank
▶ nm franc
● The **franc** is the unit of currency in Switzerland and many former French colonies. The euro replaced the franc in France, Belgium and Luxembourg in 2002.

français, e adj French
▶ nm French ▷ Il parle français couramment. He speaks French fluently.
▶ nm/f **un Français** a Frenchman; **une Française** a Frenchwoman; **les Français** the French

France nf France; **en France** in France ▷ Je suis né en France. I was born in France. **(2)** to France ▷ Je pars en France pour Noël. I'm going to France for Christmas.

franche adj see **franc**

franchement adv ❶ frankly ❷ really

franchir [39] vb to get over

franchise nf frankness

francophone adj French-speaking

frange nf fringe

frangipane nf almond cream

frapper [29] vb to strike ▷ Il l'a frappée au visage. He struck her in the face.

fredonner [29] vb to hum

freezer nm freezing compartment

frein nm brake; **le frein à main** handbrake

freiner [29] vb to brake

frêle adj frail

frelon nm hornet

frémir [39] *vb* shudder

fréquemment *adv* frequently

fréquent, e *adj* frequent

fréquenté, e *adj* busy ▷ *une rue très fréquentée* a very busy street; **un bar mal fréquenté** a rough pub

fréquenter [29] *vb* (person) to see ▷ *Je ne le fréquente pas beaucoup.* I don't see him often.

frère *nm* brother

friand *nm* **un friand au fromage** a cheese puff

friandise *nf* sweet

fric *nm* (*informal*) cash

frigidaire ® *nm* refrigerator

frigo *nm* (*informal*) fridge

frileux (*f* frileuse) *adj* **être frileux (frileuse)** to feel the cold

frimer [29] *vb* (*informal*) to show off

fringues *nfpl* (*informal*) clothes

fripé, e *adj* crumpled

frire [81] *vb* **faire frire** to fry

frisé, e *adj* curly

frisson *nm* shiver

frissonner [29] *vb* to shiver

frit, e *adj* fried

frites *nfpl* chips

friture *nf* ❶ fried food ❷ fried fish

froid, e *adj* cold
  ▶ *nm* cold; **Il fait froid.** It's cold.; **avoir froid** to be cold ▷ *Est-ce que tu as froid?* Are you cold?

se froisser [29] *vb* ❶ to crease ▷ *Ce tissu se froisse très facilement.* This material creases very easily. ❷ to take offence ▷ *Paul se froisse très facilement.* Paul's very quick to take offence.; **se froisser un muscle** to strain a muscle

frôler [29] *vb* ❶ to brush against ▷ *Le chat m'a frôlé au passage.* The cat brushed against me as it went past. ❷ to narrowly avoid ▷ *Nous avons frôlé la catastrophe.* We narrowly avoided disaster.

fromage *nm* cheese; **du fromage blanc** soft white cheese

froment *nm* wheat; **une crêpe de froment** (*made with wheat flour*) a pancake

froncer [13] *vb* **froncer les sourcils** to frown

front *nm* forehead

frontière *nf* border

frotter [29] *vb* to rub ▷ *se frotter les yeux* to rub one's eyes; **frotter une allumette** to strike a match

fruit *nm* fruit; **un fruit** a piece of fruit; **les fruits de mer** seafood

fruité, e *adj* fruity

frustrer [29] *vb* to frustrate

fugue *nf* **faire une fugue** to run away

fuir [40] *vb* ❶ to flee ▷ *fuir devant un danger* to flee from danger ❷ to drip ▷ *Le robinet fuit.* The tap's dripping.

fuite *nf* ❶ leak ❷ (*escape*) flight; **être en fuite** to be on the run

fumé, e *adj* smoked ▷ *du saumon fumé* smoked salmon

fumée *nf* smoke

fumer [29] *vb* to smoke

fumeur (*f* fumeuse) *nm/f* smoker

fur **au fur et à mesure** *adv* as you go along ▷ *Je vérifie mon travail au fur et à mesure.* I check my work as I go along.; **au fur et à mesure que** as

▷ *Je réponds à mon courrier au fur et à mesure que je le reçois.* I answer my mail as I receive it.

furet *nm* ferret

fureur *nf* fury; **faire fureur** to be all the rage

furieux (*f* furieuse) *adj* furious

furoncle *nm* (*on skin*) boil

fus *vb see* être

fuseau (*pl* fuseaux) *nm* ski pants

fusée *nf* rocket

fusil *nm* gun

fut *vb see* être

futé, e *adj* crafty

futsal *nm* indoor football

futur *nm* future

g

gâcher [29] *vb* to waste ▷ *Je n'aime pas gâcher la nourriture.* I don't like to waste food.

gâchis *nm* waste

gaffe *nf* **faire une gaffe** to do something stupid; **Fais gaffe!** (*informal*) Watch out!

gage *nm* (*in a game*) forfeit

gagnant (*f* gagnante) *nm/f* winner

gagner [29] *vb* to win ▷ *Qui a gagné?* Who won?; **gagner du temps** to gain time; **Il gagne bien sa vie.** He makes a good living.

gai, e *adj* cheerful

gaieté *nf* cheerfulness

galerie *nf* gallery; **une galerie marchande** a shopping arcade; **une galerie de jeux d'arcade** an amusement arcade

galet nm pebble

galette nf ❶ round flat cake ▷ une galette de blé noir a buckwheat pancake ❷ biscuit ▷ des galettes pur beurre shortbread biscuits; **la galette des Rois**

- A **galette des Rois** is a cake
- eaten on Twelfth Night
- containing a figurine. The
- person who finds it is the king (or
- queen) and gets a paper crown.
- They then choose someone else
- to be their queen (or king).

Galles nf le pays de Galles Wales; **le prince de Galles** the Prince of Wales

gallois, e adj Welsh
  ▶ nm/f un Gallois a Welshman; une Galloise a Welshwoman; les Gallois the Welsh

galop nm gallop

galoper [29] vb to gallop

gamin (f gamine) nm/f (informal) kid

gamme nf (in music) scale; **une gamme de produits** a range of products

gammée adj la croix gammée the swastika

gant nm glove; **un gant de toilette** a face cloth

garage nm garage

garagiste nmf ❶ garage owner ❷ mechanic

garantie nf guarantee

garantir [39] vb to guarantee

garçon nm ❶ boy ❷ (in a café) waiter ▷ Garçon! Waiter!; **un vieux garçon** a bachelor

garde nm ❶ (in prison) warder ❷ security man; **un garde du corps** a bodyguard
  ▶ nf ❶ guarding ❷ guard; **être de garde** to be on duty ▷ La pharmacie de garde ce week-end est ... The duty chemist this weekend is ...; **mettre en garde** to warn

garde-côte (pl garde-côtes) nm coastguard

garder [29] vb ❶ to keep ▷ Tu as gardé toutes ses lettres? Have you kept all his letters? ❷ to look after ▷ Je garde ma nièce samedi après-midi. I'm looking after my niece on Saturday afternoon. ❸ to guard ▷ Ils ont pris un gros chien pour garder la maison. They got a big dog to guard the house.; **garder le lit** to stay in bed; **se garder** to keep ▷ Ces crêpes se gardent bien. These pancakes keep well.

garderie nf nursery

garde-robe nf (clothes) wardrobe

gardien (f gardienne) nm/f ❶ caretaker ❷ (in a museum) attendant; **un gardien de but** a goalkeeper; **un gardien de la paix** a police officer

gare nf station ▷ la gare routière the bus station
  ▶ excl Gare aux serpents! Watch out for snakes!

garer [29] vb to park; **se garer** to park

garni, e adj un plat garni (vegetables, chips, rice etc) a dish served with accompaniments

gars nm (informal) guy

gaspiller [29] vb to waste

gâteau (pl gâteaux) nm cake; **les gâteaux secs** biscuits

gâter [29] vb to spoil ▷ Il aime gâter ses petits enfants. He likes to spoil his grandchildren.; **se gâter** to go bad ▷ Le temps va se gâter. The weather's going to break.

gauche adj left ▷ le côté gauche the left-hand side
▶ nf left ▷ sur votre gauche on your left; **à gauche (1)** on the left ▷ la deuxième rue à gauche the second street on the left **(2)** to the left ▷ à gauche de l'armoire to the left of the cupboard ▷ Tournez à gauche. Turn left.; **la voie de gauche** the left-hand lane; **la gauche** (in politics) the left

gaucher (f gauchère) adj left-handed

gaufre nf waffle

gaufrette nf wafer

Gaulois (f Gauloise) nm/f Gaul ▷ Astérix le Gaulois Asterix the Gaul

gaulois, e adj Gallic

gaz nm gas

gazeux (f gazeuse) adj **une boisson gazeuse** a fizzy drink; **de l'eau gazeuse** sparkling water

gazole nm (fuel) diesel

gazon nm lawn

GDF nm (= Gaz de France) French gas company

géant nm giant

gel nm frost

gelée nf jelly

geler [44] vb to freeze ▷ Il a gelé

cette nuit. There was a frost last night.

gélule nf (containing medicine) capsule

Gémeaux nmpl Gemini

gémir [39] vb to moan

gênant, e adj awkward

gencive nf (in mouth) gum

gendarme nm policeman

gendarmerie nf ❶ police force ❷ police station

gendre nm son-in-law

gêné, e adj embarrassed

gêner [29] vb ❶ to bother ▷ Je ne voudrais pas vous gêner. I don't want to bother you. ❷ to feel awkward ▷ Son regard la gênait. The way he was looking at her made her feel awkward.

général, e (mpl généraux) adj general; **en général** usually
▶ nm (pl généraux) general

généralement adv generally

généraliste nmf family doctor

génération nf generation

généreux (f généreuse) adj generous

générosité nf generosity

genêt nm (bush) broom

génétique nf genetics

génétiquement adv genetically ▷ les aliments génétiquement modifiés GM foods

Genève n Geneva

génial, e (mpl géniaux) adj (informal) great

genou (pl genoux) nm knee

genre nm kind

gens nmpl people

gentil (f **gentille**) adj ❶ nice
❷ kind

gentillesse nf kindness

gentiment adv ❶ nicely ❷ kindly

géographie nf geography

géométrie nf geometry

gérant (f **gérante**) nm/f manager

gérer [35] vb to manage

germain, e adj **un cousin germain**
a first cousin

geste nm gesture; **Ne faites pas
un geste!** Don't move!

gestion nf management

gestionnaire de site nmf
webmaster

gifle nf slap across the face

gifler [29] vb to slap across the face

gigantesque adj gigantic

gigot nm leg of lamb

gilet nm ❶ waistcoat ❷ cardigan;
un gilet de sauvetage a life jacket

gingembre nm ginger

girafe nf giraffe

gitan (f **gitane**) nm/f gipsy

gîte nm **un gîte rural** a holiday
house

glace nf ❶ ice ❷ ice cream ▷ **une
glace à la fraise** a strawberry ice
cream ❸ mirror

glacé, e adj ❶ icy ❷ iced ▷ **un thé
glacé** an iced tea

glacial, e (mpl **glaciaux**) adj icy

glaçon nm ice cube

glissant, e adj slippery

glisser [29] vb ❶ to slip ❷ to be
slippery

global, e (mpl **globaux**) adj total

gloire nf glory

godasse nf (informal) shoe

goéland nm seagull

golf nm ❶ golf ❷ golf course

golfe nm gulf; **le golfe de
Gascogne** the Bay of Biscay

gomme nf rubber

gommer [29] vb to rub out

gonflé, e adj ❶ (arm, finger,
stomach) swollen ❷ (ball, tyre)
inflated; **Il est gonflé!** He's got
a nerve!

gonfler [29] vb ❶ to blow up
▷ **gonfler un ballon** to blow up a
balloon ❷ to pump up ▷ **Tu devrais
gonfler ton pneu arrière.** You should
pump up your back tyre.

gorge nf ❶ throat ▷ **J'ai mal à
la gorge.** I've got a sore throat.
❷ gorge ▷ **les gorges du Tarn** the
Tarn gorges

gorgée nf sip

gorille nm gorilla

gosse nmf (informal) kid

goudron nm tar

gouffre nm chasm; **Cette voiture
est un vrai gouffre!** This car eats
up money!

gourde nf water bottle

gourmand, e adj greedy

gourmandise nf greed

gousse nf **une gousse d'ail** a clove
of garlic

goût nm taste

goûter [29] vb ❶ to taste ❷ (in
the afternoon) to have a snack ▷ **Les
enfants goûtent généralement vers
quatre heures.** The children usually
have a snack around 4 o'clock.
▶ nm afternoon snack

goutte nf drop

gouvernement nm government

gouverner [29] vb to govern

grâce nf grâce à thanks to

gracieux (f gracieuse) adj graceful

gradins nmpl (in stadium) terraces

graduel (f graduelle) adj gradual

graffiti nmpl graffiti

grain nm grain; **un grain de beauté** a beauty spot; **un grain de café** a coffee bean; **un grain de raisin** a grape

graine nf seed

graisse nf fat

grammaire nf grammar

gramme nm gramme

grand, e adj, adv ❶ tall ▷ Il est grand pour son âge. He's tall for his age. ❷ big ▷ C'est sa grande sœur. She's his big sister. ❸ long ▷ un grand voyage a long journey; **les grandes vacances** the summer holidays ❹ great ▷ C'est un grand ami à moi. He's a great friend of mine.; **un grand magasin** a department store; **une grande surface** a hypermarket; **les grandes écoles** (at university level) top ranking colleges; **au grand air** out in the open air; **grand ouvert** wide open

grand-chose pron pas grand-chose not much

Grande-Bretagne nf Britain

grandeur nf size

grandir [39] vb to grow ▷ Il a beaucoup grandi. He's grown a lot.

grand-mère (pl grands-mères) nf grandmother

grand-peine: à grand-peine adv with great difficulty

grand-père (pl grands-pères) nm grandfather

grands-parents nmpl grandparents

grange nf barn

grappe nf une grappe de raisin a bunch of grapes

gras (f grasse) adj ❶ (food) fatty ❷ greasy ❸ oily; **faire la grasse matinée** to have a lie-in

gratis adj, adv free

gratte-ciel (pl gratte-ciel) nm skyscraper

gratter [29] vb ❶ to scratch ❷ to be itchy

gratuit, e adj free ▷ entrée gratuite entrance free

grave adj ❶ serious ❷ deep ▷ Il a une voix grave. He's got a deep voice.; **Ce n'est pas grave.** It doesn't matter.

gravement adv seriously

graveur nm un graveur de CD CD burner

grec (f grecque) adj Greek
  ▶ nm Greek ▷ J'apprends le grec. I'm learning Greek.
  ▶ nm/f un Grec (man) a Greek; une Grecque (woman) a Greek; les Grecs the Greeks

Grèce nf Greece; **en Grèce (1)** in Greece **(2)** to Greece

grêle nf hail

grêler [29] vb Il grêle. It's hailing.

grelotter [29] vb to shiver

grenade nf ❶ pomegranate ❷ grenade

grenier nm attic

grenouille nf frog

grève nf ❶ strike; **en grève** on strike; **faire grève** to be on strike ❷ shore

gréviste nmf striker

grièvement adv **grièvement blessé** seriously injured

griffe nf ❶ claw ❷ label

griffer [29] vb to scratch ▷ Le chat m'a griffé. The cat scratched me.

grignoter [29] vb to nibble

grillade nf grilled food

grille nf ❶ wire fence ❷ metal gate

grille-pain (pl grille-pain) nm toaster

griller [29] vb ❶ to toast; **du pain grillé** toast ❷ to grill ▷ des saucisses grillées grilled sausages

grimace nf **faire des grimaces** to make faces

grimper [29] vb to climb

grincer [13] vb to creak

grincheux (f grincheuse) adj grumpy

grippe nf flu; **avoir la grippe** to have flu

grippé, e adj **être grippé(e)** to have flu

gris, e adj grey

Groenland nm Greenland

grogner [29] vb ❶ to growl ❷ to complain

gronder [29] vb **se faire gronder** to get a telling off ▷ Tu vas te faire gronder par ton père! You're going to get a telling off from your father!

gros (f grosse) adj ❶ big ▷ une grosse pomme a big apple ❷ fat ▷ Je suis trop grosse pour porter ça! I'm too fat to wear that!

groseille nf **la groseille rouge** redcurrant; **la groseille à maquereau** gooseberry

grossesse nf pregnancy

grossier (f grossière) adj rude; **une erreur grossière** a bad mistake

grossir [39] vb to put on weight ▷ Il a beaucoup grossi. He's put on a lot of weight.

grosso modo adv roughly

grotte nf cave

groupe nm group

grouper [29] vb to group; **se grouper** to gather ▷ Nous nous sommes groupés autour du feu. We gathered round the fire.

guépard nm cheetah

guêpe nf wasp

guérir [39] vb to recover ▷ Il est maintenant complètement guéri. He's now completely recovered.

guérison nf recovery

guerre nf war ▷ la Deuxième Guerre mondiale the Second World War

guetter [29] vb to look out for

gueule nf mouth (rude when used for people): **Ta gueule!** (rude) Shut your face!; **avoir la gueule de bois** (informal) to have a hangover

gueuler [29] vb (informal) to bawl

guichet nm (in bank, booking office) counter

guide nm guide

guider [29] vb to guide

guidon *nm* handlebars
guillemets *nmpl* inverted commas
guirlande *nf* tinsel; **des**
  guirlandes en papier paper chains
guitare *nf* guitar
gym *nf* (*informal*) PE
gymnase *nm* gym
gymnastique *nf* gymnastics

habile *adj* skilful
habillé, e *adj* ❶ dressed ▷ *Il n'est pas encore habillé.* He's not dressed yet. ❷ smart ▷ *Cette robe fait très habillé.* This dress looks very smart.
s' **habiller** [29] *vb* ❶ to get dressed ▷ *Je me suis rapidement habillé.* I got dressed quickly. ❷ to dress up ▷ *Est-ce qu'il faut s'habiller pour la réception?* Do you have to dress up to go to the party?
l' **habitant** (*f* **habitante**) *nm/f* inhabitant
habiter [29] *vb* to live ▷ *Il habite à Montpellier.* He lives in Montpellier.
les **habits** *nmpl* clothes
l' **habitude** *nf* habit; **avoir l'habitude de quelque chose** to be used to something; **d'habitude**

usually; **comme d'habitude** as usual

habituel (f **habituelle**) adj usual

s' **habituer** [29] vb **s'habituer à quelque chose** to get used to something

le **hachis** nm mince; **le hachis Parmentier** shepherd's pie

la **haie** nf hedge

la **haine** nf hatred

haïr [41] vb to hate

l' **haleine** nf breath ▷ *être hors d'haleine* to be out of breath

les **halles** nfpl covered market

la **halte** nf stop; **Halte!** Stop!

l' **haltérophilie** nf weightlifting

le **hamburger** nm hamburger

l' **hameçon** nm fish hook

le **hamster** nm hamster

la **hanche** nf hip

le **handball** nm handball

le **handicapé** nm handicapped man

l' **handicapée** nf handicapped woman

le **harcèlement** nm harassment

le **hareng** nm herring; **un hareng saur** a kipper

le **haricot** nm bean; **les haricots verts** runner beans; **les haricots blancs** haricot beans

l' **harmonica** nm mouth organ

la **harpe** nf harp

le **hasard** nm coincidence; **au hasard** at random; **par hasard** by chance; **à tout hasard** (1) just in case (2) on the off chance

la **hâte** nf **à la hâte** hurriedly; **J'ai hâte de te voir.** I can't wait to see you.

la **hausse** nf ❶ increase ❷ rise

hausser [29] vb **hausser les épaules** to shrug one's shoulders

haut, e adj, adv ❶ high ▷ *une haute montagne* a high mountain ❷ aloud ▷ *penser tout haut* to think aloud
▶ nm top; **un mur de trois mètres de haut** a wall 3 metres high; **en haut** (1) upstairs (2) at the top

la **hauteur** nf height

le **haut-parleur** nm loudspeaker

l' **hebdomadaire** nm (magazine) weekly

l' **hébergement** nm accommodation

héberger [46] vb to put up ▷ *Mon cousin a dit qu'il nous hébergerait.* My cousin said he would put us up.

hein? excl eh?; **Hein? Qu'est-ce que tu dis?** Eh? What did you say?

hélas adv unfortunately

l' **hélicoptère** nm helicopter

l' **hémorragie** nf haemorrhage

l' **herbe** nf grass; **les herbes de Provence** mixed herbs

le **hérisson** nm hedgehog

hériter [29] vb to inherit

l' **héritier** nm heir

l' **héritière** nf heiress

hermétique adj airtight

l' **héroïne** nf ❶ heroine ❷ (drug) heroin

le **héros** nm hero

l' **hésitation** nf hesitation

hésiter [29] vb to hesitate ▷ *J'ai hésité entre le pull vert et le cardigan jaune.* I couldn't decide between the green pullover and the yellow cardigan.; **sans hésiter** without hesitating

l' **heure** nf ❶ hour ▷ *Le trajet dure six heures.* The journey lasts six hours. ❷ time ▷ *Vous avez l'heure?* Have you got the time?; **Quelle heure est-il?** What time is it?; **À quelle heure?** What time?; **deux heures du matin** 2 o'clock in the morning; **être à l'heure** to be on time; **une heure de français** a period of French

heureusement adv luckily

heureux (f **heureuse**) adj happy

heurter [29] vb to hit

l' **hexagone** nm hexagon; **l'Hexagone** France
- France is often referred to as
- **l'Hexagone** because of its six-sided shape.

le **hibou** (pl**hiboux**) nm owl

hier adv yesterday; **avant-hier** the day before yesterday

la **hi-fi** nf stereo; **une chaîne hi-fi** a stereo system

hippique adj un club hippique a riding centre; **un concours hippique** a horse show

l' **hippopotame** nm hippopotamus

l' **hirondelle** nf (bird) swallow

l' **histoire** nf ❶ history ▷ *un cours d'histoire* a history lesson ❷ story ▷ *Ce roman raconte l'histoire de deux enfants.* This novel tells the story of two children.; **Ne fais pas d'histoires!** Don't make a fuss!

historique adj historic

l' **hiver** nm winter; **en hiver** in winter

l' **HLM** nf (= habitation à loyer modéré) council flat; **des HLM** council housing

le **hockey** nm hockey; **le hockey sur glace** ice hockey

hollandais, e adj Dutch
- ▶ nm Dutch ▷ *J'apprends le hollandais.* I'm learning Dutch.
- ▶ nm/f un Hollandais a Dutch man; **une Hollandaise** a Dutch woman; **les Hollandais** the Dutch

la **Hollande** nf Holland; **en Hollande** (1) in Holland (2) to Holland

le **homard** nm lobster

homéopathique adj homeopathic

l' **hommage** nm tribute

l' **homme** nm man; **un homme d'affaires** a businessman

homosexuel (f **homosexuelle**) adj homosexual

la **Hongrie** nf Hungary

hongrois, e adj Hungarian

honnête adj honest

l' **honnêteté** nf honesty

l' **honneur** nm honour

la **honte** nf shame ▷ *avoir honte de quelque chose* to be ashamed of something

l' **hôpital** (pl**hôpitaux**) nm hospital

le **hoquet** nm avoir le hoquet to have hiccups

l' **horaire** nm timetable; **les horaires de train** the train timetable

l' **horizon** nm horizon

horizontal, e (*mpl* **horizontaux**) *adj* horizontal

l' **horloge** *nf* clock

l' **horreur** *nf* horror ▷ *un film d'horreur* a horror film; **avoir horreur de** to hate ▷ *J'ai horreur du chou.* I hate cabbage.

horrible *adj* horrible

hors *prep* **hors de** out of ▷ *Elle est hors de danger maintenant.* She's out of danger now.; **hors taxes** duty-free

le **hors-d'œuvre** (*pl* **hors-d'œuvre**) *nm* (food) starter

hospitalier (f **hospitalière**) *adj* hospitable; **les services hospitaliers** hospital services

l' **hospitalité** *nf* hospitality

hostile *adj* hostile

l' **hôte** *nmf* ❶ host ❷ guest

l' **hôtel** *nm* hotel; **l'hôtel de ville** the town hall

l' **hôtesse** *nf* hostess; **une hôtesse de l'air** a stewardess

la **housse** *nf* cover ▷ *une housse de couette* a quilt cover ▷ *une housse de téléphone* a phone cover

le **houx** *nm* holly

l' **huile** *nf* oil; **l'huile solaire** suntan oil

huit *num* eight ▷ *Il a huit ans.* He's eight.; **le huit février** the eighth of February; **dans huit jours** in a week's time

huitaine *nf* **une huitaine de jours** about a week

huitième *adj* eighth ▷ *au huitième étage* on the eighth floor

l' **huître** *nf* oyster

humain, e *adj* human
  ▶ *nm* human being

l' **humeur** *nf* mood ▷ *Il est de bonne humeur.* He's in a good mood.

humide *adj* damp

humilier [**20**] *vb* to humiliate

humoristique *adj* humorous; **des dessins humoristiques** cartoons

l' **humour** *nm* humour ▷ *Il n'a pas beaucoup d'humour.* He hasn't got much sense of humour.

hurler [**29**] *vb* to howl

la **hutte** *nf* hut

hydratant, e *adj* **une crème hydratante** a moisturizing cream

l' **hygiène** *nf* hygiene

hygiénique *adj* hygienic; **une serviette hygiénique** a sanitary towel; **le papier hygiénique** toilet paper

l' **hymne** *nm* **l'hymne national** the national anthem

l' **hypermarché** *nm* hypermarket

hypermétrope *adj* long-sighted

hypocrite *adj* hypocritical

l' **hypothèse** *nf* hypothesis

a
b
c
d
e
f
g
h
i
j
k
l
m
n
o
p
q
r
s
t
u
v
w
x
y
z

iceberg nm iceberg

ici adv here ▷ Les assiettes sont ici. The plates are here.; **La mer monte parfois jusqu'ici.** The sea sometimes comes in as far as this.; **Jusqu'ici nous n'avons eu aucun problème avec la voiture.** So far we haven't had any problems with the car.

icône nf icon

idéal, e(mpl **idéaux**) adj ideal

idée nf idea

identifiant nm ❶ login ❷ username

identifier [20] vb to identify

identique adj identical

identité nf identity; **une pièce d'identité** a form of identification

idiot, e adj ❶ stupid ❷ silly
▶ nm/f idiot

ignoble adj horrible

ignorant, e adj ignorant

ignorer [29] vb ❶ not to know ▷ J'ignore son nom. I don't know his name. ❷ to ignore ▷ Il m'a complètement ignoré. He completely ignored me.

il pron ❶ he ▷ Il est parti ce matin de bonne heure. He left early this morning. ❷ it ▷ Méfie-toi de ce chien: il mord. Be careful of that dog: it bites. ▷ Il pleut. It's raining.

île nf island; **les îles Anglo-Normandes** the Channel Islands; **les îles Britanniques** the British Isles; **les îles Féroé** the Faroe Islands

illégal, e(mpl **illégaux**) adj illegal

illimité, e adj unlimited

illisible adj illegible

illuminer [29] vb to floodlight

illusion nf illusion

illustration nf illustration

illustré, e adj illustrated
▶ nm comic

illustrer [29] vb to illustrate

ils pron they ▷ Ils nous ont appelés hier soir. They phoned us last night.

image nf picture

imagination nf imagination

imaginer [29] vb to imagine

imbécile nmf idiot

imitation nf imitation

imiter [29] vb to imitate

immatriculation nf une plaque d'immatriculation (of car) a numberplate

immédiat nm dans l'immédiat for the moment

immédiatement adv immediately

immense adj ❶ huge ❷ tremendous

immeuble nm block of flats

immigration nf immigration

immigré(f **immigrée**) nm/f immigrant

immobile adj motionless

immobilier(f **immobilière**) adj une agence immobilière an estate agent's

immobiliser [29] vb to immobilize

immunisé, e adj immunized

impact nm impact

impair, e adj odd

impardonnable adj unforgivable

impasse nf cul-de-sac

impatience nf impatience

impatient, e adj impatient

impeccable adj ❶ immaculate ❷ perfect

imper nm (informal) mac

impératif nm imperative

impératrice nf empress

imperméable nm raincoat

impertinent, e adj cheeky

impitoyable adj merciless

impliquer [29] vb to mean ▷ Si tu vas à l'université, ça implique que tu vas devoir nous quitter. If you go to university, it'll mean that you have to leave us.; **être impliqué dans** to be involved in

impoli, e adj rude

importance nf importance

important, e adj ❶ important ❷ considerable

importation nf import

importer [29] vb ❶ to import ❷ (goods) to matter ▷ Peu importe. It doesn't matter.

imposant, e adj imposing

imposer [29] vb to impose; **imposer quelque chose à quelqu'un** to make somebody do something

impossible adj impossible ▶ nm **Nous ferons l'impossible pour finir à temps.** We'll do our utmost to finish in time.

impôt nm tax

imprécis, e adj imprecise

impression nf impression

impressionnant, e adj impressive

impressionner [29] vb to impress

imprévisible adj unpredictable

imprévu, e adj unexpected

imprimante nf (for computer) printer

imprimé, e adj printed

imprimer [29] vb to print

impropre adj impropre à la consommation unfit for human consumption

improviser [29] vb to improvise

improviste adv arriver à l'improviste to arrive unexpectedly

imprudence nf carelessness; **Ne fais pas d'imprudences!** Don't do anything silly!

imprudent, e adj ❶ unwise ❷ careless

impuissant, e adj helpless

impulsif(f **impulsive**) adj impulsive

inabordable adj prohibitive

inaccessible adj inaccessible

inachevé, e adj unfinished

inadmissible adj intolerable

inanimé, e adj unconscious

inaperçu, e adj **passer inaperçu** to go unnoticed

inattendu, e adj unexpected

inattention nf **une faute d'inattention** a careless mistake

inaugurer [**29**] vb (an exhibition) to open

incapable adj incapable

incassable adj unbreakable

incendie nm fire ▷ *un incendie de forêt* a forest fire

incertain, e adj ❶ uncertain ❷ unsettled ▷ *Le temps est incertain.* The weather is unsettled.

incident nm incident

inciter [**29**] vb **inciter quelqu'un à faire quelque chose** to encourage somebody to do something

inclure [**14**] vb to enclose ▷ *Veuillez inclure une enveloppe timbrée libellée à votre adresse.* Please enclose a stamped addressed envelope.; **jusqu'au dix mars inclus** until 10th March inclusive

incohérent, e adj incoherent

incollable adj **être incollable sur quelque chose** (informal) to know everything there is to know about something; **le riz incollable** non-stick rice

incolore adj colourless

incompétent, e adj incompetent

incompris, e adj misunderstood

inconnu (finconnue) nm/f stranger
▶ nm **l'inconnu** the unknown

inconsciemment adv unconsciously

inconscient, e adj unconscious

incontestable adj indisputable

incontournable adj inevitable

inconvénient nm disadvantage; **si vous n'y voyez pas d'inconvénient** if you have no objection

incorrect, e adj ❶ incorrect ❷ rude

incroyable adj incredible

inculper [**29**] vb **inculper de** to charge with

Inde nf India

indécis, e adj ❶ indecisive ❷ undecided

indéfiniment adv indefinitely

indélicat, e adj tactless

indemne adj unharmed

indemniser [**29**] vb to compensate

indépendamment adv independently; **indépendamment de** irrespective of

indépendance nf independence

indépendant, e adj independent

index nm ❶ index finger ❷ (in book) index

indicatif (findicative) adj **à titre indicatif** for your information
▶ nm ❶ dialling code ❷ (of verb) indicative ❸ (of TV programme) theme tune

indications nfpl instructions

indice nm clue

indien (f**indienne**) adj Indian
▶ nm/f **un Indien** (man) an Indian;
une Indienne (woman) an Indian

indifférence nf indifference

indifférent, e adj indifferent

indigène nmf native

indigeste adj indigestible

indigestion nf indigestion

indigne adj unworthy

indigner [29] vb **s'indigner de
quelque chose** to get indignant
about something

indiqué, e adj advisable

indiquer [29] vb to point out ▷ Il
m'a indiqué la mairie. He pointed out
the town hall.

indirect, e adj indirect

indiscipliné, e adj unruly

indiscret (f**indiscrète**) adj
indiscreet

indispensable adj indispensable

indisposé, e adj indisposed; **être
indisposée** to be having one's
period

individu nm individual

individuel (f**individuelle**) adj
individual; **Vous aurez une
chambre individuelle.** You'll have
a room of your own.

indolore adj painless

Indonésie nf Indonesia

indulgent, e adj indulgent; **Elle est
trop indulgente avec son fils.** She's
not firm enough with her son.

industrie nf industry

industriel (f**industrielle**) adj
industrial
▶ nm industrialist

inédit, e adj unpublished

inefficace adj ① (treatment)
ineffective ② inefficient

inégal, e (mpl **inégaux**) adj
① unequal ② uneven

inévitable adj unavoidable;
C'était inévitable! That was
bound to happen!

inexact, e adj inaccurate

in extremis adv **Il a réussi à
attraper son train in extremis.**
He just managed to catch his
train.; **Ils ont évité un accident
in extremis.** They avoided an
accident by the skin of their teeth.

infarctus nm coronary

infatigable adj indefatigable

infect, e adj (meal) revolting

s' infecter [29] vb to go septic

infection nf infection

inférieur, e adj lower

infernal, e (mpl **infernaux**) adj
terrible

infini nm **à l'infini** indefinitely

infinitif nm infinitive

infirme nmf disabled person

infirmerie nf medical room

infirmier (f**infirmière**) nm/f nurse

inflammable adj inflammable

influence nf influence

influencer [13] vb to influence

informaticien (f
informaticienne) nm/f computer
scientist

informations nfpl ① (on
TV) news ▷ les informations de
vingt heures the 8 o'clock news
② information ▷ Je voudrais
quelques informations, s'il vous

plaît. I'd like some information, please.; **une information** a piece of information

informatique *nf* computing

informer [29] *vb* to inform; **s'informer** to find out

infuser [29] *vb* ❶ (*tea*) to brew ❷ (*herbal tea*) to infuse

infusion *nf* herbal tea

ingénieur *nm* engineer

ingrat, e *adj* ungrateful

ingrédient *nm* ingredient

inhabituel (*f* inhabituelle) *adj* unusual

inhumain, e *adj* inhuman

initial, e (*mpl* initiaux) *adj* initial

initiale *nf* initial

initiation *nf* introduction

initiative *nf* initiative ▷ **avoir de l'initiative** to have initiative

injecter [29] *vb* to inject

injection *nf* injection

injure *nf* ❶ insult ❷ abuse

injurier [20] *vb* to insult

injurieux (*f* injurieuse) *adj* (*language*) abusive

injuste *adj* unfair

innocent, e *adj* innocent

innombrable *adj* innumerable

innover [29] *vb* to break new ground

inoccupé, e *adj* empty ▷ **un appartement inoccupé** an empty flat

inoffensif (*f* inoffensive) *adj* harmless

inondation *nf* flood

inoubliable *adj* unforgettable

inoxydable *adj* **l'acier inoxydable** stainless steel

inquiet (*f* inquiète) *adj* worried

inquiétant, e *adj* worrying

s' inquiéter [35] *vb* to worry ▷ *Ne t'inquiète pas!* Don't worry!

inquiétude *nf* anxiety

insatisfait, e *adj* dissatisfied

inscription *nf* (*for school, course*) registration

s' inscrire [31] *vb* **s'inscrire à (1)** to join ▷ *Je me suis inscrit au club de tennis.* I've joined the tennis club. **(2)** to register ▷ *N'attends pas trop pour t'inscrire à la fac.* Don't leave it too long to register at the university.

insecte *nm* insect

insensible *adj* insensitive

insigne *nm* badge

insignifiant, e *adj* insignificant

insister [29] *vb* to insist; **N'insiste pas!** Don't keep on!

insolation *nf* sunstroke

insolent, e *adj* cheeky

insouciant, e *adj* carefree

insoutenable *adj* unbearable

inspecter [29] *vb* to inspect

inspecteur (*f* inspectrice) *nm/f* inspector

inspection *nf* inspection

inspirer [29] *vb* ❶ to inspire; **s'inspirer de** to take one's inspiration from ❷ to breathe in ▷ *Inspirez! Expirez!* Breathe in! Breathe out!

instable *adj* ❶ (*piece of furniture*) unsteady ❷ (*person*) unstable

installations *nfpl* facilities

installer [29] *vb* ❶ (*shelves*) to put up ❷ (*gas, telephone*) to install;

s'installer to settle in; **Installez-vous, je vous en prie.** Have a seat please.

instant nm moment ▷ **pour l'instant** for the moment

instantané, e adj instant ▷ **du café instantané** instant coffee

instinct nm instinct

institut nm institute

instituteur (f **institutrice**) nm/f primary school teacher

institution nf institution

instruction nf ❶ instruction ❷ education

s'**instruire** [24] vb to educate oneself

instruit, e adj educated

instrument nm instrument ▷ **un instrument de musique** a musical instrument

insuffisant, e adj insufficient; "**travail insuffisant**" (on school report) "must make more effort"

insuline nf insulin

insultant, e adj insulting

insulte nf insult

insulter [29] vb to insult

insupportable adj unbearable

intact, e adj intact

intégral, e (mpl **intégraux**) adj **le texte intégral** unabridged version; **un remboursement intégral** a full refund

intégrisme nm fundamentalism

intelligence nf intelligence

intelligent, e adj intelligent

intense adj intense

intensif (f **intensive**) adj intensive; **un cours intensif** a crash course

intention nf intention; **avoir l'intention de faire quelque chose** to intend to do something

interdiction nf "**interdiction de stationner**" "no parking"; "**interdiction de fumer**" "no smoking"

interdire [28] vb to forbid

interdit, e adj forbidden

intéressant, e adj interesting; **On lui a fait une offre intéressante.** They made him an attractive offer.; **On trouve des CD à des prix très intéressants dans ce magasin.** You can get very cheap CDs in this shop.

intéresser [29] vb to interest; **s'intéresser à** to be interested in

intérêt nm interest; **avoir intérêt à faire quelque chose** to do well to do something

intérieur nm inside

interlocuteur (f **interlocutrice**) nm/f **son interlocuteur** the man he/she's speaking to; **son interlocutrice** the woman he/she's speaking to

intermédiaire nm intermediary; **par l'intermédiaire de** through

internat nm boarding school

international, e (mpl **internationaux**) adj international

internaute nmf internet user

interne nmf boarder

Internet nm internet ▷ **sur Internet** on the internet

interphone nm intercom

interprète nmf interpreter

interpréter [35] vb to interpret
interrogatif (f **interrogative**) adj interrogative
interrogation nf ❶ question ❷ test ▷ *une interrogation écrite* a written test
interrogatoire nm questioning; **C'est un interrogatoire ou quoi?** Am I being cross-examined?
interroger [46] vb to question
interrompre [76] vb to interrupt
interrupteur nm switch
interruption nf interruption; **sans interruption** without stopping
intervalle nm interval; **dans l'intervalle** in the meantime
intervenir [90] ❶ vb to intervene ❷ to take action ▷ *La police est intervenue.* The police took action.
intervention nf intervention; **une intervention chirurgicale** a surgical operation
interview nf (on radio, TV) interview
intestin nm intestine
intime adj intimate; **un journal intime** a diary
intimider [29] vb to intimidate
intimité nf dans l'intimité in private; **Le mariage a eu lieu dans l'intimité.** The wedding ceremony was private.
intitulé, e adj entitled
intolérable adj intolerable
intoxication nf **une intoxication alimentaire** food poisoning
Intranet nm Intranet

intransigeant, e adj uncompromising
intrigue nf (of book, film) plot
introduction nf introduction
introduire [24] vb to introduce
intuition nf intuition
inusable adj hard-wearing
inutile adj useless
invalide nmf disabled person
invasion nf invasion
inventer [29] vb ❶ to invent ❷ to make up ▷ *inventer une excuse* to make up an excuse
inventeur nm inventor
invention nf invention
inverse adj dans l'ordre inverse in reverse order; **en sens inverse** in the opposite direction
▶ nm reverse; **Tu t'es trompé, c'est l'inverse.** You've got it wrong, it's the other way round.
investissement nm investment
invisible adj invisible
invitation nf invitation
invité (f **invitée**) nm/f guest
inviter [29] vb to invite
involontaire adj unintentional
invraisemblable adj unlikely
iPod® nm iPod®
ira, irai, iraient, irais vb see aller; **J'irai demain au supermarché.** I'll go to the supermarket tomorrow.
Irak nm Iraq
Iran nm Iran
iras, irez vb see aller
irlandais, e adj Irish
▶ nm/f **un Irlandais** an Irishman; **une Irlandaise** an Irishwoman; **les Irlandais** the Irish

Irlande nf Ireland; **en Irlande** (1) in Ireland (2) to Ireland; **la République d'Irlande** the Irish Republic; **l'Irlande du Nord** Northern Ireland

ironie nf irony

ironique adj ironical

irons, iront vb see **aller**; **Nous irons à la plage cet après-midi.** We'll go to the beach this afternoon.

irrationnel (**firrationnelle**) adj irrational

irréel (**firréelle**) adj unreal

irrégulier (**firrégulière**) adj irregular

irrésistible adj irresistible

irritable adj irritable

irriter [29] vb to irritate

islamique adj Islamic

Islande nf Iceland

isolé, e adj isolated

Israël nm Israel

israélien (**fisraélienne**) adj Israeli
▶ nm/f **un Israélien** (man) an Israeli; **une Israélienne** (woman) an Israeli; **les Israéliens** the Israelis

israélite adj Jewish

issue nf **une voie sans issue** a dead end; **l'issue de secours** emergency exit

Italie nf Italy; **en Italie** (1) in Italy (2) to Italy

italien (**fitalienne**) adj Italian
▶ nm Italian ▷ *J'apprends l'italien.* I'm learning Italian.
▶ nm/f **un Italien** (man) an Italian; **une Italienne**; **les Italiens** the Italians

itinéraire nm route

IUT nm (= Institut universitaire de technologie) (at university level) institute of technology

ivre adj drunk

ivrogne nmf drunkard

a
b
c
d
e
f
g
h
i
j
k
l
m
n
o
p
q
r
s
t
u
v
w
x
y
z

j

j' pron see **je**

jalousie nf jealousy

jaloux (f **jalouse**) adj jealous

jamais adv ❶ never ▷ Il ne boit jamais d'alcool. He never drinks alcohol. ❷ ever

> Phrases with **jamais** meaning **ever** use a verb in the subjunctive.
> ▷ C'est la plus belle chose que j'aie jamais vue. It's the most beautiful thing I've ever seen.

jambe nf leg

jambon nm ham; **le jambon cru** Parma ham

jambonneau (pl **jambonneaux**) nm knuckle of ham

janvier nm January; **en janvier** in January

Japon nm Japan; **au Japon (1)** in Japan **(2)** to Japan

japonais, e adj Japanese .
  ▶ nm Japanese ▷ Elle parle japonais. She speaks Japanese.
  ▶ nm/f **un Japonais** (man) a Japanese; **une Japonaise** (woman) a Japanese; **les Japonais** the Japanese

jardin nm garden ▷ un jardin potager a vegetable garden

jardinage nm gardening

jardinier (f **jardinière**) nm/f gardener

jaune adj yellow
  ▶ nm yellow; **un jaune d'œuf** an egg yolk

jaunir [**39**] vb to turn yellow

jaunisse nf jaundice

Javel n l'eau de Javel bleach

jazz nm jazz

J.-C. abbr (= Jésus-Christ): **44 avant J.-C.** 44 BC; **115 après J.-C.** 115 AD

je pron I

> **je** changes to **j'** before a vowel and most words beginning with "h".
> ▷ Je t'appellerai ce soir. I'll phone you this evening. ▷ J'arrive! I'm coming!
> ▷ J'hésite. I'm not sure.

jean nm jeans

jeannette nf Brownie

Jésus-Christ nm Jesus Christ

jet nm ❶ (of water) jet; **un jet d'eau** a fountain ❷ jet plane

jetable adj disposable

jetée nf jetty

jeter [**42**] vb ❶ to throw ▷ Il a jeté son sac sur le lit. He threw his bag onto the bed. ❷ to throw away

▷ *Ils ne jettent jamais rien.* They never throw anything away.; **jeter un coup d'œil** to have a look

jeton *nm* (in board game) counter

jeu (pl **jeux**) *nm* game ▷ *Je n'aime pas les jeux de société.* I don't like board games.; **un jeu d'arcade** a video game; **un jeu de cartes** (1) a pack of cards (2) a card game; **un jeu de mots** a pun; **un jeu électronique** an electronic game; **les jeux vidéo** video games; **en jeu** at stake

jeudi *nm* ● Thursday ▷ *Aujourd'hui, nous sommes jeudi.* It's Thursday today. ● on Thursday; **le jeudi** on Thursdays; **tous les jeudis** every Thursday; **jeudi dernier** last Thursday; **jeudi prochain** next Thursday

jeun: à jeun *adv* on an empty stomach

jeune *adj* young ▷ *un jeune homme* a young man; **une jeune fille** a girl
▶ *nmf* young person ▷ *les jeunes* young people

jeunesse *nf* youth

job *nm* (informal) job

jogging *nm* ● jogging ● tracksuit

joie *nf* joy

joindre [43] *vb* ● to put together ▷ *On va joindre les deux tables.* We're going to put the two tables together. ● to contact ▷ *Vous pouvez le joindre chez lui.* You can contact him at home.; **joindre un fichier à un mail** to attach a file to an email

joint, e *adj* **une pièce jointe** (1) (in letter) an enclosure (2) (in email) an attachment

joli, e *adj* pretty

jonc *nm* rush

jonquille *nf* daffodil

joue *nf* cheek

jouer [29] *vb* ● to play; **jouer de** (instrument) to play ▷ *Il joue de la guitare et du piano.* He plays the guitar and the piano.; **jouer à** (sport, game) to play ▷ *Elle joue au tennis.* She plays tennis. ▷ *jouer aux cartes* to play cards ● to act ▷ *Je trouve qu'il joue très bien dans ce film.* I think he acts very well in this film.; **On joue Hamlet au Théâtre de la Ville.** Hamlet is on at the Théâtre de la Ville.

jouet *nm* toy

joueur (f **joueuse**) *nm/f* player; **être mauvais joueur** to be a bad loser

jour *nm* day; **Il fait jour.** It's daylight.; **mettre quelque chose à jour** to update something; **le jour de l'An** New Year's Day; **un jour de congé** a day off; **un jour férié** a public holiday; **dans huit jours** in a week; **dans quinze jours** in a fortnight

journal (pl **journaux**) *nm*
● newspaper; **le journal télévisé** the television news ● diary

journalier (f **journalière**) *adj* daily

journalisme *nm* journalism

journaliste *nmf* journalist

journée *nf* day

joyeux (f **joyeuse**) *adj* happy; **Joyeux anniversaire!** Happy birthday!; **Joyeux Noël!** Merry Christmas!

judo *nm* judo

juge nm judge

juger [46] vb to judge

juif (f juive) adj Jewish
▶ nm/f **un juif** (man) a Jew; **une juive** (woman) a Jew

juillet nm July; **en juillet** in July

juin nm June; **en juin** in June

jumeau (pl jumeaux) nm twin

jumeler [5] vb to twin ▷ Saint-Brieuc est jumelée avec Aberystwyth. Saint-Brieuc is twinned with Aberystwyth.

jumelle nf twin

jumelles nfpl binoculars

jument nf mare

jungle nf jungle

jupe nf skirt

jurer [29] vb to swear ▷ Je jure que c'est vrai! I swear it's true!

juridique adj legal

jury nm jury

jus nm juice; **un jus de fruit** a fruit juice

jusqu'à prep ❶ as far as ▷ Nous avons marché jusqu'au village. We walked as far as the village. ❷ until ▷ Il fait généralement chaud jusqu'à la mi-août. It's usually hot until mid-August.; **jusqu'à ce que** until; **jusqu'à présent** so far

jusque prep as far as ▷ Je l'ai raccompagnée jusque chez elle. I went with her as far as her house.

juste adj, adv ❶ fair ▷ Il est sévère, mais juste. He's strict but fair. ❷ tight ▷ Cette veste est un peu juste. This jacket is a bit tight.; **juste assez** just enough; **chanter juste** to sing in tune

justement adv just

justesse nf **de justesse** only just

justice nf justice

justifier [20] vb to justify

juteux (f juteuse) adj juicy

juvénile adj youthful

KO *adj* knocked out; **mettre quelqu'un KO** to knock somebody out; **Je suis complètement KO.** (*informal*) I'm knackered.
K-way® *nm* cagoule

K7 *nf* (= *cassette*) cassette
kaki *adj inv* khaki
kangourou *nm* kangaroo
karaté *nm* karate
kermesse *nf* fair
kidnapper [29] *vb* to kidnap
kilo *nm* kilo
kilogramme *nm* kilogramme
kilomètre *nm* kilometre
kinésithérapeute *nmf* physiotherapist
kiosque *nm* **un kiosque à journaux** a news stand
kit *nm* kit ▷ **en kit** in kit form ▷ **un kit mains libres** a hands-free kit
klaxon *nm* (*of car*) horn
klaxonner [29] *vb* to sound the horn
km *abbr* (= *kilomètre*): **km/h** kph (*kilometres per hour*)

l' *art, pron see* **la, le**

la *art, pron*

> la changes to **l'** before a vowel and most words beginning with "h".

❶ the ▷ *la maison* the house ▷ *l'actrice* the actress ▷ *l'herbe* the grass ▷ her ▷ *Je la connais depuis longtemps.* I've known her for a long time. ❷ it ▷ *C'est une bonne émission: je la regarde tous les jours.* It's a good programme: I watch it every day. ❸ one's; **se mordre la langue** to bite one's tongue ▷ *Je me suis mordu la langue.* I've bitten my tongue.; **six euros la douzaine** six euros a dozen

▶ *nm* ❶ A ▷ *en la bémol* in A flat ❷ la ▷ *sol, la, si, do* so, la, ti, do

là *adv* ❶ there ▷ *Ton livre est là, sur la table.* Your book's there, on the table. ❷ here ▷ *Elle n'est pas là.* She isn't here.; **C'est là que …** (1) That's where … ▷ *C'est là que je suis né.* That's where I was born. (2) That's when … ▷ *C'est là que j'ai réalisé que je m'étais trompé.* That's when I realized that I had made a mistake.

là-bas *adv* over there

labo *nm* (*informal*) lab

laboratoire *nm* laboratory

labourer [29] *vb* to plough

labyrinthe *nm* maze

lac *nm* lake

lacer [13] *vb* (shoes) to do up

lacet *nm* lace; **des chaussures à lacets** lace-up shoes

lâche *adj* ❶ loose ▷ *Le nœud est trop lâche.* The knot's too loose. ❷ cowardly; **Il est lâche.** He's a coward.

▶ *nm* coward

lâcher [29] *vb* ❶ to let go of ▷ *Il n'a pas lâché ma main de tout le film.* He didn't let go of my hand until the end of the film. ❷ to drop ▷ *Il a été tellement surpris qu'il a lâché son verre.* He was so surprised that he dropped his glass. ❸ to fail ▷ *Les freins ont lâché.* The brakes failed.

lâcheté *nf* cowardice

lacrymogène *adj* **le gaz lacrymogène** tear gas

lacune *nf* gap

là-dedans *adv* in there

là-dessous *adv* ❶ under there ❷ behind it

là-dessus adv on there

là-haut adv up there

laid, e adj ugly

laideur nf ugliness

lainage nm woollen garment

laine nf wool; **une laine polaire** (jacket) a fleece

laïque adj **une école laïque** a state school

laisse nf lead ▷ *Tenez votre chien en laisse.* Keep your dog on a lead.

laisser [29] vb ❶ to leave ▷ *J'ai laissé mon parapluie à la maison.* I've left my umbrella at home. ❷ to let ▷ *Laisse-le parler.* Let him speak.; **Elle se laisse aller.** She's letting herself go.

laisser-aller nm carelessness

lait nm milk; **un café au lait** a white coffee

laitue nf lettuce

lambeaux nmpl **en lambeaux** tattered

lame nf blade

lamelle nf thin strip

lamentable adj appalling

se lamenter [29] vb to moan

lampadaire nm standard lamp

lampe nf lamp; **une lampe de poche** a torch

lance nf spear

lancement nm launch

lancer [13] vb ❶ to throw ▷ *Lance-moi le ballon!* Throw me the ball! ❷ to launch; **se lancer** to embark on

▶ nm **le lancer de poids** putting the shot

lancinant, e adj **une douleur**

lancinante a shooting pain

landau nm pram

lande nf moor

langage nm language

langouste nf crayfish

langue nf ❶ tongue; **sa langue maternelle** his mother tongue ❷ language ▷ *une langue étrangère* a foreign language

lanière nf strap

lapin nm rabbit

laps nm **un laps de temps** a space of time

laque nf hair spray

laquelle (pl **lesquelles**) pron ❶ which ▷ *Laquelle de ces photos préfères-tu?* Which of these photos do you prefer? ❷ whom ▷ *la personne à laquelle vous faites référence* the person to whom you are referring

> **laquelle** is often not translated in English.

▷ *la personne à laquelle je pense* the person I'm thinking of

lard nm streaky bacon

lardons nmpl chunks of bacon

large adj ❶ wide; **voir large** to allow a bit extra

▶ nm **cinq mètres de large** 5 m wide; **le large** the open sea; **au large de** off the coast of

largement adv **Vous avez largement le temps.** You have plenty of time.; **C'est largement suffisant.** That's ample.

largeur nf width

larme nf tear

laryngite nf laryngitis

laser nm laser; **une chaîne laser** a compact disc player; **un disque laser** a compact disc

lasser [29] vb **se lasser de** to get tired of

latin nm Latin

laurier nm laurel tree ▷ *une feuille de laurier* a bay leaf

lavable adj washable

lavabo nm washbasin

lavage nm wash

lavande nf lavender

lave-linge (pl **lave-linge**) nm washing machine

laver [29] vb to wash; **se laver** to wash ▷ *se laver les mains* to wash one's hands

laverie nf **une laverie automatique** a launderette

lave-vaisselle (pl **lave-vaisselle**) nm dishwasher

le art, pron

> le changes to **l'** before a vowel and most words beginning with "h".

❶ the ▷ *le livre* the book ▷ *l'arbre* the tree ▷ *l'hélicoptère* the helicopter ❷ him ▷ *Daniel est un vieil ami: je le connais depuis plus de vingt ans.* Daniel is an old friend: I've known him for over 20 years. ❸ it ▷ *Où est mon stylo? Je ne le trouve plus.* Where's my pen? I can't find it. ❹ one's; **se laver le visage** to wash one's face ▷ *Évitez de vous laver le visage avec du savon.* Avoid washing your face with soap.; **dix euros le kilo** 10 euros a kilo; **Il est arrivé le douze mai.** He arrived on 12 May.

lécher [35] vb to lick

lèche-vitrine nm **faire du lèche-vitrine** to go window-shopping

leçon nf lesson

lecteur (f **lectrice**) nm/f ❶ reader ❷ (at a university) foreign language assistant

> ▶ nm **un lecteur de cassettes** a cassette player; **un lecteur de CD** a CD player

lecture nf reading

> Be careful! The French word **lecture** does not mean **lecture**.

légal, e (mpl **légaux**) adj legal

légende nf ❶ legend ❷ (of map) key ❸ (of picture) caption

léger (f **légère**) adj ❶ light ❷ slight; **à la légère** thoughtlessly

légèrement adv ❶ lightly ❷ slightly ▷ *Il est légèrement plus grand que son frère.* He's slightly taller than his brother.

législatives nfpl general election

légume nm vegetable

lendemain nm next day ▷ *le lendemain de son arrivée* the day after he arrived; **le lendemain matin** the next morning

lent, e adj slow

lentement adv slowly

lenteur nf slowness

lentille nf ❶ contact lens ❷ lentil

léopard nm leopard

lequel (f **laquelle**, mpl **lesquels**, fpl **lesquelles**) pron ❶ which ▷ *Lequel de ces films as-tu préféré?* Which of the films did you prefer? ❷ whom ▷ *l'homme avec lequel elle a été* va pour la dernière fois the man with whom she was last seen

▎**lequel** is often not translated in English.

▷ le garçon avec lequel elle est sortie the boy she went out with

les adj, pron ❶ the ▷ les arbres the trees ❷ them ▷ Elle les a invités à dîner. She invited them to dinner. ❸ one's; **se brosser les dents** to brush one's teeth ▷ Elle s'est brossé les dents. She brushed her teeth.; **dix euros les cinq** 10 euros for 5

lesbienne nf lesbian

lesquels (**flesquelles**) pron

❶ which ▷ Lesquelles de ces photos préfères-tu? Which of the photos do you prefer? ❷ whom ▷ les personnes avec lesquelles il est associé the people with whom he is in partnership

▎**lesquels** is often not translated in English.

▷ les gens chez lesquels nous avons dîné the people we had dinner with

lessive nf ❶ washing powder ❷ wash; **faire la lessive** to do the washing

leste adj nimble

Lettonie nf Latvia

lettre nf letter

lettres nfpl arts ▷ la faculté de lettres the Faculty of Arts

leur adj, pron ❶ their ▷ leur ami their friend ❷ them ▷ Je leur ai dit la vérité. I told them the truth.; **le leur** theirs ▷ Ma voiture est rouge, la leur est bleue. My car's red, theirs is blue.

leurs adj, pron their ▷ leurs amis their friends; **les leurs** theirs ▷ tes livres et les leurs your books and theirs

levé, e adj **être levé(e)** to be up

levée nf (of mail) collection

lever [44] vb to raise ▷ Levez la main! Put your hand up!; **lever les yeux** to look up; **se lever (1)** to get up ▷ Il se lève tous les jours à six heures. He gets up at 6 o'clock every day. ▷ Lève-toi! Get up! **(2)** to rise ▷ Le soleil se lève actuellement à cinq heures. At the moment the sun rises at 5 o'clock. **(3)** to stand up ▷ Levez-vous! Stand up!

▶ nm **le lever du soleil** sunrise

levier nm lever

lèvre nf lip

lévrier nm greyhound

levure nf yeast; **la levure chimique** baking powder

lexique nm word list

lézard nm lizard

liaison nf affair

libellule nf dragonfly

libérer [35] vb to free; **se libérer** to find time

liberté nf freedom; **mettre en liberté** to release

libraire nmf bookseller

librairie nf bookshop

▎Be careful **librairie** does not mean **library**.

libre adj ❶ free ▷ Est-ce que cette place est libre? Is this seat free?; **Avez-vous une chambre de libre?** Have you got a free room? ❷ clear ▷ La route est libre: vous pouvez *traverser*. The road is clear: you can cross.; **une école libre** a private school

libre-service (*pl* **libres-services**) *nm* self-service store

Libye *nf* Libya

licence *nf* ❶ degree ❷ licence

licencié (*f* **licenciée**) *nm/f* graduate

licenciement *nm* redundancy

licencier [20] *vb* to make redundant

liège *nm* cork; **un bouchon en liège** (*for bottle*) a cork

lien *nm* ❶ connection; **un lien de parenté** a family tie ❷ (*in computing*) link

lier [20] *vb* **lier conversation avec quelqu'un** to get into conversation with somebody; **se lier avec quelqu'un** to make friends with somebody

lierre *nm* ivy

lieu (*pl* **lieux**) *nm* place; **avoir lieu** to take place ▷ *La cérémonie a eu lieu dans la salle des fêtes.* The ceremony took place in the village hall.; **au lieu de** instead of

lièvre *nm* hare

ligne *nf* ❶ (*phone, train*) line ▷ *la ligne de bus numéro six* the number 6 bus; **en ligne** (*computing*) on-line ❷ figure ▷ *C'est mauvais pour la ligne.* It's bad for your figure.

ligoter [29] *vb* to tie up

ligue *nf* league

lilas *nm* lilac

limace *nf* slug

lime *nf* **une lime à ongles** a nail file

limitation *nf* **la limitation de vitesse** the speed limit

limite *nf* ❶ (*of property, football pitch*) boundary ❷ limit; **À la limite, on pourrait prendre le bus.** At a pinch we could go by bus.; **la date limite** the deadline; **la date limite de vente** the sell-by-date

limiter [29] *vb* to limit

limonade *nf* lemonade

lin *nm* linen

linge *nm* ❶ linen ❷ washing ▷ *laver le linge* to do the washing; **du linge de corps** underwear

lingerie *nf* (*women's*) underwear

lion *nm* lion; **le Lion** Leo

lionne *nf* lioness

liqueur *nf* liqueur

liquide *adj* liquid
  ▶ *nm* liquid; **payer quelque chose en liquide** to pay cash for something

lire [45] *vb* to read ▷ *Tu as lu "Madame Bovary"?* Have you read "Madame Bovary"?

lis, lisent, lisez *vb see* **lire**; **Je lis beaucoup.** I read a lot.

lisible *adj* legible

lisse *adj* smooth

liste *nf* list; **faire la liste de** to make a list of

lit *nm* bed ▷ *un grand lit* a double bed; **aller au lit** to go to bed; **faire son lit** to make one's bed; **un lit de camp** a campbed
  ▶ *vb see* **lire**

literie *nf* bedding

litière *nf* ❶ (*for cat*) litter ❷ (*of caged pet*) bedding

litre nm litre

littéraire adj **une œuvre littéraire** a work of literature

littérature nf literature

littoral (pl **littoraux**) nm coast

Lituanie nf Lithuania

livraison nf delivery; **la livraison des bagages** baggage reclaim

livre nm book; **un livre de poche** a paperback
▶ nf pound
● The French **livre** is 500 grams.
▷ une livre de beurre a pound of butter; **la livre sterling** the pound sterling

livrer [29] vb to deliver

livret nm booklet; **le livret scolaire** the school report book

livreur nm delivery man

local, e (mpl **locaux**) adj local
▶ nm (pl **locaux**) premises

locataire nmf ❶ tenant ❷ lodger

location nf location de voitures car rental; **location de skis** ski hire
■ Be careful! The French word **location** does not mean **location**.

locomotive nf locomotive

loge nf dressing room

logement nm ❶ housing ❷ accommodation

loger [46] vb to stay; **trouver à se loger** to find somewhere to live

logiciel nm software

logique adj logical
▶ nf logic

loi nf law

loin adv ❶ far ▷ La gare n'est pas très loin d'ici. The station is not very far from here. ❷ far off ▷ Noël n'est plus tellement loin. Christmas isn't far off now. ❸ a long time ago ▷ Les vacances paraissent déjà tellement loin! The holidays already seem such a long time ago!; **au loin** in the distance; **de loin** (1) from a long way away ▷ On voit l'église de loin. You can see the church from a long way away. (2) by far ▷ C'est de loin l'élève la plus brillante. She is by far the brightest pupil.; **C'est plus loin que la gare.** It's further on than the station.

lointain, e adj distant
▶ nm **dans le lointain** in the distance

loir nm dormouse; **dormir comme un loir** to sleep like a log

loisirs nmpl ❶ free time ▷ Qu'est-ce que vous faites pendant vos loisirs? What do you do in your free time? ❷ hobby

Londonien (f **Londonienne**) nm/f Londoner

Londres nf London; **à Londres** (1) in London (2) to London

long (f **longue**) adj long
▶ nm **un bateau de trois mètres de long** a boat 3 m long; **tout le long de** all along; **marcher de long en large** to walk up and down

longer [46] vb **La route longe la forêt.** The road runs along the edge of the forest.; **Nous avons longé la Seine à pied.** We walked along the Seine.

longtemps adv a long time; **pendant longtemps** for a long time; **mettre longtemps à faire quelque chose** to take a long time to do something

longue *nf* **à la longue** in the end
▸ *adj see* **long**

longuement *adv* at length

longueur *nf* length; **à longueur de journée** all day long

look *nm* look

loques *nfpl* **être en loques** to be torn to bits

lors de *prep* during

lorsque *conj* when

lot *nm* prize; **le gros lot** the jackpot

loterie *nf* **①** lottery **②** raffle

lotion *nf* lotion; **une lotion après-rasage** an aftershave; **une lotion démaquillante** cleansing milk

lotissement *nm* housing estate

loto *nm* lottery; **le loto sportif** the pools

loubard *nm* (*informal*) lout

louche *adj* fishy
▸ *nf* ladle

loucher [29] *vb* to squint

louer [29] *vb* **①** to let; **"à louer"** "to let" **②** to rent ▸ Je loue un petit appartement au centre-ville. I rent a little flat in the centre of town. **③** to hire ▸ Nous allons louer une voiture. We're going to hire a car.

loup *nm* wolf

loupe *nf* magnifying glass

louper [29] *vb* (*informal*) to miss

lourd, e *adj* heavy
▸ *adv* (*weather*) close

loutre *nf* otter

loyauté *nf* loyalty

loyer *nm* rent

lu *vb see* **lire**

lucarne *nf* skylight

luge *nf* sledge

lugubre *adj* gloomy

lui *pron* **①** him ▸ Il a été très content du cadeau que je lui ai offert. He was very pleased with the present I gave him. ▸ C'est bien lui! It's definitely him! **②** to him ▸ Mon père est d'accord: je lui ai parlé ce matin. My father said yes: I spoke to him this morning. **①** her ▸ Elle a été très contente du cadeau que je lui ai offert. She was very pleased with the present I gave her. **②** to her ▸ Ma mère est d'accord: je lui ai parlé ce matin. My mother said yes: I spoke to her this morning. **③** it ▸ Qu'est-ce que tu donnes à ton chat? — Je lui donne de la viande crue. What do you give your cat? — I give it raw meat.

▪ **lui** is also used for emphasis.
▸ Lui, il est toujours en retard! Oh HE's always late!; **lui-même** himself ▸ Il a construit son bateau lui-même. He built his boat himself.

lumière *nf* light; **la lumière du jour** daylight

lumineux (**lumineuse**) *adj* **une enseigne lumineuse** a neon sign

lunatique *adj* temperamental

lundi *nm* **①** Monday ▸ Aujourd'hui, nous sommes lundi. It's Monday today. **②** on Monday; **le lundi** on Mondays; **tous les lundis** every Monday; **lundi dernier** last Monday; **lundi prochain** next Monday; **le lundi de Pâques** Easter Monday

lune nf moon; **la lune de miel** honeymoon

lunettes nfpl glasses; **des lunettes de soleil** sunglasses; **des lunettes de plongée** swimming goggles

lutte nf ❶ fight ❷ wrestling

lutter [29] vb to fight

luxe nm luxury; **de luxe** luxury

luxueux (**luxueuse**) adj luxurious

lycée nm secondary school; **lycée technique** technical college

- In France pupils go to a **collège** between the ages of 11 and 15, and then to a **lycée** until the age of 18.

lycéen (**lycéenne**) nm/f secondary school pupil

M. abbr (= Monsieur) Mr ▷ **M. Bernard** Mr Bernard

m' pron see **me**

ma adj my ▷ **ma mère** my mother ▷ **ma montre** my watch

macaronis nmpl macaroni

Macédoine nf Macedonia

macédoine nf **la macédoine de fruits** fruit salad; **la macédoine de légumes** mixed vegetables

mâcher [29] vb to chew

machin nm (informal) thingy

machinalement adv **Elle a regardé sa montre machinalement.** She looked at her watch without thinking.

machine nf machine; **une machine à laver** a washing machine; **une machine à écrire** a typewriter; **une machine à**

coudre a sewing machine; **une machine à sous** a fruit machine

machiste nm male chauvinist

macho nm (informal) male chauvinist pig

mâchoire nf jaw

mâchonner [29] vb to chew

maçon nm bricklayer

Madame (pl **Mesdames**) nf ❶ Mrs ▷ Madame Legall Mrs Legall ❷ lady ▷ Occupez-vous de Madame. Could you look after this lady? ❸ (in letter) Madam ▷ Madame, ... Dear Madam, ...

Mademoiselle (pl **Mesdemoiselles**) nf ❶ Miss ▷ Mademoiselle Delacroix Miss Delacroix ❷ (in letter) Madam ▷ Mademoiselle, ... Dear Madam, ...

magasin nm shop; **faire les magasins** to go shopping

magazine nm magazine

magicien (f **magicienne**) nm/f magician

magie nf magic ▷ un tour de magie a magic trick

magique adj magic ▷ une baguette magique a magic wand

magistral, e (mpl **magistraux**) adj **un cours magistral** (at university) a lecture

magnétique adj magnetic

magnétophone nm tape recorder; **un magnétophone à cassettes** a cassette recorder

magnétoscope nm video recorder

magnifique adj superb

mai nm May; **en mai** in May

maigre adj ❶ skinny ❷ (meat) lean ❸ (cheese, yoghurt) low-fat

maigrir [39] vb to lose weight

maillot de bain nm ❶ swimsuit ❷ swimming trunks

main nf hand; **serrer la main à quelqu'un** to shake hands with somebody; **se serrer la main** to shake hands; **sous la main** to hand

main-d'œuvre nf workforce; **la main-d'œuvre immigrée** immigrant labour

maintenant adv ❶ now ▷ Qu'est-ce que tu veux faire maintenant? What do you want to do now? ❷ nowadays

maintenir [84] vb to maintain; **se maintenir** to hold

maire nm mayor

mairie nf town hall

mais conj but ▷ C'est cher mais de très bonne qualité. It's expensive, but very good quality.

maïs nm ❶ maize ❷ sweetcorn

maison nf house; **une maison des jeunes** a youth club; **des maisons mitoyennes** (1) semi-detached houses (2) terraced houses; **à la maison** (1) at home ▷ Je serai à la maison cet après-midi. I'll be at home this afternoon. (2) at home ▷ Elle est rentrée à la maison. She's gone home.

▶ adj inv home-made

maître nm ❶ (in primary school) teacher ❷ (of dog) master; **un maître d'hôtel** (in restaurant) a head waiter; **un maître nageur** a lifeguard

maîtresse nf ❶ (in primary school) teacher ❷ mistress

maîtrise nf master's degree; **la maîtrise de soi** self-control

maîtriser [29] vb **se maîtriser** to control oneself

majestueux (f majestueuse) adj majestic

majeur, e adj **être majeur(e)** to be 18; **la majeure partie** most

majorité nf majority; **la majorité et l'opposition** the government and the opposition

Majorque nf Majorca

majuscule nf capital letter

mal (f+pl mal) adv, adj ❶ badly ❷ wrong ▷ *C'est mal de mentir.* It's wrong to tell lies.; **aller mal** to be ill; **pas mal** quite good
▶ nm (pl maux) ❶ ache ▷ *J'ai mal à la tête.* I've got a headache. ▷ *J'ai mal aux dents.* I've got toothache. ▷ *J'ai mal au dos.* My back hurts. ▷ *Est-ce que vous avez mal à la gorge?* Have you got a sore throat?; **Ça fait mal.** It hurts.; **Où est-ce que tu as mal?** Where does it hurt?; **faire mal à quelqu'un** to hurt somebody; **se faire mal** to hurt oneself ▷ *Je me suis fait mal au bras.* I hurt my arm.; **se donner du mal pour faire quelque chose** to go to a lot of trouble to do something; **avoir le mal de mer** to be seasick; **avoir le mal du pays** to be homesick ❷ evil; **dire du mal de quelqu'un** to speak ill of somebody

malade adj ill; **tomber malade** to fall ill

▶ nmf patient

maladie nf illness

maladif (f maladive) adj sickly

maladresse nf clumsiness

maladroit, e adj clumsy

malaise nm avoir un malaise to feel faint; **Son arrivée a créé un malaise parmi les invités.** Her arrival made the guests feel uncomfortable.

malchance nf bad luck

mâle adj male

malédiction nf curse

mal en point adj inv Il avait l'air mal en point quand je l'ai vu hier soir. He didn't look too good when I saw him last night.

malentendu nm misunderstanding

malfaiteur nm criminal

mal famé, e adj **un quartier mal famé** a seedy area

malgache adj from Madagascar

malgré prep in spite of; **malgré tout** all the same

malheur nm tragedy; **faire un malheur** (informal) to be a smash hit

malheureusement adv unfortunately

malheureux (f malheureuse) adj miserable

malhonnête adj dishonest

malice nf mischief

malicieux (f malicieuse) adj mischievous

> Be careful! malicieux does not mean malicious.

malin (f maligne) adj crafty; **C'est malin!** (informal) That's clever!

malle nf trunk

malodorant, e adj foul-smelling

malpropre adj dirty

malsain, e adj unhealthy

Malte nm Malta

maltraiter [29] vb to ill-treat; **des enfants maltraités** battered children

malveillant, e adj malicious

maman nf mum

mamie nf granny

mammifère nm mammal

manche nf ❶ (of clothes) sleeve ❷ (of game) leg; **la Manche** the Channel
▶ nm (of pan) handle

mandarine nf mandarin orange

manège nm merry-go-round

manette nf lever

mangeable adj edible

manger [46] vb to eat

mangue nf mango

maniaque adj fussy

manie nf ❶ obsession; **avoir la manie de** to be obsessive about ❷ habit

manier [20] vb to handle

manière nf ❶ way; **de manière à** so as to; **de toute manière** in any case

maniéré, e adj affected

manières nfpl ❶ manners ❷ fuss ▷ Ne fais pas de manières: mange ta soupe! Don't make a fuss: eat your soup!

manifestant (f manifestante) nm/f demonstrator

manifestation nf demonstration

manifester [29] vb to demonstrate

manipuler [29] vb ❶ to handle ❷ to manipulate

mannequin nm model

manœuvrer [29] vb to manœuvre

manque nm withdrawal; **le manque de** lack of

manqué, e adj **un garçon manqué** a tomboy

manquer [29] vb to miss ▷ Il manque des pages à ce livre. There are some pages missing from this book.; **Mes parents me manquent.** I miss my parents.; **Ma sœur me manque.** I miss my sister.; **Il manque encore dix euros.** We are still 10 euros short.; **manquer de** to lack; **Il a manqué se tuer.** He nearly got killed.

manteau (pl manteaux) nm coat

manuel (f manuelle) adj manual
▶ nm ❶ textbook ❷ handbook

maquereau (pl maquereaux) nm mackerel

maquette nf model

maquillage nm make-up

se maquiller [29] vb to put on one's make-up

marais nm marsh

marbre nm marble

marchand (f marchande) nm/f ❶ shopkeeper; **un marchand de journaux** a newsagent; **une marchande de fruits et légumes** a greengrocer ❷ stallholder (in market)

marchander [29] vb to haggle

marchandise nf goods

marche nf ❶ step ▷ *Fais attention à la marche!* Mind the step! ❷ walking ▷ *La marche me fait du bien.* Walking does me good.; **être en état de marche** to be in working order; **Ne montez jamais dans un train en marche.** Never try to get into a moving train.; **mettre en marche** to start; **la marche arrière** reverse gear; **faire marche arrière** to reverse ❸ march ▷ *une marche militaire* a military march

marché nm market; **un marché aux puces** a flea market; **le marché noir** the black market

marcher [29] vb ❶ to walk ▷ *Elle marche cinq kilomètres par jour.* She walks 5 kilometres every day. ❷ to run ▷ *Le métro marche normalement aujourd'hui.* The underground is running normally today. ❸ to work ▷ *Est-ce que l'ascenseur marche?* Is the lift working? ❹ to go well; **Alors les études, ça marche?** (informal) How are you getting on at school?; **faire marcher quelqu'un** to pull somebody's leg

marcheur (f **marcheuse**) nm/f walker

mardi nm ❶ Tuesday ▷ *Aujourd'hui, nous sommes mardi.* It's Tuesday today. ❷ on Tuesday; **le mardi** on Tuesdays; **tous les mardis** every Tuesday; **mardi dernier** last Tuesday; **mardi prochain** next Tuesday; **Mardi gras** Shrove Tuesday

mare nf pond

marécage nm marsh

marée nf tide; **une marée noire** an oil slick

margarine nf margarine

marge nf margin

mari nm husband

mariage nm ❶ marriage ❷ wedding

marié, e adj married
▶ nm bridegroom; **les mariés** the bride and groom
▶ nf la mariée the bride

se marier [20] vb to marry

marin, e adj sea; **un pull marin** a sailor's jersey
▶ nm sailor

marine adj inv **bleu marine** navy-blue
▶ nf navy; **la marine nationale** the French navy

marionnette nf puppet

marketing nm marketing

marmelade nf stewed fruit; **la marmelade de pommes** stewed apple; **la marmelade d'oranges** marmalade

marmite nf cooking pot

marmonner [29] vb to mumble

Maroc nm Morocco

marocain, e adj Moroccan

maroquinerie nf leather goods shop

marquant, e adj significant

marque nf ❶ mark ❷ make ❸ brand; **l'image de marque** the public image; **une marque déposée** a registered trademark; **A vos marques! prêts! partez!** Ready, steady, go!

a b c d e f g h i j k l **m** n o p q r s t u v w x y z

marquer [29] *vb* ❶ to mark ❷ to score ▷ *L'équipe irlandaise a marqué dix points.* The Irish team scored ten points. ❸ to celebrate ▷ *On va sortir au restaurant pour marquer ton anniversaire.* We'll eat out to celebrate your birthday.

marraine *nf* godmother

marrant, e *adj* (*informal*) funny

marre *adv* (*informal*): **en avoir marre de quelque chose** to be fed up with something

se marrer [29] *vb* (*informal*) to have a good laugh

marron *nm* chestnut ▷ *la crème de marrons* chestnut purée ▶ *adj inv* brown

marronnier *nm* chestnut tree

mars *nm* March; **en mars** in March

marteau (*pl* **marteaux**) *nm* hammer

martyriser [29] *vb* to batter

masculin, e *adj* ❶ men's ▷ *la mode masculine* men's fashion ❷ masculine ▷ *"chat" est un nom masculin.* "chat" is a masculine noun.

masque *nm* mask

massacre *nm* massacre

massacrer [29] *vb* to massacre

massage *nm* massage

masse *nf* **une masse de** (*informal*) masses of; **produire en masse** to mass-produce; **venir en masse** to come en masse

masser [29] *vb* to massage; **se masser** to gather

massif (*f* **massive**) *adj* ❶ (*gold, silver, wood*) solid ❷ massive

▷ *une dose massive d'antibiotiques* a massive dose of antibiotics ❸ mass ▷ *des départs massifs* a mass exodus

mat, e *adj* matt; **être mat** (*chess*) to be checkmate

match *nm* match; **le match aller** the first leg; **le match retour** the second leg; **faire match nul** to draw

matelas *nm* mattress; **un matelas pneumatique** an air bed

matelassé, e *adj* quilted

matelot *nm* sailor

matériaux *nmpl* materials

matériel *nm* ❶ equipment ❷ gear

maternel (*f* **maternelle**) *adj* motherly; **ma grand-mère maternelle** my mother's mother; **mon oncle maternel** my mother's brother

maternelle *nf* nursery school

● The **maternelle** is a state school
● for 2–6 year-olds.

maternité *nf* **le congé de maternité** maternity leave

mathématiques *nfpl* mathematics

maths *nfpl* (*informal*) maths

matière *nf* subject ▷ *Le latin est une matière facultative.* Latin is an optional subject.; **sans matières grasses** fat-free; **les matières premières** raw materials

matin *nm* morning ▷ *à trois heures du matin* at 3 o'clock in the morning; **Je suis du matin.** I'm at my best in the morning.; **de bon matin** early in the morning

matinal, e (mpl **matinaux**) adj morning; **être matinal** to be up early

matinée nf morning

matou nm tomcat

matrimonial, e (mpl **matrimoniaux**) adj **une agence matrimoniale** a marriage bureau

maudire [47] vb to curse

maudit, e adj (informal) blasted

maussade adj sullen

mauvais, e adj, adv ❶ bad ▷ une mauvaise note a bad mark; **Il fait mauvais.** The weather's bad.; **être mauvais en** to be bad at ▷ Je suis mauvais en allemand. I'm bad at German. ❷ poor ▷ Il est en mauvaise santé. His health is poor.; **Tu as mauvaise mine.** You don't look well. ❸ wrong ▷ Vous avez fait le mauvais numéro. You've dialled the wrong number.; **des mauvaises herbes** weeds; **sentir mauvais** to smell

maux nmpl **des maux de ventre** stomachache; **des maux de tête** headache

maximal, e (mpl **maximaux**) adj maximum

maximum nm maximum; **au maximum (1)** as much as one can **(2)** at the very most

mayonnaise nf mayonnaise

mazout nm fuel oil

me pron

■ me changes to **m'** before a vowel and most words beginning with "h".

❶ me ▷ Elle me téléphone tous les jours. She phones me every day. ▷ Il m'attend depuis une heure. He's been waiting for me for an hour. ❷ to me ▷ Il me parle en allemand. He talks to me in German. ❸ myself ▷ Je vais me préparer quelque chose à manger. I'm going to make myself something to eat.

■ With reflexive verbs, **me** is often not translated.
▷ Je me lève à sept heures tous les matins. I get up at 7 every morning.

mec nm (informal) guy

mécanicien nm mechanic

mécanique nf ❶ mechanics ❷ (of watch, clock) mechanism

mécanisme nm mechanism

méchamment adv nastily

méchanceté nf nastiness

méchant, e adj nasty; **"Attention, chien méchant"** "Beware of the dog"

mèche nf (of hair) lock

mécontent, e adj **mécontent de** unhappy with

mécontentement nm displeasure

médaille nf medal

médecin nm doctor

médecine nf (subject) medicine

médias nmpl media

médical, e (mpl **médicaux**) adj medical; **passer une visite médicale** to have a medical

médicament nm (drug) medicine

médiéval, e (mpl **médiévaux**) adj medieval

médiocre adj poor

Méditerranée nf Mediterranean

méditerranéen
(f **méditerranéenne**) adj
Mediterranean

méduse nf jellyfish

méfiance nf mistrust

méfiant, e adj mistrustful

se méfier [20] vb **se méfier de
quelqu'un** to distrust somebody

mégarde nf **par mégarde** by
mistake

mégot nm cigarette end

meilleur, e adj, adv, nm/f better;
le meilleur the best; **le meilleur
des deux** the better of the two;
meilleur marché cheaper

mél nm email

mélancolique adj melancholy

mélange nm mixture

mélanger [46] vb ❶ to mix ❷ to
muddle up

mêlée nf scrum

mêler [29] vb **se mêler** to mix;
Mêle-toi de ce qui te regarde!
(informal) Mind your own business!

mélodie nf melody

melon nm melon

membre nm ❶ limb ❷ member
▷ un membre de la famille a member
of the family

mémé nf (informal) granny

même adj, adv, pron ❶ same; **en
même temps** at the same time;
moi-même myself ▷ Je l'ai fait moi-
même. I did it myself.; **toi-même**
yourself; **eux-mêmes** themselves
❷ even ▷ Il n'a même pas pleuré. He
didn't even cry.

mémoire nf memory

menace nf threat

menacer [13] vb to threaten

ménage nm housework; **une
femme de ménage** a cleaning
woman

ménager (f **ménagère**) adj **les
travaux ménagers** housework

ménagère nf housewife

mendiant (f **mendiante**) nm/f
beggar

mendier [20] vb to beg

mener [44] vb to lead; **Cela ne
vous mènera à rien!** That will get
you nowhere!

méningite nf meningitis

menottes nfpl handcuffs

mensonge nm lie

mensualité nf monthly payment

mensuel (f **mensuelle**) adj
monthly

mensurations nfpl
measurements

mentalité nf mentality

menteur (f **menteuse**) nm/f liar

menthe nf mint

mention nf grade

mentionner [29] vb to mention

mentir [78] vb to lie ▷ Tu mens!
You're lying!

menton nm chin

menu, e nm menu ▷ le menu du jour
today's menu
▶ adj, adv ❶ slim ▷ Elle est menue.
She's slim. ❷ very fine ▷ Les oignons
doivent être coupés menu. The onions
have to be cut up very fine.

menuiserie nf woodwork

menuisier nm joiner

mépris nm contempt

méprisant, e adj contemptuous

mépriser [29] *vb* to despise

mer *nf* ❶ sea; **au bord de la mer** at the seaside; **la mer du Nord** the North Sea ❷ tide

mercerie *nf* ❶ haberdashery ❷ haberdasher's shop

merci *excl* thank you ▷ *Merci de m'avoir raccompagné.* Thank you for taking me home.; **merci beaucoup** thank you very much

mercredi *nm* ❶ Wednesday ▷ *Aujourd'hui, nous sommes mercredi.* It's Wednesday today. ❷ on Wednesday; **le mercredi** on Wednesdays; **tous les mercredis** every Wednesday; **mercredi dernier** last Wednesday; **mercredi prochain** next Wednesday

merde *nf* (rude) shit

mère *nf* mother

merguez *nf* spicy sausage

méridional, e (*mpl* **méridionaux**) *adj* southern

meringue *nf* meringue

mériter [29] *vb* to deserve

merlan *nm* whiting

merle *nm* blackbird

merveille *nf* **Cet ordinateur est une vraie merveille!** This computer's really wonderful!; **à merveille** wonderfully

merveilleux (*f* **merveilleuse**) *adj* marvellous

mes *adj* my ▷ **mes parents** my parents

Mesdames *nfpl* ladies

Mesdemoiselles *nfpl* ladies

mesquin, e *adj* mean

message *nm* message; **un message SMS** a text message

messagerie *nf* **la messagerie vocale** voicemail; **la messagerie électronique** email

messe *nf* mass

messieurs *nmpl* gentlemen; **Messieurs, ...** (in letter) Dear Sirs, ...

mesure *nf* ❶ measurement; **sur mesure** tailor-made ❷ measure; **au fur et à mesure** as one goes along; **être en mesure de faire quelque chose** to be in a position to do something

mesurer [29] *vb* to measure; **Il mesure un mètre quatre-vingts.** He's 1 m 80 tall.

met *vb see* **mettre**

métal (*pl* **métaux**) *nm* metal

métallique *adj* metallic

météo *nf* weather forecast

méthode *nf* ❶ method ❷ tutor ▷ *une méthode de guitare* a guitar tutor

métier *nm* job

mètre *nm* metre; **un mètre ruban** a tape measure

métro *nm* underground

mets *vb see* **mettre**

metteur en scène (*pl* **metteurs en scène**) *nm* ❶ (of play) producer ❷ (of film) director

mettre [48] *vb* ❶ to put ▷ *Où est-ce que tu as mis tes clés?* Where have you put the keys? ❷ to put on ▷ *Je mets mon manteau et j'arrive.* I'll put on my coat and then I'll be ready. ❸ to wear ▷ *Elle ne met pas souvent de jupe.* She doesn't often wear a skirt. ❹ **to take** ▷ *Combien de temps as-tu mis pour aller à Lille?* How long did it take you to get to Lille?; **mettre en marche** to start; **Vous pouvez vous mettre là.** You can sit there.; **se mettre au lit** to get into bed; **se mettre en maillot de bain** to put on one's swimsuit; **se mettre à** to start

meuble *nm* piece of furniture

meublé ❶ furnished flat ❷ furnished room

meubler [29] *vb* to furnish

meurtre *nm* murder

meurtrier *nm* murderer

meurtrière *nf* murderess

Mexico *nf* Mexico City

Mexique *nm* Mexico

mi *nm* ❶ E ▷ *mi bémol* E flat ❷ mi ▷ *do, ré, mi ... do, re, mi ...*

mi- *prefix* ❶ half- ▷ *mi-clos* half-shut ❷ mid- ▷ *à la mi-janvier* in mid-January

miauler [29] *vb* to mew

miche *nf* loaf

mi-chemin : à mi-chemin *adv* halfway

micro *nm* microphone

microbe *nm* germ

micro-ondes *nm* microwave oven

micro-ordinateur *nm* microcomputer

microscope *nm* microscope

midi *nm* ❶ midday ▷ *à midi* at midday; **midi et demi** half past twelve ▷ *lunchtime* ▷ *On a bien mangé à midi.* We had a good meal at lunchtime.; **le Midi** the South of France

mie *nf* breadcrumbs

miel *nm* honey

mien *pron* **le mien** mine

mienne *pron* **la mienne** mine

miennes *pron* **les miennes** mine

miens *pron* **les miens** mine

miette *nf* (of bread, cake) crumb

mieux *adv, adj, nm* better; **Il vaut mieux que tu appelles ta mère.** You'd better phone your mother.; **le mieux** the best; **faire de son mieux** to do one's best; **de mieux en mieux** better and better; **au mieux** at best

mignon (*f* mignonne) *adj* sweet

migraine *nf* migraine

mijoter [29] *vb* to simmer

milieu (*pl* milieux) *nm* ❶ middle; **au milieu de** in the middle of; **au beau milieu de** in the middle of ❷ background ▷ *le milieu familial* the family background ❸ environment ▷ *le milieu marin* the marine environment

militaire *adj* military

▶ *nm* serviceman; **un militaire de carrière** a professional soldier

mille *num* a thousand ▷ *mille euros* a thousand euros ▷ *deux mille personnes* two thousand people

millefeuille *nm* vanilla slice

millénaire *nm* millennium

millénium *nm* millennium

milliard *nm* thousand million

milliardaire *nmf* multimillionaire

millier *nm* thousand; **par milliers** by the thousand

milligramme *nm* milligramme

millimètre *nm* millimetre

million *nm* million

millionnaire *nmf* millionaire

mime *nmf* mime artist

mimer [29] *vb* to mimic

minable *adj* ❶ shabby ❷ pathetic

mince *adj* ❶ thin ❷ slim; **Mince alors!** *(informal)* Oh bother!

minceur *nf* ❶ thinness ❷ slimness

mine *nf* ❶ expression ❷ look ▷ **Tu as bonne mine.** You look well. ❸ appearance ❹ *(of pencil)* lead ❺ mine ▷ *une mine de charbon* a coal mine; **faire mine de faire quelque chose** to pretend to do something; **mine de rien** somehow or other

minéral, e *(mpl* **minéraux)** *adj* mineral

minéralogique *adj* **une plaque minéralogique** a number plate

minet *nm* pussycat

minette *nf (female)* pussycat

mineur, e *adj* minor
▶ *nm* ❶ boy under 18; **les mineurs** the under-18s ❷ miner
▶ *nf* girl under 18

minidisque *nm* Minidisc®

minijupe *nf* miniskirt

minimal, e *(mpl* **minimaux)** *adj* minimum

minimum *nm* minimum; **au minimum** at the very least

ministère *nm* ministry

ministre *nm* minister

Minitel® *nm*

- Minitel is France Telecom's
- online data service. You can use
- it instead of a phone directory,
- and to make bookings for
- transport, exhibitions etc.

minorité *nf* minority

Minorque *nf* Minorca

minuit *nm* midnight ▷ *à minuit et quart* at a quarter past midnight

minuscule *adj* tiny
▶ *nf* small letter

minute *nf* minute; **à la minute** just this minute

minutieux (f minutieuse) *adj* meticulous; **C'est un travail minutieux.** It's a fiddly job.

mirabelle *nf* small yellow plum

miracle *nm* miracle

miroir *nm* mirror

mis, e *adj* **bien mis** well turned out
▶ *vb see* **mettre**

miser [29] *vb (informal)* to bank on

misérable *adj* shabby-looking

misère *nf* extreme poverty; **un salaire de misère** starvation wages

missionnaire *nmf* missionary

mit *vb see* **mettre**

mi-temps *nf* ❶ *(of match)* half ▷ *la première mi-temps* the first half ❷ half-time; **travailler à mi-temps** to work part-time

mitraillette *nf* submachine gun

mixte *adj* **une école mixte** a mixed school

Mlle *(pl* **Mlles)** *abbr (=* Mademoiselle) Miss ▷ *Mlle Renoir* Miss Renoir

Mme *(pl* **Mmes)** *abbr (=* Madame) Mrs ▷ *Mme Leroy* Mrs Leroy

mobile *nm* ❶ motive ❷ *(telephone)* mobile (phone)

mobilier *nm* furniture

mobinaute *nmf* mobile internet user

a
b
c
d
e
f
g
h
i
j
k
l
m
n
o
p
q
r
s
t
u
v
w
x
y
z

mobylette® nf moped

moche adj (informal) awful

mode nf fashion
▶ nm **le mode d'emploi** directions for use; **le mode de vie** the way of life

modèle nm model

modéré, e adj moderate

moderne adj modern

moderniser [29] vb to modernize

modeste adj modest

modestie nf modesty

moelleux (f **moelleuse**) adj soft

mœurs nfpl social attitudes; **l'évolution des mœurs** changing attitudes

moi pron me ▷ Coucou, c'est moi! Hello, it's me!; **Moi, je pense que tu as tort.** I personally think you're wrong.; **à moi** mine ▷ Ce livre n'est pas à moi. This book isn't mine. ▷ un ami à moi a friend of mine

moi-même pron myself

moindre adj **le moindre** the slightest

moine nm monk

moineau (pl **moineaux**) nm sparrow

moins adv, prep ❶ less ▷ Ça coûte moins de deux euros cinquante. It costs less than 200 euros. ❷ fewer ▷ Il y a moins de gens aujourd'hui. There are fewer people today.; **Il est cinq heures moins dix.** It's 10 to 5. ❸ minus ▷ quatre moins trois 4 minus 3; **de moins** the least; **de moins en moins** less and less; **Il a trois ans de moins que moi.** He's three years younger than me.;

au moins at least; **à moins que** unless

 à moins que is followed by a verb in the subjunctive.

▷ Je te retrouverai à dix heures à moins que le train n'ait du retard. I'll meet you at 10 o'clock unless the train's late.

mois nm month

moisi nm **Ça sent le moisi.** It smells musty.

moisir [39] vb to go mouldy

moisson nf harvest

moite adj sweaty

moitié nf half; **la moitié du temps** half the time; **à la moitié de** halfway through; **à moitié** half ▷ à moitié plein half-full; **partager moitié moitié** to go halves

molaire nf back tooth

Moldavie nf Moldova

molle adj lethargic

mollet nm (of leg) calf
▶ adj **un œuf mollet** a soft-boiled egg

môme nmf (informal) kid

moment nm moment; **en ce moment** at the moment; **pour le moment** for the moment; **au moment où** just as; **à ce moment-là** (1) at that point (2) in that case; **à tout moment** (1) at any moment (2) constantly; **sur le moment** at the time; **par moments** at times

momentané, e adj momentary

momie nf (Egyptian) mummy

mon (f ma, pl mes) adj my ▷ mon ami my friend

monarchie nf monarchy

monastère nm monastery

monde nm world; **Il y a du monde.** There are a lot of people.; **beaucoup de monde** a lot of people; **peu de monde** not many people

mondial, e (mpl **mondiaux**) adj ❶ world ▷ la population mondiale the world population ❷ world-wide

mondialisation nf globalization

moniteur nm ❶ instructor ❷ monitor

monitrice nf instructor

monnaie nf **une pièce de monnaie** a coin; **avoir de la monnaie** to have change; **rendre la monnaie à quelqu'un** to give somebody their change

monotone adj monotonous

Monsieur (pl **Messieurs**) nm ❶ Mr ▷ Monsieur Dupont Mr Dupont ❷ man ▷ Il y a un monsieur qui veut te voir. There's a man to see you. ❸ (in letter) Sir ▷ Monsieur, ... Dear Sir, ...

monstre nm monster
▶ adj **Nous avons un travail monstre.** We've got a terrific amount of work.

mont nm mount; **le mont Everest** Mount Everest; **le mont Blanc** Mont Blanc

montagne nf mountain; **les montagnes russes** roller coaster

montagneux (f **montagneuse**) adj mountainous

montant, e adj rising ▷ la marée montante the rising tide

monter [49] vb ❶ to go up ▷ Elle a du mal à monter les escaliers. She has difficulty going upstairs. ❷ to assemble ▷ Est-ce que ces étagères sont difficiles à monter? Are these shelves difficult to assemble?; **monter dans** to get on; **monter sur** to stand on; **monter à cheval** to ride

montre nf watch

montrer [29] vb to show

monture nf (of glasses) frames

monument nm monument

se moquer [29] vb **se moquer de** (1) to make fun of; **se moquer de** (2) (informal) not to care about

moquette nf fitted carpet

moqueur (f **moqueuse**) adj mocking

moral nm **Elle a le moral.** She's in good spirits.; **J'ai le moral à zéro.** I'm feeling really down.

morale nf moral; **faire la morale à quelqu'un** to lecture somebody

morceau (pl **morceaux**) nm piece

mordre [50] vb to bite

mordu, e adj **Il est mordu de jazz.** (informal) He's crazy about jazz.

morgue nf mortuary

morse nm walrus

morsure nf bite

mort, e adj dead; **Il était mort de peur.** He was scared to death.; **Je suis morte de fatigue.** I'm dead tired.
▶ nf death

mortel (f **mortelle**) adj ❶ deadly ❷ fatal

morue nf cod

Moscou n Moscow

mosquée nf mosque

mot nm ❶ word ▷ *mot à mot* word for word; **des mots croisés** a crossword; **le mot de passe** the password ❷ note

motard nm ❶ biker ❷ (informal) motorcycle cop

moteur nm engine; **un bateau à moteur** a motor boat; **un moteur de recherche** a search engine

motif nm pattern; **sans motif** for no reason

motivé, e adj motivated

moto nf motorbike

motocycliste nmf motorcyclist

mou (f **molle**) adj ❶ soft ❷ lethargic

mouche nf fly; **prendre la mouche** to get into a huff

se moucher [29] vb to blow one's nose

moucheron nm midge

mouchoir nm handkerchief; **un mouchoir en papier** a tissue

moudre [51] vb to grind

moue nf pout; **faire la moue** to pout

mouette nf seagull

moufle nf mitt

mouillé, e adj wet

mouiller [29] vb to get wet; **se mouiller** to get wet

moulant, e adj figure-hugging

moule nf mussel
　▶ nm **un moule à gâteaux** a cake tin

moulin nm mill

moulu vb see **moudre**

mourir [52] vb to die; **mourir de faim** to starve; **Je meurs de faim!** I'm starving!; **mourir de froid** to die of exposure; **Je meurs de froid!** I'm freezing!; **mourir d'envie de faire quelque chose** to be dying to do something

mousse nf ❶ moss ❷ (on beer) froth ❸ (of soap, shampoo) lather ❹ mousse ▷ *une mousse au chocolat* a chocolate mousse; **la mousse à raser** shaving foam

mousseux (f **mousseuse**) adj **un vin mousseux** a sparkling wine

moustache nf mustache; **les moustaches** whiskers

moustique nm mosquito

moutarde nf mustard

mouton nm ❶ sheep ❷ mutton

mouvement nm movement

mouvementé, e adj eventful

moyen (f **moyenne**) adj ❶ average ❷ medium ▷ *Elle est de taille moyenne.* She's of medium height.; **le moyen âge** the Middle Ages
　▶ nm way ▷ *Quel est le meilleur moyen de le convaincre?* What's the best way of convincing him?; **Je n'en ai pas les moyens.** I can't afford it.; **un moyen de transport** a means of transport; **par tous les moyens** by every possible means

moyenne nf avoir la moyenne to get a pass mark; **en moyenne** on average; **la moyenne d'âge** the average age

Moyen-Orient nm Middle East

muet (f **muette**) adj dumb; **un film muet** a silent film

muguet nm lily of the valley

multiple adj numerous

multiplier [20] vb to multiply

municipal, e (mpl municipaux) adj **la bibliothèque municipale** the public library

municipalité nf town council

munir [39] vb **munir quelqu'un de** to equip someone with; **se munir de** to equip oneself with

munitions nfpl ammunition

mur nm wall

mûr, e adj ❶ (fruit) ripe ❷ (person) mature

mûre nf bramble

mûrir [39] vb ❶ to ripen ❷ to make mature ▷ *Cette expérience l'a beaucoup mûrie.* That experience has made her much more mature.

murmurer [29] vb to whisper

muscade nf nutmeg

muscat nm ❶ muscat grape ❷ (wine) muscatel

muscle nm muscle

musclé, e adj muscular

museau (pl museaux) nm muzzle

musée nm museum

musical, e (mpl musicaux) adj musical; **avoir l'oreille musicale** to be musical

music-hall nm variety

musicien (f musicienne) nm/f musician

musique nf music

musulman, e adj Muslim ▶ nm/f **un musulman** (man) a Muslim; **une musulmane** (woman) a Muslim

mutation nf transfer

myope adj short-sighted

mystère nm mystery

mystérieux (f mystérieuse) adj mysterious

mythe nm myth

a
b
c
d
e
f
g
h
i
j
k
l
m
n
o
p
q
r
s
t
u
v
w
x
y
z

n

n' *pron see* **ne**

nage *nf* traverser une rivière à la nage to swim across a river; être en nage to be sweating profusely

nageoire *nf* fin

nager [**46**] *vb* to swim

nageur (f **nageuse**) *nm* swimmer

naïf (f **naïve**) *adj* naïve

nain *nm* dwarf

naissance *nf* birth; votre date de naissance your date of birth

naître [**53**] *vb* to be born; Il est né en 1982. He was born in 1982.

naïve *adj see* **naïf**

nana *nf* (*informal*) girl

nappe *nf* tablecloth

narine *nf* nostril

natal, e *adj* native

natation *nf* swimming; faire de la natation to go swimming

nation *nf* nation

national, e (*mpl* **nationaux**) *adj* national; la fête nationale espagnole the national day of Spain

nationale *nf* main road

nationalité *nf* nationality

natte *nf* plait

nature *nf* nature

   ▶ *adj* plain

naturel (f **naturelle**) *adj* natural

naturellement *adv* of course

naufrage *nm* shipwreck

nautique *adj* water; les sports nautiques water sports; le ski nautique water-skiing

navet *nm* turnip

navette *nf* shuttle; faire la navette to commute

navigateur *nm* (*on computer*) browser

navigation *nf* La navigation est interdite ici. Boats are not allowed here.

naviguer [**29**] *vb* to sail

navire *nm* ship

ne *adv*

> **ne** is combined with words such as **pas**, **personne**, **plus** and **jamais** to form negative phrases.

> ▷ Je ne peux pas venir. I can't come.

> **ne** changes to **n'** before a vowel and most words beginning with "h".

> ▷ Je n'ai pas d'argent. I haven't got any money.

> **ne** is sometimes not translated.

▷ *C'est plus loin que je ne le croyais.* It's further than I thought.

né *vb see* **naître** born ▷ *Elle est née en 1980.* She was born in 1980.

néanmoins *adv* nevertheless

nécessaire *adj* necessary

nectar *nm* le nectar d'abricot apricot drink

néerlandais, e *adj* Dutch
▶ *nm* Dutch ▷ *Manon parle néerlandais.* Manon speaks Dutch.
▶ *nm/f* un Néerlandais a Dutchman; une Néerlandaise a Dutchwoman; les Néerlandais the Dutch

négatif (f**négative**) *adj* negative
▶ *nm* (of photo) negative

négligé, e *adj* scruffy

négliger [46] *vb* to neglect

négocier [20] *vb* to negotiate

neige *nf* snow; un bonhomme de neige a snowman

neiger [46] *vb* to snow

nénuphar *nm* water lily

néon *nm* neon

néo-zélandais, e *adj* New Zealand
▶ *nm/f* un Néo-Zélandais (man) a New Zealander; une Néo-Zélandaise (woman) a New Zealander

nerf *nm* nerve; taper sur les nerfs de quelqu'un to get on somebody's nerves

nerveux (f**nerveuse**) *adj* nervous

nervosité *nf* nervousness

n'est-ce pas *adv*

■ **n'est-ce pas** is used to check that something is true.

▷ *Nous sommes le douze aujourd'hui, n'est-ce pas?* It's the 12th today, isn't it? ▷ *Elle aura dix-huit ans en octobre, n'est-ce pas?* She'll be 18 in October, won't she?

Net *nm* the Net

net (f**nette**) *adj, adv* ❶ clear ❷ net ▷ *Poids net: 500 g.* Net weight: 500 g. ❸ flatly ▷ *Il a refusé net de nous aider.* He flatly refused to help us.; s'arrêter net to stop dead

nettement *adv* much

nettoyage *nm* cleaning; le nettoyage à sec dry cleaning

nettoyer [54] *vb* to clean

neuf *num* nine ▷ *Claire a neuf ans.* Claire's nine.; le neuf février the ninth of February
▶ *adj* (f**neuve**) new

neutre *adj* neutral

neuve *adj see* **neuf**

neuvième *adj* ninth

neveu (pl**neveux**) *nm* nephew

nez *nm* nose; se trouver nez à nez avec quelqu'un to come face to face with somebody

ni *conj* ni ... ni ... neither ... nor ...

niche *nf* kennel

nid *nm* nest

nièce *nf* niece

nier [20] *vb* to deny

n'importe *adv* n'importe quel any old; n'importe qui anybody; n'importe quoi anything; Tu dis n'importe quoi. You're talking rubbish.; n'importe où anywhere; Ne laisse pas tes affaires n'importe où. Don't leave

your things lying everywhere.;
n'importe quand any time;
n'importe comment any
old how

niveau(pl niveaux) nm ❶ level
❷ standard; **le niveau de vie** the
standard of living

noble adj noble

noblesse nf nobility

noce nf wedding; **un repas de
noce** a wedding reception; **Leurs
noces d'or.** Their golden wedding
anniversary.

nocif(f nocive) adj harmful

nocturne adj ❶ nocturnal ❷ by
night ▷ Découvrez le Paris nocturne!
Discover Paris by night!
▶ nf late-night opening

Noël nm Christmas; **Joyeux Noël!**
Merry Christmas!

nœud nm ❶ knot ❷ bow; **un
nœud papillon** a bow tie

▌ Word for word, the French
means "butterfly knot".

noir, e adj ❶ black ❷ dark ▷ Il fait
noir dehors. It's dark outside.
▶ nm dark ▷ J'ai peur du noir. I'm
afraid of the dark.; **le travail au
noir** moonlighting

Noir nm black man; **les Noirs** black
people

Noire nf black woman

noisette nf hazelnut

noix(pl noix) nf walnut; **une noix
de coco** a coconut; **les noix de
cajou** cashew nuts; **une noix de
beurre** a knob of butter

nom nm ❶ name; **mon nom de
famille** my surname; **son nom de**

jeune fille her maiden name
❷ (in grammar) noun

nombre nm number

nombreux(f nombreuse) adj
❶ many ❷ large ▷ une famille
nombreuse a large family; **peu
nombreux** few

nombril nm navel

nommer [29] vb ❶ to name ❷ to
appoint

non adv no; **non seulement** not
only; **moi non plus** neither do I

non alcoolisé, e adj non-alcoholic

non-fumeur nm non-smoker;
une voiture non-fumeurs a no-
smoking carriage

nord nm north; **vers le nord**
northwards; **au nord de Paris**
north of Paris; **l'Afrique du Nord**
North Africa; **le vent du nord** the
north wind
▶ adj ❶ north; **le pôle Nord** the
North Pole ❷ northern

nord-est nm north-east

nord-ouest nm north-west

normal, e(mpl normaux) adj
❶ normal ❷ natural ▷ C'est tout à
fait normal. It's perfectly natural.;
Vous trouvez que c'est normal?
Does that seem right to you?

normalement adv normally;
**Normalement, elle doit arriver
à huit heures.** She's supposed to
arrive at 8 o'clock.

normand, e adj **un village
normand** a village in Normandy;
la côte normande the coast of
Normandy

Normandie nf Normandy

Norvège nf Norway

norvégien (f **norvégienne**) adj Norwegian

▶ nm **Elle parle norvégien.** She speaks Norwegian.

▶ nm/f **un Norvégien** (man) a Norwegian; **une Norvégienne** (woman) a Norwegian

nos adj our ▷ **Où sont nos affaires?** Where are our things?

notaire nm solicitor

note nf ❶ note ▷ **J'ai pris des notes pendant la conférence.** I took notes at the lecture. ❷ mark ▷ **Vincent a de bonnes notes en maths.** Vincent's got good marks in maths. ❸ bill ▷ **Il n'a pas payé sa note.** He didn't pay his bill.

noter [29] vb to make a note of

notions nfpl basics

notre (pl **nos**) adj our ▷ **Voici notre maison.** Here's our house.

nôtre pron le nôtre ours

nôtres pron les nôtres ours

nouer [29] vb to tie

nouilles nfpl noodles

nounours nm teddy bear

nourrir [39] vb to feed

nourriture nf food

nous pron ❶ we ▷ **Nous avons deux enfants.** We have two children. ❷ us ▷ **Viens avec nous.** Come with us.; **nous-mêmes** ourselves

nouveau (msg also **nouvel**, f **nouvelle**, mpl **nouveaux**) adj new ▷ **une nouvelle voiture** a new car.

> **nouveau** changes to **nouvel** before a vowel and most words beginning with "h".

▷ **le nouvel élève dans ma classe** The new boy in my class; **le nouvel an** New Year

▶ nm new pupil; **de nouveau** again

nouveau-né nm newborn child

nouveauté nf novelty

nouvel, nouvelle adj see **nouveau**

nouvelle nf ❶ news ❷ short story; **les nouvelles** the news; **avoir des nouvelles de quelqu'un** to hear from somebody ❸ new pupil

Nouvelle-Zélande nf New Zealand

novembre nm November; **en novembre** in November

noyau (pl **noyaux**) nm (of fruit) stone

noyer nm walnut tree

se noyer [54] vb to drown

nu, e adj ❶ naked ❷ bare

nuage nm cloud; **un nuage de lait** a drop of milk

nuageux (f **nuageuse**) adj cloudy

nucléaire adj nuclear

nudiste nmf nudist

nuit nf night; **Il fait nuit.** It's dark.; **cette nuit** tonight; **Bonne nuit!** Good night!; **de nuit** by night

nul (f **nulle**) adj rubbish; **Ce film est nul.** (informal) This film's rubbish.; **être nul** to be no good ▷ **Je suis nul en maths.** I'm no good at maths.; **un match nul** (in sport) a draw; **nulle part** nowhere

numérique adj digital ▷ **un appareil photo numérique** a digital camera

numéro *nm* number; **mon numéro de téléphone** my phone number; **le numéro de compte** the account number

nu-pieds *adj, adv* barefoot

nuque *nf* nape of the neck

nylon *nm* nylon

obéir [**39**] *vb* to obey; **obéir à quelqu'un** to obey somebody

obéissant, e *adj* obedient

objet *nm* object; **les objets de valeur** valuables; **les objets trouvés** the lost property office

obligatoire *adj* compulsory

obliger [**46**] *vb* **obliger quelqu'un à faire quelque chose** to force somebody to do something; **Je suis bien obligé d'accepter.** I can't really refuse.

obscur, e *adj* dark

obscurité *nf* darkness

obsédé *nm* sex maniac; **un obsédé sexuel** a sex maniac

obséder [**35**] *vb* to obsess

observation *nf* comment

observer [**29**] *vb* ❶ to watch ▷ *Il observait les canards sur le lac.* He

watched the ducks on the lake.
❷ to observe

obstacle nm ❶ obstacle ❷ (*in show jumping*) fence; **une course d'obstacles** an obstacle race

obstiné, e adj stubborn

obtenir [84] vb ❶ to get ▷ *Ils ont obtenu cinquante pour cent des voix.* They got 50% of the votes. ❷ to achieve ▷ *Nous avons obtenu de bons résultats.* We achieved good results.

occasion nf ❶ opportunity ❷ occasion ❸ bargain; **d'occasion** second-hand

Occident nm West; **en Occident** in the West

occidental, e (*mpl* occidentaux) adj western; **les pays occidentaux** the West

occupation nf occupation

occupé, e adj ❶ busy ❷ taken ▷ *Est-ce que cette place est occupée?* Is this seat taken? ❸ engaged ▷ *Les toilettes sont occupées.* The toilet's engaged.

occuper [29] vb to occupy; **s'occuper de quelque chose** (1) to be in charge of something (2) to deal with something; **On s'occupe de vous?** (*in a shop*) Are you being attended to?

océan nm ocean

octobre nm October; **en octobre** in October

odeur nf smell

odieux (f odieuse) adj horrible

œil (*pl* yeux) nm eye; **à l'œil** (*informal*) for free

œillet nm carnation

œuf nm egg; **un œuf à la coque** a soft-boiled egg; **un œuf dur** a hard-boiled egg; **un œuf au plat** a fried egg; **les œufs brouillés** scrambled eggs; **un œuf de Pâques** an Easter egg

œuvre nf work; **une œuvre d'art** a work of art

offert vb see **offrir**

office nm **un office du tourisme** a tourist office

officiel (f officielle) adj official

officier nm officer

offre nf offer; **"offres d'emploi"** "situations vacant"

offrir [55] vb **offrir quelque chose** (1) to offer something ▷ *Elle lui a offert à boire.* She offered him a drink. (2) to give something ▷ *Il lui a offert des roses.* He gave her roses.; **s'offrir quelque chose** to treat oneself to something

oie nf goose

oignon nm onion

oiseau (*pl* oiseaux) nm bird

olive nf olive

olympique adj **les Jeux olympiques** the Olympic Games

ombre nf ❶ shade ❷ shadow; **l'ombre à paupières** eye shadow

omelette nf omelette

omnibus nm local train

on pron ❶ we ▷ *On va à la plage demain.* We're going to the beach tomorrow. ❷ someone ▷ *On m'a volé mon sac.* Someone has stolen my bag.; **On m'a dit d'attendre.** I was told to wait.; **On vous**

demande au téléphone. There's a phone call for you. ❸ **you** ▷ *On peut visiter le château en été.* You can visit the castle in the summer.

oncle *nm* uncle

onde *nf* (on radio) wave

ongle *nm* nail; **se couper les ongles** to cut one's nails

ont *vb see* **avoir**; **Ils ont beaucoup d'argent.** They've got lots of money.; **Elles ont passé de bonnes vacances.** They had a good holiday.

ONU *nf* (= Organisation des Nations unies) UN (United Nations)

onze *num* eleven ▷ *Il a onze ans.* She's eleven.; **le onze février** the eleventh of February

onzième *adj* eleventh

opéra *nm* opera

opération *nf* operation

opérer [35] *vb* to operate on ▷ *Elle a été opérée de l'appendicite.* She was operated on for appendicitis.; **se faire opérer** to have an operation

opinion *nf* opinion

opposé, e *adj* opposite; **être opposé à quelque chose** to be opposed to something
▶ *nm* the opposite

opposer [29] *vb* opposer quelqu'un à quelqu'un to pit somebody against somebody; **s'opposer** to conflict ▷ *Ces deux points de vue s'opposent.* These two points of view conflict.; **s'opposer à quelque chose** to oppose something

opposition *nf* opposition; **par opposition à** as opposed to; **faire opposition à un chèque** to stop a cheque

opticien (*f* opticienne) *nm/f* optician

optimiste *adj* optimistic

option *nf* option; **une matière en option** an optional subject

or *nm* gold ▷ *un bracelet en or* a gold bracelet
▶ *conj* and yet ▷ *Il était sûr de gagner, or il a perdu.* He was sure he would win, and yet he lost.

orage *nm* thunderstorm

orageux (*f* orageuse) *adj* stormy

oral, e (*mpl* oraux) *adj* **une épreuve orale** an oral exam; **à prendre par voie orale** to be taken orally
▶ *nm* (*pl* oraux) (*exam*) oral

orange *nf* (*fruit*) orange
▶ *adj inv* (*in colour*) orange

orchestre *nm* ❶ orchestra ❷ band

ordinaire *adj* ❶ ordinary ❷ standard
▶ *nm* two-star (petrol); **sortir de l'ordinaire** to be out of the ordinary

ordinateur *nm* computer

ordonnance *nf* prescription

ordonné, e *adj* tidy

ordonner [29] *vb* ordonner à quelqu'un de faire quelque chose to order somebody to do something

ordre *nm* order; **dans l'ordre** in order; **mettre en ordre** to tidy up; **jusqu'à nouvel ordre** until further notice

ordures nfpl rubbish; **jeter quelque chose aux ordures** to throw something in the bin

oreille nf ear

oreiller nm pillow

oreillons nmpl mumps

organe nm (in body) organ

organisateur (f **organisatrice**) nm/f organizer

organisation nf organization

organiser [29] vb to organize; **s'organiser** to get organized

organisme nm (organization) body

orgue nm organ

orgueilleux (f **orgueilleuse**) adj proud

Orient nm East; **en Orient** in the East

oriental, e (mpl **orientaux**) adj ① oriental ② eastern

orientation nf orientation; **avoir le sens de l'orientation** to have a good sense of direction; **l'orientation professionnelle** careers advice

originaire adj **Elle est originaire de Paris.** She's from Paris.

original, e (mpl **originaux**) adj original

▶ nm (pl **originaux**) original; **un vieil original** an old eccentric

origine nf origin; **à l'origine** originally

orphelin (f **orpheline**) nm/f orphan

orteil nm toe

orthographe nf spelling

os nm bone

oser [29] vb to dare; **oser faire quelque chose** to dare to do something

otage nm hostage

ôter [29] vb ① to take off ▷ **Elle a ôté son manteau.** She took off her coat. ② to take away

ou conj or; **ou ... ou ...** either ... or ...; **ou bien** or else ▷ **On pourrait aller au cinéma ou bien rentrer directement.** We could go to the cinema or else go straight home.

où pron, adv ① where ▷ **Où est Nick?** Where's Nick? ▷ **Où allez-vous?** Where are you going? ▷ **Je sais où il est.** I know where he is. ② that ▷ **Le jour où il est parti, tout le monde a pleuré.** The day that he left, everyone cried.; **Par où allons-nous passer?** Which way are we going to go?

ouate nf cotton wool

oublier [20] vb ① to forget ▷ **N'oublie pas de fermer la porte.** Don't forget to shut the door. ② to leave ▷ **J'ai oublié mon sac chez Sabine.** I left my bag at Sabine's.

ouest nm west; **à l'ouest de Paris** west of Paris; **vers l'ouest** westwards; **l'Europe de l'Ouest** Western Europe; **le vent d'ouest** the west wind

▶ adj inv ① west ② western

ouf excl phew!

oui adv yes

ouragan nm hurricane

ourlet nm seam

ours nm bear; **un ours en peluche** a teddy bear

outil nm tool

outré, e adj outraged

ouvert, e adj ❶ open ▷ *Le magasin est ouvert.* The shop's open. ❷ on ▷ *Il a laissé le robinet ouvert.* He left the tap on.; **avoir l'esprit ouvert** to be open-minded
▶ vb see **ouvrir**

ouverture nf opening

ouvre-boîte nm tin opener

ouvre-bouteille nm bottle-opener

ouvreuse nf usherette

ouvrier (f ouvrière) nm/f worker

ouvrir [56] vb to open ▷ *Ouvrez!* Open up! ▷ *Elle a ouvert la porte.* She opened the door.; **s'ouvrir** to open

ovale adj oval

ovni nm (= objet volant non identifié) UFO

oxygène nm oxygen

ozone nm ozone

p

Pacifique nm Pacific

pacifiste nm pacifist

page nf page; **la page d'accueil** (*internet*) the home page

paie nf wages

paiement nm payment

paillasson nm doormat

paille nf straw

pain nm ❶ bread ❷ loaf; **le pain complet** wholemeal bread; **le pain d'épice** gingerbread; **le pain de mie** sandwich loaf; **le pain grillé** toast

pair, e adj even ▷ *un nombre pair* an even number; **une jeune fille au pair** an au pair

paire nf pair

paisible adj peaceful

paix nf peace; **faire la paix (1)** to

make peace (2) to make up; **avoir la paix** to have peace and quiet; **Fiche-lui la paix!** (*informal*) Leave him alone!

palais nm ❶ palace ❷ (*in mouth*) palate

pâle *adj* pale

Palestine nf Palestine

pâleur nf paleness

palier nm landing

pâlir [39] *vb* to go pale

palme nf (*for swimming*) flipper

palmé, e *adj* webbed

palmier nm palm tree

palpitant, e *adj* thrilling

pamplemousse nm grapefruit

panaché, e nm shandy

pancarte nf sign

pané, e *adj* fried in breadcrumbs

panier nm basket

panique nf panic

paniquer [29] *vb* to panic

panne nf breakdown; **être en panne** to have broken down; **tomber en panne** to break down; **une panne de courant** a power cut

panneau (*pl* **panneaux**) nm sign; **panneau d'affichage** (1) advertising hoarding (2) (*in station*) arrivals and departures board (3) (*on internet*) a bulletin board

panorama nm panorama

pansement nm ❶ (*bandage*) dressing ❷ sticking plaster

pantalon nm trousers; **un pantalon de ski** a pair of ski pants

panthère nf panther

pantoufle nf slipper

PAO *abbr* (= *publication assistée par ordinateur*) DTP (desktop publishing)

paon nm peacock

papa nm dad

pape nm pope

papeterie nf stationer's

papi nm (*informal*) granddad

papier nm paper; **Vos papiers, s'il vous plaît.** Your identity papers, please.; **les papiers d'identité** identity papers; **le papier à lettres** writing paper; **le papier hygiénique** toilet paper; **le papier peint** wallpaper

papillon nm butterfly

paquebot nm liner

pâquerette nf daisy

Pâques nm Easter; **les œufs de Pâques** Easter eggs

● In France, Easter eggs are said
● to be brought by the Easter bells
● or **cloches de Pâques** which fly
● from Rome and drop them in
● people's gardens.

paquet nm ❶ packet ❷ parcel

paquet-cadeau (*pl* **paquets-cadeaux**) nm gift-wrapped parcel

par *prep* ❶ by ▷ *L'Amérique a été découverte par Christophe Colomb.* America was discovered by Christopher Columbus.; **deux par deux** two by two ❷ with ▷ *Son nom commence par un H.* His name begins with H. ❸ out of ▷ *Elle regardait par la fenêtre.* She was looking out of the window. ❹ via ▷ *Nous sommes passés par Lyon pour aller à Grenoble.* We went via Lyons to Grenoble. ❺ through ▷ *Il faut* *passer par la douane avant de prendre l'avion.* You have to go through customs before boarding the plane. ❷ *per* ▷ *Prenez trois cachets par jour.* Take three tablets per day.; **par ici (1)** this way ▷ *Il faut passer par ici pour y arriver.* You have to go this way to get there. **(2)** round here ▷ *Il y a beaucoup de touristes par ici.* There are lots of tourists round here.; **par-ci, par-là** here and there

parachute nm parachute

parachutiste nmf parachutist

paradis nm heaven

parages nmpl **dans les parages** in the area

paragraphe nm paragraph

paraître [57] vb ❶ to seem ▷ *Ça paraît incroyable.* It seems unbelievable. ❷ to look ▷ *Elle paraît plus jeune que son frère.* She looks younger than her brother.; **il paraît que** it seems that

parallèle nm parallel
▶ nf parallel line

paralysé, e adj paralysed

parapluie nm umbrella

parasol nm parasol

parc nm ❶ park; **un parc d'attractions** an amusement park ❷ grounds

parce que conj because ▷ *Il n'est pas venu parce qu'il n'avait pas de voiture.* He didn't come because he didn't have a car.

parcmètre nm parking meter

parcourir [17] vb ❶ to cover ▷ *Gavin a parcouru cinquante kilomètres à vélo.* Gavin covered

50 kilometres on his bike. ❷ to glance through ▷ *J'ai parcouru le journal d'aujourd'hui.* I glanced through today's newspaper.

parcours nm journey

par-dessous adv underneath

pardessus nm overcoat

par-dessus adv, prep ❶ on top ❷ over ▷ *Elle a sauté par-dessus le mur.* She jumped over the wall.; **en avoir par-dessus la tête** to have had enough

pardon excl ❶ sorry! ▷ *Oh, pardon! J'espère que je ne vous ai pas fait mal.* Oh, sorry! I hope I didn't hurt you.; **demander pardon à quelqu'un** to apologize to somebody; **Je vous demande pardon.** I'm sorry. ❷ excuse me! ▷ *Pardon, madame! Pouvez-vous me dire où se trouve la poste?* Excuse me! Could you tell me where the post office is? ❸ pardon? ▷ *Pardon? Je n'ai pas compris ce que vous avez dit.* Pardon? I didn't understand what you said.
▶ nm forgiveness

pardonner [29] vb to forgive

pare-brise (pl pare-brise) nm windscreen

pare-chocs nm bumper

pareil (f pareille) adj ❶ the same ▷ *Ces deux maisons ne sont pas pareilles.* These two houses aren't the same. ❷ like that ▷ *J'aime bien sa voiture. J'en voudrais une pareille.* I like his car. I'd like one like that. ❸ such ▷ *Je refuse d'écouter des bêtises pareilles.* I won't listen to such nonsense.; **sans pareil** unequalled

parenthèse nf bracket

parents nmpl ❶ (mother and father) parents ❷ relatives

paresse nf laziness

paresseux (f **paresseuse**) adj lazy

parfait, e adj perfect

parfaitement adv perfectly

parfois adv sometimes

parfum nm ❶ perfume ❷ flavour

parfumé, e adj ❶ fragrant ❷ flavoured

parfumerie nf perfume shop

pari nm bet

parier [20] vb to bet

Paris n Paris; **à Paris (1)** in Paris **(2)** to Paris

parisien (f **parisienne**) adj ❶ Parisian ❷ Paris ▷ le métro parisien the Paris metro ▶ nm/f un Parisien (man) a Parisian; une Parisienne (woman) a Parisian

parking nm car park

Be careful! The French word **parking** does not mean **parking**.

parlement nm parliament

parler [29] vb ❶ to speak ▷ Vous parlez français? Do you speak French? ❷ to talk ▷ Nous étions en train de parler quand le directeur est entré. We were talking when the headmaster came in.; **parler de quelque chose à quelqu'un** to tell somebody about something

parmi prep among ▷ Ils étaient parmi les meilleurs de la classe. They were among the best pupils in the class.

paroi nf wall

paroisse nf parish

parole nf ❶ speech ❷ word; **les paroles** lyrics

parquet nm (wooden) floor

parrain nm godfather

parrainer [29] vb to sponsor ▷ Cette entreprise parraine notre équipe de rugby. This firm is sponsoring our rugby team.

pars vb see **partir**

part nf ❶ share ❷ piece ▷ une part de gâteau a piece of cake; **prendre part à quelque chose** to take part in something; **de la part de (1)** on behalf of (1) from; **à part** except

partager [46] vb ❶ to share ▷ Ils partagent un appartement. They share a flat. ❷ to divide ▷ Janet a partagé le gâteau en quatre. Janet divided the cake into four.

partenaire nmf partner

parti nm party

participant (f **participante**) nm/f participant

participation nf participation

participe nm participle; **le participe passé** the past participle; **le participe présent** the present participle

participer [29] vb **participer à quelque chose (1)** to take part in something ▷ André va participer à la course. André is going to take part in the race. **(2)** to contribute to something ▷ Je voudrais participer aux frais. I would like to contribute to the cost.

particularité nf characteristic

particulier (f **particulière**) adj
① private ▷ *une maison particulière*
a private house **②** distinctive
③ particular; **en particulier**
(1) particularly (2) in private

particulièrement adv
particularly

partie nf **①** part ▷ *Une partie du
groupe partira en Italie.* Part of the
group will go to Italy. **②** game
▷ *une partie de cartes* a game of
cards; **en partie** partly; **en grande
partie** largely; **faire partie de** to
be part of

partiel (f **partielle**) adj partial

partir [58] vb **①** to go ▷ *Je lui ai
téléphoné mais il était déjà parti.*
I phoned him but he'd already
gone.; **partir en vacances** to go
on holiday; **partir de** to leave ▷ *Il
est parti de Nice à sept heures.* He left
Nice at 7.; **à partir de** from

partition nf (in music) score

partout adv everywhere

paru vb see **paraître**

parution nf publication

parvenir [90] vb **parvenir à
faire quelque chose** to manage
to do something; **faire parvenir
quelque chose à quelqu'un** to
send something to somebody

pas adv ne ... pas not ▷ *Il ne pleut
pas.* It's not raining. ▷ *Elle n'est pas
venue.* She didn't come.; **Vous
viendrez à notre soirée, n'est-ce
pas?** You're coming to our party,
aren't you?; **pas moi** not me; **pas
du tout** not at all; **pas mal** not
bad; **pas mal de** quite a lot of

▶ nm **①** pace **②** step **③** footstep;
au pas at walking pace; **faire les
cent pas** to pace up and down

passage nm passage; **Il a été
éclaboussé au passage de la
voiture.** He was soaked by a
passing car.; **de passage** passing
through; **un passage à niveau** a
level crossing; **un passage clouté**
a pedestrian crossing; **un passage
protégé** a pedestrian crossing; **un
passage souterrain** a subway

passager (f **passagère**) adj
temporary
▶ nm/f passenger; **un passager
clandestin** a stowaway

passant (f **passante**) nm/f
passer-by

passé, e adj **①** last ▷ *Je l'ai vu la
semaine passée.* I saw him last
week. **②** past ▷ *Il est minuit passé.*
It's past midnight.
▶ nm **①** past **②** past tense; **le
passé composé** the perfect tense;
le passé simple the past historic

passeport nm passport

passer [59] vb **①** to cross ▷ *Nous
avons passé la frontière belge.* We
crossed the Belgian border. **②** to
go through ▷ *Il faut passer la douane
en sortant.* You have to go through
customs on the way out. **③** to
take ▷ *Gordon a passé ses examens la
semaine dernière.* Gordon took his
exams last week.

> Be careful! **passer un examen**
> does not mean **to pass an
> exam.**

④ to spend ▷ *Ils passent toujours*

leurs vacances au Danemark. They always spend their holidays in Denmark. ❸ **to pass** ▷ *Passe-moi le sel, s'il te plaît.* Pass me the salt, please. ❹ **to show** ▷ *On passe "Le Kid" au cinéma cette semaine.* They're showing "The Kid" at the cinema this week. ❺ **to call in** ▷ *Je passerai chez vous ce soir.* I'll call in this evening.; **passer à la radio** to be on the radio; **passer à la télévision** to be on the television; **Ne quittez pas, je vous passe Madame Chevalier.** Hold on please, I'm putting you through to Mrs Chevalier.; **passer par** to go through ▷ *Ils sont passés par Paris pour aller à Tours.* They went through Paris to get to Tours.; **en passant** in passing; **laisser passer** to let through ▷ *Il m'a laissé passer.* He let me through.; **se passer (1)** to take place ▷ *Cette histoire se passe au moyen âge.* This story takes place in the Middle Ages. **(2)** to go ▷ *Comment se sont passés tes examens?* How did your exams go? **(3)** to happen ▷ *Que s'est-il passé? Un accident?* What happened? Was there an accident?; **Qu'est-ce qui se passe? Pourquoi qu'elle pleure?** What's the matter? Why is she crying?; **se passer de** to do without

passerelle *nf* ❶ (over river) footbridge ❷ (onto plane, boat) gangway

passe-temps *nm* pastime

passif (*f* **passive**) *adj* passive

▶ *nm* passive

passion *nf* passion

passionnant, e *adj* fascinating

passionné, e *adj* keen; **Il est passionné de voile.** He's a sailing fanatic.

passionner [29] *vb Son travail le passionne.* He's passionate about his work.; **se passionner pour quelque chose** to have a passion for something

passoire *nf* sieve

pastèque *nf* watermelon

pasteur *nm* (priest) minister

pastille *nf* cough sweet

patate *nf* (informal) potato; **une patate douce** a sweet potato

pâte *nf* ❶ pastry ❷ dough ❸ cake mixture; **la pâte à crêpes** pancake batter; **la pâte à modeler** Plasticine®; **la pâte d'amandes** marzipan

pâté *nm* pâté; **un pâté de maisons** a block (of houses)

paternel (*f* **paternelle**) *adj* ma grand-mère paternelle my father's mother; **mon oncle paternel** my father's brother

pâtes *nfpl* pasta

patience *nf* patience

patient, e *adj* patient

▶ *nm/f* patient

patienter [29] *vb* to wait ▷ *Veuillez patienter un instant, s'il vous plaît.* Please wait a moment.

patin *nm* ❶ skate ❷ skating; **les patins à glace** ice skates; **les patins en ligne** Rollerblades®; **les patins à roulettes** roller skates

a
b
c
d
e
f
g
h
i
j
k
l
m
n
o
p
q
r
s
t
u
v
w
x
y
z

patinage nm skating; **le patinage artistique** figure skating

patiner [29] vb to skate

patineur (f **patineuse**) nm skater

patinoire nf ice rink

pâtisserie nf cake shop; **faire de la pâtisserie** to bake; **les pâtisseries** cakes

pâtissier (f **pâtissière**) nm confectioner

patrie nf homeland

patron nm ❶ boss ❷ (for dressmaking) pattern

patronne nf boss; **Elle est patronne de café.** She runs a café.

patronner [29] vb to sponsor
▷ Le festival est patronné par des entreprises locales. The festival is sponsored by local businesses.

patrouille nf patrol

patte nf ❶ (of dog, cat) paw ❷ (of bird, animal) leg

paumer [29] vb (informal) to lose
▷ J'ai paumé mes clefs. I've lost my keys.

paupière nf eyelid

pause nf ❶ break ▷ une pause de midi a lunch break ❷ pause

pauvre adj poor

pauvreté nf poverty

pavé, e adj cobbled

pavillon nm house

payant, e adj paying; **C'est payant.** You have to pay.

paye nf wages

payer [60] vb ❶ to pay for
▷ Combien as-tu payé ta voiture? How much did you pay for your car?; **J'ai payé ce T-shirt vingt euros.** I paid

20 euros for this T-shirt. ❷ to pay
▷ Elle a été payée aujourd'hui. She got paid today.; **faire payer quelque chose à quelqu'un** to charge somebody for something ▷ Il me l'a fait payer dix euros. He charged me 10 euros for it.; **payer quelque chose à quelqu'un** to buy somebody something ▷ Allez, je vous paye un verre. Come on, I'll buy you a drink.

pays nm country; **du pays** local

paysage nm landscape

paysan (f **paysanne**) nm/f farmer

Pays-Bas nmpl Netherlands; **aux Pays-Bas** (1) in the Netherlands (2) to the Netherlands

pays de Galles nm Wales; **au pays de Galles** (1) in Wales (2) to Wales

PC nm PC (personal computer)
▶ abbr (= Parti communiste) Communist Party

PDG nm (= président-directeur général) MD (managing director)

péage nm ❶ toll ▷ Nous avons payé vingt euros de péage. We paid a toll of 20 euros. ❷ tollbooth
● French motorways charge a toll.

peau (pl **peaux**) nf skin

Peau-Rouge (pl **Peaux-Rouges**) nmf Red Indian

pêche nf ❶ peach ❷ fishing; **aller à la pêche** to go fishing; **la pêche à la ligne** angling

péché nm sin

pêcher [29] vb ❶ to fish for ▷ Ils sont partis pêcher la truite. They've gone fishing for trout. ❷ to catch

▷ *Jacques a pêché deux saumons.* Jacques caught two salmon.

pêcheur nm fisherman; **un pêcheur à la ligne** an angler

pédagogique adj educational

pédale nf pedal

pédalo nm pedalo

pédestre adj **une randonnée pédestre** a ramble

peigne nm comb

peigner [29] vb to comb ▷ *Elle peigne sa poupée.* She's combing her doll's hair.; **se peigner** to comb one's hair

peignoir nm dressing gown; **un peignoir de bain** a bathrobe

peindre [61] vb to paint

peine nf trouble; **avoir de la peine à faire quelque chose** to have trouble doing something; **se donner de la peine** to make a real effort; **prendre la peine de faire quelque chose** to go to the trouble of doing something; **faire de la peine à quelqu'un** to upset somebody; **ce n'est pas la peine** there's no point; **à peine (1)** hardly **(2)** only just

peintre nm painter

peinture nf ❶ painting ❷ paint; "peinture fraîche" "wet paint"

pêle-mêle adv higgledy-piggledy

peler [44] vb to peel

pelle nf ❶ shovel ❷ spade

pellicule nf film

pellicules nfpl dandruff

pelote nf ball

pelouse nf lawn

peluche nf **un animal en peluche** a soft toy

penchant nm **avoir un penchant pour quelque chose** to have a liking for something

pencher [29] vb to tilt ▷ *Ce tableau penche vers la droite.* The picture's tilting to the right.; **se pencher (1)** to lean over ▷ *Françoise s'est penchée sur son cahier.* Françoise leant over her exercise book. **(2)** to bend down ▷ *Il s'est penché pour ramasser sa casquette.* He bent down to pick his cap up. **(3)** to lean out ▷ *Annick s'est penchée par la fenêtre.* Annick leant out of the window.

pendant prep during ▷ *Ça s'est passé pendant l'été.* It happened during the summer.; **pendant que** while

pendentif nm pendant

penderie nf (for hanging clothes) wardrobe

pendre [89] vb to hang ▷ *Il a pendu sa veste dans l'armoire.* He hung his jacket in the wardrobe.; **pendre quelqu'un** to hang somebody ▷ *L'assassin a été pendu.* The murderer was hanged.

pendule nf clock

pénétrer [35] vb ❶ to enter ▷ *Ils ont pénétré dans la maison en passant par le jardin.* They entered the house through the garden. ❷ to penetrate ▷ *L'armée a pénétré sur le territoire ennemi.* The army penetrated enemy territory.

pénible adj hard; **Il est vraiment pénible.** He's a real nuisance.

péniblement adv with difficulty

péniche nf barge

pénis nm penis

pénombre nf half-light

pensée nf thought

penser [29] vb to think ▷ Je pense que Yann a eu raison de partir. I think Yann was right to leave.; **penser à quelque chose** to think about something; **faire penser quelqu'un à quelque chose** to remind someone of something ▷ Cette photo me fait penser à la Grèce. This photo reminds me of Greece.; **faire penser quelqu'un à faire quelque chose** to remind someone to do something ▷ Fais-moi penser à téléphoner à Claire. Remind me to phone Claire.; **penser faire quelque chose** to be planning to do something ▷ Ils pensent partir en Espagne en juillet. They're planning to go to Spain in July.

pension nf ❶ boarding school ❷ pension ❸ boarding house; **la pension complète** full board

pensionnaire nmf boarder

pensionnat nm boarding school

pente nf slope; **en pente** sloping

Pentecôte nf Whitsun

pépin nm ❶ pip ❷ (informal) problem ▷ avoir un pépin to have a slight problem

perçant, e adj ❶ sharp ▷ Il a une vue perçante. He has very sharp eyes. ❷ piercing ▷ un cri perçant a piercing cry

percer [13] vb to pierce ▷ Elle s'est fait percer les oreilles. She's had her ears pierced.

percuter [29] vb to smash into

perdant (f **perdante**) nm/f loser

perdre [62] vb to lose ▷ Cécile a perdu ses clés. Cécile's lost her keys.; **J'ai perdu mon chemin.** I've lost my way.; **perdre un match** to lose a match; **perdre du temps** to waste time ▷ J'ai perdu beaucoup de temps ce matin. I've wasted a lot of time this morning.; **se perdre** to get lost ▷ Je me suis perdu en route. I got lost on the way here.

perdu vb see **perdre**

père nm father; **le père Noël** Father Christmas

perfectionné, e adj sophisticated

perfectionner [29] vb to improve ▷ Elle a besoin de perfectionner son anglais. She needs to improve her English.

périmé, e adj out-of-date; **Ces yaourts sont périmés.** These yoghurts are past their use-by date.

période nf period

périodique adj periodic

périphérique adj outlying ▶ nm ring road

perle nf pearl

permanence nf assurer une permanence to operate a basic service; **être de permanence** to be on duty; **en permanence** permanently

permanent, e adj ❶ permanent ❷ continuous

permanente nf perm

permettre [48] vb to allow; **permettre à quelqu'un de faire**

quelque chose to allow somebody to do something ▷ *Sa mère lui permet de sortir le soir.* His mother allows him to go out at night.

permis nm permit; **le permis de conduire** driving licence; **un permis de séjour** a residence permit; **un permis de travail** a work permit

permission nf permission; **avoir la permission de faire quelque chose** to have permission to do something; **être en permission** (*from the army*) to be on leave

Pérou nm Peru

perpétuel (*f* **perpétuelle**) adj perpetual

perplexe adj puzzled

perroquet nm parrot

perruche nf budgie

perruque nf wig

persil nm parsley

personnage nm ❶ figure ▷ *les grands personnages de l'histoire de France* the important figures in French history ❷ character ▷ *le personnage principal du film* the main character in the film

personnalité nf ❶ personality ❷ prominent figure

personne nf person ▷ *une personne âgée* an elderly person; **en personne** in person
▶ pron ❶ nobody ▷ *Il n'y a personne à la maison.* There's nobody at home. ❷ anybody ▷ *Elle ne veut voir personne.* She doesn't want to see anybody.

personnel (*f* **personnelle**) adj personal
▶ nm staff; **le service du personnel** the personnel department

personnellement adv personally

perspective nf prospect; **perspectives d'avenir** prospects; **en perspective** (1) in prospect (2) in perspective

persuader [29] vb to persuade; **persuader quelqu'un de faire quelque chose** to persuade somebody to do something

perte nf ❶ loss ❷ waste

perturber [29] vb to disrupt

pèse-personne nm bathroom scales

peser [44] vb to weigh ▷ *Elle pèse cent kilos.* She weighs 100 kilos.

pessimiste adj pessimistic

pétale nm petal

pétanque nf
- pétanque is a type of bowls
- played in France, especially in
- the south.

pétard nm firecracker

péter [35] vb (*rude*) to fart

pétillant, e adj sparkling

petit, e adj ❶ small ▷ *Sonia habite une petite ville.* Sonia lives in a small town. ❷ little ▷ *Elle a une jolie petite maison.* She has a nice little house.; **petit à petit** bit by bit; **un petit ami** a boyfriend; **une petite amie** a girlfriend; **le petit déjeuner** breakfast ▷ *prendre le petit déjeuner* to have breakfast; **un petit pain** a bread roll; **les petites annonces**

the small ads; **des petits pois**
garden peas; **les petits** (of animal)
young

petite-fille (pl **petites-filles**) nf
granddaughter

petit-fils (pl **petits-fils**) nm
grandson

petits-enfants nmpl
grandchildren

pétrole nm oil

> Be careful! **pétrole** does not
> mean petrol.

peu adv, nm not much; **un peu** a
bit; **un petit peu** a little bit; **peu
de** (1) not many (2) not much; **à
peu près** (1) more or less (2) about;
peu à peu little by little; **peu
avant** shortly before; **peu après**
shortly afterwards; **de peu** only
just

peuple nm people

peur nf fear; **avoir peur de** to
be afraid of; **avoir peur de faire
quelque chose** to be frightened
of doing something; **faire peur à
quelqu'un** to frighten somebody

peureux (f **peureuse**) adj fearful

peut vb see **pouvoir**; **Il ne peut pas
venir.** He can't come.

peut-être adv perhaps; **peut-être
que** perhaps

peuvent, peux vb see **pouvoir**; **Je
ne peux pas le faire.** I can't do it.

p. ex. abbr (= par exemple) e.g.

phare nm ❶ lighthouse
❷ headlight ▷ Il a laissé les phares
de sa voiture allumés. He left his
headlights on.

pharmacie nf chemist's

> Chemist's shops in France are
> identified by a special green
> cross outside the shop.

pharmacien (f **pharmacienne**)
nm pharmacist

phasme nm stick insect

phénomène nm phenomenon

philosophie nf philosophy

phoque nm (animal) seal

photo nf photograph; **en photo** in
photographs; **prendre quelqu'un
en photo** to take a photo of
somebody; **une photo d'identité**
a passport photograph

photocopie nf photocopy

photocopier [20] vb to
photocopy

photocopieuse nf photocopier

photographe nmf photographer

photographie nf ❶ photography
❷ photograph

photographier [20] vb to
photograph

phrase nf sentence

physique adj physical
▶ nm Il a un physique agréable.
He's quite good-looking.
▶ nf physics

pianiste nmf pianist

piano nm piano

pic nm peak; **à pic** (1) vertically ▷ La
falaise tombe à pic dans la mer. The
cliff drops vertically into the sea.
(2) just at the right time ▷ Tu es
arrivé à pic. You arrived just at the
right time.

pièce nf ❶ room; **un cinq-pièces**
a five-roomed flat ❷ play ▷ une
pièce de Shakespeare a play by

165 | **pique-nique**

Shakespeare ❶ part ▷ *une pièce du moteur* an engine part ❹ *coin* ▷ *des pièces d'un euro* some one-euro coins; **cinquante euros pièce** 50 euros each; **un maillot une pièce** a one-piece swimsuit; **un maillot deux-pièces** a bikini; **Avez-vous une pièce d'identité?** Have you got any identification?; **une pièce jointe** an email attachment

pied *nm* foot; **à pied** on foot; **avoir pied** to be able to touch the bottom

pied-noir (*pl* **pieds-noirs**) *nm*
- A pied-noir is a French person
- born in Algeria; most of them
- moved to France during the
- Algerian war in the 1950s.

piège *nm* trap; **prendre quelqu'un au piège** to trap somebody

piéger [67] *vb* to trap; **un colis piégé** a parcel bomb; **une voiture piégée** a car bomb

pierre *nf* stone; **une pierre précieuse** a precious stone

piéton (*f* **piétonne**) *nm/f* pedestrian

piétonnier (*f* **piétonnière**) *adj* **une rue piétonnière** a pedestrianized street; **un quartier piétonnier** a pedestrianized area

pieuvre *nf* octopus

pigeon *nm* pigeon

piger [46] *vb* (*informal*) to understand

pile *nf* ❶ pile ▷ *une pile de disques* a pile of records ❷ battery ▷ *La pile de ma montre est usée.* The battery in my watch has run out.

▶ *adv* **à deux heures pile** at two on the dot; **jouer à pile ou face** to toss up; **Pile ou face?** Heads or tails?

pilote *nm* pilot; **un pilote de course** a racing driver; **un pilote de ligne** an airline pilot

piloter [29] *vb* (*a plane*) to fly

pilule *nf* pill; **prendre la pilule** to be on the pill

piment *nm* chilli

pin *nm* pine

pinard *nm* (*informal*) wine

pince *nf* ❶ (*tool*) pliers ❷ (*of crab*) pincer; **une pince à épiler** tweezers; **une pince à linge** a clothes peg

pinceau (*pl* **pinceaux**) *nm* paintbrush

pincée *nf* **une pincée de sel** a pinch of salt

pincer [13] *vb* to pinch

pingouin *nm* penguin

ping-pong *nm* table tennis

pintade *nf* guinea fowl

pion *nm* ❶ (*in chess*) pawn ❷ (*in draughts*) piece ❸ (*man*) supervisor
- In French secondary schools, the
- teachers are not responsible for
- supervising the pupils outside
- class. This job is done by people
- called **pions** or **surveillants**.

pionne *nf* (*woman*) supervisor

pipe *nf* pipe

piquant, e *adj* ❶ prickly ❷ spicy

pique *nm* spades
▶ *nf* cutting remark

pique-nique *nm* picnic

piquer [29] vb ❶ to bite ▷ Nous avons été piqués par les moustiques. We were bitten by mosquitoes. ❷ to burn ▷ Cette sauce me pique la langue. This sauce is burning my tongue. ❸ (informal) to steal ▷ On m'a piqué mon porte-monnaie. I've had my purse stolen.; **se piquer** to prick oneself

piquet nm ❶ post ❷ peg ▷ Il nous manque un des piquets de la tente. One of our tent pegs is missing.

piqûre nf ❶ injection ❷ bite ❸ sting

pirate nm pirate; **un pirate informatique** a hacker

pire adj worse
  ▶ nm **le pire** the worst; **le pire de** the worst of

piscine nf swimming pool

pisser [29] vb (informal) to have a pee

pistache nf pistachio

piste nf ❶ lead ▷ La police est sur une piste. The police are following a lead. ❷ runway ❸ ski run; **une piste artificielle** a dry ski slope; **la piste de danse** the dance floor; **une piste cyclable** a cycle lane

pistolet nm pistol

pistonner [29] vb Il a été pistonné pour avoir ce travail. They pulled some strings to get him this job.

pitié nf pity; **Il me fait pitié.** I feel sorry for him.; **avoir pitié de quelqu'un** to feel sorry for somebody

pittoresque adj picturesque

pizza nf pizza

placard nm cupboard

place nf ❶ place ❷ square ❶ space ▷ Il ne reste plus de place pour se garer. There's no more space to park. ❹ seat ▷ Il y a vingt places assises. There are 20 seats.; **remettre quelque chose en place** to put something back in its place; **sur place** on the spot; **à la place** instead; **à la place de** instead of

placer [13] vb ❶ to seat ▷ Nous étions placés à côté du directeur. We were seated next to the manager. ❷ to invest ▷ Il a placé ses économies en Bourse. He invested his money on the Stock Exchange.

plafond nm ceiling

plage nf beach

plaie nf wound

plaindre [18] vb plaindre quelqu'un to feel sorry for somebody ▷ Je te plains. I feel sorry for you.; **se plaindre** to complain ▷ Il n'arrête pas de se plaindre. He never stops complaining.; **se plaindre à quelqu'un** to complain to somebody; **se plaindre de quelque chose** to complain about something

plaine nf (level area) plain

plainte nf complaint; **porter plainte** to lodge a complaint

plaire [63] vb Ce cadeau me plaît beaucoup. I like this present a lot.; **Ce film plaît beaucoup aux jeunes.** The film is very popular with young people.; **Ça t'a plu d'aller en Italie?** Did you enjoy going to Italy?; **Elle lui plaît.** He fancies her.; **s'il te plaît** please; **s'il vous plaît** please

plaisanter [29] vb to joke

plaisanterie nf joke

plaisir nm pleasure; **faire plaisir à quelqu'un** to please somebody

plaît vb see **plaire**

plan nm plan; **un plan de la ville** a street map; **au premier plan** in the foreground

planche nf plank; **une planche à repasser** an ironing board; **une planche à roulettes** a skateboard; **une planche à voile** a sailboard

plancher nm floor

planer [29] vb ❶ to glide ▷ L'avion planait dans le ciel. The plane was gliding in the sky. ❷ (informal) to have one's head in the clouds ▷ Ce garçon plane complètement. He's not with us at all.

planète nf planet

plante nf plant

planter [29] vb ❶ to plant ▷ Jean-Pierre a planté un clou dans le mur. Jean-Pierre hammered a nail into the wall. ❷ to pitch ▷ André a planté sa tente au bord du lac. André pitched his tent next to the lake.; **Ne reste pas planté là!** Don't just stand there!; **se planter** (informal) to fail ❸ (computer) to crash

plaque nf (metal) plate; **une plaque de verglas** a patch of ice; **une plaque de chocolat** a bar of chocolate

plaqué, e adj plaqué or

gold-plated; **plaqué argent** silver-plated

plaquer [29] vb ❶ (informal) to ditch ▷ Elle a plaqué son copain. She ditched her boyfriend. ❷ to pack in ▷ Il a plaqué son boulot. He packed in his job.

plaquette nf **une plaquette de chocolat** a bar of chocolate; **une plaquette de beurre** a pack of butter

plastique nm plastic

plat, e adj flat; **être à plat ventre** to be lying face down; **l'eau plate** still water

▶ nm ❶ dish ❷ course ▷ le plat principal the main course; **un plat cuisiné** a pre-cooked meal; **le plat de résistance** the main course; **le plat du jour** the dish of the day

platane nm plane tree

plateau (pl plateaux) nm ❶ tray; **un plateau de fromages** a selection of cheeses ❷ plateau

platine nm platinum

▶ nf (of record player) turntable; **une platine laser** a CD player

plâtre nm plaster

plein, e adj full; **à plein temps** full-time; **plein de** (informal) lots of; **Il y a plein de gens dans la rue.** The street is full of people.; **en plein air** in the open air; **en pleine nuit** in the middle of the night; **en plein jour** in broad daylight

▶ nm **faire le plein** (petrol tank) to fill up

pleurer [29] vb to cry

pleut vb see **pleuvoir**

pleuvoir [64] vb to rain ▷ Il pleut. It's raining.

pli nm ❶ fold ❷ pleat ❸ crease

pliant, e adj folding

plier [20] vb ❶ to fold ▷ Elle a plié sa serviette. She folded her towel. ❷ to bend ▷ Elle a plié le bras. She bent her arm.

plomb nm ❶ lead ❷ fuse; l'essence sans plomb unleaded petrol

plombier nm plumber; Il est plombier. He's a plumber.

plongée nf diving

plongeoir nm diving board

plongeon nm dive

plonger [46] vb to dive; J'ai plongé ma main dans l'eau. I plunged my hand into the water.; être plongé dans son travail to be absorbed in your work; se plonger dans un livre to get absorbed in a book

plu vb see plaire, pleuvoir

pluie nf rain

plume nf feather; un stylo à plume a fountain pen

plupart: la plupart pron most (of them) ▷ La plupart ont moins de quinze ans. Most of them are under 15.; la plupart des most ▷ La plupart des gens ont vu ce film. Most people have seen this film.; la plupart du temps most of the time

pluriel nm plural; au pluriel in the plural

plus adv, prep ne ... plus (1) not ... any more ▷ Je ne veux plus le voir. I don't want to see him any more.

(2) no longer ▷ Il ne travaille plus ici. He's no longer working here.; Je n'ai plus de pain. I've got no bread left.; plus ... que more ... than ▷ Il est plus intelligent que son frère. He's more intelligent than his brother.; C'est le plus grand de la famille. He's the tallest in his family.; plus ... plus ... the more ... the more ...; plus de (1) more ▷ Il nous faut plus de pain. We need more bread. (2) more than ▷ Il y avait plus de dix personnes. There were more than 10 people.; de plus more ▷ Il nous faut un joueur de plus. We need one more player.; en plus more ▷ J'ai apporté quelques gâteaux en plus. I brought a few more cakes.; de plus en plus more and more; un peu plus difficile a bit more difficult.; plus ou moins more or less; Quatre plus deux égalent six. 4 plus 2 is 6.

plusieurs pron several ▷ Elle a acheté plusieurs chemises. She bought several shirts.

plus-que-parfait nm pluperfect

plutôt adv ❶ quite ▷ Elle est plutôt jolie. She's quite pretty. ❷ rather ▷ L'eau est plutôt froide. The water's rather cold. ❸ instead ▷ Demande-leur plutôt de venir avec toi. Ask them to come with you instead.; plutôt que rather than

pluvieux (f pluvieuse) adj rainy

pneu nm tyre

pneumonie nf pneumonia; la pneumonie atypique SARS (Severe Acute Respiratory Syndrome)

poche nf pocket; **l'argent de poche** pocket money; **un livre de poche** a paperback

podcast nm podcast

podcaster vb to podcast

poêle nf frying pan; **une poêle à frire** a frying pan

poème nm poem

poésie nf ❶ poetry ❷ poem

poète nm poet

poids nm weight; **prendre du poids** to put on weight; **perdre du poids** to lose weight; **un poids lourd** a lorry

poignée nf ❶ handful ❷ handle; **une poignée de main** a handshake

poignet nm ❶ wrist ❷ (of shirt) cuff

poil nm ❶ hair ❷ fur; **à poil** (informal) stark naked

poilu, e adj hairy

poinçonner [29] vb to punch ▷ Le contrôleur a poinçonné les billets. The conductor punched the tickets.

poing nm fist; **un coup de poing** a punch

point nm ❶ point; **point de vue** point of view ❷ full stop; **un point d'exclamation** an exclamation mark; **un point d'interrogation** a question mark; **point com** dotcom; **être sur le point de faire quelque chose** to be just about to do something; **mettre au point** to finalize; Ce n'est pas encore au point. It's not finalized yet.; **à point** medium ▷ Comment voulez-vous votre steak? — À point.

How would you like your steak? — Medium.; **un point noir** a blackhead

pointe nf point; **être à la pointe du progrès** to be in the forefront of progress; **sur la pointe des pieds** on tiptoe; **les heures de pointe** peak hours

pointillé nm dotted line

pointu, e adj pointed

pointure nf size (of shoes) ▷ Quelle est votre pointure? What size shoes do you take?

point-virgule (pl points-virgules) nm semicolon

poire nf pear

poireau (pl poireaux) nm leek

pois nm pea; **les petits pois** peas; **les pois chiches** chickpeas; **à pois** spotted

poison nm poison

poisson nm fish; **les Poissons** Pisces; **Poisson d'avril!** April fool!

  ● Pinning a paper fish to
  ● somebody's back is a traditional
  ● April fool joke in France.

un poisson rouge a goldfish

poissonnerie nf fish shop

poissonnier nm fishmonger

poitrine nf ❶ chest ❷ bust

poivre nm (spice) pepper

poivron nm (vegetable) pepper

pôle nm pole; **le pôle Nord** the North Pole; **le pôle Sud** the South Pole

poli, e adj polite

police nf police; **police secours** emergency services; **une police d'assurance** an insurance policy

policier (f **policière**) adj un roman policier a detective novel
▶ nm policeman

politesse nf politeness

politique nf politics; un homme politique a politician

pollué, e adj polluted

polluer [29] vb to pollute

pollution nf pollution

polo nm polo shirt

Pologne nf Poland

polonais, e adj Polish
▶ nm Polish ▷ Elle parle polonais. She speaks Polish.
▶ nm/f un Polonais (man) a Pole; une Polonaise (woman) a Pole; les Polonais the Poles

Polynésie nf Polynesia

pommade nf ointment

pomme nf apple; les pommes de terre potatoes; les pommes frites chips; les pommes vapeur boiled potatoes

pompe nf pump; une pompe à essence a petrol pump; les pompes funèbres undertakers

pompier nm fireman

pompiste nm petrol pump attendant

ponctuel (f **ponctuelle**) adj ❶ punctual ❷ occasional; On a rencontré quelques problèmes ponctuels. We've had the occasional problem.

pondre [70] vb (eggs) to lay

poney nm pony

pont nm ❶ bridge ❷ (of ship) deck; faire le pont to take a long weekend

populaire adj ❶ popular ❷ working-class

population nf population

porc nm ❶ pig ❷ pork

porcelaine nf china

port nm ❶ harbour ❷ port

portable nm ❶ (telephone) mobile phone ❷ (computer) laptop

portail nm gate

portatif (f **portative**) adj portable

porte nf ❶ door; la porte d'entrée the front door ❷ gate; mettre quelqu'un à la porte to sack somebody

porte-bagages nm luggage rack

porte-clés nm key ring

portée nf à portée de la main within arm's reach; hors de portée out of reach

portefeuille nm wallet

portemanteau (pl **portemanteaux**) nm ❶ coat hanger ❷ coat rack

porte-monnaie (pl **porte-monnaie**) nm purse

porter [29] vb ❶ to carry ▷ Il portait une valise. He was carrying a suitcase. ❷ to wear ▷ Elle porte une robe bleue. She's wearing a blue dress.; se porter bien to be well; se porter mal to be unwell

porteur nm porter

portière nf (of car) door

portion nf portion

porto nm (wine) port

portrait nm portrait

portugais, e adj Portuguese
▶ nm Portuguese ▷ Il parle portugais. He speaks Portuguese.

▶ nm/f un Portugais (man) a Portuguese; une Portugaise (woman) a Portuguese; les Portugais the Portuguese

Portugal nm Portugal; au Portugal (1) in Portugal (2) to Portugal

poser [29] vb ① to put down ▷ J'ai posé la cafetière sur la table. I put the coffee pot down on the table. ② to pose ▷ Cela pose un problème. That poses a problem.; poser une question à quelqu'un to ask somebody a question; se poser to land

positif (f **positive**) adj positive

position nf position

posséder [35] vb to own ▷ Ils possèdent une jolie maison. They own a lovely house.

possibilité nf possibility

possible adj possible; le plus de gens possible as many people as possible; le plus tôt possible as early as possible; le moins d'argent possible as little money as possible; Il travaille le moins possible. He works as little as possible.; dès que possible as soon as possible; faire son possible to do all one can

poste nf ① post ② post office; mettre une lettre à la poste to post a letter

▶ nm ① post ② (phone) extension ③ set ▷ un poste de radio a radio set; un poste de police a police station

poster [29] vb to post

▶ nm poster

When **poster** is a noun, the ending sounds like "air".

postérieur, e adj ① later ② back

pot nm jar; prendre un pot (informal) to have a drink; un pot de fleurs a plant pot

potable adj eau potable drinking water; "eau non potable" "not drinking water"

potage nm soup

potager nm vegetable garden

pot-au-feu (pl pot-au-feu) nm beef stew

pot-de-vin (pl pots-de-vin) nm bribe

pote nm (informal) mate

poteau (pl poteaux) nm post; un poteau indicateur a signpost

potentiel (f **potentielle**) adj potential

poterie nf ① pottery ② piece of pottery

potier nm potter

pou (pl poux) nm louse

poubelle nf dustbin

pouce nm ① thumb ② inch; manger sur le pouce to have a quick snack

poudre nf ① powder ② face powder; la poudre à laver washing powder; le lait en poudre powdered milk; le café en poudre instant coffee

poulain nm foal

poule nf hen

poulet nm ① chicken ② (informal) cop

pouls nm pulse

poumon nm lung

poupée nf doll

pour prep for ▷ Qu'est-ce que tu veux pour ton petit déjeuner? What would you like for breakfast?; **pour faire quelque chose** to do something ▷ Je lui ai téléphoné pour l'inviter. I phoned him to invite him.; **Pour aller à Strasbourg, s'il vous plaît?** Which way is it to Strasbourg, please?; **pour que** so that

▌ **pour que** is followed by a verb in the subjunctive.

▷ Je lui ai prêté mon pull pour qu'elle n'ait pas froid. I lent her my jumper so that she wouldn't be cold.; **pour cent** per cent

pourboire nm tip

pourcentage nm percentage

pourquoi adv, conj why

pourra, pourrai, pourras, pourrez vb see **pouvoir**

pourri, e adj rotten

pourrir [39] vb to go bad ▷ Ces poires ont pourri. These pears have gone bad.

pourrons, pourront vb see **pouvoir**

poursuite nf chase; **se lancer à la poursuite de quelqu'un** to chase after somebody

poursuivre [82] vb to carry on with ▷ Ils ont poursuivi leur travail. They carried on with their work.; **se poursuivre** to go on ▷ Le concert s'est poursuivi très tard. The concert went on very late.

pourtant adv yet; **C'est pourtant facile!** But it's easy!

pourvu adj pourvu que ... let's hope that ...

▌ **pourvu que** is followed by a verb in the subjunctive.

▷ Pourvu qu'il ne pleuve pas! Let's hope it doesn't rain!

pousser [29] vb ① to push ▷ Ils ont dû pousser la voiture. They had to push the car. ② to grow ▷ Mes cheveux poussent vite. My hair grows quickly.; **pousser un cri** to give a cry; **se pousser** to move over ▷ Pousse-toi, je ne vois rien. Move over, I can't see a thing.

poussette nf pushchair

poussière nf ① dust ② speck of dust

poussiéreux (f poussiéreuse) adj dusty

poussin nm chick

pouvoir [65] vb can ▷ Je peux lui téléphoner si tu veux. I can phone her if you want. ▷ J'ai fait tout ce que j'ai pu. I did all I could.; **Je n'en peux plus.** I'm exhausted.; **Il se peut que ...** It's possible that ...

▌ **il se peut que** is followed by a verb in the subjunctive.

▷ Il se peut que j'y aille. I might go.
▶ nm power

prairie nf meadow

pratique nf practice
▶ adj practical

pratiquement adv virtually

pratiquer [29] vb to practise; **Pratiquez-vous un sport?** Do you do any sport?

pré nm meadow

précaution nf precaution; **par**

précaution as a precaution; **avec précaution** cautiously; "à manipuler avec précaution" "handle with care"

précédemment adv previously

précédent, e adj previous

précieux (f **précieuse**) adj precious; **une pierre précieuse** a precious stone; **de précieux conseils** invaluable advice

précipice nm ravine

précipitamment adv hurriedly

précipitation nf haste

se **précipiter** [29] vb to rush

précis, e adj precise; **à huit heures précises** at exactly eight o'clock

précisément adv precisely

préciser [29] vb ① to be more specific about ▷ Pouvez-vous préciser ce que vous voulez dire? Can you be more specific about what you want to say? ② to specify

précision nf ① precision ② detail

préfecture nf
● A **préfecture** is the headquarters
● of a **département**, one of the 96
● administrative areas of France.
la préfecture de police the police headquarters

préférable adj preferable

préféré, e adj favourite

préférence nf preference; **de préférence** preferably

préférer [35] vb to prefer ▷ Je préfère manger à la cantine. I prefer to eat in the canteen.; **Je préférerais du thé.** I'd rather have tea.; **préférer quelqu'un à quelqu'un** to prefer somebody to

somebody ▷ Je le préfère à son frère. I prefer him to his brother.

préhistorique adj prehistoric

préjugé nm prejudice

premier (f **première**) adj first ▷ au premier étage on the first floor ▷ le premier mai the first of May ▷ Il est arrivé premier. He came first.; **le Premier ministre** the Prime Minister

première nf ① first class ▷ Nous avons voyagé en première. We travelled first class. ② first gear ● lower sixth form
● In French secondary schools,
● years are counted from the
● **sixième** (youngest) to **première**
● and **terminale** (oldest).
▷ Ma sœur est en première. My sister's in the lower sixth.

premièrement adv firstly

prendre [66] vb to take ▷ Prends tes affaires et viens avec moi. Take your things and come with me.; **prendre quelque chose à quelqu'un** to take something from somebody; **Nous avons pris le train de huit heures.** We took the eight o'clock train.; **Je prends toujours le train pour aller à Paris.** I always go to Paris by train.; **passer prendre** to pick up ▷ Je dois passer prendre Richard. I have to pick up Richard.; **prendre à gauche** to turn left ▷ Prenez à gauche en arrivant au rond-point. Turn left at the roundabout.; **Il se prend pour Napoléon.** He thinks he's Napoleon.; **s'en prendre à**

quelqu'un (*verbally*) to lay into somebody; **s'y prendre** to set about it ▷ *Tu t'y prends mal!* You're setting about it the wrong way!

prénom *nm* first name

préoccupé, e *adj* worried

préparation *nf* preparation

préparer [29] *vb* ❶ to prepare ▷ *Elle prépare le dîner.* She's preparing dinner. ❷ to make ▷ *Je vais préparer le café.* I'm going to make the coffee. ❸ to prepare for ▷ *Laure prépare son examen d'économie.* Laure's preparing for her economics exam.; **se préparer** to get ready

préposition *nf* preposition

près *adv* **tout près** nearby; **près de** (1) near (to) (2) next to; **de près** closely; **à peu de chose près** more or less

présence *nf* ❶ presence ❷ attendance

présent, e *adj* present ▶ *nm* present tense; **à présent** now

présentation *nf* presentation; **faire les présentations** to do the introductions

présenter [29] *vb* to present; **présenter quelqu'un à quelqu'un** to introduce somebody to somebody ▷ *Il m'a présenté à sa sœur.* He introduced me to his sister.; **Marc, je te présente Anaïs.** Marc, this is Anaïs.; **se présenter** (1) to introduce oneself ▷ *Elle s'est présentée à ses collègues.* She introduced herself

to her colleagues. (2) to arise ▷ *Si l'occasion se présente, nous irons en Écosse.* If the chance arises, we'll go to Scotland. (3) to stand ▷ *Monsieur Legros se présente encore aux élections.* Mr Legros is standing for election again.

préservatif *nm* condom

préserver [29] *vb* to protect

président *nm* ❶ president ❷ chairman; **le président directeur général** the chairman and managing director

présider [29] *vb* ❶ to chair ❷ to be the guest of honour

presque *adv* nearly; **presque rien** hardly anything; **presque pas** hardly at all; **presque pas de** hardly any

presqu'île *nf* peninsula

presse *nf* press

pressé, e *adj* ❶ in a hurry ❷ urgent; **une orange pressée** a fresh orange juice

presser [29] *vb* ❶ to squeeze ▷ *Tu peux me presser un citron?* Can you squeeze me a lemon? ❷ to be urgent ▷ *Est-ce que ça presse?* Is it urgent?; **se presser** to hurry up; **Rien ne presse.** There's no hurry.

pressing *nm* dry-cleaner's

pression *nf* ❶ pressure; **faire pression sur quelqu'un** to put pressure on somebody ❷ (*informal*) draught beer

prêt, e *adj* ready ▶ *nm* loan

prêt-à-porter *nm* ready-to-wear clothes

prétendre [89] *vb* **prétendre que** to claim that ▷ *Il prétend qu'il ne la connaît pas.* He claims he doesn't know her.

> Be careful **prétendre** does not mean **to pretend**.

prétendu, e *adj* so-called

prétentieux (*f* **prétentieuse**) *adj* pretentious

prêter [29] *vb* **prêter quelque chose à quelqu'un** to lend something to someone ▷ *Il m'a prêté sa voiture.* He lent me his car.; **prêter attention à quelque chose** to pay attention to something

prétexte *nm* excuse; **sous aucun prétexte** on no account

prétexter [29] *vb* to give as an excuse

prêtre *nm* priest

preuve *nf* ❶ evidence ❷ proof; **faire preuve de courage** to show courage; **faire ses preuves** to prove oneself

prévenir [90] *vb* **prévenir quelqu'un** to warn somebody ▷ *Je te préviens, il est de mauvaise humeur.* I'm warning you, he's in a bad mood.

prévention *nf* prevention; **des mesures de prévention** preventative measures; **la prévention routière** road safety

prévision *nf* **les prévisions météorologiques** the weather forecast; **en prévision de quelque chose** in anticipation of something

prévoir [93] *vb* ❶ to plan ▷ *Nous prévoyons un pique-nique pour dimanche.* We're planning to have a picnic on Sunday.; **Le départ est prévu pour dix heures.** The departure's scheduled for 10 o'clock. ❷ to allow ▷ *J'ai prévu assez à manger pour quatre.* I allowed enough food for four. ❸ to foresee ▷ *J'avais prévu qu'il serait en retard.* I'd foreseen that he'd be late.; **Je prévois qu'il me faudra une heure de plus.** I reckon it taking me another hour.

prier [20] *vb* to pray to; **prier quelqu'un de faire quelque chose** to ask somebody to do something ▷ *Elle l'a prié de sortir.* She asked him to leave.; **je vous en prie (1)** please do ▷ *Je peux m'asseoir? — Je vous en prie.* May I sit down? — Please do. **(2)** please ▷ *Je vous en prie, ne me laissez pas seule.* Please, don't leave me alone. **(3)** don't mention it ▷ *Merci pour votre aide. — Je vous en prie.* Thanks for your help. — Don't mention it.

prière *nf* prayer; **"prière de ne pas fumer"** "no smoking please"

primaire *nm* primary education; **l'école primaire** primary school

prime *nf* bonus

primevère *nf* primrose

prince *nm* prince

princesse *nf* princess

principal, e (*mpl* **principaux**) *adj* main

▶ *nm* (*pl* **principaux**)
❶ headmaster ❷ main thing

▷ *Personne n'a été blessé; c'est le principal.* Nobody was injured; that's the main thing.

principe nm principle; **pour le principe** on principle; **en principe (1)** as a rule **(2)** in theory

printemps nm spring; **au printemps** in spring

priorité nf ❶ priority ❷ right of way

pris, e adj ❶ taken ▷ *Est-ce que cette place est prise?* Is this seat taken? ❷ busy ▷ *Je serai très pris demain.* I'll be very busy tomorrow.; **avoir le nez pris** to have a stuffy nose; **être pris de panique** to be panic-stricken
▶ vb see **prendre**

prise nf ❶ plug ❷ socket; **une prise de courant** a power point; **une prise multiple** an adaptor; **une prise de sang** a blood test

prison nf prison

prisonnier (f **prisonnière**) adj captive
▶ nm/f prisoner

prit vb see **prendre**

privé, e adj private; **en privé** in private

priver [29] vb **priver quelqu'un de quelque chose** to deprive somebody of something; **Tu seras privé de dessert!** You won't get any pudding!

prix nm ❶ price ❷ prize; **hors de prix** exorbitantly priced; **à aucun prix** not at any price; **à tout prix** at all costs

probable adj likely; **C'est peu probable.** That's unlikely.

probablement adv probably

problème nm problem

procédé nm process

procès nm trial; **Il est en procès avec son employeur.** He's involved in a lawsuit with his employer.

prochain, e adj next; **la prochaine fois** next time; **la semaine prochaine** next week; **À la prochaine!** See you!

prochainement adv soon

proche adj ❶ near ❷ close; **proche de** near to; **le Proche-Orient** the Middle East

proches nmpl close relatives

proclamer [29] vb to proclaim

procurer [29] vb **procurer quelque chose à quelqu'un** to get something for somebody; **se procurer quelque chose** to get something

producteur (f **productrice**) nm/f producer

production nf production

produire [24] vb to produce; **se produire** to take place

produit nm product

prof nm (informal) teacher

professeur nm ❶ teacher ❷ professor; **un professeur de faculté** a university lecturer

profession nf profession; **"sans profession"** "unemployed"

professionnel (f **professionnelle**) adj professional

profil nm ❶ (of person) profile ❷ (of object) contours

profit nm profit; **tirer profit de quelque chose** to profit from something; **au profit de** in aid of

profiter [29] vb profiter de quelque chose to take advantage of something; **Profitez-en bien!** Make the most of it!

profond, e adj deep; peu profond shallow

profondeur nf depth

programme nm ❶ programme ❷ syllabus ❸ program ▷ un programme informatique a computer program

programmer [29] vb ❶ to show ▷ Ce film est programmé dimanche soir. The film is scheduled for Sunday evening. ❷ to program

programmeur (f **programmeuse**) nm/f programmer

progrès nm progress

progresser [29] vb to progress

progressif (f **progressive**) adj progressive

projecteur nm ❶ projector ❷ spotlight

projet nm ❶ plan ❷ draft; un projet de loi (in parliament) a bill

projeter [42] vb ❶ to plan ▷ Ils projettent d'acheter une maison. They're planning to buy a house. ❷ to cast ▷ une ombre projetée sur le mur a shadow cast onto the wall; **Elle a été projetée hors de la voiture.** She was thrown out of the car.

prolonger [46] vb ❶ to prolong ❷ to extend ▷ Je vais prolonger mon abonnement. I'm going to extend my subscription.; **se prolonger** to go on ▷ La réunion s'est prolongée tard. The meeting went on late.

promenade nf walk; **faire une promenade** to go for a walk; **faire une promenade en voiture** to go for a drive; **faire une promenade à vélo** to go for a bike ride

promener [44] vb to take for a walk ▷ Cordelia promène son chien tous les jours. Cordelia takes her dog for a walk every day.; **se promener** to go for a walk

promesse nf promise

promettre [48] vb to promise

promotion nf promotion; **être en promotion** to be on special offer

pronom nm pronoun

prononcer [13] vb ❶ to pronounce ▷ Le russe est difficile à prononcer. Russian is difficult to pronounce. ❷ to deliver ▷ prononcer un discours to deliver a speech; **se prononcer** to be pronounced ▷ Le "e" final ne se prononce pas. The final "e" isn't pronounced.

prononciation nf pronunciation

propagande nf propaganda

se propager [46] vb to spread

proportion nf proportion

propos nm à propos by the way; **à propos de quelque chose** about something

proposer [29] vb proposer quelque chose à quelqu'un (1) to suggest something to somebody ▷ Nous lui avons proposé une promenade en bateau. We suggested going on a boat ride to him. (2) to offer somebody something ▷ Ils m'ont proposé des chocolats. They offered me some chocolates.

a
b
c
d
e
f
g
h
i
j
k
l
m
n
o
p
q
r
s
t
u
v
w
x
y
z

proposition nf offer
propre adj ❶ clean ❷ own
▷ *Gordon l'a fabriqué de ses propres mains.* Gordon made it with his own hands.; **propre à** characteristic of
▶ nm **recopier quelque chose au propre** to make a fair copy of something
proprement adv ❶ properly; **le village proprement dit** the village itself; **à proprement parler** strictly speaking
propreté nf cleanliness
propriétaire nm ❶ owner ❷ landlord
▶ nf ❶ owner ❷ landlady
propriété nf property
prospectus nm leaflet
prospère adj prosperous
prostituée nf prostitute
protecteur (f **protectrice**) adj ❶ protective ❷ patronizing
protection nf protection
protéger [67] vb to protect
protéine nf protein
protestant, e adj Protestant; **Il est protestant.** He's a Protestant.
protestation nf protest
protester [29] vb to protest ▷ *Ils protestent contre leurs conditions de travail.* They're protesting about their working conditions.
prouver [29] vb to prove
provenance nf origin; **un avion en provenance de Berlin** a plane arriving from Berlin
provenir [90] vb **provenir de** (1) to come from ▷ *Ces tomates*

proviennent d'Espagne. These tomatoes come from Spain. **(2)** to be the result of ▷ *Cela provient d'un manque d'organisation.* This is the result of a lack of organization.
proverbe nm proverb
province nf province; **en province** in the provinces
proviseur nm *(of state secondary school)* headteacher
provision nf supply
provisions nfpl food
provisoire adj temporary
provoquer [29] vb ❶ to provoke ❷ to cause ▷ *Cet accident a provoqué la mort de quarante personnes.* The accident caused the death of 40 people.
proximité nf proximity; **à proximité** nearby
prudemment adv ❶ carefully ❷ wisely ❸ cautiously
prudence nf caution; **avec prudence** carefully
prudent, e adj ❶ careful ❷ wise
prune nf plum
> Be careful! The French word **prune** does not mean **prune**.

pruneau (pl **pruneaux**) nm prune
psychiatre nmf psychiatrist
psychologie nf psychology
psychologique adj psychological
psychologue nmf psychologist
pu vb see **pouvoir**; **Je n'ai pas pu venir.** I couldn't come.
pub nf ❶ *(informal)* advertising ❷ adverts
public (f **publique**) adj public; **une école publique** a state school

▶ nm ❶ public ❷ audience; **en public** in public

publicitaire adj **une agence publicitaire** an advertising agency; **un film publicitaire** a publicity film

publicité nf ❶ advertising ❷ advert; **faire de la publicité pour quelque chose** to publicize something

publier [20] vb to publish

publique adj see **public**

puce nf ❶ flea ❷ chip; **une carte à puce** a smart card

puces nfpl flea market

puer [29] vb to stink

puéril, e adj childish

puis vb see **pouvoir**; **Puis-je venir vous voir samedi?** May I come and see you on Saturday?
▶ adv then

puisque conj since

puissance nf power

puissant, e adj powerful

puits nm well

pull nm jumper

pull-over nm jumper

pulvérisateur nm spray

pulvériser [29] vb ❶ to pulverize ❷ to spray

punaise nf drawing pin

punir [39] vb to punish ▷ *Il a été puni pour avoir menti.* He was punished for lying.

punition nf punishment

pupitre nm (for pupil) desk

pur, e adj ❶ pure ❷ (undiluted) neat; **c'est de la folie pure** it's sheer madness

purée nf mashed potatoes; **la purée de marrons** chestnut purée

putain nf (rude) whore

puzzle nm jigsaw puzzle

PV nm (= *procès-verbal*) parking ticket

pyjama nm pyjamas

pyramide nf pyramid

Pyrénées nfpl Pyrenees; **dans les Pyrénées** in the Pyrenees

a
b
c
d
e
f
g
h
i
j
k
l
m
n
o
p
q
r
s
t
u
v
w
x
y
z

q

QI nm (= quotient intellectuel) IQ
quai nm ❶ quay ❷ platform
qualifié, e adj qualified
qualifier [20] vb **se qualifier** to qualify ▷ Bob s'est qualifié pour la demi-finale. Bob has qualified for the semifinal.
qualité nf quality
quand conj, adv when ▷ Quand est-ce que tu pars en vacances? When are you going on holiday?; **quand même** all the same ▷ Je ne voulais pas de dessert, mais j'en ai mangé quand même. I didn't want any dessert, but I had some all the same.
quant à prep regarding ▷ Quant au problème de chauffage … Regarding the problem with the heating … ▷ Quant à moi, … As for me, …

quantité nf amount; **des quantités de** a great deal of
quarantaine nf about forty; **Elle a la quarantaine.** She's in her forties.
quarante num forty; **quarante et un** forty-one; **quarante-deux** forty-two
quart nm quarter; **le quart de** a quarter of; **trois quarts** three quarters; **un quart d'heure** a quarter of an hour; **deux heures et quart** a quarter past two; **dix heures moins le quart** a quarter to ten; **Un quart d'eau minérale, s'il vous plaît.** A small bottle of mineral water, please.
quartier nm ❶ (of town) area; **un cinéma de quartier** a local cinema ❸ piece ▷ un quartier d'orange a piece of orange
quartz nm **une montre à quartz** a quartz watch
quasi adv nearly
quasiment adv nearly; **quasiment jamais** hardly ever
quatorze num fourteen; **le quatorze février** the fourteenth of February
quatre num four ▷ Il a quatre ans. He's four.; **le quatre février** the fourth of February; **faire les quatre cents coups** to be a bit wild
quatre-vingts num eighty

quatre-vingts is spelt with an **-s** when it is followed by a noun, but not when it is followed by another number.

▷ quatre-vingts euros eighty euros

▷ *Elle a quatre-vingt-deux ans.* She's eighty-two.; **quatre-vingt-dix** ninety; **quatre-vingt-onze** ninety-one; **quatre-vingt-quinze** ninety-five; **quatre-vingt-dix-huit** ninety-eight

quatrième *adj* fourth ▷ *au quatrième étage* on the fourth floor
▶ *nf* year 9
● In French secondary schools,
● years are counted from the
● **sixième** (youngest) to **première**
● and **terminale** (oldest).
● *Mon frère est en quatrième.* My
● brother's in year 9.

que *conj, pron, adv* ❶ that ▷ *Il sait que tu es là.* He knows that you're here.; **Je veux que tu viennes.** I want you to come. ❷ what ▷ *Que fais-tu?* What are you doing?; **Qu'est-ce que ...?** What ...? ▷ *Qu'est-ce que tu fais?* What are you doing? ▷ *Qu'est-ce que c'est?* What's that?; **plus ... que** more ... than ▷ *Il est plus grand que moi.* He's bigger than me.; **aussi ... que** as ... as ▷ *Elle est aussi jolie que sa sœur.* She's as pretty as her sister.; **ne ... que** only ▷ *Il ne boit que de l'eau.* He only drinks water.; **Qu'il est bête!** He's so silly!

quel (f **quelle**) *adj* ❶ who ▷ *Quel est ton chanteur préféré?* Who's your favourite singer? ❷ what ▷ *Quelle heure est-il?* What time is it? ❸ which ▷ *Quel groupe préfères-tu?* Which band do you like best?; **quel que soit (1)** whoever **(2)** whatever

quelle *adj see* **quel**

quelque *adj, adv* ❶ some ▷ *Il a quelques amis à Paris.* He has some friends in Paris. ❷ a few ▷ *Il reste quelques bouteilles.* There are a few bottles left. ❸ few ▷ *Ils ont fini les quelques bouteilles qui restaient.* They finished the few bottles that were left.; **quelque chose (1)** something ▷ *J'ai quelque chose pour toi.* I've got something for you. **(2)** anything ▷ *Avez-vous quelque chose à déclarer?* Have you got anything to declare?; **quelque part (1)** somewhere **(2)** anywhere

quelquefois *adv* sometimes

quelques-uns (f **quelques-unes**) *pron* some ▷ *As-tu vu ses films? J'en ai vu quelques-uns.* Have you seen his films? I've seen some of them.

quelqu'un *pron* ❶ somebody ▷ *Il y a quelqu'un à la porte.* There's somebody at the door. ❷ anybody ▷ *Est-ce que quelqu'un a vu mon parapluie?* Has anybody seen my umbrella?

querelle *nf* quarrel

qu'est-ce que *see* **que**

qu'est-ce qui *see* **qui**

question *nf* question; **Il n'en est pas question.** There's no question of it.; **De quoi est-il question?** What's it about?; **Il est question de l'organisation du concert.** It's about the organization of the concert.; **hors de question** out of the question

questionnaire *nm* questionnaire

questionner [29] *vb* to question

queue nf ❶ <u>tail</u>; **faire la queue**
to queue; **une queue de cheval**
a ponytail

  Word for word, the French
  means "horse's tail".

❷ <u>rear</u> ❸ <u>bottom</u> ❹ (of fruit,
leaf) <u>stalk</u>

qui pron ❶ <u>who</u> ▷ *Qui a téléphoné?*
Who phoned? ❷ <u>whom</u> ▷ *C'est la
personne à qui j'ai parlé hier.* It's the
person whom I spoke to yesterday.
❸ <u>that</u> ▷ *Donne-moi la veste qui est
sur la chaise.* Give me the jacket
that's on the chair.; **Qui est-ce
qui ...?** Who ...? ▷ *Qui est-ce qui
t'emmène au spectacle?* Who's taking
you to the show?; **Qui est-ce
que ...?** Who ...? ▷ *Qui est-ce que
tu as vu à cette soirée?* Who did you see
at the party?; **Qu'est-ce qui ...?**
What ...? ▷ *Qu'est-ce qui est sur la
table?* What's on the table? ▷ *Qu'est-
ce qui te prend?* What's the matter
with you?; **À qui est ce sac?** Whose
bag is this?; **À qui parlais-tu?** Who
were you talking to?

quille nf **un jeu de quilles** skittles

quincaillerie nf <u>ironmonger's
(shop)</u>

quinquennat nm

  Le **quinquennat** is the five-year
  term of office of the French
  President.

quinzaine nf <u>about fifteen</u>; **une
quinzaine de jours** a fortnight

quinze num <u>fifteen</u>; **le quinze
février** the fifteenth of February;
dans quinze jours in a fortnight's
time

quittance nf ❶ <u>receipt</u> ❷ <u>bill</u>

quitter [29] vb to <u>leave</u> ▷ *J'ai quitté
la maison à huit heures.* I left the
house at 8 o'clock.; **se quitter** to
part ▷ *Les deux amis se sont quittés
devant le café.* The two friends
parted in front of the café.; **Ne
quittez pas.** (on telephone) Hold
the line.

quoi pron <u>what?</u> ▷ *À quoi penses-tu?*
What are you thinking about?;
Quoi de neuf? What's new?; **As-tu
de quoi écrire?** Have you got
anything to write with?; **Je n'ai
pas de quoi acheter une voiture.**
I can't afford to buy a car.; **Quoi
qu'il arrive.** Whatever happens.;
Il n'y a pas de quoi. Don't mention
it.; **Il n'y a pas de quoi s'énerver.**
There's no reason for getting
worked up.; **En quoi puis-je vous
aider?** How may I help you?

quoique conj <u>even though</u>

  quoique is followed by a verb
  in the subjunctive.

▷ *Il va l'acheter quoique ce soit cher.*
He's going to buy it even though
it's expensive.

quotidien (f **quotidienne**) adj
<u>daily</u>; **la vie quotidienne** everyday
life

▶ nm <u>daily paper</u>

r

rab nm (informal: of meal) seconds

rabais nm (in price) reduction; **au rabais** at a discount

racaille nf riff-raff

raccompagner [29] vb to take home ▷ *Tu peux me raccompagner?* Can you take me home?

raccourci nm shortcut

raccrocher [29] vb to hang up (telephone)

race nf ❶ race ❷ breed; **de race** pedigree

racheter [2] vb ❶ to buy another ▷ *J'ai racheté un portefeuille.* I've bought another wallet. ▷ *racheter du lait* to buy more milk ❷ to buy ▷ *Il m'a racheté ma moto.* He bought my bike from me.

racine nf root

racisme nm racism

raciste adj racist

raconter [29] vb **raconter quelque chose à quelqu'un** to tell somebody about something; **Qu'est-ce que tu racontes?** What are you talking about?

radar nm radar

radiateur nm radiator; **un radiateur électrique** an electric heater

radin, e adj (informal) stingy

radio nf ❶ radio ❷ X-ray; **passer une radio** to have an X-ray

radio-réveil (pl radios-réveils) nm clock radio

radis nm radish

raffoler [29] vb **raffoler de** to be crazy about

rafraîchir [39] vb to cool down; **se rafraîchir** (1) to get cooler ▷ *Le temps se rafraîchit.* The weather's getting cooler. (2) to freshen up ▷ *Il a pris une douche pour se rafraîchir.* He had a shower to freshen up.

rafraîchissant, e adj refreshing

rage nf rabies; **une rage de dents** raging toothache

ragoût nm stew

raide adj ❶ steep ❷ straight ▷ *Laure a les cheveux raides.* Laure has straight hair. ❸ stiff

raie nf ❶ (fish) skate ❷ (in hair) parting

rail nm rail

raisin nm grapes; **des raisins secs** raisins

raison nf reason; **Ce n'est pas une raison.** That's no excuse.; **avoir**

raison to be right; **en raison de** because of

raisonnable *adj* sensible

raisonnement *nm* reasoning

rajouter [29] *vb* to add

ralentir [39] *vb* to slow down

râler [29] *vb* (informal) to moan

ramassage *nm* **le ramassage scolaire** the school bus service

ramasser [29] *vb* ❶ to pick up ▷ Il a ramassé son crayon. He picked up his pencil. ❷ to take in ▷ Il a ramassé les copies. He took in the exam papers.

rame *nf* ❶ (of boat) oar ❷ (on the underground) train

rameau (*pl* **rameaux**) *nm* branch; **le dimanche des Rameaux** Palm Sunday

ramener [44] *vb* ❶ to bring back ▷ Je t'ai ramené un souvenir de Grèce. I've brought you back a present from Greece. ❷ to take home ▷ Tu me ramènes? Will you take me home?

ramer [29] *vb* to row

rampe *nf* banister

rancune *nf* **garder rancune à quelqu'un** to bear somebody a grudge; **Sans rancune!** No hard feelings!

rancunier (*f* **rancunière**) *adj* vindictive

randonnée *nf* **une randonnée à vélo** a bike ride; **une randonnée pédestre** a ramble; **faire de la randonnée** to go hiking

randonneur (*f* **randonneuse**) *nm/f* hiker

rang *nm* (line) row

rangée *nf* (line) row

ranger [46] *vb* ❶ to put away ▷ J'ai rangé tes affaires. I've put your things away. ❷ to tidy up ▷ Va ranger ta chambre. Go and tidy up your room.

rap *nm* rap

râper [29] *vb* to grate ▷ le fromage râpé grated cheese

rapide *adj* ❶ fast ❷ quick

rapidement *adv* quickly

rappel *nm* ❶ (vaccination) booster ❷ curtain call

rappeler [5] *vb* to call back ▷ Je te rappelle dans cinq minutes. I'll call you back in 5 minutes.; **rappeler quelque chose à quelqu'un** to remind somebody of something; **rappeler à quelqu'un de faire quelque chose** to remind somebody to do something; **se rappeler** to remember ▷ Il s'est rappelé qu'il avait une course à faire. He remembered he had some shopping to do.

rapport *nm* ❶ report ❷ connection ▷ Je ne vois pas le rapport. I can't see the connection.; **par rapport à** in comparison with ▶ *nmpl* relations; **les rapports sexuels** sexual intercourse

rapporter [29] *vb* to bring back

rapporteur (*f* **rapporteuse**) *nm/f* ▶ *nm* (in geometry) protractor

rapprocher [29] *vb* ❶ to bring together ▷ Cet accident a rapproché les deux frères. The accident brought

the two brothers together.
❷ to bring closer ▷ Il a rapproché
le fauteuil de la télé. He brought
the armchair closer to the TV.;
se rapprocher to come closer
▷ Rapproche-toi, tu verras mieux.
Come closer, you'll see better.

raquette nf ❶ (tennis) racket
❷ (table tennis) bat

rare adj rare

rarement adv rarely

ras, e adj, adv short; **à ras bords**
to the brim; **en avoir ras le bol de
quelque chose** (informal) to be fed
up with something; **un pull ras du
cou** a crew-neck jumper

raser [29] vb to shave off; **se raser**
to shave

rasoir nm razor
▸ adj inv (informal) dead boring

rassembler [29] vb to assemble
▷ Il a rassemblé les enfants dans la
cour. He assembled the children in
the playground.; **se rassembler** to
gather together

rassurer [29] vb to reassure;
Je suis rassuré. I don't need to
worry any more.; **se rassurer** to
be reassured ▷ Rassure-toi! Don't
worry!

rat nm rat

raté, e adj unsuccessful

râteau (pl râteaux) nm rake

rater [29] vb ❶ to miss ▷ Chantal
a raté son train. Chantal missed
her train. ❷ to fail ▷ J'ai raté mon
examen de maths. I failed my maths
exam.

RATP nf Paris transport authority

rattacher [29] vb to tie up again

rattraper [29] vb ❶ to recapture
❷ to catch up with ▷ Je vais
rattraper Cécile. I'll catch up with
Cécile. ❸ to make up for ▷ Il
faut rattraper le temps perdu. We
must make up for lost time.; **se
rattraper** to make up for it

rature nf correction

ravi, e adj être ravi(e) to be
delighted

se **raviser** [29] vb to change your
mind ▷ Il allait accepter, mais il s'est
ravisé. He was going to accept, but
he changed his mind.

ravissant, e adj lovely

rayé, e adj striped

rayer [60] vb ❶ to scratch ❷ to
cross off ▷ Son nom a été rayé de la
liste. His name has been crossed
off the list.

rayon nm ❶ ray ▷ un rayon de soleil
a ray of sunshine ❷ radius ❸ shelf
▷ les rayons d'une bibliothèque
the shelves of a bookcase
❹ department ▷ le rayon hi-fi vidéo
the hi-fi and video department; **les
rayons X** X-rays

rayure nf stripe

ré nm ❶ D ❷ re

réaction nf reaction

réagir [39] vb to react

réalisateur (f réalisatrice) nm/f
director (of film)

réaliser [29] vb ❶ to carry out ▷ Ils
ont réalisé leur projet. They carried
out their plan. ❷ to fulfil ▷ Il a
réalisé son rêve. He has fulfilled his
dream. ❸ to realize ❹ to make

▷ *réaliser un film* to make a film;
se réaliser to come true
réaliste *adj* realistic
réalité *nf* reality; **en réalité** in fact
rebelle *nmf* rebel
rebondir [39] *vb* to bounce
rebord *nm* edge; **le rebord de la
fenêtre** the window ledge
recaler [29] *vb* (informal): *J'ai été
recalé en maths.* I failed maths.
récemment *adv* recently
récent, e *adj* recent
récepteur *nm* receiver
réception *nf* reception desk
réceptionniste *nmf* receptionist
recette *nf* recipe
recevoir [68] *vb* ❶ to receive ▷ *J'ai
reçu une lettre.* I received a letter.
❷ to see ▷ *Il a déjà reçu trois clients.*
He has already seen three clients.
❸ to have round ▷ *Je reçois des
amis à dîner.* I'm having friends for
dinner.; **être reçu à un examen** to
pass an exam
rechange *nm* **de rechange**
(battery, bulb) spare
recharge *nf* refill
réchaud *nm* stove
réchauffer [29] *vb* ❶ to reheat
▷ *Je vais réchauffer les légumes.* I'll
reheat the vegetables. ❷ to warm
up ▷ *Un bon café va te réchauffer.*
A nice cup of coffee will warm
you up.; **se réchauffer** to warm
oneself
recherche *nf* research; **être à
la recherche de quelque chose**
to be looking for something; **les
recherches** search

recherché, e *adj* much sought-
after
rechercher [29] *vb* to look for ▷ *La
police recherche l'assassin.* The police
are looking for the killer.
rechute *nf* relapse
récipient *nm* container
récit *nm* story
réciter [29] *vb* to recite
réclamation *nf* complaint; **les
réclamations** the complaints
department
réclame *nf* advert; **en réclame** on
special offer
réclamer [29] *vb* ❶ to demand
▷ *Nous réclamons la semaine de trente
heures.* We demand a 30-hour
week. ❷ to complain ▷ *Elles
sont toujours en train de réclamer.*
They're always complaining about
something.
reçois *vb see* **recevoir**
récolte *nf* harvest
récolter [29] *vb* ❶ to harvest ❷ to
collect ▷ *Ils ont récolté deux cents
euros.* They collected 200 euros.
❸ (informal) to get ▷ *Il a récolté une
amende.* He got a fine.
recommandé *nm* **en
recommandé** by registered mail
recommander [29] *vb* to
recommend
recommencer [13] *vb* ❶ to start
again ▷ *Il a recommencé à pleuvoir.*
It's started raining again. ❷ to
do again ▷ *S'il n'est pas puni, il va
recommencer.* If he's not punished
he'll do it again.
récompense *nf* reward

récompenser [29] vb to reward

réconcilier [20] vb **se réconcilier avec quelqu'un** to be make it up with somebody ▷ Il s'est réconcilié avec sa sœur. He has made it up with his sister.

reconnaissant, e adj grateful

reconnaître [15] vb ❶ to recognize ▷ Je ne l'ai pas reconnu. I didn't recognize him. ❷ to admit ▷ Je reconnais que j'ai eu tort. I admit I was wrong.

reconstruire [24] vb to rebuild

record nm record

recouvrir [56] vb to cover ▷ La neige recouvre le sol. The ground is covered in snow.

récréation nf break; **la cour de récréation** the playground (of school)

rectangle nm rectangle

rectangulaire adj rectangular

rectifier [20] vb to correct

reçu nm receipt

▶ vb see **recevoir**; J'ai reçu un colis ce matin. I received a parcel this morning.; **être reçu à un examen** to pass an exam

reculer [29] vb ❶ to step back ▷ Il a reculé pour la laisser entrer. He stepped back to let her in. ❷ to reverse ▷ J'ai reculé pour laisser passer le camion. I reversed to let the lorry past. ❸ to postpone ▷ Ils ont reculé la date du spectacle. They postponed the show.

reculons: à reculons adv backwards

récupérer [35] vb ❶ to get back ▷ Je vais récupérer ma voiture au garage. I'm going to get my car

back from the garage. ❷ to make up ▷ J'ai des heures à récupérer. I've got time to make up. ❸ to recover ▷ J'ai besoin de récupérer. I need to recover.

recycler [29] vb to recycle

rédaction nf essay

redemander [29] vb ❶ to ask again for ▷ Je vais lui redemander son adresse. I'll ask him for his address again. ❷ to ask for more ▷ Je vais redemander des carottes. I'm going to ask for more carrots.

redescendre [25] vb ❶ to go back down ▷ Il est redescendu au premier étage. He went back down to the first floor. ▷ Elle a redescendu l'escalier. She went back down the stairs.

rédiger [46] vb (an essay) to write

redoubler [29] vb to repeat a year ▷ Il a raté son examen et doit redoubler. He's failed his exam and will have to repeat the year.
- In French schools you sometimes have to repeat a year
- if you've not done well.

réduction nf ❶ reduction ❷ discount

réduire [24] vb to cut ▷ Ils ont réduit leurs prix. They've cut their prices.

réel (f **réelle**) adj real

réellement adv really

refaire [37] vb ❶ to do again ▷ Je dois refaire ce rapport. I've got to do this report again. ❷ to take up again ▷ Je voudrais refaire de la gym. I'd like to take up gymnastics again.

réfectoire nm refectory

référence nf reference; **faire référence à quelque chose** to refer to something; **Ce n'est pas une référence!** That's no recommendation!

réfléchi, e adj (verb) reflexive; **C'est tout réfléchi.** My mind's made up.

réfléchir [39] vb to think ▷ Il est en train de réfléchir. He's thinking.; **réfléchir à quelque chose** to think about something

reflet nm reflection

refléter [35] vb to reflect

réflexe nm reflex

réflexion nf ❶ thought ❷ remark; **réflexion faite** on reflection

refrain nm chorus (of song)

réfrigérateur nm refrigerator

refroidir [39] vb to cool ▷ Laissez le gâteau refroidir. Leave the cake to cool.; **se refroidir** to get colder ▷ Le temps se refroidit. It's getting colder.

se réfugier [20] vb to take shelter

refus nm refusal; **Ce n'est pas de refus.** I wouldn't say no.

refuser [29] vb to refuse ▷ Il a refusé de payer sa part. He refused to pay his share.; **Je refuse qu'on me parle ainsi!** I won't let anybody talk to me like that!

se régaler [29] vb Merci beaucoup: je me suis régalé! Thank you very much: it was absolutely delicious!

regard nm look; **Tous les regards se sont tournés vers lui.** All eyes turned towards him.

regarder [29] vb ❶ to look at ▷ Il regardait ses photos de vacances. He was looking at his holiday photos. ❷ to watch ▷ Je regarde la télévision. I'm watching television. ❸ to concern ▷ Ça ne nous regarde pas. It doesn't concern us.; **ne pas regarder à la dépense** to spare no expense

régime nm ❶ regime (of a country) ❷ diet; **un régime de bananes** a bunch of bananas

région nf region

régional, e (mpl régionaux) adj regional

registre nm register

règle nf ❶ ruler ❷ rule; **être en règle** to be in order; **les règles** (menstruation) period

règlement nm rules

régler [35] vb ❶ to adjust ❷ to tune ▷ J'ai réglé ma radio sur 99 FM. I tuned my radio to 99 FM. ❸ to set ▷ J'ai réglé le thermostat à vingt degrés. I've set the thermostat to 20 degrees. ❹ to solve ▷ Le problème est réglé. The problem's solved. ❺ to settle ▷ Elle a réglé sa facture. She's settled her bill.

réglisse nf liquorice

règne nm reign

régner [35] vb to reign

regret nm regret; **à regret** reluctantly

regretter [29] vb ❶ to regret; **Je regrette.** I'm sorry. ▷ Je regrette, je ne peux pas vous aider. I'm sorry, I can't help you. ❷ to miss ▷ Je regrette mon ancien travail. I miss my old job.

regrouper [29] vb to group together; **se regrouper** to gather together

régulier (f **régulière**) adj ❶ regular ❷ steady ▷ à un rythme régulier at a steady rate ❸ scheduled ▷ des vols réguliers pour Marseille scheduled flights to Marseilles

régulièrement adv regularly

rein nm kidney; **les reins** (of body) back

reine nf queen

rejoindre [43] vb to go back to ▷ J'ai rejoint mes amis. I went back to my friends.; **Je te rejoins au café.** I'll see you at the café.; **se rejoindre** to meet up ▷ Elles se sont rejointes une heure après. They met up an hour later.

relâcher [29] vb (prisoner, animal) to release; **se relâcher** to get slack ▷ Il se relâche dans son travail. His work is getting careless.

relais nm relay race; **prendre le relais** to take over

relation nf relationship; **les relations franco-britanniques** Anglo-French relations

se relaxer [29] vb to relax

se relayer [60] vb **se relayer pour faire quelque chose** to take it in turns to do something

relevé nm **un relevé de compte** a bank statement

relever [44] vb ❶ to collect ▷ Je relève les copies dans cinq minutes. I'll collect the papers in five minutes. ❷ to react to ▷ Je n'ai pas relevé sa réflexion. I didn't react to his

remark.; **relever la tête** to look up; **se relever** to get up ▷ Il est tombé mais s'est relevé aussitôt. He fell, but got up immediately.

religieuse nf ❶ nun ❷ choux cream bun

religieux (f **religieuse**) adj religious

religion nf religion

relire [45] vb ❶ to read over ❷ to read again

remarquable adj remarkable

remarque nf ❶ remark ❷ comment

remarquer [29] vb to notice ▷ J'ai remarqué qu'elle avait l'air triste. I noticed she was looking sad.; **faire remarquer quelque chose à quelqu'un** to point something out to somebody ▷ Je lui ai fait remarquer que c'était un peu cher. I pointed out to him that it was rather expensive.; **Remarquez, il n'est pas si bête que ça.** Mind you, he's not as stupid as all that.; **se remarquer** to be noticeable; **se faire remarquer** to call attention to oneself

remboursement nm refund

rembourser [29] vb to pay back ▷ Il m'a remboursé l'argent qu'il me devait. He paid me back the money he owed me.; **"satisfait ou remboursé"** "satisfaction or your money back"

remède nm ❶ medicine ❷ cure

remercier [20] vb to thank ▷ Je te remercie pour ton cadeau. Thank you for your present.; **remercier**

quelqu'un d'avoir fait quelque chose to thank somebody for doing something ▷ *Je vous remercie de m'avoir invité.* Thank you for inviting me.

remettre [48] vb ❶ to put back on ▷ *Il a remis son pull.* He put his sweater back on. ❷ to put back ▷ *Il a remis sa veste dans l'armoire.* He put his jacket back in the wardrobe. ❸ to put off ▷ *J'ai dû remettre mon rendez-vous.* I've had to put my appointment off.; **se remettre** (*from illness*) to recover

remonte-pente nm ski-lift

remonter [49] vb ❶ to go back up ▷ *Il est remonté au premier étage.* He has gone back up to the first floor. ❷ to go up ▷ *Ils ont remonté la pente.* They went up the hill. ❸ to buck up ▷ *Cette nouvelle m'a un peu remonté.* The news bucked me up a bit.; **remonter le moral à quelqu'un** to cheer somebody up

remords nm **avoir des remords** to feel remorse

remorque nf (*of car*) trailer

remparts nmpl city walls

remplaçant (f remplaçante) nm/f supply teacher

remplacer [13] vb to replace ▷ *Il remplace le prof de maths.* He's replacing the maths teacher.; **remplacer par** to replace with

rempli, e adj busy; **rempli de** full of

remplir [39] vb ❶ to fill up ▷ *Elle a rempli son verre de vin.* She filled her glass with wine. ❷ to fill in ▷ *Tu as rempli ton formulaire?* Have you

filled in your form?; **se remplir** to fill up

remuer [29] vb ❶ to move ▷ *Elle a remué le bras.* She moved her arm. ❷ to stir ▷ *Remuez la sauce pendant deux minutes.* Stir the sauce for two minutes.; **se remuer** (*informal*) to go to a lot of trouble ▷ *Ils se sont beaucoup remués pour organiser cette soirée.* They went to a lot of trouble organizing this party.

renard nm fox

rencontre nf **faire la rencontre de quelqu'un** to meet somebody; **aller à la rencontre de quelqu'un** to go and meet somebody

rencontrer [29] vb to meet; **se rencontrer** to meet ▷ *Ils se sont rencontrés il y a deux ans.* They met two years ago.

rendez-vous nm ❶ appointment; **prendre rendez-vous avec quelqu'un** to make an appointment with somebody ❷ date ▷ *Tu sors ce soir? — Oui, j'ai un rendez-vous.* Are you going out tonight? — Yes, I've got a date.; **donner rendez-vous à quelqu'un** to arrange to meet somebody

rendre [8] vb ❶ to give back ▷ *J'ai rendu ses disques à Christine.* I've given Christine her records back. ❷ to take back ▷ *J'ai rendu mes livres à la bibliothèque.* I've taken my books back to the library.; **rendre quelqu'un célèbre** to make somebody famous; **se rendre** to give oneself up ▷ *Le meurtrier s'est rendu à la police.* The murderer gave himself up to the police.; **se rendre compte de quelque chose** to realize something

renfermé nm **sentir le renfermé** to smell stuffy

renifler [29] vb to sniff

renne nm reindeer

renommé, e adj renowned

renoncer [13] vb **renoncer à** to give up ▷ Ils ont renoncé à leur projet. They've given up their plan.; **renoncer à faire quelque chose** to give up the idea of doing something

renouvelable adj (energy) renewable

renouveler [5] vb (passport, contract) to renew; **se renouveler** to happen again ▷ J'espère que ça ne se renouvellera pas. I hope that won't happen again.

renseignement nm piece of information; **les renseignements** (1) information ▷ Il m'a donné des renseignements. He gave me some information. (2) information desk (3) directory inquiries

renseigner [29] vb **renseigner quelqu'un sur quelque chose** to give somebody information about something; **Est-ce que je peux vous renseigner?** Can I help you?; **se renseigner** to find out

rentable adj profitable

rentrée nf **la rentrée (des classes)** the start of the new school year

rentrer [69] vb ❶ to come in ▷ Rentre, tu vas prendre froid. Come in, you'll catch cold. ❷ to go in ▷ Elle est rentrée dans le magasin.

She went into the shop. ❸ to get home ▷ Je suis rentré à sept heures hier soir. I got home at 7 o'clock last night. ❹ to put away ▷ Tu as rentré la voiture? Have you put the car away?; **rentrer dans** to crash into ▷ Sa voiture est rentrée dans un arbre. He crashed into a tree.; **rentrer dans l'ordre** to get back to normal

renverse nf **tomber à la renverse** to fall backwards

renverser [29] vb ❶ to knock over ▷ J'ai renversé mon verre. I knocked my glass over. ❷ to knock down ▷ Elle a été renversée par une voiture. She was knocked down by a car. ❸ to spill ▷ Il a renversé de l'eau partout. He has spilt water everywhere.; **se renverser** (glass, vase) to fall over

renvoyer [34] vb ❶ to send back ▷ Je t'ai renvoyé ton courrier. I've sent your mail back to you. ❷ to dismiss ▷ On a renvoyé deux employés. Two employees have been dismissed.

répandu, e adj common; **du vin répandu sur la table** wine spilt on the table; **des papiers répandus sur le sol** papers scattered over the floor

réparateur nm repairman

réparation nf repair

réparer [29] vb to repair

repartir [58] vb to set off again ▷ Il était là tout à l'heure, mais il est reparti. He was here a moment ago, but he's gone again.; **repartir à zéro** to start again from scratch

repas nm meal; **le repas de midi**
lunch; **le repas du soir** dinner

repassage nm ironing

repasser [29] vb ❶ to come back
▷ Je repasserai demain. I'll come back
tomorrow. ❷ to go back ▷ Je dois
repasser au magasin. I've got to go
back to the shop. ❸ to iron ▷ J'ai
repassé ma chemise. I've ironed my
shirt. ❹ to resit ▷ Elle doit repasser son
examen. She's got to resit her exam.

repérer [35] vb ❶ to spot ▷ J'ai
repéré deux fautes. I spotted two
mistakes.; **se repérer** to find one's
way around ▷ J'ai du mal à me repérer
de nuit. I have difficulty finding my
way around when it's dark.

répertoire nm directory

répéter [35] vb ❶ to repeat ▷ Elle
répète toujours la même chose.
She keeps repeating the same
thing. ❷ to rehearse ▷ Les acteurs
répètent une scène. The actors are
rehearsing a scene.; **se répéter**
to happen again ▷ J'espère que cela
ne se répétera pas! I hope this won't
happen again!

répétition nf ❶ repetition; **des
grèves à répétition** repeated
strikes ❷ rehearsal; **la répétition
générale** the dress rehearsal

répondeur nm answering
machine

répondre [70] vb to answer
▷ répondre à quelqu'un to answer
somebody

réponse nf answer

reportage nm ❶ report ❷ story

reporter nm reporter

repos nm rest

reposer [29] vb to put back down
▷ Elle a reposé son verre sur la table.
She put her glass back down on the
table.; **se reposer** to have a rest
▷ Tu pourras te reposer demain. You'll
be able to have a rest tomorrow.

repousser [29] vb ❶ to grow
again ▷ Ses cheveux ont repoussé.
Her hair has grown again. ❷ to
postpone ▷ Le voyage est repoussé.
The trip's been postponed.

reprendre [66] vb ❶ to take back
▷ Il a repris son livre. He's taken his
book back. ❷ to go back to ▷ Elle
a repris le travail. She went back to
work. ❸ to start again ▷ La réunion
reprendra à deux heures. The meeting
will start again at 2 o'clock.;
reprendre du pain to take more
bread; **reprendre la route** to set
off again; **reprendre son souffle**
to get one's breath back

représentant (f **représentante**)
nm/f rep

représentation nf performance

représenter [29] vb to show ▷ Le
tableau représente un enfant et un
chat. The picture shows a child
with a cat.; **se représenter** to
arise again ▷ Cette occasion ne se
représentera pas. This opportunity
won't arise again.

reproche nm **faire des reproches
à quelqu'un** to reproach
somebody

reprocher [29] vb **reprocher
quelque chose à quelqu'un**
to reproach somebody for

something; **Qu'est-ce que tu lui reproches?** What have you got against him?

reproduction nf reproduction

reproduire [24] vb to reproduce; **se reproduire** to happen again ▷ Je te promets que ça ne se reproduira pas! I promise it won't happen again!

républicain, e adj republican

république nf republic

répugnant, e adj repulsive

réputation nf reputation

requin nm shark

RER nm Greater Paris high-speed train service

réseau (pl réseaux) nm network

réservation nf reservation

réserve nf stock; **mettre quelque chose en réserve** to put something aside

réservé, e adj reserved

réserver [29] vb ❶ to reserve ▷ Cette table est réservée. This table is reserved. ❷ to book ▷ Nous avons réservé une chambre. We've booked a room. ❸ to save ▷ Je t'ai réservé une part de gâteau. I've saved you a piece of cake.

réservoir nm petrol tank

résidence nf block of flats; **une résidence secondaire** a second home

résistant, e adj ❶ hard-wearing ❷ robust

résister [29] vb to resist

résolu vb see **résoudre**

résoudre [71] vb to solve

respect nm respect

respecter [29] vb to respect

respiration nf breathing

respirer [29] vb to breathe

responsabilité nf responsibility

responsable adj responsible ▷ être responsable de quelque chose to be responsible for something
▶ nmf ❶ person in charge ❷ person responsible

ressembler [29] vb **ressembler à** (1) to look like ▷ Elle ne ressemble pas à sa sœur. She doesn't look like her sister. (2) to be like ▷ Ça ressemble à un conte de fées. It's like a fairy tale.; **se ressembler** (1) to look alike ▷ Les deux frères ne se ressemblent pas. The two brothers don't look alike. (2) to be alike ▷ Ces deux pays ne se ressemblent pas. These two countries aren't alike.

ressort nm (metal) spring

ressortir [80] vb to go out again

restaurant nm restaurant

reste nm rest; **un reste de poulet** some left-over chicken; **les restes** the left-overs

rester [72] vb ❶ to stay ▷ Je reste à la maison ce week-end. I'm staying at home this weekend. ❷ to be left ▷ Il reste du pain. There's some bread left.; **Il ne me reste plus qu'à ...** I've just got to ... ▷ Il ne me reste plus qu'à ranger mes affaires. I've just got to put my things away.; **Restons-en là.** Let's leave it at that.

résultat nm result

résumé nm summary

résumer [29] vb to summarize
  ▌ Be careful! **résumer** does not mean **to resume**.

a
b
c
d
e
f
g
h
i
j
k
l
m
n
o
p
q
r
s
t
u
v
w
x
y
z

se **rétablir** [39] *vb* to get well

retard *nm* delay; **avoir du retard** to be late; **être en retard de deux heures** to be two hours late; **prendre du retard** to be delayed

retarder [29] *vb* **❶** to be slow ▷ *Ma montre retarde.* My watch is slow. **❷** to put back ▷ *Je dois retarder la pendule d'une heure.* I've got to put the clock back an hour.; **être retardé** to be delayed

retenir [84] *vb* **❶** to remember ▷ *Tu as retenu leur adresse?* Do you remember their address? **❷** to book ▷ *J'ai retenu une chambre à l'hôtel.* I've booked a room at the hotel.; **retenir son souffle** to hold one's breath

retenu, e *adj* **❶** reserved ▷ *Cette place est retenue.* This seat is reserved. **❷** held up

retenue *nf* detention

retirer [29] *vb* **❶** to withdraw ▷ *Elle a retiré de l'argent.* She withdrew some money. **❷** to take off ▷ *Il a retiré son pull.* He took off his sweater.

retour *nm* return; **être de retour** to be back

retourner [73] *vb* **❶** to go back ▷ *Est-ce que tu es retourné à Londres?* Have you been back to London? **❷** to turn over ▷ *Elle a retourné la crêpe.* She turned the pancake over.; **se retourner (1)** to turn round ▷ *Janet s'est retournée.* Janet turned round. **(2)** to turn over ▷ *La voiture s'est retournée.* The car turned over.

retraite *nf* **être à la retraite** to be retired; **prendre sa retraite** to retire

retraité, e *adj* retired
▷ *nm/f* pensioner

rétrécir [39] *vb* to shrink ▷ *Son pull a rétréci au lavage.* Her sweater shrank in the wash.; **se rétrécir** to get narrower ▷ *La rue se rétrécit.* The street gets narrower.

retrouver [29] *vb* **❶** to find ▷ *J'ai retrouvé mon portefeuille.* I've found my wallet. **❷** to meet up with ▷ *Je te retrouve au café à trois heures.* I'll meet you at the café at 3 o'clock.; **se retrouver (1)** to meet up ▷ *Ils se sont retrouvés devant le cinéma.* They met up in front of the cinema. **(2)** to find one's way around ▷ *Je n'arrive pas à me retrouver.* I can't find my way around.

rétroviseur *nm* rear-view mirror

réunion *nf* meeting

se **réunir** [39] *vb* to meet ▷ *Ils se sont réunis à cinq heures.* They met at 5 o'clock.

réussi, e *adj* successful; **être réussi** to be a success

réussir [39] *vb* to be successful ▷ *Tous ses enfants ont très bien réussi.* All her children are very successful.; **réussir à faire quelque chose** to succeed in doing something; **réussir à un examen** to pass an exam

réussite *nf* success

revanche *nf* return match; **prendre sa revanche** to get one's own back; **en revanche** on the other hand

rêve nm dream; **de rêve** fantastic

réveil nm alarm clock; **mettre le réveil à huit heures** to set the alarm for eight o'clock

réveille-matin (pl **réveille-matin**) nm alarm clock

réveiller [29] vb to wake up ▷ *réveiller quelqu'un* to wake somebody up; **se réveiller** to wake up

réveillon nm **le réveillon du premier de l'an** New Year's Eve celebrations; **le réveillon de Noël** Christmas Eve celebrations

réveillonner [29] vb ❶ to celebrate New Year's Eve ❷ to celebrate Christmas Eve

revenir [74] vb to come back ▷ *Reviens vite!* Come back soon!; **Je n'en reviens pas!** I can't get over it!; **revenir sur ses pas** to retrace one's steps

revenu nm income

rêver [29] vb to dream; **rêver de quelque chose** to dream of something

réverbère nm street lamp

revers nm ❶ backhand ❷ (of jacket) lapel; **le revers de la médaille** the other side of the coin

revient vb see **revenir**

réviser [29] vb ❶ to revise ▷ *Je dois réviser mon anglais.* I've got to revise my English. ❷ to service ▷ *Je dois faire réviser ma voiture.* I must have my car serviced.

révision nf revision

revoir [93] vb ❶ to see again ▷ *J'ai revu Sophie hier soir.* I saw Sophie again last night. ❷ to revise ▷ *Il est en train de revoir sa géographie.* He's revising his geography.; **au revoir** goodbye

révolution nf revolution

revolver nm revolver

revue nf magazine

rez-de-chaussée nm ground floor

Rhin nm Rhine

rhinocéros nm rhinoceros

Rhône nm Rhone

rhubarbe nf rhubarb

rhum nm rum

rhume nm cold; **un rhume de cerveau** a head cold; **le rhume des foins** hay fever

ri vb see **rire**; **Nous avons bien ri.** We had a good laugh.

riche adj ❶ well-off ❷ rich

rideau (pl **rideaux**) nm curtain

ridicule adj ridiculous

rien pron ❶ nothing ▷ *Qu'est-ce que tu as acheté? — Rien.* What have you bought? — Nothing. ▷ *Ça n'a rien à voir.* It has nothing to do with it.; **rien d'intéressant** nothing interesting; **rien d'autre** nothing else; **rien du tout** nothing at all ❷ anything ▷ *Il n'a rien dit.* He didn't say anything.; **rien que** (1) just ▷ *rien que pour lui faire plaisir* just to please him (2) nothing but ▷ *rien que la vérité* nothing but the truth; **De rien!** Not at all! ▷ *Merci beaucoup! — De rien!* Thank you very much! — Not at all!

▶ *nm* **pour un rien** at the slightest thing; **en un rien de temps** in no time at all

rigoler [29] *vb* ① (informal) to laugh ▷ *Elle a rigolé en le voyant tomber.* She laughed when she saw him fall. ▷ *On a bien rigolé hier soir.* We had good fun last night. ② to be joking ▷ *Ne te fâche pas, je rigolais.* Don't get upset, I was only joking.; **pour rigoler** for a laugh

rigolo (*f* **rigolote**) *adj* (informal) funny

rincer [13] *vb* to rinse

rire [75] *vb* to laugh ▷ *Nous avons bien ri.* We had a good laugh.; **pour rire** for a laugh
▶ *nm* laughter

risque *nm* ① risk ② danger

risqué, e *adj* risky

risquer [29] *vb* to risk; **Ça ne risque rien.** It's quite safe.; **Il risque de se tuer.** He could get himself killed.; **C'est ce qui risque de se passer.** That's what might well happen.

rivage *nm* shore

rivière *nf* river

riz *nm* rice

RMI *nm* Income Support

RN *nf* (= route nationale) A road

robe *nf* dress; **une robe de soirée** an evening dress; **une robe de mariée** a wedding dress; **une robe de chambre** a dressing gown

robinet *nm* tap

robot *nm* robot

roche *nf* (stone) rock

rocher *nm* rock

rock *nm* (music) rock

rôder [29] *vb* to loiter ▷ *Il y a un homme louche qui rôde autour de l'école.* There's a suspicious man loitering around the school.

rognons *nmpl* (in cooking) kidneys

roi *nm* king; **le jour des Rois** Twelfth Night

rôle *nm* role

rollers *nmpl* Rollerblades®

romain, e *adj* Roman

roman *nm* novel; **un roman policier** a detective story; **un roman d'espionnage** a spy story

romancier *nm* novelist

romantique *adj* romantic

rompre [76] *vb* ① to split up ▷ *Paul et Justine ont rompu.* Paul and Justine have split up. ② to break off ▷ *Ils ont rompu leurs fiançailles.* They've broken off their engagement.

ronces *nfpl* brambles

ronchonner [29] *vb* (informal) to grouse

rond, e *adj* ① round ▷ *La Terre est ronde.* The Earth is round.; **ouvrir des yeux ronds** to stare in amazement ② chubby ▷ *Il a les joues rondes.* He has chubby cheeks. ③ (informal) drunk
▶ *nm* circle; **en rond** in a circle; **tourner en rond** to go round in circles; **Je n'ai plus un rond.** (informal) I haven't a penny left.

rondelle *nf* slice

rond-point (*pl* **ronds-points**) *nm* roundabout

ronfler [29] vb to snore

rosbif nm roast beef

rose nf rose
  ▶ adj pink

rosé nm rosé (wine)

rosier nm rosebush

rôti nm roast meat; **un rôti de bœuf** a joint of beef

rôtir [39] vb to roast ▷ faire rôtir quelque chose to roast something

roue nf wheel ▷ une roue de secours a spare wheel

rouge adj red
  ▶ nm ① red ▷ Le rouge est ma couleur préférée. Red is my favourite colour. ② red wine; **passer au rouge (1)** to change to red ▷ Le feu est passé au rouge. The light changed to red. **(2)** to go through a red light ▷ Il est passé au rouge. He went through a red light.; **un rouge à lèvres** a lipstick

  Word for word, the French means "red for lips".

rougeole nf measles

rougir [39] vb ① to blush ▷ Il a rougi en me voyant. He blushed when he saw me. ② to flush ▷ Il a rougi de colère. He flushed with anger.

rouille nf rust

rouillé, e adj rusty

rouiller [29] vb to go rusty

roulant, e adj **un fauteuil roulant** a wheelchair; **une table roulante** a trolley

rouleau (pl rouleaux) nm roll; **un rouleau à pâtisserie** a rolling pin

rouler [29] vb ① to go ▷ Le train roulait à 250 km/h. The train was going at 250 km an hour. ② to drive ▷ Il a roulé sans s'arrêter. He drove without stopping. ③ to roll ▷ Gilles a roulé une cigarette. Gilles rolled a cigarette. ④ to roll up ▷ Il a roulé le tapis. He rolled the carpet up. ⑤ (informal) to con ▷ Ils se sont fait rouler. They were conned.; **Alors, ça roule?** (informal) How's it going?

Roumanie nf Romania

rouquin (f rouquine) nm/f (informal) redhead

rousse adj, nf see **roux**

route nf ① road; **une route nationale** an A road ② way ▷ Je ne connais pas la route. I don't know the way.; **Il y a trois heures de route.** It's a 3-hour journey.; **en route** on the way; **mettre en route** to start up; **se mettre en route** to set off

routier nm ① lorry driver ② transport café

routine nf routine

roux (f rousse) adj ① red ② red-haired
  ▶ nm/f redhead

royal, e (mpl royaux) adj royal

royaume nm kingdom; **le Royaume-Uni** the United Kingdom

ruban nm ribbon; **le ruban adhésif** adhesive tape

rubéole nf German measles

ruche nf hive

rudement adv (informal) terribly

rue nf street

ruelle nf alley

rugby nm rugby

rugueux (f **rugueuse**) adj rough

ruine nf ruin

ruiner [29] vb to ruin

ruisseau (pl **ruisseaux**) nm stream

rumeur nf rumour

rupture nf break-up

ruse nf trickery

rusé, e adj cunning

russe adj Russian
> ▶ nm Russian ▷ Il parle russe. He speaks Russian.
> ▶ nm/f un **Russe** (man) a Russian; une **Russe** (woman) a Russian; les **Russes** the Russians

Russie nf Russia

rythme nm ❶ rhythm ❷ pace

S

s' pron see **se**

sa adj ❶ his ▷ Paul est allé voir sa grand-mère. Paul's gone to see his grandmother. ❷ her ▷ Elle a embrassé sa mère. She kissed her mother. ❸ its ▷ Remets la télécommande à sa place. Put the remote control back in its place.

sable nm sand; des **sables mouvants** quicksand

sablé nm shortbread biscuit

sabot nm ❶ clog ❷ (of horse) hoof

sac nm bag; un **sac de voyage** a travel bag; un **sac de couchage** a sleeping bag; un **sac à main** a handbag; un **sac à dos** a rucksack; **voyager sac au dos** to go backpacking

sachet nm (of sugar, coffee) sachet;

du potage en sachet packet soup;
un sachet de thé a tea bag

sacoche nf bag; **une sacoche de
bicyclette** a saddlebag

sacré, e adj sacred

sage adj ❶ (well-behaved) good
❷ (sensible) wise

sagesse nf wisdom; **une dent de
sagesse** a wisdom tooth

Sagittaire nm Sagittarius

saignant, e adj (meat) rare

saigner [29] vb to bleed; **saigner
du nez** to have a nosebleed

sain, e adj healthy; **sain et sauf**
safe and sound

saint, e adj holy; **la Sainte Vierge**
the Blessed Virgin; **le vendredi
saint** Good Friday; **la Saint-
Sylvestre** New Year's Eve
▶ nm/f saint
- Every day on a French calendar
  belongs to a saint. On March
- 15th, St Louise's day, people say
  "Bonne fête Louise!" to anyone
- with that name. Girls called
- Louise might get presents too.

sais vb see **savoir**; **Je ne sais pas.**
I don't know.

saisir [39] vb to take hold of; **saisir
l'occasion de faire quelque chose**
to seize the opportunity to do
something

saison nf season; **la saison des
vendanges** harvest time

sait vb see **savoir**; **Il sait que ...** He
knows that ...; **On ne sait jamais!**
You never know!

salade nf ❶ lettuce ❷ salad

saladier nm salad bowl

salaire nm salary

salami nm salami

salarié (f salariée) nm/f salaried
employee

salaud nm (rude) bastard

sale adj dirty

salé, e adj ❶ salty ❷ salted
❸ savoury

saler [29] vb to put salt in ▷ J'ai
oublié de saler la soupe. I forgot to
put salt in the soup.

saleté nf dirt; **faire des saletés** to
make a mess

salir [39] vb **salir quelque chose** to
get something dirty; **se salir** to get
oneself dirty

salle nf ❶ room ❷ (in hospital)
ward; **la salle à manger** the
dining room; **la salle de séjour**
the living room; **la salle de bains**
the bathroom; **la salle d'attente**
the waiting room; **une salle de
classe** a classroom; **la salle des
professeurs** the staffroom; **une
salle de concert** a concert hall;
la salle d'embarquement the
departure lounge

salon nm lounge; **un salon de thé**
a tearoom; **un salon de coiffure** a
hair salon; **un salon de beauté** a
beauty salon

salope nf (rude) bitch

salopette nf ❶ dungarees
❷ overalls

saluer [29] vb **saluer quelqu'un**
(1) to say hello to somebody ▷ Je l'ai
croisé dans la rue et il m'a salué. I met
him in the street and he said hello.
(2) to say goodbye to somebody

a
b
c
d
e
f
g
h
i
j
k
l
m
n
o
p
q
r
s
t
u
v
w
x
y
z

▷ *Il nous a salués et il est parti.* He said goodbye and left.

salut *excl* (informal) Hi!

salutation *nf* greeting

samedi *nm* ❶ Saturday
▷ *Aujourd'hui, nous sommes samedi.* It's Saturday today. ❷ on Saturday; **le samedi** on Saturdays; **tous les samedis** every Saturday; **samedi dernier** last Saturday; **samedi prochain** next Saturday

SAMU *nm* ambulance service

sandale *nf* sandal

sandwich *nm* sandwich

sang *nm* blood; **en sang** covered in blood

sang-froid *nm* **garder son sang-froid** to keep calm; **perdre son sang-froid** to lose one's cool; **faire quelque chose de sang-froid** to do something in cold blood

sanglier *nm* wild boar

sanglot *nm* **éclater en sanglots** to burst into tears

sans *prep* without ▷ *Elle est venue sans son frère.* She came without her brother.; **un pull sans manches** a sleeveless sweater

sans-abri (*pl* sans-abri) *nmf* homeless person

sans-gêne *adj* inconsiderate

santé *nf* health; **Santé!** Cheers!

saoudien (*f* saoudienne) *adj* Saudi Arabian
▶ *nm/f* **un Saoudien** (man) a Saudi Arabian; **une Saoudienne** (woman) a Saudi Arabian

sapeur-pompier (*pl* sapeurs-pompiers) *nm* fireman; **les**

sapeurs-pompiers the fire brigade

sapin *nm* fir tree; **un sapin de Noël** a Christmas tree

Sardaigne *nf* Sardinia

sardine *nf* sardine

satellite *nm* satellite

satisfaire [37] *vb* to satisfy

satisfaisant, e *adj* satisfactory

satisfait, e *adj* satisfied

sauce *nf* ❶ sauce ❷ gravy

saucisse *nf* sausage

saucisson *nm* salami

sauf *prep* except ▷ *Tout le monde est venu sauf lui.* Everyone came except him.; **sauf si** unless; **sauf que** except that

saumon *nm* salmon

saur *adj* **un hareng saur** a kipper

saut *nm* jump; **le saut en longueur** the long jump; **le saut en hauteur** the high jump; **le saut à la perche** the pole vault; **le saut à l'élastique** bungee jumping; **un saut périlleux** a somersault

sauter [29] *vb* to jump ▷ *Nous avons sauté par-dessus la barrière.* We jumped over the gate.; **sauter à la corde** to skip (with a rope); **faire sauter quelque chose** to blow something up

sauterelle *nf* grasshopper

sauvage *adj* ❶ wild ▷ *les animaux sauvages* wild animals; **une région sauvage** an unspoiled area ❷ shy ▷ *Il est sauvage.* He's shy.

sauvegarder [29] *vb* (file on computer) to save

sauver [29] *vb* to save; **se sauver** (1) to run away ▷ *Il s'est sauvé à* *toutes jambes.* He ran away as fast as he could. **(2)** (*informal*) to be off ▷ *Allez, je me sauve!* Right, I'm off.

sauvetage *nm* rescue

sauveur *nm* saviour

savais, savait *vb see* **savoir**; *Je ne savais pas qu'il devait venir.* I didn't know he was going to come.

savant *nm* scientist

savent *vb see* **savoir**; *Ils ne savent pas ce qu'ils veulent.* They don't know what they want.

saveur *nf* flavour

savez *vb see* **savoir**; *Est-ce que vous savez où elle habite?* Do you know where she lives?

savoir [77] *vb* to know ▷ *Je ne sais pas où il est allé.* I don't know where he's gone.; *Tu sais nager?* Can you swim?

savon *nm* soap

savonnette *nf* bar of soap

savons *vb see* **savoir**

savoureux (*f* **savoureuse**) *adj* tasty

saxo *nm* ① (*informal*) sax ② sax player
▶ *nf* (*informal*) sax player

scandale *nm* scandal; **faire scandale** to cause a scandal

scandaleux (*f* **scandaleuse**) *adj* outrageous

Scandinave *nmf* Scandinavian

scandinave *adj* Scandinavian

Scandinavie *nf* Scandinavia

scarabée *nm* beetle

scène *nf* ① scene; **une scène de ménage** a domestic row ② stage; **être sur scène** to be on stage

sceptique *adj* sceptical

schéma *nm* diagram

schématique *adj* l'explication schématique d'une théorie the broad outline of a theory; *Cette interprétation est un peu trop schématique.* This interpretation is a bit oversimplified.

scie *nf* saw; **une scie à métaux** a hacksaw

science *nf* science; *Elle est forte en sciences.* She is good at science.; **les sciences physiques** physics; **les sciences naturelles** biology; **les sciences économiques** economics; **sciences po** (*informal*) politics

science-fiction *nf* science fiction

scientifique *adj* scientific
▶ *nf* ① scientist ② science student

scier [20] *vb* to saw

scolaire *adj* school ▷ *l'année scolaire* the school year ▷ *les vacances scolaires* the school holidays

Scorpion *nm* Scorpio

Scotch® *nm* adhesive tape

scrupule *nm* scruple

sculpter [29] *vb* to sculpt

sculpteur *nm* sculptor

sculpture *nf* sculpture

SDF *nmf* (= *sans domicile fixe*) homeless person; **les SDF** the homeless

se *pron*

se forms part of reflexive constructions.

① himself ▷ *Il se regarde dans la glace.* He's looking at himself in the mirror. ② herself ▷ *Elle se regarde dans la glace.* She's looking

at herself in the mirror. ❸ itself
▷ Le chien s'est fait mal. The dog
hurt itself. ❹ oneself ▷ se regarder
dans une glace to look at oneself in
a mirror ❺ themselves ▷ Ils se sont
regardés dans la glace. They looked
at themselves in the mirror.

> se changes to s' before a vowel
> and most words beginning
> with "h".

▷ Elle s'admire dans sa nouvelle robe.
She's admiring herself in her new
dress. ❻ each other ▷ Ils s'aiment.
They love each other.

séance nf ❶ session ❷ (at the
cinema) showing

seau (pl seaux) nm bucket

sec (f sèche) adj ❶ dry ❷ dried

sèche-cheveux (pl sèche-
cheveux) nm hair dryer

sèche-linge (pl sèche-linge) nm
tumble dryer

sécher [35] vb ❶ to dry
❷ (informal) to be stumped ▷ J'ai
complètement séché à l'interrogation
de maths. I was completely
stumped in the maths test.; **se
sécher** to dry oneself ▷ Sèche-toi
avec cette serviette. Dry yourself
with this towel.

sécheresse nf drought

séchoir nm dryer

second, e adj second
▶ nm second floor
▶ nf ❶ second ❷ year 11
⦿ In French secondary schools,
⦿ years are counted from the
⦿ **sixième** (youngest) to **première**
⦿ and **terminale** (oldest).

▷ Ma sœur est en seconde. My sister's
in year 11. ❷ second class ▷ voyager
en seconde to travel second-class

secondaire adj secondary; **des
effets secondaires** side effects

secouer [29] vb to shake ▷ secouer
la tête to shake one's head

secourir [17] vb to rescue

secourisme nm first aid

secours nm help ▷ Au secours!
Help!; **les premiers secours**
first aid; **une sortie de secours**
an emergency exit; **la roue de
secours** the spare wheel

secret nm secret
▶ adj (f secrète) secret

secrétaire nm ❶ secretary
❷ writing desk
▶ nf secretary

secrétariat nm secretary's office

secteur nm sector

section nf (of school) department

sécu nf (informal) Social Security

sécurité nf ❶ safety; **être en
sécurité** to be safe; **la sécurité
routière** road safety; **une ceinture
de sécurité** a seatbelt ❷ security;
la sécurité sociale Social Security;
la sécurité de l'emploi job security

séduisant, e adj attractive

seigle nm rye

seigneur nm lord; **le Seigneur**
the Lord

sein nm breast; **au sein de** within

seize num sixteen ▷ Elle a seize ans.
She's sixteen.; **le seize février** the
sixteenth of February

seizième adj sixteenth

séjour nm stay ▷ J'ai fait un séjour

d'une semaine en Italie. I stayed in Italy for a week.

sel nm salt

sélectionner [29] vb to select

self nm (informal) self-service restaurant

self-service nm self-service restaurant

selle nf saddle

selon prep according to ▷ *selon lui* according to him

semaine nf week; **en semaine** on weekdays

semblable adj similar

semblant nm **faire semblant de faire quelque chose** to pretend to do something

sembler [29] vb to seem ▷ *Le temps semble s'améliorer.* The weather seems to be improving.

semelle nf ❶ sole ❷ insole

semoule nf semolina

sens nm ❶ sense ▷ *avoir le sens de l'humour* to have a sense of humour; **le bon sens** common sense ❷ direction; **sens dessus dessous** upside down; **un sens interdit** a one-way street; **un sens unique** a one-way street

sensation nf feeling

sensationnel (f **sensationnelle**) adj sensational

sensé, e adj sensible

sensible adj ❶ sensitive ❷ visible

Be careful! The French word **sensible** does not mean **sensible**.

sensiblement adv ❶ visibly ❷ approximately

sentence nf (judgement) sentence

sentier nm path

sentiment nm feeling

sentimental, e (mpl **sentimentaux**) adj sentimental

sentir [78] vb ❶ to smell ▷ *Ça sent bon.* That smells good. ▷ *Ça sent mauvais.* It smells bad. ❷ to smell of ▷ *Ça sent les frites ici.* It smells of chips in here. ❸ to taste ▷ *Tu sens l'ail dans le rôti?* Can you taste the garlic in the roast? ❹ to feel ▷ *Je n'ai rien senti.* I didn't feel a thing. ▷ *Je ne me sens pas bien.* I don't feel well.; **Il ne peut pas la sentir.** (informal) He can't stand her.

séparé, e adj separated

séparément adv separately

séparer [29] vb to separate; **se séparer** to separate

sept num seven ▷ *Elle a sept ans.* She's seven.; **le sept février** the seventh of February

septembre nm September; **en septembre** in September

septième adj seventh

sera, serai, seras, serez vb see **être**; **Je serai de retour à dix heures.** I'll be back at 10 o'clock.

série nf series

sérieusement adv seriously

sérieux (f **sérieuse**) adj ❶ serious ❷ responsible

▶ nm **garder son sérieux** to keep a straight face; **prendre quelque chose au sérieux** to take something seriously; **prendre quelqu'un au sérieux** to take somebody seriously; **Il manque**

un peu de sérieux. He's not very
responsible.

seringue nf syringe

séronégatif (f**séronégative**) adj
HIV-negative

serons, seront vb see **être**

séropositif (f**séropositive**) adj
HIV-positive

serpent nm snake

serre nf greenhouse; **l'effet de
serre** the greenhouse effect

serré, e adj tight ▷ Mon pantalon est
trop serré. My trousers are too tight.

serrer [29] vb Ce pantalon me
serre trop. These trousers are too
tight for me.; **serrer la main à
quelqu'un** to shake hands with
somebody; **se serrer** to squeeze
up ▷ Serrez-vous un peu pour que je
puisse m'asseoir. Squeeze up a bit so
I can sit down.; **serrer quelqu'un
dans ses bras** to hug somebody;
"Serrer à droite" "Keep right"

serrure nf lock

sers, sert vb see **servir**

serveur nm ❶ (in café) waiter
❷ (computer) server

serveuse nf waitress

serviable adj helpful

service nm ❶ (in restaurant) service
▷ Le service est compris. Service
is included.; **être de service** to
be on duty; **hors service** out of
order; **faire le service** (at table) to
serve ❷ favour; **rendre service
à quelqu'un** to do somebody a
favour ❸ (sport) serve ▷ Il a un bon
service. He's a good serve.; **le
service militaire** military service;

les **services sociaux** the social
services; les **services secrets** the
secret service

serviette nf ❶ towel; une
serviette hygiénique a sanitary
towel ❷ (napkin) serviette
❸ briefcase

servir [79] vb to serve ▷ On vous
sert? Are you being served?; À
toi de servir. (tennis) It's your
serve.; **se servir** to help oneself
▷ Servez-vous. Help yourself.; **se
servir de** to use ▷ Tu te sers souvent
de ton vélo? Do you use your bike a
lot?; **servir à quelqu'un** to be of
use to somebody; **À quoi ça sert?**
What's it for?; **Ça ne sert à rien.**
It's no use.

ses adj ❶ his ▷ Il est parti voir ses
grands-parents. He's gone to see his
grandparents. ❷ her ▷ Delphine
a oublié ses baskets. Delphine's
forgotten her trainers. ❸ its ▷ la
ville et ses alentours the town and its
surroundings

set nm ❶ (on table) tablemat ❷ (in
tennis) set

seuil nm doorstep

seul, e adj, adv ❶ alone ❷ by
oneself; **faire quelque chose tout
seul** to do something by oneself;
se sentir seul to feel lonely; **un
seul livre** one book only; **Il reste
une seule nectarine.** There's only
one nectarine left.; **le seul livre
que ...** the only book that ...; **le
seul** the only one

seulement adv only; **non
seulement ..., mais** not only ..., but

sévère adj strict

sexe nm sex

sexuel (f **sexuelle**) adj sexual

shampooing nm shampoo; **se faire un shampooing** to wash one's hair

short nm shorts

si conj, adv ❶ if ▷ si tu veux if you like ▷ si seulement if only ❷ so ▷ Elle est si gentille. She's so kind. ❸ yes ▷ Tu n'es pas allé à l'école habillé comme ça? — Si. You didn't go to school dressed like that? — Yes I did.
▶ nm ❶ B ▷ en si bémol in B flat ❷ ti ▷ la, si, do la, ti, do

Sicile nf Sicily

sida nm AIDS

siècle nm century

siège nm ❶ (in vehicle) seat ❷ head office

sien pron **le sien** (1) his (2) hers

sienne pron **la sienne** (1) his (2) hers

siennes pron **les siennes** (1) his (2) hers

siens pron **les siens** (1) his (2) hers

sieste nf nap

siffler [29] vb to whistle

sifflet nm whistle

sigle nm acronym

signal (pl **signaux**) nm signal

signature nf signature

signe nm sign; **faire un signe de la main** to wave; **faire signe à quelqu'un d'entrer** to beckon to somebody to come in; **les signes du zodiaque** the signs of the zodiac

signer [29] vb to sign

signet nm bookmark

signification nf meaning

signifier [20] vb to mean ▷ Que signifie ce mot? What does this word mean?

silence nm silence; **Silence!** Be quiet!

silencieux (f **silencieuse**) adj ❶ silent ❷ quiet

silhouette nf figure

similaire adj similar

simple adj simple
▶ nm (tennis) singles

simplement adv simply

simuler [29] vb to simulate

simultané, e adj simultaneous

sincère adj sincere

sincèrement adv sincerely

sincérité nf sincerity

singe nm monkey

singulier nm singular

sinistre adj sinister

sinon conj otherwise

sinusite nf sinusitis

sirène nf mermaid; **la sirène d'alarme** the fire alarm

sirop nm syrup; **le sirop contre la toux** cough mixture

site nm setting; **un site pittoresque** a beauty spot; **un site touristique** a tourist attraction; **un site archéologique** an archaeological site; **un site Web** a website

sitôt adv sitôt dit, sitôt fait no sooner said than done; **pas de sitôt** not for a long time

situation nf ❶ situation; **la situation de famille** marital status ❷ job

a
b
c
d
e
f
g
h
i
j
k
l
m
n
o
p
q
r
s
t
u
v
w
x
y
z

se **situer** [29] vb to be situated
▷ *Versailles se situe à l'ouest de Paris.* Versailles is situated to the west of Paris.; **bien situé** well situated

six num six ▷ *Il a six ans.* He's six.; **le six février** the sixth of February

sixième adj sixth ▷ *au sixième étage* on the sixth floor
▶ nf year 7
● In French secondary schools, years are counted from the **sixième** (youngest) to **première** and **terminale** (oldest).
▷ *Mon frère est en sixième.* My brother's in year 7.

ski nm ❶ ski ❷ skiing; **le ski de fond** cross-country skiing; **le ski nautique** water-skiing; **le ski de piste** downhill skiing; **le ski de randonnée** cross-country skiing

skier [20] vb to ski

skieur (f **skieuse**) nm skier

slip nm pants; **un slip de bain** swimming trunks

Slovaquie nf Slovakia

Slovénie nf Slovenia

SMIC nm guaranteed minimum wage

smoking nm dinner suit

SNCF nf (= *Société nationale des chemins de fer français*) French railways

snob adj inv snobbish

sobre adj ❶ sober ❷ plain

social, e (mpl **sociaux**) adj social

socialiste nmf socialist

société nf ❶ society ❷ company

sociologie nf sociology

socquette nf ankle sock

sœur nf sister; **une bonne sœur** (informal) a nun

soi pron oneself ▷ *avoir confiance en soi* to have confidence in oneself; **rester chez soi** to stay at home; **Ça va de soi.** It goes without saying.

soi-disant adv, adj supposedly; **un soi-disant poète** a so-called poet

soie nf silk

soif nf thirst; **avoir soif** to be thirsty

soigner [29] vb (ill person, animal) to look after

soigneux (f **soigneuse**) adj careful

soi-même pron oneself ▷ *Il vaut mieux le faire soi-même.* It's better to do it oneself.

soin nm care; **prendre soin de quelque chose** to take care of something

soins nmpl treatment; **les premiers soins** first aid; **"aux bons soins de Madame Martin"** (on letter) "c/o Mrs Martin"

soir nm evening; **à sept heures du soir** at 7 p.m.; **demain soir** tomorrow night; **hier soir** last night

soirée nf evening

sois vb see **être**; **Sois tranquille!** Be quiet!

soit conj soit ..., soit ... either ... or ... ▷ *soit lundi, soit mardi* either Monday or Tuesday

soixantaine nf about sixty; **Elle a la soixantaine.** She's in her sixties.

soixante num sixty; **soixante et onze** seventy-one; **soixante-quinze** seventy-five

soixante-dix num seventy

soja nm soya; **des germes de soja** beansprouts

sol nm ❶ floor; **à même le sol** on the floor ❷ soil ❸ G ⊳ sol dièse G sharp ❹ so ⊳ do, ré, mi, fa, sol ... do, re, mi, fa, so ...

solaire adj solar; **la crème solaire** sun cream

soldat nm soldier

solde nm **être en solde** to be reduced; **les soldes** the sales ⊳ faire les soldes to go round the sales

soldé, e adj **être soldé(e)** to be reduced

sole nf (fish) sole

soleil nm sun; **Il y a du soleil.** It's sunny.

solfège nm musical theory

solidaire adj **être solidaire de quelqu'un** to back somebody up

solide adj ❶ (person) strong ❷ (object) solid

solitaire adj solitary
▶ nmf loner

solitude nf loneliness

solution nf solution; **une solution de facilité** an easy way out

sombre adj dark

sommaire nm summary

somme nf sum
▶ nm nap

sommeil nm sleep; **avoir sommeil** to be sleepy

sommes vb see **être**; **Nous sommes en vacances.** We're on holiday.

sommet nm summit

somnifère nm sleeping pill

somptueux (f **somptueuse**) adj sumptuous

son (f **sa**, pl **ses**) adj ❶ his ⊳ son père his father ❷ her ⊳ son père her father ❸ its ⊳ Le chien est dans son panier. The dog is in its basket.
▶ nm ❶ sound ⊳ baisser le son to turn the sound down ❷ bran; **le pain de son** brown bread

sondage nm survey; **un sondage d'opinion** an opinion poll

sonner [29] vb to ring ⊳ Le téléphone a sonné. The phone rang.

sonnerie nf (electric) bell

sonnette nf bell

sono nf (informal) sound system

sont vb see **être**; **Ils sont en vacances.** They're on holiday.

sophistiqué, e adj sophisticated

sorcière nf witch

sort nm ❶ spell; **un mauvais sort** a curse ❷ fate; **tirer au sort** to draw lots

sorte nf sort

sortie nf way out; **la sortie de secours** the emergency exit; **Attends-moi à la sortie de l'école.** Meet me after school.

sortir [80] vb ❶ to go out ⊳ J'aime sortir. I like going out. ❷ to come out ⊳ Elle sort de l'hôpital demain. She's coming out of hospital tomorrow. ❸ to take out ⊳ Je vais sortir la voiture du garage. I'll get the car out of the garage.; **sortir avec quelqu'un** to be going out with somebody ⊳ Tu sors avec lui? Are you going out with him?; **s'en**

sortir to manage ▷ *Ne t'en fais pas, tu t'en sortiras.* Don't worry, you'll manage OK.

sottise *nf* **Ne fais pas de sottises.** Don't do anything silly.; **Ne dis pas de sottises.** Don't talk nonsense.

sou *nm* **une machine à sous** a fruit machine; **Je n'ai pas un sou sur moi.** I haven't got a penny on me.; **être près de ses sous** (*informal*) to be tight-fisted

souci *nm* worry; **se faire du souci** to worry

soucieux (*f* **soucieuse**) *adj* worried

soucoupe *nf* saucer; **une soucoupe volante** a flying saucer

soudain, e *adj* sudden
▷ *adv* suddenly

souffle *nm* breath; **à bout de souffle** out of breath

soufflé *nm* soufflé

souffler [29] *vb* ❶ to blow ▷ *Le vent soufflait fort.* The wind was blowing hard. ❷ to blow out ▷ *Souffle les bougies!* Blow out the candles!

souffrance *nf* suffering

souffrant, e *adj* unwell

souffrir [55] *vb* to be in pain

souhait *nm* wish; **Atchoum! — À tes souhaits!** Atchoo! — Bless you!

souhaiter [29] *vb* to wish

soûl, e *adj* (*informal*) drunk

soulager [46] *vb* to relieve

soulever [44] *vb* to lift ▷ *Je n'arrive pas à soulever cette valise.* I can't lift this suitcase.

soulier *nm* shoe

souligner [29] *vb* to underline

soupçon *nm* suspicion; **un soupçon de** a dash of

soupçonner [29] *vb* to suspect

soupe *nf* soup

souper [29] *vb* to have supper

soupir *nm* sigh

soupirer [29] *vb* to sigh

souple *adj* ❶ (*person*) supple ❷ (*system*) flexible

source *nf* spring

sourcil *nm* eyebrow

sourd, e *adj* deaf

souriant, e *adj* cheerful

sourire [75] *vb* to smile ▷ *sourire à quelqu'un* to smile at somebody
▶ *nm* smile

souris *nf* mouse; **la petite souris** the tooth fairy
● French children believe that a
● little mouse (**la petite souris**)
● comes at night to take their
● tooth from under the pillow and
● replace it with money.

sournois, e *adj* sly

sous *prep* under; **sous terre** underground; **sous la pluie** in the rain

sous-entendu, e *adj* implied
▶ *nm* insinuation

sous-marin, e *adj* underwater
▶ *nm* submarine

sous-sol *nm* basement

sous-titre *nm* subtitle

sous-titré, e *adj* with subtitles

soustraction *nf* subtraction

sous-vêtements *nmpl* underwear

soutenir [84] *vb* to support; **soutenir que** to maintain that

souterrain, e adj underground
▶ nm underground passage

soutien nm support

soutien-gorge (pl **soutiens-gorge**) nm bra

souvenir nm ❶ memory
❷ souvenir; **Garde ce livre en souvenir de moi.** Keep the book: it'll remind you of me.

se souvenir [84] vb **se souvenir de quelque chose** to remember something ▷ Je ne me souviens pas de son adresse. I can't remember his address.; **se souvenir que** to remember that ▷ Je me souviens qu'il neigeait. I remember it was snowing.

souvent adv often

soyez, soyons vb see **être**; **Soyons clairs!** Let's be clear about this!

SPA nf (= Société protectrice des animaux) RSPCA

spacieux (f **spacieuse**) adj spacious

spaghettis nmpl spaghetti

spam nm (email) spam

sparadrap nm sticking plaster

speaker (f **speakerine**) nm/f announcer

spécial, e (mpl **spéciaux**) adj
❶ special; **les effets spéciaux** special effects ❷ peculiar

spécialement adv ❶ specially
❷ particularly

se spécialiser [29] vb **se spécialiser dans quelque chose** to specialize in something

spécialiste nmf specialist

spécialité nf speciality

spécifier [20] vb to specify

spectacle nm show

spectaculaire adj spectacular

spectateur (f **spectatrice**) nm/f
❶ member of the audience
❷ spectator

spéléologie nf potholing

spirituel (f **spirituelle**) adj
❶ spiritual ❷ witty

splendide adj magnificent

spontané, e adj spontaneous

sport nm sport; **les sports d'hiver** winter sports
▶ adj inv casual

sportif (f **sportive**) adj ❶ sporty
▷ Elle est très sportive. She's very sporty. ❷ sports ▷ un club sportif a sports club
▶ nm sportsman
▶ nf sportswoman

spot nm spotlight; **un spot publicitaire** a commercial break

square nm public gardens

squelette nm skeleton

SRAS nm (= syndrome respiratoire aigu sévère) SARS

stable adj stable; **un emploi stable** a steady job

stade nm stadium

stage nm ❶ training course
❷ work experience; **faire un stage en entreprise** to do a work placement

⎸ Be careful! The French word
⎸ stage does not mean stage.

stagiaire nmf trainee
▶ adj trainee ▷ un professeur stagiaire a trainee teacher

stand nm ❶ (at exhibition) stand ❷ (at fair) stall

standardiste nmf operator

station nf une station de métro an underground station; une station de taxis a taxi rank; une station de ski a ski resort

stationnement nm parking; "stationnement interdit" "no parking"

stationner [29] vb to park

station-service (pl stations-service) nf service station

statistique nf statistic

steak nm steak; un steak frites steak and chips; un steak haché a hamburger

sténo nf shorthand

sténodactylo nf shorthand typist

stérile adj sterile

stimulant, e adj stimulating

stimuler [29] vb to stimulate

stop nm stop sign; faire du stop to hitchhike

stopper [29] vb to stop

store nm ❶ (on window) blind ❷ awning

strapontin nm foldaway seat

stratégie nf strategy

stratégique adj strategic

stressant, e adj stressful

stressé, e adj stressed out

strict, e adj ❶ (person) strict ❷ (clothes) severe; le strict minimum the bare minimum

strophe nf stanza

studieux (f studieuse) adj studious

studio nm ❶ studio flat ❷ studio

stupéfait, e adj astonished

stupéfiants nmpl narcotics

stupéfier [20] vb to astonish
▷ Sa réponse m'a stupéfié. I was astonished by his answer.

stupide adj stupid

style nm style

styliste nmf designer

stylo nm pen; un stylo plume a fountain pen; un stylo bille a ballpoint pen; un stylo-feutre a felt-tip pen

su vb see savoir; Si j'avais su ... If I'd known ...

subir [39] vb (defeat) to suffer; subir une opération to have an operation

subit, e adj sudden

subitement adv suddenly

subjectif (f subjective) adj subjective

subjonctif nm subjunctive

substituer [29] vb to substitute
▷ substituer un mot à un autre to substitute one word for another

subtil, e adj subtle

subvention nf subsidy

subventionner [29] vb to subsidize

succès nm success ▷ avoir du succès to be successful

successeur nm successor

succursale nf (of company) branch

sucer [13] vb to suck

sucette nf lollipop

sucre nm sugar; un sucre a sugar-lump; du sucre en morceaux lump sugar; un sucre d'orge a barley sugar; du sucre en poudre caster sugar; **du sucre glace** icing sugar

sucré, e adj ❶ sweet ❷ sweetened

sucreries nfpl sweet things

sucrier nm sugar bowl

sud nm south; **vers le sud** southwards; **au sud de Paris** south of Paris; **l'Amérique du Sud** South America; **le vent du sud** the south wind
▶ adj inv ❶ south; **le pôle sud** the South Pole ❷ southern

sud-africain, e adj South African

sud-américain, e adj South American

sud-est nm south-east

sud-ouest nm south-west

Suède nf Sweden

suédois, e adj Swedish
▶ nm Swedish ▷ **Ils parlent suédois.** They speak Swedish.
▶ nm/f **un Suédois** (man) a Swede; **une Suédoise** (woman) a Swede; **les Suédois** the Swedes

suer [29] vb to sweat

sueur nf sweat; **en sueur** sweating

suffire [81] vb to be enough ▷ **Tiens, voilà dix euros. Ça te suffit?** Here's ten euros. Is that enough for you?; **Ça suffit!** That's enough!

suffisamment adv enough

suffisant, e adj sufficient

suffoquer [29] vb to suffocate

suggérer [35] vb to suggest

se suicider [29] vb to commit suicide

suis vb see **être**; **suivre**; **Je suis écossais.** I'm Scottish.; **Suis-moi.** Follow me.

suisse adj Swiss ▷ **le franc suisse** the Swiss franc

Suisse nf Switzerland
▶ nm/f **un Suisse** a Swiss man; **une Suisse** a Swiss woman; **les Suisses** the Swiss

suite nf ❶ rest ❷ (to book, film) sequel; **tout de suite** straightaway; **de suite** in succession; **par la suite** subsequently

suivant, e adj following; **Au suivant!** Next!

suivre [82] vb ❶ to follow ▷ **Il m'a suivie jusque chez moi.** He followed me home. ❷ to do ▷ **Je suis un cours d'anglais à la fac.** I'm doing an English course at uni. ❸ to keep up ▷ **Il n'arrive pas à suivre en maths.** He can't keep up in maths.; **"à suivre"** "to be continued"; **suivre un régime** to be on a diet

sujet nm subject; **au sujet de** about; **un sujet de conversation** a topic of conversation; **un sujet d'examen** an examination question; **un sujet de plaisanterie** something to joke about

super adj inv great
▶ nm (petrol) super

superficiel (f **superficielle**) adj superficial

superflu, e adj superfluous

supérieur, e adj ❶ upper ▷ **la lèvre supérieure** the upper lip ❷ superior ▷ **qualité supérieure** superior quality; **supérieur à** greater than
▶ nm superior

supermarché nm supermarket

superposé, e adj des lits superposés bunk beds

superstitieux (f superstitieuse) adj superstitious

suppléant (f suppléante) nm/f supply teacher

supplément nm payer un supplément to pay an additional charge; **Le vin est en supplément.** Wine is extra.; **un supplément de travail** extra work

supplémentaire adj additional; **faire des heures supplémentaires** to do overtime

supplice nm torture

supplier [20] vb supplier quelqu'un de faire quelque chose to beg somebody to do something ▷ Je t'en supplie! I'm begging you!

supportable adj bearable

supporter [29] vb (tolerate) to stand ▷ Je ne peux pas la supporter. I can't stand her.

> Be careful! **supporter** does not mean to support.

supposer [29] vb to suppose

supprimer [29] vb ❶ to cut ▷ Deux mille emplois ont été supprimés. Two thousand jobs have been cut. ❷ to cancel ▷ Le train de Londres a été supprimé. The train to London has been cancelled. ❸ to get rid of ▷ Ils ont supprimé les témoins gênants. They got rid of the awkward witnesses.

sur prep ❶ on ▷ Pose-le sur la table. Put it down on the table. ❷ in ▷ une personne sur dix 1 person in 10 ❸ out of ▷ J'ai eu onze sur vingt en maths. I got 11 out of 20 in maths. ● Tests and homework are usually marked out of 20 in French schools. ● by ▷ quatre mètres sur deux 4 metres by 2

sûr, e adj ❶ sure ▷ Tu es sûr? Are you sure?; **sûr et certain** absolutely certain ❷ reliable ❸ safe; **sûr de soi** self-confident

sûrement adv certainly

sûreté nf mettre quelque chose en sûreté to put something in a safe place

surf nm surfing

surface nf surface; **les grandes surfaces** the supermarkets

surfer [29] vb to go surfing; **surfer sur le Net** to surf the Net

surgelé, e adj frozen

surgelés nmpl frozen food

surhumain, e adj superhuman

sur-le-champ adv immediately

surlendemain nm le surlendemain de son arrivée two days after he arrived; **le surlendemain dans la matinée** two days later, in the morning

se surmener [44] vb to work too hard

surmonter [49] vb to overcome

surnaturel (f surnaturelle) adj supernatural

surnom nm nickname

surnommer nmf to nickname

surpeuplé, e adj overpopulated

surprenant, e adj surprising

surprendre [66] vb to surprise; surprendre quelqu'un en train

de faire quelque chose to catch somebody doing something

surpris, e adj surprised

surprise nf surprise ▷ **faire une surprise à quelqu'un** to give somebody a surprise

sursauter [29] vb to jump ▷ **J'ai sursauté en entendant mon nom.** I jumped when I heard my name.

surtout adv ❶ especially ❷ above all

surveillant (f **surveillante**) nm/f supervisor

- In French secondary schools, the
- teachers are not responsible for
- supervising the pupils outside
- class. This job is done by people
- called **surveillants** or **pions**.

surveiller [29] vb ❶ to keep an eye on ❷ to keep a watch on ❸ to supervise; **surveiller un examen** to invigilate an exam; **surveiller sa ligne** to watch one's figure

survêtement nm tracksuit

survie nf survival

survivant (f **survivante**) nm/f survivor

survivre [92] vb to survive ▷ **survivre à un accident** to survive an accident

survoler [29] vb to fly over

sus adv **en sus** in addition

susceptible adj touchy

suspect, e adj suspicious

suspecter [29] vb to suspect

suspense nm suspense; **un film à suspense** a thriller

suture nf **un point de suture** a stitch

svelte adj slender

SVP abbr (= **s'il vous plaît**) please

sweat nm sweatshirt

syllabe nf syllable

symbole nm symbol

symbolique adj symbolic

symboliser [29] vb to symbolize

symétrique adj symmetrical

sympa adj inv (informal) nice

sympathie nf **J'ai beaucoup de sympathie pour lui.** I like him a lot.

sympathique adj nice

⬛ Be careful! **sympathique** does not mean **sympathetic**.

sympathiser [29] vb to get on well ▷ **Nous avons immédiatement sympathisé avec nos voisins.** We got on well with our neighbours straight away.

symptôme nm symptom

synagogue nf synagogue

syndicat nm trade union; **le syndicat d'initiative** the tourist information office

synonyme adj synonymous ▷ nm synonym

synthétique adj synthetic

Syrie nf Syria

syrien (f **syrienne**) adj Syrian

systématique adj systematic

système nm system

t

t' pron see te

ta adj your ▷ J'ai vu ta sœur hier. I saw your sister yesterday.

tabac nm ❶ tobacco ❷ smoking ▷ Le tabac est mauvais pour la santé. Smoking is bad for you.

table nf table; **mettre la table** to lay the table; **se mettre à table** to sit down to eat; **À table!** Dinner's ready!; **une table de nuit** a bedside table; **"table des matières"** "contents"

tableau (pl **tableaux**) nm painting; **le tableau d'affichage** the notice board; **le tableau noir** the blackboard

tablette nf **une tablette de chocolat** a bar of chocolate

tableur nm spreadsheet

tablier nm apron

tabouret nm stool

tache nf (stain) mark; **des taches de rousseur** freckles

tâche nf task; **les tâches ménagères** housework

tacher [29] vb to leave a stain

tâcher [29] vb **tâcher de faire quelque chose** to try to do something

tact nm tact

tactique nf tactics; **changer de tactique** to try something different

taie nf **une taie d'oreiller** a pillowcase

taille nf ❶ waist ❷ height ▷ un homme de taille moyenne a man of average height ❸ size ▷ Avez-vous ma taille? Have you got my size?

taille-crayon nm pencil sharpener

tailleur nm ❶ tailor ❷ (lady's) suit; **Il est assis en tailleur.** He's sitting cross-legged.

se taire [83] vb to stop talking; **Taisez-vous!** Be quiet!

talon nm heel

tambour nm drum

Tamise nf Thames

tampon nm pad; **un tampon hygiénique** a tampon

tamponneuse adj **les autos tamponneuses** dodgems

tandis que conj while ▷ Il a toujours de bonnes notes, tandis que les miennes sont mauvaises. He always gets good marks, while mine are poor.

tant adv so much ▷ Je l'aime tant! I love him so much!; **tant de (1)** so

much (2) so many; **tant que**
(1) until (2) while; **tant mieux** so
much the better; **tant pis** never
mind

tante nf aunt

tantôt adv sometimes

tapage nm ❶ racket ❷ fuss

taper [29] vb to beat down ▷ *Le
soleil tape.* The sun's really beating
down.; **taper quelqu'un** to
hit somebody ▷ *Maman, il m'a
tapé!* Mum, he hit me!; **taper
sur quelque chose** to bang on
something; **taper des pieds** to
stamp one's feet; **taper des mains**
to clap one's hands; **taper à la
machine** to type

tapis nm ❶ carpet; **le tapis
roulant** (for people) the Travelator®
❷ (in factory) the conveyer belt
❸ (at baggage reclaim) the carousel;
un tapis de souris a mouse mat

tapisser [29] vb to paper

tapisserie nf ❶ wallpaper
❷ tapestry

taquiner [29] vb to tease

tard adv late; **plus tard** later on;
au plus tard at the latest

tardif (f **tardive**) adj late

tarif nm **le tarif des
consommations** (in café) the price
list; **une communication à tarif
réduit** an off-peak phone call;
un billet de train à tarif réduit
a concessionary train ticket; **un
billet de train à plein tarif** a full-
price train ticket; **Est-ce que vous
faites un tarif de groupe?** Is there
a reduction for groups?

tarte nf tart

tartine nf slice of bread ▷ *une
tartine de confiture* a slice of bread
and jam

tartiner [29] vb to spread; **le
fromage à tartiner** cheese spread

tas nm heap; **un tas de** (informal)
loads of

tasse nf cup

taureau (pl **taureaux**) nm bull;
le Taureau Taurus

taux nm rate

taxe nf tax; **la boutique hors
taxes** the duty-free shop

taxi nm taxi

tchèque adj Czech; **la République
tchèque** the Czech Republic

te pron ❶ you ▷ *Je te vois.* I can
see you.

> **te** changes to **t'** before a vowel
> and most words beginning
> with "h".

▷ *Il t'a vu?* Did he see you? ❷ to you
▷ *Elle t'a parlé?* Did she speak to
you? ❸ yourself ▷ *Tu vas te rendre
malade.* You'll make yourself sick.

> With reflexive verbs, **te** is often
> not translated.

▷ *Comment tu t'appelles?* What's
your name?

technicien (f **technicienne**) nm/f
technician

technique adj technical
▶ nf technique

techno nf techno music

technologie nf technology

teint nm complexion

teinte nf (colour) shade

teinturier nm dry cleaner's

tel (f **telle**) adj Il a un tel enthousiasme! He's got such enthusiasm!; **rien de tel** nothing like; J'ai tout laissé tel quel. I left everything as it was.; **tel que** such as

télé nf telly ▷ à la télé on telly

télécarte nf phonecard

télécharger [46] vb to download

télécommande nf remote control

téléconférence nf video conference

télécopie nf fax

télégramme nm telegram

téléphérique nm cable car

téléphone nm telephone ▷ Elle est au téléphone. She's on the phone.

téléphoner [29] vb to phone ▷ Je vais téléphoner à Claire. I'll phone Claire.

téléréalité nf reality TV

télésiège nm chairlift

téléski nm ski-tow

téléspectateur (f **téléspectatrice**) nm (TV) viewer

téléviseur nm television set

télévision nf television; la télévision en circuit fermé CCTV; la télévision numérique digital TV

telle adj J'ai n'ai jamais eu une telle peur. I've never had such a fright.; **telle que** such as

tellement adv ① so ▷ Andrew est tellement gentil. Andrew's so nice. ② so much ③ so many

telles adj such

tels adj such

témoignage nm testimony

témoigner [29] vb to testify

témoin nm witness

température nf temperature

tempête nf storm

temple nm ① (Protestant) church ② (Hindu, Sikh, Buddhist) temple

temporaire adj temporary

temps nm ① weather ▷ Quel temps fait-il? What's the weather like? ② time ▷ Je n'ai pas le temps. I haven't got time.; **juste à temps** just in time; **de temps en temps** from time to time; **en même temps** at the same time; **à temps** in time; **à plein temps** full time; **à temps complet** full time; **à temps partiel** part time; **dans le temps** at one time ③ (of verb) tense

tenais, tenait vb see **tenir**

tendance nf avoir tendance à faire quelque chose to tend to do something

tendre [89] vb to stretch out ▷ Ils ont tendu une corde entre deux arbres. They stretched out a rope between two trees.; **tendre quelque chose à quelqu'un** to hold something out to somebody; **tendre la main** to hold out one's hand; **tendre le bras** to reach out; **tendre un piège à quelqu'un** to set a trap for someone
▷ adj tender

tendrement adv tenderly

tendresse nf tenderness

tendu, e adj tense

tenir [84] vb to hold ▷ Tu peux tenir la lampe, s'il te plaît? Can you hold the torch, please?; **Tenez votre chien**

en laisse. Keep your dog on the lead.; **tenir à quelqu'un** to be attached to somebody; **tenir à faire quelque chose** to be determined to do something ▷ *Elle tient à y aller.* She's determined to go.; **tenir de quelqu'un** to take after somebody ▷ *Il tient de son père.* He takes after his father.; **Tiens, voilà un stylo.** Here's a pen.; **Tiens, c'est Alain là-bas!** Look, that's Alain over there!; **Tiens?** Really?; **se tenir (1)** to stand ▷ *Il se tenait près de la porte.* He was standing by the door. **(2)** to be held ▷ *La foire va se tenir place du marché.* The fair will be held in the market place.; **se tenir droit (1)** to stand up straight ▷ *Tiens-toi droit!* Stand up straight! **(2)** to sit up straight ▷ *Arrête de manger le nez dans ton assiette, tiens-toi droit.* Don't slouch while you're eating, sit up straight.; **Tiens-toi bien!** Behave yourself!

tennis *nm* ❶ tennis; **le tennis de table** table tennis ❷ tennis court; **les tennis** trainers

tentant, e *adj* tempting

tentation *nf* temptation

tentative *nf* attempt

tente *nf* tent

tenter [29] *vb* to tempt ▷ *J'ai été tenté de tout abandonner.* I was tempted to give up. ▷ *Ça ne me tente vraiment pas d'aller à la piscine.* I don't really fancy going to the swimming pool.; **tenter de faire quelque chose** to try to do something

tenu *vb see* **tenir**

tenue *nf* clothes; **en tenue de soirée** in evening dress

terme *nm* **à court terme** short-term; **à long terme** long-term

terminale *nf* upper sixth ▷ *Je suis en terminale.* I'm in the upper sixth.
▪ In French secondary schools, ▪ years are counted from the ▪ **sixième** (youngest) to **première** ▪ and **terminale** (oldest).

terminer [29] *vb* to finish; **se terminer** to end ▷ *Les vacances se terminent demain.* The holidays end tomorrow.

terminus *nm* terminus

terrain *nm* land; **un terrain de camping** a campsite; **un terrain de football** a football pitch; **un terrain de golf** a golf course; **un terrain de jeu** a playground; **un terrain de sport** a sports ground; **un terrain vague** a piece of waste ground

terrasse *nf* terrace; **Si on s'asseyait en terrasse?** (*at café*) Shall we sit outside?

terre *nf* earth; **la Terre** the Earth; **Elle s'est assise par terre.** She sat on the floor.; **Il est tombé par terre.** He fell down.; **la terre cuite** terracotta; **la terre glaise** clay

terrible *adj* terrible; **pas terrible** (*informal*) nothing special

terrine *nf* pâté

territoire *nm* territory

terrorisé, e *adj* terrified

terrorisme *nm* terrorism

terroriste *nmf* terrorist

a b c d e f g h i j k l m n o p q r s t u v w x y z

tes adj your ▷ J'aime bien tes baskets. I like your trainers.

test nm test

testament nm will

tester [29] vb to test

tétanos nm tetanus

têtard nm tadpole

tête nf head; **se laver la tête** to wash one's hair; **la tête la première** headfirst; **tenir tête à quelqu'un** to stand up to somebody; **faire la tête** to sulk; **en avoir par-dessus la tête** to be fed up

têtu, e adj stubborn

texte nm text

TGV nm (= train à grande vitesse) high-speed train

thé nm tea

théâtre nm theatre; **faire du théâtre** to act

théière nf teapot

thème nm ❶ subject ❷ prose (translation into the foreign language)

théorie nf theory

thermomètre nm thermometer

thon nm tuna

thune nf (informal) dosh

tibia nm ❶ shinbone ❷ shin

tic nm nervous twitch

ticket nm ticket; **le ticket de caisse** the till receipt

tiède adj ❶ (water, air) warm ❷ (food, drink) lukewarm

tien pron **le tien** yours

tienne pron **la tienne** yours; **À la tienne!** Cheers!

tiennes pron **les tiennes** yours

tiens pron **les tiens** yours

tiens, tient vb see tenir

tiers nm third; **le tiers monde** the Third World

tige nf stem

tigre nm tiger

tilleul nm lime tea

timbre nm stamp

timbre-poste nm postage stamp

timide adj shy

timidement adv shyly

timidité nf shyness

tir nm shooting; **le tir à l'arc** archery

tirage nm **par tirage au sort** by drawing lots

tire-bouchon nm corkscrew

tirelire nf money box

tirer [29] vb ❶ to pull ▷ Elle a tiré un mouchoir de son sac. She pulled a handkerchief out of her bag. ▷ "Tirer" "Pull" ❷ to draw; **tirer les rideaux** to draw the curtains; **tirer un trait** to draw a line; **tirer des conclusions** to draw conclusions; **tirer au sort** to draw lots ❸ to fire ▷ Il a tiré sur les policiers. He fired at the police.; **Tu t'en tires bien.** You're doing well.

tiret nm (hyphen) dash

tiroir nm drawer

tisane nf herbal tea

tisser [29] vb to weave

tissu nm material; **un sac en tissu** a cloth bag

titre nm title; **les gros titres** the headlines; **un titre de transport** a travel ticket

tituber [29] vb to stagger

TNT nf (= Télévision numérique terrestre) digital television

toast nm ❶ piece of toast ❷ toast ▷ *porter un toast à quelqu'un* to drink a toast to somebody

toboggan nm slide

toi pron you ▷ *Ça va?* — *Oui, et toi?* How are you? — Fine, and you? ▷ *J'ai faim, pas toi?* I'm hungry, aren't you?; *Assieds-toi.* Sit down.; *C'est à toi de jouer.* It's your turn to play.; *Est-ce que ce stylo est à toi?* Is this pen yours?

toile nf *un pantalon de toile* cotton trousers; *un sac de toile* a canvas bag; *une toile cirée* an oilcloth; *une toile d'araignée* a cobweb

toilette nf wash ▷ *faire sa toilette* to have a wash

toilettes nfpl toilet

toi-même pron yourself ▷ *Tu as fait ça toi-même?* Did you do it yourself?

toit nm roof; *un toit ouvrant* a sunroof

tolérant, e adj tolerant

tolérer [35] vb to tolerate

tomate nf tomato

tombe nf grave

tombeau (pl tombeaux) nm tomb

tombée nf *à la tombée de la nuit* at nightfall

tomber [85] vb to fall ▷ *Attention, tu vas tomber!* Be careful, you'll fall!; *laisser tomber* (1) to drop ▷ *Elle a laissé tomber son stylo.* She dropped her pen. (2) to give up ▷ *Il a laissé tomber le piano.* He gave up the piano. (3) to let down ▷ *Il ne laisse jamais tomber ses amis.* He never

lets his friends down.; **tomber sur quelqu'un** to bump into someone; *Ça tombe bien.* That's lucky.; *Il tombe de sommeil.* He's asleep on his feet.

ton (f ta, pl tes) adj your ▷ *C'est ton stylo?* Is this your pen?
  ▶ nm tone of voice

tonalité nf dialling tone

tondeuse nf lawnmower

tondre [70] vb to mow

tonique adj fortifying

tonne nf tonne

tonneau (pl tonneaux) nm barrel

tonnerre nm thunder

tonus nm *avoir du tonus* to be energetic

torchon nm tea towel

tordre [50] vb *se tordre la cheville* to twist one's ankle

tordu, e adj ❶ bent ❷ crazy ▷ *une histoire complètement tordue* a crazy story

torrent nm mountain stream

torse nm chest

tort nm *avoir tort* to be wrong; *donner tort à quelqu'un* to lay the blame on somebody

torticolis nm stiff neck

tortue nf tortoise

torture nf torture

torturer [29] vb to torture

tôt adv early; *au plus tôt* at the earliest; *tôt ou tard* sooner or later

total, e (mpl totaux) adj total
  ▶ nm (pl totaux) total; *au total* in total

totalement adv totally

totalité | 220

FRENCH > ENGLISH

totalité nf **la totalité des profs** all the teachers; **la totalité du personnel** the entire staff

touchant, e adj touching

toucher [29] vb ❶ to touch ▷ Ne touche pas à mes livres! Don't touch my books!; **Nos deux jardins se touchent.** Our gardens are next to each other. ❷ to feel ▷ Ce pull a l'air doux. Je peux toucher? That sweater looks soft. Can I feel it? ❸ to hit ▷ La balle l'a touché en pleine poitrine. The bullet hit him right in the chest. ❹ to affect ▷ Ces nouvelles réformes ne nous touchent pas. The new reforms don't affect us. ❺ to receive ▷ Il a touché une grosse somme d'argent. He received a large sum of money.

toujours adv ❶ always ▷ Il est toujours très gentil. He's always very nice.; **pour toujours** forever ❷ still ▷ Quand on est revenus, Pierre était toujours là. When we got back Pierre was still there.

toupet nm (informal): **avoir du toupet** to have a nerve

tour nf ❶ tower ▷ la Tour Eiffel the Eiffel Tower ❷ tower block ▶ nm turn ▷ C'est ton tour de jouer. It's your turn to play.; **faire un tour** to go for a walk; **faire un tour en voiture** to go for a drive; **faire un tour à vélo** to go for a ride; **faire le tour du monde** to travel round the world; **à tour de rôle** alternately

tourbillon nm whirlpool

tourisme nm tourism

touriste nm tourist

touristique adj tourist

se **tourmenter** [29] vb to fret

tournant nm ❶ bend ❷ turning point

tournée nf ❶ round ▷ C'est ma tournée. It's my round. ❷ tour ▷ Il est en tournée aux États-Unis. He's on tour in the United States.

tourner [29] vb ❶ to turn ▷ Tournez à droite au prochain feu. Turn right at the lights. ❷ to go sour ▷ Le lait a tourné. The milk's gone sour.; **mal tourner** to go wrong ▷ Ça a mal tourné. It all went wrong.; **tourner le dos à quelqu'un** to have one's back to somebody; **tourner un film** to make a film

tournesol nm sunflower

tournevis nm screwdriver

tournoi nm tournament

tourte nf pie

tous adj, pron see **tout**

Toussaint nf All Saints' Day

tousser [29] vb to cough

tout (mpl **tous**, fpl **toutes**) adj, adv, pron ❶ all ▷ tout le lait all the milk ▷ toute la nuit all night ▷ tous les livres all the books ▷ toute la journée all day ▷ tout le temps all the time ▷ C'est tout. That's all.; **Il est tout seul.** He's all alone.; **pas du tout** not at all; **tout de même** all the same ❷ every ▷ tous les jours every day; **tout le monde** everybody; **tous les deux** both; **tous les trois** all three ❸ everything ▷ Il a tout organisé. He organized everything. ❹ very ▷ Elle habite tout près.

She lives very close.; **tout en haut** right at the top; **tout droit** straight ahead; **tout d'abord** first of all; **tout à coup** suddenly; **tout à fait** absolutely; **tout à l'heure (1)** just now **(2)** in a moment; **À tout à l'heure!** See you later!; **tout de suite** straight away; **Il a fait son travail tout en chantant.** He sang as he worked.

toutefois adv however

toutes adj, pron see **tout**

toux nf cough

toxicomane nmf drug addict

toxicomanie nf drug addiction

TP nm (= travaux pratiques) practical class

trac nm **avoir le trac** to be feeling nervous

tracasser [29] vb to worry ▷ La santé de mon père me tracasse. My dad's health worries me.; **se tracasser** to worry

trace nf ① trace ② mark ▷ des traces de doigts finger marks; **des traces de pas** footprints

tracer [13] vb to draw ▷ tracer un trait to draw a line

tracteur nm tractor

tradition nf tradition

traditionnel (f **traditionnelle**) adj traditional

traducteur (f **traductrice**) nm/f translator

traduction nf translation

traduire [24] vb to translate

trafic nm traffic; **le trafic de drogue** drug trafficking

trafiquant nm **un trafiquant de drogue** a drug trafficker

tragique adj tragic

trahir [39] vb to betray

trahison nf betrayal

train nm train; **un train électrique** a train set; **Il est en train de manger.** He's eating.

traîneau (pl **traîneaux**) nm sledge

traîner [29] vb ① to wander around ▷ J'ai vu des jeunes qui traînaient en ville. I saw some young people wandering around town. ② to hang about ▷ Dépêche-toi, ne traîne pas! Hurry up, don't hang about! ③ to drag on ▷ La réunion a traîné jusqu'à midi. The meeting dragged on till 12 o'clock.; **traîner des pieds** to drag one's feet; **laisser traîner qch** to leave sth lying around

train-train nm humdrum routine

traire [86] vb to milk

trait nm ① line ▷ Tracez un trait. Draw a line. ② feature ▷ Elle a les traits fins. She has delicate features.; **boire quelque chose d'un trait** to drink something down in one gulp; **un trait d'union** a hyphen

traitement nm treatment; **le traitement de texte** word processing

traiter [29] vb to treat; **Il m'a traité d'imbécile.** He called me an idiot.; **traiter de** to be about ▷ Cet article traite des sans-abri. This article is about the homeless.

traiteur nm caterer

trajet nm ❶ journey ▷ J'ai une heure de trajet pour aller au travail. My journey to work takes an hour. ❷ route ▷ C'est le trajet le plus court. It's the shortest route.

tramway nm tram

tranchant, e adj (knife) sharp

tranche nf slice

tranquille adj quiet; **Sois tranquille, il ne va rien lui arriver.** Don't worry, nothing will happen to him.; **Tiens-toi tranquille!** Be quiet!; **Laisse-moi tranquille.** Leave me alone.; **Laisse ça tranquille.** Leave it alone.

tranquillement adv quietly; **Je peux travailler tranquillement cinq minutes?** Can I have five minutes to myself to work in peace?

tranquillité nf peace and quiet

transférer [35] vb to transfer

transformer [29] vb ❶ to transform ❷ to convert ▷ Ils ont transformé la grange en garage. They've converted the barn into a garage.; **se transformer en** to turn into

transfusion nf une transfusion sanguine a blood transfusion

transiger [46] vb to compromise

transmettre [48] vb transmettre quelque chose à quelqu'un to pass something on to somebody

transpercer [13] vb to go through ▷ La pluie a transpercé mes vêtements. The rain went through my clothes.

transpiration nf perspiration

transpirer [29] vb to perspire

transport nm transport; **les transports en commun** public transport

transporter [29] vb ❶ to carry ▷ Le train transportait des marchandises. The train was carrying freight. ❷ to move ▷ Je ne sais pas comment je vais transporter mes affaires. I don't know how I'm going to move my stuff.

traumatiser [29] vb to traumatize

travail (pl **travaux**) nm ❶ work ▷ J'ai beaucoup de travail. I've got a lot of work. ❷ job ▷ Il a un travail intéressant. He's got an interesting job.; **Il est sans travail depuis un an.** He has been out of work for a year.; **le travail au noir** moonlighting

travailler [29] vb to work

travailleur (f **travailleuse**) adj hard-working

▶ nm/f worker

travaillistes nmpl the Labour Party

travaux nmpl ❶ work ▷ des travaux de construction building work ❷ roadworks; **être en travaux** to be undergoing alterations; **les travaux dirigés** supervised practical work; **les travaux manuels** handicrafts; **les travaux ménagers** housework; **les travaux pratiques** practical work

travers nm **en travers de** across; **de travers** crooked; **comprendre de travers** to misunderstand; **J'ai avalé de travers.** Something went down the wrong way.; **à travers** through

traversée nf crossing

traverser [29] vb ❶ to cross
▷ *Traversez la rue.* Cross the street.
❷ to go through ▷ *Nous avons traversé la France pour aller en Espagne.* We went through France on the way to Spain.

traversin nm bolster

trébucher [29] vb to trip up

trèfle nm ❶ clover ❷ (at cards) clubs

treize num thirteen ▷ *Il a treize ans.* He's thirteen.; **le treize février** the thirteenth of February

treizième adj thirteenth

tréma nm diaeresis

tremblement de terre nm earthquake

trembler [29] vb to shake
▷ *trembler de peur* to shake with fear; **trembler de froid** to shiver

trempé, e adj soaking wet;
trempé jusqu'aux os soaked to the skin

tremper [29] vb to soak; **tremper sa main dans l'eau** to dip one's hand in the water

tremplin nm springboard

trentaine nf about thirty; **Il a la trentaine.** He's in his thirties.

trente num thirty; **le trente janvier** the thirtieth of January;
trente et un thirty-one; **trente-deux** thirty-two

trentième adj thirtieth

très adv very

trésor nm treasure

tresse nf plait

triangle nm triangle

tribu nf tribe

tribunal (pl **tribunaux**) nm court

tricher [29] vb to cheat

tricolore adj three-coloured; **le drapeau tricolore** the French tricolour

- le drapeau tricolore is the French flag which is blue, white and red.

tricot nm ❶ knitting ❷ sweater

tricoter [29] vb to knit

trier [20] vb to sort out

trimestre nm term

trinquer [29] vb to clink glasses

triomphe nm triumph

triompher [29] vb to triumph

tripes nfpl tripe

triple nm **Ça m'a coûté le triple.**
It cost me three times as much.; **Il gagne le triple de mon salaire.** He earns three times my salary.

tripler [29] vb to treble

triplés nmpl triplets

triste adj sad

tristesse nf sadness

trognon nm core

trois num three ▷ *Elle a trois ans.*
She's three.; **le trois février** the third of February

troisième adj third
▶ nf year 10
- In French secondary schools, years are counted from the **sixième** (youngest) to **première** and **terminale** (oldest).
▷ *Mon frère est en troisième.* My brother's in year 10.

trois-quarts nmpl three-quarters
trombone nm ❶ trombone
❷ paper clip
trompe nf trunk
tromper [29] vb to deceive; **se tromper** to make a mistake; **se tromper de jour** to get the wrong day; **Vous vous êtes trompé de numéro.** You've got the wrong number.
trompette nf trumpet; **Il a le nez en trompette.** He's got a turned-up nose.
tronc nm trunk
trop adv ❶ too ▷ **Il conduit trop vite.** He drives too fast. ❷ too much ▷ **J'ai trop mangé.** I've eaten too much.; **trop de (1)** too much **(2)** too many; **trois personnes de trop** 3 people too many
tropique nm tropic
trottoir nm pavement
trou nm hole; **J'ai eu un trou de mémoire.** My mind went blank.
trouble adj, adv cloudy; **Sans mes lunettes je vois trouble.** Without my glasses I can't see properly.
troubles nmpl **une période de troubles politiques** a period of political instability
trouer [29] vb to make a hole in
trouille nf **avoir la trouille** (informal) to be scared to death
troupe nf troop; **une troupe de théâtre** a theatre company
troupeau (pl troupeaux) nm **un troupeau de moutons** a flock of sheep; **un troupeau de vaches** a herd of cows

trousse nf pencil case; **une trousse de secours** a first-aid kit; **une trousse de toilette** a toilet bag
trouver [29] vb ❶ to find ▷ **Je ne trouve pas mes lunettes.** I can't find my glasses. ❷ to think ▷ **Je trouve que c'est bête.** I think it's stupid.; **se trouver** to be ▷ **Où se trouve la poste?** Where is the post office? ▷ **Nice se trouve dans le sud de la France.** Nice is in the South of France.; **se trouver mal** to pass out
truc nm ❶ (informal) thing ▷ **un truc en plastique** a thing made of plastic ❷ trick
truite nf trout
T-shirt nm T-shirt
TSVP abbr (= tournez s'il vous plaît) PTO (please turn over)
tu pron you ▷ **Est-ce que tu as un animal familier?** Have you got a pet?
tuba nm ❶ tuba ❷ snorkel
tube nm ❶ tube ▷ **un tube de dentifrice** a tube of toothpaste; **un tube de rouge à lèvres** a lipstick ❷ hit ▷ **Ça va être le tube de l'été.** It's going to be this summer's hit.
tuer [29] vb to kill; **se tuer** to get killed
tue-tête: **à tue-tête** adv at the top of one's voice
tuile nf tile
tunique nf tunic
Tunisie nf Tunisia
tunisien (f **tunisienne**) adj Tunisian

tunnel *nm* tunnel; **le tunnel sous la Manche** the Channel Tunnel

turbulent, e *adj* boisterous

turc (*f* **turque**) *adj* Turkish
▶ *nm* Turkish ▷ **Il parle turc.** He speaks Turkish.
▶ *nm/f* **un Turc** (**man**) a Turk; **une Turque** (**woman**) a Turk

Turquie *nf* Turkey

tutoyer [54] *vb* **tutoyer quelqu'un** to address somebody as "tu"

  tutoyer quelqu'un means to
  call someone **tu** rather than
  vous. Use **tu** when talking to
  someone of your own age or
  whom you know well; use **vous**
  to everyone else or when talking
  to more than one person. If in
  doubt use **vous**.

  On se tutoie? Shall we use "tu" to each other?

tuyau (*pl* **tuyaux**) *nm* ❶ pipe; **un tuyau d'arrosage** a hosepipe ❷ (*informal*) tip

TVA *nf* (= *taxe sur la valeur ajoutée*) VAT

tympan *nm* eardrum

type *nm* (*informal*) guy

typique *adj* typical

tyran *nm* tyrant

tzigane *nmf* gipsy

u

UE *nf* (= *Union européenne*) the EU (European Union)

un *art, pron, adj* ❶ a, an ▷ **un garçon** a boy ▷ **un œuf** an egg ❷ one ▷ **l'un des meilleurs** one of the best ▷ **un citron et deux oranges** one lemon and two oranges; **l'un ..., l'autre ...** one ..., the other ... ▷ **L'un est grand, l'autre est petit.** One is tall, the other is short.; **les uns ..., les autres ...** some ..., others ... ▷ **Les uns marchaient, les autres couraient.** Some were walking, others were running.; **l'un ou l'autre** either of them ▷ **Prends l'un ou l'autre, ça m'est égal.** Take either of them, I don't mind.; **un par un** one by one

unanime *adj* unanimous

unanimité *nf* **à l'unanimité** unanimously

une art, pron, adj ❶ a, an ▷ *une fille* a girl ▷ *une pomme* an apple ❷ one ▷ *une pomme et deux bananes* one apple and two bananas ▷ *à une heure du matin* at one in the morning ▷ *l'une des meilleures* one of the best; **l'une ..., l'autre ...** one ..., the other ... ▷ *L'une est grande, l'autre est petite.* One is tall, the other is short.; **les unes..., les autres...** some ..., others ... ▷ *Les unes marchaient, les autres couraient.* Some were walking, others were running.; **l'une ou l'autre** either of them ▷ *Prends l'une ou l'autre, ça m'est égal.* Take either of them, I don't mind.; **une par une** one by one

uni, e adj ❶ plain ❷ close-knit

uniforme nm uniform

union nf union; **l'Union européenne** the European Union; **l'ex-Union soviétique** the former Soviet Union

unique adj unique; **Il est fils unique.** He's an only child.; **Elle est fille unique.** She's an only child.

uniquement adv only

unité nf ❶ unity ❷ unit

univers nm universe

universitaire adj university; **faire des études universitaires** to study at university

université nf university

urgence nf C'est une urgence. It's urgent.; **Il n'y a pas urgence.** It's not urgent.; **le service des urgences** the accident and emergency department; **Il a été**

transporté d'urgence à l'hôpital. He was rushed to hospital.; **Téléphonez d'urgence.** Phone as soon as possible.

urgent, e adj urgent

urine nf urine

USA nmpl USA; **aux USA (1)** in the USA **(2)** to the USA

usage nm use; **hors d'usage** out of action

usagé, e adj ❶ old ❷ used

usager nm user ▷ *les usagers de la route* road users

usé, e adj worn

s'user [29] vb to wear out ▷ *Mes baskets se sont usées en quinze jours.* My trainers wore out in two weeks.

usine nf factory

ustensile nm un ustensile de cuisine a kitchen utensil

usuel (fuselle) adj everyday

utile adj useful

utilisation nf use

utiliser [29] vb to use

utilité nf use

V

va *vb see* **aller**

vacances *nfpl* holidays ▷ *aller en vacances* to go on holiday ▷ *être en vacances* to be on holiday; **les vacances de Noël** the Christmas holidays; **les vacances de Pâques** the Easter holidays; **les grandes vacances** the summer holidays

vacancier (*f* **vacancière**) *nm* holiday-maker

vacarme *nm* racket

vaccin *nm* vaccine

vaccination *nf* vaccination

vacciner [29] *vb* to vaccinate

vache *nf* cow
▶ *adj* (*informal*) mean ▷ *Il est vache.* He's a mean sod.

vachement *adv* (*informal*) really

vagabond *nm* tramp

vagin *nm* vagina

vague *nf* (*in sea*) wave; **une vague de chaleur** a heat wave
▶ *adj* vague

vain *adj* **en vain** in vain

vaincre [87] *vb* ① to defeat ② to overcome

vainqueur *nm* winner

vais *vb see* **aller**; *Je vais écrire à mes cousins.* I'm going to write to my cousins.

vaisseau (*pl* **vaisseaux**) *nm* **un vaisseau spatial** a spaceship; **un vaisseau sanguin** a blood vessel

vaisselle *nf* ① washing-up ▷ *Je vais faire la vaisselle.* I'll do the washing-up. ② dishes

valable *adj* valid

valet *nm* (*in card games*) jack

valeur *nf* value; **des objets de valeur** valuables

valider [29] *vb* to stamp ▷ *Vous devez faire valider votre billet avant votre départ.* You must get your ticket stamped before you leave.

valise *nf* suitcase; **faire sa valise** to pack

vallée *nf* valley

valoir [88] *vb* to be worth ▷ *Ça vaut combien?* How much is it worth?; **Ça vaut mieux.** That would be better. ▷ *Il vaut mieux ne rien dire.* It would be better to say nothing.; **valoir la peine** to be worth it ▷ *Ça vaudrait la peine d'essayer.* It would be worth a try.

vampire *nm* vampire

vandalisme *nm* vandalism

vanille *nf* vanilla

vanité *nf* vanity

vaniteux (f **vaniteuse**) adj conceited

se **vanter** [29] vb to boast

vapeur nf steam

varappe nf rock climbing

variable adj (weather) changeable

varicelle nf chickenpox

varié, e adj varied

varier [20] vb to vary; Le menu varie tous les jours. The menu changes every day.

variété nf variety; une émission de variétés a television variety show

vas vb see **aller**

vase nm vase
▶ nf mud

vaste adj vast

vaudrait, vaut vb see **valoir**

vautour nm vulture

veau (pl **veaux**) nm ❶ (animal) calf ❷ (meat) veal

vécu vb see **vivre**; Il a vécu à Paris pendant dix ans. He lived in Paris for ten years.

vedette nf ❶ star ▷ une vedette de cinéma a film star ❷ motor boat; une vedette de police a police launch

végétal, e (mpl **végétaux**) adj vegetable

végétarien (f **végétarienne**) adj vegetarian

végétation nf vegetation

véhicule nm vehicle

veille nf the day before ▷ la veille au soir the previous evening; la veille de Noël Christmas Eve; la veille du jour de l'An New Year's Eve

veiller [29] vb to stay up; veiller sur quelqu'un to watch over somebody

veinard, e adj (informal): Qu'est-ce qu'il est veinard! He's such a lucky devil!

veine nf vein; avoir de la veine (informal) to be lucky

véliplanchiste nmf windsurfer

vélo nm bike; un vélo tout-terrain a mountain bike

vélomoteur nm moped

velours nm velvet; le velours côtelé corduroy

vendanges nfpl grape harvest

vendeur (f **vendeuse**) nm/f shop assistant

vendre [89] vb to sell; vendre quelque chose à quelqu'un to sell somebody something; "à vendre" "for sale"

vendredi nm ❶ Friday ▷ Aujourd'hui, nous sommes vendredi. It's Friday today. ❷ on Friday; le vendredi on Fridays; tous les vendredis every Friday; vendredi dernier last Friday; vendredi prochain next Friday; le Vendredi saint Good Friday

vénéneux (f **vénéneuse**) adj (plant) poisonous

vengeance nf revenge

se **venger** [46] vb to get revenge

venimeux (f **venimeuse**) adj (animal) poisonous

venin nm poison

venir [90] vb to come ▷ Il viendra demain. He'll come tomorrow. ▷ Il est venu nous voir. He came to see us.; **venir de** to have just ▷ *Je viens de le voir.* I've just seen him.; **faire venir quelqu'un** to call somebody out

vent nm wind

vente nf sale; **en vente** on sale; **la vente par téléphone** telesales; **une vente aux enchères** an auction

ventilateur nm (for cooling) fan

ventre nm stomach

venu vb see **venir**

ver nm worm; **un ver de terre** an earthworm

verbe nm verb

verdict nm verdict

verger nm orchard

verglacé, e adj icy

verglas nm black ice

véridique adj truthful

vérification nf check

vérifier [20] vb to check

véritable adj real; **en cuir véritable** made of real leather

vérité nf truth

verni, e adj varnished; **des chaussures vernies** patent leather shoes

vernir [39] vb to varnish

vernis nm varnish

verra, verrai, verras vb see **voir**; **on verra** ... we'll see ...

verre nm ❶ glass ▷ *une table en verre* a glass table ▷ *un verre d'eau* a glass of water; **boire un verre** to have a drink ❷ (of spectacles) lens ▷ *des verres de contact* contact lenses

verrez, verrons, verront vb see **voir**

verrou nm (on door) bolt

verrouiller [29] vb to bolt

verrue nf wart

vers nm (of poetry) line
   ▶ prep ❶ towards ▷ *Il allait vers la gare.* He was going towards the station. ❷ at about ▷ *Il est rentré chez lui vers cinq heures.* He went home at about 5 o'clock.

verse: **à verse** adv Il pleut à verse. It's pouring with rain.

Verseau nm Aquarius

versement nm instalment

verser [29] vb to pour ▷ *Est-ce que tu peux me verser un verre d'eau?* Could you pour me a glass of water?

version nf ❶ version ❷ (from the foreign language) translation; **un film en version originale** a film in the original language

verso nm (of sheet of paper) back; **voir au verso** see overleaf

vert, e adj green

vertèbre nf vertebra

vertical, e (mpl **verticaux**) adj vertical

vertige nm vertigo

verveine nf verbena tea

vessie nf bladder

veste nf jacket

vestiaire nm ❶ (in theatre, museum) cloakroom ❷ (at sports ground) changing room

vestibule nm hall

vêtement nm garment; **les vêtements** clothes

vétérinaire nmf vet

veuf nm widower

a
b
c
d
e
f
g
h
i
j
k
l
m
n
o
p
q
r
s
t
u
v
w
x
y
z

veuille, veuillez, veuillons, veulent, veut vb see **vouloir**; **Veuillez fermer la porte en sortant.** Please shut the door when you go out.

veuve nf widow

veux vb see **vouloir**

vexer [29] vb **vexer quelqu'un** to hurt somebody's feelings; **se vexer** to be offended

viande nf meat; **la viande hachée** mince

vibrer [29] vb to vibrate

vice nm vice

vicieux (f **vicieuse**) adj lecherous

victime nf victim

victoire nf victory

vide adj empty
　▶ nm vacuum; **avoir peur du vide** to be afraid of heights

vidéo nf video
　▶ adj inv video ▷ **une cassette vidéo** a video cassette ▷ **un jeu vidéo** a video game ▷ **une caméra vidéo** a video camera

vidéoclip nm music video

vidéoclub nm video shop

vider [29] vb to empty

vie nf life; **être en vie** to be alive

vieil adj
　　　vieil is used with a masculine singular noun in place of **vieux** when the noun begins with a vowel sound.

　old ▷ **un vieil arbre** an old tree ▷ **un vieil homme** an old man

vieillard nm old man

vieille adj f old; **une vieille fille** an old maid

　▶ nf old woman; **Eh bien, ma vieille ...** (informal) Well, my dear ...

vieillesse nf old age

vieillir [39] vb to age

viendrai, vienne, viens vb see **venir**; **Je viendrai dès que possible.** I'll come as soon as possible.; **Je voudrais que tu viennes.** I'd like you to come.; **Viens ici!** Come here!

Vierge nf Virgo; **la Vierge** the Virgin Mary
　▶ adj ❶ virgin ❷ blank ▷ **une cassette vierge** a blank cassette

Viêt-Nam nm Vietnam

vietnamien (f **vietnamienne**) adj Vietnamese
　▶ nm/f **un Vietnamien** (man) a Vietnamese; **une Vietnamienne** (woman) a Vietnamese; **les Vietnamiens** the Vietnamese

vieux (msg also **vieil**, f **vieille**) adj old; **un vieux garçon** a bachelor
　▶ nm old man; **les vieux** old people

vieux jeu adj inv old-fashioned

vif (f **vive**) adj ❶ (mentally) sharp; **avoir l'esprit vif** to be quick-witted ❷ crisp ▷ **L'air est plus vif à la campagne.** The air is crisper in the country. ❸ (colour) bright

vigne nf vine; **des champs de vigne** vineyards

vigneron nm wine grower

vignette nf tax disc

vignoble nm vineyard

vilain, e adj ❶ naughty ❷ ugly ▷ **Il n'est pas vilain.** He's not bad-looking.

villa nf villa

village nm village

villageois (f **villageoise**) nm/f villager

ville nf town ▷ Je vais en ville. I'm going into town.; **une grande ville** a city

vin nm wine

vinaigre nm vinegar

vinaigrette nf French dressing

vingt num twenty; **le vingt février** the twentieth of February; **vingt et un** twenty-one; **vingt-deux** twenty-two

vingtaine nf about twenty; **Il a une vingtaine d'années.** He's about twenty.

vingtième adj twentieth

viol nm rape

violemment adv violently

violence nf violence

violent, e adj violent

violer [29] vb to rape

violet (f **violette**) adj purple

violette nf (flower) violet

violon nm violin

violoncelle nm cello

violoniste nmf violinist

vipère nf viper

virage nm bend

virgule nf ① comma ② decimal point

virus nm virus

vis vb see **vivre**; **Je vis en Écosse.** I live in Scotland.
　▶ nf screw

visa nm visa

visage nm face

vis-à-vis de prep with regard to ▷ Ce n'est pas très juste vis-à-vis de lui.

It's not very fair to him.

viser [29] vb to aim at

visibilité nf visibility

visible adj visible

visière nf (of cap) peak

visite nf visit; **rendre visite à quelqu'un** to visit somebody; **avoir de la visite** to have visitors; **une visite guidée** a guided tour; **une visite médicale** a medical examination

visiter [29] vb to visit

visiteur (f **visiteuse**) nm visitor

vison nm (fur) mink

vit vb see **vivre**; **Il vit chez ses parents.** He lives with his parents.

vital, e (mpl **vitaux**) adj vital

vitamine nf vitamin

vite adv ① quick; **Le temps passe vite.** Time flies. ② fast ▷ Il roule trop vite. He drives too fast. ③ soon ▷ Il va vite oublier. He'll soon forget.; **Il a vite compris.** He understood immediately.

vitesse nf ① speed ② gear

viticulteur nm wine grower

vitrail (pl **vitraux**) nm stained-glass window

vitre nf window

vitrine nf shop window

vivant, e adj ① living ▷ les êtres vivants living creatures ② lively ▷ Elle est très vivante. She's very lively.

vive (msg **vif**) adj ① (mentally) sharp ② (colour) bright; **à vive allure** at a brisk pace; **de vive voix** in person
　▶ excl **Vive le roi!** Long live the king!

vivement excl **Vivement les vacances!** Roll on the holidays!

vivre [92] vb to live ▷ J'aimerais vivre à l'étranger. I'd like to live abroad.

vlan excl wham!

VO nf **un film en VO** a film in the original language

vocabulaire nm vocabulary

vocation nf vocation

vœu (pl **vœux**) nm ❶ wish ▷ Meilleurs vœux de bonne année! Best wishes for the New Year!

vogue nf fashion

voici prep ❶ this is ▷ Voici mon frère et voilà ma sœur. This is my brother and that's my sister. ❷ here is ▷ Tu as perdu ton stylo? Tiens, en voici un autre. Have you lost your pen? Here's another one.; **Le voici!** Here he is!

voie nf lane; **par voie buccale** orally; **la voie ferrée** the railway track

voilà prep ❶ there is ▷ Tiens! Voilà Paul. Look! There's Paul.; **Les voilà!** There they are! ❷ that is ▷ Voilà ma sœur. That's my sister.

voile nm veil
▶ nf ❶ sail ❷ sailing; **un bateau à voiles** a sailing boat

voilier nm sailing boat

voir [93] vb to see ▷ Venez me voir quand vous serez à Paris. Come and see me when you're in Paris.; **faire voir quelque chose à quelqu'un** to show somebody something; **se voir** to be obvious ▷ Est-ce que cette tache se voit? Does that stain show?; **avoir quelque chose à**

voir avec to have something to do with; **Je ne peux vraiment pas la voir.** (informal) I really can't stand her.

voisin (f **voisine**) nm/f neighbour

voisinage nm **dans le voisinage** in the vicinity

voiture nf car

voix (pl **voix**) nf ❶ voice; **à haute voix** aloud ❷ vote

vol nm ❶ flight; **à vol d'oiseau** as the crow flies; **le vol à voile** gliding ❷ theft

volaille nf poultry

volant nm ❶ steering wheel ❷ shuttlecock

volcan nm volcano

volée nf (in tennis) volley; **rattraper une balle à la volée** to catch a ball in mid-air

voler [29] vb ❶ to fly ▷ J'aimerais savoir voler. I'd like to be able to fly. ❷ to steal ▷ On a volé mon appareil photo. My camera's been stolen.; **voler quelque chose à quelqu'un** to steal something from somebody; **voler quelqu'un** to rob somebody

volet nm shutter

voleur (f **voleuse**) nm/f thief; **Au voleur!** Stop thief!

volley nm volleyball

volontaire nm volunteer

volonté nf willpower; **la bonne volonté** goodwill; **la mauvaise volonté** lack of goodwill

volontiers adv ❶ gladly ❷ yes please

volume nm volume

volumineux (f **volumineuse**)
  adj bulky

vomir [39] *vb* to vomit

vont *vb* see **aller**

vos *adj* your ▷ *Rangez vos jouets, les enfants!* Children, put your toys away!

vote *nm* vote

voter [29] *vb* to vote

votre (pl **vos**) *adj* your

vôtre *pron* le **vôtre** yours; À la **vôtre!** Cheers!

vôtres *pron* les **vôtres** yours

voudra, voudrai, voudrais, voudras, voudrez, voudrons, voudront *vb* see **vouloir**; Je **voudrais** … I'd like … ▷ *Je voudrais deux litres de lait, s'il vous plaît.* I'd like two litres of milk, please.

vouloir [94] *vb* to want ▷ *Elle veut un vélo pour Noël.* She wants a bike for Christmas. ▷ *On va au cinéma? — Si tu veux.* Shall we go to the cinema? — If you like.; Je **veux bien.** I'll be happy to.; **Voulez-vous une tasse de thé? — Je veux bien.** Would you like a cup of tea? — Yes please.; **sans le vouloir** without meaning to; **en vouloir à quelqu'un** to be angry at somebody; **vouloir dire** to mean ▷ *Qu'est-ce que ça veut dire?* What does that mean?

voulu *vb* see **vouloir**

vous *pron* ❶ you ▷ *Vous aimez la pizza?* Do you like pizza? ❷ to you ▷ *Je vous écrirai bientôt.* I'll write to you soon. ❸ yourself ▷ *Vous vous êtes fait mal?* Have you hurt

yourself?; **vous-même** yourself ▷ *Vous l'avez fait vous-même?* Did you do it yourself?

vouvoyer [54] *vb* **vouvoyer quelqu'un** to address somebody as "vous"

  • **vouvoyer quelqu'un** means
  • to call someone **vous** rather
  • than **tu**. Use **tu** when talking
  • to someone of your own age or
  • whom you know well; use **vous**
  • to everyone else or when talking
  • to more than one person. If in
  • doubt use **vous**.

Est-ce que je dois vouvoyer ta sœur? Should I use "vous" to your sister?

voyage *nm* journey ▷ *Avez-vous fait bon voyage?* Did you have a good journey?; **Bon voyage!** Have a good trip!

voyager [46] *vb* to travel

voyageur (f **voyageuse**) *nm* passenger

voyaient, voyais, voyait *vb* see **voir**

voyelle *nf* vowel

voyez, voyiez, voyions *vb* see **voir**

voyons *vb* see **voir** ❶ let's see ▷ *Voyons ce qu'on peut faire.* Let's see what we can do. ❷ come on ▷ *Voyons, sois raisonnable!* Come on, be reasonable!

voyou *nm* hooligan

vrac: en vrac *adv* loose

vrai, e *adj* true; **à vrai dire** to tell the truth; **Vrai ou faux?** True or false?

vraiment *adv* really

vraisemblable *adj* likely

VTT *nm* (= vélo tout-terrain) mountain bike

vu *vb see* **voir**; **être bien vu** (person) to be popular ▷ *Est-ce qu'il est bien vu à l'école?* Is he popular at school?; **être mal vu** to be disapproved of ▷ *C'est mal vu de fumer ici.* They don't like people smoking here.

vue *nf* ❶ eyesight ▷ *J'ai une mauvaise vue.* I've got bad eyesight. ❷ view ▷ *Il y a une belle vue d'ici.* There's a lovely view from here.; **à vue d'œil** visibly

vulgaire *adj* vulgar

wagon *nm* railway carriage

wagon-lit (pl wagons-lits) *nm* (on train) sleeper

wagon-restaurant (pl wagons-restaurants) *nm* restaurant car

walkman® *nm* Walkman®

wallon (f wallonne) *adj* (French-speaking Belgian) Walloon
▶ *nm/f* **les Wallons** the French-speaking Belgians

Wallonie *nf* French-speaking Belgium

W.-C. *nmpl* toilet

The French word **W.-C.** is pronounced "vay-say".

Web *nm* Web

webcam *nf* webcam

webmaster *nm* webmaster

webzine *nm* webzine

week-end *nm* weekend

western *nm* *(film)* western
whisky *(pl* **whiskies)** *nm* whisky
wifi *nm* Wi-Fi

xénophobe *adj* prejudiced against
  foreigners
xénophobie *nf* prejudice against
  foreigners
xylophone *nm* xylophone

Yougoslavie *nf* Yugoslavia;
l'**ex-Yougoslavie** the former
Yugoslavia
youpi *excl* Yippee!
yoyo *nm* yo-yo

y *pron* there ▷ *Nous y sommes allés
l'été dernier.* We went there last
summer. ▷ *Regarde dans le tiroir:
je pense que les clés y sont.* Look in
the drawer: I think the keys are
in there.

> **y** replaces phrases with **à** in
> constructions like the ones
> below:

**Je pensais à l'examen. — Mais
arrête d'y penser!** I was thinking
about the exam. —Well,
stop thinking about it!; **Je ne
m'attendais pas à ça. — Moi, je
m'y attendais.** I wasn't expecting
that. —I was expecting it.
yaourt *nm* yoghurt
yeux *(sg œil) nmpl* eyes
yoga *nm* yoga
yoghourt *nm* yoghurt

Z

zapper [**29**] *vb* to channel hop
zèbre *nm* zebra
zéro *nm* zero; **Ils ont gagné trois à zéro.** They won three-nil.
zézayer [**60**] *vb* to lisp ▷ *Il zézaie.* He's got a lisp.
zigzag *nm* **faire des zigzags** to zigzag
zone *nf* zone; **une zone industrielle** an industrial estate; **une zone piétonne** a pedestrian precinct
zoo *nm* zoo
zoologique *adj* zoological
zut *excl* Oh heck!

a

a *indef art*

Use **un** for masculine nouns, **une** for feminine nouns.

un (f une) ▷ *a book* un livre ▷ *an apple* une pomme

You do not translate **a** when you want to describe somebody's job in French.

▷ *She's a doctor.* Elle est médecin.; **once a week** une fois par semaine; **10 km an hour** dix kilomètres à l'heure; **30 pence a kilo** trente pence le kilo; **a hundred pounds** cent livres

abandon *vb* abandonner

abbey *n* abbaye *f*

abbreviation *n* abréviation *f*

ability *n* **to have the ability to do something** être capable de faire quelque chose

able *adj* **to be able to do something** être capable de faire quelque chose

abolish *vb* abolir

abortion *n* avortement *m*; **She had an abortion.** Elle s'est fait avorter.

about *prep, adv* ❶ (*concerning*) à propos de ▷ *I'm phoning you about tomorrow's meeting.* Je vous appelle à propos de la réunion de demain. ❷ (*approximately*) environ ▷ *It takes about 10 hours.* Ça prend dix heures environ.; **about a hundred pounds** une centaine de livres; **at about 11 o'clock** vers onze heures ❸ (*around*) dans ▷ *to walk about the town* se promener dans la ville ❹ sur ▷ *a book about London* un livre sur Londres; **to be about to do something** être sur le point de faire quelque chose ▷ *I was about to go out.* J'étais sur le point de sortir.; **to talk about something** parler de quelque chose; **What's it about?** De quoi s'agit-il?; **How about going to the cinema?** Et si nous allions au cinéma?

above *prep, adv* ❶ (*higher than*) au-dessus de ▷ *He put his hands above his head.* Il a mis ses mains au-dessus de sa tête.; **the flat above** l'appartement du dessus; **mentioned above** mentionné ci-dessus; **above all** par-dessus tout ❷ (*more than*) plus de ▷ *above 40 degrees* plus de quarante degrés

abroad *adv* à l'étranger ▷ *to go abroad* partir à l'étranger

absence n absence f

absent adj absent(e)

absent-minded adj distrait(e)
▷ She's a bit absent-minded. Elle est un peu distraite.

absolutely adv ❶ (completely) tout à fait ▷ Chantal's absolutely right. Chantal a tout à fait raison. ❷ absolument ▷ Do you think it's a good idea? — Absolutely! Tu trouves que c'est une bonne idée? — Absolument!

abuse n (misuse) abus m; **to shout abuse at somebody** insulter quelqu'un; **the issue of child abuse** la question des enfants maltraités; **the problem of drug abuse** le problème de la drogue ▶ vb ❶ (child, woman) maltraiter ▷ abused children les enfants maltraités; **to be abused** être maltraité ❷ (insult) injurier; **to abuse drugs** se droguer

academic adj universitaire ▷ the academic year l'année universitaire

academy n collège m ▷ a military academy un collège militaire

accelerate vb accélérer

accelerator n accélérateur m

accent n accent m ▷ He's got a French accent. Il a l'accent français.

accept vb accepter

acceptable adj acceptable

access n ❶ accès ▷ He has access to confidential information. Il a accès à des renseignements confidentiels. ❷ droit m de visite ▷ Her ex-husband has access to the children. Son ex-mari a le droit de visite.

accessory n accessoire m ▷ fashion accessories les accessoires de mode

accident n accident m ▷ to have an accident avoir un accident; **by accident (1)** (by mistake) accidentellement ▷ The burglar killed him by accident. Le cambrioleur l'a tué accidentellement. **(2)** (by chance) par hasard ▷ She met him by accident. Elle l'a rencontré par hasard.

accidental adj accidentel (f accidentelle)

accommodation n logement m

accompany vb accompagner

according to prep selon ▷ According to him, everyone had gone. Selon lui, tout le monde était parti.

account n ❶ compte ▷ a bank account un compte en banque; **to do the accounts** tenir la comptabilité ❷ (report) compte m rendu (pl comptes rendus) ▷ He gave a detailed account of what happened. Il a donné un compte rendu détaillé des événements.; **to take something into account** tenir compte de quelque chose; **on account of** à cause de ▷ We couldn't go out on account of the bad weather. Nous n'avons pas pu sortir à cause du mauvais temps.

accountant n comptable mf ▷ She's an accountant. Elle est comptable.

accuracy n exactitude f

accurate adj précis(e) ▷ *accurate information* les renseignements précis

accurately adv avec précision

accuse vb **to accuse somebody of something** accuser quelqu'un de quelque chose ▷ *The police are accusing her of murder.* La police l'accuse de meurtre.

ace n as m ▷ *the ace of hearts* l'as de cœur

ache n douleur f
▷ vb **My leg's aching.** J'ai mal à la jambe.

achieve vb ❶ (*an aim*) atteindre ❷ (*victory*) remporter

achievement n exploit m ▷ *That was quite an achievement.* C'était un véritable exploit.

acid n acide m

acid rain n pluies fpl acides

acne n acné f

acrobat n acrobate mf ▷ *He's an acrobat.* Il est acrobate.

across prep, adv de l'autre côté de ▷ *the shop across the road* la boutique de l'autre côté de la rue; **to walk across the road** traverser la rue; **to run across the road** traverser la rue en courant; **across from** (*opposite*) en face de ▷ *He sat down across from her.* Il s'est assis en face d'elle.

act vb ❶ (*in play, film*) jouer ▷ *He acts really well.* Il joue vraiment bien. ❷ (*take action*) agir ▷ *The police acted quickly.* La police a agi rapidement.; **She acts as** his interpreter. Elle lui sert d'interprète.
▷ n (*in play*) acte m ▷ *in the first act* au premier acte

action n action f ▷ *The film was full of action.* Il y avait beaucoup d'action dans le film.; **to take firm action against** prendre des mesures énergiques contre

active adj actif (f active) ▷ *He's a very active person.* Il est très actif.; **an active volcano** un volcan en activité

activity n activité f ▷ *outdoor activities* les activités de plein air

actor n acteur m ▷ *Brad Pitt is a well-known actor.* Brad Pitt est un acteur connu.

actress n actrice f ▷ *Julia Roberts is a well-known actress.* Julia Roberts est une actrice connue.

actual adj réel (f réelle) ▷ *The film is based on actual events.* Le film repose sur des faits réels.; **What's the actual amount?** Quel est le montant exact?

⚠ Be careful not to translate **actual** by actuel.

actually adv ❶ (*really*) vraiment ▷ *Did it actually happen?* Est-ce que c'est vraiment arrivé? ❷ (*in fact*) en fait ▷ *Actually, I don't know him at all.* En fait, je ne le connais pas du tout.

⚠ Be careful not to translate **actually** by actuellement.

ad n ❶ (*in paper*) annonce f ❷ (*on TV, radio*) pub f

AD abbr J.-C. (*après Jésus-Christ*) ▷ *in 800 AD* en huit cents après Jésus-Christ

adapt vb adapter ▷ *His novel was adapted for television.* Son roman a été adapté pour la télévision.; **to adapt to something** (*get used to*) s'adapter à quelque chose ▷ *He adapted to his new school very quickly.* Il s'est adapté très vite à sa nouvelle école.

adaptor n adaptateur m

add vb ajouter ▷ *Add two eggs to the mixture.* Ajoutez deux œufs au mélange.; **to add up** additionner ▷ *Add the figures up.* Additionnez les chiffres.

addict n (*drug addict*) drogué m, droguée f; **Jean-Pierre's a football addict.** Jean-Pierre est un mordu de football.

addicted adj **to be addicted to** (*drug*) s'adonner à ▷ *She's addicted to heroin.* Elle s'adonne à l'héroïne.; **She's addicted to soap operas.** C'est une mordue des soaps.

addition n **in addition** en plus ▷ *He's broken his leg and, in addition, he's caught a cold.* Il s'est cassé la jambe et en plus, il a attrapé un rhume.; **in addition to** en plus de ▷ *In addition to the price of the CD, there's a charge for postage.* En plus du prix du CD, il y a des frais de port.

address n adresse f ▷ *What's your address?* Quelle est votre adresse?

adjective n adjectif m

adjust vb régler ▷ *You can adjust the height of the chair.* Tu peux régler la hauteur de la chaise.; **to adjust to something** (*get used to*) s'adapter

à quelque chose ▷ *He adjusted to his new school very quickly.* Il s'est adapté très vite à sa nouvelle école.

adjustable adj réglable

administration n administration f

admiral n amiral m

admire vb admirer

admission n entrée f ▷ *"admission free"* "entrée gratuite"

admit vb **①** (*agree*) admettre ▷ *I must admit that …* Je dois admettre que … **②** (*confess*) reconnaître ▷ *He admitted that he'd done it.* Il a reconnu qu'il l'avait fait.

adolescent n adolescent m, adolescente f

adopt vb adopter ▷ *Phil was adopted.* Phil a été adopté.

adopted adj adoptif (f adoptive) ▷ *an adopted son* un fils adoptif

adoption n adoption f

adore vb adorer

Adriatic Sea n mer f Adriatique

adult n adulte m f; **adult education** l'enseignement pour adultes

advance vb **①** (*move forward*) avancer ▷ *The troops are advancing.* Les troupes avancent. **②** (*progress*) progresser ▷ *Technology has advanced a lot.* La technologie a beaucoup progressé.

▶ n **in advance** à l'avance ▷ *They bought the tickets in advance.* Ils ont acheté les billets à l'avance.

advanced adj avancé(e)

advantage n avantage m ▷ *Going to university has many advantages.*

Aller à l'université présente de nombreux avantages.; **to take advantage of something** profiter de quelque chose ▷ *He took advantage of the good weather to go for a walk.* Il a profité du beau temps pour faire une promenade.; **to take advantage of somebody** exploiter quelqu'un ▷ *The company was taking advantage of its employees.* La société exploitait ses employés.

adventure n aventure f

adverb n adverbe m

advert, advertisement n ❶ (on TV) publicité f ❷ (in newspaper) annonce f

advertise vb faire de la publicité pour ▷ *They're advertising the new model.* Ils font de la publicité pour leur nouveau modèle.; **Jobs are advertised in the paper.** Le journal publie des annonces d'emplois.

advertising n publicité f

advice n conseils mpl ▷ *to give somebody advice* donner des conseils à quelqu'un; **a piece of advice** un conseil ▷ *He gave me a good piece of advice.* Il m'a donné un bon conseil.

advise vb conseiller ▷ *He advised me to wait.* Il m'a conseillé d'attendre. ▷ *He advised me not to go there.* Il m'a conseillé de ne pas y aller.

aerial n antenne f

aerobics npl aérobic f ▷ *I'm going to aerobics tonight.* Je vais au cours d'aérobic ce soir.

aeroplane n avion m

aerosol n bombe f

affair n ❶ (romantic) aventure f ▷ *to have an affair with somebody* avoir une aventure avec quelqu'un ❷ (event) affaire f

affect vb affecter

affectionate adj affectueux (f affectueuse)

afford vb avoir les moyens d'acheter ▷ *I can't afford a new pair of jeans.* Je n'ai pas les moyens d'acheter un nouveau jean.; **We can't afford to go on holiday.** Nous n'avons pas les moyens de partir en vacances.

afraid adj **to be afraid of something** avoir peur de quelque chose ▷ *I'm afraid of spiders.* J'ai peur des araignées.; **I'm afraid I can't come.** Je crains de ne pouvoir venir.; **I'm afraid so.** Hélas oui.; **I'm afraid not.** Hélas non.

Africa n Afrique f; **in Africa** en Afrique

African adj africain(e) ▶ n Africain m, Africaine f

after prep, adv, conj après ▷ *after dinner* le dîner ▷ *He ran after me.* Il a couru après moi. ▷ *soon after* peu après; **after I'd had a rest** après m'être reposé; **after having asked** après avoir demandé; **after all** après tout

afternoon n après-midi mf ▷ *3 o'clock in the afternoon* trois heures de l'après-midi ▷ *this afternoon* cet après-midi ▷ *on Saturday afternoon* samedi après-midi

afters n dessert m

aftershave n après-rasage m

afterwards adv après ▷ She left not long afterwards. Elle est partie peu de temps après.

again adv ❶ (once more) de nouveau ▷ They're friends again. Ils sont de nouveau amis. ❷ (one more time) encore une fois ▷ Can you tell me again? Tu peux me le dire encore une fois?; **not ... again** ne ... plus ▷ I won't go there again. Je n'y retournerai plus.; **Do it again!** Refais-le!; **again and again** à plusieurs reprises

against prep contre ▷ He leant against the wall. Il s'est appuyé contre le mur. ▷ I'm against nuclear testing. Je suis contre les essais nucléaires.

age n âge m ▷ at the age of 16 à l'âge de seize ans; **I haven't been to the cinema for ages.** Ça fait une éternité que je ne suis pas allé au cinéma.

agenda n ordre m du jour ▷ on the agenda à l'ordre du jour

> Be careful not to translate **agenda** by the French word **agenda**.

agent n agent m ▷ an estate agent un agent immobilier

aggressive adj agressif (f agressive)

ago adv **two days ago** il y a deux jours; **two years ago** il y a deux ans; **not long ago** il n'y a pas longtemps; **How long ago did it happen?** Il y a combien de temps que c'est arrivé?

agony n **to be in agony** souffrir le martyre ▷ He was in agony. Il souffrait le martyre.

agree vb **to agree with** être d'accord avec ▷ I agree with Carol. Je suis d'accord avec Carol.; **to agree to do something** accepter de faire quelque chose ▷ He agreed to go and pick her up. Il a accepté d'aller la chercher.; **to agree that ...** admettre que ... ▷ I agree that it's difficult. J'admets que c'est difficile.; **Garlic doesn't agree with me.** Je ne supporte pas l'ail.

agreement n accord m; **to be in agreement** être d'accord ▷ Everybody was in agreement with Ray. Tout le monde était d'accord avec Ray.

agricultural adj agricole

agriculture n agriculture f

ahead adv devant ▷ She looked straight ahead. Elle regardait droit devant elle.; **ahead of time** en avance; **to plan ahead** organiser à l'avance; **The French are 5 points ahead.** Les Français ont cinq points d'avance.; **Go ahead!** Allez-y!

aid n **in aid of charity** au profit d'associations caritatives

AIDS n sida m

aim vb **to aim at** braquer sur ▷ He aimed a gun at me. Il a braqué un revolver sur moi.; **The film is aimed at children.** Le film est destiné aux enfants.; **to aim to do something** avoir l'intention de faire quelque chose ▷ Janice aimed

to leave at 5 o'clock. Janice avait l'intention de partir à cinq heures.
▶ *n* objectif *m* ▷ *The aim of the festival is to raise money.* L'objectif du festival est de collecter des fonds.

air *n* air *m* ▷ *to get some fresh air* prendre l'air; **by air** en avion ▷ *I prefer to travel by air.* Je préfère voyager en avion.

air-conditioned *adj* climatisé(e)

air conditioning *n* climatisation *f*

Air Force *n* armée *f* de l'air

air hostess *n* hôtesse *f* de l'air
▷ *She's an air hostess.* Elle est hôtesse de l'air.

airline *n* compagnie *f* aérienne

airmail *n* **by airmail** par avion

airplane *n* (US) avion *m*

airport *n* aéroport *m*

aisle *n* allée *f* centrale

alarm *n* (*warning*) alarme *f*; **a fire alarm** un avertisseur d'incendie

alarm clock *n* réveil *m*

album *n* album *m*

alcohol *n* alcool *m*

alcoholic *n* alcoolique *mf* ▷ *He's an alcoholic.* C'est un alcoolique.
▶ *adj* alcoolisé(e) ▷ *alcoholic drinks* des boissons alcoolisées

alert *adj* ❶ (*bright*) vif (*f* vive) ▷ *a very alert baby* un bébé très vif
❷ (*paying attention*) vigilant(e)
▷ *We must stay alert.* Nous devons rester vigilants.

A levels *npl* baccalauréat *m*
  ● The **baccalauréat** (or **bac** for short) is taken at the age of 17 or 18. Students have to sit one of a variety of set subject

  combinations, rather than being
  able to choose any combination
  of subjects they want. If you
  pass you have the right to a
  place at university.

Algeria *n* Algérie *f*; **in Algeria** en Algérie

alien *n* (*from outer space*) extra-terrestre *mf*

alike *adv* **to look alike** se ressembler ▷ *The two sisters look alike.* Les deux sœurs se ressemblent.

alive *adj* vivant(e)

all *adj, pron, adv* tout(e) (*mpl* tous)
▷ *all the time* tout le temps ▷ *I ate all of it.* J'ai tout mangé. ▷ *all day* toute la journée ▷ *all the books* tous les livres ▷ *all the girls* toutes les filles; **All of us went.** Nous y sommes tous allés.; **after all** après tout ▷ *After all, nobody can make us go.* Après tout, personne ne peut nous obliger à y aller.; **all alone** tout seul ▷ *She's all alone.* Elle est toute seule.; **not at all** pas du tout ▷ *I'm not tired at all.* Je ne suis pas du tout fatigué.; **The score is 5 all.** Le score est de cinq partout.

allergic *adj* allergique; **to be allergic to something** être allergique à quelque chose ▷ *I'm allergic to cats' hair.* Je suis allergique aux poils de chat.

allergy *n* allergie *f*

allow *vb* **to be allowed to do something** être autorisé à faire quelque chose ▷ *He's not allowed to go out at night.* Il n'est pas autorisé à sortir le soir.; **to allow somebody to do something** permettre à quelqu'un de faire quelque chose ▷ *His mum allowed him to go out.* Sa mère lui a permis de sortir.

all right *adv* ❶ *(okay)* bien ▷ *Everything turned out all right.* Tout s'est bien terminé.; **Are you all right?** Ça va? ❷ *(not bad)* pas mal ▷ *The film was all right.* Le film n'était pas mal. ❸ *(when agreeing)* d'accord ▷ *We'll talk about it later. — All right.* On en reparlera plus tard. — D'accord.; **Is that all right with you?** Tu es d'accord?

almond *n* amande *f*

almost *adv* presque ▷ *I've almost finished.* J'ai presque fini.

alone *adj, adv* seul(e) ▷ *She lives alone.* Elle habite seule.; **to leave somebody alone** laisser quelqu'un tranquille ▷ *Leave her alone!* Laisse-la tranquille!; **to leave something alone** ne pas toucher à quelque chose ▷ *Leave my things alone!* Ne touche pas à mes affaires!

along *prep, adv* le long de ▷ *Chris was walking along the beach.* Chris se promenait le long de la plage.; **all along** depuis le début ▷ *He was lying to me all along.* Il m'a menti depuis le début.

aloud *adv* à haute voix ▷ *He read the poem aloud.* Il a lu le poème à haute voix.

alphabet *n* alphabet *m*

Alps *npl* Alpes *fpl*

already *adv* déjà ▷ *Liz had already gone.* Liz était déjà partie.

also *adv* aussi

alter *vb* changer

alternate *adj* **on alternate days** tous les deux jours

alternative *n* choix *m* ▷ *You have no alternative.* Tu n'as pas le choix.; **Fruit is a healthy alternative to chocolate.** Les fruits sont plus sains que le chocolat.; **There are several alternatives.** Il y a plusieurs possibilités.
▶ *adj* autre ▷ *They made alternative plans.* Ils ont pris d'autres dispositions.; **an alternative solution** une solution de rechange; **alternative medicine** la médecine douce

alternatively *adv* **Alternatively, we could just stay at home.** On pourrait aussi rester à la maison.

although *conj* bien que

　　bien que has to be followed by a verb in the subjunctive.

▷ *Although she was tired, she stayed up late.* Bien qu'elle soit fatiguée, elle s'est couchée tard.

altogether *adv* ❶ *(in total)* en tout ▷ *You owe me £20 altogether.* Tu me dois vingt livres en tout. ❷ *(completely)* tout à fait ▷ *I'm not altogether happy with your work.* Je ne suis pas tout à fait satisfait de votre travail.

aluminium *(US* aluminum*)* *n* aluminium *m*

always *adv* toujours ▷ *He's always moaning.* Il est toujours en train de ronchonner.

am *vb see* **be**

a.m. abbr du matin ▷ at 4 a.m. à quatre heures du matin

amateur n amateur m

amaze vb **to be amazed** être stupéfait(e) ▷ She was amazed that she managed to do it. Elle était stupéfaite d'avoir réussi.

amazing adj ① (surprising) stupéfiant(e) ▷ That's amazing news! C'est une nouvelle stupéfiante! ② (excellent) exceptionnel (f exceptionnelle) ▷ Vivian's an amazing cook. Vivian est une cuisinière exceptionnelle.

ambassador n ambassadeur m, ambassadrice f

ambition n ambition f

ambitious adj ambitieux (f ambitieuse) ▷ She's very ambitious. Elle est très ambitieuse.

ambulance n ambulance f

amenities npl aménagements mpl; **The hotel has very good amenities.** L'hôtel est très bien aménagé.

America n Amérique f; **in America** en Amérique; **to America** en Amérique

American adj américain(e) ▷ She's American. Elle est américaine. ▶ n Américain m, Américaine f; **the Americans** les Américains

among prep parmi ▷ There were six children among them. Il y avait six enfants parmi eux.; **We were among friends.** Nous étions entre amis.; **among other things** entre autres

amount n ① somme f ▷ a large amount of money une grosse somme d'argent ② quantité f ▷ a huge amount of rice une énorme quantité de riz

amp n ① (of electricity) ampère m ② (for hi-fi) ampli m

amplifier n (for hi-fi) amplificateur m

amuse vb amuser ▷ He was most amused by the story. L'histoire l'a beaucoup amusé.

amusement arcade n salle f de jeux électroniques

an indef art see **a**

anaesthetic n anesthésique m

analyse vb analyser

analysis n analyse f

ancestor n ancêtre mf

anchor n ancre f

ancient adj ① (civilization) antique ▷ ancient Greece la Grèce antique ② (custom, building) ancien (f ancienne) ▷ an ancient monument un monument ancien

and conj et ▷ you and me toi et moi; **Please try and come!** Essaie de venir!; **He talked and talked.** Il n'a pas arrêté de parler.; **better and better** de mieux en mieux

angel n ange m

anger n colère f

angle n angle m

angry adj en colère ▷ Dad looks very angry. Papa a l'air très en colère.; **to be angry with somebody** être furieux contre quelqu'un ▷ Mum's really angry with you. Maman est vraiment furieuse contre toi.; **to get angry** se fâcher

animal n animal m (pl animaux)

ankle n cheville f

anniversary n anniversaire m ▷ a wedding anniversary un anniversaire de mariage

announce vb annoncer

announcement n annonce f

annoy vb agacer ▷ He's really annoying me. Il m'agace vraiment.; **to get annoyed** se fâcher ▷ Don't get so annoyed! Ne vous fâchez pas!

annoying adj agaçant(e) ▷ It's really annoying. C'est vraiment agaçant.

annual adj annuel (f annuelle) ▷ an annual meeting une réunion annuelle

anorak n anorak m

anorexia n anorexie f

another adj un autre (f une autre) ▷ Would you like another piece of cake? Tu veux un autre morceau de gâteau?

answer vb répondre à ▷ Can you answer my question? Peux-tu répondre à ma question? ▷ to answer the phone répondre au téléphone; **to answer the door** aller ouvrir ▷ Can you answer the door please? Tu peux aller ouvrir s'il te plaît?
▶ n ❶ (to question) réponse f ❷ (to problem) solution f

answering machine n répondeur m

ant n fourmi f

Antarctic n Antarctique f

anthem n the national anthem l'hymne m national

antibiotic n antibiotique m

antique n (furniture) meuble m ancien

antique shop n magasin n d'antiquités

antiseptic n antiseptique m

antivirus n (program) antivirus m

anxious adj inquiet (f inquiète)

any adj, pron, adv

Use **du, de la** or **des** to translate **any** according to the gender of the French noun that follows it. **du** and **de la** become **de l'** when they're followed by a noun starting with a vowel.

❶ du, de la, de l' (pl des) ▷ Would you like any bread? Voulez-vous du pain? ▷ Would you like any beer? Voulez-vous de la bière? ▷ Have you got any mineral water? Avez-vous de l'eau minérale? ▷ Have you got any Madonna CDs? Avez-vous des CD de Madonna?

If you want to say you haven't got any of something, use **de** whatever the gender of the following noun is. **de** becomes **d'** when it comes before a noun starting with a vowel.

❷ de, d' ▷ I haven't got any books. Je n'ai pas de livres. ▷ I haven't got any money. Je n'ai pas d'argent.

Use **en** where there is no noun after **any**.

❸ en ▷ Sorry, I haven't got any. Désolé, je n'en ai pas.; **any more** (1) (additional) encore de ▷ Would you like any more coffee? Est-ce que tu veux encore du café? **(2)** (no longer) ne ... plus ▷ I don't love him any more. Je ne l'aime plus.

anybody pron **①** (in question) quelqu'un ▷ Has anybody got a pen? Est-ce que quelqu'un a un stylo? **②** (no matter who) n'importe qui ▷ Anybody can learn to swim. N'importe qui peut apprendre à nager.

> Use **ne ... personne** in a negative sentence. **ne** comes before the verb, **personne** after it.

① ne ... personne ▷ I can't see anybody. Je ne vois personne.

anyhow adv = **anyway**
anyone pron = **anybody**
anything pron **①** (in question) quelque chose ▷ Would you like anything to eat? Tu veux manger quelque chose? **②** (no matter what) n'importe quoi ▷ Anything could happen. Il pourrait arriver n'importe quoi.

> Use **ne ... rien** in a negative sentence. **ne** comes before the verb, **rien** after it.

① ne ... rien ▷ I can't hear anything. Je n'entends rien.

anyway adv de toute façon ▷ He doesn't want to go out and anyway he's not allowed. Il ne veut pas sortir et de toute façon il n'y est pas autorisé.

anywhere adv **①** (in question) quelque part ▷ Have you seen my coat anywhere? Est-ce que tu as vu mon manteau quelque part?
② n'importe où ▷ You can buy

stamps almost anywhere. On peut acheter des timbres presque n'importe où.

> Use **ne ... nulle part** in a negative sentence. **ne** comes before the verb, **nulle part** after it.

① ne ... nulle part ▷ I can't find it anywhere. Je ne le trouve nulle part.

apart adv The two towns are 10 kilometres apart. Les deux villes sont à dix kilomètres l'une de l'autre.; apart from à part ▷ Apart from that, everything's fine. À part ça, tout va bien.

apartment n appartement m
apologize vb s'excuser ▷ He apologized for being late. Il s'est excusé de son retard.; I apologize! Je vous prie de m'excuser.
apology n excuses fpl
apostrophe n apostrophe f
apparent adj apparent(e)
apparently adv apparemment
appeal vb lancer un appel ▷ They appealed for help. Ils ont lancé un appel au secours.; Greece doesn't appeal to me. Ça ne me tente pas d'aller en Grèce.; Does that appeal to you? Ça te tente?
▶ n appel m ▷ They have launched an appeal. Ils ont lancé un appel.

appear vb **①** (come into view) apparaître ▷ The bus appeared around the corner. Le bus est apparu au coin de la rue.; to appear on TV passer à la télé **②** (seem) paraître ▷ She appeared to be asleep. Elle paraissait dormir.

appendicitis n appendicite f
appetite n appétit m
applaud vb applaudir
applause n applaudissements mpl
apple n pomme f; **an apple tree** un pommier
applicant n candidat m, candidate f ▷ There were a hundred applicants for the job. Il y avait cent candidats pour ce poste.
application n a job application une candidature
application form n ❶ (for job) dossier m de candidature ❷ (for university) dossier m d'inscription
apply vb to apply for a job poser sa candidature à un poste; **to apply to** (be relevant) s'appliquer à ▷ This rule doesn't apply to us. Ce règlement ne s'applique pas à nous.
appointment n rendez-vous m ▷ I've got a dental appointment. J'ai rendez-vous chez le dentiste.
appreciate vb être reconnaissant de ▷ I really appreciate your help. Je vous suis extrêmement reconnaissant de votre aide.
apprentice n apprenti m, apprentie f
approach vb ❶ (get nearer to) s'approcher de ▷ He approached the house. Il s'est approché de la maison. ❷ (tackle) aborder ▷ to approach a problem aborder un problème
appropriate adj approprié(e) ▷ That dress isn't very appropriate for an interview. Cette robe n'est pas très appropriée pour un entretien.

approval n approbation f
approve vb to approve of approuver ▷ I don't approve of his choice. Je n'approuve pas son choix.; **They didn't approve of his girlfriend.** Sa copine ne leur a pas plu.
approximate adj approximatif (f approximative)
apricot n abricot m
April n avril m; **in April** en avril; **April Fool's Day** le premier avril
● Pinning a paper fish to
● somebody's back is a traditional
● April Fool joke in France.
apron n tablier m
Aquarius n Verseau m ▷ I'm Aquarius. Je suis Verseau.
Arab adj arabe ▷ the Arab countries les pays arabes
▷ n Arabe mf
Arabic n arabe m
arch n arc m
archaeologist n archéologue mf ▷ He's an archaeologist. Il est archéologue.
archaeology n archéologie f
archbishop n archevêque m
archeologist n (US) = **archaeologist**
archeology n (US) = **archaeology**
architect n architecte mf ▷ She's an architect. Elle est architecte.
architecture n architecture f
Arctic n Arctique m
are vb see **be**
area n ❶ région f ▷ She lives in the Paris area. Elle habite dans la région parisienne. ❷ quartier m ▷ My

favourite area of Paris is Montmartre. Montmartre est le quartier de Paris que je préfère. ❸ **superficie** f ▷ The field has an area of 1500m². Le champ a une superficie de mille cinq cent mètres carrés.

Argentina n Argentine f; **in Argentina** en Argentine

Argentinian adj argentin(e)

argue vb se disputer ▷ They never stop arguing. Ils n'arrêtent pas de se disputer.

argument n **to have an argument** se disputer ▷ They had an argument. Ils se sont disputés.

Aries n Bélier m ▷ I'm Aries. Je suis Bélier.

arithmetic n arithmétique f

arm n bras m

armchair n fauteuil m

army n armée f

around prep, adv ❶ autour de ▷ She wore a scarf around her neck. Elle portait une écharpe autour du cou. ❷ (approximately) environ ▷ It costs around £100. Cela coûte environ cent livres. ❸ (date, time) vers ▷ Let's meet at around 8 p.m. Retrouvons-nous vers vingt heures.; **around here (1)** (nearby) près d'ici ▷ Is there a chemist's around here? Est-ce qu'il y a une pharmacie près d'ici? **(2)** (in this area) dans les parages ▷ He lives around here. Il habite dans les parages.

arrange vb **to arrange to do something** prévoir de faire quelque chose ▷ They arranged to go out together on Friday. Ils ont prévu

de sortir ensemble vendredi.; **to arrange a meeting** convenir d'un rendez-vous ▷ Can we arrange a meeting? Pouvons-nous convenir d'un rendez-vous?; **to arrange a party** organiser une fête

arrangement n (plan) arrangement m; **They made arrangements to go out on Friday night.** Ils ont organisé une sortie vendredi soir.

arrest vb arrêter ▷ The police have arrested 5 people. La police a arrêté cinq personnes.
▶ n arrestation f ▷ You're under arrest! Vous êtes en état d'arrestation!

arrival n arrivée f

arrive vb arriver ▷ I arrived at 5 o'clock. Je suis arrivé à cinq heures.

arrow n flèche f

art n art m

artery n artère f

art gallery n musée m

article n article m ▷ a newspaper article un article de journal

artificial adj artificiel (f artificielle)

artist n artiste mf ▷ She's an artist. C'est une artiste.

artistic adj artistique

as conj, adv ❶ (while) au moment où ▷ He came in as I was leaving. Il est arrivé au moment où je partais. ❷ (since) puisque ▷ As it's Sunday, you can have a lie-in. Tu peux faire la grasse matinée, puisque c'est dimanche.; **as ... as** aussi ... que ▷ Pierre's as tall as Michel. Pierre est aussi grand que Michel.; **twice**

a
b
c
d
e
f
g
h
i
j
k
l
m
n
o
p
q
r
s
t
u
v
w
x
y
z

as ... as deux fois plus ... que ▷ *Her coat costs twice as much as mine.* Son manteau a coûté deux fois plus cher que le mien.; **as much ... as** autant ... que ▷ *I haven't got as much money as you.* Je n'ai pas autant d'argent que toi.; **as soon as possible** dès que possible ▷ *I'll do it as soon as possible.* Je le ferai dès que possible.; **as from tomorrow** à partir de demain ▷ *As from tomorrow, the shop will stay open until 10 p.m.* À partir de demain, le magasin restera ouvert jusqu'à vingt-deux heures.; **as though** comme si ▷ *She acted as though she hadn't seen me.* Elle a fait comme si elle ne m'avait pas vu.; **as if** comme si; **He works as a waiter in the holidays.** Il travaille comme serveur pendant les vacances.

ash n ① (*dust*) cendre f ② (*ash tree*) frêne m

ashamed adj **to be ashamed** avoir honte ▷ *You should be ashamed of yourself!* Tu devrais avoir honte!

ashtray n cendrier m

Asia n Asie f; **in Asia** en Asie

Asian adj asiatique ▷ *He's Asian.* C'est un Asiatique.
  ▶ n Asiatique mf

ask vb ① (*inquire, request*) demander ▷ *"Have you finished?" she asked.* "Tu as fini?" a-t-elle demandé.; **to ask somebody something** demander quelque chose à quelqu'un ▷ *He asked her how old she was.* Il lui a demandé quel âge elle avait.; **to ask for something** demander quelque

chose ▷ *He asked for a cup of tea.* Il a demandé une tasse de thé.; **to ask somebody to do something** demander à quelqu'un de faire quelque chose ▷ *She asked him to do the shopping.* Elle lui a demandé de faire les courses.; **to ask about something** se renseigner sur quelque chose ▷ *I asked about train times to Leeds.* Je me suis renseigné sur les horaires des trains pour Leeds.; **to ask somebody a question** poser une question à quelqu'un ② **inviter** ▷ *Have you asked Matthew to the party?* Est-ce que tu as invité Matthew à la fête?; **He asked her out.** (*on a date*) Il l'a demandé de sortir avec lui.

asleep adj **to be asleep** dormir ▷ *He's asleep.* Il dort.; **to fall asleep** s'endormir ▷ *I fell asleep in front of the TV.* Je me suis endormi devant la télé.

asparagus n asperges fpl

aspirin n aspirine f

assembly n (*in school*) rassemblement m
  ● There is no assembly in French schools.

assignment n (*in school*) devoir m

assistance n aide f

assistant n ① (*in shop*) vendeur m, vendeuse f ② (*helper*) assistant m, assistante f

association n association f

assortment n assortiment m

assume vb supposer ▷ *I assume she won't be coming.* Je suppose qu'elle ne viendra pas.

assure vb assurer ▷ He assured me he was coming. Il m'a assuré qu'il viendrait.

asterisk n astérisque m

asthma n asthme m ▷ I've got asthma. J'ai de l'asthme.

astonished adj étonné(e)

astonishing adj étonnant(e)

astrology n astrologie f

astronaut n astronaute mf

astronomy n astronomie f

at prep

▌ à + le becomes **au**, à + les becomes **aux**.

à, au, à la, à l' (pl aux) ▷ at 4 o'clock à quatre heures ▷ at Christmas à Noël ▷ at the office au bureau ▷ at home à la maison ▷ at school à l'école ▷ at the races aux courses; **at night** la nuit; **What are you doing at the weekend?** Qu'est-ce que tu fais ce week-end?; **at sign** (@) arobase f

ate vb see **eat**

Athens n Athènes; **in Athens** à Athènes

athlete n athlète mf

athletic adj athlétique

athletics n athlétisme m ▷ I like watching the athletics on TV. J'aime bien regarder les épreuves d'athlétisme à la télé.

Atlantic n océan m Atlantique

atlas n atlas m

atmosphere n atmosphère f

atom n atome m

atomic adj atomique

attach vb fixer ▷ He attached a rope to the car. Il a fixé une corde à la voiture.; **Please find attached ...**

Veuillez trouver ci-joint ...; **to attach a file to an email** joindre un fichier à un mail

attached adj **to be attached to** être attaché à ▷ He's very attached to his family. Il est très attaché à sa famille.

attachment n (email) pièce f jointe

attack vb attaquer ▷ The dog attacked her. Le chien l'a attaquée.

▶ n attaque f

attempt n tentative f ▷ She gave up after several attempts. Elle y a renoncé après plusieurs tentatives.

▶ vb **to attempt to do something** essayer de faire quelque chose ▷ I attempted to write a song. J'ai essayé d'écrire une chanson.

attend vb assister à ▷ to attend a meeting assister à une réunion

▌ Be careful not to translate to **attend** by **attendre**.

attention n attention f; **to pay attention to** faire attention à ▷ He didn't pay attention to what I was saying. Il ne faisait pas attention à ce que je disais.

attic n grenier m

attitude n (way of thinking) attitude f ▷ I really don't like your attitude! Je n'aime pas du tout ton attitude!

attorney n (US) avocat m, avocate f

attract vb attirer ▷ The Lake District attracts lots of tourists. La région des lacs attire de nombreux touristes.

attraction n attraction f ▷ a
tourist attraction une attraction
touristique
attractive adj séduisant(e)
▷ She's very attractive. Elle est très
séduisante.
aubergine n aubergine f
auction n vente f aux enchères
audience n (in theatre) spectateurs
mpl
August n août m; **in August**
en août
aunt, aunty n tante f ▷ my aunt
ma tante
au pair n jeune fille f au pair ▷ She's
an au pair. Elle est jeune fille au pair.
Australia n Australie f; **in
Australia** en Australie; **to
Australia** en Australie
Australian adj australien
(f australienne) ▷ He's Australian.
Il est australien.
  ▶ Australien m, Australienne f;
  the Australians les Australiens
Austria n Autriche f; **in Austria**
en Autriche
Austrian adj autrichien
(f autrichienne) ▷ She's Austrian.
Elle est autrichienne.
  ▶ Autrichien m, Autrichienne f;
  the Austrians les Autrichiens
author n auteur m ▷ She's a famous
author. C'est un auteur connu.
autobiography n
autobiographie f
autograph n autographe m
automatic adj automatique
▷ an automatic door une porte
automatique

automatically adv
automatiquement
autumn n automne m; **in autumn**
en automne
availability n disponibilité f
available adj disponible ▷ Free
brochures are available on request.
Des brochures gratuites sont
disponibles sur demande. ▷ Is Mr
Cooke available today? Est-ce que
Monsieur Cooke est disponible
aujourd'hui?
avalanche n avalanche f
avenue n avenue f
average n moyenne f ▷ on average
en moyenne
  ▶ adj moyen (f moyenne) ▷ the
  average price le prix moyen
avocado n avocat m
avoid vb éviter ▷ He avoids her
when she's in a bad mood. Il l'évite
lorsqu'elle est de mauvaise
humeur.; **to avoid doing
something** éviter de faire quelque
chose ▷ Avoid going out on your own
at night. Évite de sortir seul le soir.
awake adj **to be awake** être
réveillé ▷ Is she awake? Elle est
réveillée?; **He was still awake.**
Il ne dormait pas encore.
award n prix m ▷ He's won an award.
Il a remporté un prix.
aware adj **to be aware of
something** être conscient de
quelque chose
away adj, adv (not here) absent(e)
▷ André's away today. André est
absent aujourd'hui.; **He's away
for a week.** Il est parti pour

une semaine.; **The town's 2 kilometres away.** La ville est à deux kilomètres d'ici.; **The coast is 2 hours away by car.** La côte est à deux heures de route.; **Go away!** Va-t'en!; **to put something away** ranger quelque chose ▷ *He put his toys away in the cupboard.* Il a rangé ses jouets dans le placard.

away match n match m à l'extérieur (pl matchs à l'extérieur)

awful adj affreux (f affreuse) ▷ *That's awful!* C'est affreux!; **an awful lot of …** énormément de …

awkward adj ❶ (difficult to deal with) délicat(e) ▷ *an awkward situation* une situation délicate ❷ (embarrassing) gênant(e) ▷ *an awkward question* une question gênante; **It's a bit awkward for me to come and see you.** Ce n'est pas très pratique pour moi de venir vous voir.

axe n hache f

baby n bébé m

babysit vb faire du baby-sitting

babysitter n baby-sitter mf

babysitting n baby-sitting m

bachelor n célibataire m ▷ *He's a bachelor.* Il est célibataire.

back n ❶ (of person, horse, book) dos m ❷ (of car, house) arrière m ▷ *in the back* à l'arrière ❸ (of page) verso m ▷ *on the back* au verso ❹ (of room, garden) fond m ▷ *at the back* au fond ▶ adj, adv arrière inv ▷ *the back seat* le siège arrière; **the back door** la porte de derrière; **to get back** rentrer ▷ *What time did you get back?* À quelle heure est-ce que tu es rentré?; **We went there by bus and walked back.** Nous y sommes allés en bus et nous sommes rentrés à pied.; **He's not back**

yet. Il n'est pas encore rentré.;
to call somebody back rappeler
quelqu'un ▷ I'll call back later. Je
rappellerai plus tard.
▶ vb (support) soutenir ▷ I'm backing
Tony Blair. Je soutiens Tony Blair.;
to back a horse parier sur un
cheval; **to back out** se désister
▷ They promised to help and then
backed out. Ils avaient promis de
nous aider et ils se sont désistés.;
to back somebody up soutenir
quelqu'un

backache n mal m au dos ▷ to have
backache avoir mal au dos

backbone n colonne f vertébrale

backfire vb (go wrong) échouer

background n ❶ (of picture)
arrière-plan m ▷ a house in the
background une maison à l'arrière-
plan; **background noise** les bruits
de fond ❷ milieu m (pl milieux) ▷
his family background son milieu
familial

backhand n revers m

backing n (support) soutien m

backpack n sac m à dos

backpacker n ❶ (globe-
trotter) routard m, routarde f
❷ (hill-walker) randonneur m,
randonneuse f

backside n derrière m

backstroke n dos m crawlé

backup n (support) soutien m; **a
backup file** une sauvegarde

backwards adv en arrière ▷ to take
a step backwards faire un pas en
arrière; **to fall backwards** tomber
à la renverse

bacon n ❶ (French type) lard m
❷ (British type) bacon m ▷ bacon
and eggs des œufs au bacon

bad adj ❶ mauvais(e) ▷ to be in
a bad mood être de mauvaise
humeur; **to be bad at something**
être mauvais en quelque chose
▷ I'm really bad at maths. Je suis
vraiment mauvais en maths. ❷
(serious) grave ▷ a bad accident
un accident grave ❸ (naughty)
vilain(e) ▷ You bad boy! Vilain!; **to
go bad** (food) se gâter; **I feel bad
about it.** Ça m'ennuie.; **not bad**
pas mal ▷ That's not bad at all. Ce
n'est pas mal du tout.

badge n badge m

badly adv mal ▷ badly paid mal
payé; **badly wounded** grièvement
blessé; **He badly needs a rest.** Il a
sérieusement besoin de se reposer.

badminton n badminton m ▷ to
play badminton jouer au badminton

bad-tempered adj **to be
bad-tempered (1)** (by nature) avoir
mauvais caractère ▷ He's a really
bad-tempered person. Il a vraiment
mauvais caractère. **(2)** (temporarily)
être de mauvaise humeur ▷ He was
really bad-tempered yesterday. Il était
vraiment de mauvaise humeur hier.

bag n sac m; **an old bag** (person)
une vieille peau

baggage n bagages mpl

baggage reclaim n livraison f des
bagages

bagpipes npl cornemuse f ▷ Ed
plays the bagpipes. Ed joue de la
cornemuse.

bake vb **to bake a cake** faire un gâteau

baked adj cuit(e) au four ▷ baked potatoes pommes de terre cuites au four; **baked beans** haricots blancs en sauce

baker n boulanger m, boulangère f ▷ He's a baker. Il est boulanger.

bakery n boulangerie f

balance n équilibre m ▷ to lose one's balance perdre l'équilibre

balanced adj équilibré(e)

balcony n balcon m

bald adj chauve

ball n ❶ (tennis, golf, cricket) balle f ❷ (football, rugby) ballon m

ballet n ballet m ▷ We went to a ballet. Nous sommes allés voir un ballet.; **ballet lessons** les cours de danse

ballet dancer n danseur m classique, danseuse f classique

ballet shoes npl chaussons mpl de danse

balloon n (for parties) ballon m; **a hot-air balloon** une montgolfière

ballpoint pen n stylo m à bille

ban n interdiction f
▶ vb interdire

banana n banane f ▷ a banana skin une peau de banane

band n ❶ (rock band) groupe m ❷ (brass band) fanfare f

bandage n bandage m
▶ vb mettre un bandage à ▷ The nurse bandaged his arm. L'infirmière lui a mis un bandage au bras.

Band-Aid® n (US) pansement m adhésif

bang n ❶ détonation f ▷ I heard a loud bang. J'ai entendu une forte détonation. ❷ coup m ▷ a bang on the head un coup sur la tête; **Bang!** Pan!
▶ vb (part of body) se cogner ▷ I banged my head. Je me suis cogné la tête.; **to bang the door** claquer la porte; **to bang on the door** cogner à la porte

Bangladesh n Bangladesh m; **from Bangladesh** du Bangladesh

bank n ❶ (financial) banque f ❷ (of river, lake) bord m

bank account n compte m en banque

bank card n carte f d'identité bancaire

banker n banquier m

bank holiday n jour m férié

banknote n billet m de banque

bar n ❶ (pub) bar m ❷ (counter) comptoir m; **a bar of chocolate** une tablette de chocolat; **a bar of soap** une savonnette

barbecue n barbecue m

bare adj nu(e)

barefoot adj, adv nu-pieds inv ▷ The children go around barefoot. Les enfants se promènent nu-pieds.; **to be barefoot** avoir les pieds nus ▷ She was barefoot. Elle avait les pieds nus.

barely adv à peine ▷ I could barely hear what she was saying. J'entendais à peine ce qu'elle disait.

bargain n affaire f ▷ It was a bargain! C'était une affaire!

barge n péniche f

bark vb aboyer

barmaid n barmaid f ▷ She's a barmaid. Elle est barmaid.

barman n barman m ▷ He's a barman. Il est barman.

barn n grange f

barrel n tonneau m (pl tonneaux)

barrier n barrière f

base n base f

baseball n base-ball m; **a baseball cap** une casquette de base-ball

based adj based on fondé(e) sur

basement n sous-sol m

bash vb to bash something taper sur quelque chose
▷ n **I'll have a bash.** Je vais essayer.

basic adj ❶ de base ▷ It's a basic model. C'est un modèle de base. ❷ rudimentaire ▷ The accommodation is pretty basic. Le logement est plutôt rudimentaire.

basically adv tout simplement ▷ Basically, I just don't like him. Tout simplement, je ne l'aime pas.

basics npl rudiments mpl

basin n (washbasin) lavabo m

basis n on a daily basis quotidiennement; **on a regular basis** régulièrement

basket n panier m

basketball n basket m

bass n ❶ (guitar, singer) basse f ▷ He plays the bass. Il joue de la basse.; **a bass guitar** une guitare basse ❷ (on hi-fi) graves mpl

bass drum n grosse caisse f

bassoon n basson m ▷ I play the bassoon. Je joue du basson.

bat n ❶ (for cricket, rounders) batte f ❷ (for table tennis)

raquette f ❸ (animal) chauve-souris f (pl chauves-souris)

bath n ❶ bain m ▷ to have a bath prendre un bain; **a hot bath** un bain chaud ❷ (bathtub) baignoire f ▷ There's a spider in the bath. Il y a une araignée dans la baignoire.

bathe vb se baigner

bathroom n salle f de bains

bath towel n serviette f de bain

batter n pâte f à frire

battery n ❶ (for torch, toy) pile f ❷ (of car) batterie f

battle n bataille f ▷ the Battle of Hastings la bataille de Hastings; **It was a battle, but we managed in the end.** Il a fallu se battre, mais on a fini par y arriver.

bay n baie f

BC abbr (= before Christ) av. J.-C. (avant Jésus-Christ) ▷ in 200 BC en deux cents avant Jésus-Christ

be vb être ▷ I'm tired. Je suis fatigué. ▷ I've been ill. J'ai été malade.; **It's the 28th of October today.** Nous sommes le vingt-huit octobre.; **Have you been to Greece before?** Est-ce que tu es déjà allé en Grèce?; **I've never been to Paris.** Je ne suis jamais allé à Paris.; **to be killed** être tué

> When you are saying what somebody's occupation is, you leave out the "a" in French.

▷ He's a student. Il est étudiant.

> With certain adjectives, such as "cold", "hot", "hungry" and "thirsty", use avoir instead of être.

I'm cold. J'ai froid.; **I'm hungry.**
J'ai faim.

When saying how old somebody
is, use **avoir** not **être**.

I'm fourteen. J'ai quatorze ans.;
How old are you? Quel âge as-tu?

When referring to the weather,
use **faire**.

It's cold. Il fait froid.; **It's too hot.**
Il fait trop chaud.; **It's a nice day.**
Il fait beau.

beach n plage f
bead n perle f
beak n bec m
beam n rayon m
beans npl ❶ haricots mpl ❷ (baked
beans) haricots mpl blancs à la
sauce tomate ▷ I had beans on toast.
J'ai mangé des haricots blancs à la
sauce tomate sur du pain grillé.;
broad beans fèves fpl; **green
beans** haricots verts; **kidney
beans** haricots rouges
bear n ours m
▶ vb **I can't bear it!** C'est
insupportable!; **to bear up** tenir le
coup; **Bear up!** Tiens bon!
beard n barbe f; **He's got a beard.**
Il est barbu.; **a man with a beard**
un barbu
bearded adj barbu(e)
beat n rythme m
▶ vb (informal) battre ▷ We beat
them 3-0. On les a battus trois
à zéro.; **Beat it!** Fiche le camp!
(informal); **to beat somebody up**
tabasser quelqu'un
beautiful adj beau (f belle, mpl
beaux)

beautifully adv admirablement
beauty n beauté f
became vb see **become**
because conj parce que ▷ I did it
because ... Je l'ai fait parce que ...;
because of à cause de ▷ because of
the weather à cause du temps
become vb devenir ▷ He became
a famous writer. Il est devenu un
grand écrivain.
bed n lit m ▷ in bed au lit; **to go to
bed** aller se coucher; **to go to bed
with somebody** coucher avec
quelqu'un
bed and breakfast n chambre
f d'hôte ▷ We stayed in a bed and
breakfast. Nous avons logé dans
une chambre d'hôte.
bedclothes npl draps mpl et
couvertures fpl
bedding n literie f
bedroom n chambre f
bedsit n chambre f meublée
bedspread n dessus-de-lit m (pl
dessus-de-lit)
bedtime n **Ten o'clock is my
bedtime.** Je me couche à dix
heures.; **Bedtime!** Au lit!
bee n abeille f
beech n hêtre m
beef n bœuf m; **roast beef** le rosbif
beefburger n hamburger m
been vb see **be**
beer n bière f
beetle n scarabée m
beetroot n betterave f rouge
before prep, conj, adv ❶ avant
▷ before Tuesday avant mardi
❷ avant de ▷ I'll phone before I

leave. J'appellerai avant de partir.
❸ *(already)* déjà ▷ *I've seen this film before.* J'ai déjà vu ce film.; **the day before** la veille; **the week before** la semaine précédente
beforehand *adv* à l'avance
beg *vb* ❶ *(for money)* mendier
❷ supplier ▷ *He begged me to stop.* Il m'a supplié d'arrêter.
began *vb see* **begin**
beggar *n* mendiant *m*, mendiante *f*
begin *vb* commencer; **to begin doing something** commencer à faire quelque chose
beginner *n* débutant *m*, débutante *f* ▷ *I'm just a beginner.* Je ne suis qu'un débutant.
beginning *n* début *m* ▷ *in the beginning* au début
begun *vb see* **begin**
behalf *n* **on behalf of somebody** pour quelqu'un
behave *vb* se comporter ▷ *He behaved like an idiot.* Il s'est comporté comme un idiot. ▷ *She behaved very badly.* Elle s'est très mal comportée.; **to behave oneself** être sage ▷ *Did the children behave themselves?* Est-ce que les enfants ont été sages?; **Behave!** Sois sage!
behaviour(US **behavior**) *n* comportement *m*
behind *prep, adv* derrière ▷ *behind the television* derrière la télévision; **to be behind** *(late)* avoir du retard ▷ *I'm behind with my revision.* J'ai du retard dans mes révisions.
▶ *n* derrière *m*
beige *adj* beige

Belgian *adj* belge ▷ *She's Belgian.* Elle est belge.
▶ *n* Belge *mf*; **the Belgians** les Belges
Belgium *n* Belgique *f*; **in Belgium** en Belgique
believe *vb* croire ▷ *I don't believe you.* Je ne te crois pas.; **to believe in something** croire à quelque chose ▷ *Do you believe in ghosts?* Tu crois aux fantômes?; **to believe in God** croire en Dieu
bell *n* ❶ *(doorbell)* sonnette *f*; **to ring the bell** sonner à la porte
❷ *(in church)* cloche *f* ❸ *(in school)* sonnerie *f* ❹ *(bell)* clochette *f* ▷ *Our cat has a bell on its neck.* Notre chat a une clochette sur son collier.
belong *vb* **to belong to somebody** être à quelqu'un ▷ *Who does it belong to?* C'est à qui? ▷ *That belongs to me.* C'est à moi.; **Do you belong to any clubs?** Est-ce que tu es membre d'un club?; **Where does this belong?** Où est-ce que ça va?
belongings *npl* affaires *fpl*
below *prep, adv* ❶ au-dessous de ▷ *below the castle* au-dessous du château ❷ en dessous ▷ *on the floor below* à l'étage en dessous; **10 degrees below freezing** moins dix
belt *n* ceinture *f*
bench *n* ❶ *(seat)* banc *m* ❷ *(for woodwork)* établi *m*
bend *n* ❶ *(in road)* virage *m* ❷ *(in river)* coude *m*
▶ *vb* ❶ *(back)* courber ❷ *(leg, arm)* plier ▷ *I can't bend my arm.* Je n'arrive pas à plier le bras.; **"do not bend"**

"ne pas plier" ❸ (object) tordre
▸ You've bent it. Tu l'as tordu. ❹ se
tordre ▸ It bends easily. Ça se tord
facilement.; **to bend down** se
baisser.; **to bend over** se pencher

beneath prep sous

benefit n (advantage) avantage m;
unemployment benefit les
allocations de chômage
▸ vb **He'll benefit from the change.**
Le changement lui fera du bien.

bent vb see **bend**
▸ adj tordu(e) ▸ a bent fork une
fourchette tordue

beret n béret m

berth n couchette f

beside prep à côté de ▸ beside the
television à côté de la télévision; **He
was beside himself.** Il était hors
de lui.; **That's beside the point.**
Cela n'a rien à voir.

besides adv en plus ▸ Besides, it's
too expensive. En plus, c'est trop
cher.

best adj, adv ❶ meilleur(e) ▸ He's
the best player in the team. Il est
le meilleur joueur de l'équipe.
▸ Janet's the best at maths. Janet est
la meilleure en maths. ❷ le mieux
▸ Emma sings best. C'est Emma qui
chante le mieux. ▸ That's the best I
can do. Je ne peux pas faire mieux.;
to do one's best faire de son mieux
▸ It's not perfect, but I did my best.
Ça n'est pas parfait, mais j'ai fait
de mon mieux.; **to make the best
of it** s'en contenter ▸ We'll have to
make the best of it. Il va falloir nous
en contenter.

best man n garçon m d'honneur

bet n pari m ▸ **to make a bet** faire
un pari
▸ vb parier ▸ I bet he forgot. Je parie
qu'il a oublié.

better adj, adv ❶ meilleur(e) ▸ This
one's better than that one. Celui-ci
est meilleur que celui-là. ▸ a better
way to do it une meilleure façon de
le faire ❷ mieux ▸ That's better!
C'est mieux comme ça.; **better
still** encore mieux ▸ Go and see her
tomorrow, or better still, go today.
Va la voir demain, ou encore
mieux, vas-y aujourd'hui.; **to get
better (1)** (improve) s'améliorer
▸ My French is getting better. Mon
français s'améliore. **(2)** (from illness)
se remettre ▸ I hope you get better
soon. J'espère que tu vas vite te
remettre.; **to feel better** se sentir
mieux ▸ Are you feeling better now?
Tu te sens mieux maintenant?;
You'd better do it straight away.
Vous feriez mieux de le faire
immédiatement.; **I'd better go
home.** Je ferais mieux de rentrer.

between prep entre ▸ Stroud is
between Oxford and Bristol. Stroud
est entre Oxford et Bristol.
▸ between 15 and 20 minutes entre
quinze et vingt minutes

beyond prep au-delà de ▸ There was
a lake beyond the mountain. Il y avait
un lac au-delà de la montagne.;
beyond belief incroyable; **beyond
repair** irréparable

Bible n Bible f

bicycle n vélo m

big adj ❶ grand(e) ▷ *a big house* une
grande maison ▷ *my big brother*
mon grand frère; **He's a big guy.**
C'est un grand gaillard. ❷ (*car,
animal, book, parcel*) gros (f grosse)
▷ *a big car* une grosse voiture
bigheaded adj **to be bigheaded**
avoir la grosse tête
bike n vélo m ▷ *by bike* en vélo
bikini n bikini m
bilingual adj bilingue
bill n ❶ (*in restaurant*) addition f
▷ *Can we have the bill, please?*
L'addition, s'il vous plaît. ❷ (*for gas,
electricity*) facture f ❸ (US) billet m
▷ *a five-dollar bill* un billet de cinq
dollars
billiards n billard m ▷ **to play
billiards** jouer au billard
billion n milliard m
bin n poubelle f
binoculars npl jumelles fpl; **a pair
of binoculars** des jumelles
biochemistry n biochimie f
biography n biographie f
biology n biologie f
bird n oiseau m (pl oiseaux)
birdwatching n **My hobby's
birdwatching.** Mon passe-temps
favori est d'observer les oiseaux.;
to go birdwatching aller observer
les oiseaux
Biro® n bic® m
birth n naissance f ▷ *date of birth* la
date de naissance
birth certificate n acte m de
naissance
birth control n contraception f
birthday n anniversaire m ▷ *When's*

your birthday? Quelle est la date
de ton anniversaire?; **a birthday
cake** un gâteau d'anniversaire;
a birthday card une carte
d'anniversaire; **I'm going to have
a birthday party.** Je vais faire une
fête pour mon anniversaire.
biscuit n gâteau m sec
bishop n évêque m
bit n morceau m (pl morceaux)
▷ *Would you like another bit?* Est-ce
que tu en veux un autre morceau?;
a bit of (1) (*piece of*) un morceau
de ▷ *a bit of cake* un morceau de
gâteau **(2)** (*a little*) un peu de ▷ *a bit
of music* un peu de musique; **It's a
bit of a nuisance.** C'est ennuyeux.;
a bit un peu ▷ *a bit too hot* un peu
trop chaud; **to fall to bits** se
désintégrer; **to take something
to bits** démonter quelque chose;
bit by bit petit à petit
▷ vb see **bite**
bite vb ❶ (*person, dog*) mordre
❷ (*insect*) piquer ▷ *I got bitten by
mosquitoes.* Je me suis fait piquer
par des moustiques.; **to bite one's
nails** se ronger les ongles
▷ n ❶ (*insect bite*) piqûre f
❷ (*animal bite*) morsure f; **to have
a bite to eat** manger un morceau
bitten vb see **bite**
bitter adj ❶ amer (f amère)
❷ (*weather, wind*) glacial(e) (mpl
glaciaux) ▷ *It's bitter today.* Il fait un
froid glacial aujourd'hui.
▷ n bière f brune
black adj noir(e) ▷ *a black jacket* une
veste noire

blackberry n mûre f

blackbird n merle m

blackboard n tableau m noir

blackcurrant n cassis m

blackmail n chantage m ▷ *That's blackmail!* C'est du chantage! ▶ vb **to blackmail somebody** faire chanter quelqu'un ▷ *He blackmailed her.* Il l'a fait chanter.

black pudding n boudin m

blade n lame f

blame vb **Don't blame me!** Ça n'est pas ma faute!; **I blame the police.** À mon avis, c'est la faute de la police.; **He blamed it on my sister.** Il a dit que c'était la faute de ma sœur.

blank adj **①** *(paper)* blanc *(f* blanche) **②** *(cassette, video, page)* vierge; **My mind went blank.** J'ai eu un trou. ▶ n blanc m ▷ *Fill in the blanks.* Remplissez les blancs.

blanket n couverture f

blast n **a bomb blast** une explosion

blaze n incendie m

blazer n blazer m

bleach n eau f de Javel

bleed vb saigner ▷ *My nose is bleeding.* Je saigne du nez.

blender n mixer m

bless vb *(religiously)* bénir; **Bless you!** *(after sneezing)* À tes souhaits!

blew vb see **blow**

blind adj aveugle ▶ n *(for window)* store m

blink vb cligner des yeux

blister n ampoule f

blizzard n tempête f de neige

block n immeuble m ▷ *He lives in our block.* Il habite dans notre immeuble.; **a block of flats** un immeuble ▶ vb bloquer

blonde adj blond(e) ▷ *She's got blonde hair.* Elle a les cheveux blonds.

blood n sang m

blood pressure n **to have high blood pressure** faire de la tension

blood test n prise f de sang

blouse n chemisier m

blow n coup m ▶ vb *(wind, person)* souffler; **to blow one's nose** se moucher; **to blow a whistle** siffler; **to blow out a candle** éteindre une bougie; **to blow up (1)** faire sauter ▷ *The terrorists blew up a police station.* Les terroristes ont fait sauter un commissariat de police. **(2)** gonfler ▷ *to blow up a balloon* gonfler un ballon; **The house blew up.** La maison a sauté.

blow-dry n brushing m; **A cut and blow-dry, please.** Une coupe brushing, s'il vous plaît.

blown vb see **blow**

blue adj bleu(e) ▷ *a blue dress* une robe bleue; **a blue film** un film pornographique; **It came out of the blue.** C'était complètement inattendu.

blues npl blues m

blunder n gaffe f

blunt adj **①** *(person)* brusque **②** *(knife)* émoussé(e)

blush vb rougir

board n ❶ (wooden) planche f
❷ (blackboard) tableau m (pl
tableaux) ▷ on the board au tableau
❸ (noticeboard) panneau m (pl
panneaux) ❹ (for board games) jeu
m (pl jeux) ❺ (for chess) échiquier
m; **on board** à bord; **"full board"**
"pension complète"

boarder n interne mf

board game n jeu m de société (pl
jeux de société)

boarding card n carte f
d'embarquement

boarding school n pensionnat
m; **I go to boarding school.** Je suis
interne.

boast vb se vanter ▷ Stop boasting!
Arrête de te vanter!; **to boast
about something** se vanter de
quelque chose

boat n bateau m (pl bateaux)

body n corps m

bodybuilding n culturisme m

bodyguard n garde m du corps

boil n furoncle m
▶ vb ❶ faire bouillir ▷ to boil some
water faire bouillir de l'eau; **to
boil an egg** faire cuire un œuf
❷ bouillir ▷ The water's boiling.
L'eau bout. ▷ The water's boiled.
L'eau a bouilli.; **to boil over**
déborder

boiled adj à l'eau ▷ boiled potatoes
des pommes de terre à l'eau;
a boiled egg un œuf à la coque

boiling adj **It's boiling in here!**
Il fait une chaleur torride ici!;
boiling hot torride ▷ a boiling hot
day une journée torride

bolt n ❶ (on door) verrou m ❷ (with
nut) boulon m

bomb n bombe f
▶ vb bombarder

bomber n bombardier m

bombing n attentat m à la bombe

bone n ❶ (of human, animal) os m
❷ (of fish) arête f

bonfire n feu m (pl feux)

bonnet n (of car) capot m

bonus n ❶ (extra payment) prime f
❷ (added advantage) plus m

book n livre m
▶ vb réserver ▷ We haven't booked.
Nous n'avons pas réservé.

bookcase n bibliothèque f

booklet n brochure f

bookshelf n étagère f à livres

bookshop n librairie f

boot n ❶ (of car) coffre m ❷ (fashion
boot) botte f ❸ (for hiking)
chaussure f de marche; **football
boots** des chaussures de foot

border n frontière f

bore vb see **bear**

bored adj **to be bored** s'ennuyer ▷ I
was bored. Je m'ennuyais.; **to get
bored** s'ennuyer

boring adj ennuyeux (f ennuyeuse)

born adj **to be born** naître ▷ I was
born in 1982. Je suis né en mille neuf
cent quatre-vingt-deux.

borrow vb emprunter ▷ Can I
borrow your pen? Je peux emprunter
ton stylo?; **to borrow something
from somebody** emprunter
quelque chose à quelqu'un ▷ I
borrowed some money from a friend.
J'ai emprunté de l'argent à un ami.

Bosnia n Bosnie f
Bosnian adj bosniaque
boss n patron m, patronne f
boss around vb to boss
somebody around donner des
ordres à quelqu'un
bossy adj autoritaire
both adj, pron tous les deux (f
toutes les deux) ▷ We both went.
Nous y sommes allés tous les deux.
▷ Both of your answers are wrong.
Vos réponses sont toutes les deux
mauvaises. ▷ Both of them have
left. Ils sont partis tous les deux.
▷ Both of us went. Nous y sommes
allés tous les deux. ▷ Both Maggie
and John are against it. Maggie et
John sont tous les deux contre.; **He
speaks both German and Italian.**
Il parle allemand et italien.
bother vb ❶ (worry) tracasser
▷ What's bothering you? Qu'est-ce
qui te tracasse? ❷ (disturb)
déranger ▷ I'm sorry to bother you.
Je suis désolé de vous déranger.;
no bother aucun problème; **Don't
bother!** Ça n'est pas la peine!; **to
bother to do something** prendre
la peine de faire quelque chose
▷ He didn't bother to tell me about it.
Il n'a pas pris la peine de m'en
parler.
bottle n bouteille f
bottle bank n conteneur m à verre
bottle-opener n ouvre-bouteille m
bottom n ❶ (of container, bag, sea)
fond m ❷ (buttocks) derrière m
❸ (of page, list) bas m
▶ adj inférieur(e) ▷ the bottom shelf

l'étagère inférieure; **the bottom
sheet** le drap de dessous
bought vb see **buy**
bounce vb rebondir
bouncer n videur m
bound adj He's bound to fail. Il va
sûrement échouer.
boundary n frontière f
bow n ❶ (knot) nœud m ▷ to tie a
bow faire un nœud ❷ arc m ▷ a bow
and arrows un arc et des flèches
▶ vb faire une révérence
bowl n (for soup, cereal) bol m
▶ vb (in cricket) lancer la balle
bowling n bowling m; **to go
bowling** jouer au bowling; **a
bowling alley** un bowling
bow tie n nœud m papillon
box n boîte f ▷ a box of matches une
boîte d'allumettes; **a cardboard
box** un carton
boxer n boxeur m
boxer shorts npl caleçon m
boxing n boxe f
Boxing Day n lendemain m de
Noël ▷ on Boxing Day le lendemain
de Noël

> Word for word, the French
> means "the day after
> Christmas".

boy n garçon m
boyfriend n copain m ▷ Have you
got a boyfriend? Est-ce que tu as
un copain?
bra n soutien-gorge m (pl soutiens-
gorge)
brace n (on teeth) appareil m ▷ She
wears a brace. Elle a un appareil.
bracelet n bracelet m

brackets npl in brackets entre parenthèses

brain n cerveau m (pl cerveaux)

brainy adj intelligent(e)

brake n frein m
▶ vb freiner

branch n ❶ (of tree) branche f
❷ (of bank) agence f

brand n marque f ▷ a well-known brand of coffee une marque de café bien connue

brand-new adj tout neuf (f toute neuve)

brandy n cognac m

brass n cuivre m; **the brass section** les cuivres

brass band n fanfare f

brave adj courageux (f courageuse)

Brazil n Brésil m; **in Brazil** au Brésil

bread n pain m ▷ brown bread pain complet ▷ white bread pain blanc; **bread and butter** les tartines de pain beurrées

break n ❶ (rest) pause f ▷ to take a break faire une pause ❷ (at school) récréation f ▷ during morning break pendant la récréation du matin; **the Christmas break** les vacances de Noël; **Give me a break!** Laissemoi tranquille!
▶ vb ❶ casser ▷ Careful, you'll break something! Attention, tu vas casser quelque chose! ❷ (get broken) se casser ▷ Careful, it'll break! Attention, ça va se casser!; **to break one's leg** se casser la jambe ▷ I broke my leg. Je me suis cassé la jambe.; **He broke his arm.** Il s'est cassé le bras.; **to break a promise**

rompre une promesse; **to break a record** battre un record; **to break the law** violer la loi

break down vb tomber en panne
▷ The car broke down. La voiture est tombée en panne.

break in vb entrer par effraction

break out vb ❶ (fire) se déclarer ❷ (war) éclater ❸ (prisoner) s'évader; **to break out in a rash** être couvert de boutons

break up vb ❶ (crowd) se disperser ❷ (meeting, party) se terminer ❸ (couple) se séparer; **to break up a fight** mettre fin à une bagarre; **We break up next Wednesday.** Nos vacances commencent mercredi.

breakdown n ❶ (in vehicle) panne f ▷ to have a breakdown tomber en panne ❷ (mental) dépression f ▷ to have a breakdown faire une dépression

breakfast n petit déjeuner m
▷ What would you like for breakfast? Qu'est-ce vous voulez pour le petit déjeuner?

break-in n cambriolage m

breast n (of woman) sein m; **chicken breast** le blanc de poulet

breaststroke n brasse f

breath n haleine f ▷ to have bad breath avoir mauvaise haleine; **to be out of breath** être essoufflé; **to get one's breath back** reprendre son souffle

breathe vb respirer

breathe in vb inspirer

breathe out vb expirer

breed vb (reproduce) se reproduire; **to breed dogs** faire de l'élevage de chiens
▶ n race f

breeze n brise f

brewery n brasserie f

bribe vb soudoyer

brick n brique f; **a brick wall** un mur en brique

bride n mariée f

bridegroom n marié m

bridesmaid n demoiselle f d'honneur

bridge n ❶ pont m ▷ a suspension bridge un pont suspendu ❷ bridge m ▷ to play bridge jouer au bridge

brief adj bref (f brève)

briefcase n serviette f

briefly adv brièvement

briefs npl slip m; **a pair of briefs** un slip

bright adj ❶ (colour, light) vif (f vive) ▷ a bright colour une couleur vive; **bright blue** bleu vif ▷ a bright blue car une voiture bleu vif ❷ intelligent(e) ▷ He's not very bright. Il n'est pas très intelligent.

brilliant adj ❶ (wonderful) génial(e) (mpl géniaux) ▷ Brilliant! Génial! ❷ (clever) brillant(e) ▷ a brilliant scientist un savant brillant

bring vb ❶ apporter ▷ Bring warm clothes. Apportez des vêtements chauds. ❷ (person) amener ▷ Can I bring a friend? Est-ce que je peux amener un ami?

bring back vb rapporter

bring up vb élever ▷ She brought up 5 children on her own. Elle a élevé cinq enfants toute seule.

Britain n Grande-Bretagne f; **in Britain** en Grande-Bretagne; **to Britain** en Grande-Bretagne; **I'm from Britain.** Je suis britannique.; **Great Britain** la Grande-Bretagne

British adj britannique ▷ the British les Britanniques; **the British Isles** les îles fpl Britanniques

Brittany n Bretagne f; **in Brittany** en Bretagne; **to Brittany** en Bretagne; **She's from Brittany.** Elle est bretonne.

broad adj (wide) large; **in broad daylight** en plein jour

broadband n ADSL m ▷ We're getting broadband. On va avoir l'ADSL.

broad bean n fève f

broadcast n émission f
▶ vb diffuser ▷ The interview was broadcast all over the world. L'interview a été diffusé dans le monde entier.; **to broadcast live** retransmettre en direct

broccoli n brocolis mpl

brochure n brochure f

broke vb see **break**
▶ adj **to be broke** (without money) être fauché(e)

broken adj cassé(e) ▷ It's broken. C'est cassé. ▷ He's got a broken arm. Il a le bras cassé.

bronchitis n bronchite f

bronze n bronze m ▷ the bronze medal la médaille de bronze

brooch n broche f

broom n balai m

brother n frère m ▷ my brother mon frère ▷ my big brother mon grand frère

brother-in-law n beau-frère m (pl beaux-frères)

brought vb see **bring**

brown adj ❶ (clothes) marron inv ❷ (hair) brun(e) ❸ (tanned) bronzé(e); **brown bread** pain complet

browse vb (on internet) parcourir le Net

bruise n bleu m

brush n ❶ brosse f ❷ (paintbrush) pinceau m (pl pinceaux)
▶ vb brosser; **to brush one's hair** se brosser les cheveux ▷ I brushed my hair. Je me suis brossé les cheveux.; **to brush one's teeth** se brosser les dents ▷ I brush my teeth every night. Je me brosse les dents tous les soirs.

Brussels n Bruxelles; **in Brussels** à Bruxelles; **to Brussels** à Bruxelles

Brussels sprouts npl choux mpl de Bruxelles

bubble n bulle f

bubble bath n bain m moussant

bubble gum n chewing-gum m

bucket n seau m (pl seaux)

buckle n (on belt, watch, shoe) boucle f

Buddhism n bouddhisme m

Buddhist adj bouddhiste

budgie n perruche f

buffet n buffet m

buffet car n voiture-bar f

bug n ❶ (insect) insecte m ❷ (infection) microbe m ▷ There's a

bug going round. Il y a un microbe qui traîne.; **a stomach bug** une gastroentérite ❸ (in computer) bug m

build vb construire ▷ He's building a garage. Il construit un garage.; **to build up** (increase) s'accumuler

builder n ❶ (owner of firm) entrepreneur m ❷ (worker) maçon m

building n bâtiment m

built vb see **build**

bulb n (electric) ampoule f

Bulgaria n Bulgarie f

bull n taureau m (pl taureaux)

bullet n balle f

bullfighting n tauromachie f

bully n brute f ▷ He's a big bully. C'est une brute.
▶ vb tyranniser

bum n (bottom) derrière m

bum bag n banane f

bump n ❶ (lump) bosse f ❷ (minor accident) accrochage m ▷ We had a bump. Nous avons eu un accrochage.

bump into vb **to bump into something** rentrer dans quelque chose ▷ We bumped into his car. Nous sommes rentrés dans sa voiture.; **to bump into somebody** (1) (literally) rentrer dans quelqu'un ▷ He stopped suddenly and I bumped into him. Il s'est arrêté subitement et je lui suis rentré dedans.
(2) (meet by chance) rencontrer par hasard; **I bumped into Jane in the supermarket.** J'ai rencontré Jane par hasard au supermarché.

bumper n pare-chocs m (pl pare-chocs)

bumpy adj cahoteux (f cahoteuse)

bun n petit pain m au lait

bunch n **a bunch of flowers** un bouquet de fleurs; **a bunch of grapes** une grappe de raisin; **a bunch of keys** un trousseau de clés

bunches npl couettes fpl ▷ She has her hair in bunches. Elle a des couettes.

bungalow n bungalow m

bunk n couchette f; **bunk beds** lits superposés

burger n hamburger m

burglar n cambrioleur m, cambrioleuse f

burglary n cambriolage m

burgle vb cambrioler ▷ Her house was burgled. Sa maison a été cambriolée.

burn n brûlure f
▶ vb ❶ (rubbish, documents) brûler ❷ (food) faire brûler ▷ I burned the cake. J'ai fait brûler le gâteau.; **to burn oneself** se brûler ▷ I burned myself on the oven door. Je me suis brûlé sur la porte du four.; **I've burned my hand.** Je me suis brûlé la main.; **to burn down** brûler ▷ The factory burned down. L'usine a brûlé.

burst vb éclater ▷ The balloon burst. Le ballon a éclaté.; **to burst a balloon** faire éclater un ballon; **to burst out laughing** éclater de rire; **to burst into flames** prendre feu; **to burst into tears** fondre en larmes

bury vb enterrer

bus n autobus m ▷ a bus stop un arrêt d'autobus; **the school bus** le car scolaire; **a bus pass** une carte d'abonnement pour le bus; **a bus station** une gare routière; **a bus ticket** un ticket de bus

bush n buisson m

business n ❶ (firm) entreprise f ▷ He's got his own business. Il a sa propre entreprise. ❷ (commerce) affaires fpl ▷ He's away on business. Il est en voyage d'affaires.; **a business trip** un voyage d'affaires; **It's none of my business.** Ça ne me regarde pas.

businessman n homme m d'affaires

businesswoman n femme f d'affaires

bust n (chest) poitrine f

busy adj ❶ (person, phone line) occupé(e) ❷ (day, schedule) chargé(e) ❸ (shop, street) très fréquenté(e)

but conj mais ▷ I'd like to come, but I'm busy. J'aimerais venir mais je suis occupé.

butcher n boucher m ▷ He's a butcher. Il est boucher.

butcher's n boucherie f

butter n beurre m

butterfly n papillon m

button n bouton m

buy vb acheter ▷ He bought me an ice cream. Il m'a acheté une glace.; **to buy something from somebody** acheter quelque chose à quelqu'un ▷ I bought a watch from

a
b
c
d
e
f
g
h
i
j
k
l
m
n
o
p
q
r
s
t
u
v
w
x
y
z

him. Je lui ai acheté une montre.
▶ *n* **It was a good buy.** C'était une bonne affaire.

by *prep* **①** par ▷ *The thieves were caught by the police.* Les voleurs ont été arrêtés par la police. **②** de ▷ *a painting by Picasso* un tableau de Picasso **③** en ▷ *by car* en voiture ▷ *by train* en train ▷ *by bus* en autobus **④** (*close to*) à côté de ▷ *Where's the bank? — It's by the post office.* Où est la banque? — Elle est à côté de la poste. **⑤** (*not later than*) avant ▷ *We have to be there by 4 o'clock.* Nous devons y être avant quatre heures.; **by the time ...** quand ... ▷ *By the time I got there it was too late.* Quand je suis arrivé il était déjà trop tard.; **That's fine by me.** Ça me va.; **all by himself** seul; **all by herself** toute seule; **I did it all by myself.** Je l'ai fait tout seul.; **by the way** au fait

bye *excl* salut!

bypass *n* route f de contournement

C

cab *n* taxi *m*

cabbage *n* chou *m* (*pl* choux)

cabin *n* (*on ship*) cabine f

cable *n* câble *m*

cable car *n* téléphérique *m*

cable television *n* télévision f par câble

cactus *n* cactus *m*

café *n* café *m*

  ● Cafés in France sell both
  ● alcoholic and non-alcoholic
  ● drinks.

cafeteria *n* cafétéria f

cage *n* cage f

cagoule *n* K-way® *m*

cake *n* gâteau *m* (*pl* gâteaux)

calculate *vb* calculer

calculation *n* calcul *m*

calculator *n* machine f à calculer

calendar *n* calendrier *m*

calf n ❶ (of cow) veau m (pl veaux) ❷ (of leg) mollet m

call n (by phone) appel m ▷ Thanks for your call. Merci de votre appel.; **a phone call** un coup de téléphone; **to be on call** (doctor) être de permanence ▷ He's on call this evening. Il est de permanence ce soir.

▶ vb appeler ▷ I'll tell him you called. Je lui dirai que vous avez appelé. ▷ We called the police. Nous avons appelé la police. ▷ Everyone calls him Jimmy. Tout le monde l'appelle Jimmy.; **to be called** s'appeler ▷ What's she called? Elle s'appelle comment?; **to call somebody names** insulter quelqu'un; **He called me an idiot.** Il m'a traité d'idiot.

call back vb (phone again) rappeler ▷ I'll call back at 6 o'clock. Je rappellerai à six heures.

call for vb passer prendre ▷ I'll call for you at 2.30. Je passerai te prendre à deux heures et demie.

call off vb annuler ▷ The match was called off. Le match a été annulé.

call box n cabine f téléphonique

call centre n centre m d'appels

calm adj calme

calm down vb se calmer ▷ Calm down! Calme-toi!

calorie n calorie f

calves npl see **calf**

Cambodia n Cambodge m; **in Cambodia** au Cambodge

camcorder n caméscope m

came vb see **come**

camel n chameau m (pl chameaux)

camera n ❶ (for photos) appareil m photo (pl appareils photo) ❷ (for filming, TV) caméra f

cameraman n caméraman m

camp vb camper
▶ n camp m; **a camp bed** un lit de camp

campaign n campagne f

camper n ❶ (person) campeur m, campeuse f ❷ (van) camping-car m

camping n camping m; **to go camping** faire du camping ▷ We went camping in Cornwall. Nous avons fait du camping en Cornouailles.

campsite n terrain m de camping

can n ❶ (tin) boîte f ▷ a can of beer une boîte de bière ❷ (jerry can) bidon m ▷ a can of petrol un bidon d'essence

▶ vb ❶ (be able to, be allowed to) pouvoir ▷ I can't come. Je ne peux pas venir. ▷ Can I help you? Est-ce que je peux vous aider? ▷ You could hire a bike. Tu pourrais louer un vélo. ▷ I couldn't sleep because of the noise. Je ne pouvais pas dormir à cause du bruit.

| **can** is sometimes not translated.

▷ I can't hear you. Je ne t'entends pas. ▷ Can you speak French? Parlez-vous français? ❷ (have learnt how to) savoir ▷ I can swim. Je sais nager.; **That can't be true!** Ce n'est pas possible!; **You could be right.** Vous avez peut-être raison.

Canada n Canada m; **in Canada** au Canada; **to Canada** au Canada

Canadian adj canadien (f canadienne)
▶ n Canadien m, Canadienne f

canal n canal m (pl canaux)

Canaries npl **the Canaries** les îles fpl Canaries

canary n canari m

cancel vb annuler ▷ The match was cancelled. Le match a été annulé.

cancer n ① cancer m ▷ He's got cancer. Il a le cancer. ② Cancer m ▷ I'm Cancer. Je suis Cancer.

candidate n candidat m, candidate f

candle n bougie f

candy n (US) bonbons mpl; **a candy** un bonbon

candyfloss n barbe à papa

canned adj (food) en conserve

cannot vb see **can**

canoe n canoë m

canoeing n **to go canoeing** faire du canoë ▷ We went canoeing. Nous avons fait du canoë.

can-opener n ouvre-boîte m

can't vb see **can**

canteen n cantine f

canter vb aller au petit galop

canvas n toile f

cap n ① (hat) casquette f ② (of bottle, tube) bouchon m

capable adj capable

capacity n capacité f

capital n ① capitale f ▷ Cardiff is the capital of Wales. Cardiff est la capitale du pays de Galles. ② (letter) majuscule f ▷ Write your address in capitals. Écris ton adresse en majuscules.

capitalism n capitalisme m

Capricorn n Capricorne m ▷ I'm Capricorn. Je suis Capricorne.

captain n capitaine m ▷ She's captain of the hockey team. Elle est capitaine de l'équipe de hockey.

capture vb capturer

car n voiture f; **to go by car** aller en voiture ▷ We went by car. Nous y sommes allés en voiture.; **a car crash** un accident de voiture

caramel n caramel m

caravan n caravane f ▷ a caravan site un camping pour caravanes

carbon footprint n empreinte f écologique

card n carte f; **a card game** un jeu de cartes

cardboard n carton m

cardigan n cardigan m

cardphone n téléphone m à carte

care n soin m ▷ with care avec soin; **to take care of** s'occuper de ▷ I take care of the children on Saturdays. Le samedi, je m'occupe des enfants.; **Take care! (1)** (Be careful!) Fais attention! **(2)** (Look after yourself!) Prends bien soin de toi!
▶ vb **to care about** se soucier de ▷ They don't care about their image. Ils se soucient peu de leur image.; **I don't care!** Ça m'est égal! ▷ She doesn't care. Ça lui est égal.; **to care for somebody** (patients, old people) s'occuper de quelqu'un

career n carrière f; **a careers adviser** un conseiller d'orientation

careful adj Be careful! Fais attention!

carefully adv ❶ soigneusement ▷ She carefully avoided talking about it. Elle évitait soigneusement d'en parler. ❷ (safely) prudemment ▷ Drive carefully! Conduisez prudemment!; **Think carefully!** Réfléchis bien!

careless adj ❶ (work) peu soigné(e); **a careless mistake** une faute d'inattention ❷ (person) peu soigneux (f peu soigneuse) ▷ She's very careless. Elle est bien peu soigneuse. ❸ imprudent(e) ▷ a careless driver un conducteur imprudent

caretaker n gardien m, gardienne f

car-ferry n ferry m

cargo n cargaison f

car hire n location f de voitures

Caribbean adj antillais(e) ▷ Caribbean food la cuisine antillaise ▶ n ❶ (islands) Caraïbes fpl ▷ We're going to the Caribbean. Nous allons aux Caraïbes.; **He's from the Caribbean.** Il est antillais. ❷ (sea) mer f des Caraïbes

carnation n œillet m

carnival n carnaval m

carol n a Christmas carol un chant de Noël

car park n parking m

carpenter n charpentier m ▷ He's a carpenter. Il est charpentier.

carpentry n menuiserie f

carpet n ❶ tapis m ▷ a Persian carpet un tapis persan ❷ (fitted) moquette f

car rental n (US) location f de voitures

carriage n voiture f

carrier bag n sac m en plastique

carrot n carotte f

carry vb ❶ porter ▷ I'll carry your bag. Je vais porter ton sac. ❷ transporter ▷ a plane carrying 100 passengers un avion transportant cent passagers

carry on vb continuer ▷ She carried on talking. Elle a continué à parler.

carrycot n porte-bébé m

cart n charrette f

carton n (of milk, juice) brique f

cartoon n ❶ (film) dessin animé ❷ (in newspaper) dessin humoristique; **a strip cartoon** une bande dessinée

cartridge n cartouche f

carve vb (meat) découper

case n ❶ valise f ▷ I've packed my case. J'ai fait ma valise. ❷ cas m (pl cas) ▷ in some cases dans certains cas; **in that case** dans ce cas ▷ I don't want it. — In that case, I'll take it. Je n'en veux pas. — Dans ce cas, je le prends.; **in case** au cas où ▷ in case it rains au cas où il pleuvrait; **just in case** à tout hasard ▷ Take some money, just in case. Prends de l'argent à tout hasard.

cash n argent m ▷ I'm a bit short of cash. Je suis un peu à court d'argent.; **in cash** en liquide ▷ £2000 in cash deux mille livres en liquide; **to pay cash** payer comptant; **a cash card** une carte de retrait; **the cash desk** la caisse;

a cash dispenser un distributeur automatique de billets; **a cash register** une caisse

cashew n noix f de cajou

cashier n caissier m, caissière f

cashmere n cachemire m ▷ a cashmere sweater un pull en cachemire

casino n casino m

cassette n cassette f; **a cassette player** un lecteur de cassettes; **a cassette recorder** un magnétophone

cast n acteurs mpl ▷ After the play, we met the cast. Après la représentation, nous avons rencontré les acteurs.

castle n château m (pl châteaux)

casual adj ① décontracté(e) ▷ casual clothes les vêtements décontractés ② désinvolte ▷ a casual attitude une attitude désinvolte ③ en passant ▷ It was just a casual remark. C'était juste une remarque en passant.

casualty n (in hospital) urgences fpl

cat n chat m, chatte f ▷ Have you got a cat? Est-ce que tu as un chat?

catalogue n catalogue m

catastrophe n catastrophe f

catch vb ① attraper ▷ to catch a thief attraper un voleur; **to catch somebody doing something** attraper quelqu'un en train de faire quelque chose ▷ If they catch you smoking ... S'ils t'attrapent en train de fumer ...; **to catch a cold** attraper un rhume ② (bus, train) prendre ▷ We caught the last bus.

On a pris le dernier bus. ③ (hear) saisir ▷ I didn't catch his name. Je n'ai pas saisi son nom.; **to catch up** rattraper son retard ▷ I've got to catch up: I was away last week. Je dois rattraper mon retard: j'étais absent la semaine dernière.

category n catégorie f

catering n restauration f

cathedral n cathédrale f

Catholic adj catholique
▶ n catholique mf ▷ I'm a Catholic. Je suis catholique.

cattle npl bétail m

caught vb see **catch**

cauliflower n chou-fleur m (pl choux-fleurs)

cause n cause f
▶ vb provoquer ▷ to cause an accident provoquer un accident

cautious adj prudent(e)

cave n grotte f

CD n CD m (pl CD)

CD burner n graveur m de CD

CD player n platine f laser

CD-ROM n CD-ROM m (pl CD-ROM)

ceiling n plafond m

celebrate vb (birthday) fêter

celebrity n célébrité f

celery n céleri m

cell n cellule f

cellar n cave f ▷ a wine cellar une cave à vins

cello n violoncelle m ▷ I play the cello. Je joue du violoncelle.

cell phone n téléphone m portable

cement n ciment m

cemetery n cimetière m

cent n cent m ▷ twenty cents vingt cents

centenary n centenaire m

center n (US) = **centre**

centigrade adj centigrade ▷ 20 degrees centigrade vingt degrés centigrade

centimetre (US **centimeter**) n centimètre m

central adj central(e) (mpl centraux)

central heating n chauffage m central

centre n centre m ▷ a sports centre un centre sportif

century n siècle m ▷ the 21st century le vingt et unième siècle

cereal n céréales fpl ▷ I have cereal for breakfast. Je prends des céréales au petit déjeuner.

ceremony n cérémonie f

certain adj certain(e) ▷ a certain person une certaine personne ▷ I'm certain it was him. Je suis certain que c'était lui.; **I don't know for certain.** Je n'en suis pas certain.; **to make certain** s'assurer ▷ I made certain the door was locked. Je me suis assuré que la porte était fermée à clé.

certainly adv vraiment ▷ I certainly expected something better. Je m'attendais vraiment à quelque chose de mieux.; **Certainly not!** Certainement pas!; **So it was a surprise? — It certainly was!** C'était donc une surprise? — Ça oui alors!

certificate n certificat m

chain n chaîne f

chair n ❶ chaise f ▷ a table and 4 chairs une table et quatre chaises ❷ (armchair) fauteuil m

chairlift n télésiège m

chairman n président m

chalet n chalet m

chalk n craie f

challenge n défi m

▶ vb **She challenged me to a race.** Elle m'a proposé de faire la course avec elle.

champagne n champagne m

champion n champion m, championne f

championship n championnat m

chance n ❶ chance f ▷ Do you think I've got any chance? Tu crois que j'ai une chance?; **No chance!** Pas question! ❷ occasion f ▷ I'd like to have a chance to travel. J'aimerais avoir l'occasion de voyager.; **I'll write when I get the chance.** J'écrirai quand j'aurai un moment.; **by chance** par hasard ▷ We met by chance. Nous nous sommes rencontrés par hasard.; **to take a chance** prendre un risque ▷ I'm taking no chances! Je ne veux prendre aucun risque!

change vb ❶ changer ▷ The town has changed a lot. La ville a beaucoup changé. ▷ I'd like to change £50. Je voudrais changer cinquante livres.

Use **changer de** when you change one thing for another.

❷ changer de ▷ You have to change trains in Paris. Il faut changer de

a b c d e f g h i j k l m n o p q r s t u v w x y z

train à Paris. ▷ *He wants to change his job.* Il veut changer d'emploi.;
to change one's mind changer d'avis ▷ *I've changed my mind.* J'ai changé d'avis.; **to change gear** changer de vitesse ❺ se changer ▷ *She's changing to go out.* Elle est en train de se changer pour sortir.; **to get changed** se changer ▷ *I'm going to get changed.* Je vais me changer. ❻ (*swap*) échanger ▷ *Can I change this sweater? It's too small.* Est-ce que je peux échanger ce pull? Il est trop petit.
▶ *n* ❶ changement *m* ▷ *There's been a change of plan.* Il y a eu un changement de programme. ❷ (*money*) monnaie *f* ▷ *I haven't got any change.* Je n'ai pas de monnaie.; **a change of clothes** des vêtements de rechange; **for a change** pour changer ▷ *Let's play tennis for a change.* Si on jouait au tennis pour changer?
changing room *n* ❶ (*in shop*) salon *m* d'essayage ❷ (*for sport*) vestiaire *m*
channel *n* (*TV*) chaîne *f* ▷ *There's football on the other channel.* Il y a du football sur l'autre chaîne.; **the Channel** la Manche; **the Channel Islands** les îles *f* Anglo-Normandes; **the Channel Tunnel** le tunnel sous la Manche
chaos *n* chaos *m*
chapel *n* (*part of church*) chapelle *f*
chapter *n* chapitre *m*
character *n* ❶ caractère *m* ▷ *Give me some idea of his character.*

Décris-moi un peu son caractère.; **She's quite a character.** C'est un drôle de numéro. ❷ (*in play, film*) personnage *m* ▷ *The character played by Depardieu ...* Le personnage joué par Depardieu ...
characteristic *n* caractéristique *f*
charcoal *n* charbon *m* de bois
charge *n* frais *mpl* ▷ *Is there a charge for delivery?* Est-ce qu'il y a des frais de livraison?; **an extra charge** un supplément; **free of charge** gratuit; **to reverse the charges** appeler en P.C.V. ▷ *I'd like to reverse the charges.* Je voudrais appeler en P.C.V.; **to be on a charge** être inculpé ▷ *He's on a charge of murder.* Il est inculpé de meurtre.; **to be in charge** être responsable ▷ *Mrs Munday was in charge of the group.* Madame Munday était responsable du groupe.
▶ *vb* ❶ (*money*) prendre ▷ *They charge £10 an hour.* Ils prennent dix livres de l'heure. ❷ (*with crime*) inculper ▷ *The police have charged him with murder.* La police l'a inculpé de meurtre.
charity *n* association *f* caritative ▷ *He gave the money to charity.* Il a donné l'argent à une association caritative.
charm *n* charme *m* ▷ *He's got a lot of charm.* Il a beaucoup de charme.
charming *adj* charmant(e)
chart *n* tableau *m* (*pl* tableaux) ▷ *The chart shows the rise of unemployment.* Le tableau indique la progression du chômage.;

the charts le hit-parade ▷ *This album is number one in the charts.* Cet album est numéro un au hit-parade.

charter flight n charter m

chase vb pourchasser
▶ n poursuite f ▷ *a car chase* une poursuite en voiture

chat n **to have a chat** bavarder
▶ vb bavarder; **to chat somebody up** draguer quelqu'un (*informal*)
▷ *He's not very good at chatting up girls.* Il n'est pas très doué pour draguer les filles.

chatroom n forum m de discussion

chat show n talk-show m

chauvinist n **a male chauvinist** un machiste

cheap adj bon marché inv ▷ *a cheap T-shirt* un T-shirt bon marché

cheaper adj moins cher (f moins chère) ▷ *It's cheaper by bus.* C'est moins cher en bus.

cheat vb tricher ▷ *You're cheating!* Tu triches!
▶ n tricheur m, tricheuse f

check n ① contrôle m ▷ *a security check* un contrôle de sécurité ② (*US*) chèque m ▷ *to write a check* faire un chèque ③ (*US*) addition f ▷ *Can we have the check, please?* L'addition, s'il vous plaît.
▶ vb vérifier ▷ *I'll check the time of the train.* Je vais vérifier l'heure du train.; **to check in** (1) (*at airport*) se présenter à l'enregistrement ▷ *What time do I have to check in?* À quelle heure est-ce que je dois me présenter à l'enregistrement?

(2) (*in hotel*) se présenter à la réception; **to check out** (*from hotel*) régler sa note

checked adj (*fabric*) à carreaux

checkers n (*US*) dames fpl ▷ **to play checkers** jouer aux dames

check-in n enregistrement m

checkout n caisse f

check-up n examen m de routine

cheek n ① joue f ▷ *He kissed her on the cheek.* Il l'a embrassée sur la joue. ② culot m ▷ *What a cheek!* Quel culot!

cheeky adj effronté(e) ▷ *Don't be cheeky!* Ne sois pas effronté!; **a cheeky smile** un sourire malicieux

cheer n hourras mpl; **to give a cheer** pousser des hourras; **Cheers!** (1) (*good health*) À la vôtre! (2) (*thanks*) Merci!
▶ vb applaudir; **to cheer somebody up** remonter le moral à quelqu'un ▷ *I was trying to cheer him up.* J'essayais de lui remonter le moral.; **Cheer up!** Ne te laisse pas abattre!

cheerful adj gai(e)

cheese n fromage m

chef n chef m

chemical n produit m chimique

chemist n ① (*dispenser*) pharmacien m, pharmacienne f ② (*shop*) pharmacie f ▷ *You get it from the chemist.* C'est vendu en pharmacie.
● Chemist's shops in France are
● identified by a special green
● cross outside the shop.
③ (*scientist*) chimiste mf

a
b
c
d
e
f
g
h
i
j
k
l
m
n
o
p
q
r
s
t
u
v
w
x
y
z

chemistry n chimie f ▷ *the chemistry lab* le laboratoire de chimie

cheque n chèque m ▷ *to write a cheque* faire un chèque

chequebook n carnet m de chèques

cherry n cerise f

chess n échecs mpl ▷ *to play chess* jouer aux échecs

chessboard n échiquier m

chest n (of person) poitrine f ▷ *his chest measurement* son tour de poitrine; **a chest of drawers** une commode

chestnut n marron m ▷ *We have turkey with chestnuts.* Nous mangeons de la dinde aux marrons.

chew vb mâcher

chewing gum n chewing-gum m

chick n poussin m ▷ *a hen and her chicks* une poule et ses poussins

chicken n poulet m

chickenpox n varicelle f

chickpeas npl pois mpl chiches

chief n chef m ▷ *the chief of security* le chef de la sécurité
▶ adj principal(e) ▷ *His chief reason for resigning was the low pay.* La principale raison de sa démission était son mauvais salaire.

child n enfant mf ▷ *all the children* tous les enfants

childish adj puéril(e)

child minder n nourrice f

children npl see **child**

Chile n Chili m; **in Chile** au Chili

chill vb mettre au frais ▷ *Put the*

wine in the fridge to chill. Mets le vin au frais dans le réfrigérateur.

chilli n piment m

chilly adj froid(e)

chimney n cheminée f

chin n menton m

china n porcelaine f ▷ *a china plate* une assiette en porcelaine

China n Chine f; **in China** en Chine

Chinese adj chinois(e) ▷ *a Chinese restaurant* un restaurant chinois; **a Chinese man** un Chinois; **a Chinese woman** une Chinoise
▶ n (language) chinois m; **the Chinese** (people) les Chinois

chip n ❶ (food) frite f ▷ *We bought some chips.* Nous avons acheté des frites. ❷ (in computer) puce f

chiropodist n pédicure mf ▷ *He's a chiropodist.* Il est pédicure.

chives npl ciboulette f

chocolate n chocolat m ▷ *a chocolate cake* un gâteau au chocolat; **hot chocolate** le chocolat chaud

choice n choix m ▷ *I had no choice.* Je n'avais pas le choix.

choir n chorale f ▷ *I sing in the school choir.* Je chante dans la chorale de l'école.

choke vb s'étrangler ▷ *He choked on a fishbone.* Il s'est étranglé avec une arête de poisson.

choose vb choisir ▷ *It's difficult to choose.* C'est difficile de choisir.

chop vb émincer ▷ *Chop the onions.* Émincez les oignons.
▶ n côte f ▷ *a pork chop* une côte de porc

chopsticks npl baguettes fpl

chose, chosen vb see **choose**

Christ n Christ m ▷ the birth of Christ la naissance du Christ

christening n baptême m

Christian n chrétien m, chrétienne f
▶ adj chrétien (f chrétienne)

Christian name n prénom m

Christmas n Noël m ▷ Happy Christmas! Joyeux Noël!;
Christmas Day le jour de Noël;
Christmas Eve la veille de Noël;
a Christmas tree un arbre de Noël; **a Christmas card** une carte de Noël

- The French more often send
- greetings cards (**une carte de**
- **vœux**) in January rather than at
- Christmas, with best wishes for
- the New Year.

Christmas dinner le repas de Noël

- Most French people have their
- Christmas meal (**réveillon**
- **de Noël**) on the evening of
- Christmas Eve, though some
- have a **repas de Noël** on
- Christmas Day.

Christmas pudding

- The French usually have a
- Yule log (**une bûche de Noël**)
- for pudding at the Christmas
- meal. You could explain what
- Christmas pudding is using the
- example given.

▷ Christmas pudding is made with dried fruit and spices, and steamed. Le "Christmas pudding" est un

gâteau avec des raisins secs, parfumé avec des épices et cuit à la vapeur.

chunk n gros morceau m (pl gros morceaux) ▷ Cut the meat into chunks. Coupez la viande en gros morceaux.

church n église f ▷ I don't go to church every Sunday. Je ne vais pas à l'église tous les dimanches.;
the Church of England l'Église anglicane

cider n cidre m

cigar n cigare m

cigarette n cigarette f

cigarette lighter n briquet m

cinema n cinéma m ▷ I'm going to the cinema this evening. Je vais au cinéma ce soir.

cinnamon n cannelle f

circle n cercle m

circular adj circulaire

circumflex n accent m circonflexe

circumstances npl circonstances fpl

circus n cirque m

citizen n citoyen m, citoyenne f ▷ a French citizen un citoyen français

citizenship n citoyenneté f

city n ville f; **the city centre** le centre-ville ▷ It's in the city centre. C'est au centre-ville.

civilization n civilisation f

civil servant n fonctionnaire mf

civil war n guerre f civile

claim vb ❶ prétendre ▷ He claims to have found the money. Il prétend avoir trouvé l'argent. ❷ (receive) percevoir ▷ She's claiming *unemployment benefit.* Elle perçoit des allocations chômage.; **She can't claim unemployment benefit.** Elle n'a pas droit aux allocations chômage.; **to claim on one's insurance** se faire rembourser par son assurance ▷ *We claimed on our insurance.* On s'est fait rembourser par notre assurance.

▶ *n* (on insurance policy) demande f d'indemnité ▷ *to make a claim* faire une demande d'indemnité

clap *vb* (applaud) applaudir; **to clap one's hands** frapper dans ses mains ▷ *I've trained my dog to sit when I clap my hands.* J'ai dressé mon chien à s'asseoir quand je frappe dans mes mains.

clarinet *n* clarinette f ▷ *I play the clarinet.* Je joue de la clarinette.

clash *vb* ❶ (colours) jurer ▷ *These two colours clash.* Ces deux couleurs jurent. ❷ (events) tomber en même temps ▷ *The concert clashes with Ann's party.* Le concert tombe en même temps que la soirée d'Ann.

clasp *n* (of necklace) fermoir m

class *n* ❶ (group) classe f ▷ *We're in the same class.* Nous sommes dans la même classe. ❷ (lesson) cours m ▷ *I go to dancing classes.* Je vais à des cours de danse.

classic *adj* classique ▷ *a classic example* un cas classique
▶ *n* (book, film) classique m

classical *adj* classique ▷ *I like classical music.* J'aime la musique classique.

classmate *n* camarade m de classe, camarade f de classe

classroom *n* classe f

classroom assistant *n* aide-éducateur m, aide-éducatrice f

claw *n* ❶ (of cat, dog) griffe f ❷ (of bird) serre f ❸ (of crab, lobster) pince f

clay *n* argile f

clean *adj* propre ▷ *a clean shirt* une chemise propre
▶ *vb* nettoyer

cleaner *n* ❶ (woman) femme f de ménage ❷ (man) agent m d'entretien

cleaner's *n* teinturerie f

cleansing lotion *n* lotion f démaquillante

clear *adj* ❶ clair(e) ▷ *It's clear you don't believe me.* Il est clair que tu ne me crois pas. ❷ (road, way) libre ▷ *The road's clear now.* La route est libre maintenant.
▶ *vb* dégager ▷ *The police are clearing the road after the accident.* La police dégage la route après l'accident. ❷ (fog, mist) se dissiper ▷ *The mist cleared.* La brume s'est dissipée.; **to be cleared of a crime** être reconnu non coupable d'un crime ▷ *She was cleared of murder.* Elle a été reconnue non coupable du meurtre.; **to clear the table** débarrasser la table ▷ *I'll clear the table.* Je vais débarrasser la table.; **to clear up** ranger ▷ *Who's going to clear all this up?* Qui va ranger tout ça?; **I think it's going to clear up.**

(weather) Je pense que le temps
va se lever.

clearly adv ❶ clairement ▷ She
explained it very clearly. Elle
l'a expliqué très clairement.
❷ nettement ▷ The French coast
was clearly visible. On distinguait
nettement la côte française.
❸ distinctement ▷ to speak clearly
parler distinctement

clementine n clémentine f

clever adj ❶ intelligent(e) ▷ She's
very clever. Elle est très intelligente.
❷ (ingenious) astucieux (f
astucieuse) ▷ a clever system un
système astucieux; **What a clever
idea!** Quelle bonne idée!

click n (of door, camera) petit bruit m
▶ vb (with mouse) cliquer; **to click
on an icon** cliquer sur une icône

client n client m, cliente f

cliff n falaise f

climate n climat m

climb vb ❶ escalader ▷ We're going
to climb Snowdon. Nous allons
escalader le Snowdon. ❷ (stairs)
monter

climber n grimpeur m,
grimpeuse f

climbing n escalade f; **to go
climbing** faire de l'escalade ▷ We're
going climbing in Scotland. Nous
allons faire de l'escalade en Écosse.

Clingfilm® n film m alimentaire

clinic n centre m médical (pl centres
médicaux)

clip n ❶ (for hair) barrette f ❷ (film)
court extrait m ▷ some clips from
Brad Pitt's latest film quelques

courts extraits du dernier film de
Brad Pitt

cloakroom n ❶ (for coats) vestiaire
m ❷ (toilet) toilettes fpl

clock n ❶ horloge f ▷ the
church clock l'horloge de l'église
❷ (smaller) pendule f; **an alarm
clock** un réveil; **a clock-radio** un
radio-réveil

close adj, adv ❶ (near) près ▷ The
shops are very close. Les magasins
sont tout près.; **close to** près de
▷ The youth hostel is close to the
station. L'auberge de jeunesse est
près de la gare.; **Come closer.**
Rapproche-toi. ❸ (in relationship)
proche ▷ We're just inviting close
relations. Nous n'invitons que les
parents proches. ▷ She's a close
friend of mine. C'est une proche
amie. ❸ (contest) très serré(e) ▷ It's
going to be very close. Ça va être
très serré. ❸ (weather) lourd ▷ It's
close this afternoon. Il fait lourd cet
après-midi.
▶ vb ❶ fermer ▷ The shops close at
5.30. Les magasins ferment à cinq
heures et demie. ❷ se fermer ▷ The
doors close automatically. Les portes
se ferment automatiquement.

closed adj fermé(e) ▷ The bank's
closed. La banque est fermée.

closely adv (look, examine) de près

cloth n (material) tissu m; **a cloth**
un chiffon ▷ Wipe it with a damp
cloth. Nettoyez-le avec un chiffon
humide.

clothes npl vêtements mpl ▷ new
clothes des vêtements neufs;

a clothes line un fil à linge; **a clothes peg** une pince à linge

clothing n = **clothes**

cloud n nuage m

cloudy adj nuageux (f nuageuse)

clove n **a clove of garlic** une gousse d'ail

clown n clown m

club n club m ▷ *a golf club* (society and for playing golf) un club de golf; **the youth club** la maison des jeunes; **clubs** (in cards) le trèfle ▷ *the ace of clubs* l'as de trèfle

clubbing n **to go clubbing** sortir en boîte

clue n indice m ▷ *an important clue* un indice important; **I haven't a clue.** Je n'en ai pas la moindre idée.

clumsy adj maladroit(e)

clutch n (of car) pédale f d'embrayage

clutter n désordre m ▷ *There's too much clutter in here.* Il y a trop de désordre ici.

coach n ❶ car m ▷ *We went there by coach.* Nous y sommes allés en car.; **the coach station** la gare routière; **a coach trip** une excursion en car ❷ (trainer) entraîneur m ▷ *the French coach* l'entraîneur de l'équipe de France

coal n charbon m; **a coal mine** une mine de charbon; **a coal miner** un mineur

coarse adj ❶ (surface, fabric) rugueux (f rugueuse) ▷ *The bag was made of coarse cloth.* Le sac était fait d'un tissu rugueux. ❷ (vulgar)

grossier (f grossière) ▷ *coarse language* un langage grossier

coast n côte f ▷ *It's on the west coast of Scotland.* C'est sur la côte ouest de l'Écosse.

coastguard n garde-côte m (pl garde-côtes)

coat n manteau m (pl manteaux) ▷ *a warm coat* un manteau chaud; **a coat of paint** une couche de peinture

coat hanger n cintre m

cobweb n toile f d'araignée

cocaine n cocaïne f

cockerel n coq m

cocoa n cacao m ▷ *a cup of cocoa* une tasse de cacao

coconut n noix f de coco

code n code m

coffee n café m; **A cup of coffee, please.** Un café, s'il vous plaît.

coffee table n table f basse

coffin n cercueil m

coin n pièce f de monnaie; **a 2 euro coin** une pièce de deux euros

coincidence n coïncidence f

Coke® n coca m ▷ *a can of Coke®* une boîte de coca

colander n passoire f

cold adj froid(e) ▷ *The water's cold.* L'eau est froide.; **It's cold today.** Il fait froid aujourd'hui.; **to be cold** (person) avoir froid ▷ *I'm cold.* J'ai froid.
   ▶ n ❶ froid m ▷ *I can't stand the cold.* Je ne supporte pas le froid. ❷ rhume m ▷ *to catch a cold* attraper un rhume; **to have a cold** avoir un rhume ▷ *I've got a bad cold.*

J'ai un gros rhume.; **a cold sore** un bouton de fièvre

coleslaw n salade f de chou cru à la mayonnaise

collapse vb s'effondrer ▷ He collapsed. Il s'est effondré.

collar n ❶ (of coat, shirt) col m ❷ (for animal) collier m

collarbone n clavicule f ▷ I broke my collarbone. Je me suis cassé la clavicule.

colleague n collègue mf

collect vb ❶ ramasser ▷ They collect the rubbish twice a week. Ils ramassent les ordures deux fois par semaine. ❷ faire collection de ▷ I collect stamps. Je fais collection de timbres. ❸ aller chercher ▷ Their mothers collect them from school. Leur mère va les chercher à l'école. ❹ faire une collecte ▷ They're collecting for charity. Ils font une collecte pour une association caritative.

collection n ❶ collection f ▷ my CD collection ma collection de CD ❷ collecte f ▷ a collection for charity une collecte pour une association caritative ❸ (of mail) levée f ▷ Next collection: 5pm Prochaine levée: 17 heures

collector n collectionneur m, collectionneuse f

college n collège m ▷ a technical college un collège d'enseignement technique

collide vb entrer en collision

collie n colley m

collision n collision f

colon n (punctuation mark) deux points mpl

colonel n colonel m

colour (US color) n couleur f ▷ What colour is it? C'est de quelle couleur?; **a colour film** (for camera) une pellicule en couleur

colourful (US colorful) adj coloré(e)

column n colonne f

comb n peigne m
  ▶ vb **to comb one's hair** se peigner ▷ You haven't combed your hair. Tu ne t'es pas peigné.

combination n combinaison f

combine vb ❶ allier ▷ The film combines humour with suspense. Le film allie l'humour au suspense. ❷ concilier ▷ It's difficult to combine a career with a family. Il est difficile de concilier carrière et vie de famille.

come vb ❶ venir ▷ I'll come with you. Je viens avec toi. ❷ (arrive) arriver ▷ I'm coming! J'arrive! ▷ They came late. Ils sont arrivés en retard.; **to come back** revenir ▷ Come back! Reviens!; **to come down** (1) (person, lift) descendre (2) (prices) baisser; **to come from** venir de ▷ Where do you come from? Tu viens d'où?; **to come in** entrer ▷ Come in! Entrez!; **Come on!** Allez!; **to come out** sortir ▷ It's just come out on video. Ça vient de sortir en vidéo.; **None of my photos came out.** Mes photos n'ont rien donné.; **to come round** (after faint, operation) reprendre connaissance;

to come up ▷ monter ▷ *Come up here!* Monte!; **to come up to somebody (1)** s'approcher de quelqu'un ▷ *She came up to me and kissed me.* Elle s'est approchée de moi et m'a embrassé. **(2)** (*to speak to them*) aborder quelqu'un ▷ *A man came up to me and said …* Un homme m'a abordé et m'a dit …

comedian n comique m

comedy n comédie f

comfortable adj ❶ (*bed, chair*) confortable ❷ (*person*) à l'aise ▷ *I'm very comfortable, thanks.* Je suis parfaitement à l'aise, merci.

comic n (*magazine*) illustré m

comic strip n bande f dessinée

comma n virgule f

command n ordre m

comment n commentaire m ▷ *He made no comment.* Il n'a fait aucun commentaire.; **No comment!** Je n'ai rien à dire!
▶ vb **to comment on something** faire des commentaires sur quelque chose

commentary n (*on TV, radio*) reportage m en direct

commentator n commentateur m sportif, commentatrice f sportive

commercial n spot m publicitaire

commit vb **to commit a crime** commettre un crime; **to commit oneself** s'engager ▷ *I don't want to commit myself.* Je ne veux pas m'engager.; **to commit suicide** se suicider ▷ *He committed suicide.* Il s'est suicidé.

committee n comité m

common adj courant(e) ▷ *"Smith" is a very common surname.* "Smith" est un nom de famille très courant.; **in common** en commun ▷ *We've got a lot in common.* Nous avons beaucoup de choses en commun.

Commons npl **the House of Commons** la Chambre des communes

common sense n bon sens m ▷ *Use your common sense!* Sers-toi de ton bon sens!

communicate vb communiquer

communication n communication f

communion n communion f ▷ *my First Communion* ma première communion

communism n communisme m

community n communauté f

commute vb faire la navette ▷ *She commutes between Liss and London.* Elle fait la navette entre Liss et Londres.

compact disc n disque m compact; **a compact disc player** une platine laser

company n ❶ société f ▷ *He works for a big company.* Il travaille pour une grosse société. ❷ compagnie f ▷ *an insurance company* une compagnie d'assurance; **to keep somebody company** tenir compagnie à quelqu'un ▷ *I'll keep you company.* Je vais te tenir compagnie.

comparatively adv relativement

compare vb comparer ▷ *People always compare him with his brother.* On le compare toujours à son frère.; **compared with** en comparaison de ▷ *Oxford is small compared with London.* Oxford est une petite ville en comparaison de Londres.

comparison n comparaison f

compartment n compartiment m

compass n boussole f

compatible adj compatible

compensation n indemnité f ▷ *They got £2000 compensation.* Ils ont reçu une indemnité de deux mille livres.

compete vb participer ▷ *I'm competing in the marathon.* Je participe au marathon.; **to compete for something** se disputer quelque chose ▷ *There are 50 students competing for 6 places.* Ils sont cinquante étudiants à se disputer six places.

competent adj compétent(e)

competition n concours m ▷ *a singing competition* un concours de chant

competitive adj compétitif (f compétitive) ▷ *a very competitive price* un prix très compétitif; **to be competitive** (person) avoir l'esprit de compétition ▷ *He's a very competitive person.* Il a vraiment l'esprit de compétition.

competitor n concurrent m, concurrente f

complain vb se plaindre ▷ *I'm going to complain to the manager.* Je vais

me plaindre au directeur.

complaint n plainte f ▷ *There were lots of complaints about the food.* Il y a eu beaucoup de plaintes à propos de la nourriture.

complete adj complet (f complète)

completely adv complètement

complexion n teint m

complicated adj compliqué(e)

compliment n compliment m
▶ vb complimenter ▷ *They complimented me on my French.* Ils m'ont complimenté sur mon français.

composer n compositeur m, compositrice f

comprehension n
❶ (understanding) compréhension f
❷ (school exercise) exercice m de compréhension

comprehensive adj complet (f complète) ▷ *a comprehensive guide* un guide complet

> Be careful not to translate **comprehensive** by **compréhensif**.

comprehensive school n
❶ collège m ❷ lycée m
- In France pupils go to a **collège**
- between the ages of 11 and 15,
- and then to a **lycée** until the
- age of 18.

compulsory adj obligatoire

computer n ordinateur m

computer game n jeu m électronique (pl jeux électroniques)

computer programmer n programmeur m, programmeuse f

▷ *She's a computer programmer.* Elle est programmeuse.
computer science n informatique f
computing n informatique f
concentrate vb se concentrer ▷ *I couldn't concentrate.* Je n'arrivais pas à me concentrer.
concentration n concentration f
concern n (preoccupation) inquiétude f ▷ *They expressed concern about the image of the school.* Ils ont exprimé leur inquiétude concernant l'image de l'école.
concerned adj **to be concerned** s'inquiéter ▷ *His mother is concerned about him.* Sa mère s'inquiète à son sujet.; **as far as I'm concerned** en ce qui me concerne
concerning prep concernant ▷ *For further information concerning the job, contact Mr Ross Hutchinson.* Pour plus d'informations concernant cet emploi, contacter M. Ross Hutchinson.
concert n concert m
conclusion n conclusion f
concrete n béton m
condemn vb condamner ▷ *The government has condemned the decision.* Le gouvernement a condamné cette décision.
condition n ① condition f ▷ *I'll do it, on one condition ...* Je veux bien le faire, à une condition ... ② état m ▷ *in bad condition* en mauvais état
conditional n conditionnel m
conditioner n (for hair) baume m démêlant

condom n préservatif m
conduct vb (orchestra) diriger
conductor n chef m d'orchestre
cone n cornet m ▷ *an ice-cream cone* un cornet de glace
conference n conférence f
confess vb avouer ▷ *He confessed to the murder.* Il a avoué avoir commis le meurtre.
confession n confession f
confidence n ① confiance f ▷ *I've got confidence in you.* J'ai confiance en toi. ② assurance f ▷ *She lacks confidence.* Elle manque d'assurance.
confident adj sûr(e) ▷ *I'm confident everything will be okay.* Je suis sûr que tout ira bien.; **She's seems quite confident.** Elle a l'air sûre d'elle.
confidential adj confidentiel (f confidentielle)
confirm vb (booking) confirmer
confuse vb **to confuse somebody** embrouiller les idées de quelqu'un ▷ *Don't confuse me!* Ne m'embrouille pas les idées!
confused adj désorienté(e)
confusing adj **The traffic signs are confusing.** Les panneaux de signalisation ne sont pas clairs.
confusion n confusion f
congratulate vb féliciter ▷ *My friends congratulated me on passing the test.* Mes amis m'ont félicité d'avoir réussi à l'examen.
congratulations npl félicitations fpl ▷ *Congratulations*

on your new job! Félicitations pour votre nouveau poste!

conjunction n conjonction f

conjurer n prestidigitateur m

connection n ❶ rapport m
▷ There's no connection between the two events. Il n'y a aucun rapport entre les deux événements. ❷ (electrical) contact m ▷ There's a loose connection. Il y a un mauvais contact. ❸ (of trains, planes) correspondance f ▷ We missed our connection. Nous avons raté la correspondance.

conscience n conscience f

conscious adj conscient(e)

consciousness n connaissance f; **to lose consciousness** perdre connaissance ▷ I lost consciousness. J'ai perdu connaissance.

consequence n conséquence f ▷ What are the consequences for the environment? Quelles sont les conséquences pour l'environnement?; **as a consequence** en conséquence

consequently adv par conséquent

conservation n protection f

conservative adj conservateur (f conservatrice); **the Conservative Party** le Parti conservateur

conservatory n jardin m d'hiver

consider vb ❶ considérer ▷ He considers it a waste of time. Il considère que c'est une perte de temps. ❷ envisager ▷ We

considered cancelling our holiday. Nous avons envisagé d'annuler nos vacances.; **I'm considering the idea.** J'y songe.

considerate adj délicat(e)

considering prep ❶ étant donné ▷ Considering we were there for a month ... Étant donné que nous étions là pour un mois ... ❷ tout compte fait ▷ I got a good mark, considering. J'ai eu une bonne note, tout compte fait.

consist vb **to consist of** être composé de ▷ The band consists of three guitarists and a drummer. Le groupe est composé de trois guitaristes et un batteur.

consonant n consonne f

constant adj constant(e)

constantly adv constamment

constipated adj constipé(e)

construct vb construire

construction n construction f

consult vb consulter

consumer n consommateur m, consommatrice f

contact n contact m ▷ I'm in contact with her. Je suis en contact avec elle.
▶ vb joindre ▷ Where can we contact you? Où pouvons-nous vous joindre?

contact lenses npl verres mpl de contact

contain vb contenir

container n récipient m

contents npl ❶ (of container) contenu m ❷ (of book) table f des matières

a
b
c
d
e
f
g
h
i
j
k
l
m
n
o
p
q
r
s
t
u
v
w
x
y
z

contest n concours m

contestant n concurrent m, concurrente f

context n contexte m

continent n continent m ▷ *How many continents are there?* Combien y a-t-il de continents?; **the Continent** l'Europe ▷ *I've never been to the Continent.* Je ne suis jamais allé en Europe.

continental breakfast n petit déjeuner m à la française

continue vb ❶ continuer ▷ *She continued talking to her friend.* Elle a continué à parler à son amie. ❷ (*after interruption*) reprendre ▷ *We continued working after lunch.* Nous avons repris le travail après le déjeuner.

continuous adj continu(e); **continuous assessment** le contrôle continu

contraceptive n contraceptif m

contract n contrat m

contradict vb contredire

contrary n contraire m; **on the contrary** au contraire

contrast n contraste m

contribute vb ❶ (*to success, achievement*) contribuer ▷ *The treaty will contribute to world peace.* Le traité va contribuer à la paix dans le monde. ❷ (*share in*) participer ▷ *He didn't contribute to the discussion.* Il n'a pas participé à la discussion. ❸ (*give*) donner ▷ *She contributed £10.* Elle a donné dix livres.

contribution n ❶ contribution f

❷ (*to pension, national insurance*) cotisation f

control n (*of vehicle*) contrôle m; **to lose control** (*of machine*) perdre le contrôle ▷ *He lost control of the car.* Il a perdu le contrôle de son véhicule.; **the controls** les commandes; **to be in control** être maître de la situation; **to keep control** (*of people*) se faire obéir ▷ *He can't keep control of the class.* Il n'arrive pas à se faire obéir de sa classe.; **out of control** (*child, class*) déchaîné m

▶ vb ❶ (*country, organization*) diriger ❷ se faire obéir de ▷ *He can't control the class.* Il n'arrive pas à se faire obéir de sa classe. ❸ maîtriser ▷ *I couldn't control the horse.* Je ne suis pas arrivé à maîtriser le cheval.; **to control oneself** se contrôler

controversial adj controversé(e) ▷ *a controversial book* un livre controversé

convenient adj (*place*) bien situé(e) ▷ *The hotel's convenient for the airport.* L'hôtel est bien situé par rapport à l'aéroport.; **It's not a convenient time for me.** C'est une heure qui ne m'arrange pas.; **Would Monday be convenient for you?** Est-ce que lundi vous conviendrait?

conventional adj conventionnel (f conventionnelle)

conversation n conversation f ▷ *a French conversation class* un cours de conversation française

convert vb transformer ▷ We've converted the loft into a spare room. Nous avons transformé le grenier en chambre d'amis.

convince vb persuader ▷ I'm not convinced. Je n'en suis pas persuadé.

cook vb ❶ faire la cuisine ▷ I can't cook. Je ne sais pas faire la cuisine. ❷ préparer ▷ She's cooking lunch. Elle est en train de préparer le déjeuner. ❸ faire cuire ▷ Cook the pasta for 10 minutes. Faites cuire les pâtes pendant dix minutes.; **to be cooked** être cuit ▷ When the potatoes are cooked ... Lorsque les pommes de terre sont cuites ...
▶ n cuisinier m, cuisinière f
▷ Matthew's an excellent cook. Matthew est un excellent cuisinier.

cooker n cuisinière f ▷ a gas cooker une cuisinière à gaz

cookery n cuisine f

cookie n (US) gâteau m sec

cooking n cuisine f ▷ I like cooking. J'aime bien faire la cuisine.

cool adj frais (f fraîche) ▷ a cool place un endroit frais; **to stay cool** (keep calm) garder son calme ▷ He stayed cool. Il a gardé son calme.

cooperation n coopération f

cop n (informal) flic m

cope vb se débrouiller ▷ It was hard, but we coped. C'était dur, mais nous nous sommes débrouillés.; **to cope with** faire face à ▷ She's got a lot of problems to cope with. Elle doit faire face à de nombreux problèmes.

copper n ❶ cuivre m ▷ a copper bracelet un bracelet en cuivre ❷ (informal: policeman) flic m

copy n ❶ (of letter, document) copie f ❷ (of book) exemplaire m
▶ vb copier ▷ The teacher accused him of copying. Le professeur l'a accusé d'avoir copié.; **to copy and paste** copier-coller

core n (of fruit) trognon m ▷ an apple core un trognon de pomme

cork n ❶ (of bottle) bouchon m ❷ (material) liège m ▷ a cork table mat un set de table en liège

corkscrew n tire-bouchon m

corn n ❶ (wheat) blé m ❷ (sweetcorn) maïs m; **corn on the cob** épi de maïs

corner n ❶ coin m ▷ in a corner of the room dans un coin de la pièce; **the shop on the corner** la boutique au coin de la rue; **He lives just round the corner.** Il habite tout près d'ici. ❷ (in football) corner m

cornflakes npl corn-flakes mpl

Cornwall n Cornouailles f; **in Cornwall** en Cornouailles

corpse n cadavre m

correct adj exact(e) ▷ That's correct. C'est exact.; **the correct choice** le bon choix; **the correct answer** la bonne réponse
▶ vb corriger

correction n correction f

correctly adv correctement

corridor n couloir m

corruption n corruption f

Corsica n Corse f; **in Corsica** en Corse

cosmetics *npl* produits *mpl* de beauté

cosmetic surgery *n* chirurgie *f* esthétique

cost *vb* coûter ▷ *It costs too much.* Ça coûte trop cher.
▶ *n* coût *m*; **the cost of living** le coût de la vie; **at all costs** à tout prix

costume *n* costume *m*

cosy *adj* douillet (*f* douillette)

cot *n* lit *m* d'enfant

cottage *n* cottage *m*; **a thatched cottage** une chaumière

cotton *n* coton *m* ▷ *a cotton shirt* une chemise en coton; **cotton wool** le coton hydrophile

couch *n* canapé *m*

cough *vb* tousser
▶ *n* toux *f* ▷ *a bad cough* une mauvaise toux; **I've got a cough.** Je tousse.; **a cough sweet** une pastille

could *vb see* **can**

council *n* conseil *m*
  ● The nearest French equivalent
  ● of a local council would be
  ● a **conseil municipal**, which
  ● administers a **commune**.
He's on the council. Il fait partie du conseil municipal.; **a council estate** une cité HLM; **a council house** une HLM
  ● **HLM** stands for **habitation à**
  ● **loyer modéré** which means
  ● "low-rent home".

councillor *n* **She's a local councillor.** Elle fait partie du conseil municipal.

count *vb* compter; **to count on** compter sur ▷ *You can count on me.* Tu peux compter sur moi.

counter *n* ● (*in shop*) comptoir *m* ● (*in post office, bank*) guichet *m* ● (*in game*) jeton *m*

country *n* ● pays *m* ▷ *the border between the two countries* la frontière entre les deux pays ● campagne *f* ▷ *I live in the country.* J'habite à la campagne.; **country dancing** la danse folklorique

countryside *n* campagne *f*

county *n* comté *m*
  ● The nearest French equivalent
  ● of a county would be a
  ● **département**.
the county council
  ● The nearest French equivalent
  ● of a county council would
  ● be a **conseil général**, which
  ● administers a **département**.

couple *n* couple *m* ▷ *the couple who live next door* le couple qui habite à côté; **a couple** deux ▷ *a couple of hours* deux heures; **Could you wait a couple of minutes?** Pourriez-vous attendre quelques minutes?

courage *n* courage *m*

courgette *n* courgette *f*

courier *n* ● (*for tourists*) accompagnateur *m*, accompagnatrice *f* ● (*delivery service*) coursier *m* ▷ *They sent it by courier.* Ils l'ont envoyé par coursier.

  ▌ Be careful not to translate
  ▌ **courier** by the French word
  ▌ **courrier**.

course n ❶ cours m ▷ *to go on a course* suivre un cours ❷ plat m ▷ *the main course* le plat principal; **the first course** l'entrée f ❸ terrain m ▷ *a golf course* un terrain de golf; **of course** bien sûr ▷ *Do you love me?* — *Of course I do!* Tu m'aimes? — Bien sûr que oui!

court n ❶ (of law) tribunal m (pl tribunaux) ▷ *He was in court last week.* Il est passé devant le tribunal la semaine dernière. ❷ (tennis) court m ▷ *There are tennis and squash courts.* Il y a des courts de tennis et de squash.

courtyard n cour f

cousin n cousin m, cousine f

cover n ❶ (of book) couverture f ❷ (of duvet) housse f
▶ vb ❶ couvrir ▷ *My face was covered with mosquito bites.* J'avais le visage couvert de piqûres de moustique. ❷ prendre en charge ▷ *Our insurance didn't cover it.* Notre assurance ne l'a pas pris en charge.; **to cover up a scandal** étouffer un scandale

cow n vache f

coward n lâche m ▷ *She's a coward.* Elle est lâche.

cowboy n cow-boy m

crab n crabe m

crack n ❶ (in wall) fissure f ❷ (in cup, window) fêlure f ❸ (drug) crack m; **I'll have a crack at it.** Je vais tenter le coup.
▶ vb (nut, egg) casser; **to crack a joke** sortir une blague

cracked adj (cup, window) fêlé(e)

cracker n ❶ (biscuit) cracker m ❷ (Christmas cracker) diablotin m

craft n travaux mpl manuels ▷ *We do craft at school.* Nous avons des cours de travaux manuels à l'école.; **a craft centre** un centre artisanal

crammed adj crammed with bourré(e) de ▷ *Her bag was crammed with books.* Son sac était bourré de livres.

crane n (machine) grue f

crash vb avoir un accident ▷ *He's crashed his car.* Il a eu un accident de voiture.; **The plane crashed.** L'avion s'est écrasé.
▶ n ❶ (of car) collision f ❷ (of plane) accident m; **a crash helmet** un casque; **a crash course** un cours intensif

crawl vb (baby) marcher à quatre pattes
▶ n crawl m ▷ *to do the crawl* nager le crawl

crazy adj fou (f folle)

cream adj (colour) crème inv
▶ n crème f ▷ *strawberries and cream* les fraises à la crème; **a cream cake** un gâteau à la crème; **cream cheese** le fromage à la crème; **sun cream** la crème solaire

crease n pli m

creased adj froissé(e)

create vb créer

creative adj créatif (f créative)

creature n créature f

crèche n crèche f

credit n crédit m ▷ *on credit* à crédit

credit card n carte f de crédit

creeps npl It gives me the creeps. Ça me donne la chair de poule.

creep up vb s'approcher à pas de loup; **to creep up on somebody** s'approcher de quelqu'un à pas de loup

crept vb see **creep up**

crew n ① équipage m ② (of ship, plane) équipe f ▷ a film crew une équipe de tournage

crew cut n cheveux mpl en brosse

cricket n ① cricket m ▷ I play cricket. Je joue au cricket.; **a cricket bat** une batte de cricket ② (insect) grillon m

crime n ① délit m ▷ Murder is a crime. Le meurtre est un délit. ② (lawlessness) criminalité f; **Crime is rising.** La criminalité augmente.

criminal n criminel m, criminelle f ▶ adj criminel (f criminelle) ▷ It's criminal! C'est criminel!; **It's a criminal offence.** C'est un crime puni par la loi.; **to have a criminal record** avoir un casier judiciaire

crisis n crise f

crisp adj (food) croquant(e)

crisps npl chips fpl ▷ a bag of crisps un paquet de chips

critical adj critique; **a critical remark** une critique

criticism n critique f

criticize vb critiquer

Croatia n Croatie f; **in Croatia** en Croatie

crochet vb crocheter

crocodile n crocodile m

crook n (criminal) escroc m

crooked adj courbé(e)

crop n récolte f ▷ a good crop of apples une bonne récolte de pommes

cross n croix f ▶ adj fâché(e) ▷ to be cross about something être fâché à propos de quelque chose ▶ vb (street, bridge) traverser; **to cross out** barrer; **to cross over** traverser

cross-country n (race) cross m; **cross-country skiing** le ski de fond

crossing n ① (by boat) traversée f ▷ the crossing from Dover to Calais la traversée de Douvres à Calais ② (for pedestrians) passage m clouté

crossroads n carrefour m

crossword n mots mpl croisés ▷ I like doing crosswords. J'aime faire les mots croisés.

crouch down vb s'accroupir

crow n corbeau m (pl corbeaux)

crowd n foule f; **the crowd** (at sports match) les spectateurs

crowded adj bondé(e)

crown n couronne f

crude adj (vulgar) grossier (f grossière)

cruel adj cruel (f cruelle)

cruise n croisière f ▷ to go on a cruise faire une croisière

crumb n miette f

crunchy adj croquant(e)

crush vb écraser

crutch n béquille f

cry n cri m ▷ He gave a cry of surprise. Il a poussé un cri de surprise.; Go

on, have a good cry! Vas-y, pleure un bon coup!
▸ vb pleurer ▷ The baby's crying. Le bébé pleure.

crystal n cristal m (pl cristaux)

cub n ① (animal) petit m ② (scout) louveteau m (pl louveteaux)

cube n cube m

cubic adj **a cubic metre** un mètre cube

cucumber n concombre m

cuddle n câlin m ▷ Come and give me a cuddle. Viens me faire un câlin.

cue n (for snooker, pool) queue f de billard

culture n culture f

cunning adj ① (person) rusé(e) ② (plan, idea) astucieux (f astucieuse)

cup n ① tasse f ▷ a china cup une tasse en porcelaine; **a cup of coffee** un café ② (trophy) coupe f

cupboard n placard m

cure vb guérir
▸ n remède m

curious adj curieux (f curieuse)

curl n (in hair) boucle f

curly adj ① (loosely curled) bouclé(e) ② (tightly curled) frisé(e)

currant n (dried fruit) raisin m de Corinthe

currency n devise f ▷ foreign currency les devises étrangères

current n courant m ▷ The current is very strong. Le courant est très fort.
▸ adj actuel (f actuelle) ▷ the current situation la situation actuelle

current affairs npl actualité f

curriculum n programme m

curriculum vitae n curriculum vitae m

curry n curry m

cursor n (computing) curseur m

curtain n rideau m (pl rideaux); **to draw the curtains** tirer les rideaux

cushion n coussin m

custard n (for pouring) crème f anglaise

custody n (of child) garde f

custom n coutume f ▷ It's an old custom. C'est une ancienne coutume.

customer n client m, cliente f

customs npl douane f

customs officer n douanier m, douanière f

cut n ① coupure f ▷ He's got a cut on his forehead. Il a une coupure au front. ② coupe f ▷ a cut and blow-dry une coupe brushing ③ (in price, spending) réduction f
▸ vb ① couper ▷ I'll cut some bread. Je vais couper du pain.; **to cut oneself** se couper ▷ I cut my foot on a piece of glass. Je me suis coupé au pied avec un morceau de verre. ② (price, spending) réduire; **to cut down** abattre; **to cut off** couper ▷ The electricity was cut off. L'électricité a été coupée.; **to cut up** hacher

cute adj mignon (f mignonne)

cutlery n couverts mpl

CV n C.V. m

cybercafé n cybercafé m

cycle vb faire de la bicyclette ▷ I like cycling. J'aime faire de la bicyclette.;

I cycle to school. Je vais à l'école à bicyclette.
▸ *n* bicyclette *f*; **a cycle ride** une promenade à bicyclette; **a cycle lane** une piste cyclable

cycling *n* cyclisme *m*

cyclist *n* cycliste *mf*

cylinder *n* cylindre *m*

Cyprus *n* Chypre; **in Cyprus** à Chypre; **We went to Cyprus.** Nous sommes allés à Chypre.

Czech *adj* tchèque; **the Czech Republic** la République tchèque
▸ *n* ❶ *(person)* Tchèque *mf*
❷ *(language)* tchèque *m*

dad *n* ❶ père *m* ▷ *my dad* mon père
❷ papa *m*

> Use **papa** only when you are talking to your father or using it as his name; otherwise use **père**.

Dad! Papa! ▷ *I'll ask Dad.* Je vais demander à papa.

daffodil *n* jonquille *f*

daft *adj* idiot(e)

daily *adj, adv* ❶ quotidien (*f* quotidienne) ▷ *It's part of my daily routine.* Ça fait partie de mes occupations quotidiennes. ❷ tous les jours ▷ *The pool is open daily.* La piscine est ouverte tous les jours.

dairy products *npl* produits *mpl* laitiers

daisy *n* pâquerette *f*

dam *n* barrage *m*

damage n dégâts mpl ▷ The storm did a lot of damage. La tempête a fait beaucoup de dégâts.
▶ vb endommager

damp adj humide

dance n ❶ danse f ▷ The last dance was a waltz. La dernière danse était une valse. ❷ bal m ▷ Are you going to the dance tonight? Tu vas au bal ce soir?
▶ vb danser; **to go dancing** aller danser ▷ Let's go dancing! Si on allait danser?

dancer n danseur m, danseuse f

dandruff n pellicules fpl

Dane n Danois m, Danoise f

danger n danger m; **in danger** en danger ▷ His life is in danger. Sa vie est en danger.; **to be in danger of** risquer de ▷ We were in danger of missing the plane. Nous risquions de rater l'avion.

dangerous adj dangereux (f dangereuse)

Danish adj danois(e)
▶ n (language) danois m

dare vb oser; **to dare to do something** oser faire quelque chose ▷ I didn't dare to tell my parents. Je n'ai pas osé le dire à mes parents.; **I dare say it'll be okay.** Je suppose que ça va aller.

daring adj audacieux (f audacieuse)

dark adj ❶ (room) sombre ▷ It's dark. (inside) Il fait sombre.; **It's dark outside.** Il fait nuit dehors.; **It's getting dark.** La nuit tombe. ❷ (colour) foncé ▷ She's got dark hair.

Elle a les cheveux foncés. ▷ a dark green sweater un pull vert foncé
▶ n noir m ▷ I'm afraid of the dark. J'ai peur du noir.; **after dark** après la tombée de la nuit

darkness n obscurité f ▷ The room was in darkness. La chambre était dans l'obscurité.

darling n chéri m, chérie f ▷ Thank you, darling! Merci, chéri!

dart n fléchette f ▷ to play darts jouer aux fléchettes

data npl données fpl

database n (on computer) base f de données

date n ❶ date f ▷ my date of birth ma date de naissance; **What's the date today?** Quel jour sommes-nous?; **to have a date with somebody** sortir avec quelqu'un ▷ She's got a date with Ian tonight. Elle sort avec Ian ce soir.; **out of date** (1) (passport) périmé(e) (2) (technology) dépassé(e) (3) (clothes) démodé(e) ❷ (fruit) datte f

daughter n fille f

daughter-in-law n belle-fille f (pl belles-filles)

dawn n aube f ▷ at dawn à l'aube

day n

Use **jour** to refer to the whole 24-hour period. **journée** only refers to the time when you are awake.

❶ jour m ▷ We stayed in Nice for three days. Nous sommes restés trois jours à Nice.; **every day** tous les jours ❷ journée f ▷ I stayed at home all day. Je suis resté à la maison toute la journée.; **the day before** la veille ▷ *the day before my birthday* la veille de mon anniversaire; **the day after** le lendemain; **the day after tomorrow** après-demain ▷ *We're leaving the day after tomorrow.* Nous partons après-demain.; **the day before yesterday** avant-hier ▷ *He arrived the day before yesterday.* Il est arrivé avant-hier.

dead adj, adv ❶ mort(e) ▷ *He was already dead when the doctor came.* Il était déjà mort quand le docteur est arrivé.; **He was shot dead.** Il a été abattu. ❷ (totally) absolument ▷ *You're dead right!* Tu as absolument raison!; **dead on time** à l'heure pile ▷ *The train arrived dead on time.* Le train est arrivé à l'heure pile.

dead end n impasse f

deadline n date limite f ▷ *The deadline for entries is May 2nd.* La date limite d'inscription est le deux mai.

deaf adj sourd(e)

deafening adj assourdissant(e)

deal n marché m; **It's a deal!** Marché conclu!; **a great deal** beaucoup ▷ *a great deal of money* beaucoup d'argent
▶ vb (cards) donner ▷ *It's your turn to deal.* C'est à toi de donner.; **to deal with something** s'occuper de quelque chose ▷ *He promised to deal with it immediately.* Il a promis de s'en occuper immédiatement.

dealer n marchand m, marchande f ▷ *a drug dealer* un dealer

dealt vb see **deal**

dear adj ❶ cher (f chère) ▷ *Dear Mrs Duval* Chère Madame Duval; **Dear Sir/Madam** (in a circular) Madame, Monsieur ❷ (expensive) coûteux (f coûteuse)

death n mort f ▷ *after his death* après sa mort; **I was bored to death.** Je me suis ennuyé à mourir.

debate n débat m
▶ vb débattre

debt n dette f ▷ *He's got a lot of debts.* Il a beaucoup de dettes.; **to be in debt** avoir des dettes

decade n décennie f

decaffeinated adj décaféiné(e)

December n décembre m; **in December** en décembre

decent adj convenable ▷ *a decent education* une éducation convenable

decide vb ❶ décider ▷ *I decided to write to her.* J'ai décidé de lui écrire. ▷ *I decided not to go.* J'ai décidé de ne pas y aller. ❷ se décider ▷ *I can't decide.* Je n'arrive pas à me décider.; **to decide on something** se mettre d'accord sur quelque chose ▷ *They haven't decided on a name yet.* Ils ne se sont pas encore mis d'accord sur un nom.

decimal adj décimal(e) ▷ *the decimal system* le système décimal

decision n décision f; **to make a decision** prendre une décision

deck n ❶ (of ship) pont m; **on**

deck sur le pont ❷ (of cards) jeu m (pl jeux)

deckchair n chaise f longue

declare vb déclarer

decorate vb ❶ décorer ▷ I decorated the cake with glacé cherries. J'ai décoré le gâteau avec des cerises confites. ❷ (paint) peindre ❸ (wallpaper) tapisser

decrease n diminution f ▷ a decrease in the number of unemployed people une diminution du nombre de chômeurs

▶ vb diminuer

dedication n ❶ (commitment) dévouement m ❷ (in book, on radio) dédicace f

deduct vb déduire

deep adj ❶ (water, hole, cut) profond(e) ▷ Is it deep? Est-ce que c'est profond?; **How deep is the lake?** Quelle est la profondeur du lac?; **a hole 4 metres deep** un trou de quatre mètres de profondeur ❷ (layer) épais (f épaisse) ▷ The snow was really deep. Il y avait une épaisse couche de neige.; **He's got a deep voice.** Il a la voix grave.; **to take a deep breath** respirer à fond

deeply adv (depressed) profondément

deer n ❶ (red deer) cerf m ❷ (fallow deer) daim m ❸ (roe deer) chevreuil m

defeat n défaite f

▶ vb battre

defect n défaut m

defence n défense f

defend vb défendre

defender n défenseur m

define vb définir

definite adj ❶ précis(e) ▷ I haven't got any definite plans. Je n'ai pas de projets précis. ❷ net (f nette) ▷ It's a definite improvement. Cela constitue une nette amélioration. ❸ sûr(e) ▷ Perhaps we'll go to Spain, but it's not definite. Nous irons peut-être en Espagne, mais ce n'est pas sûr.; **He was definite about it.** Il a été catégorique.

definitely adv vraiment ▷ He's definitely the best player. C'est vraiment lui le meilleur joueur.; **He's the best player. — Definitely!** C'est le meilleur joueur. — C'est sûr!; **I definitely think he'll come.** Je suis sûr qu'il va venir.

definition n définition f

degree n ❶ degré m ▷ a temperature of 30 degrees une température de trente degrés ❷ licence f ▷ a degree in English une licence d'anglais

delay vb ❶ retarder ▷ We decided to delay our departure. Nous avons décidé de retarder notre départ. ❷ tarder ▷ Don't delay! Ne tarde pas!; **to be delayed** être retardé ▷ Our flight was delayed. Notre vol a été retardé.

▶ n retard m ▷ There will be delays to trains on the London-Brighton line. Il y aura des retards sur la ligne Londres-Brighton.

⎸ Be careful not to translate **delay** by **délai**.

delete vb (on computer, tape) effacer

deliberate adj délibéré(e)

deliberately adv exprès ▷ She did it deliberately. Elle l'a fait exprès.

delicate adj délicat(e)

delicatessen n épicerie f fine

delicious adj délicieux (f délicieuse)

delight n to her delight à sa plus grande joie

delighted adj ravi(e) ▷ He'll be delighted to see you. Il sera ravi de vous voir.

deliver vb ❶ livrer ▷ I deliver newspapers. Je livre les journaux. ❷ (mail) distribuer

delivery n livraison f

demand vb exiger

> Be careful not to translate **to demand** by **demander**.

▶ n (for product) demande f

democracy n démocratie f

democratic adj démocratique

demolish vb démolir

demonstrate vb ❶ (show) faire une démonstration de ▷ She demonstrated the technique. Elle a fait une démonstration de la technique. ❷ (protest) manifester; **to demonstrate against something** manifester contre quelque chose

demonstration n ❶ (of method, technique) démonstration f ❷ (protest) manifestation f

demonstrator n (protester) manifestant m, manifestante f

denim n jean m ▷ a denim jacket une veste en jean

Denmark n Danemark m; **in Denmark** au Danemark; **to**

Denmark au Danemark

dense adj ❶ (crowd, fog) dense ❷ (smoke) épais (f épaisse); **He's so dense!** Il est vraiment bouché!

dent n bosse f

▶ vb cabosser

dental adj dentaire; **dental floss** le fil dentaire

dentist n dentiste mf ▷ Catherine is a dentist. Catherine est dentiste.

deny vb nier ▷ She denied everything. Elle a tout nié.

deodorant n déodorant m

depart vb partir

department n ❶ (in shop) rayon m ▷ the shoe department le rayon chaussures ❷ (university, school) département m ▷ the English department le département d'anglais

department store n grand magasin m

departure n départ m

departure lounge n hall m des départs

depend vb **to depend on** dépendre de ▷ The price depends on the quality. Le prix dépend de la qualité.; **depending on the weather** selon le temps; **It depends.** Ça dépend.

deposit n ❶ (part payment) arrhes fpl ▷ You have to pay a deposit when you book. Il faut verser des arrhes lors de la réservation. ❷ (when hiring something) caution f ▷ You get the deposit back when you return the bike. On vous remboursera la caution quand vous ramènerez le vélo. ❸ (on bottle) consigne f

depressed adj déprimé(e) ▷ I'm feeling depressed. Je suis déprimé.

depressing adj déprimant(e)

depth n profondeur f

deputy head n directeur m adjoint, directrice f adjointe

descend vb descendre

describe vb décrire

description n description f

desert n désert m

desert island n île f déserte

deserve vb mériter

design n ❶ conception f ▷ It's a completely new design. C'est une conception entièrement nouvelle. ❷ motif m ▷ a geometric design un motif géométrique; **fashion design** le stylisme
▶ vb (clothes, furniture) dessiner

designer n (of clothes) styliste mf; **designer clothes** les vêtements griffés

desire n désir m
▶ vb désirer

desk n ❶ (in office) bureau m (pl bureaux) ❷ (for pupil) pupitre m ❸ (in hotel) réception f ❹ (at airport) comptoir m

despair n désespoir m; **I was in despair.** J'étais désespéré.

desperate adj désespéré(e) ▷ a desperate situation une situation désespérée; **to get desperate** désespérer ▷ I was getting desperate. Je commençais à désespérer.

desperately adv ❶ terriblement ▷ We're desperately worried. Nous sommes terriblement inquiets. ❷ désespérément ▷ He was

desperately trying to persuade her. Il essayait désespérément de la persuader.

despise vb mépriser

despite prep malgré

dessert n dessert m ▷ for dessert comme dessert

destination n destination f

destroy vb détruire

destruction n destruction f

detached house n pavillon m

detail n détail m ▷ in detail en détail

detailed adj détaillé(e)

detective n inspecteur m de police; **a private detective** un détective privé; **a detective story** un roman policier

detention n to get a detention être consigné

detergent n ❶ détergent m ❷ (US) lessive f

determined adj déterminé(e); **to be determined to do something** être déterminé à faire quelque chose ▷ She's determined to succeed. Elle est déterminée à réussir.

detour n détour m

devastated adj anéanti(e) ▷ I was devastated. J'étais anéanti.

develop vb ❶ développer ▷ to get a film developed faire développer un film ❷ se développer ▷ Girls develop faster than boys. Les filles se développent plus vite que les garçons.; **to develop into** se transformer en ▷ The argument developed into a fight. La dispute s'est transformée en bagarre.; **a developing country** un pays en voie de développement

development n développement
m ▷ the latest developments les
derniers développements

devil n diable m ▷ Poor devil! Pauvre
diable!

devoted adj dévoué(e) ▷ He's
completely devoted to her. Il lui est
très dévoué.

diabetes n diabète m

diabetic n diabétique mf ▷ I'm a
diabetic. Je suis diabétique.

diagonal adj diagonal(e) (mpl
diagonaux)

diagram n diagramme m

dial vb (number) composer

dialling tone n tonalité f

dialogue n dialogue m

diamond n diamant m ▷ a diamond
ring une bague en diamant;
diamonds (at cards) le carreau

diaper n (US) couche f

diarrhoea n diarrhée f ▷ I've got
diarrhoea. J'ai la diarrhée.

diary n ❶ agenda m ▷ I've got her
phone number in my diary. J'ai son
numéro de téléphone dans mon
agenda. ❷ journal m (pl journaux)
▷ I keep a diary. Je tiens un journal.

dice n dé m

dictation n dictée f

dictionary n dictionnaire m

did vb see do

die vb mourir ▷ He died last year. Il
est mort l'année dernière.; **to be
dying to do something** mourir
d'envie de faire quelque chose ▷ I'm
dying to see you. Je meurs d'envie
de te voir.

diesel n ❶ (fuel) gazole m ▷ 30 litres

of diesel trente litres de gazole
❷ (car) voiture f diesel ▷ My car's a
diesel. J'ai une voiture diesel.

diet n régime m ▷ I'm on a diet. Je
suis au régime.
▶ vb faire un régime ▷ I've been
dieting for two months. Je fais un
régime depuis deux mois.

difference n différence f
▷ There's not much difference in age
between us. Il n'y a pas une grande
différence d'âge entre nous.;
It makes no difference. Ça revient
au même.

different adj différent(e) ▷ Paris
is different from London. Paris est
différent de Londres.

difficult adj difficile ▷ It's difficult to
choose. C'est difficile de choisir.

difficulty n difficulté f ▷ without
difficulty sans difficulté; **to have
difficulty doing something** avoir
du mal à faire quelque chose

dig vb ❶ (hole) creuser ❷ (garden)
bêcher; **to dig something up**
déterrer quelque chose

digestion n digestion f

digital camera n appareil m
photo numérique

digital radio n radio f numérique

digital television n télévision f
numérique

digital watch n montre f à
affichage numérique

dim adj ❶ (light) faible ❷ (stupid)
limité(e)

dimension n dimension f

din n vacarme m

diner n (US) snack m

dinghy n **a rubber dinghy** un canot pneumatique; **a sailing dinghy** un dériveur

dining room n salle f à manger

> Word for word, the French means "room for eating".

dinner n ❶ (at midday) déjeuner m ❷ (in the evening) dîner m

dinner lady n dame f de service

dinner party n dîner m

dinner time n ❶ (midday) heure f du déjeuner ❷ (in the evening) heure f du dîner

dinosaur n dinosaure m

diploma n diplôme m

direct adj, adv direct(e) ▷ **the most direct route** le chemin le plus direct ▷ **You can't fly to Nice direct from Cork.** Il n'y a pas de vols directs de Cork à Nice.

► vb ❶ (film, programme) réaliser ❷ (play, show) mettre en scène

direction n direction f ▷ **We're going in the wrong direction.** Nous allons dans la mauvaise direction.; **to ask somebody for directions** demander son chemin à quelqu'un

director n ❶ (of company) directeur m, directrice f ❷ (of play) metteur m en scène (pl metteurs en scène) ❸ (of film, programme) réalisateur m, réalisatrice f

directory n ❶ (phone book) annuaire m ❷ (computing) répertoire m

dirt n saleté f

dirty adj sale; **to get dirty** se salir; **to get something dirty** salir quelque chose

disabled adj handicapé(e); **the disabled** les handicapés

disadvantage n désavantage m

disagree vb **We always disagree.** Nous ne sommes jamais d'accord.; **I disagree!** Je ne suis pas d'accord!; **He disagrees with me.** Il n'est pas d'accord avec moi.

disagreement n désaccord m

disappear vb disparaître

disappearance n disparition f

disappointed adj déçu(e)

disappointment n déception f

disaster n désastre m

disastrous adj désastreux (f désastreuse)

disc n disque m

discipline n discipline f

disc jockey n disc-jockey m

disco n soirée f disco ▷ **There's a disco at the school tonight.** Il y a une soirée disco à l'école ce soir.

disconnect vb ❶ (electrical equipment) débrancher ❷ (telephone, water supply) couper

discount n réduction f ▷ **a discount for students** une réduction pour les étudiants

discourage vb décourager; **to get discouraged** se décourager ▷ **Don't get discouraged!** Ne te décourage pas!

discover vb découvrir

discrimination n discrimination f ▷ **racial discrimination** la discrimination raciale

discuss vb ❶ discuter de ▷ **I'll discuss it with my parents.** Je vais en discuter avec mes parents.

❷ (topic) discuter sur ▷ We
discussed the problem of pollution.
Nous avons discuté du problème
de la pollution.
discussion n discussion f
disease n maladie f
disgraceful adj scandaleux (f
scandaleuse)
disguise vb déguiser ▷ He was
disguised as a policeman. Il était
déguisé en policier.
disgusted adj dégoûté(e) ▷ I
was absolutely disgusted. J'étais
complètement dégoûté.
disgusting adj ❶ (food, smell)
dégoûtant(e) ▷ It looks disgusting.
Ça a l'air dégoûtant. ❷ (disgraceful)
honteux (f honteuse) ▷ That's
disgusting! C'est honteux!
dish n plat m ▷ a vegetarian dish un
plat végétarien; **to do the dishes**
faire la vaisselle ▷ He never does the
dishes. Il ne fait jamais la vaisselle.
dishonest adj malhonnête
dishwasher n lave-vaisselle m (pl
lave-vaisselle)
disinfectant n désinfectant m
disk n disque m; **a floppy disk**
une disquette; **the hard disk** le
disque dur
dismal adj lugubre
dismiss vb (employee) renvoyer
disobedient adj désobéissant(e)
display n étalage m ▷ There was a
lovely display of fruit in the window.
Il y avait un superbe étalage de
fruits en vitrine.; **to be on display**
être exposé ▷ Her best paintings
were on display. Ses meilleurs

tableaux étaient exposés.;
a firework display un feu d'artifice
▶ vb ❶ montrer ▷ She proudly
displayed her medal. Elle a montré
sa médaille avec fierté. ❷ (in shop
window) exposer
disposable adj jetable
disqualify vb disqualifier; **to be
disqualified** être disqualifié ▷ He
was disqualified. Il a été disqualifié.
disrupt vb perturber ▷ Protesters
disrupted the meeting. Des
manifestants ont perturbé la
réunion.
dissolve vb dissoudre
distance n distance f ▷ a distance
of 40 kilometres une distance de
quarante kilomètres; **It's within
walking distance.** On peut y
aller à pied.; **in the distance**
au loin
distant adj lointain(e) ▷ in the
distant future dans un avenir
lointain
distract vb distraire
distribute vb distribuer
district n ❶ (of town) quartier m
❷ (of country) région f
disturb vb déranger ▷ I'm sorry to
disturb you. Je suis désolé de vous
déranger.
ditch n fossé m
▶ vb (informal) plaquer ▷ She's just
ditched her boyfriend. Elle vient de
plaquer son copain.
dive n plongeon m
▶ vb plonger
diver n plongeur m, plongeuse f
diversion n (for traffic) déviation f

divide vb ❶ diviser ▷ *Divide the pastry in half.* Divisez la pâte en deux. ▷ *12 divided by 3 is 4.* Douze divisé par trois égalent quatre. ❷ se diviser ▷ *We divided into two groups.* Nous nous sommes divisés en deux groupes.

diving n plongée f; **a diving board** un plongeoir

division n division f

divorce n divorce m

divorced adj divorcé(e) ▷ *My parents are divorced.* Mes parents sont divorcés.

DIY n bricolage m ▷ *to do DIY* faire du bricolage

dizzy adj **to feel dizzy** avoir la tête qui tourne ▷ *I feel dizzy.* J'ai la tête qui tourne.

DJ n disc-jockey m

do vb ❶ faire ▷ *I haven't done my homework.* Je n'ai pas fait mes devoirs. ▷ *I'll do my best.* Je ferai de mon mieux.; **to do well** marcher bien ▷ *She's doing well at school.* Ses études marchent bien. ❷ (be enough) aller ▷ *It's not very good, but it'll do.* Ce n'est pas très bon, mais ça ira.; **That'll do, thanks.** Ça ira, merci.

> In English **do** is used to make questions. In French questions are made either with **est-ce que** or by reversing the order of verb and subject.

▷ *Where does he live?* Où est-ce qu'il habite? ▷ *Do you speak English?* Parlez-vous anglais? ▷ *What do you do in your free time?* Qu'est-ce que

vous faites pendant vos loisirs? ▷ *Where did you go for your holidays?* Où es-tu allé pendant tes vacances?

> Use **ne ... pas** in negative sentences for **don't**.

▷ *I don't understand.* Je ne comprends pas.

> **do** is not translated when it is used in place of another verb.

▷ *I hate maths. —So do I.* Je déteste les maths. — Moi aussi. ▷ *I didn't like the film. —Neither did I.* Je n'ai pas aimé le film. — Moi non plus.

> Use **n'est-ce pas** to check information.

▷ *You go swimming on Fridays, don't you?* Tu fais de la natation le vendredi, n'est-ce pas?; **How do you do?** Enchanté!; **to do up (1)** (shoes) lacer ▷ *Do up your shoes!* Lace tes chaussures! **(2)** (renovate) retaper ▷ *They're doing up an old cottage.* Ils retapent une vieille maison. **(3)** (shirt, cardigan) boutonner; **Do up your zip!** (on trousers) Ferme ta braguette!; **to do without** se passer de ▷ *I couldn't do without my computer.* Je ne pourrais pas me passer de mon ordinateur.

doctor n médecin m ▷ *She's a doctor.* Elle est médecin.

document n document m

documentary n documentaire m

dodge vb (attacker) échapper à

dodgems npl autos fpl tamponneuses ▷ *to go on the dodgems* aller faire un tour d'autos tamponneuses

does vb see **do**

doesn't = **does not**

dog n (female) chien m, chienne f ▷ Have you got a dog? Est-ce que tu as un chien?

do-it-yourself n bricolage m

dole n allocations fpl chômage; **to be on the dole** toucher le chômage ▷ A lot of people are on the dole. Beaucoup de gens touchent le chômage.; **to go on the dole** s'inscrire au chômage

doll n poupée f

dollar n dollar m

dolphin n dauphin m

dominoes npl **to have a game of dominoes** faire une partie de dominos

donate vb donner

done vb see **do**

donkey n âne m

don't = **do not**

door n ❶ porte f ▷ the first door on the right la première porte à droite ❷ (of car, train) portière f

doorbell n sonnette f; **to ring the doorbell** sonner; **Suddenly the doorbell rang.** Soudain, on a sonné.

doorstep n pas m de la porte

dormitory n dortoir m

dot n (on letter "i", in email address) point m; **on the dot** à l'heure pile ▷ He arrived at 9 o'clock on the dot. Il est arrivé à neuf heures pile.

dotcom n point m com

double vb doubler ▷ The number of attacks has doubled. Le nombre d'agressions a doublé.

▶ adj, adv double ▷ a double helping une double portion; **to cost double** coûter le double ▷ First-class tickets cost double. Les billets de première classe coûtent le double.; **a double bed** un grand lit; **a double room** une chambre pour deux personnes; **a double-decker bus** un autobus à impériale

double bass n contrebasse f ▷ I play the double bass. Je joue de la contrebasse.

double-click vb double-cliquer ▷ to double-click on an icon double-cliquer sur une icône

double glazing n double m vitrage

doubles npl (in tennis) double m ▷ to play mixed doubles jouer en double mixte

doubt n doute m ▷ I have my doubts. J'ai des doutes.

▶ vb douter de; **I doubt it.** J'en doute.; **to doubt that** douter que

> ⏐ **douter que** has to be followed by a verb in the subjunctive.

▷ I doubt he'll agree. Je doute qu'il soit d'accord.

doubtful adj **to be doubtful about doing something** hésiter à faire quelque chose ▷ I'm doubtful about going by myself. J'hésite à y aller tout seul.; **It's doubtful.** Ce n'est pas sûr.; **You sound doubtful.** Tu n'as pas l'air sûr.

dough n pâte f

doughnut n beignet m ▷ a jam doughnut un beignet à la confiture

Dover n Douvres ▷ We went from Dover to Boulogne. Nous sommes allés de Douvres à Boulogne.; **in Dover** à Douvres

down adv, adj, prep ❶ (below) en bas ▷ His office is down on the first floor. Son bureau est en bas, au premier étage.; **It's down there.** C'est là-bas. ❷ (to the ground) à terre ▷ He threw down his racket. Il a jeté sa raquette à terre.; **They live just down the road.** Ils habitent tout à côté.; **to come down** descendre ▷ Come down here! Descends!; **to go down** descendre ▷ The rabbit went down the hole. Le lapin est descendu dans le terrier.; **to sit down** s'asseoir ▷ Sit down! Asseyez-vous!; **to feel down** avoir le cafard ▷ I'm feeling a bit down. J'ai un peu le cafard.; **The computer's down.** L'ordinateur est en panne.

download vb télécharger ▷ to download a file télécharger un fichier

downstairs adv, adj ❶ au rez-de-chaussée ▷ The bathroom's downstairs. La salle de bain est au rez-de-chaussée. ❷ du rez-de-chaussée ▷ the downstairs bathroom la salle de bain du rez-de-chaussée; **the people downstairs** les voisins du dessous

downtown adj (US) dans le centre

doze vb sommeiller; **to doze off** s'assoupir

dozen n douzaine f ▷ two dozen deux douzaines ▷ a dozen eggs une douzaine d'œufs; **I've told you that dozens of times.** Je te l'ai dit ça des centaines de fois.

draft n (US) = **draught**

drag vb (thing, person) traîner ▶ n **It's a real drag!** (informal) C'est la barbe!; **in drag** travesti ▷ He was in drag. Il était travesti.

dragon n dragon m

drain n égout m ▷ The drains are blocked. Les égouts sont bouchés. ▶ vb (vegetables, pasta) égoutter

drama n art m dramatique ▷ Drama is my favourite subject. L'art dramatique est ma matière préférée.; **drama school** l'école d'art dramatique ▷ I'd like to go to drama school. J'aimerais entrer dans une école d'art dramatique.; **Greek drama** le théâtre grec

dramatic adj spectaculaire ▷ a dramatic improvement une amélioration spectaculaire; **dramatic news** une nouvelle extraordinaire

drank vb see **drink**

drapes npl (US) rideaux mpl

draught n courant m d'air

draughts n dames fpl ▷ to play draughts jouer aux dames

draw vb ❶ dessiner ▷ He's good at drawing. Il dessine bien.; **to draw a picture** faire un dessin; **to draw a picture of somebody** faire le portrait de quelqu'un; **to draw a line** tirer un trait ❷ (sport) faire match nul ▷ We drew 2–2. Nous avons fait match nul deux à deux.; **to draw the curtains** tirer les rideaux; **to draw lots** tirer au sort

▶ n ① (sport) match m nul ▷ The game ended in a draw. La partie s'est soldée par un match nul. ② (in lottery) tirage m au sort ▷ The draw takes place on Saturday. Le tirage au sort a lieu samedi.

drawback n inconvénient m

drawer n tiroir m

drawing n dessin m

drawing pin n punaise f

drawn vb see **draw**

dreadful adj ① terrible ▷ a dreadful mistake une terrible erreur ② affreux (f affreuse) ▷ The weather was dreadful. Il a fait un temps affreux.; **I feel dreadful.** Je ne me sens vraiment pas bien.; **You look dreadful.** (ill) Tu as une mine affreuse.

dream vb rêver ▷ I dreamed I was in Belgium. J'ai rêvé que j'étais en Belgique.

▶ n rêve m ▷ It was just a dream. Ce n'était qu'un rêve.; **a bad dream** un cauchemar

drench vb to get drenched se faire tremper ▷ We got drenched. Nous nous sommes fait tremper.

dress n robe f

▶ vb s'habiller ▷ I got up, dressed, and went downstairs. Je me suis levé, je me suis habillé et je suis descendu.; **to dress somebody** habiller quelqu'un ▷ She dressed the children. Elle a habillé les enfants.; **to get dressed** s'habiller ▷ I got dressed quickly. Je me suis habillé rapidement.; **to dress up** se déguiser ▷ I dressed up as a ghost. Je me suis déguisé en fantôme.

dressed adj habillé(e) ▷ I'm not dressed yet. Je ne suis pas encore habillé.; **She was dressed in a green sweater and jeans.** Elle portait un pull vert et un jean.

dresser n (furniture) vaisselier m

dressing gown n robe f de chambre

dressing table n coiffeuse f

drew vb see **draw**

dried vb see **dry**

drier n séchoir m

drift n a snow drift une congère

▶ vb ① (boat) aller à la dérive ② (snow) s'amonceler

drill n perceuse f

▶ vb percer

drink vb boire ▷ What would you like to drink? Qu'est-ce que vous voulez boire?; **I don't drink.** Je ne bois pas d'alcool.

▶ n ① boisson f ▷ a cold drink une boisson fraîche ② (alcoholic) verre m ▷ They've gone out for a drink. Ils sont allés prendre un verre.; **to have a drink** prendre un verre

drive n ① tour m en voiture; **to go for a drive** faire un tour en voiture ▷ We went for a drive in the country. Nous sommes allés faire un tour à la campagne.; **We've got a long drive tomorrow.** Nous avons une longue route à faire demain. ② (of house) allée f ▷ He parked his car in the drive. Il a garé sa voiture dans l'allée.

▶ vb ① (a car) conduire ▷ Can you drive? Tu sais conduire? ② (go by car) aller en voiture ▷ Did you go by train? — No, we drove. Vous êtes partis en train? — Non, nous y sommes allés en voiture. ❷ **emmener en voiture** ▷ *My mother drives me to school.* Ma mère m'emmène à l'école en voiture.; **to drive somebody home** raccompagner quelqu'un ▷ *He offered to drive me home.* Il m'a proposé de me raccompagner.; **to drive somebody mad** rendre quelqu'un fou ▷ *He drives her mad.* Il la rend folle.

driver n ❶ conducteur m, conductrice f ▷ *She's an excellent driver.* C'est une excellente conductrice. ❷ *(of taxi, bus)* chauffeur m ▷ *He's a bus driver.* Il est chauffeur d'autobus.

driver's license n (US) = **driving licence**

driving instructor n moniteur m d'auto-école ▷ *He's a driving instructor.* Il est moniteur d'auto-école.

driving lesson n leçon f de conduite

driving licence n permis m de conduire

driving test n **to take one's driving test** passer son permis de conduire ▷ *He's taking his driving test tomorrow.* Il passe son permis de conduire demain.; **She's just passed her driving test.** Elle vient d'avoir son permis.

drop n goutte f ▷ *a drop of water* une goutte d'eau

▶ vb ❶ laisser tomber ▷ *I dropped*

the glass and it broke. J'ai laissé tomber le verre et il s'est cassé. ▷ *I'm going to drop chemistry.* Je vais laisser tomber la chimie. ❷ déposer ▷ *Could you drop me at the station?* Pouvez-vous me déposer à la gare?

drought n sécheresse f

drove vb see **drive**

drown vb se noyer ▷ *A boy drowned here yesterday.* Un jeune garçon s'est noyé ici hier.

drug n ❶ *(medicine)* médicament m ▷ *They need food and drugs.* Ils ont besoin de nourriture et de médicaments. ❷ *(illegal)* drogue f ▷ *hard drugs* les drogues dures; **to take drugs** se droguer; **a drug addict** un drogué ▷ *She's a drug addict.* C'est une droguée.; **a drug pusher** un dealer; **a drug smuggler** un trafiquant de drogue; **the drugs squad** la brigade antidrogue

drugstore n (US) drugstore m

drum n tambour m ▷ *an African drum* un tambour africain; **a drum kit** une batterie; **drums** batterie f ▷ *I play drums.* Je joue de la batterie.

drummer n *(in rock group)* batteur m, batteuse f

drunk adj ivre ▷ *He was drunk.* Il était ivre.

▶ n ivrogne mf ▷ *The streets were full of drunks.* Les rues étaient pleines d'ivrognes.

dry adj ❶ sec (f sèche) ▷ *The paint isn't dry yet.* La peinture n'est pas encore sèche. ❷ *(weather)* sans

<u>pluie</u> ▷ *a long dry period* une longue période sans pluie

▶ vb ❶ <u>sécher</u> ▷ *The washing will dry quickly in here.* Le linge va sécher vite au soleil.; **to dry one's hair** se sécher les cheveux ▷ *I haven't dried my hair yet.* Je ne me suis pas encore séché les cheveux. ❷ *(clothes)* <u>faire sécher</u> ▷ *There's nowhere to dry clothes here.* Il n'y a pas d'endroit où faire sécher les vêtements ici.; **to dry the dishes** essuyer la vaisselle

dry-cleaner's n teinturerie f

dryer n *(for clothes)* séchoir m; **a tumble dryer** un séchoir à linge; **a hair dryer** un sèche-cheveux

dubbed adj doublé(e) ▷ *The film was dubbed into French.* Le film était doublé en français.

duck n canard m

due adj, adv **to be due to do something** devoir faire quelque chose ▷ *He's due to arrive tomorrow.* Il doit arriver demain.; **The plane's due in half an hour.** L'avion doit arriver dans une demi-heure.; **When's the baby due?** Le bébé est prévu pour quand?; **due to** à cause de ▷ *The trip was cancelled due to bad weather.* Le voyage a été annulé à cause du mauvais temps.

dug vb see **dig**

dull adj ❶ ennuyeux *(f* ennuyeuse*)* ▷ *He's nice, but a bit dull.* Il est sympathique, mais un peu ennuyeux. ❷ *(weather, day)* maussade

dumb adj ❶ muet *(f* muette*)*; **She's deaf and dumb.** Elle est

sourde-muette. ❷ *(stupid)* bête ▷ *That was a really dumb thing I did!* C'était vraiment bête de ma part!

dummy n *(for baby)* tétine f

dump n **It's a real dump!** C'est un endroit minable!; **a rubbish dump** une décharge

▶ vb ❶ *(waste)* déposer ▷ *"no dumping"* "défense de déposer des ordures" ❷ *(informal)* plaquer ▷ *He's just dumped his girlfriend.* Il vient de plaquer sa copine.

dungarees npl salopette f

dungeon n cachot m

during prep pendant ▷ *during the day* pendant la journée

dusk n crépuscule m ▷ *at dusk* au crépuscule

dust n poussière f

▶ vb épousseter ▷ *I dusted the shelves.* J'ai épousseté les étagères.; **I hate dusting!** Je déteste faire les poussières!

dustbin n poubelle f

dustman n éboueur m ▷ *He's a dustman.* Il est éboueur.

dusty adj poussiéreux *(f* poussiéreuse*)*

Dutch adj hollandais(e) ▷ *She's Dutch.* Elle est hollandaise.

▶ n *(language)* hollandais m; **the Dutch** les Hollandais

Dutchman n Hollandais m

Dutchwoman n Hollandaise f

duty n devoir m ▷ *It was his duty to tell the police.* C'était son devoir de prévenir la police.; **to be on duty (1)** *(policeman)* être de service **(2)** *(doctor, nurse)* être de garde

duty-free adj hors taxes; **the duty-free shop** la boutique hors taxes

duvet n couette f

DVD n DVD m (pl DVD) ▷ I've got that film on DVD. J'ai ce film en DVD.

DVD player n lecteur m de DVD

dwarf n nain m, naine f

dying vb see **die**

dynamic adj dynamique

dyslexia n dyslexie f

dyslexic adj dyslexique

e

each adj, pron ❶ chaque ▷ each day chaque jour ❷ chacun(e) ▷ The girls each have their own bedroom. Les filles ont chacune leur chambre. ▷ They have 10 points each. Ils ont dix points chacun. ▷ He gave each of us £10. Il nous a donné dix livres à chacun.

> Use a reflexive verb to translate **each other**.

They hate each other. Ils se détestent.; **We wrote to each other.** Nous nous sommes écrit.; **They don't know each other.** Ils ne se connaissent pas.

eagle n aigle m

ear n oreille f

earache n **to have earache** avoir mal aux oreilles

earlier adv ❶ tout à l'heure ▷ I saw him earlier. Je l'ai vu tout à l'heure.

❷ (in the morning) plus tôt ▷ I ought to get up earlier. Je devrais me lever plus tôt.

early adv, adj ❶ (early in the day) tôt ▷ I have to get up early. Je dois me lever tôt.; **to have an early night** se coucher tôt ❷ (ahead of time) en avance ▷ I came early to get a good seat. Je suis venu en avance pour avoir une bonne place.

earn vb gagner ▷ She earns £5 an hour. Elle gagne cinq livres de l'heure.

earnings npl salaire m

earring n boucle f d'oreille

earth n terre f

earthquake n tremblement m de terre

easily adv facilement

east adj, adv ❶ est inv ▷ the east coast la côte est; **an east wind** un vent d'est; **east of** à l'est de ▷ It's east of London. C'est à l'est de Londres. ❷ vers l'est ▷ We were travelling east. Nous allions vers l'est.
▶ n est m ▷ in the east dans l'est

Easter n Pâques f ▷ at Easter à Pâques ▷ We went to my grandparents' for Easter. Nous sommes allés chez mes grands-parents à Pâques.

Easter egg n œuf m de Pâques

eastern adj **the eastern part of the island** la partie est de l'île; **Eastern Europe** l'Europe de l'Est

easy adj facile

eat vb manger; **Would you like something to eat?** Est-ce que tu veux manger quelque chose?

echo n écho m

eco-friendly adj respectueux de l'environnement (f respectueuse de l'environnement)

ecological adj écologique

ecology n écologie f

economic adj (profitable) rentable

economical adj ❶ (person) économe ❷ (method, car) économique

economics n économie f ▷ He's studying economics. Il étudie les sciences économiques.

economy n économie f

ecstasy n (drug) ecstasy f; **to be in ecstasy** s'extasier

eczema n eczéma m

edge n bord m

Edinburgh n Édimbourg

editor n (of newspaper) rédacteur m en chef, rédactrice f en chef

education n ❶ éducation f ▷ There should be more investment in education. On devrait investir plus dans l'éducation. ❷ (teaching) enseignement m ▷ She works in education. Elle travaille dans l'enseignement.

educational adj (experience, toy) éducatif (f éducative) ▷ It was very educational. C'était très éducatif.

effect n effet m ▷ special effects les effets spéciaux

effective adj efficace

effectively adv efficacement
▮ Be careful not to translate **effectively** by effectivement.

efficient adj efficace

effort n effort m

e.g. abbr p. ex. (par exemple)

egg n œuf m ▷ a hard-boiled egg un œuf dur ▷ a fried egg un œuf sur le plat; **scrambled eggs** les œufs brouillés

egg cup n coquetier m

eggplant n (US) aubergine f

Egypt n Égypte f; **in Egypt** en Égypte

Eiffel Tower n tour f Eiffel

eight num huit ▷ She's eight. Elle a huit ans.

eighteen num dix-huit ▷ She's eighteen. Elle a dix-huit ans.

eighteenth adj dix-huitième ▷ her eighteenth birthday son dix-huitième anniversaire ▷ the eighteenth floor le dix-huitième étage; **the eighteenth of August** le dix-huit août

eighth adj huitième ▷ the eighth floor le huitième étage; **the eighth of August** le huit août

eighty num quatre-vingts

Eire n République f d'Irlande; **in Eire** en République d'Irlande

either adv, conj, pron non plus ▷ I don't like milk, and I don't like eggs either. Je n'aime pas le lait, et je n'aime pas les œufs non plus. ▷ I've never been to Spain. — I haven't either. Je ne suis jamais allé en Espagne. — Moi non plus.; **either ... or ...** soit ... soit ... ▷ You can have either ice cream or yoghurt. Tu peux prendre soit une glace soit un yaourt.; **either of them** l'un ou l'autre ▷ Take either of them. Prends l'un ou l'autre.; **I don't like either of**

them. Je n'aime ni l'un ni l'autre.

elastic n élastique m

elastic band n élastique m

elbow n coude m

elder adj aîné(e) ▷ my elder sister ma sœur aînée

elderly adj âgé(e); **the elderly** les personnes âgées

eldest adj aîné(e) ▷ my eldest sister ma sœur aînée ▷ He's the eldest. C'est l'aîné.

elect vb élire

election n élection f

electric adj électrique ▷ an electric fire un radiateur électrique ▷ an electric guitar une guitare électrique; **an electric blanket** une couverture chauffante

electrical adj électrique; **an electrical engineer** un ingénieur électricien

electrician n électricien m ▷ He's an electrician. Il est électricien.

electricity n électricité f

electronic adj électronique

electronics n électronique f ▷ My hobby is electronics. Ma passion, c'est l'électronique.

elegant adj élégant(e)

elementary school n (US) école f primaire

elephant n éléphant m

elevator n (US) ascenseur m

eleven num onze ▷ She's eleven. Elle a onze ans.

eleventh adj onzième ▷ the eleventh floor le onzième étage; **the eleventh of August** le onze août

a
b
c
d
e
f
g
h
i
j
k
l
m
n
o
p
q
r
s
t
u
v
w
x
y
z

else adv d'autre ▷ somebody else quelqu'un d'autre ▷ nobody else personne d'autre ▷ nothing else rien d'autre; **something else** autre chose; **anything else** autre chose ▷ Would you like anything else? Désirez-vous autre chose?; **I don't want anything else.** Je ne veux rien d'autre.; **somewhere else** ailleurs; **anywhere else** autre part

email n courrier m électronique; **email address** adresse f e-mail ▷ My email address is: ... Mon adresse e-mail, c'est: ...
▶ vb **to email somebody** envoyer un e-mail à quelqu'un

embankment n talus m

embarrassed adj gêné(e) ▷ I was really embarrassed. J'étais vraiment gêné.

embarrassing adj gênant(e) ▷ It was so embarrassing. C'était tellement gênant.

embassy n ambassade f ▷ the British Embassy l'ambassade de Grande-Bretagne ▷ the French Embassy l'ambassade de France

embroider vb broder

embroidery n broderie f ▷ I do embroidery. Je fais de la broderie.

emergency n urgence f ▷ This is an emergency! C'est une urgence!; **in an emergency** en cas d'urgence; **an emergency exit** une sortie de secours; **an emergency landing** un atterrissage forcé; **the emergency services** les services d'urgence

emigrate vb émigrer

emotion n émotion f

emotional adj (person) émotif (f émotive)

emperor n empereur m

emphasize vb **to emphasize something** insister sur quelque chose; **to emphasize that ...** souligner que ...

empire n empire m

employ vb employer ▷ The factory employs 600 people. L'usine emploie six cents personnes.

employee n employé m, employée f

employer n employeur m

employment n emploi m

empty adj vide
▶ vb vider; **to empty something out** vider quelque chose

enclose vb (in letter etc) joindre; **please find enclosed** veuillez trouver ci-joint

encourage vb encourager; **to encourage somebody to do something** encourager quelqu'un à faire quelque chose

encouragement n encouragement m

encyclopedia n encyclopédie f

end n ❶ fin f ▷ the end of the film la fin du film; **in the end** en fin de compte ▷ In the end I decided to stay at home. En fin de compte j'ai décidé de rester à la maison.; **It turned out all right in the end.** Ça s'est bien terminé. ❷ bout m ▷ at the end of the street au bout de la rue; **for hours on end** des heures entières
▶ vb finir ▷ What time does the film

end? À quelle heure est-ce que le film finit?; **to end up doing something** finir par faire quelque chose ▷ I ended up walking home. J'ai fini par rentrer chez moi à pied.

ending n fin f ▷ It was an exciting film, especially the ending. C'était un film passionnant, surtout la fin.

endless adj interminable ▷ The journey seemed endless. Le voyage a paru interminable.

enemy n ennemi m, ennemie f

energetic adj (person) énergique

energy n énergie f

engaged adj ❶ (busy, in use) occupée f ▷ I phoned, but it was engaged. J'ai téléphoné, mais c'était occupé. ❷ (to be married) fiancé(e) ▷ She's engaged to Brian. Elle est fiancée à Brian.; **to get engaged** se fiancer

engagement n fiançailles fpl ▷ an engagement ring une bague de fiançailles

engine n moteur m

Be careful not to translate **engine** by the French word **engin**.

engineer n ingénieur m ▷ He's an engineer. Il est ingénieur.

engineering n ingénierie f

England n Angleterre f; **in England** en Angleterre; **to England** en Angleterre; **I'm from England.** Je suis anglais.

English adj anglais(e) ▷ I'm English. Je suis anglais.; **English people** les Anglais; **the English Channel** la Manche

▶ n (language) anglais m ▷ Do you speak English? Est-ce que vous parlez anglais?; **the English** les Anglais

Englishman n Anglais m

Englishwoman n Anglaise f

enjoy vb aimer ▷ Did you enjoy the film? Est-ce que vous avez aimé le film?; **to enjoy oneself** s'amuser ▷ I really enjoyed myself. Je me suis vraiment bien amusé.

enjoyable adj agréable

enlargement n (of photo) agrandissement m

enormous adj énorme

enough pron, adj assez de ▷ enough time assez de temps ▷ I didn't have enough money. Je n'avais pas assez d'argent. ▷ I've had enough! J'en ai assez!; **big enough** suffisamment grand; **warm enough** suffisamment chaud; **That's enough.** Ça suffit.

enquire vb to enquire about something se renseigner sur quelque chose ▷ I am going to enquire about train times. Je vais me renseigner sur les horaires de trains.

enquiry n to make enquiries (about something) se renseigner (sur quelque chose) ▷ "enquiries" "renseignements"

enter vb entrer; **to enter a room** entrer dans une pièce; **to enter a competition** s'inscrire à une compétition

entertain vb (guests) recevoir

entertaining adj amusant(e)

a b c d e f g h i j k l m n o p q r s t u v w x y z

enthusiasm n enthousiasme m

enthusiast n a railway enthusiast un passionné des trains; She's a DIY enthusiast. C'est une passionnée de bricolage.

enthusiastic adj enthousiaste

entire adj entier (f entière) ▷ the entire world le monde entier

entirely adv entièrement

entrance n entrée f; an entrance exam un concours d'entrée; entrance fee le prix d'entrée

entry n entrée f; "no entry" (1) (on door) "défense d'entrer" (2) (on road sign) "sens interdit"; an entry form une feuille d'inscription

entry phone n interphone m

envelope n enveloppe f

envious adj envieux (f envieuse)

environment n environnement m

environmental adj écologique

environment-friendly adj écologique

envy n envie f
▶ vb envier ▷ I don't envy you! Je ne t'envie pas!

epileptic n épileptique mf

episode n épisode m

equal adj égal(e) (mpl égaux)
▶ vb égaler

equality n égalité f

equalize vb (in sport) égaliser

equator n équateur m

equipment n équipement m
▷ fishing equipment l'équipement de pêche ▷ skiing equipment l'équipement de ski

equipped adj equipped with

équipé(e) de; to be well equipped être bien équipé(e)

error n erreur f

escalator n escalier m roulant

escape n (from prison) évasion f
▶ vb s'échapper ▷ A lion has escaped. Un lion s'est échappé.; to escape from prison s'évader de prison

escort n escorte f ▷ a police escort une escorte de police

especially adv surtout ▷ It's very hot there, especially in the summer. Il fait très chaud là-bas, surtout en été.

essay n dissertation f ▷ a history essay une dissertation d'histoire

essential adj essentiel (f essentielle) ▷ It's essential to bring warm clothes. Il est essentiel d'apporter des vêtements chauds.

estate n (housing estate) cité f ▷ I live on an estate. J'habite dans une cité.

estate agent n agent m immobilier

estate car n break m

estimate vb estimer ▷ They estimated it would take three weeks. Ils ont estimé que cela prendrait trois semaines.

etc abbr (= et cetera) etc.

Ethiopia n Éthiopie f; in Ethiopia en Éthiopie

ethnic adj ❶ (racial) ethnique ▷ an ethnic minority une minorité ethnique ❷ (clothes, music) folklorique

EU n (= European Union) Union f européenne

euro n euro m ▷ 50 euros 50 euros

euro cent n centime m d'euro

Europe n Europe f; **in Europe** en Europe; **to Europe** en Europe

European adj européen (f européenne)
▶ n (person) Européen m, Européenne f

European Union n Union f européenne

eurozone n eurozone f

eve n **Christmas Eve** la veille de Noël; **New Year's Eve** la Saint-Sylvestre

even adv même ▷ I like all animals, even snakes. J'aime tous les animaux, même si tu me le serpents.; **even if** même si ▷ I'd never do that, even if you asked me. Je ne ferais jamais ça, même si tu me le demandais.; **not even** même pas ▷ He never stops working, not even at the weekend. Il n'arrête jamais de travailler, même pas le week-end.; **even though** bien que

bien que has to be followed by a verb in the subjunctive.

▷ He's never got any money, even though his parents are quite rich. Il n'a jamais d'argent, bien que ses parents soient assez riches.; **even more** encore plus ▷ I liked Boulogne even more than Paris. J'ai encore plus aimé Boulogne que Paris.
▶ adj régulier (f régulière) ▷ an even layer of snow une couche régulière de neige; **an even number** un nombre pair; **to get even with somebody** prendre sa revanche sur quelqu'un ▷ He wanted to get

even with her. Il voulait prendre sa revanche sur elle.

evening n soir m ▶ in the evening le soir ▷ yesterday evening hier soir ▷ tomorrow evening demain soir; **all evening** toute la soirée; **Good evening!** Bonsoir!

evening class n cours m du soir (pl cours du soir)

event n événement m; **a sporting event** une épreuve sportive

eventful adj mouvementé(e)

eventual adj final(e)

Be careful not to translate eventual by éventuel.

eventually adv finalement

Be careful not to translate eventually by éventuellement.

ever adv **Have you ever been to Germany?** Est-ce que tu es déjà allé en Allemagne?; **Have you ever seen her?** Vous l'avez déjà vue?; **I haven't ever done that.** Je ne l'ai jamais fait.; **the best I've ever seen** le meilleur que j'aie jamais vu; **for the first time ever** pour la première fois; **ever since** depuis que ▷ ever since I met him depuis que je l'ai rencontré; **ever since then** depuis ce moment-là

every adj chaque ▷ every pupil chaque élève; **every time** chaque fois ▷ Every time I see him he's depressed. Chaque fois que je le vois il est déprimé.; **every day** tous les jours; **every week** toutes les semaines; **every now and then** de temps en temps

everybody pron tout le monde
▷ *Everybody had a good time.* Tout le monde s'est bien amusé.

everyone pron = **everybody**

everything pron tout ▷ *You've thought of everything!* Tu as pensé à tout!; **Have you remembered everything?** Est-ce que tu n'as rien oublié?; **Money isn't everything.** L'argent ne fait pas le bonheur.

everywhere adv partout ▷ *I looked everywhere, but I couldn't find it.* J'ai regardé partout, mais je n'ai pas pu le trouver.

evil adj mauvais(e)

exact adj exact(e)

exactly adv exactement ▷ *exactly the same* exactement le même ▷ *not exactly.* pas exactement.; **It's exactly 10 o'clock.** Il est dix heures précises.

exaggerate vb exagérer

exaggeration n exagération f

exam n examen m ▷ *a French exam* un examen de français ▷ *the exam results* les résultats des examens

examination n examen m

examine vb examiner ▷ *He examined her passport.* Il a examiné son passeport.

examiner n examinateur m, examinatrice f

example n exemple m; **for example** par exemple

excellent adj excellent(e) ▷ *Her results were excellent.* Elle a eu d'excellents résultats.; **It was excellent fun.** C'était vraiment super.

except prep sauf ▷ *everyone except me* tout le monde sauf moi; **except for** sauf; **except that** sauf que ▷ *The weather was great, except that it was a bit cold.* Il a fait un temps superbe, sauf qu'il a fait un peu froid.

exception n exception f; **to make an exception** faire une exception

exchange vb échanger ▷ *I exchanged the book for a video.* J'ai échangé le livre contre une vidéo.

exchange rate n taux m de change

excited adj excité(e)

excitement n excitation f

exciting adj passionnant(e)

exclamation mark n point m d'exclamation

excuse n excuse f
▶ vb **Excuse me!** Pardon!

exercise n exercice m; **an exercise bike** un vélo d'appartement; **an exercise book** un cahier

exhausted adj épuisé(e)

exhaust fumes npl gaz mpl d'échappement

exhaust pipe n tuyau m d'échappement

exhibition n exposition f

exist vb exister

exit n sortie f

expect vb ① attendre ▷ *I'm expecting him for dinner.* Je l'attends pour dîner. ▷ *She's expecting a baby.* Elle attend un enfant. ② s'attendre à ▷ *I was expecting the worst.* Je m'attendais au pire. ③ supposer ▷ *I expect it's a mistake.* Je suppose qu'il s'agit d'une erreur.

expedition n expédition f

expel vb **to get expelled** (from school) se faire renvoyer

expenses npl frais mpl

expensive adj cher (f chère)

experience n expérience f

experienced adj expérimenté(e)

experiment n expérience f

expert n spécialiste m, spécialiste f ▷ He's a computer expert. C'est un spécialiste en informatique.; **He's an expert cook.** Il cuisine très bien.

expire vb expirer

explain vb expliquer

explanation n explication f

explode vb exploser

explore vb (place) explorer

explosion n explosion f

export vb exporter
▶ n exportation f

express vb exprimer; **to express oneself** s'exprimer ▷ It's not easy to express oneself in a foreign language. Ce n'est pas facile de s'exprimer dans une langue étrangère.

expression n expression f ▷ It's an English expression. C'est une expression anglaise.

expressway n (US) autoroute f urbaine

extension n ❶ (of building) annexe f ❷ (telephone) poste m

In France phone numbers are broken into groups of two digits where possible.

Extension 3137, please. Poste trente et un trente-sept, s'il vous plaît.

extent n **to some extent** dans une certaine mesure

exterior adj extérieur(e)

extinct adj **to become extinct** disparaître; **to be extinct** avoir disparu ▷ The species is almost extinct. Cette espèce a presque disparu.

extinguisher n (fire extinguisher) extincteur m

extra adj, adv supplémentaire ▷ an extra blanket une couverture supplémentaire; **to pay extra** payer un supplément; **Breakfast is extra.** Il y a un supplément pour le petit déjeuner.; **It costs extra.** Il y a un supplément.

extraordinary adj extraordinaire

extravagant adj (person) dépensier (f dépensière)

extreme adj extrême

extremely adv extrêmement

extremist n extrémiste mf

eye n œil m (pl yeux) ▷ I've got green eyes. J'ai les yeux verts.; **to keep an eye on something** surveiller quelque chose

eyebrow n sourcil m

eyelash n cil m

eyelid n paupière f

eyeliner n eye-liner m

eye shadow n ombre f à paupières

eyesight n vue f

f

fabric n tissu m

fabulous adj formidable ▷ The show was fabulous. Le spectacle était formidable.

face n ① (of person) visage m ② (of clock) cadran m ③ (of cliff) paroi f; **on the face of it** à première vue; **in the face of these difficulties** face à ces difficultés; **face to face** face à face; **a face cloth** un gant de toilette

▶ vb (place, problem) faire face à; **to face up to something** faire face à quelque chose ▷ You must face up to your responsibilities. Vous devez faire face à vos responsabilités.

face cloth n gant m de toilette
- The French traditionally wash with a towelling glove rather than a flannel.

facilities npl équipement m ▷ This school has excellent facilities. Cette école dispose d'un excellent équipement.; **toilet facilities** les toilettes; **cooking facilities** la cuisine équipée

fact n fait m; **in fact** en fait

factory n usine f

fail vb ① rater ▷ I failed the history exam. J'ai raté l'examen d'histoire. ② échouer ▷ In our class, no one failed. Dans notre classe, personne n'a échoué. ③ lâcher ▷ My brakes failed. Mes freins ont lâché.; **to fail to do something** ne pas faire quelque chose ▷ She failed to return her library books. Elle n'a pas rendu ses livres à la bibliothèque.

▶ n **without fail** sans faute

failure n ① échec m ▷ feelings of failure sentiment m d'échec ② raté m, ratée f ▷ He's a failure. C'est un raté. ③ défaillance f ▷ a mechanical failure une défaillance mécanique

faint adj faible ▷ His voice was very faint. Sa voix était très faible.; **to feel faint** se trouver mal

▶ vb s'évanouir ▷ All of a sudden she fainted. Tout à coup elle s'est évanouie.

fair adj ① juste ▷ That's not fair. Ce n'est pas juste.; **fair trade** le commerce équitable ② (hair) blond(e) ▷ He's got fair hair. Il a les cheveux blonds. ③ (skin) clair ▷ people with fair skin les gens qui ont la peau claire ④ (weather) beau (f belle, mpl beaux) ▷ The weather was fair. Il faisait beau. ⑤ (good

enough) <u>assez bon</u> (f assez bonne)
▷ I have a fair chance of winning. J'ai
d'assez bonnes chances de gagner.
❺ (sizeable) <u>considérable</u> ▷ That's
a fair distance. Ça représente une
distance considérable.
▶ n <u>foire</u> f ▷ They went to the fair. Ils
sont allés à la foire.; **a trade fair**
une foire commerciale
fairground n <u>champ</u> m <u>de foire</u>
fairly adv ❶ <u>équitablement</u> ▷ The
cake was divided fairly. Le gâteau
a été partagé équitablement.
❷ (quite) <u>assez</u> ▷ That's fairly good.
C'est assez bien.
fairy n <u>fée</u> f
fairy tale n <u>conte</u> m <u>de fées</u> (pl
contes de fées)
faith n ❶ <u>foi</u> f ▷ the Catholic faith
la foi catholique ❷ <u>confiance</u>
f ▷ People have lost faith in the
government. Les gens ont perdu
confiance dans le gouvernement.
faithful adj <u>fidèle</u>
faithfully adv Yours faithfully ...
(in letter) Veuillez agréer mes
salutations distinguées ...
fake n <u>faux</u> m ▷ The painting was a
fake. Le tableau était un faux.
▶ adj <u>faux</u> (f fausse) ▷ She wore
fake fur. Elle portait une fausse
fourrure.
fall ❶ <u>chute</u> f ▷ She had a nasty
fall. Elle a fait une mauvaise
chute.; **the Niagara Falls** les
chutes du Niagara ❷ (US: autumn)
<u>automne</u> m
▶ vb ❶ <u>tomber</u> ▷ He tripped and
fell. Il a trébuché et il est tombé.

❷ <u>baisser</u> ▷ Prices are falling.
Les prix baissent.; **to fall down**
(1) (person) tomber ▷ She's fallen
down. Elle est tombée. **(2)** (building)
s'écrouler ▷ The house is slowly
falling down. La maison est en
train de s'écrouler.; **to fall for**
(1) se laisser prendre à ▷ They fell
for it. Ils s'y sont laissé prendre.
(2) tomber amoureux de ▷ She's
falling for him. Elle est en train de
tomber amoureuse de lui.; **to
fall off** tomber de ▷ The book fell
off the shelf. Le livre est tombé de
l'étagère.; **to fall out**; **to fall out
with somebody** se fâcher avec
quelqu'un ▷ Sarah's fallen out with
her boyfriend. Sarah s'est fâchée
avec son copain.; **to fall through**
tomber à l'eau ▷ Our plans have
fallen through. Nos projets sont
tombés à l'eau.
fallen vb see **fall**
false adj <u>faux</u> (f fausse); **a false
alarm** une fausse alerte; **false
teeth** les fausses dents
fame n <u>renommée</u> f
familiar adj <u>familier</u> (f familière)
▷ a familiar face un visage familier;
to be familiar with something
bien connaître quelque chose ▷ I'm
familiar with his work. Je connais
bien ses œuvres.
family n <u>famille</u> f; **the Cooke
family** la famille Cooke
famine n <u>famine</u> f
famous adj <u>célèbre</u>
fan n ❶ (hand-held) <u>éventail</u> m
❷ (electric) <u>ventilateur</u> m ❸ (of

person, band) fan mf ▷ I'm a fan of U2. Je suis une fan de U2. ❸ (of sport) supporter mf f ▷ football fans les supporters de football

fanatic n fanatique mf

fancy vb to fancy something avoir envie de quelque chose ▷ I fancy an ice cream. J'ai envie d'une glace.; **to fancy doing something** avoir envie de faire quelque chose; **He fancies her.** Elle lui plaît.

fancy dress n déguisement m ▷ He was wearing fancy dress. Il portait un déguisement.; **a fancy-dress ball** un bal costumé

fantastic adj fantastique

FAQs npl (= frequently asked questions) foire f aux questions

far adj, adv loin ▷ Is it far? Est-ce que c'est loin?; **far from** loin de ▷ It's not far from London. Ce n'est pas loin de Londres.; **How far is it?** C'est à quelle distance?; **How far is it to Geneva?** Combien y a-t-il jusqu'à Genève?; **How far have you got?** (with a task) Où en êtes-vous?; **at the far end** à l'autre bout ▷ at the far end of the room à l'autre bout de la pièce; **far better** beaucoup mieux; **as far as I know** pour autant que je sache

fare n ❶ (on trains, buses) prix m du billet ❷ (in taxi) prix m de la course; **half fare** le demi-tarif; **full fare** le plein tarif

Far East n Extrême-Orient m; **in the Far East** en Extrême-Orient

farm n ferme f

farmer n agriculteur m, agricultrice f ▷ He's a farmer. Il est agriculteur.

farmhouse n ferme f

farming n agriculture f

fascinating adj fascinant(e)

fashion n mode f ▷ a fashion show un défilé de mode; **in fashion** à la mode

fashionable adj à la mode ▷ Jane wears fashionable clothes. Jane porte des vêtements à la mode.

fast adj, adv ❶ vite b ▷ He can run fast. Il sait courir vite. ❷ rapide ▷ a fast car une voiture rapide; **That clock's fast.** Cette pendule avance.; **He's fast asleep.** Il est profondément endormi.

fast food n fast-food m

fat adj gros (f grosse) ▶ n ❶ (on meat, in food) gras m ▷ It's very high in fat. C'est très gras. ❷ (for cooking) matière f grasse

fatal adj ❶ (causing death) mortel (f mortelle) ▷ a fatal accident un accident mortel ❷ (disastrous) fatal ▷ He made a fatal mistake. Il a fait une erreur fatale.

father n père m ▷ my father mon père

father-in-law n beau-père m (pl beaux-pères)

faucet n (US) robinet m

fault n ❶ (mistake) faute f ▷ It's my fault. C'est de ma faute. ❷ (defect) défaut m ▷ There's a fault in this material. Ce tissu a un défaut.; **a mechanical fault** une défaillance mécanique

favour (US **favor**) n service m; **to do somebody a favour** rendre service à quelqu'un ▷ Could you do me a favour? Tu peux me rendre service?; **to be in favour of something** être pour quelque chose ▷ I'm in favour of nuclear disarmament. Je suis pour le désarmement nucléaire.

favourite (US **favorite**) adj favori (f favorite) ▷ Blue's my favourite colour. Le bleu est ma couleur favorite.
▶ n favori m (f favorite) ▷ Liverpool are favourites to win the Cup. L'équipe de Liverpool est favorite pour la coupe.

fax n fax m; **to send somebody a fax** envoyer un fax à quelqu'un
▶ vb **to fax somebody** envoyer un fax à quelqu'un

fear n peur f
▶ vb craindre ▷ You have nothing to fear. Vous n'avez rien à craindre.

feather n plume f

feature n (of person, object) caractéristique f ▷ an important feature une caractéristique essentielle

February n février m; **in February** en février

fed vb see **feed**

fed up adj **to be fed up with something** en avoir marre de quelque chose ▷ I'm fed up of waiting for him. J'en ai marre de l'attendre.

feed vb donner à manger à ▷ Have you fed the cat? Est-ce que tu as donné à manger au chat?; **He worked hard to feed his family.** Il travaillait dur pour nourrir sa famille.

feel vb ❶ se sentir ▷ I don't feel well. Je ne me sens pas bien. ▷ I feel a bit lonely. Je me sens un peu seul. ❷ sentir ▷ I didn't feel much pain. Je n'ai presque rien senti. ❸ toucher ▷ The doctor felt his forehead. Le docteur lui a touché le front.; **I was feeling hungry.** J'avais faim.; **I was feeling cold, so I went inside.** J'avais froid, alors je suis rentré.; **I feel like ...** (want) J'ai envie de ... ▷ Do you feel like an ice cream? Tu as envie d'une glace?

feeling n ❶ (physical) sensation f ▷ a burning feeling une sensation de brûlure ❷ (emotional) sentiment m ▷ a feeling of satisfaction un sentiment de satisfaction

feet npl see **foot**

fell vb see **fall**

felt vb see **feel**

felt-tip pen n stylo-feutre m

female adj ❶ femelle ▷ a female animal un animal femelle ❷ féminin(e) ▷ the female sex le sexe féminin
▶ n (animal) femelle f

feminine adj féminin(e)

feminist n féministe mf

fence n barrière f

fern n fougère f

ferry n ferry m

festival n festival m ▷ a jazz festival un festival de jazz

fetch vb ❶ aller chercher ▷ Fetch the bucket. Va chercher le seau.

❷ (sell for) se vendre ▷ His painting
fetched £5000. Son tableau s'est
vendu cinq mille livres.

fever n (temperature) fièvre f

few adj, pron (not many) peu
de ▷ few books peu de livres; **a
few** (1) quelques ▷ a few hours
quelques heures (2) quelques-uns
(f quelques-unes) ▷ How many
apples do you want? — A few. Tu
veux combien de pommes? —
Quelques-unes.; **quite a few
people** pas mal de monde

fewer adj moins de ▷ There are
fewer pupils in this class. Il y a moins
d'élèves dans cette classe.

fiancé n fiancé m ▷ He's my fiancé.
C'est mon fiancé.

fiancée n fiancée f ▷ She's my
fiancée. C'est ma fiancée.

fiction n (novels) romans mpl

field n ❶ (in countryside) champ
m ▷ a field of wheat un champ de
blé ❷ (for sport) terrain m ▷ a
football field un terrain de football
❸ (subject) domaine m ▷ He's an
expert in his field. C'est un expert
dans son domaine.

fierce adj ❶ féroce ▷ The dog looked
very fierce. Le chien avait l'air très
féroce. ❷ violent ▷ a fierce attack
une attaque violente

fifteen num quinze ▷ I'm fifteen.
J'ai quinze ans.

fifteenth adj quinzième ▷ the
fifteenth floor le quinzième étage;
the fifteenth of August le quinze
août

fifth adj cinquième ▷ the fifth floor

le cinquième étage; **the fifth of
August** le cinq août

fifty num cinquante ▷ He's fifty. Il a
cinquante ans.

fight n ❶ bagarre f ▷ There was a
fight in the pub. Il y a eu une bagarre
au pub. ❷ lutte f ▷ the fight against
cancer la lutte contre le cancer
▶ vb ❶ se battre ▷ They were
fighting. Ils se battaient. ❷ lutter
contre ▷ The doctors tried to fight the
disease. Les médecins ont essayé de
lutter contre la maladie.

figure n ❶ (number) chiffre m ▷ Can
you give me the exact figures? Pouvez-
vous me donner les chiffres exacts?
❷ (outline of person) silhouette f
▷ Hélène saw the figure of a man on
the bridge. Hélène a vu la silhouette
d'un homme sur le pont.; **She's
got a good figure.** Elle est bien
faite.; **I have to watch my figure.**
Je dois faire attention à ma ligne.
❸ (personality) personnage m
▷ She's an important political figure.
C'est un personnage politique
important.

figure out vb ❶ calculer ▷ I'll try to
figure out how much it'll cost. Je vais
essayer de calculer combien ça va
coûter. ❷ voir ▷ I couldn't figure out
what it meant. Je n'arrivais pas à voir
ce que ça voulait dire. ❸ cerner ▷ I
can't figure him out at all. Je n'arrive
pas du tout à le cerner.

file n ❶ (document) dossier m ▷ Have
we got a file on the suspect? Est-ce
que nous avons un dossier sur le
suspect? ❷ (folder) chemise f ▷ She

keeps all her letters in a cardboard file.
Elle garde toutes ses lettres dans
une chemise en carton. ❸ (ring
binder) classeur m ❹ (on computer)
fichier m ❺ (for nails, metal) lime f
▶ vb ❶ (papers) classer ❷ (nails,
metal) limer ▷ to file one's nails se
limer les ongles

fill vb remplir ▷ She filled the glass
with water. Elle a rempli le verre
d'eau.; **to fill in (1)** remplir ▷ Can
you fill this form in please? Est-ce que
vous pouvez remplir ce formulaire
s'il vous plaît? **(2)** boucher ▷ He
filled the hole in with soil. Il a bouché
le trou avec de la terre.; **to fill
up** remplir ▷ He filled the cup up to
the brim. Il a rempli la tasse à ras
bords.; **Fill it up, please.** (at petrol
station) Le plein, s'il vous plaît.

filling n (for tooth) plombage m

film n ❶ (movie) film m ❷ (for
camera) pellicule f

film star n vedette f de cinéma
▷ He's a film star. C'est une vedette
de cinéma.

filthy adj dégoûtant(e)

final adj ❶ (last) dernier (f dernière)
▷ our final farewells nos derniers
adieux ❷ (definite) définitif
(f définitive) ▷ a final decision une
décision définitive; **I'm not going
and that's final.** Je n'y vais pas, un
point c'est tout.
▶ n finale f ▷ Federer is in the final.
Federer va disputer la finale.

finally adv ❶ (lastly) enfin
▷ Finally, I would like to say ... Enfin,
je voudrais dire ... ❷ (eventually)

finalement ▷ They finally decided to
leave on Saturday instead of Friday.
Ils ont finalement décidé de partir
samedi au lieu de vendredi.

find vb ❶ trouver ▷ I can't find the
exit. Je ne trouve pas la sortie.
❷ (something lost) retrouver ▷ Did
you find your pen? Est-ce que tu
as retrouvé ton crayon?; **to find
something out** découvrir quelque
chose ▷ I'm determined to find out
the truth. Je suis décidé à découvrir
la vérité.; **to find out about
(1)** (make enquiries) se renseigner
sur ▷ Try to find out about the cost of
a hotel. Essaye de te renseigner sur
le prix d'un hôtel. **(2)** (by chance)
apprendre ▷ I found out about their
affair. J'ai appris leur liaison.

fine adj, adv ❶ (very good)
excellent(e) ▷ He's a fine musician.
C'est un excellent musicien.; **to be
fine** aller bien ▷ How are you? — I'm
fine. Comment ça va? — Ça va
bien.; **I feel fine.** Je me sens bien.;
The weather is fine today. Il fait
beau aujourd'hui. ❷ (not coarse)
fin(e) ▷ She's got very fine hair. Elle a
les cheveux très fins.
▶ n ❶ amende f ▷ She got a £50
fine. Elle a eu une amende de
cinquante livres. ❷ (for traffic
offence) contravention f ▷ I got a fine
for driving through a red light. J'ai eu
une contravention pour avoir grillé
un feu rouge.

finger n doigt m; **my little finger**
mon petit doigt

fingernail n ongle m

finish n (of race) arrivée f ▷ We saw the finish of the London Marathon. Nous avons vu l'arrivée du marathon de Londres.
▶ vb ❶ finir ▷ I've finished! J'ai fini!; **to finish doing something** finir de faire quelque chose ❷ terminer ▷ I've finished the book. J'ai terminé ce livre. ▷ The film has finished. Le film est terminé.

Finland n Finlande f; **in Finland** en Finlande; **to Finland** en Finlande

Finn n Finlandais m, Finlandaise f

Finnish adj finlandais(e)
▶ n (language) finnois m

fire n ❶ feu m (pl feux) ▷ He made a fire to warm himself up. Il a fait du feu pour se réchauffer.; **to be on fire** être en feu ❷ (accidental) incendie m ▷ The house was destroyed by fire. La maison a été détruite par un incendie. ❸ (heater) radiateur m ▷ Turn the fire on. Allume le radiateur.; **the fire brigade** les pompiers; **a fire alarm** un avertisseur d'incendie; **a fire engine** une voiture de pompiers; **a fire escape** un escalier de secours; **a fire extinguisher** un extincteur; **a fire station** une caserne de pompiers
▶ vb (shoot) tirer ▷ She fired twice. Elle a tiré deux fois.; **to fire at somebody** tirer sur quelqu'un ▷ The terrorist fired at the crowd. Le terroriste a tiré sur la foule.; **to fire a gun** tirer un coup de feu; **to fire somebody** mettre quelqu'un à la porte ▷ He was fired from his job. Il a

été mis à la porte.

firefighter n pompier m ▷ She's a firefighter. Elle est pompier.

fireman n pompier m ▷ He's a fireman. Il est pompier.

fireplace n cheminée f

fireworks npl feu m d'artifice ▷ Are you going to see the fireworks? Est-ce que tu vas voir le feu d'artifice?

firm adj ferme ▷ to be firm with somebody se montrer ferme avec quelqu'un
▶ n entreprise f ▷ He works for a large firm in London. Il travaille pour une grande entreprise à Londres.

first adj, adv ❶ premier (f première) ▷ the first of September le premier septembre ▷ the first time la première fois; **to come first** (in exam, race) arriver premier ▷ Rachel came first. Rachel est arrivée première. ❷ d'abord ▷ I want to get a job, but first I have to pass my exams. Je veux trouver du travail, mais d'abord je dois réussir à mes examens.; **first of all** tout d'abord
▶ n premier m, première f ▷ She was the first to arrive. Elle est arrivée la première.; **at first** au début

first aid n premiers secours mpl; **a first aid kit** une trousse de secours

first-class adj ❶ de première classe ▷ She has booked a first-class ticket. Elle a réservé un billet de première classe. ❷ excellent ▷ a first-class meal un excellent repas; **a first-class stamp**

• In France there is no first-class or second-class postage. However letters cost more to send than postcards, so you have to say what you are sending when buying stamps.

firstly adv premièrement ▷ *Firstly, let's see what the book is about.* Premièrement, voyons de quoi parle ce livre.

first name n prénom m

fir tree n sapin m

fish n poisson m ▷ *I caught three fish.* J'ai pêché trois poissons. ▷ *I don't like fish.* Je n'aime pas le poisson.
▶ vb pêcher; **to go fishing** aller à la pêche ▷ *We went fishing in the River Dee.* Nous sommes allés à la pêche sur la Dee.

fisherman n pêcheur m ▷ *He's a fisherman.* Il est pêcheur.

fishing n pêche f ▷ *My hobby is fishing.* La pêche est mon passe-temps favori.

fishing boat n bateau m de pêche

fishing rod n canne f à pêche

fishing tackle n matériel m de pêche

fist n poing m

fit vb ❶ (be the right size) être la bonne taille ▷ *Does it fit?* Est-ce que c'est la bonne taille?

> In French you usually specify whether something is too big, small, tight etc.

These trousers don't fit me.
(1) (too big) Ce pantalon est trop grand pour moi. **(2)** (too small) Ce pantalon est trop petit pour

moi. ❷ (fix up) installer ▷ *He fitted an alarm in his car.* Il a installé une alarme dans sa voiture. ❸ (attach) adapter ▷ *She fitted a plug to the hair dryer.* Elle a adapté une prise au sèche-cheveux.; **to fit in**
(1) (match up) correspondre ▷ *That story doesn't fit in with what he told us.* Cette histoire ne correspond pas à ce qu'il nous a dit. **(2)** (person) s'adapter ▷ *She fitted in well at her new school.* Elle s'est bien adaptée à sa nouvelle école.
▶ adj (in condition) en forme ▷ *He felt relaxed and fit after his holiday.* Il se sentait détendu et en forme après ses vacances.
▶ n **to have a fit (1)** (epileptic) avoir une crise d'épilepsie **(2)** (be angry) piquer une crise de nerfs ▷ *My Mum will have a fit when she sees the carpet!* Ma mère va piquer une crise de nerfs quand elle va voir la moquette!

fitted carpet n moquette f

five num cinq ▷ *He's five.* Il a cinq ans.

fix vb ❶ (mend) réparer ▷ *Can you fix my bike?* Est-ce que tu peux réparer mon vélo? ❷ (decide) fixer ▷ *Let's fix a date for the party.* Fixons une date pour la soirée. ❸ préparer ▷ *Janice fixed some food for us.* Janice nous a préparé à manger.

fizzy adj gazeux (f gazeuse) ▷ *I don't like fizzy drinks.* Je n'aime pas les boissons gazeuses.

flag n drapeau m (pl drapeaux)

flame n flamme f

flan n ❶ (sweet) tarte f ▷ a raspberry flan une tarte aux framboises ❷ (savoury) quiche f ▷ a cheese and onion flan une quiche au fromage et aux oignons

flap vb battre de ▷ The bird flapped its wings. L'oiseau battait des ailes.

flash n flash m (pl flashes) ▷ Has your camera got a flash? Est-ce que ton appareil photo a un flash?; a flash of lightning un éclair; in a flash en un clin d'œil
▷ vb ❶ clignoter ▷ The police car's blue light was flashing. Le gyrophare de la voiture de police clignotait. ❷ projeter ▷ They flashed a torch in his face. Ils lui ont projeté la lumière d'une torche en plein visage.; She flashed her headlights. Elle a fait un appel de phares.

flask n (vacuum flask) thermos m

flat adj ❶ plat(e) ▷ flat shoes des chaussures plates ❷ (tyre) crevé ▷ I've got a flat tyre. J'ai un pneu crevé.
▷ n appartement m ▷ She lives in a flat. Elle habite un appartement.

flatter vb flatter

flavour n ❶ (taste) goût m ▷ It has a very strong flavour. Ça a un goût très fort. ❷ (variety) parfum m ▷ Which flavour of ice cream would you like? Quel parfum de glace est-ce que tu veux?

flew vb see fly

flexible adj flexible ▷ flexible working hours des horaires flexibles

flick vb to flick through a book feuilleter un livre

flight n vol m ▷ What time is the flight to Paris? À quelle heure est le vol pour Paris?; a flight of stairs un escalier

flight attendant n ❶ (woman) hôtesse f de l'air ❷ (man) steward m

fling vb jeter ▷ He flung the book onto the floor. Il a jeté le livre par terre.

flippers n palmes fpl

float vb flotter ▷ A leaf was floating on the water. Une feuille flottait sur l'eau.

flood n ❶ inondation f ▷ The rain has caused many floods. La pluie a provoqué de nombreuses inondations. ❷ flot m ▷ He received a flood of letters. Il a reçu un flot de lettres.
▷ vb inonder ▷ The river has flooded the village. La rivière a inondé le village.

floor n ❶ sol m ▷ a tiled floor un sol carrelé; on the floor par terre ❷ (storey) étage m ▷ the first floor le premier étage; the ground floor le rez-de-chaussée; on the third floor au troisième étage

floppy disk n disquette f

florist n fleuriste mf

flour n farine f

flow vb (river) couler

flower n fleur f
▷ vb fleurir

flown vb see fly

flu n grippe f ▷ She's got flu. Elle a la grippe.

fluent adj He speaks fluent French. Il parle couramment le français.

flung vb see **fling**

flush n (of toilet) chasse f d'eau
▶ vb **to flush the toilet** tirer la chasse

flute n flûte f ▷ I play the flute. Je joue de la flûte.

fly n (insect) mouche f
▶ vb ❶ voler ▷ The plane flies at a speed of 400 km per hour. L'avion vole à quatre cents kilomètres à l'heure. ❷ (passenger) aller en avion ▷ He flew from Paris to New York. Il est allé de Paris à New York en avion.; **to fly away** s'envoler ▷ The bird flew away. L'oiseau s'est envolé.

focus n **to be out of focus** être flou ▷ The house is out of focus in this photo. La maison est floue sur cette photo.
▶ vb mettre au point ▷ Try to focus the binoculars. Essaye de mettre les jumelles au point.; **to focus on something** (1) (with camera, telescope) régler la mise au point sur quelque chose ▷ The cameraman focused on the bird. Le caméraman a réglé la mise au point sur l'oiseau. (2) (concentrate) se concentrer sur quelque chose ▷ Let's focus on the plot of the play. Concentrons-nous sur l'intrigue de la pièce.

fog n brouillard m

foggy adj **It's foggy.** Il y a du brouillard.; **a foggy day** un jour de brouillard

foil n (kitchen foil) papier m d'aluminium ▷ She wrapped the meat in foil. Elle a enveloppé la viande dans du papier d'aluminium.

fold n pli m
▶ vb plier ▷ He folded the newspaper in half. Il a plié le journal en deux.; **to fold something up** plier quelque chose; **to fold one's arms** croiser ses bras ▷ She folded her arms. Elle a croisé les bras.

folder n ❶ chemise f ▷ She kept all her letters in a folder. Elle gardait toutes ses lettres dans une chemise. ❷ (ring binder) classeur m

follow vb suivre ▷ She followed him. Elle l'a suivi.

following adj suivant(e) ▷ the following day le jour suivant

fond adj **to be fond of somebody** aimer beaucoup quelqu'un ▷ I'm very fond of her. Je l'aime beaucoup.

food n nourriture f; **We need to buy some food.** Nous devons acheter à manger.; **cat food** la nourriture pour chat; **dog food** la nourriture pour chien

fool n idiot m, idiote f

foot n ❶ (of person) pied m ▷ My feet are aching. J'ai mal aux pieds. ❷ (of animal) patte f ▷ The dog's foot was injured. Le chien était blessé à la patte.; **on foot** à pied ❸ (12 inches) pied m

• In France measurements are in metres and centimetres rather than feet and inches. A foot is about 30 centimetres.

Dave is 6 foot tall. Dave mesure un mètre quatre-vingt.; **That mountain is 5000 feet high.** Cette montagne fait mille six cents mètres de haut.

football n ❶ (game) football m ▷ I like playing football. J'aime jouer au football. ❷ (ball) ballon m ▷ Paul threw the football over the fence. Paul a envoyé le ballon par dessus la clôture.

footballer n footballeur m, footballeuse f

footie n foot m

footpath n sentier m ▷ Jane followed the footpath through the forest. Jane a suivi le sentier à travers la forêt.

for prep

There are several ways of translating **for**. Scan the examples to find one that is similar to what you want to say.

❶ pour ▷ a present for me un cadeau pour moi ▷ the train for London le train pour Londres ▷ I'll do it for you. Je vais le faire pour toi. ▷ Are you for or against the idea? Êtes-vous pour ou contre cette idée?

When referring to periods of time, use **pendant** for the future and completed actions in the past, and **depuis** (with the French verb in the present tense) for something that started in the past and is still going on.

❷ pendant ▷ She will be away for a month. Elle sera absente pendant un mois. ▷ There are road works for three kilometres. Il y a des travaux pendant trois kilomètres.

❸ depuis ▷ He's been learning French for two years. Il apprend le français depuis deux ans.

When talking about amounts of money, you do not translate **for**.

▷ I sold it for £5. Je l'ai vendu cinq livres.; **What's the French for "lion"?** Comment dit-on "lion" en français?; **It's time for lunch.** C'est l'heure du déjeuner.; **What for?** Pour quoi faire? ▷ Give me some money! —What for? Donne-moi de l'argent! — Pour quoi faire?; **What's it for?** Ça sert à quoi?; **for sale** à vendre ▷ The factory's for sale. L'usine est en vente.

forbid vb défendre; **to forbid somebody to do something** défendre à quelqu'un de faire quelque chose ▷ I forbid you to go out tonight! Je te défends de sortir ce soir.

forbidden adj défendu(e) ▷ Smoking is strictly forbidden. Il est strictement défendu de fumer.

force n force f ▷ the force of the explosion la force de l'explosion; **in force** en vigueur ▷ No-smoking rules are now in force. Un règlement qui interdit de fumer est maintenant en vigueur.
▶ vb forcer ▷ They forced him to open the safe. Ils l'ont obligé à ouvrir le coffre-fort.

forecast n the weather forecast la météo

forehead n front m

foreign adj étranger (f étrangère)

foreigner n étranger m, étrangère f

forest n forêt f

forever adv ❶ pour toujours ▷ He's gone forever. Il est parti pour toujours. ❷ (always) toujours ▷ She's forever complaining. Elle est toujours en train de se plaindre.

forgave vb see **forgive**

forge vb contrefaire ▷ She tried to forge his signature. Elle a essayé de contrefaire sa signature.

forged adj faux (ffausse) ▷ forged banknotes des faux billets

forget vb oublier ▷ I've forgotten his name. J'ai oublié son nom.

forgive vb to forgive somebody pardonner à quelqu'un ▷ I forgive you. Je te pardonne.; to forgive somebody for doing something pardonner à quelqu'un d'avoir fait quelque chose ▷ She forgave him for forgetting her birthday. Elle lui a pardonné d'avoir oublié son anniversaire.

forgot, forgotten vb see **forget**

fork n ❶ (for eating) fourchette f ❷ (for gardening) fourche f ❸ (in road) bifurcation f

form n ❶ (paper) formulaire m ▷ to fill in a form remplir un formulaire ❷ (type) forme f ▷ I'm against hunting in any form. Je suis contre la chasse sous toutes ses formes.; in top form en pleine forme; She's in the fourth form. Elle est en troisième.

formal adj ❶ (occasion) officiel (fofficielle) ▷ a formal dinner un dîner officiel ❷ (person) guindé(e) ❸ (language) soutenu(e) ▷ In English, "residence" is a formal term. En anglais, "residence" est un terme soutenu.; **formal clothes** une tenue habillée; **He's got no formal education.** Il n'a pas fait beaucoup d'études.

former adj ancien (fancienne) ▷ a former pupil un ancien élève

fortnight n a fortnight quinze jours ▷ I'm going on holiday for a fortnight. Je pars en vacances pendant quinze jours.

> Word for word, **quinze jours** means 15 days.

fortunate adj to be fortunate avoir de la chance ▷ He was extremely fortunate to survive. Il a eu énormément de chance de survivre.; **It's fortunate that I remembered the map.** C'est une chance que j'aie pris la carte.

fortunately adv heureusement ▷ Fortunately, it didn't rain. Heureusement, il n'a pas plu.

fortune n fortune f ▷ Kate earns a fortune! Kate gagne une fortune!; to tell somebody's fortune dire la bonne aventure à quelqu'un

forty num quarante ▷ He's forty. Il a quarante ans.

forward adv to move forward avancer
▶ vb faire suivre ▷ He forwarded all Janette's letters. Il a fait suivre toutes les lettres de Janette.

forward slash n barre f oblique

foster child n enfant m adoptif, enfant f adoptive

fought vb see **fight**

foul adj infect(e) ⊳ The weather was foul. Le temps était infect.
▶ n faute f ⊳ Ferguson committed a foul. Ferguson a fait une faute.

fountain n fontaine f

fountain pen n stylo m à encre

four num quatre ⊳ She's four. Elle a quatre ans.

fourteen num quatorze ⊳ I'm fourteen. J'ai quatorze ans.

fourteenth adj quatorzième ⊳ the fourteenth floor le quatorzième étage; **the fourteenth of August** le quatorze août

fourth adj quatrième ⊳ the fourth floor le quatrième étage; **the fourth of July** le quatre juillet

fox n renard m

fragile adj fragile

frame n (for picture) cadre m

France n France f; **in France** en France; **to France** en France; **He's from France.** Il est français.

frantic adj I was going frantic. J'étais dans tous mes états.; **to be frantic with worry** être folle d'inquiétude

fraud n ❶ (crime) fraude f ⊳ He was jailed for fraud. On l'a mis en prison pour fraude. ❷ (person) imposteur m ⊳ He's not a real doctor, he's a fraud. Ce n'est pas un vrai médecin, c'est un imposteur.

freckles npl taches fpl de rousseur

free adj ❶ (free of charge) gratuit(e) ⊳ a free brochure une brochure gratuite ❷ (not busy, not taken) libre ⊳ Is this seat free? Est-ce que cette place est libre? ⊳ Are you free

after school? Tu es libre après l'école?
▶ vb libérer

freedom n liberté f

freeway n (US) autoroute f

freeze vb ❶ geler ⊳ The water had frozen. L'eau avait gelé. ❷ (food) congeler ⊳ She froze the rest of the raspberries. Elle a congelé le reste des framboises.

freezer n congélateur m

freezing adj It's freezing! (informal) Il fait un froid de canard! (informal); **I'm freezing!** Je suis gelé! (informal); **3 degrees below freezing** moins trois

French adj français(e) ⊳ She's French. Elle est française.
▶ n (language) français m ⊳ Do you speak French? Est-ce que tu parles français?; **the French** (people) les Français

French beans npl haricots mpl verts

French fries npl frites fpl

French kiss n baiser m profond

Frenchman n Français m

French windows npl porte-fenêtre f (pl portes-fenêtres)

Frenchwoman n Française f

frequent adj fréquent(e) ⊳ frequent showers des averses fréquentes; **There are frequent buses to the town centre.** Il y a beaucoup de bus pour le centre ville.

fresh adj frais (f fraîche); **I need some fresh air.** J'ai besoin de prendre l'air.

Friday n vendredi m ⊳ on Friday

vendredi n > on Fridays le vendredi
> every Friday tous les vendredis

fridge n frigo m

fried adj frit(e) > fried vegetables des
légumes frits; **a fried egg** un œuf
sur le plat

friend n ami m, amie f

friendly adj ❶ gentil (f
gentille) > She's really friendly.
Elle est vraiment gentille.
❷ accueillant(e) > Liverpool is a very
friendly city. Liverpool est une ville
très accueillante.

friendship n amitié f

fright n peur f > I got a terrible fright!
Ça m'a fait une peur terrible!

frighten vb faire peur à > Horror
films frighten me. Les films
d'horreur lui font peur.

frightened adj to be frightened
avoir peur > I'm frightened! J'ai peur!;
to be frightened of something
avoir peur de quelque chose
> Anna's frightened of spiders. Anna a
peur des araignées.

frightening adj effrayant(e)

fringe n (of hair) frange f > She's got
a fringe. Elle a une frange.

frog n grenouille f; frogs' legs les
cuisses de grenouille

from prep de > Where do you come
from? D'où venez-vous? > I come
from Perth. Je viens de Perth.;
from ... to ... de ... à ... > He flew from
London to Paris. Il a pris l'avion de
Londres à Paris.; **from ... onwards**
à partir de ... > We'll be at home from
7 o'clock onwards. Nous serons chez
nous à partir de sept heures.

front n devant m > the front of the
house le devant de la maison; **in
front** devant > the car in front la
voiture de devant; **in front of**
devant > in front of the house devant
la maison > the car in front of us la
voiture devant nous; **in the front**
(of car) à l'avant > I was sitting in the
front. J'étais assis à l'avant.; **at the
front of the train** à l'avant du train
▶ adj ❶ de devant > the front row
la rangée de devant ❷ avant > the
front seats of the car les sièges avant
de la voiture; **the front door** la
porte d'entrée

frontier n frontière f

frost n gel m

frosty adj It's frosty today. Il gèle
aujourd'hui.

frown vb froncer les sourcils > He
frowned. Il a froncé les sourcils.

froze vb see **freeze**

frozen adj (food) surgelé(e) > frozen
chips des frites surgelées

fruit n fruit m; fruit juice le jus de
fruits; **a fruit salad** une salade
de fruits

fruit machine n machine f à sous

frustrated adj frustré(e)

fry vb faire frire > Fry the onions for
5 minutes. Faites frire les oignons
pendant cinq minutes.

frying pan n poêle f

fuel n (for car, aeroplane) carburant
m > to run out of fuel avoir une
panne de carburant

full adj, adv ❶ plein(e) > The
tank's full. Le réservoir est plein.
❷ complet (f complète) > He asked

for full information on the job. Il a demandé des renseignements complets sur le poste.; **your full name** vos nom et prénoms ▷ *My full name is Ian John Marr.* Je m'appelle Ian John Marr.; **I'm full.** *(after meal)* J'ai bien mangé.; **at full speed** à toute vitesse ▷ *He drove at full speed.* Il conduisait à toute vitesse.; **There was a full moon.** C'était la pleine lune.

full stop n point m

full-time adj, adv à plein temps ▷ *She's got a full-time job.* Elle a un travail à plein temps. ▷ *She works full-time.* Elle travaille à plein temps.

fully adv complètement ▷ *He hasn't fully recovered from his illness.* Il n'est pas complètement remis de sa maladie.

fumes npl **exhaust fumes** les gaz d'échappement

fun adj **marrant(e)** ▷ *She's a fun person.* Elle est marrante.
▶ n **to have fun** s'amuser ▷ *We had great fun playing in the snow.* Nous nous sommes bien amusés à jouer dans la neige.; **for fun** pour rire ▷ *He entered the competition just for fun.* Il a participé à la compétition juste pour rire.; **to make fun of somebody** se moquer de quelqu'un ▷ *They made fun of him.* Ils se sont moqués de lui.; **It's fun!** C'est chouette!; **Have fun!** Amuse-toi bien!

funds npl **fonds** mpl ▷ **to raise funds** collecter des fonds

funeral n **enterrement** m

funfair n **fête f foraine**

funny adj ① *(amusing)* **drôle** ▷ *It was really funny.* C'était vraiment drôle. ② *(strange)* **bizarre** ▷ *There's something funny about him.* Il est un peu bizarre.

fur n ① **fourrure** f ▷ *a fur coat* un manteau de fourrure ② **poil** m ▷ *the dog's fur* le poil du chien

furious adj **furieux** (f **furieuse**) ▷ *Dad was furious with me.* Papa était furieux contre moi.

furniture n **meubles** mpl ▷ *a piece of furniture* un meuble

further adv, adj **plus loin** ▷ *London is further from Manchester than Leeds is.* Londres est plus loin de Manchester que Leeds.; **How much further is it?** C'est encore loin?

further education n **enseignement** m **postscolaire**

fuse n **fusible** m ▷ *The fuse has blown.* Le fusible a sauté.

fuss n **agitation** f ▷ *What's all the fuss about?* Qu'est-ce que c'est que toute cette agitation?; **to make a fuss** faire des histoires ▷ *He's always making a fuss about nothing.* Il fait toujours des histoires pour rien.

fussy adj **difficile** ▷ *She is very fussy about her food.* Elle est très difficile sur la nourriture.

future n ① **avenir** m ▷ *What are your plans for the future?* Quels sont vos projets pour l'avenir?; **in future** à l'avenir ▷ *Be more careful in future.*

Sois plus prudent à l'avenir.
❷ *(in grammar)* futur m ▷ *Put this sentence into the future.* Mettez cette phrase au futur.

gadget *n* gadget m

gain *vb* **to gain weight** prendre du poids; **to gain speed** prendre de la vitesse

gallery *n* musée m ▷ *an art gallery* un musée d'art

gamble *vb* jouer ▷ *He gambled £100 at the casino.* Il a joué cent livres au casino.

gambling *n* jeu m ▷ *He likes gambling.* Il aime le jeu.

game *n* ❶ jeu m (pl jeux) ▷ *The children were playing a game.* Les enfants jouaient à un jeu. ❷ *(sport)* match m ▷ *a game of football* un match de football; **a game of cards** une partie de cartes

gang *n* bande f

gangster *n* gangster m

gap n ❶ trou m ▷ *There's a gap in the hedge.* Il y a un trou dans la haie. ❷ intervalle m ▷ *a gap of four years* un intervalle de quatre ans

gap year n année f sabbatique avant l'université

garage n garage m

garbage n ordures fpl

garden n jardin m

gardener n jardinier m ▷ *He's a gardener.* Il est jardinier.

gardening n jardinage m ▷ *Margaret loves gardening.* Margaret aime le jardinage.

garlic n ail m

garment n vêtement m

gas n ❶ gaz m; **a gas cooker** une cuisinière à gaz; **a gas cylinder** une bouteille de gaz; **a gas fire** un radiateur à gaz; **a gas leak** une fuite de gaz ❷ (US: petrol) essence f

gasoline n (US) essence f

gate n ❶ (of garden) portail m ❷ (of field) barrière f ❸ (at airport) porte f

gather vb (assemble) se rassembler ▷ *People gathered in front of Buckingham Palace.* Les gens se sont rassemblés devant Buckingham Palace.; **to gather speed** prendre de la vitesse ▷ *The train gathered speed.* Le train a pris de la vitesse.

gave vb see **give**

gay adj homosexuel (f homosexuelle)

GCSE n brevet m des collèges

gear n ❶ (in car) vitesse f ▷ *in first gear* en première vitesse ▷ *to change gear* changer de vitesse ❷ matériel

m ▷ *camping gear* le matériel de camping; **your sports gear** (clothes) tes affaires de sport

gear lever n levier m de vitesse

gearshift n (US) = **gear lever**

geese npl see **goose**

gel n gel m; **hair gel** le gel pour les cheveux

Gemini n Gémeaux mpl ▷ *I'm Gemini.* Je suis Gémeaux.

gender n ❶ (of person) sexe m ❷ (of noun) genre m

general n général m (pl généraux) ▶ adj général(e) (mpl généraux); **in general** en général

general election n élections fpl législatives

general knowledge n connaissances fpl générales

generally adv généralement ▷ *I generally go shopping on Saturday.* Généralement, je fais mes courses le samedi.

generation n génération f ▷ *the younger generation* la nouvelle génération

generous adj généreux (f généreuse) ▷ *That's very generous of you.* C'est très généreux de votre part.

genetically-modified adj génétiquement modifié(e)

genetics n génétique f

Geneva n Genève; **in Geneva** à Genève; **to Geneva** à Genève; **Lake Geneva** le lac Léman

genius n génie m ▷ *She's a genius!* C'est un génie!

gentle adj doux (f douce)

gentleman n monsieur m (pl messieurs)

gently adv doucement

gents n toilettes fpl pour hommes ▷ Can you tell me where the gents is, please? Pouvez-vous me dire où sont les toilettes, s'il vous plaît?; **"gents"** (on sign) "messieurs"

genuine adj ❶ (real) véritable ▷ These are genuine diamonds. Ce sont de véritables diamants. ❷ (sincere) sincère ▷ She's a very genuine person. C'est quelqu'un de très sincère.

geography n géographie f

geometry n géométrie f

gerbil n gerbille f

germ n microbe m

German adj allemand(e)
▶ n ❶ (person) Allemand m, Allemande f ❷ (language) allemand m ▷ Do you speak German? Parlez-vous allemand?

Germany n Allemagne f; **in Germany** en Allemagne; **to Germany** en Allemagne

get vb

> There are several ways of translating **get**. Scan the examples to find one that is similar to what you want to say.

❶ (have, receive) avoir ▷ I got lots of presents. J'ai eu beaucoup de cadeaux. ▷ He got first prize. Il a eu le premier prix. ▷ How many have you got? Combien en avez-vous? ❷ (fetch) aller chercher ▷ Quick, get help! Allez vite chercher de l'aide!

❸ (catch) attraper ▷ They've got the thief. Ils ont attrapé le voleur. ❹ (train, bus) prendre ▷ I'm getting the bus into town. Je prends le bus pour aller en ville. ❺ (understand) comprendre ▷ I don't get it. Je ne comprends pas. ❻ (go) aller ▷ How do you get to the castle? Comment est-ce qu'on va au château? ❼ (arrive) arriver ▷ He should get here soon. Il devrait arriver bientôt. ❽ (become) devenir ▷ to get old devenir vieux; **to get something done** faire faire quelque chose ▷ to get one's hair cut se faire couper les cheveux; **to get something for somebody** trouver quelque chose pour quelqu'un ▷ The librarian got the book for me. Le bibliothécaire m'a trouvé le livre.; **to have got to do something** devoir faire quelque chose ▷ I've got to tell him. Je dois le lui dire.; **to get away** s'échapper ▷ One of the burglars got away. L'un des cambrioleurs s'est échappé.; **to get back (1)** rentrer ▷ What time did you get back? Tu es rentré à quelle heure? **(2)** récupérer ▷ He got his money back. Il a récupéré son argent.; **to get in** rentrer ▷ What time did you get in last night? Tu es rentré à quelle heure hier soir?; **to get into** monter dans ▷ Sharon got into the car. Sharon est montée dans la voiture.; **to get off** descendre de ▷ Isobel got off the train. Isobel est descendue du train.; **to get on (1)** (vehicle) monter dans ▷ Phyllis got on the bus. Phyllis est montée dans le bus. **(2)** (bike) enfourcher ▷ Carol got on her bike. Carol a enfourché son vélo.; **to get on with somebody** s'entendre avec quelqu'un ▷ We got on really well. Nous nous sommes très bien entendus.; **to get out** sortir ▷ Hélène got out of the car. Hélène est sortie de la voiture.; **to get something out** sortir quelque chose ▷ She got the map out. Elle a sorti la carte.; **to get over (1)** se remettre ▷ It took her a long time to get over the illness. Il lui a fallu longtemps pour se remettre de sa maladie. **(2)** surmonter ▷ He managed to get over the problem. Il a réussi à résoudre le problème.; **to get together** se retrouver ▷ Could we get together this evening? Pourrait-on se retrouver ce soir?; **to get up** se lever ▷ What time do you get up? Tu te lèves à quelle heure?

ghost n fantôme m

giant adj énorme ▷ They ate a giant meal. Ils ont mangé un énorme repas.
  ▶ n géant m, géante f

gift n **①** (present) cadeau m (pl cadeaux) **②** (talent) don m; **to have a gift for something** être doué pour quelque chose ▷ Dave has a gift for painting. Dave est doué pour la peinture.

gin n gin m

ginger n gingembre m ▷ Add a teaspoon of ginger. Ajoutez une cuillère à café de gingembre.

  ▶ adj roux (f rousse) ▷ Chris has ginger hair. Chris a les cheveux roux.

giraffe n girafe f

girl n **①** fille f ▷ They've got a girl and two boys. Ils ont une fille et deux garçons. **②** (young) petite fille f ▷ a five-year-old girl une petite fille de cinq ans **③** (older) jeune fille f ▷ a sixteen-year-old girl une jeune fille de seize ans ▷ an English girl une jeune Anglaise

girlfriend n **①** (lover) copine f ▷ Damon's girlfriend is called Justine. La copine de Damon s'appelle Justine. **②** (friend) amie f ▷ She often went out with her girlfriends. Elle sortait souvent avec ses amies.

give vb (in traffic) donner; **to give something to somebody** donner quelque chose à quelqu'un ▷ He gave me £10. Il m'a donné dix livres.; **to give something back to somebody** rendre quelque chose à quelqu'un ▷ I gave the book back to him. Je lui ai rendu le livre.; **to give something out** distribuer quelque chose ▷ The teacher gave out the books. Le professeur a distribué les livres.; **to give in** céder ▷ His Mum gave in and let him go out. Sa mère a cédé et l'a laissé sortir.; **to give out** distribuer ▷ He gave out the exam papers. Il a distribué les sujets d'examen.; **to give up** laisser tomber ▷ I couldn't do it, so I gave up. Je n'arrivais pas à le faire, alors j'ai laissé tomber.; **to give up doing something** arrêter de faire quelque chose ▷ *He gave up smoking.* Il a arrêté de fumer.; **to give oneself up** se rendre ▷ *The thief gave himself up.* Le voleur s'est rendu.; **to give way** céder la priorité

glad adj content(e) ▷ *She's glad she's done it.* Elle est contente de l'avoir fait.

glamorous adj ❶ (person) glamour inv ▷ *She's very glamorous.* Elle est très glamour. ❷ (job) prestigieux (f prestigieuse); **to have a glamorous lifestyle** vivre comme une star

glass n verre m ▷ *a glass of milk* un verre de lait

glasses npl lunettes fpl ▷ *Jean-Pierre wears glasses.* Jean-Pierre porte des lunettes.

glider n planeur m

global adj mondial(e) (mpl mondiaux); **on a global scale** à l'échelle mondiale

global warming n réchauffement m de la planète

globe n globe m

gloomy adj ❶ morose ▷ *She's been feeling very gloomy recently.* Elle se sent très morose ces derniers temps. ❷ lugubre ▷ *He lives in a small gloomy flat.* Il habite un petit appartement lugubre.

glorious adj magnifique

glove n gant m

glue n colle f
▷ vb ❶ coller

GM adj (= genetically modified) génétiquement modifié(e) ▷ *GM*

foods les aliments génétiquement modifiés

go n **to have a go at doing something** essayer de faire quelque chose ▷ *He had a go at making a cake.* Il a essayé de faire un gâteau.; **Whose go is it?** À qui le tour?
▷ vb ❶ aller ▷ *I'm going to the cinema tonight.* Je vais au cinéma ce soir. ❷ (leave) partir ▷ *Where's Pierre? — He's gone.* Où est Pierre? — Il est parti. ❸ (go away) s'en aller ▷ *I'm going now.* Je m'en vais. ❹ (vehicle) marcher ▷ *My car won't go.* Ma voiture ne marche pas.; **to go home** rentrer à la maison ▷ *I go home at about 4 o'clock.* Je rentre à la maison vers quatre heures.; **to go for a walk** aller se promener ▷ *Shall we go for a walk?* Si on allait se promener?; **How did it go?** Comment est-ce que ça s'est passé?; **I'm going to do it tomorrow.** Je vais le faire demain.; **It's going to be difficult.** Ça va être difficile.

go after vb suivre ▷ *Quick, go after them!* Vite, suivez-les!

go away vb s'en aller ▷ *Go away!* Allez-vous-en!

go back vb

> Use **rentrer** only when you are entering a building, usually your home; otherwise use **retourner**.

❶ retourner ▷ *We went back to the same place.* Nous sommes retournés au même endroit.

❷ rentrer ▷ Is he still here? — No, he's gone back home. Est-ce qu'il est encore là? — Non, il est rentré chez lui.

go by vb ❶ (person) passer ▷ Two policemen went by. Deux policiers sont passés.

go down vb ❶ (person) descendre ▷ to go down the stairs descendre l'escalier ❷ (decrease) baisser ▷ The price of computers has gone down. Le prix des ordinateurs a baissé. ❸ (deflate) se dégonfler ▷ My airbed kept going down. Mon matelas pneumatique se dégonflait constamment.; **My brother's gone down with flu.** Mon frère a attrapé la grippe.

go in vb entrer ▷ He knocked on the door and went in. Il a frappé à la porte et il est entré.

go off vb ❶ (bomb) exploser ▷ The bomb went off. La bombe a explosé. ❷ (alarm, gun) se déclencher ▷ The fire alarm went off. L'avertisseur d'incendie s'est déclenché. ❸ (alarm clock) sonner ▷ My alarm clock goes off at seven every morning. Mon réveil sonne à sept heures tous les matins. ❹ (food) tourner ▷ The milk's gone off. Le lait a tourné. ❺ (go away) partir ▷ He went off in a huff. Il est parti de mauvaise humeur.

go on vb ❶ (happen) se passer ▷ What's going on? Qu'est-ce qui se passe? ❷ (carry on) continuer ▷ The concert went on until 11 o'clock at night. Le concert a continué jusqu'à onze heures du soir.; **to go**

on doing something continuer à faire quelque chose ▷ He went on reading. Il a continué à lire.; **to go on at somebody** être sur le dos de quelqu'un ▷ My parents always go on at me. Mes parents sont toujours sur mon dos.; **Go on!** Allez! ▷ Go on, tell me what the problem is! Allez, dis-moi quel est le problème!

go out vb ❶ (person) sortir ▷ Are you going out tonight? Tu sors ce soir?; **to go out with somebody** sortir avec quelqu'un ▷ Are you going out with him? Est-ce que tu sors avec lui? ❷ (light, fire, candle) s'éteindre ▷ Suddenly the lights went out. Soudain, les lumières se sont éteintes.

go past vb **to go past something** passer devant quelque chose ▷ He went past the shop. Il est passé devant la boutique.

go round vb **to go round a corner** prendre un tournant; **to go round to somebody's house** aller chez quelqu'un; **to go round a museum** visiter un musée; **to go round the shops** faire les boutiques; **There's a bug going round.** Il y a un microbe qui circule.

go through vb traverser ▷ We went through Paris to get to Rennes. Nous avons traversé Paris pour aller à Rennes.

go up vb ❶ (person) monter ▷ to go up the stairs monter l'escalier ❷ (increase) augmenter ▷ The price has gone up. Le prix a augmenté.; **to go up in flames** s'embraser

▷ *The whole factory went up in flames.* L'usine toute entière s'est embrasée.

go with vb aller avec ▷ *Does this blouse go with that skirt?* Est-ce que ce chemisier va avec cette jupe?

goal n but m ▷ *to score a goal* marquer un but

goalkeeper n gardien m de but

goat n chèvre f; **goat's cheese** le fromage de chèvre

god n dieu m (pl dieux) ▷ *I believe in God.* Je crois en Dieu.

goddaughter n filleule f

godfather n parrain m

godmother n marraine f

godson n filleul m

goggles npl ❶ (of welder, mechanic etc) lunettes fpl de protection ❷ (of swimmer) lunettes fpl de plongée

gold n or m ▷ *a gold necklace* un collier en or

goldfish n poisson m rouge ▷ *I've got five goldfish.* J'ai cinq poissons rouges.

golf n golf m ▷ *My dad plays golf.* Mon père joue au golf.; **a golf club** un club de golf

golf course n terrain m de golf

gone vb see **go**

good adj ❶ bon (f bonne) ▷ *It's a very good film.* C'est un très bon film. ▷ *Vegetables are good for you.* Les légumes sont bons pour la santé.; **to be good at something** être bon en quelque chose ▷ *Jane's very good at maths.* Jane est très bonne en maths. ❷ (kind) gentil (f gentille) ▷ *That's very good of you.* C'est

très gentil de votre part. ❸ (not naughty) sage ▷ *Be good!* Sois sage!; **for good** pour de bon ▷ *One day he left for good.* Un jour il est parti pour de bon.; **Good morning!** Bonjour!; **Good afternoon!** Bonjour!; **Good evening!** Bonsoir!; **Good night!** Bonne nuit!; **It's no good complaining.** Cela ne sert à rien de se plaindre.

goodbye excl au revoir!

Good Friday n Vendredi m saint

good-looking adj beau (f belle, mpl beaux) ▷ *He's very good-looking.* Il est très beau.

goods npl (in shop) marchandises fpl; **a goods train** un train de marchandises

goose n oie f

gorgeous adj ❶ superbe ▷ *She's gorgeous!* Elle est superbe! ❷ splendide ▷ *The weather was gorgeous.* Il a fait un temps splendide.

gorilla n gorille m

gossip n ❶ (rumours) cancans mpl ▷ *Tell me the gossip!* Raconte-moi les cancans! ❷ (woman) commère f ▷ *She's such a gossip!* C'est une vraie commère! ❸ (man) bavard m ▷ *What a gossip!* Quel bavard!
▶ vb ❶ (chat) bavarder ▷ *They were always gossiping.* Elles étaient tout le temps en train de bavarder. ❷ (about somebody) faire des commérages ▷ *They gossiped about her.* Elles faisaient des commérages à son sujet.

got vb see **get**

gotten vb (US) see **get**

government n gouvernement m

GP n médecin m généraliste

grab vb saisir

graceful adj élégant(e)

grade n (at school) note f ▷ He got good grades in his exams. Il a eu de bonnes notes à ses examens.

grade school n (US) école f primaire

gradual adj progressif (f progressive)

gradually adv peu à peu ▷ We gradually got used to it. Nous nous y sommes habitués peu à peu.

graffiti npl graffiti mpl

grain n grain m

gram n gramme m

grammar n grammaire f

grammar school n ① collège m ② lycée m
- In France pupils go to a **collège** between the ages of 11 and 15, and then to a **lycée** until the age of 18. French schools are mostly non-selective.

grammatical adj grammatical(e) (mpl grammaticaux)

gramme n gramme m ▷ 500 grammes of cheese cinq cents grammes de fromage

grand adj somptueux (f somptueuse) ▷ Samantha lives in a very grand house. Samantha habite une maison somptueuse.

grandchild n petit-fils m, petite-fille f; **my grandchildren** mes petits-enfants

granddad n papi m ▷ my granddad mon papi

granddaughter n petite-fille f (pl petites-filles)

grandfather n grand-père m (pl grands-pères) ▷ my grandfather mon grand-père

grandma n mamie f ▷ my grandma ma mamie

grandmother n grand-mère f (pl grands-mères) ▷ my grandmother ma grand-mère

grandpa n papi m ▷ my grandpa mon papi

grandparents npl grands-parents mpl ▷ my grandparents mes grands-parents

grandson n petit-fils m (pl petits-fils)

granny n mamie f ▷ my granny ma mamie

grape n raisin m

grapefruit n pamplemousse m

graph n graphique m

graphics npl images fpl de synthèse ▷ I designed the graphics, she wrote the text. J'ai conçu les images de synthèse, elle a écrit le texte.; **He works in computer graphics.** Il fait de l'infographie.

grass n herbe f ▷ The grass is long. L'herbe est haute.; **to cut the grass** tondre le gazon

grasshopper n sauterelle f

grate vb râper ▷ to grate some cheese râper du fromage

grateful adj reconnaissant(e)

grave n tombe f

gravel n gravier m

graveyard n cimetière m

gravy n sauce f au jus de viande

grease n lubrifiant m

greasy adj gras (f grasse) ▷ He has greasy hair. Il a les cheveux gras.

great adj ❶ génial(e) (mpl géniaux) ▷ That's great! C'est génial!

❷ grand(e) ▷ a great mansion un grand manoir

Great Britain n Grande-Bretagne f; **in Great Britain** en Grande-Bretagne; **to Great Britain** en Grande-Bretagne; **I'm from Great Britain.** Je suis britannique.

great-grandfather n arrière-grand-père m (pl arrière-grands-pères)

great-grandmother n arrière-grand-mère f (pl arrière-grands-mères)

Greece n Grèce f; **in Greece** en Grèce; **to Greece** en Grèce

greedy adj ❶ (for food) gourmand(e) ▷ I want some more cake. — Don't be so greedy! Je veux encore du gâteau. — Ne sois pas si gourmand! ❷ (for money) avide

Greek adj grec (f grecque) ▷ She's Greek. Elle est grecque.
▶ n ❶ (person) Grec m, Grecque f
❷ (language) grec m

green adj ❶ vert(e) ▷ a green light un feu vert ▷ a green salad une salade verte ❷ (movement, candidate) écologiste ▷ the Green Party le parti écologiste
▶ n vert m ▷ a dark green un vert foncé; **greens** (vegetables) les légumes verts; **the Greens** (party) les Verts

greengrocer's n marchand m de fruits et légumes

greenhouse n serre f; **the greenhouse effect** l'effet de serre

Greenland n Groenland m

greetings card n carte f de vœux

grew vb see **grow**

grey adj gris(e) ▷ She's got grey hair. Elle a les cheveux gris.; **He's going grey.** Il grisonne.

grey-haired adj grisonnant(e)

grid n ❶ (in road) grille f ❷ (of electricity) réseau m (pl réseaux)

grief n chagrin m

grill n (of cooker) gril m; **a mixed grill** les grillades
▶ vb **to grill something** faire griller quelque chose

grin vb sourire ▷ Dave grinned at me. Dave m'a souri.
▶ n large sourire m

grip vb saisir

grit n gravillon m

groan vb gémir ▷ He groaned with pain. Il a gémi sous l'effet de la douleur.
▶ n (of pain) gémissement m

grocer n épicier m ▷ He's a grocer. Il est épicier.

groceries npl provisions fpl

grocer's (shop) n épicerie f

grocery store n (US) épicerie f

groom n (bridegroom) marié m ▷ the groom and his best man le marié et son témoin

gross adj (revolting) dégoûtant(e) ▷ It was really gross! C'était vraiment dégoûtant!

ground n ❶ (earth) sol m ▷ The ground's wet. Le sol est mouillé. ❷ (for sport) terrain m ▷ a football ground un terrain de football ❸ (reason) raison f ▷ We've got grounds for complaint. Nous avons des raisons de nous plaindre.; **on the ground** par terre ▷ We sat on the ground. Nous nous sommes assis par terre.; **ground coffee** le café moulu

ground floor n rez-de-chaussée m; **on the ground floor** au rez-de-chaussée

group n groupe m

grow vb ❶ (plant) pousser ▷ Grass grows quickly. L'herbe pousse vite. ❷ (person, animal) grandir ▷ Haven't you grown! Comme tu as grandi! ❸ (increase) augmenter ▷ The number of unemployed people has grown. Le nombre de chômeurs a augmenté. ❹ (cultivate) faire pousser ▷ My Dad grows potatoes. Mon père fait pousser des pommes de terre.; **to grow a beard** se laisser pousser la barbe; **to grow up** grandir ▷ Oh, grow up! Ne fais pas l'enfant!; **He's grown out of his jacket.** Sa veste est devenue trop petite pour lui.

growl vb grogner

grown vb see **grow**

grown-up n adulte mf

growth n croissance f ▷ economic growth la croissance économique

grudge n rancune f; **to bear a grudge against somebody** garder rancune à quelqu'un

gruesome adj horrible

guarantee n garantie f; **a five-year guarantee** une garantie de cinq ans
▶ vb garantir ▷ I can't guarantee he'll come. Je ne peux pas garantir qu'il viendra.

guard vb garder ▷ They guarded the palace. Ils gardaient le palais.; **to guard against something** protéger contre quelque chose
▶ n (of train) chef m de train; **a security guard** un vigile; **a guard dog** un chien de garde

guess vb deviner ▷ Can you guess what it is? Devine ce que c'est!; **to guess wrong** se tromper ▷ Janice guessed wrong. Janice s'est trompée.
▶ n supposition f ▷ It's just a guess. C'est une simple supposition.; **Have a guess!** Devine!

guest n ❶ invité m, invitée f ▷ We have guests staying with us. Nous avons des invités. ❷ (of hotel) client m, cliente f

guesthouse n pension f de famille

guide n ❶ (book, person) guide m ▷ We bought a guide to Paris. Nous avons acheté un guide sur Paris. ▷ The guide showed us round the castle. Le guide nous a fait visiter le château. ❷ (girl guide) éclaireuse f; **the Guides** les Éclaireuses

guidebook n guide m

guide dog n chien m d'aveugle

guilty adj coupable ▷ to feel guilty se sentir coupable ▷ She was found guilty. Elle a été reconnue coupable.

guinea pig n cobaye m

guitar n guitare f ▷ I play the guitar. Je joue de la guitare.

gum n (sweet) chewing-gum m; **gums** (in mouth) les gencives fpl

gun n ❶ (small) revolver m ❷ (rifle) fusil m

gunpoint n at gunpoint sous la menace d'une arme

guy n type m ▷ He's a nice guy. C'est un type sympa.

gym n gym f ▷ I go to the gym every day. Je vais tous les jours à la gym.; **gym classes** les cours de gym

gymnast n gymnaste mf ▷ She's a gymnast. Elle est gymnaste.

gymnastics n gymnastique f ▷ to do gymnastics faire de la gymnastique

gypsy n Tzigane mf

h

habit n habitude f ▷ a bad habit une mauvaise habitude

had vb see **have**

hadn't = **had not**

hail n grêle f
▶ vb grêler ▷ It's hailing. Il grêle.

hair n ❶ cheveux mpl ▷ She's got long hair. Elle a les cheveux longs.; **to brush one's hair** se brosser les cheveux ▷ I'm brushing my hair. Je me brosse les cheveux.; **to wash one's hair** se laver les cheveux ▷ I need to wash my hair. Il faut que je me lave les cheveux.; **to have one's hair cut** se faire couper les cheveux ▷ I've just had my hair cut. Je viens de me faire couper les cheveux.; **a hair (1)** (from head) un cheveu **(2)** (from body) un poil ❷ (fur of animal) pelage m

hairbrush n brosse f à cheveux
haircut n coupe f; **to have a haircut** se faire couper les cheveux ▷ I've just had a haircut. Je viens de me faire couper les cheveux.
hairdresser n coiffeur m, coiffeuse f ▷ He's a hairdresser. Il est coiffeur.
hairdresser's n coiffeur m ▷ at the hairdresser's chez le coiffeur
hair dryer n sèche-cheveux m (pl sèche-cheveux)
hair gel n gel m pour les cheveux
hairgrip n pince f à cheveux
hair spray n laque f
hairstyle n coiffure f
half n ① moitié f ▷ half of the cake la moitié du gâteau ② (ticket) billet m demi-tarif ▷ A half to York, please. Un billet demi-tarif pour York, s'il vous plaît.; **two and a half** deux et demi; **half an hour** une demi-heure; **half past ten** dix heures et demie; **half a kilo** cinq cents grammes; **to cut something in half** couper quelque chose en deux ▶ adj, adv ① demi(e) ▷ a half chicken un demi-poulet ② à moitié ▷ He was half asleep. Il était à moitié endormi.
half-brother n demi-frère m
half-hour n demi-heure f
half-price adj, adv **at half-price** à moitié prix
half-sister n demi-sœur f
half-term n vacances fpl
• There are two half-term holidays
• in France: **les vacances de**
• **la Toussaint** (in October/

November) and **les vacances de février** (in February).
half-time n mi-temps f
halfway adv ① à mi-chemin ▷ halfway between Oxford and London à mi-chemin entre Oxford et Londres ② à la moitié ▷ halfway through the chapter à la moitié du chapitre
hall n ① (in house) entrée f ② salle f ▷ the village hall la salle des fêtes
Hallowe'en n veille f de la Toussaint
hallway n vestibule m
ham n jambon m; **a ham sandwich** un sandwich au jambon
hamburger n hamburger m
hammer n marteau m (pl marteaux)
hamster n hamster m
hand n ① (of person) main f; **to give somebody a hand** donner un coup de main à quelqu'un ▷ Can you give me a hand? Tu peux me donner un coup de main?; **on the one hand ..., on the other hand ...** d'une part ..., d'autre part ... ② (of clock) aiguille f
▶ vb passer ▷ He handed me the book. Il m'a passé le livre.; **to hand something in** rendre quelque chose ▷ He handed his exam paper in. Il a rendu sa copie d'examen.; **to hand something out** distribuer quelque chose ▷ The teacher handed out the books. Le professeur a distribué les livres.; **to hand something over** remettre quelque

chose ▷ *She handed the keys over to me.* Elle m'a remis les clés.
handbag *n* sac *m* à main (*pl* sacs à main)
handcuffs *npl* menottes *fpl*
handkerchief *n* mouchoir *m*
handle *n* ❶ (*of door*) poignée *f* ❷ (*of cup*) anse *f* ❸ (*of knife*) manche *m* ❹ (*of saucepan*) queue *f* ▶ *vb* **He handled it well.** Il s'en est bien tiré.; **Kath handled the travel arrangements.** Kath s'est occupée de l'organisation du voyage.; **She's good at handling children.** Elle sait bien s'y prendre avec les enfants.
handlebars *npl* guidon *m*
handmade *adj* fait(e) à la main
hands-free kit *n* (*phone*) kit *m* mains libres
handsome *adj* beau (*f* belle, *mpl* beaux) ▷ *He's handsome.* Il est beau.
handwriting *n* écriture *f*
handy *adj* ❶ pratique ▷ *This knife's very handy.* Ce couteau est très pratique. ❷ sous la main ▷ *Have you got a pen handy?* Est-ce que tu as un stylo sous la main?
hang *vb* ❶ accrocher ▷ *Mike hung the painting on the wall.* Mike a accroché le tableau au mur. ❷ pendre ▷ *They hanged the criminal.* Ils ont pendu le criminel.; **to hang around** traîner ▷ *On Saturdays we hang around in the park.* Le samedi nous traînons dans le parc.; **to hang on** patienter ▷ *Hang on a minute please.* Patientez une

minute s'il vous plaît.; **to hang up** **(1)** (*clothes*) accrocher ▷ *Hang your jacket up on the hook.* Accrochez votre veste au portemanteau. **(2)** (*phone*) raccrocher ▷ *I tried to phone him but he hung up on me.* J'ai essayé de l'appeler, mais il m'a raccroché au nez.
hanger *n* (*coat hanger*) cintre *m*
hangover *n* gueule *f* de bois ▷ *to have a hangover* avoir la gueule de bois
happen *vb* se passer ▷ *What's happened?* Qu'est-ce qui s'est passé?; **as it happens** justement ▷ *As it happens, I don't want to go.* Justement, je ne veux pas y aller.
happily *adv* ❶ joyeusement ▷ *"Don't worry!" he said happily.* "Ne te fais pas de souci" dit-il joyeusement. ❷ (*fortunately*) heureusement ▷ *Happily, everything went well.* Heureusement, tout s'est bien passé.
happiness *n* bonheur *m*
happy *adj* heureux (*f* heureuse) ▷ *Janet looks happy.* Janet a l'air heureuse.; **I'm very happy with your work.** Je suis très satisfait de ton travail.; **Happy birthday!** Bon anniversaire!
harassment *n* harcèlement *m* ▷ *police harassment* le harcèlement policier
harbour (*US* **harbor**) *n* port *m*
hard *adj, adv* ❶ dur(e) ▷ *This cheese is very hard.* Ce fromage est très dur. ▷ *He's worked very hard.* Il a travaillé très dur. ❷ difficile ▷ *This question's*

a
b
c
d
e
f
g
h
i
j
k
l
m
n
o
p
q
r
s
t
u
v
w
x
y
z

too hard for me. Cette question est trop difficile pour moi.

hard disk n (of computer) disque m dur

hardly adv **I've hardly got any money.** Je n'ai presque pas d'argent.; **I hardly know you.** Je te connais à peine.; **hardly ever** presque jamais

hard up adj fauché(e)

harm vb **to harm somebody** faire du mal à quelqu'un ▷ I didn't mean to harm you. Je ne voulais pas te faire de mal.; **to harm something** nuire à quelque chose ▷ Chemicals harm the environment. Les produits chimiques nuisent à l'environnement.

harmful adj nuisible ▷ harmful chemicals des produits chimiques nuisibles

harmless adj inoffensif (f inoffensive) ▷ Most spiders are harmless. La plupart des araignées sont inoffensives.

has vb see **have**

hasn't = **has not**

hat n chapeau m (pl chapeaux)

hate vb détester ▷ I hate maths. Je déteste les maths.

hatred n haine f

haunted adj hanté(e); **a haunted house** une maison hantée

have vb ❶ avoir ▷ Have you got a sister? Tu as une sœur? ▷ He's got blue eyes. Il a les yeux bleus. ▷ I've got a cold. J'ai un rhume. ▷ He's done it, hasn't he? Il l'a fait, non?

> The perfect tense of some verbs is formed with **être**.

❷ être ▷ They have arrived. Ils sont arrivés. ❸ prendre ▷ He had his breakfast. Il a pris son petit déjeuner.; **to have got to do something** devoir faire quelque chose ▷ She's got to do it. Elle doit le faire.; **to have a party** faire une fête; **to have one's hair cut** se faire couper les cheveux

haven't = **have not**

hay n foin m

hay fever n rhume m des foins ▷ Do you get hay fever? Est-ce que vous êtes sujet au rhume des foins?

hazelnut n noisette f

he pron il ▷ He loves dogs. Il aime les chiens.

head n ❶ (of person) tête f ▷ The wine went to my head. Le vin m'est monté à la tête. ❷ (of private or primary school) directeur m, directrice f ❸ (of state secondary school) proviseur m ❹ (leader) chef m ▷ a head of state un chef d'État; **to have a head for figures** être doué pour les chiffres; **Heads or tails? — Heads.** Pile ou face? — Face.
▶ vb **to head for something** se diriger vers quelque chose ▷ They headed for the church. Ils se sont dirigés vers l'église.

headache n **I've got a headache.** J'ai mal à la tête.

headlight n phare m

headline n titre m

headmaster n ❶ (of private or primary school) directeur m ❷ (of state secondary school) proviseur m

headmistress n ❸ (of private or primary school) directrice f ❷ (of state secondary school) proviseur m

headphones npl écouteurs mpl

headquarters npl (of organization) siège m

headteacher n ❶ (of private or primary school) directeur m, directrice f ❷ (of state secondary school) proviseur m ▷ She's a headteacher. Elle est proviseur.

heal vb cicatriser ▷ The wound soon healed. La blessure a vite cicatrisé.

health n santé f

healthy adj ❶ (person) en bonne santé ▷ Lesley's a healthy person. Lesley est en bonne santé. ❷ (climate, food) sain(e) ▷ a healthy diet une alimentation saine

heap n tas m ▷ a rubbish heap un tas d'ordures

hear vb ❶ entendre ▷ He heard the dog bark. Il a entendu le chien aboyer.; **to hear about something** entendre parler de quelque chose ▷ Did you hear the good news? Est-ce que tu as appris la bonne nouvelle?; **to hear from somebody** avoir des nouvelles de quelqu'un ▷ I haven't heard from him recently. Je n'ai pas eu de ses nouvelles récemment.

heart n cœur m; **to learn something by heart** apprendre quelque chose par cœur; **the ace of hearts** l'as de cœur

heart attack n crise f cardiaque

heartbroken adj **to be heartbroken** avoir le cœur brisé

heat n chaleur f
▶ vb faire chauffer ▷ Heat gently for 5 minutes. Faire chauffer à feu doux pendant cinq minutes.; **to heat up (1)** (cooked food) faire réchauffer ▷ He heated the soup up. Il a fait réchauffer la soupe. **(2)** (water, oven) chauffer ▷ The water is heating up. L'eau chauffe.

heater n radiateur m ▷ an electric heater un radiateur électrique

heather n bruyère f

heating n chauffage m

heaven n paradis m

heavy adj ❶ lourd(e) ▷ This bag's very heavy. Ce sac est très lourd.; **heavy rain** une grosse averse ❷ (busy) chargé(e) ▷ I've got a very heavy week ahead. Je vais avoir une semaine très chargée.; **to be a heavy drinker** être un gros buveur

he'd = he would; he had

hedge n haie f

hedgehog n hérisson m

heel n talon m

height n ❶ (of person) taille f ❷ (of object) hauteur f ❸ (of mountain) altitude f

held vb see **hold**

helicopter n hélicoptère m

hell n enfer m

he'll = he will; he shall

hello excl bonjour!

helmet n casque m

help vb aider ▷ Can you help me? Est-ce que vous pouvez m'aider?; **Help!** Au secours!; **Help yourself!**

Servez-vous!; **He can't help it.**
Il n'y peut rien.

▶ *n* aide f ▷ *Do you need any help?*
Vous avez besoin d'aide?

helpful *adj* serviable ▷ *He was very helpful.* Il a été très serviable.

hen *n* poule f

her *adj* son (f sa, pl ses) ▷ *her father* son père ▷ *her mother* sa mère ▷ *her parents* ses parents

▌ **sa** becomes **son** before a vowel sound.

her friend (1) (*male*) son ami
(2) (*female*) son amie

▌ Do not use **son/sa/ses** with parts of the body.

▷ *She's going to wash her hair.* Elle va se laver les cheveux. ▷ *She's cleaning her teeth.* Elle se brosse les dents.
▷ *She's hurt her foot.* Elle s'est fait mal au pied.

▶ *pron*

▌ **la** becomes **l'** before a vowel sound.

❶ la, l' ▷ *I can see her.* Je la vois.
▷ *I saw her.* Je l'ai vue.

▌ Use **lui** when **her** means **to her.**

❷ lui ▷ *I gave her a book.* Je lui ai donné un livre. ▷ *I told her the truth.* Je lui ai dit la vérité.

▌ Use **elle** after prepositions.

❸ elle ▷ *I'm going with her.* Je vais avec elle.

▌ **elle** is also used in comparisons.
▷ *I'm older than her.* Je suis plus âgé qu'elle.

herb *n* herbe; **herbs** les fines herbes ▷ *What herbs do you use in*
this sauce? Quelles fines herbes utilise-t-on pour cette sauce?

here *adv* ici ▷ *I live here.* J'habite ici.;
here is … voici … ▷ *Here's Helen.*
Voici Helen. ▷ *Here he is!* Le voici!;
here are … voici … ▷ *Here are the books.* Voici les livres.

hero *n* héros m ▷ *He's a real hero!*
C'est un véritable héros!

heroin *n* héroïne f ▷ *Heroin is a hard drug.* L'héroïne est une drogue dure.; **a heroin addict** un héroïnomane ▷ *She's a heroin addict.*
C'est une héroïnomane.

heroine *n* héroïne f ▷ *the heroine of the novel* l'héroïne du roman

hers *pron* le sien msg (fsg la sienne, mpl les siens, fpl les siennes) ▷ *Is this her coat?* — *No, hers is black.*
C'est son manteau? — Non, le sien est noir. ▷ *Is this her car?* — *No, hers is white.* C'est sa voiture? — Non, la sienne est blanche.; **Is this hers?**
C'est à elle? ▷ *This book is hers.* Ce livre est à elle.

herself *pron* ❶ se ▷ *She's hurt herself.* Elle s'est blessée. ❷ (*after preposition*) elle ▷ *She talked mainly about herself.* Elle a surtout parlé d'elle. ❸ elle-même ▷ *She did it herself.* Elle l'a fait elle-même.;
by herself toute seule ▷ *She doesn't like travelling by herself.* Elle n'aime pas voyager toute seule.

he's = he is; he has

hesitate *vb* hésiter

heterosexual *adj* hétérosexuel
(f hétérosexuelle)

hi *excl* salut!

hiccups npl **to have hiccups** avoir le hoquet

hide vb se cacher ▷ He hid behind a bush. Il s'est caché derrière un buisson.; **to hide something** cacher quelque chose ▷ Paula hid the present. Paula a caché le cadeau.

hide-and-seek n **to play hide-and-seek** jouer à cache-cache

hi-fi n chaîne f hi-fi (pl chaînes hi-fi)

high adj, adv ❶ haut(e) ▷ It's too high. C'est trop haut.; **How high is the wall?** Quelle est la hauteur du mur?; **The wall's 2 metres high.** Le mur fait deux mètres de haut. ❷ élevé(e) ▷ a high price un prix élevé; **at high speed** à grande vitesse; **It's very high in fat.** C'est très gras.; **She's got a very high voice.** Elle a la voix très aiguë.; **to be high** (on drugs) être défoncé (informal); **to get high** se défoncer (informal); **to get high on crack** se défoncer au crack

higher education n enseignement m supérieur

Highers npl (in Scottish schools) baccalauréat m

- The **baccalauréat** (or **bac** for
- short) is taken at the age of
- 17 or 18. Students have to sit
- one of a variety of set subject
- combinations, rather than being
- able to choose any combination
- of subjects they want. If you
- pass you have the right to a
- place at university.

high-heeled adj à hauts talons;

high-heeled shoes des chaussures à hauts talons

high jump n saut m en hauteur

high-rise n tour f ▷ I live in a high-rise. J'habite dans une tour.

high school n lycée m

hijack vb détourner

hijacker n pirate m de l'air

hiking n **to go hiking** faire une randonnée

hilarious adj hilarant(e) ▷ It was hilarious! C'était hilarant!

hill n colline f ▷ She walked up the hill. Elle a gravi la colline.

hill-walking n randonnée f de basse montagne ▷ to go hill-walking faire de la randonnée de basse montagne

him pron

■ **le** becomes **l'** before a vowel sound.

❶ le, l' ▷ I can see him. Je le vois. ▷ I saw him. Je l'ai vu.

■ Use **lui** when **him** means **to him**, and after prepositions.

❷ lui ▷ I gave him a book. Je lui ai donné un livre. ▷ I'm going with him. Je vais avec lui.

■ **lui** is also used in comparisons. ▷ I'm older than him. Je suis plus âgé que lui.

himself pron ❶ se ▷ He's hurt himself. Il s'est blessé. ❷ lui ▷ He talked mainly about himself. Il a surtout parlé de lui. ❸ lui-même ▷ He did it himself. Il l'a fait lui-même.; **by himself** tout seul ▷ He was travelling by himself. Il voyageait tout seul.

Hindu adj hindou(e) ▷ a Hindu temple un temple hindou

hip n hanche f

hippie n hippie mf

hippo n hippopotame m

hire vb ❶ louer ▷ to hire a car louer une voiture ❷ (person) engager ▷ They hired a cleaner. Ils ont engagé une femme de ménage.
▶ n location f; car hire location de voitures; for hire à louer

his adj son (fsa, pl ses) ▷ his father son père ▷ his mother sa mère ▷ his parents ses parents

　　sa becomes **son** before a vowel sound.

　　his friend (1) (male) son ami **(2)** (female) son amie

　　Do not use **son/sa/ses** with parts of the body.

▷ He's going to wash his hair. Il va se laver les cheveux. ▷ He's cleaning his teeth. Il se brosse les dents. ▷ He's hurt his foot. Il s'est fait mal au pied.
▶ pron le sien msg (fsg la sienne, mpl les siens, fpl les siennes) ▷ Is this his coat? — No, his is black. C'est son manteau? — Non, le sien est noir. ▷ Is this his car? — No, his is white. C'est sa voiture? — Non, la sienne est blanche.; **Is this his?** C'est à lui? ▷ This book is his. Ce livre est à lui.

history n histoire f

hit vb ❶ frapper ▷ Andrew hit him. Andrew l'a frappé. ❷ renverser ▷ He was hit by a car. Il a été renversé par une voiture. ❸ toucher ▷ The arrow hit the target. La flèche a touché la cible.; **to hit it off with**

somebody bien s'entendre avec quelqu'un ▷ She hit it off with his parents. Elle s'est bien entendue avec ses parents.
▶ n ❶ (song) tube m ▷ U2's latest hit le dernier tube de U2 ❷ (success) succès m ▷ The film was a massive hit. Le film a eu un immense succès.

hitch n contretemps m ▷ There's been a slight hitch. Il y a eu un léger contretemps.

hitchhike vb faire de l'auto-stop

hitchhiker n auto-stoppeur m, auto-stoppeuse f

hitchhiking n auto-stop m ▷ Hitchhiking can be dangerous. Il peut être dangereux de faire de l'auto-stop.

HIV-negative adj séronégatif (f séronégative)

HIV-positive adj séropositif (f séropositive)

hobby n passe-temps m favori ▷ What are your hobbies? Quels sont tes passe-temps favoris?

hockey n hockey m ▷ I play hockey. Je joue au hockey.

hold vb ❶ (hold on to) tenir ▷ She held the baby. Elle tenait le bébé. ❷ (contain) contenir ▷ This bottle holds one litre. Cette bouteille contient un litre.; **to hold a meeting** avoir une réunion; **Hold the line!** (on telephone) Ne quittez pas!; **Hold it!** (wait) Attendis!; **to get hold of something** (obtain) trouver quelque chose ▷ I couldn't get hold of it. Je n'ai pas réussi à en trouver.

hold on vb ❶ (keep hold) tenir bon ▷ The cliff was slippery but he managed to hold on. La falaise était glissante, mais il est parvenu à tenir bon.; **to hold on to something** se cramponner à quelque chose ▷ He held on to the chair. Il se cramponnait à la chaise. ❷ (wait) attendre ▷ Hold on, I'm coming! Attends, je viens!; **Hold on!** (on telephone) Ne quittez pas!

hold up vb **to hold up one's hand** lever la main ▷ Pierre held up his hand. Pierre a levé la main.; **to hold somebody up** (delay) retenir quelqu'un ▷ I was held up at the office. J'ai été retenu au bureau.; **to hold up a bank** (rob) braquer une banque (informal)

hold-up n ❶ (at bank) hold-up m ❷ (delay) retard m ❸ (traffic jam) bouchon m

hole n trou m

holiday n ❶ vacances fpl ▷ our holidays in France nos vacances en France; **on holiday** en vacances ▷ to go on holiday partir en vacances; **the school holidays** les vacances scolaires ❷ (public holiday) jour m férié ▷ Next Wednesday is a holiday. Mercredi prochain est un jour férié. ❸ (day off) jour m de congé ▷ He took a day's holiday. Il a pris un jour de congé.; **a holiday camp** un camp de vacances

Holland n Hollande f; **in Holland** en Hollande; **to Holland** en Hollande

hollow adj creux (f creuse)

holly n houx m ▷ a sprig of holly un brin de houx

holy adj saint(e)

home n maison f; **at home** à la maison; **Make yourself at home.** Faites comme chez vous.
▸ adv à la maison ▷ I'll be home at 5 o'clock. Je serai à la maison à cinq heures.; **to get home** rentrer ▷ What time did he get home? Il est rentré à quelle heure?

homeland n patrie f

homeless adj sans abri inv; **the homeless** les sans-abri

home match n match m à domicile

home page n page f d'accueil

homesick adj **to be homesick** avoir le mal du pays

homework n devoirs mpl ▷ Have you done your homework? Est-ce que tu as fait tes devoirs? ▷ my geography homework mes devoirs de géographie

homosexual adj homosexuel (f homosexuelle)
▸ n homosexuel m, homosexuelle f

honest adj ❶ (trustworthy) honnête ▷ She's a very honest person. Elle est très honnête. ❷ (sincere) franc (f franche) ▷ He was very honest with her. Il a été très franc avec elle.

honestly adv franchement ▷ I honestly don't know. Franchement, je n'en sais rien.

honesty n honnêteté f

honey n miel m

honeymoon n lune f de miel

honour (US honor) n honneur m

hood n ❶ (on coat) capuche f
❷ (US: of car) capot m

hook n crochet m ▷ He hung the painting on the hook. Il a suspendu le tableau au crochet.; **to take the phone off the hook** décrocher le téléphone; **a fish-hook** un hameçon

hooligan n voyou m (pl voyous)

hooray excl hourra!

Hoover® n aspirateur m

hoover vb passer l'aspirateur ▷ to hoover the lounge passer l'aspirateur dans le salon

hope vb espérer ▷ I hope he comes. J'espère qu'il va venir. ▷ I'm hoping for good results. J'espère avoir de bons résultats.; **I hope so.** Je l'espère.; **I hope not.** J'espère que non.
▶ n espoir m; **to give up hope** perdre espoir ▷ Don't give up hope! Ne perds pas espoir!

hopefully adv avec un peu de chance ▷ Hopefully he'll make it in time. Avec un peu de chance, il arrivera à temps.

hopeless adj nul (f nulle) ▷ I'm hopeless at maths. Je suis nul en maths.

horizon n horizon m

horizontal adj horizontal(e) (mpl horizontaux)

horn n ❶ klaxon m ▷ He sounded his horn. Il a klaxonné. ❷ cor m ▷ I play the horn. Je joue du cor.

horoscope n horoscope m

horrible adj horrible ▷ What a horrible dress! Quelle robe horrible!

horrifying adj effrayant(e)

horror n horreur f

horror film n film m d'horreur

horse n cheval m (pl chevaux)

horse-racing n courses fpl de chevaux

hose n tuyau m (pl tuyaux) ▷ a garden hose un tuyau d'arrosage

hospital n hôpital m (pl hôpitaux) ▷ in hospital à l'hôpital

hospitality n hospitalité f

host n hôte m, hôtesse f ▷ Don't forget to write and thank your hosts. N'oublie pas d'écrire à tes hôtes pour les remercier.

hostage n otage m; **to take somebody hostage** prendre quelqu'un en otage

hostel n (for refugees, homeless people) foyer m; **a youth hostel** une auberge de jeunesse

hot adj ❶ (warm) chaud(e) ▷ a hot bath un bain chaud ▷ a hot country un pays chaud

> When you are talking about a person being hot, you use **avoir chaud**.

▷ I'm hot. J'ai chaud.

> When you mean that the weather is hot, you use **faire chaud**.

▷ It's hot. Il fait chaud. ❷ (spicy) épicé(e) ▷ a very hot curry un curry très épicé

hot dog n hot-dog m

hotel n hôtel m ▷ We stayed in a hotel. Nous avons logé à l'hôtel.

hour n heure f ▷ She always takes hours to get ready. Elle passe toujours des heures à se préparer.; **a quarter of an hour** un quart d'heure; **half an hour** une demi-heure; **two and a half hours** deux heures et demie

hourly adj, adv toutes les heures ▷ There are hourly buses. Il y a des bus toutes les heures.; **to be paid hourly** être payé à l'heure

house n maison f; **at his house** chez lui; **We stayed at their house.** Nous avons séjourné chez eux.

housewife n femme f au foyer ▷ She's a housewife. Elle est femme au foyer.

housework n ménage m; **to do the housework** faire le ménage

hovercraft n aéroglisseur m

how adv comment ▷ How are you? Comment allez-vous?; **How many?** Combien?; **How many ...?** Combien de ...? ▷ How many pupils are there in the class? Combien d'élèves y a-t-il dans la classe?; **How much?** Combien?; **How much ...?** Combien de ...? ▷ How much sugar do you want? Combien de sucres voulez-vous?; **How old are you?** Quel âge as-tu?; **How far is it to Edinburgh?** Combien y a-t-il de kilomètres d'ici à Édimbourg?; **How long have you been here?** Depuis combien de temps êtes-vous là?; **How do you say "apple" in French?** Comment dit-on "apple" en français?

however conj pourtant ▷ This, however, isn't true. Pourtant, ce n'est pas vrai.

hug vb serrer dans ses bras ▷ He hugged her. Il l'a serrée dans ses bras.
▶ n to give somebody a hug serrer quelqu'un dans ses bras ▷ She gave them a hug. Elle les a serrés dans ses bras.

huge adj immense

hum vb fredonner

human adj humain(e) ▷ the human body le corps humain

human being n être m humain

humour (US humor) n humour m; **to have a sense of humour** avoir le sens de l'humour

hundred num **a hundred** cent ▷ a hundred euros cent euros; **five hundred** cinq cents; **five hundred and one** cinq cent un; **hundreds of people** des centaines de personnes

hung vb see **hang**

Hungarian n ❶ (person) Hongrois m, Hongroise f ❷ (language) hongrois m
▶ adj hongrois(e) ▷ She's Hungarian. Elle est hongroise.

Hungary n Hongrie f; **in Hungary** en Hongrie; **to Hungary** en Hongrie

hunger n faim f

hungry adj to be hungry avoir faim ▷ I'm hungry. J'ai faim.

hunt vb ❶ (animal) chasser ▷ People used to hunt wild boar. On chassait le sanglier autrefois.; **to go hunting**

aller à la chasse ❷ *(criminal)*
pourchasser ▷ *The police are hunting
the killer.* La police pourchasse le
criminel.; **to hunt for something**
(search) chercher quelque chose
partout ▷ *I hunted everywhere for that
book.* J'ai cherché ce livre partout.
hunting *n* chasse *f* ▷ *I'm against
hunting.* Je suis contre la chasse.;
fox-hunting la chasse au renard
hurdle *n* obstacle *m*
hurricane *n* ouragan *m*
hurry *vb* se dépêcher ▷ *Sharon
hurried back home.* Sharon s'est
dépêchée de rentrer chez elle.;
Hurry up! Dépêche-toi!
▶ *n* **to be in a hurry** être pressé;
to do something in a hurry faire
quelque chose en vitesse; **There's
no hurry.** Rien ne presse.
hurt *vb* **to hurt somebody**
(1) *(physically)* faire mal à quelqu'un
▷ *You're hurting me!* Tu me fais mal!
(2) *(emotionally)* blesser quelqu'un
▷ *His remarks really hurt me.* Ses
remarques m'ont vraiment blessé.;
to hurt oneself se faire mal ▷ *I fell
over and hurt myself.* Je me suis fait
mal en tombant.; **That hurts.** Ça
fait mal. ▷ *It hurts to have a tooth
out.* Ça fait mal de se faire arracher
une dent.; **My leg hurts.** J'ai mal
à la jambe.
▶ *adj* blessé(e) ▷ *Is he badly hurt?*
Est-ce qu'il est grièvement blessé?
▷ *I was hurt by what he said.* J'ai été
blessé par ce qu'il a dit.; **Luckily,
nobody got hurt.** Heureusement,
il n'y a pas eu de blessés.

husband *n* mari *m*
hut *n* hutte *f*
hymn *n* cantique *m*
hypermarket *n* hypermarché *m*
hyphen *n* trait *m* d'union

I pron ① je ▷ *I speak French.* Je parle français.

    je changes to **j'** before a vowel and most words beginning with "h".

    ▷ *I love cats.* J'aime les chats. ② moi ▷ *Ann and I* Ann et moi

ice n ① glace f ▷ *There was ice on the lake.* Il y avait de la glace sur le lac. ② (on road) verglas m

iceberg n iceberg m

ice cream n glace f ▷ *vanilla ice cream* la glace à la vanille

ice cube n glaçon m

ice hockey n hockey m sur glace

Iceland n Islande f; **in Iceland** en Islande; **to Iceland** en Islande

ice rink n patinoire f

ice-skating n patinage m sur glace; **to go ice-skating** faire du patin à glace

icing n (on cake) glaçage m; **icing sugar** le sucre glace

icon n icône f

ICT n informatique f

icy adj glacial(e) (mpl glaciaux) ▷ *There was an icy wind.* Il y avait un vent glacial.; **The roads are icy.** Il y a du verglas sur les routes.

I'd = **I had**; **I would**

idea n idée f ▷ *Good idea!* Bonne idée!

ideal adj idéal(e) (mpl idéaux)

identical adj identique

identification n identification f

identify vb identifier

identity card n carte f d'identité

idiot n idiot m, idiote f

idiotic adj stupide

i.e. abbr c.-à-d. (c'est-à-dire)

if conj si ▷ *You can have it if you like.* Tu peux le prendre si tu veux.

    si changes to **s'** before **il** and **ils**.

    ▷ *Do you know if he's there?* Savez-vous s'il est là?; **if only** si seulement ▷ *If only I had more money!* Si seulement j'avais plus d'argent!; **if not** sinon ▷ *Are you coming? If not, I'll go with Mark.* Est-ce que tu viens? Sinon, j'irai avec Mark.

ignore vb **to ignore something** ne tenir aucun compte de quelque chose ▷ *She ignored my advice.* Elle n'a tenu aucun compte de mes conseils.; **to ignore somebody** ignorer quelqu'un ▷ *She saw me, but she ignored me.* Elle m'a vu, mais elle m'a ignoré.; **Just ignore him!** Ne fais pas attention à lui!

ill adj (sick) malade; **to be taken ill** tomber malade ▷ *She was taken ill while on holiday.* Elle est tombée malade pendant qu'elle était en vacances.

I'll = I will

illegal adj illégal(e) (mpl illégaux)

illness n maladie f

illusion n illusion f

illustration n illustration f

image n image f ▷ *The company has changed its image.* La société a changé d'image.

imagination n imagination f

imagine vb imaginer ▷ *You can imagine how I felt!* Tu peux imaginer ce que j'ai ressenti! ▷ *Is he angry? — I imagine so.* Est-ce qu'il est en colère? — J'imagine que oui.

imitate vb imiter

imitation n imitation f

immediate adj immédiat(e)

immediately adv immédiatement ▷ *I'll do it immediately.* Je vais le faire immédiatement.

immigrant n immigré m, immigrée f

immigration n immigration f

impatience n impatience f

impatient adj impatient(e); **to get impatient** s'impatienter ▷ *People are getting impatient.* Les gens commencent à s'impatienter.

impatiently adv avec impatience ▷ *We waited impatiently.* Nous avons attendu avec impatience.

import vb importer
▶ n importation f

importance n importance f

important adj important(e)

impossible adj impossible

impress vb impressionner ▷ *She's trying to impress you.* Elle essaie de t'impressionner.

impressed adj impressionné(e) ▷ *I'm very impressed!* Je suis très impressionné!

impression n impression f ▷ *I was under the impression that …* J'avais l'impression que …

impressive adj impressionnant(e)

improve vb ❶ (make better) améliorer ▷ *They have improved the service.* Ils ont amélioré le service. ❷ (get better) s'améliorer ▷ *My French has improved.* Mon français s'est amélioré.

improvement n ❶ (of condition) amélioration f ▷ *It's a great improvement.* C'est une nette amélioration. ❷ (of learner) progrès m ▷ *There's been an improvement in his French.* Il a fait des progrès en français.

in prep, adv

> There are several ways of translating **in**. Scan the examples to find one that is similar to what you want to say. For other expressions with **in**, see the verbs **go**, **come**, **get**, **give** etc.

❶ dans ▷ *in the house* dans la maison ▷ *in the sixties* dans les années soixante ▷ *I'll see you in three weeks.* Je te verrai dans trois semaines. ② à ▷ *in the country* à la campagne ▷ *in school* à l'école ▷ *in London* à Londres ▷ *in spring* au printemps ▷ *in a loud voice* à voix haute ▷ *the boy in the blue shirt* le garçon à la chemise bleue ▷ *It was written in pencil.* C'était écrit au crayon. ③ en ▷ *in French* en français ▷ *in summer* en été ▷ *in town* en ville ▷ *in good condition* en bon état

> When **in** refers to a country which is feminine, use **en**; when the country is masculine, use **au**; when the country is plural, use **aux**.

▷ *in France* en France ▷ *in Portugal* au Portugal ▷ *in the United States* aux États-Unis ④ de ▷ *the best pupil in the class* le meilleur élève de la classe ▷ *at 6 in the morning* à six heures du matin; **in the afternoon** l'après-midi; **You look good in that dress.** Tu es jolie avec cette robe.; **in time** à temps ▷ *We arrived in time for dinner.* Nous sommes arrivés à temps pour le dîner.; **in here** ici ▷ *It's hot in here.* Il fait chaud ici.; **in the rain** sous la pluie; **one person in ten** une personne sur dix; **to be in** (*at home, work*) être là ▷ *He wasn't in.* Il n'était pas là.; **to ask somebody in** inviter quelqu'un à entrer

include vb comprendre ▷ *Service is not included.* Le service n'est pas compris.

including prep compris ▷ *It will be 200 euros, including tax.* Ça coûtera deux cents euros, toutes taxes comprises.

income n revenu m

income tax n impôt m sur le revenu

inconsistent adj incohérent(e)

inconvenient adj *That's very inconvenient for me.* Ça ne m'arrange pas du tout.

incorrect adj incorrect(e)

increase n augmentation f ▷ *an increase in road accidents* une augmentation des accidents de la route

▶ vb augmenter

incredible adj incroyable

indeed adv vraiment ▷ *It's very hard indeed.* C'est vraiment très difficile.; **Know what I mean? — Indeed I do.** Tu vois ce que je veux dire? — Oui, tout à fait.; **Thank you very much indeed!** Merci beaucoup!

independence n indépendance f

independent adj indépendant(e); **an independent school** une école privée

index n (*in book*) index m

index finger n index m

India n Inde f; **in India** en Inde; **to India** en Inde

Indian adj indien (f indienne)

▶ n (*person*) Indien m, Indienne f; **an American Indian** un Indien d'Amérique

indicate vb indiquer

indicator n (*on car*) clignotant m

a
b
c
d
e
f
g
h
i
j
k
l
m
n
o
p
q
r
s
t
u
v
w
x
y
z

indigestion n indigestion f;
I've got indigestion. J'ai une
indigestion.

individual adj individuel
(f individuelle)

indoor adj an indoor swimming
pool une piscine couverte; indoor
football le futsal

indoors adv à l'intérieur ▷ They're
indoors. Ils sont à l'intérieur.; to
go indoors rentrer ▷ We'd better
go indoors. Nous ferions mieux de
rentrer.

industrial adj industriel (f
industrielle)

industrial estate n zone f
industrielle

industry n industrie f ▷ the tourist
industry l'industrie du tourisme

inevitable adj inévitable

inexperienced adj
inexpérimenté(e)

infant school n
- CP (cours préparatoire) is the
- equivalent of first-year infants,
- and CE1 (cours élémentaire
- première année) the equivalent
- of second-year infants.
▷ He's just started at infant
school. Il vient d'entrer au cours
préparatoire.

infection n infection f ▷ an ear
infection une infection de l'oreille;
a throat infection une angine

infectious adj contagieux
(f contagieuse) ▷ It's not infectious.
Ce n'est pas contagieux.

infinitive n infinitif m

inflation n inflation f

inform vb informer; to inform
somebody of something informer
quelqu'un de quelque chose
▷ Nobody informed me of the new
plan. Personne ne m'a informé de
ce nouveau projet.

informal adj ❶ (person, party)
décontracté(e) ▷ "informal
dress" "tenue décontractée"
❷ (colloquial) familier (f familière)
▷ informal language le langage
familier; an informal visit une
visite non officielle

information n renseignements
mpl ▷ important information les
renseignements importants;
a piece of information un
renseignement; Could you give
me some information about
trains to Paris? Pourriez-vous
me renseigner sur les trains pour
Paris?

information office n bureau m
des renseignements

information technology n
informatique f

infuriating adj exaspérant(e)

ingredient n ingrédient m

inherit vb hériter de ▷ She inherited
her father's house. Elle a hérité de la
maison de son père.

initials npl initiales fpl ▷ Her initials
are CDT. Ses initiales sont CDT.

injection n piqûre f

injure vb blesser

injured adj blessé(e)

injury n blessure f

ink n encre f

in-laws npl beaux-parents mpl

innocent adj innocent(e)

insane adj fou (f folle)

inscription n inscription f

insect n insecte m

insect repellent n insectifuge m

insert vb insérer

inside n intérieur m
▶ adv, prep à l'intérieur ▷ inside the house à l'intérieur de la maison; **to go inside** rentrer; **Come inside!** Rentrez!

insist vb insister ▷ I didn't want to, but he insisted. Je ne voulais pas, mais il a insisté.; **to insist on doing something** insister pour faire quelque chose ▷ She insisted on paying. Elle a insisté pour payer.; **He insisted he was innocent.** Il affirmait qu'il était innocent.

inspector n (police) inspecteur m ▷ Inspector Jill Brown l'inspecteur Jill Brown; **ticket inspector** (on buses) le contrôleur

install vt installer

instalment n ❶ (payment) versement m ▷ to pay in instalments payer en plusieurs versements ❷ (episode) épisode m

instance n **for instance** par exemple

instant adj immédiat(e) ▷ It was an instant success. Ça a été un succès immédiat.; **instant coffee** le café instantané

instantly adv tout de suite

instead adv **instead of (1)** (followed by noun) à la place de ▷ He went instead of Peter. Il y est allé à la place de Peter. **(2)** (followed by verb) au

lieu de ▷ We played tennis instead of going swimming. Nous avons joué au tennis au lieu d'aller nager.; **The pool was closed, so we played tennis instead.** La piscine était fermée, alors nous avons joué au tennis.

instinct n instinct m

instruct vb **to instruct somebody to do something** donner l'ordre à quelqu'un de faire quelque chose ▷ She instructed us to wait outside. Elle nous a donné l'ordre d'attendre dehors.

instructions npl ❶ instructions fpl ▷ Follow the instructions carefully. Suivez soigneusement les instructions. ❷ (booklet) mode m d'emploi ▷ Where are the instructions? Où est le mode d'emploi?

instructor n moniteur m, monitrice f ▷ a driving instructor un moniteur d'auto-école

instrument n instrument m ▷ Do you play an instrument? Est-ce que tu joues d'un instrument?

insulin n insuline f

insult n insulte f
▶ vb insulter

insurance n assurance f ▷ his car insurance son assurance automobile; **an insurance policy** une police d'assurance

intelligent adj intelligent(e)

intend vb **to intend to do something** avoir l'intention de faire quelque chose ▷ I intend to do French at university. J'ai l'intention d'étudier le français à l'université.

intensive adj intensif (f intensive)
intention n intention f
interest n intérêt m ▷ to show an interest in something manifester de l'intérêt pour quelque chose; **What interests do you have?** Quels sont tes centres d'intérêt?; **My main interest is music.** Ce qui m'intéresse le plus c'est la musique.
▶ vb intéresser ▷ It doesn't interest me. Ça ne m'intéresse pas.; **to be interested in something** s'intéresser à quelque chose ▷ I'm not interested in politics. Je ne m'intéresse pas à la politique.
interesting adj intéressant(e)
interior n intérieur m
interior designer n designer mf
international adj international(e) (mpl internationaux)
internet n Internet m ▷ on the internet sur Internet
internet café n cybercafé m
internet user n internaute mf
interpreter n interprète mf
interrupt vb interrompre
interruption n interruption f
interval n (in play, concert) entracte m
interview n ❶ (on TV, radio) interview f ❷ (for job) entretien m
▶ vb (on TV, radio) interviewer ▷ I was interviewed on the radio. J'ai été interviewé à la radio.
interviewer n (on TV, radio) interviewer m
into prep ❶ dans ▷ He got into the car. Il est monté dans la voiture.

❷ en ▷ I'm going into town. Je vais en ville. ▷ Translate it into French. Traduisez ça en français.
introduce vb présenter ▷ He introduced me to his parents. Il m'a présenté à ses parents.
introduction n (in book) introduction f
invade vb envahir
invalid n malade mf
invent vb inventer
invention n invention f
investigation n (police) enquête f
invisible adj invisible
invitation n invitation f
invite vb inviter ▷ He's not invited. Il n'est pas invité.; **to invite somebody to a party** inviter quelqu'un à une fête
involve vb nécessiter ▷ His job involves a lot of travelling. Son travail nécessite de nombreux déplacements.; **to be involved in something** (crime, drugs) être impliqué dans quelque chose; **to be involved with somebody** (in relationship) avoir une relation avec quelqu'un
iPod® n iPod® m
Iran n Iran m; **in Iran** en Iran
Iraq n Iraq m; **in Iraq** en Iraq
Iraqi adj irakien (f irakienne)
▶ n Irakien, Irakienne f; **the Iraqis** les Irakiens
Ireland n Irlande f; **in Ireland** en Irlande; **to Ireland** en Irlande; **I'm from Ireland.** Je suis irlandais.
Irish adj irlandais(e) ▷ Irish music la musique irlandaise

▶ n (language) irlandais m; **the Irish** (people) les Irlandais

Irishman n Irlandais m

Irishwoman n Irlandaise f

iron n ❶ (metal) fer m ❷ (for clothes) fer m à repasser
▶ vb repasser

ironing n repassage m ▷ **to do the ironing** faire le repassage

ironing board n planche f à repasser

irresponsible adj (person) irresponsable ▷ **That was irresponsible of him.** C'était irresponsable de sa part.

irritating adj irritant(e)

is vb see **be**

Islam n Islam m

Islamic adj islamique ▷ **Islamic law** la loi islamique; **Islamic fundamentalists** les intégristes musulmans

island n île f

isle n **the Isle of Man** l'île de Man; **the Isle of Wight** l'île de Wight

isolated adj isolé(e)

Israel n Israël m; **in Israel** en Israël

Israeli adj israélien (f israélienne)
▶ n Israélien m, Israélienne f

issue n ❶ (matter) question f ▷ **a controversial issue** une question controversée ❷ (of magazine) numéro m
▶ vb (equipment) distribuer

IT n informatique f

it pron

> Remember to check if **it** stands for a masculine or feminine noun.

❶ il (f elle) ▷ **Where's my book?** — **It's on the table.** Où est mon livre? — Il est sur la table.

> Use **le** or **la** when **it** is the object of the sentence. **le** and **la** change to **l'** before a vowel and most words beginning with "h".

❷ le, la, l' ▷ **There's a croissant left. Do you want it?** Il reste un croissant. Tu le veux? ▷ **I don't want this apple. Take it.** Je ne veux pas de cette pomme. Prends-la. ▷ **It's a good film. Did you see it?** C'est un bon film. L'as-tu vu? ▷ **He's got a new car.** — **Yes, I saw it.** Il a une nouvelle voiture. — Oui, je l'ai vue. ▷ **It's raining.** Il pleut.; **It's 6 o'clock.** Il est six heures.; **It's Friday tomorrow.** Demain c'est vendredi.; **Who is it?** — **It's me.** Qui est-ce? — C'est moi.; **It's expensive.** C'est cher.

Italian adj italien (f italienne)
▶ n ❶ (person) Italien m, Italienne f ❷ (language) italien m

Italy n Italie f; **in Italy** en Italie; **to Italy** en Italie

itch vb **It itches.** Ça me démange.; **My head's itching.** J'ai des démangeaisons à la tête.

itchy adj **My arm is itchy.** J'ai des fourmis dans le bras.

it'd = **it had; it would**

item n (object) article m

it'll = **it will**

its adj

> Remember to check if **its** refers to a masculine, feminine or plural noun.

son (*f* sa, *pl* ses) ▷ *What's its name?*
Quel est son nom?
it's = it is; it has
itself *pron* se

> se changes to **s'** before a vowel
> and most words beginning
> with "h".
> ▷ *The heating switches itself
> off.* Le chauffage s'arrête
> automatiquement.

I've = I have

j

jack *n* ❶ (*for car*) cric *m* ❷ (*playing card*) valet *m*
jacket *n* veste *f*; **jacket potatoes** les pommes de terre en robe des champs
jail *n* prison *f*; **to go to jail** aller en prison
> ▶ *vb* emprisonner
jam *n* confiture *f* ▷ *strawberry jam* la confiture de fraises; **a traffic jam** un embouteillage
jammed *adj* coincé(e) ▷ *The window's jammed.* La fenêtre est coincée.
janitor *n* concierge *m* ▷ *He's a janitor.* Il est concierge.
January *n* janvier *m*; **in January** en janvier
Japan *n* Japon *m*; **in Japan** au Japon; **from Japan** du Japon

Japanese adj japonais(e)
▶ n ❶ (person) Japonais m,
Japonaise f; **the Japanese** les
Japonais ❷ (language) japonais m
jar n bocal m (pl bocaux) ▷ an empty
jar un bocal vide; **a jar of honey** un
pot de miel
javelin n javelot m
jaw n mâchoire f
jazz n jazz m
jealous adj jaloux (f jalouse)
jeans npl jean m
Jello® n (US) gelée f
jelly n gelée f
jellyfish n méduse f
jersey n (pullover) pull-over m
Jesus n Jésus m
jet n (plane) jet m
**jetlag to be suffering from
jetlag** être sous le coup du
décalage horaire
Jew n Juif m, Juive f
jewel n bijou m (pl bijoux)
jeweller (US jeweler) n bijoutier
m, bijoutière f ▷ He's a jeweller. Il est
bijoutier.
jeweller's shop (US jeweler's
shop) n bijouterie f
jewellery (US jewelry) n bijoux
mpl
Jewish adj juif (f juive)
jigsaw n puzzle m
job n ❶ emploi m ▷ He's lost his
job. Il a perdu son emploi.; **I've
got a Saturday job.** Je travaille le
samedi. ❷ (chore, task) travail m (pl
travaux) ▷ That was a difficult job.
C'était un travail difficile.
jobless adj sans emploi

jockey n jockey m
jog vb faire du jogging
jogging n jogging m; **to go
jogging** faire du jogging
join vb ❶ (become member of)
s'inscrire à ▷ I'm going to join the ski
club. Je vais m'inscrire au club de
ski. ❷ se joindre à ▷ Do you mind if I
join you? Puis-je me joindre à vous?
joiner n menuisier m ▷ He's a joiner.
Il est menuisier.
joint n ❶ (in body) articulation f
❷ (of meat) rôti m ❸ (drugs)
joint m
joke n plaisanterie f; **to tell a joke**
raconter une plaisanterie
▶ vb plaisanter ▷ I'm only joking. Je
plaisante.
Jordan n (country) Jordanie f; **in
Jordan** en Jordanie
jotter n (pad) bloc-notes m (pl
blocs-notes)
journalism n journalisme m
journalist n journaliste mf ▷ She's a
journalist. Elle est journaliste.
journey n ❶ voyage m ▷ I don't like
long journeys. Je n'aime pas les longs
voyages.; **to go on a journey** faire
un voyage ❷ (to school, work) trajet
m ▷ The journey to school takes about
half an hour. Il y a une demi-heure
de trajet pour aller à l'école.; **a bus
journey** un trajet en autobus
joy n joie f
joystick n (for computer game)
manette m de jeu
judge n juge m ▷ She's a judge. Elle
est juge.
▶ vb juger

a
b
c
d
e
f
g
h
i
j
k
l
m
n
o
p
q
r
s
t
u
v
w
x
y
z

judo n judo m ▷ *My hobby is judo.* Je fais du judo.

jug n pot m

juggler n jongleur m, jongleuse f

juice n jus m ▷ *orange juice* le jus d'orange

July n juillet m; **in July** en juillet

jumble sale n vente f de charité

jump vb sauter; **to jump over something** sauter par-dessus quelque chose; **to jump out of the window** sauter par la fenêtre; **to jump off the roof** sauter du toit

jumper n (pullover) pull-over m

junction n (of roads) carrefour m

June n juin m; **in June** en juin

jungle n jungle f

junior n **the juniors** (in school) les élèves des petites classes

junior school n école f primaire

junk n (old things) bric-à-brac no pl ▷ *The attic's full of junk.* Le grenier est rempli de bric-à-brac.; **to eat junk food** manger n'importe comment; **a junk shop** un magasin de brocante

jury n jury m

just adv juste ▷ *just after Christmas* juste après Noël ▷ *just in time* juste à temps; **just here** ici; **I'm rather busy just now.** Je suis assez occupé en ce moment.; **I did it just now.** Je viens de le faire.; **He's just arrived.** Il vient d'arriver.; **I'm just coming!** J'arrive!; **It's just a suggestion.** Ce n'est qu'une suggestion.

justice n justice f

kangaroo n kangourou m

karaoke n karaoké m

karate n karaté m

kebab n ❶ (shish kebab) brochette f ❷ (doner kebab) doner kebab m

keen adj enthousiaste ▷ *He doesn't seem very keen.* Il n'a pas l'air très enthousiaste.; **She's a keen student.** C'est une étudiante assidue.; **to be keen on something** aimer quelque chose ▷ *I'm keen on maths.* J'aime les maths.; **to be keen on somebody** (fancy them) être très attiré par quelqu'un ▷ *He's keen on her.* Il est très attiré par elle.; **to be keen on doing something** avoir très envie de faire quelque chose ▷ *I'm not very keen on going.* Je n'ai pas très envie d'y aller.

keep vb ❶ (retain) garder ▷ You can keep it. Tu peux le garder. ❷ (remain) rester ▷ Keep still! Reste tranquille!; **Keep quiet!** Tais-toi!; **I keep forgetting my keys.** J'oublie tout le temps mes clés.; **to keep on doing something** (1) (continue) continuer à faire quelque chose ▷ He kept on reading. Il a continué à lire. (2) (repeatedly) ne pas arrêter de faire quelque chose ▷ The car keeps on breaking down. La voiture n'arrête pas de tomber en panne.; **"keep out"** "défense d'entrer"

keep up vb se maintenir à la hauteur de quelqu'un ▷ Matthew walks so fast I can't keep up. Matthew marche tellement vite que je n'arrive pas à me maintenir à sa hauteur.; **I can't keep up with the rest of the class.** Je n'arrive pas à suivre le reste de la classe.

kept vb see **keep**

ketchup n ketchup m

kettle n bouilloire f

key n clé f

keyboard n clavier m ▷ ... with Mike Moran on keyboards ... avec Mike Moran aux claviers

kick n coup m de pied
▶ vb **to kick somebody** donner un coup de pied à quelqu'un ▷ He kicked me. Il m'a donné un coup de pied.; **to kick off** (in football) donner le coup d'envoi

kick-off n coup m d'envoi ▷ The kick-off is at 10 o'clock. Le coup d'envoi sera donné à dix heures.

kid n (child) gosse mf
▶ vb plaisanter ▷ I'm just kidding. Je plaisante.

kidnap vb kidnapper

kidney n ❶ (human) rein m ▷ He's got kidney trouble. Il a des problèmes de reins. ❷ (to eat) rognon m ▷ I don't like kidneys. Je n'aime pas les rognons.

kill vb tuer ▷ He was killed in a car accident. Il a été tué dans un accident de voiture.; **Luckily, nobody was killed.** Il n'y a heureusement pas eu de victimes.; **Six people were killed in the accident.** L'accident a fait six morts.; **to kill oneself** se suicider ▷ He killed himself. Il s'est suicidé.

killer n ❶ (murderer) meurtrier m, meurtrière f ▷ The police are searching for the killer. La police recherche le meurtrier. ❷ (hit man) tueur m, tueuse f ▷ a hired killer un tueur à gages; **Meningitis can be a killer.** La méningite peut être mortelle.

kilo n kilo m ▷ 10 euros a kilo dix euros le kilo

kilometre (US kilometer) n kilomètre m

kilt n kilt m

kind adj gentil (f gentille); **to be kind to somebody** être gentil avec quelqu'un; **Thank you for being so kind.** Merci pour votre gentillesse.

▶ n sorte f ▷ It's a kind of sausage. C'est une sorte de saucisse.

kindness n gentillesse f

king n roi m

kingdom n royaume m

kiosk n (phone box) cabine f téléphonique

kiss n baiser m ▷ a passionate kiss un baiser passionné
▶ vb ❶ embrasser ▷ He kissed her. Il l'a embrassée. ❷ s'embrasser ▷ They kissed. Ils se sont embrassés.

kit n ❶ (clothes for sport) affaires fpl ▷ I've forgotten my gym kit. J'ai oublié mes affaires de gym. ❷ trousse f ▷ a first aid kit une trousse de secours; **a drum kit** une batterie; **a sewing kit** un nécessaire à couture

kitchen n cuisine f ▷ a fitted kitchen une cuisine aménagée; **the kitchen units** les éléments de cuisine; **a kitchen knife** un couteau de cuisine

kite n cerf-volant m (pl cerfs-volants)

kitten n chaton m

kiwi (fruit) n kiwi m

knee n genou m (pl genoux); **He was on his knees.** Il était à genoux.

kneel (down) vb s'agenouiller

knew vb see **know**

knickers npl culotte f; **a pair of knickers** une culotte

knife n couteau m (pl couteaux); **a kitchen knife** un couteau de cuisine; **a sheath knife** un couteau à gaine; **a penknife** un canif

knit vb tricoter

knitting n tricot m ▷ I like knitting. J'aime faire du tricot.

knives npl see **knife**

knob n (on door, radio, TV, radiator) bouton m

knock vb frapper ▷ Someone's knocking at the door. Quelqu'un frappe à la porte.; **to knock somebody down** renverser quelqu'un ▷ She was knocked down by a car. Elle a été renversée par une voiture.; **to knock somebody out (1)** (defeat) éliminer ▷ They were knocked out early in the tournament. Ils ont été éliminés au début du tournoi. **(2)** (stun) assommer ▷ They knocked out the watchman. Ils ont assommé le gardien.
▶ n coup m

knot n nœud m; **to tie a knot in something** faire un nœud à quelque chose

know vb

Use **savoir** for knowing facts, **connaître** for knowing people and places.

❶ savoir ▷ It's a long way. — Yes, I know. C'est loin. — Oui, je sais. ▷ I don't know. Je ne sais pas. ▷ I don't know what to do. Je ne sais pas quoi faire. ❷ connaître ▷ I know her. Je la connais. ▷ **I don't know any German.** Je ne parle pas du tout allemand.; **to know that ...** savoir que ... ▷ I know that you like chocolate. Je sais que tu aimes le chocolat.; **to know about something (1)** (be aware of) être au courant de quelque chose ▷ *Do you know about the meeting this afternoon?* Tu es au courant de la réunion de cet après-midi? **(2)** (*be knowledgeable about*) s'y connaître en quelque chose ▷ *He knows a lot about cars.* Il s'y connaît en voitures.; **to get to know somebody** apprendre à connaître quelqu'un; **How should I know?** (*I don't know!*) Comment veux-tu que je le sache?; **You never know!** On ne sait jamais!

knowledge *n* connaissance *f*
known *vb see* **know**
Koran *n* Coran *m*
Korea *n* Corée *f*; **in Korea** en Corée
kosher *adj* kascher *inv*

lab *n* (= *laboratory*) labo *m*; **a lab technician** un laborantin
label *n* étiquette *f*
labor (*US*) *n* = **labour**
laboratory *n* laboratoire *m*
labour *n* **to be in labour** être en train d'accoucher; **the labour market** le marché du travail; **the Labour Party** le parti travailliste
lace *n* ❶ (*of shoe*) lacet *m* ❷ dentelle *f* ▷ *a lace collar* un col en dentelle
lad *n* gars *m*
ladder *n* échelle *f*
lady *n* dame *f*; **a young lady** une jeune fille; **Ladies and gentlemen ...** Mesdames, Messieurs ...; **the ladies'** les toilettes pour dames
ladybird *n* coccinelle *f*

lager n bière f blonde

laid vb see **lay**

laid-back adj relaxe

lain vb see **lie**

lake n lac m; **Lake Geneva** le lac Léman

lamb n agneau m (pl agneaux); **a lamb chop** une côtelette d'agneau

lamp n lampe f

lamppost n réverbère m

lampshade n abat-jour m (pl abat-jour)

land n terre f; **a piece of land** un terrain

▶ vb (plane, passenger) atterrir

landing n ❶ (of plane) atterrissage m ❷ (of staircase) palier m

landlady n propriétaire f

landlord n propriétaire f

landscape n paysage m

lane n ❶ (in country) chemin m ❷ (on motorway) voie f

language n langue f ▷ French isn't a difficult language. Le français n'est pas une langue difficile.; **to use bad language** dire des grossièretés

language laboratory n laboratoire m de langues

lap n (sport) tour m de piste ▷ I ran ten laps. J'ai fait dix tours de piste en courant.; **on my lap** sur mes genoux

laptop n (computer) portable m

large adj ❶ grand(e) ▷ a large house une grande maison ❷ (person, animal) gros (f grosse) ▷ a large dog un gros chien

laser n laser m

last adj, adv ❶ dernier (f dernière) ▷ last Friday vendredi dernier ▷ last week la semaine dernière ▷ last summer l'été dernier ❷ en dernier ▷ He arrived last. Il est arrivé en dernier. ❸ pour la dernière fois ▷ I've lost my bag. —When did you see it last? J'ai perdu mon sac. — Quand est-ce que tu l'as vu pour la dernière fois?; **the last time** la dernière fois ▷ the last time I saw her la dernière fois que je l'ai vue; **last night (1)** (evening) hier soir ▷ I got home at midnight last night. Je suis rentré à minuit hier soir. **(2)** (sleeping hours) la nuit dernière ▷ I couldn't sleep last night. J'ai eu du mal à dormir la nuit dernière.; **at last** enfin

▶ vb durer ▷ The concert lasts two hours. Le concert dure deux heures.

lastly adv finalement ▷ Lastly, what time do you arrive? Finalement, à quelle heure arrives-tu?

late adj, adv ❶ en retard ▷ Hurry up or you'll be late! Dépêche-toi, sinon tu vas être en retard! ▷ I'm often late for school. J'arrive souvent en retard à l'école.; **to arrive late** arriver en retard ▷ She arrived late. Elle est arrivée en retard. ❷ tard ▷ I went to bed late. Je me suis couché tard.; **in the late afternoon** en fin d'après-midi; **in late May** fin mai

lately adv ces derniers temps ▷ I haven't seen him lately. Je ne l'ai pas vu ces derniers temps.

later adv plus tard ▷ I'll do it later. Je ferai ça plus tard.; **See you later!** À tout à l'heure!

latest adj dernier (f dernière) ▷ their latest album leur dernier album; **at the latest** au plus tard ▷ by 10 o'clock at the latest à dix heures au plus tard

Latin n latin m ▷ I do Latin. Je fais du latin.

Latin America n Amérique f latine; **in Latin America** en Amérique latine

Latin American adj latino-américain(e)

latter n second m, seconde f; **the former ..., the latter ...** le premier ..., le second ... ▷ The former lives in the US, the latter in Australia. Le premier habite aux États-Unis, le second en Australie.

laugh n rire m; **It was a good laugh.** (it was fun) On s'est bien amusés.
▶ vb rire; **to laugh at something** se moquer de quelque chose ▷ They laughed at her. Ils se sont moqués d'elle.

launch vb (product, rocket, boat) lancer ▷ They're going to launch a new model. Ils vont lancer un nouveau modèle.

Launderette® n laverie f

Laundromat® n (US) laverie f

laundry n (clothes) linge m

lavatory n toilettes fpl

lavender n lavande f

law n loi f ▷ The laws are very strict. Les lois sont très sévères.;

It's against the law. C'est illégal. ❷ (subject) droit m ▷ My sister's studying law. Ma sœur fait des études de droit.

lawn n pelouse f

lawnmower n tondeuse f à gazon

lawyer n avocat m, avocate f ▷ My mother's a lawyer. Ma mère est avocate.

lay vb
■ lay is also a form of lie (verb). mettre ▷ She laid the baby in her cot. Elle a mis le bébé dans son lit.; **to lay the table** mettre la table; **to lay something on (1)** (provide) organiser quelque chose ▷ They laid on extra buses. Ils ont organisé un service de bus supplémentaire. **(2)** (prepare) préparer quelque chose ▷ They laid on a special meal. Ils ont préparé un repas soigné.

lay-by n aire f de stationnement

layer n couche f ▷ the ozone layer la couche d'ozone

layout n ❶ (of newspaper article) mise f en page ❷ (of house, buildings) disposition f ▷ the layout of the school la disposition de l'école

lazy adj paresseux (f paresseuse)

lead n
■ This word has two pronunciations. Make sure you choose the right translation.
❶ (cable) fil m ❷ (for dog) laisse f; **to be in the lead** être en tête ▷ Our team is in the lead. Notre équipe est en tête. ❸ (metal) plomb m
▶ vb mener ▷ the street that leads

to the station la rue qui mène à la gare; **to lead the way** montrer le chemin; **to lead somebody away** emmener quelqu'un ▷ *The police led the man away.* La police a emmené l'homme.

leader n ❶ (*of expedition, gang*) chef m ❷ (*of political party*) dirigeant m, dirigeante f

lead-free adj lead-free petrol de l'essence sans plomb

lead singer n chanteur m principal, chanteuse f principale

leaf n feuille f

leaflet n brochure f

league n championnat m ▷ *They are at the top of the league.* Ils sont en tête du championnat.; **the Premier League** la première division

leak n fuite f ▷ *a gas leak* une fuite de gaz
▶ vb (*pipe, water, gas*) fuir

lean vb se pencher ▷ *She leant out of the window.* Elle s'est penchée par la fenêtre.; **to lean forward** se pencher en avant; **to lean on something** s'appuyer contre quelque chose ▷ *He leant on the wall.* Il s'est appuyé contre le mur.; **to be leaning against something** être appuyé contre quelque chose ▷ *The ladder was leaning against the wall.* L'échelle était appuyée contre le mur.; **to lean something against a wall** appuyer quelque chose contre un mur ▷ *He leant his bike against the wall.* Il a appuyé son vélo contre le mur.

lean out vb se pencher au dehors; **She leant out of the window.** Elle s'est penché par la fenêtre.

leap vb sauter ▷ *They leapt over the stream.* Ils ont sauté pour traverser la rivière.

leap year n année f bissextile

learn vb apprendre ▷ *I'm learning to ski.* J'apprends à skier.

learner n She's a quick learner. Elle apprend vite.; **French learners** (*people learning French*) ceux qui apprennent le français

learner driver n conducteur m débutant, conductrice f débutante

learnt vb see **learn**

least adv, adj, pron the **least** (1) (*followed by noun*) le moins de ▷ *It takes the least time.* C'est ce qui prend le moins de temps. (2) (*after a verb*) le moins ▷ *Maths is the subject I like the least.* Les maths sont la matière que j'aime le moins.

> When **least** is followed by an adjective, the translation depends on whether the noun referred to is masculine, feminine or plural ...

the least ... le moins ...
(f la moins ..., pl les moins ...) ▷ *the least expensive hotel* l'hôtel le moins cher ▷ *the least expensive seat* la place la moins chère ▷ *the least expensive hotels* les hôtels les moins chers; **It's the least I can do.** C'est le moins que je puisse faire.; **at least (1)** au moins ▷ *It'll cost at least £200.* Ça va coûter au moins deux

cents livres. (2) du moins ▷ ... *but at least nobody was hurt.* ... mais du moins personne n'a été blessé.

leather n cuir m ▷ *a black leather jacket* un blouson en cuir noir

leave n ❶ (from job) congé m ❷ (from army) permission f
▶ vb ❶ (deliberately) laisser ▷ *Don't leave your camera in the car.* Ne laisse pas ton appareil-photo dans la voiture. ❷ (by mistake) oublier ▷ *I've left my book at home.* J'ai oublié mon livre à la maison. ❸ (go) partir ▷ *The bus leaves at 8.* Le car part à huit heures. ❹ (go away from) quitter ▷ *We leave London at six o'clock.* Nous quittons Londres à six heures.; **to leave somebody alone** laisser quelqu'un tranquille ▷ *Leave me alone!* Laisse-moi tranquille!

leave out vb mettre à l'écart ▷ *Not knowing the language I felt really left out.* Comme je ne connaissais pas la langue, je me suis vraiment senti à l'écart.

leaves npl see **leaf**

Lebanon n Liban m; **in Lebanon** au Liban

lecture n ❶ (public) conférence f ❷ (at university) cours m magistral (pl cours magistraux)

> Be careful not to translate **lecture** by the French word **lecture**.

▶ vb ❶ enseigner ▷ *She lectures at the technical college.* Elle enseigne au collège technique. ❷ faire la morale ▷ *He's always lecturing*

us. Il n'arrête pas de nous faire la morale.

lecturer n professeur m d'université ▷ *She's a lecturer.* Elle est professeur d'université.

led vb see **lead**

leek n poireau m (pl poireaux)

left adj, adv ❶ (not right) gauche ▷ *my left hand* ma main gauche ❷ à gauche ▷ *Turn left at the traffic lights.* Tournez à gauche aux prochains feux.; **I haven't got any money left.** Il ne me reste plus d'argent.
▶ n gauche f; **on the left** à gauche ▷ *Remember to drive on the left.* N'oubliez pas de conduire à gauche.
▶ vb see **leave**

left-hand adj **the left-hand side** la gauche ▷ *It's on the left-hand side.* C'est à gauche.

left-handed adj gaucher (f gauchère)

left-luggage office n consigne f

leg n jambe f ▷ *She's broken her leg.* Elle s'est cassé la jambe.; **a chicken leg** une cuisse de poulet; **a leg of lamb** un gigot d'agneau

legal adj légal(e) (mpl légaux)

leggings n caleçon m

leisure n loisirs mpl ▷ *What do you do in your leisure time?* Qu'est-ce que tu fais pendant tes loisirs?

leisure centre n centre m de loisirs

lemon n citron m

lemonade n limonade f

lend vb prêter ▷ I can lend you some money. Je peux te prêter de l'argent.

length n longueur f; **It's about a metre in length.** Ça fait environ un mètre de long.

lens n ❶ (contact lens) lentille f ❷ (of spectacles) verre m ❸ (of camera) objectif m

Lent n carême m

lent vb see **lend**

lentil n lentille f

Leo n Lion m ▷ I'm Leo. Je suis Lion.

leotard n justaucorps m

lesbian n lesbienne f

less pron, adv, adj ❶ moins ▷ He's less intelligent than her. Il est moins intelligent qu'elle. ❷ moins de ▷ I've got less time for hobbies now. J'ai moins de temps pour les loisirs maintenant.; **less than (1)** (with amounts) moins de ▷ It's less than a kilometre from here. C'est à moins d'un kilomètre d'ici. ▷ less than half moins de la moitié **(2)** (in comparisons) moins que ▷ He spent less than me. Il a dépensé moins que moi.

lesson n ❶ leçon f ▷ a French lesson une leçon de français ❷ (class) cours m ▷ The lessons last forty minutes each. Chaque cours dure quarante minutes.

let vb ❶ (allow) laisser; **to let somebody do something** laisser quelqu'un faire quelque chose ▷ Let me have a look. Laisse-moi voir.; **to let somebody know** faire savoir à quelqu'un ▷ I'll let you know as soon as possible. Je vous le ferai savoir

dès que possible.; **to let down** décevoir ▷ I won't let you down. Je ne vous décevrai pas.; **to let somebody go** lâcher quelqu'un ▷ Let me go! Lâche-moi!; **to let in** laisser entrer ▷ They wouldn't let me in because I was under 18. Ils ne m'ont pas laissé entrer parce que j'avais moins de dix-huit ans.

> To make suggestions using **let's**, you can ask questions beginning with **si on**.

▷ Let's go to the cinema! Si on allait au cinéma?; **Let's go!** Allons-y!
❸ (hire out) louer; **"to let"** "à louer"

letter n lettre f

letterbox n boîte f à lettres

lettuce n salade f

leukaemia n leucémie f

level adj plan(e) ▷ A snooker table must be perfectly level. Un billard doit être parfaitement plan.
▶ n niveau m (pl niveaux) ▷ The level of the river is rising. Le niveau de la rivière monte.; **"A" levels** baccalauréat

- The French **baccalauréat** (or
- **bac** for short) is taken at the age
- of 17 or 18. Students have to sit
- one of a variety of set subject
- combinations, rather than being
- able to choose any combination
- of subjects they want. If you
- pass you have the right to a
- place at university.

level crossing n passage m à niveau

lever n levier m

liar n menteur m, menteuse f

liberal adj (opinions) libéral(e) (mpl libéraux); **the Liberal Democrats** le parti libéral-démocrate

Libra n Balance f ▷ I'm Libra. Je suis Balance.

librarian n bibliothécaire mf ▷ She's a librarian. Elle est bibliothécaire.

library n bibliothèque f

> Be careful not to translate **library** by librairie.

licence (US **license**) n permis m; **a driving licence** un permis de conduire

lick vb lécher

lid n couvercle m

lie vb (not tell the truth) mentir ▷ I know she's lying. Je sais qu'elle ment.; **to lie down** s'allonger; **He was lying on the sofa.** Il était allongé sur le canapé. ▷ When I'm on holiday I lie on the beach all day. Quand je suis en vacances, je reste allongé sur la plage toute la journée. ▶ n mensonge m; **to tell a lie** mentir; **That's a lie!** Ce n'est pas vrai!

lie-in n **to have a lie-in** faire la grasse matinée ▷ I have a lie-in on Sundays. Je fais la grasse matinée le dimanche.

lieutenant n lieutenant m

life n vie f

lifebelt n bouée f de sauvetage

lifeboat n canot m de sauvetage

lifeguard n maître nageur m

life jacket n gilet m de sauvetage

lifestyle n style m de vie

lift vb soulever ▷ It's too heavy, I can't lift it. C'est trop lourd, je ne peux pas le soulever. ▶ n ascenseur m ▷ The lift isn't working. L'ascenseur est en panne.; **He gave me a lift to the cinema.** Il m'a emmené au cinéma en voiture.; **Would you like a lift?** Est-ce que je peux vous déposer quelque part?

light adj ❶ (not heavy) léger (flégère) ▷ a light jacket une veste légère ▷ a light meal un repas léger ❷ (colour) clair ▷ a light blue sweater un pull bleu clair ▶ n ❶ lumière f ▷ to switch on the light allumer la lumière ❷ lampe f ▷ There's a light by my bed. Il y a une lampe près de mon lit.; **the traffic lights** les feux; **Have you got a light?** (for cigarette) Avez-vous du feu? ▶ vb (candle, cigarette, fire) allumer

light bulb n ampoule f

lighter n (for cigarettes) briquet m

lighthouse n phare m

lightning n éclairs mpl; **a flash of lightning** un éclair

like vb ❶ aimer ▷ I don't like mustard. Je n'aime pas la moutarde. ▷ I like riding. J'aime monter à cheval.

> Note that **aimer** also means to love, so make sure you use **aimer bien** for just liking somebody.

❷ aimer bien ▷ I like Paul, but I don't want to go out with him. J'aime bien Paul, mais je ne veux pas sortir avec lui.; **I'd like ...** Je voudrais ...

a b c d e f g h i j k l m n o p q r s t u v w x y z

▷ *I'd like an orange juice, please.* Je voudrais un jus d'orange, s'il vous plaît. ▷ *Would you like some coffee?* Voulez-vous du café?; **I'd like to ...** J'aimerais ... ▷ *I'd like to wash my hands.* J'aimerais me laver les mains.; **Would you like to go for a walk?** Tu veux aller faire une promenade?; **... if you like ...** si tu veux ▶ prep comme ▷ *It's fine like that.* C'est bien comme ça. ▷ *Do it like this.* Fais-le comme ça. ▷ *a city like Paris* une ville comme Paris; **What's the weather like?** Quel temps fait-il?; **to look like somebody** ressembler à quelqu'un ▷ *You look like my brother.* Tu ressembles à mon frère.

likely adj probable ▷ *That's not very likely.* C'est peu probable.; **She's likely to come.** Elle viendra probablement.; **She's not likely to come.** Elle ne viendra probablement pas.

lily of the valley n muguet m

lime n (fruit) citron m vert

limit n limite f ▷ *The speed limit is 70 mph.* La vitesse est limitée à cent dix kilomètres à l'heure.

limp vb boiter

line n ❶ ligne f ▷ *a straight line* une ligne droite ❷ (to divide, cancel) trait m ▷ *Draw a line under each answer.* Tirez un trait après chaque réponse. ❸ (railway track) voie f; **Hold the line, please.** Ne quittez pas.; **It's a very bad line.** La ligne est très mauvaise.; **on line** (computing) en ligne

linen n lin m ▷ *a linen jacket* une veste en lin

lining n (of jacket, skirt etc) doublure f

link n ❶ rapport m ▷ *the link between smoking and cancer* le rapport entre le tabagisme et le cancer ❷ (computing) lien m ▶ vb relier

lion n lion m

lip n lèvre f

lip-read vb lire sur les lèvres

lipstick n rouge m à lèvres
    Word for word, the French means "red for lips".

liquid n liquide m

liquidizer n mixer m

list n liste f ▶ vb faire une liste de ▷ *List your hobbies!* Fais une liste de tes hobbies!

listen vb écouter ▷ *Listen to me!* Écoutez-moi!

lit vb see **light**

liter n (US) = **litre**

literature n littérature f ▷ *I'm studying English Literature.* J'étudie la littérature anglaise.

litre n litre m

litter n ordures fpl

litter bin n poubelle f

little adj petit(e) ▷ *a little girl* une petite fille; **a little** un peu ▷ *How much would you like? — Just a little.* Combien en voulez-vous? — Juste un peu.; **very little** très peu ▷ *We've got very little time.* Nous avons très peu de temps.; **little by little** petit à petit

live adj ❶ (animal) vivant(e)
❷ (broadcast) en direct; **There's
live music on Fridays.** Il y a des
musiciens qui jouent le vendredi.
▶ vb ❶ vivre ▷ I live with my
grandmother. Je vis avec ma grand-
mère.; **to live on something**
vivre de quelque chose ▷ He lives
on benefit. Il vit de ses indemnités.
❷ (reside) habiter ▷ Where do you
live? Où est-ce que tu habites?
▷ I live in Edinburgh. J'habite à
Édimbourg.; **to live together
(1)** partager un appartement
▷ She's living with two Greek students.
Elle partage un appartement avec
deux étudiants grecs. **(2)** vivre
ensemble ▷ My parents aren't living
together any more. Mes parents ne
vivent plus ensemble.; **They're
not married, they're living
together.** Ils ne sont pas mariés,
ils vivent en concubinage.

lively adj animé(e) ▷ It was a lively
party. C'était une soirée animée.;
She's got a lively personality. Elle
est pleine de vitalité.

liver n foie m

lives npl see **life**

living n **to make a living** gagner
sa vie; **What does she do for a
living?** Qu'est-ce qu'elle fait dans
la vie?

living room n salle f de séjour

lizard n lézard m

load n loads of un tas de ▷ loads
of people un tas de gens; **You're
talking a load of rubbish!** Tu ne dis
que des bêtises!

▶ vb charger ▷ a trolley loaded
with luggage un chariot chargé de
bagages

loaf n pain m; **a loaf of bread**
un pain

loan n prêt m
▶ vb prêter

loaves npl see **loaf**

lobster n homard m

local adj local(e) (mpl locaux)
▷ the local paper le journal local;
a local call une communication
urbaine

location n endroit m ▷ A hotel set in
a beautiful location. Un hôtel situé
dans un endroit magnifique.

> Be careful not to translate
> **location** by the French word
> **location**.

loch n loch m

lock n serrure f ▷ The lock is broken.
La serrure est cassée.
▶ vb fermer à clé ▷ Make sure you
lock your door. N'oubliez pas de
fermer votre porte à clé.

locker n casier m; **the locker
room** le vestiaire; **the left-
luggage lockers** la consigne
automatique

lodger n locataire mf

loft n grenier m

log n (of wood) bûche f

log in vb se connecter

log off vb se déconnecter

log on vb se connecter

log out vb se déconnecter

logical adj logique

login n identifiant m

lollipop n sucette f

London n Londres; **in London** à Londres; **to London** à Londres; **I'm from London.** Je suis de Londres.

Londoner n Londonien m, Londonienne f

loneliness n solitude f

lonely adj seul(e); **to feel lonely** se sentir seul ▷ She feels a bit lonely. Elle se sent un peu seule.

long adj, adv long (f longue) ▷ She's got long hair. Elle a les cheveux longs. ▷ The room is 6 metres long. La pièce fait six mètres de long.; **how long?** (time) combien de temps? ▷ How long did you stay there? Combien de temps êtes-vous resté là-bas? ▷ I've been waiting a long time. J'attends depuis longtemps.; **It takes a long time.** Ça prend du temps.; **as long as** si ▷ I'll come as long as it's not too expensive. Je viendrai si ce n'est pas trop cher.

▶ vb **to long to do something** attendre avec impatience de faire quelque chose; **I'm longing to see my boyfriend again.** J'attends avec impatience de revoir mon copain.

longer adv **They're no longer going out together.** Ils ne sortent plus ensemble.; **I can't stand it any longer.** Je ne peux plus le supporter.

long jump n saut m en longueur

loo n toilettes fpl ▷ Where's the loo? Où sont les toilettes?

look n **to have a look** regarder ▷ Have a look at this! Regardez ceci!;

I don't like the look of it. Ça ne me dit rien.

▶ vb ❶ regarder ▷ Look! Regardez!; **to look at something** regarder quelque chose ▷ Look at the picture. Regardez cette image. ❷ (seem) avoir l'air ▷ She looks surprised. Elle a l'air surprise. ▷ It looks fine. Ça a l'air bien.; **to look like somebody** ressembler à quelqu'un ▷ He looks like his brother. Il ressemble à son frère.; **What does she look like?** Comment est-elle physiquement?; **Look out!** Attention!; **to look after** s'occuper de ▷ I look after my little sister. Je m'occupe de ma petite sœur.; **to look for** chercher ▷ I'm looking for my passport. Je cherche mon passeport.; **to look forward to something** attendre quelque chose avec impatience ▷ I'm looking forward to the holidays. J'attends les vacances avec impatience.; **Looking forward to hearing from you ...** J'espère avoir bientôt de tes nouvelles ...; **to look round** **(1)** (look behind) se retourner ▷ I shouted and he looked round. J'ai crié et il s'est retourné. **(2)** (have a look) jeter un coup d'œil ▷ I'm just looking round. Je jette simplement un coup d'œil.; **to look round a museum** visiter un musée; **I like looking round the shops.** J'aime faire les boutiques.; **to look up** (word, name) chercher ▷ If you don't know a word, look it up in the dictionary. Si vous ne connaissez pas un mot, cherchez-le dans le dictionnaire.

loose adj (clothes) ample; **loose change** la petite monnaie

lord n (feudal) seigneur m; **the House of Lords** la Chambre des lords; **good Lord!** mon Dieu!

lorry n camion m

lorry driver n routier m ▷ He's a lorry driver. Il est routier.

lose vb perdre ▷ I've lost my purse. J'ai perdu mon porte-monnaie.; **to get lost** se perdre ▷ I was afraid of getting lost. J'avais peur de me perdre.

loser n ❶ perdant m, perdante f; **to be a bad loser** être mauvais perdant ❷ (pathetic person) loser m ▷ He's such a loser! C'est un vrai loser!

loss n perte f

lost vb see **lose**
▷ adj perdu(e)

lost-and-found n (US) = **lost property office**

lost property office n objets mpl trouvés

> Word for word, the French means "things that have been found", not lost!

lot n **a lot** beaucoup; **a lot of** beaucoup de ▷ We saw a lot of interesting things. Nous avons vu beaucoup de choses intéressantes.; **lots of** un tas de ▷ She's got lots of money. Elle a un tas d'argent.; **What did you do at the weekend? — Not a lot.** Qu'as-tu fait ce week-end? — Pas grand-chose.; **Do you like football? — Not a lot.** Tu aimes le football?

— Pas tellement.; **That's the lot.** C'est tout.

lottery n loterie f; **to win the lottery** gagner à la loterie

loud adj fort(e) ▷ The television is too loud. La télévision est trop forte.

loudly adv fort

loudspeaker n haut-parleur m

lounge n salon m

love n ❶ amour m; **to be in love** être amoureux ▷ She's in love with Paul. Elle est amoureuse de Paul.; **to make love** faire l'amour; **Give Delphine my love.** Embrasse Delphine pour moi.; **Love, Rosemary.** Amitiés, Rosemary.
▷ vb ❶ (be in love with) aimer ▷ I love you. Je t'aime. ❷ (like a lot) aimer beaucoup ▷ Everybody loves her. Tout le monde l'aime beaucoup. ▷ I'd love to come. J'aimerais beaucoup venir. ❸ (things) adorer ▷ I love chocolate. J'adore le chocolat.

lovely adj charmant(e) ▷ What a lovely surprise! Quelle charmante surprise! ▷ She's a lovely person. Elle est charmante.; **It's a lovely day.** Il fait très beau aujourd'hui.; **Is your meal OK? — Yes, it's lovely.** Est-ce que c'est bon? — Oui, c'est délicieux.; **They've got a lovely house.** Ils ont une très belle maison.; **Have a lovely time!** Amusez-vous bien!

lover n ❶ (in relationship) amant m, maîtresse f ❷ (of hobby, wine) amateur m ▷ an art lover un amateur d'art

low adj, adv (price, level) bas
(f basse) ▷ That plane is flying very
low. Cet avion vole très bas.; **the
low season** la basse saison ▷ in the
low season en basse saison

lower sixth n première f ▷ He's in
the lower sixth. Il est en première.

loyalty n fidélité f

loyalty card n carte f de fidélité

luck n chance f ▷ She hasn't had
much luck. Elle n'a pas eu beaucoup
de chance.; **Good luck!** Bonne
chance!; **Bad luck!** Pas de chance!

luckily adv heureusement

lucky adj **to be lucky (1)** (be
fortunate) avoir de la chance ▷ He's
lucky, he's got a job. Il a de la chance,
il a un emploi. **(2)** (bring luck) porter
bonheur ▷ Black cats are lucky in
Britain. Les chats noirs portent
bonheur en Grande-Bretagne.;
a lucky horseshoe un fer à cheval
porte-bonheur

luggage n bagages mpl

lump n ❶ morceau m (pl
morceaux) ▷ a lump of butter un
morceau de beurre ❷ (swelling)
bosse f ▷ He's got a lump on his
forehead. Il a une bosse sur
le front.

lunch n déjeuner m; **to have lunch**
déjeuner ▷ We have lunch at 12.30.
Nous déjeunons à midi et demie.

lung n poumon m; **lung cancer** le
cancer du poumon

Luxembourg n ❶ (country)
Luxembourg m; **in Luxembourg**
au Luxembourg; **to Luxembourg**
au Luxembourg ❷ (city)

Luxembourg m; **in Luxembourg** à
Luxembourg

luxurious adj luxueux (f luxueuse)

luxury n luxe m ▷ It was luxury!
C'était un vrai luxe!; **a luxury hotel**
un hôtel de luxe

lying vb see **lie**

lyrics npl (of song) paroles fpl

m

macaroni n macaronis mpl

machine n machine f

machine gun n mitrailleuse f

machinery n machines fpl

mad adj ❶ (insane) fou (f folle)
▷ You're mad! Tu es fou! ❷ (angry)
furieux (f furieuse) ▷ She'll be mad
when she finds out. Elle sera furieuse
quand elle va s'en apercevoir.; **to be
mad about (1)** (sport, activity) être
enragé de ▷ He's mad about football.
Il est enragé de foot. **(2)** (person,
animal) adorer ▷ She's mad about
horses. Elle adore les chevaux.

madam n madame f ▷ Would you
like to order, Madam? Désirez-vous
commander, Madame?

made vb see **make**

madness n folie f ▷ It's absolute
madness. C'est de la pure folie.

magazine n magazine m

maggot n asticot m

magic adj ❶ (magical) magique ▷ a
magic wand une baguette magique
❷ (brilliant) super; **It was magic!**
C'était super!
▶ n magie f; **a magic trick** un tour
de magie; **My hobby is magic.** Je
fais des tours de magie.

magician n (conjurer)
prestidigitateur m

magnet n aimant m

magnifying glass n loupe f

maid n (servant) domestique f

maiden name n nom m de
jeune fille

mail n courrier m ▷ Here's your mail.
Voici ton courrier.; **email** (electronic
mail) le courrier électronique; **by
mail** par la poste

mailbox n (US) boîte f à lettres

mailman n (US) facteur m

main adj principal(e) (mpl
principaux) ▷ the main problem le
principal problème; **the main
thing is to ...** l'essentiel est de ...

mainly adv principalement

main road n grande route f ▷ I
don't like cycling on main roads. Je
n'aime pas faire du vélo sur les
grandes routes.

majesty n majesté f; **Your
Majesty** Votre Majesté

major adj majeur(e) ▷ a major
problem un problème majeur; **in C
major** en do majeur

Majorca n Majorque f ▷ We went to
Majorca in August. Nous sommes
allés à Majorque en août.

majority n majorité f
make n marque f ▷ *What make is that car?* De quelle marque est cette voiture?
  ▶ vb ❶ faire ▷ *I'm going to make a cake.* Je vais faire un gâteau. ▷ *I make my bed every morning.* Je fais mon lit tous les matins. ❷ *(manufacture)* fabriquer ▷ *made in France* fabriqué en France ❸ *(earn)* gagner ▷ *He makes a lot of money.* Il gagne beaucoup d'argent.; **to make somebody do something** obliger quelqu'un à faire quelque chose ▷ *My mother makes me do my homework.* Ma mère m'oblige à faire mes devoirs.; **to make lunch** préparer le repas ▷ *She's making lunch.* Elle prépare le repas.; **to make a phone call** donner un coup de téléphone ▷ *I'd like to make a phone call.* J'aimerais donner un coup de téléphone.; **to make fun of somebody** se moquer de quelqu'un ▷ *They made fun of him.* Ils se sont moqués de lui.; **What time do you make it?** Quelle heure avez-vous?
make up vb ❶ *(invent)* inventer ▷ *He made up the whole story.* Il a inventé cette histoire de toutes pièces. ❷ *(after argument)* se réconcilier ▷ *They had a quarrel, but soon made up.* Ils se sont disputés, mais se sont vite réconciliés.; **to make oneself up** se maquiller ▷ *She spends hours making herself up.* Elle passe des heures à se maquiller.

make-up n maquillage m
Malaysia n Malaisie f; **in Malaysia** en Malaisie
male adj ❶ *(animals, plants)* mâle ▷ *a male kitten* un chaton mâle ❷ *(person, on official forms)* masculin(e) ▷ *Sex: male.* Sexe: masculin.; **Most football players are male.** La plupart des joueurs de football sont des hommes.; **a male chauvinist** un macho; **a male nurse** un infirmier
malicious adj malveillant(e) ▷ *a malicious rumour* une rumeur malveillante

▌ Be careful not to translate **malicious** by **malicieux**.

mall n centre m commercial
Malta n Malte; **in Malta** à Malte; **to Malta** à Malte
mammal n mammifère m
man n homme m ▷ *an old man* un vieil homme
manage vb ❶ *(be in charge of)* diriger ▷ *She manages a big store.* Elle dirige un grand magasin. ❷ *(get by)* se débrouiller ▷ *It's okay, I can manage.* Ça va, je me débrouille.; **Can you manage okay?** Tu y arrives?; **to manage to do something** réussir à faire quelque chose ▷ *Luckily I managed to pass the exam.* J'ai heureusement réussi à avoir mon examen.; **I can't manage all that.** *(food)* C'est trop pour moi.
management n ❶ *(organization)* gestion f ▷ *He's responsible for the management of the company.* Il est

responsable de la gestion de la société. ❷ (people in charge) direction f ▷ "under new management" "changement de direction"

manager n ❶ (of company) directeur m, directrice f ❷ (of shop, restaurant) gérant m, gérante f ❸ (of team, performer) manager m

manageress n gérante f

mandarin n (fruit) mandarine f

mango n mangue f

mania n manie f

maniac n fou m, folle f ▷ He drives like a maniac. Il conduit comme un fou.; **a religious maniac** un fanatique religieux

mankind n humanité f

manner n façon f; **She behaves in an odd manner.** Elle se comporte de façon étrange.; **He has a confident manner.** Il a de l'assurance.

manners npl manières fpl ▷ good manners les bonnes manières; **It's bad manners to speak with your mouth full.** Ce n'est pas poli de parler la bouche pleine.

mansion n manoir m

mantelpiece n cheminée f

manual n manuel m

manufacture vb fabriquer

manufacturer n fabricant m

many adj, pron beaucoup de ▷ He hasn't got many friends. Il n'a pas beaucoup d'amis. ▷ Were there many people at the concert? Est-ce qu'il y avait beaucoup de gens au concert?; **very many** beaucoup

de ▷ I haven't got very many CDs. Je n'ai pas beaucoup de CD.; **not many** pas beaucoup; **How many?** Combien? ▷ How many do you want? Combien en veux-tu?; **how many ...?** combien de ...? ▷ How many euros do you get for £1? Combien d'euros a-t-on pour une livre?; **too many** trop ▷ That's too many. C'est trop.; **too many ...** trop de ... ▷ She makes too many mistakes. Elle fait trop d'erreurs.; **so many** autant ▷ I didn't know there would be so many. Je ne pensais pas qu'il y en aurait autant.; **so many ...** autant de ... ▷ I've never seen so many policemen. Je n'ai jamais vu autant de policiers.

map n ❶ (of country, area) carte f ❷ (of town) plan m

marathon n marathon m ▷ the London marathon le marathon de Londres

marble n marbre m ▷ a marble statue une statue en marbre; **to play marbles** jouer aux billes

March n mars m; **in March** en mars

march n (demonstration) manifestation f
▶ vb ❶ (soldiers) marcher au pas ❷ (protesters) défiler

mare n jument f

margarine n margarine f

margin n marge f ▷ Write notes in the margin. Écrivez vos notes dans la marge.

marijuana n marijuana f

mark n ❶ (in school) note f ▷ I get good marks for French. J'ai de bonnes notes en français. ❷ (*stain*) tache f ▷ *You've got a mark on your skirt.* Tu as une tache sur ta jupe. ▶ vb corriger ▷ *The teacher hasn't marked my homework yet.* Le professeur n'a pas encore corrigé mon devoir.

market n marché m

marketing n marketing m

marmalade n confiture f d'oranges

marriage n mariage m

married adj marié(e) ▷ *They are not married.* Ils ne sont pas mariés. ▷ *They have been married for 15 years.* Ils sont mariés depuis quinze ans.

marry vb épouser ▷ *He wants to marry her.* Il veut l'épouser.; **to get married** se marier ▷ *My sister's getting married in June.* Ma sœur se marie en juin.

marvellous (*US* **marvelous**) adj ❶ excellent(e) ▷ *She's a marvellous cook.* C'est une excellente cuisinière. ❷ superbe ▷ *The weather was marvellous.* Il a fait un temps superbe.

marzipan n pâte f d'amandes

mascara n mascara m

masculine adj masculin(e)

mashed potatoes npl purée f ▷ *sausages and mashed potatoes* des saucisses avec de la purée

mask n masque m

mass n ❶ multitude f ▷ *a mass of books and papers* une multitude de livres et de papiers ❷ (*in church*) messe f ▷ *We go to mass on Sunday.* Nous allons à la messe le dimanche.; **the mass media** les médias

massage n massage m

massive adj énorme

master vb maîtriser

masterpiece n chef-d'œuvre m (pl chefs-d'œuvre)

mat n (*doormat*) paillasson m; **a table mat** un set de table; **a beach mat** un tapis de plage

match n ❶ allumette f ▷ *a box of matches* une boîte d'allumettes ❷ (*sport*) match m (pl matchs) ▷ *a football match* un match de foot ▶ vb être assorti à ▷ *The jacket matches the trousers.* La veste est assortie au pantalon.; **These colours don't match.** Ces couleurs ne vont pas ensemble.

mate n (*informal*) pote m ▷ *On Friday night I go out with my mates.* Vendredi soir, je sors avec mes potes.

material n ❶ (*cloth*) tissu m ❷ (*information, data*) documentation f ▷ *I'm collecting material for my project.* Je rassemble une documentation pour mon dossier.; **raw materials** les matières premières

mathematics n mathématiques fpl

maths n maths fpl

matter n question f ▷ *It's a matter of life and death.* C'est une question de vie ou de mort.; **What's the matter?** Qu'est-ce qui ne va pas?; **as a matter of fact** en fait ▶ vb **it doesn't matter (1)** (*I don't* mind) ça ne fait rien ▷ I can't give you the money today. — It doesn't matter. Je ne peux pas te donner l'argent aujourd'hui. — Ça ne fait rien. **(2)** (it makes no difference) ça n'a pas d'importance ▷ Shall I phone today or tomorrow? —Whenever, it doesn't matter. Est-ce que j'appelle aujourd'hui ou demain? — Quand tu veux, ça n'a pas d'importance.; **It matters a lot to me.** C'est très important pour moi.

mattress n matelas m

mature adj mûr(e) ▷ She's quite mature for her age. Elle est très mûre pour son âge.

maximum n maximum m
▶ adj maximum inv ▷ The maximum speed is 100 km/h. La vitesse maximum autorisée est de cent kilomètres à l'heure.; **the maximum amount** le maximum

May n mai m; **in May** en mai; **May Day** le Premier Mai

may vb He may come. Il va peut-être venir. ▷ It may rain. Il va peut-être pleuvoir.; **Are you going to the party? — I don't know, I may.** Est-ce que tu vas à la soirée? — Je ne sais pas, peut-être.; **May I smoke?** Est-ce que je peux fumer?

maybe adv peut-être ▷ maybe not peut-être pas ▷ Maybe she's at home. Elle est peut-être chez elle. ▷ Maybe he'll change his mind. Il va peut-être changer d'avis.

mayonnaise n mayonnaise f

mayor n maire m

me pron

me becomes **m'** before a vowel sound.

❶ me, m' ▷ Could you lend me your pen? Est-ce que tu peux me prêter ton stylo? ▷ Can you help me? Est-ce que tu peux m'aider?

moi is used in exclamations.
❷ moi ▷ Me too! Moi aussi! ▷ Excuse me! Excusez-moi! ▷ Wait for me! Attends-moi!

moi is also used after prepositions and in comparisons.
▷ You're after me. Tu es après moi.
▷ She's older than me. Elle est plus âgée que moi.

meal n repas m

mean vb vouloir dire ▷ I don't know what it means. Je ne sais pas ce que ça veut dire. ▷ What do you mean? Qu'est que vous voulez dire? ▷ That's not what I meant. Ce n'est pas ce que je voulais dire.; **Which one do you mean?** Duquel veux-tu parler?; **Do you really mean it?** Tu es sérieux?; **to mean to do something** avoir l'intention de faire quelque chose ▷ I didn't mean to offend you. Je n'avais pas l'intention de vous blesser.
▶ adj **❶** (with money) radin(e) ▷ He's too mean to buy Christmas presents. Il est trop radin pour acheter des cadeaux de Noël. **❷** (unkind) méchant(e) ▷ You're being mean to me. Tu es méchant avec moi.; **That's a really mean thing to say!** Ce n'est vraiment pas gentil de dire ça!

a b c d e f g h i j k l m n o p q r s t u v w x y z

meaning n sens m

meant vb see **mean**

meanwhile adv pendant ce temps

measles n rougeole f

measure vb ❶ mesurer ▷ I measured the page. J'ai mesuré la page. ❷ faire ▷ The room measures 3 metres by 4. La pièce fait trois mètres sur quatre.

measurements npl ❶ (of object) dimensions fpl ▷ What are the measurements of the room? Quelles sont les dimensions de la pièce? ❷ (of body) mensurations fpl ▷ What are your measurements? Quelles sont tes mensurations?; **my waist measurement** mon tour de taille; **What's your neck measurement?** Quel est votre tour de cou?

meat n viande f ▷ I don't eat meat. Je ne mange pas de viande.

Mecca n La Mecque

mechanic n mécanicien m ▷ He's a mechanic. Il est mécanicien.

medal n médaille f; **the gold medal** la médaille d'or

media npl médias mpl

medical adj médical(e) (mpl médicaux) ▷ medical treatment les soins médicaux; **medical insurance** l'assurance maladie; **to have medical problems** avoir des problèmes de santé; **She's a medical student.** Elle est étudiante en médecine.
▶ n **to have a medical** passer une visite médicale

medicine n ❶ (subject) médecine f ▷ I want to study medicine. Je veux faire médecine.; **alternative medicine** la médecine douce ❷ (medication) médicament m ▷ I need some medicine. J'ai besoin d'un médicament.

Mediterranean adj méditerranéen (f méditerranéenne); **the Mediterranean** la Méditerranée

medium adj moyen (f moyenne) ▷ a man of medium height un homme de taille moyenne

medium-sized adj de taille moyenne ▷ a medium-sized town une ville de taille moyenne

meet vb ❶ (by chance) rencontrer ▷ Have you met him before? Tu l'as déjà rencontré? ❷ se rencontrer ▷ We met by chance in the shopping centre. Nous nous sommes rencontrés par hasard dans le centre commercial. ❶ (by arrangement) retrouver ▷ I'm going to meet my friends. Je vais retrouver mes amis. ❷ se retrouver ▷ Let's meet in front of the tourist office. Retrouvons-nous devant l'office de tourisme.; **I like meeting new people.** J'aime faire de nouvelles connaissances. ❸ (pick up) aller chercher ▷ I'll meet you at the station. J'irai te chercher à la gare.; **to meet up** se retrouver ▷ What time shall we meet up? On se retrouve à quelle heure?

meeting n ❶ (for work) réunion f ▷ a business meeting une réunion

d'affaires ❷ (socially) rencontre f
▷ their first meeting leur première
rencontre

mega adj **He's mega rich.** Il est
hyper-riche.

megabyte n (computing) méga-
octet m

melon n melon m

melt vb fondre ▷ The snow's melting.
La neige est en train de fondre.

member n membre m; **a Member
of Parliament** un député

memorial n monument m ▷ a war
memorial un monument aux morts

memorize vb apprendre par cœur

memory n ❶ (also for computer)
mémoire f ▷ I haven't got a good
memory. Je n'ai pas une bonne
mémoire. ❷ (recollection) souvenir
m ▷ to bring back memories rappeler
des souvenirs

men npl see **man**

mend vb réparer

mental adj ❶ mental(e) (mpl
mentaux) ▷ a mental illness une
maladie mentale ❷ (mad) fou (f
folle) ▷ You're mental! Tu es fou!;
a mental hospital un hôpital
psychiatrique

mention vb mentionner; **Thank
you! — Don't mention it!** Merci! —
Il n'y a pas de quoi!

menu n menu m ▷ Could I have the
menu please? Est-ce que je pourrais
avoir le menu s'il vous plaît?

meringue n meringue f

merry adj **Merry Christmas!**
Joyeux Noël!

merry-go-round n manège m

mess n fouillis m ▷ My
bedroom's usually in a mess. Il y a
généralement du fouillis dans ma
chambre.

mess about vb **to mess about
with something** (interfere
with) tripoter quelque chose
▷ Stop messing about with my
computer! Arrête de tripoter mon
ordinateur!; **Don't mess about
with my things!** Ne touche pas à
mes affaires!

mess up vb **to mess something
up** mettre la pagaille dans quelque
chose ▷ My little brother has messed
up my CDs. Mon petit frère a mis la
pagaille dans mes CDs.

message n message m

messenger n messager m

messy adj ❶ (dirty) salissant(e)
▷ a messy job un travail salissant
❷ (untidy) en désordre ▷ Your
desk is really messy. Ton bureau est
vraiment en désordre. ❸ (person)
désordonné(e) ▷ She's so messy! Elle
est tellement désordonnée!; **My
writing is terribly messy.** J'ai une
écriture de cochon.

met vb see **meet**

metal n métal m (pl métaux)

meter n ❶ (for gas, electricity,
taxi) compteur m ❷ (parking
meter) parcmètre m ❸ (US: unit of
measurement) mètre m

method n méthode f

Methodist n méthodiste mf ▷ I'm a
Methodist. Je suis méthodiste.

metre n mètre m

metric adj métrique

Mexico n Mexique m; **in Mexico** au Mexique; **to Mexico** au Mexique

mice npl see **mouse**

microchip n puce f

microphone n microphone m

microscope n microscope m

microwave oven n four m à micro-ondes

midday n midi m; **at midday** à midi

middle n milieu m ▷ in the middle of the road au milieu de la route ▷ in the middle of the night au milieu de la nuit

middle-aged adj d'un certain âge ▷ a middle-aged man un homme d'un certain âge; **to be middle-aged** avoir la cinquantaine ▷ She's middle-aged. Elle a la cinquantaine.

middle-class adj de la classe moyenne ▷ a middle-class family une famille de la classe moyenne

Middle East n Moyen-Orient m; **in the Middle East** au Moyen-Orient

middle name n deuxième nom m

midge n moucheron m

midnight n minuit m; **at midnight** à minuit

midwife n sage-femme f (pl sages-femmes) ▷ She's a midwife. Elle est sage-femme.

might vb

■ Use **peut-être** to express possibility.

▷ He might come later. Il va peut-être venir plus tard. ▷ She might not have understood. Elle n'a peut-être pas compris.

migraine n migraine f ▷ I've got a migraine. J'ai la migraine.

mike n micro m

mild adj doux (f douce) ▷ The winters are quite mild. Les hivers sont assez doux.

mile n mille m

■ In France distances are expressed in kilometres. A mile is about 1.6 kilometres.

▷ It's 5 miles from here. C'est à huit kilomètres d'ici.; **We walked miles!** Nous avons fait des kilomètres à pied!

military adj militaire

milk n lait m ▷ tea with milk du thé au lait

▶ vb traire

milk chocolate n chocolat m au lait

milkman n

■ In France milk is not delivered to people's homes.

▷ He's a milkman. Il livre le lait à domicile.

milk shake n milk-shake m

millennium n millénaire m ▷ the third millennium le troisième millénaire; **the millennium** le millénium

millimetre (US **millimeter**) n millimètre m

million n million m

millionaire n millionnaire m

mince n viande f hachée

mind vb ❶ garder ▷ Could you mind the baby this afternoon? Est-ce que tu pourrais garder le bébé cet après-midi? ❷ (keep an eye on) surveiller ▷ Could you mind my bags? Est-ce que vous pourriez surveiller mes bagages?; **Do you mind if I open the window?** Est-ce que je pourrais ouvrir la fenêtre?; **I don't mind.** Ça ne me dérange pas. ▷ I don't mind the noise. Le bruit ne me dérange pas.; **Never mind!** Ça ne fait rien!; **Mind that bike!** Attention au vélo!; **Mind the step!** Attention à la marche!

▶ **to make up one's mind** se décider ▷ I haven't made up my mind yet. Je ne me suis pas encore décidé.; **to change one's mind** changer d'avis ▷ He's changed his mind. Il a changé d'avis.; **Are you out of your mind?** Tu as perdu la tête?

mine pron le mien (fla mienne) ▷ Is this your coat? — No, mine's black. C'est ton manteau? — Non, le mien est noir. ▷ Is this your car? — No, mine's green. C'est ta voiture? — Non, la mienne est verte.; **It's mine.** C'est à moi. ▷ This book is mine. Ce livre est à moi.

▶ n mine f ▷ a coal mine une mine de charbon ▷ a land mine une mine terrestre

miner n mineur m
mineral water n eau f minérale
miniature adj miniature ▷ a miniature version une version miniature

▶ n miniature f
minibus n minibus m
Minidisc® n minidisque m
minimum n minimum m

▶ adj minimum inv ▷ The minimum age for driving is 17. L'âge minimum pour conduire est dix-sept ans.; **the minimum amount** le minimum
miniskirt n mini-jupe f
minister n ❶ (in government) ministre m ❷ (of church) pasteur m
minor adj mineur(e) ▷ a minor problem un problème mineur; **in D minor** en ré mineur; **a minor operation** une opération bénigne
minority n minorité f
mint n ❶ (plant) menthe f ▷ mint sauce la sauce à la menthe ❷ (sweet) bonbon m à la menthe
minus prep moins ▷ 16 minus 3 is 13. Seize moins trois égale treize. ▷ It's minus two degrees outside. Il fait moins deux dehors.
minute n minute f ▷ Wait a minute! Attends une minute!

▶ adj minuscule ▷ Her flat is minute. Son appartement est minuscule.
miracle n miracle m
mirror n ❶ (on wall) glace f ❷ (in car) rétroviseur m
misbehave vb se conduire mal
miscellaneous adj divers(e)
mischief n bêtises fpl ▷ My little sister's always up to mischief. Ma petite sœur fait constamment des bêtises.
mischievous adj coquin(e)
miser n avare mf
miserable adj ❶ (person) malheureux (f malheureuse) ▷ You're looking miserable. Tu as l'air malheureux. ❷ (weather)

épouvantable ▷ *The weather was miserable.* Il faisait un temps épouvantable.; **to feel miserable** ne pas avoir le moral ▷ *I'm feeling miserable.* Je n'ai pas le moral.

misery n ❶ (unhappiness) tristesse f ▷ *All that money brought nothing but misery.* Tout cet argent n'a apporté que de la tristesse. ❷ (unhappy person) pleurnicheur m, pleurnicheuse f ▷ *She's a real misery.* C'est une vraie pleurnicheuse.

Miss n ❶ Mademoiselle (pl Mesdemoiselles) ❷ (in address) Mlle (pl Mlles)

miss vb ❶ rater ▷ *Hurry or you'll miss the bus.* Dépêche-toi ou tu vas rater le bus. ❷ manquer ▷ *to miss an opportunity* manquer une occasion; **I miss you.** Tu me manques. ▷ *I'm missing my family.* Ma famille me manque. ▷ *I miss them.* Ils me manquent.

missing adj manquant(e) ▷ *the missing part* la pièce manquante; **to be missing** avoir disparu ▷ *Two members of the group are missing.* Deux membres du groupe ont disparu.

mist n brume f

mistake n ❶ (slip) faute f ▷ *a spelling mistake* une faute d'orthographe; **to make a mistake (1)** (in writing, speaking) faire une faute **(2)** (get mixed up) se tromper ▷ *I'm sorry, I made a mistake.* Je suis désolé, je me suis trompé. ❷ (misjudgement) erreur f ▷ *It was a mistake to buy those yellow shoes.*

J'ai fait une erreur en achetant ces chaussures jaunes.; **by mistake** par erreur ▷ *I took his bag by mistake.* J'ai pris son sac par erreur.

▶ vb He mistook me for my sister. Il m'a prise pour ma sœur.

mistaken adj **to be mistaken** se tromper ▷ *If you think I'm going to get up at 6 o'clock, you're mistaken.* Si tu penses que je vais me lever à six heures, tu te trompes.

mistletoe n gui m

mistook vb see **mistake**

misty adj brumeux (f brumeuse) ▷ *a misty morning* un matin brumeux

misunderstand vb mal comprendre ▷ *Sorry, I misunderstood you.* Je suis désolé, je t'avais mal compris.

misunderstanding n malentendu m

misunderstood vb see **misunderstand**

mix n mélange m ▷ *It's a mix of science fiction and comedy.* C'est un mélange de science-fiction et de comédie.; **a cake mix** une préparation pour gâteau

▶ vb ❶ mélanger ▷ *Mix the flour with the sugar.* Mélangez la farine au sucre. ❷ combiner ▷ *He's mixing business with pleasure.* Il combine les affaires et le plaisir.; **to mix with somebody** (associate) fréquenter quelqu'un; **He doesn't mix much.** Il se tient à l'écart.; **to mix up** (people) confondre ▷ *He always mixes me up with my sister.*

Il me confond toujours avec ma sœur.; **The travel agent mixed up the bookings.** L'agence de voyage s'est embrouillée dans les réservations.; **I'm getting mixed up.** Je ne m'y retrouve plus.

mixed adj **a mixed salad** une salade composée; **a mixed school** une école mixte; **a mixed grill** un assortiment de grillades

mixer n **She's a good mixer.** Elle est très sociable.

mixture n mélange m ▷ a mixture of spices un mélange d'épices; **cough mixture** le sirop pour la toux

mix-up n confusion f

moan vb râler ▷ She's always moaning. Elle est toujours en train de râler.

mobile home n mobile home m

mobile phone n portable m

mock vb ridiculiser

▶ adj **a mock exam** un examen blanc

model n ❶ (type) modèle m ▷ His car is the latest model. Sa voiture est le tout dernier modèle. ❷ (mock-up) maquette f ▷ a model of the castle une maquette du château ❸ (fashion) mannequin m ▷ She's a famous model. C'est un mannequin célèbre.

▶ adj **a model plane** un modèle réduit d'avion; **a model railway** un modèle réduit de voie ferrée; **He's a model pupil.** C'est un élève modèle.

▶ vb **She was modelling a Lorna Bailey outfit.** Elle présentait une

tenue de la collection Lorna Bailey.

modem n modem m

moderate adj modéré(e) ▷ His views are quite moderate. Ses opinions sont assez modérées.; **a moderate amount of** un peu de; **a moderate price** un prix raisonnable

modern adj moderne

modernize vb moderniser

modern languages n langues fpl vivantes

modest adj modeste

moisturizer n ❶ (cream) crème f hydratante ❷ (lotion) lait m hydratant

moldy adj (US) = **mouldy**

mole n ❶ (animal) taupe f ❷ (on skin) grain m de beauté

moment n instant m ▷ Could you wait a moment? Pouvez-vous attendre un instant? ▷ in a moment dans un instant; **at the moment** en ce moment; **any moment now** d'un moment à l'autre ▷ They'll be arriving any moment now. Ils vont arriver d'un moment à l'autre.

Monaco n Monaco; **in Monaco** à Monaco

monarchy n monarchie f

Monday n lundi m ▷ on Monday lundi ▷ on Mondays le lundi ▷ every Monday tous les lundis

money n argent m ▷ I need to change some money. J'ai besoin de changer de l'argent.; **to make money** gagner de l'argent

mongrel n bâtard m ▷ My dog's a mongrel. Mon chien est un bâtard.

monitor n (of computer)
moniteur m

monkey n singe m

monotonous adj monotone

monster n monstre m

month n mois m ▷ this month
ce mois-ci ▷ next month le mois
prochain ▷ last month le mois
dernier ▷ every month tous les mois

monthly adj mensuel (f mensuelle)

monument n monument m

mood n humeur f; **to be in a bad
mood** être de mauvaise humeur;
to be in a good mood être de
bonne humeur

moody adj ❶ (temperamental)
lunatique ❷ (in a bad mood)
maussade

moon n lune f ▷ There's a full moon
tonight. Il y a pleine lune ce soir.

moped n cyclomoteur m

moral adj moral(e) (mpl moraux)
▶ n morale f ▷ the moral of the story
la morale de l'histoire; **morals** la
moralité

more adj, pron, adv

When comparing one amount
with another, you usually
use **plus**.

❶ plus ▷ Could you speak more
slowly? Est-ce que vous pourriez
parler plus lentement? ▷ a bit more
un peu plus ▷ There isn't any more.
Il n'y en a plus.; **more ... than**
plus ... que ▷ He's more intelligent
than me. Il est plus intelligent que
moi. ❷ (followed by noun) plus de
▷ I get more homework than you do.
J'ai plus de devoirs que toi. ▷ I spent

more than 500 euros. J'ai dépensé
plus de cinq cents euros.

When referring to an
additional amount, more than
there is already, you usually
use **encore**.

❸ encore ▷ Is there any more? Est-ce
qu'il y en a encore? ▷ Would you like
some more? Vous en voulez encore?
❹ (followed by noun) encore de ▷ Do
you want some more tea? Voulez-
vous encore du thé?; **more or less**
plus ou moins; **more than ever**
plus que jamais

morning n matin m ▷ this morning
ce matin ▷ tomorrow morning
demain matin ▷ every morning tous
les matins; **in the morning** le
matin ▷ at 7 o'clock in the morning à
sept heures du matin; **a morning
paper** un journal du matin

Morocco n Maroc m; **in Morocco**
au Maroc

mortgage n hypothèque f

Moscow n Moscou; **in Moscow**
à Moscou

Moslem n musulman m,
musulmane f ▷ He's a Moslem. Il est
musulman.

mosque n mosquée f

mosquito n moustique m; **a
mosquito bite** une piqûre de
moustique

most adv, adj, pron

Use **la plupart de** when
most (of) is followed by a
plural noun and **la majeure
partie (de)** when **most (of)** is
followed by a singular noun.

❶ la plupart de ▷ *most of my friends* la plupart de mes amis ▷ *most people* la plupart des gens; **most of them** la plupart d'entre eux; **most of the time** la plupart du temps ❷ la majeure partie de ▷ *most of the work* la majeure partie du travail ▷ *most of the night* la majeure partie de la nuit; **the most** le plus ▷ *He's the one who talks the most.* C'est lui qui parle le plus.

> When **most** is followed by adjective, the translation depends on whether the noun referred to is masculine, feminine or plural.

the most ... le plus ... (f la plus ..., pl les plus ...) ▷ *the most expensive restaurant* le restaurant le plus cher ▷ *the most expensive seat* la place la plus chère; **to make the most of something** profiter au maximum de quelque chose; **at the most** au maximum ▷ *Two hours at the most.* Deux heures au maximum.

moth n papillon m de nuit

> Word for word, the French means "butterfly of the night".

mother n mère f ▷ *my mother* ma mère; **mother tongue** langue f maternelle
mother-in-law n belle-mère f (pl belles-mères)
Mother's Day n fête f des Mères
> Mother's Day is usually on the last Sunday of May in France.
motivated adj motivé(e) ▷ *He is highly motivated.* Il est très motivé.
motivation n motivation f

motor n moteur m ▷ *The boat has a motor.* Le bateau a un moteur.
motorbike n moto f
motorboat n bateau m à moteur
motorcycle n vélomoteur m
motorcyclist n motard m
motorist n automobiliste mf
motor racing n course f automobile
motorway n autoroute f ▷ *on the motorway* sur l'autoroute
mouldy adj moisi(e)
mount vb ❶ monter ▷ *They're mounting a publicity campaign.* Ils montent une campagne publicitaire. ❷ augmenter ▷ *Tension is mounting.* La tension augmente.
mountain n montagne f; **a mountain bike** un VTT (vélo tout-terrain)
mountaineer n alpiniste mf
mountaineering n alpinisme m ▷ *I go mountaineering.* Je fais de l'alpinisme.
mountainous adj montagneux (f montagneuse)
mouse n (also for computer) souris f ▷ *white mice* des souris blanches
mouse mat n tapis m de souris
mousse n ❶ (food) mousse f ▷ *chocolate mousse* la mousse au chocolat ❷ (for hair) mousse f coiffante
moustache n moustache f ▷ *He's got a moustache.* Il a une moustache.; **a man with a moustache** un moustachu
mouth n bouche f

a
b
c
d
e
f
g
h
i
j
k
l
m
n
o
p
q
r
s
t
u
v
w
x
y
z

mouthful n bouchée f
mouth organ n harmonica m
▷ I play the mouth organ. Je joue de
l'harmonica.
move n ❶ tour m ▷ It's your move.
C'est ton tour. ❷ déménagement
m ▷ Our move from Oxford to Luton ...
Notre déménagement d'Oxford
à Luton ...; **to get a move on** se
remuer ▷ Get a move on! Remue-toi!
▷ vb ❶ bouger ▷ Don't move! Ne
bouge pas! ❷ avancer ▷ The
car was moving very slowly. La
voiture avançait très lentement.
❸ émouvoir ▷ She was very moved by
the film. Elle a été très émue par ce
film.; **to move house** déménager
▷ We're moving in July. Nous allons
déménager en juillet.; **to move
forward** avancer; **to move in**
emménager ▷ They're moving in next
week. Ils emménagent la semaine
prochaine.; **to move over** se
pousser ▷ Could you move over a
bit? Est-ce que vous pouvez vous
pousser un peu?
movement n mouvement m
movie n film m; **the movies** le
cinéma ▷ Let's go to the movies! Si on
allait au cinéma?
moving adj ❶ (not stationary) en
marche ▷ a moving bus un bus en
marche ❷ (touching) touchant(e)
▷ a moving story une histoire
touchante
MP n député m ▷ She's an MP. Elle
est député.
MP3 n MP3 m ▷ an MP3 player un
lecteur de MP3

mph abbr (= miles per hour) km/h
(kilomètres-heure) ▷ to drive at
50 mph rouler à 80 km/h
● In France, speed is expressed in
● kilometres per hour. 50 mph is
● about 80 km/h.
Mr n ❶ Monsieur (pl Messieurs)
❷ (in address) M. (pl MM.)
Mrs n ❶ Madame (pl Mesdames)
❷ (in address) Mme (pl Mmes)
MS n (= multiple sclerosis) sclérose f
en plaques ▷ She's got MS. Elle a la
sclérose en plaques.
Ms n ❶ Madame (pl Mesdames)
❷ (in address) Mme (pl Mmes)
● There isn't a direct equivalent of
● Ms in French. If you are writing
● to somebody and don't know
● whether she is married, use
● Madame.
much adj, adv, pron ❶ (with verb)
beaucoup ▷ Do you go out much?
Tu sors beaucoup? ▷ I feel much
better now. Je me sens beaucoup
mieux maintenant. ❷ (followed by
noun) beaucoup de ▷ I haven't got
much money. Je n'ai pas beaucoup
d'argent.; **very much (1)** (with verb)
beaucoup ▷ Thank you very much.
Merci beaucoup. **(2)** (followed
by noun) beaucoup de ▷ I haven't
got very much money. Je n'ai pas
beaucoup d'argent.; **not much
(1)** pas beaucoup ▷ Have you got
a lot of luggage? — No, not much.
As-tu beaucoup de bagages?
— Non, pas beaucoup. **(2)** pas
grand-chose ▷ What's on TV? — Not
much. Qu'est-ce qu'il y a à la télé?

— Pas grand-chose.; **How much?** Combien? ▷ *How much do you want?* Tu en veux combien? ▷ *How much is it?* (cost) Combien est-ce que ça coûte?; **too much** ▷ *That's too much!* C'est trop! ▷ *It costs too much.* Ça coûte trop cher. ▷ *They give us too much homework.* Ils nous donnent trop de devoirs.; **so much** autant ▷ *I didn't think it would cost so much.* Je ne pensais pas que ça coûterait autant. ▷ *I've never seen so much traffic.* Je n'ai jamais vu autant de circulation.

mud n boue f

muddle n désordre m ▷ *The photos are in a muddle.* Les photos sont en désordre.

muddle up vb (people) confondre ▷ *He muddles me up with my sister.* Il me confond avec ma sœur.; **to get muddled up** s'embrouiller ▷ *I'm getting muddled up.* Je m'embrouille.

muddy adj boueux (f boueuse)

muesli n muesli m

mug n grande tasse f ▷ *Do you want a cup or a mug?* Est-ce que vous voulez une tasse normale ou une grande tasse?; **a beer mug** une chope à bière
▶ vb agresser ▷ *He was mugged in the city centre.* Il s'est fait agresser au centre ville.

mugging n agression f

multiple choice test n QCM m (questionnaire à choix multiples)

multiplication n multiplication f

multiply vb multiplier ▷ *to multiply 6 by 3* multiplier six par trois

mum n

> You use **maman** only when you are talking to your mother or using it as her name; otherwise use **mère**.

❶ mère f ▷ *my mum* ma mère ▷ *her mum* sa mère ❷ maman f ▷ *Mum! Maman!* ▷ *I'll ask Mum.* Je vais demander à maman.

mummy n ❶ (mum) maman f ▷ *Mummy says I can go.* Maman dit que je peux y aller. ❷ (Egyptian) momie f

mumps n oreillons mpl

murder n meurtre m
▶ vb assassiner ▷ *He was murdered.* Il a été assassiné.

murderer n assassin m

muscle n muscle m

museum n musée m

mushroom n champignon m ▷ *mushroom omelette* l'omelette aux champignons

music n musique f

musical adj doué(e) pour la musique ▷ *I'm not musical.* Je ne suis pas doué pour la musique.; **a musical instrument** un instrument de musique
▶ n comédie f musicale

musician n musicien m, musicienne f

Muslim n musulman m, musulmane f ▷ *He's a Muslim.* Il est musulman.

mussel n moule f

must vb

When **must** means that you assume or suppose something, use **devoir**; when it means it's necessary to do something, eg **I must buy some presents**, use **il faut que ...**, which comes from the verb **falloir** and is followed by a verb in the subjunctive.

① (*I suppose*) devoir ▷ *You must be tired.* Tu dois être fatigué. ▷ *They must have plenty of money.* Ils doivent avoir beaucoup d'argent. ▷ *There must be some problem.* Il doit y avoir un problème. **②** il faut que ▷ *I must buy some presents.* Il faut que j'achète des cadeaux. ▷ *I really must go now.* Il faut que j'y aille.; **You mustn't forget to send her a card.** N'oublie surtout pas de lui envoyer une carte.; **You must come and see us.** (*invitation*) Venez donc nous voir.

mustard n moutarde f

mustn't = **must not**

my adj mon (f ma, pl mes) ▷ *my father* mon père ▷ *my aunt* ma tante ▷ *my parents* mes parents

ma becomes **mon** before a vowel sound.

my friend (1) (*male*) mon ami **(2)** (*female*) mon amie

Do not use **mon/ma/mes** with parts of the body.

▷ *I want to wash my hair.* Je voudrais me laver les cheveux. ▷ *I'm going to clean my teeth.* Je vais me brosser les dents. ▷ *I've hurt my foot.* Je me suis fait mal au pied.

myself pron **①** me ▷ *I've hurt myself.* Je me suis fait mal. ▷ *I really enjoyed myself.* Je me suis vraiment bien amusé. ▷ *...when I look at myself in the mirror.* ...quand je me regarde dans la glace. **②** moi ▷ *I don't like talking about myself.* Je n'aime pas parler de moi. **③** moi-même ▷ *I made it myself.* Je l'ai fait moi-même.; **by myself** tout(e) seul(e) ▷ *I don't like travelling by myself.* Je n'aime pas voyager tout seul.

mysterious adj mystérieux (f mystérieuse)

mystery n mystère m; **a murder mystery** (*novel*) un roman policier

myth n **①** (*legend*) mythe m ▷ *a Greek myth* un mythe grec **②** (*untrue idea*) idée f reçue ▷ *That's a myth.* C'est une idée reçue.

n

nag vb (scold) harceler ▷ She's always nagging me. Elle me harcèle constamment.

nail n ❶ (on finger, toe) ongle m ▷ Don't bite your nails! Ne te ronge pas les ongles! ❷ (made of metal) clou m

nailbrush n brosse f à ongles

nailfile n lime f à ongles

nail scissors npl ciseaux mpl à ongles

nail varnish n vernis m à ongles; **nail varnish remover** dissolvant m

naked adj nu(e)

name n nom m; What's your name? Comment vous appelez-vous?

nanny n garde f d'enfants ▷ She's a nanny. C'est une garde d'enfants.

napkin n serviette f

nappy n couche f

narrow adj étroit(e)

nasty adj ❶ (bad) mauvais(e) ▷ a nasty cold un mauvais rhume ❷ (unfriendly) méchant(e) ▷ He gave me a nasty look. Il m'a regardé d'un air méchant.

nation n nation f

national adj national(e) (mpl nationaux) ▷ He's the national champion. C'est le champion national.; **the national elections** les élections législatives

national anthem n hymne m national

nationality n nationalité f

National Lottery® n Loterie f nationale

national park n parc m national (pl parcs nationaux)

natural adj naturel (f naturelle)

naturally adv naturellement ▷ Naturally, we were very disappointed. Nous avons naturellement été très déçus.

nature n nature f

naughty adj vilain(e) ▷ Don't be naughty! Ne fais pas le vilain!

navy n marine f ▷ He's in the navy. Il est dans la marine.

navy-blue adj bleu marine inv ▷ a navy-blue skirt une jupe bleu marine

near adj proche ▷ It's fairly near. C'est assez proche.; **It's near enough to walk.** On peut facilement y aller à pied.; **the nearest** le plus proche ▷ The nearest shops were three kilometres away. Les

magasins les plus proches étaient à trois kilomètres.
▶ prep, adv près de ▷ near my house près de chez moi; near here près d'ici ▷ Is there a bank near here? Est-ce qu'il y a une banque près d'ici?; near to près de ▷ It's very near to the school. C'est tout près de l'école.

nearby adv à proximité ▷ There's a supermarket nearby. Il y a un supermarché à proximité.
▶ adj ❶ (close) proche ▷ a nearby garage un garage proche ❷ (neighbouring) voisin(e) ▷ We went to the nearby village of Torrance. Nous sommes allés à Torrance, le village voisin.

nearly adv presque ▷ Dinner's nearly ready. Le dîner est presque prêt. ▷ I'm nearly 15. J'ai presque quinze ans.; I nearly missed the train. J'ai failli rater le train.

neat adj soigné(e) ▷ She has very neat writing. Elle a une écriture très soignée.; a neat whisky un whisky sec

neatly adv soigneusement

necessarily adv not necessarily pas forcément

necessary adj nécessaire

neck n ❶ (of body) cou m; a stiff neck un torticolis ❷ (of garment) encolure f ▷ a V-neck sweater un pull avec une encolure en V

necklace n collier m

nectarine n nectarine f

need n avoir besoin de ▷ I need a bigger size. J'ai besoin d'une plus grande taille.; to need to do

something avoir besoin de faire quelque chose ▷ I need to change some money. J'ai besoin de changer de l'argent.
▶ n There's no need to book. Il n'est pas nécessaire de réserver.

needle n aiguille f

negative n (photo) négatif m
▶ adj négatif (f négative) ▷ He's got a very negative attitude. Il a une attitude très négative.

neglected adj (untidy) mal tenu(e) ▷ The garden is neglected. Le jardin est mal tenu.

negotiate vb négocier

neighbour (US neighbor) n voisin m, voisine f ▷ the neighbours' garden le jardin des voisins

neighbourhood (US neighborhood) n quartier m

neither pron, conj, adv aucun des deux (f aucune des deux) ▷ Neither of them is coming. Aucun des deux ne vient.; neither ... nor ... ni ... ni ... ▷ Neither Sarah nor Tamsin is coming to the party. Ni Sarah ni Tamsin ne viennent à la soirée.; Neither do I. Moi non plus. ▷ I don't like him. — Neither do I! Je ne l'aime pas. — Moi non plus!; Neither have I. Moi non plus. ▷ I've never been to Spain. — Neither have I. Je ne suis jamais allé en Espagne. — Moi non plus.

nephew n neveu m (pl neveux) ▷ my nephew mon neveu

nerve n ❶ nerf m ▷ She sometimes gets on my nerves. Elle me tape quelquefois sur les nerfs. ❷ (cheek) toupet m ▷ He's got a nerve! Il a du toupet!

nervous adj (tense) tendu(e) ▷ I bite my nails when I'm nervous. Je me ronge les ongles quand je suis tendu.; **to be nervous about something** appréhender de faire quelque chose ▷ I'm a bit nervous about flying. J'appréhende un peu de prendre l'avion.

nest n nid m

Net n Net m ▷ to surf the Net surfer sur le Net

net n filet m ▷ a fishing net un filet de pêche

netball n netball m
  ● Netball is not played in France.
  ● Both sexes play basketball or volleyball instead.

Netherlands npl Pays-Bas mpl; **in the Netherlands** aux Pays-Bas

network n réseau m (pl réseaux)

never adv ❶ jamais ▷ Have you ever been to Germany? — No, never. Est-ce que tu es déjà allé en Allemagne? — Non, jamais.

> Add ne if the sentence contains a verb.

❷ ne... jamais ▷ I have never been camping. Je n'ai jamais fait de camping. ▷ Never leave valuables in your car. Ne laissez jamais d'objets de valeur dans votre voiture.; **Never again!** Plus jamais!; **Never mind.** Ça ne fait rien.

new adj ❶ nouveau (f nouvelle, pl nouveaux) ▷ her new boyfriend son nouveau copain ❷ (brand new)

neuf (f neuve) ▷ They've got a new car. Ils ont une voiture neuve.

news n ❶ nouvelles fpl ▷ I've had some bad news. J'ai reçu de mauvaises nouvelles. ❷ (single piece of news) nouvelle f ▷ That's wonderful news! Quelle bonne nouvelle! ❸ (on TV) journal m télévisé ▷ I watch the news every evening. Je regarde le journal télévisé tous les soirs. ❹ (on radio) informations fpl ▷ I listen to the news every morning. J'écoute les informations tous les matins.

newsagent n marchand m de journaux

newspaper n journal m (pl journaux) ▷ I deliver newspapers. Je distribue des journaux.

newsreader n présentateur m, présentatrice f

New Year n Nouvel An m ▷ to celebrate New Year fêter le Nouvel An; **Happy New Year!** Bonne Année!; **New Year's Day** le premier de l'An; **New Year's Eve** la Saint-Sylvestre ▷ a New Year's Eve party un réveillon du premier de l'An

New Zealand n Nouvelle-Zélande f; **in New Zealand** en Nouvelle-Zélande

New Zealander n Néo-Zélandais m, Néo-Zélandaise f

next adj, adv, prep ❶ (in time) prochain(e) ▷ next Saturday samedi prochain ▷ next year l'année prochaine ▷ next summer l'été prochain ❷ (in sequence)

suivant(e) ▷ *the next train* le train
suivant ▷ *Next please!* Au suivant!
❶ *(afterwards)* ensuite ▷ *What
shall I do next?* Qu'est-ce que je fais
ensuite?; **next to** à côté de ▷ *next
to the bank* à côté de la banque;
the next day le lendemain ▷ *The
next day we visited Versailles.* Le
lendemain nous avons visité
Versailles.; **the next time** la
prochaine fois ▷ *the next time you
see her* la prochaine fois que tu la
verras; **next door** à côté ▷ *They live
next door.* Ils habitent à côté.; **the
next room** la pièce d'à côté
NHS n Sécurité f sociale
● In France you have to pay for
medical treatment when you
receive it, and then claim it back
from the **Sécurité sociale**.
nice adj ❶ *(kind)* gentil (f gentille)
▷ *Your parents are very nice.* Tes
parents sont très gentils.; **to be
nice to somebody** être gentil avec
quelqu'un ❷ *(pretty)* joli(e) ▷ *That's
a nice dress!* Qu'est-ce qu'elle est
jolie, cette robe! ❸ *(food)* bon
(f bonne) ▷ *a nice cup of coffee* une
bonne tasse de café; **Have a
nice time!** Amuse-toi bien!; **nice
weather** le beau temps; **It's a nice
day.** Il fait beau.
nickname n surnom m
niece n nièce f ▷ *my niece* ma nièce
Nigeria n Nigéria m; **in Nigeria**
au Nigéria
night n ❶ nuit f ▷ *I want a single
room for two nights.* Je veux une
chambre à un lit pour deux nuits.;

My mother works nights. Ma mère
travaille de nuit.; **at night** la nuit;
Goodnight! Bonne nuit!; **a night
club** une boîte de nuit ❷ *(evening)*
soir m ▷ *last night* hier soir
nightie n chemise f de nuit
nightmare n cauchemar m ▷ *It
was a real nightmare!* Ça a été un vrai
cauchemar!; **to have a nightmare**
faire un cauchemar
nil n zéro m ▷ *We won one-nil.* Nous
avons gagné un à zéro.
nine num neuf ▷ *She's nine.* Elle a
neuf ans.
nineteen num dix-neuf ▷ *She's
nineteen.* Elle a dix-neuf ans.
nineteenth adj dix-neuvième ▷ *the
nineteenth floor* le dix-neuvième
étage; **the nineteenth of August**
le dix-neuf août
ninety num quatre-vingt-dix
ninth adj neuvième ▷ *the ninth floor*
le neuvième étage; **the ninth of
August** le neuf août
no adv, adj ❶ non ▷ *Are you coming?
— No.* Est-ce que vous venez? —
Non. ❷ *(not any)* pas de ▷ *There's no
hot water.* Il n'y a pas d'eau chaude.
▷ *No problem.* Pas de problème.;
I've got no idea. Je n'en ai aucune
idée.; **No way!** Pas question!;
"no smoking" "défense de fumer"
nobody pron ❶ personne ▷ *Who's
going with you? — Nobody.* Qui
t'accompagne? — Personne.
┃ Add **ne** if the sentence
┃ contains a verb.
❷ ne ... personne ▷ *There was
nobody in the office.* Il n'y avait

personne au bureau.; **Nobody likes him.** Personne ne l'aime.

nod vb (in agreement) acquiescer d'un signe de tête; **to nod at somebody** (as greeting) saluer quelqu'un d'un signe de tête

noise n bruit m ▷ Please make less noise. Faites moins de bruit s'il vous plaît.

noisy adj bruyant(e)

nominate vb ❶ (appoint) nommer ▷ She was nominated as director. Elle a été nommée directrice. ❷ (propose) proposer ▷ I nominate Ian Alexander as president of the society. Je propose Ian Alexander comme président de la société.; **He was nominated for an Oscar.** Il a été nominé pour un Oscar.

none pron ❶ aucun(e) ▷ How many sisters have you got? — None. Tu as combien de sœurs? — Aucune.

> Add **ne** if the sentence contains a verb.

❷ aucun ... ne ▷ None of my friends wanted to come. Aucun de mes amis n'a voulu venir.; **There's none left.** Il n'y en a plus.; **There are none left.** Il n'y en a plus.

nonsense n bêtises fpl ▷ She talks a lot of nonsense. Elle dit beaucoup de bêtises.

non-smoking adj non-fumeur ▷ a non-smoking carriage une voiture non-fumeurs

non-stop adj, adv ❶ direct(e) ▷ a non-stop flight un vol direct ❷ sans arrêt ▷ He talks non-stop. Il parle sans arrêt.

noodles npl nouilles fpl

noon n midi m ▷ at noon à midi

no one pron ❶ personne ▷ Who's going with you? — No one. Qui t'accompagne? — Personne.

> Add **ne** if the sentence contains a verb.

❷ ne ... personne ▷ There was no one in the office. Il n'y avait personne au bureau.; **No one likes Christopher.** Personne n'aime Christopher.

nor conj neither ... nor ni ... ni ▷ neither the cinema nor the swimming pool ni le cinéma, ni la piscine; **Nor do I.** Moi non plus. ▷ I didn't like the film. — Nor did I. Je n'ai pas aimé le film. — Moi non plus.; **Nor have I.** Moi non plus. ▷ I haven't seen him. — Nor have I. Je ne l'ai pas vu. — Moi non plus.

normal adj ❶ (usual) habituel (f habituelle) ▷ at the normal time à l'heure habituelle ❷ (standard) normal(e) (mpl normaux) ▷ a normal car une voiture normale

normally adv ❶ (usually) généralement ▷ I normally arrive at nine o'clock. J'arrive généralement à neuf heures. ❷ (as normal) normalement ▷ In spite of the strike, the airports are working normally. Malgré la grève, les aéroports fonctionnent normalement.

Normandy n Normandie f; **in Normandy** en Normandie; **to Normandy** en Normandie

north adj, adv ❶ nord inv ▷ the north coast la côte nord; **a north**

a b c d e f g h i j k l m n o p q r s t u v w x y z

wind un vent du nord ② vers le nord ▷ *We were travelling north.* Nous allions vers le nord.; **north of** au nord de ▷ *It's north of London.* C'est au nord de Londres.
▶ *n* nord m ▷ *in the north* dans le nord

North America *n* Amérique f du Nord

northeast *n* nord-est m ▷ *in the northeast* au nord-est

northern *adj* **the northern part of the island** la partie nord de l'île; **Northern Europe** l'Europe du Nord

Northern Ireland *n* Irlande f du Nord; **in Northern Ireland** en Irlande du Nord; **to Northern Ireland** en Irlande du Nord; **I'm from Northern Ireland.** Je viens d'Irlande du Nord.

North Pole *n* pôle m Nord

North Sea *n* mer f du Nord

northwest *n* nord-ouest m ▷ *in the northwest* au nord-ouest

Norway *n* Norvège f; **in Norway** en Norvège

Norwegian *adj* norvégien (f norvégienne)
▶ *n* ① *(person)* Norvégien m, Norvégienne f ② *(language)* norvégien m

nose *n* nez m *(pl* nez)

nosebleed *n* **to have a nosebleed** saigner du nez ▷ *I often get nosebleeds.* Je saigne souvent du nez.

nosy *adj* fouineur (f fouineuse)

not *adv* ① pas ▷ *Are you coming or not?* Est-ce que tu viens ou pas?;

not really pas vraiment; **not at all** pas du tout; **not yet** pas encore ▷ *Have you finished? — Not yet.* As-tu fini? — Pas encore.
▇ Add **ne** before a verb.
② ne … pas ▷ *I'm not sure.* Je ne suis pas sûr. ▷ *It's not raining.* Il ne pleut pas. ▷ *They haven't arrived yet.* Ils ne sont pas encore arrivés. ③ non ▷ *I hope not.* J'espère que non.

note *n* ① note f ▷ *to take notes* prendre des notes ② *(letter)* mot m ▷ *I'll write her a note.* Je vais lui écrire un mot. ③ *(banknote)* billet m ▷ *a £5 note* un billet de cinq livres

notebook *n* carnet m

notepad *n* bloc-notes m *(pl* blocs-notes)

nothing *n* ① rien ▷ *What's wrong? — Nothing.* Qu'est-ce qui ne va pas? — Rien. ▷ *nothing special* rien de particulier
▇ Add **ne** if the sentence contains a verb.
② ne … rien ▷ *He does nothing.* Il ne fait rien.; **Nothing is open on Sundays.** Rien n'est ouvert le dimanche.

notice *n* *(sign)* panneau m *(pl* panneaux); **to put up a notice** mettre un panneau; **a warning notice** un avertissement; **Don't take any notice of him!** Ne fais pas attention à lui!
▶ *vb* remarquer

notice board *n* panneau m d'affichage *(pl* panneaux d'affichage)

nought *n* zéro m

noun n nom m

novel n roman m

novelist n romancier m, romancière f

November n novembre m; **in November** en novembre

now adv, conj maintenant ▷ What are you doing now? Qu'est-ce que tu fais maintenant?; **just now** en ce moment ▷ I'm rather busy just now. Je suis très occupé en ce moment.; **I did it just now.** Je viens de le faire.; **He should be there by now.** Il doit être arrivé à l'heure qu'il est.; **It should be ready by now.** Ça devrait être déjà prêt.; **now and then** de temps en temps

nowhere adv nulle part ▷ nowhere else nulle part ailleurs

nuclear adj nucléaire ▷ nuclear power l'énergie nucléaire ▷ a nuclear power station une centrale nucléaire

nuisance n It's a nuisance. C'est très embêtant.; **Sorry to be a nuisance.** Désolé de vous déranger.

numb adj engourdi(e) ▷ My leg's gone numb. J'ai les jambes engourdies.; **numb with cold** engourdi par le froid

number n ❶ (total amount) nombre m ▷ a large number of people un grand nombre de gens ❷ (of house, telephone, bank account) numéro m ▷ They live at number 5. Ils habitent au numéro cinq. ▷ What's your phone number? Quel est votre numéro de téléphone?

▷ You've got the wrong number. Vous vous êtes trompé de numéro. ❸ (figure, digit) chiffre m ▷ I can't read the second number. Je n'arrive pas à lire le deuxième chiffre.

number plate n plaque f d'immatriculation

nun n religieuse f ▷ She's a nun. Elle est religieuse.

nurse n infirmier m, infirmière f ▷ She's a nurse. Elle est infirmière.

nursery n ❶ (for children) crèche f ❷ (for plants) pépinière f

nursery school n école f maternelle
 • The **école maternelle** is a state school for 2–6 year-olds.

nut n ❶ (peanut) cacahuète f ❷ (hazelnut) noisette f ❸ (walnut) noix f (pl noix) ❹ (made of metal) écrou m

nuts adj He's nuts. Il est dingue.

nylon n nylon m

a
b
c
d
e
f
g
h
i
j
k
l
n
o
p
q
r
s
t
u
v
w
x
y
z

O

oak n chêne m ▷ an oak table une table en chêne

oar n aviron m

oats n avoine f

obedient adj obéissant(e)

obey vb **to obey the rules** respecter le règlement

object n objet m ▷ a familiar object un objet familier

objection n objection f

oboe n hautbois m ▷ I play the oboe. Je joue du hautbois.

obsessed adj obsédé(e) ▷ He's obsessed with trains. Il est obsédé par les trains.

obsession n obsession f
▷ It's getting to be an obsession with you. Ça devient une obsession chez toi.; **Football's an obsession of mine.** Le football est une de mes passions.

obtain vb obtenir

obvious adj évident(e)

obviously adv ❶ (of course) évidemment ▷ Do you want to pass the exam? — Obviously! Tu veux être reçu à l'examen? — Évidemment!; **Obviously not!** Bien sûr que non! ❷ (visibly) manifestement ▷ She was obviously exhausted. Elle était manifestement épuisée.

occasion n occasion f ▷ a special occasion une occasion spéciale; **on several occasions** à plusieurs reprises

occasionally adv de temps en temps

occupation n profession f

occupy vb occuper ▷ That seat is occupied. Cette place est occupée.

occur vb (happen) avoir lieu
▷ The accident occurred yesterday. L'accident a eu lieu hier.; **It suddenly occurred to me that ...** Il m'est soudain venu à l'esprit que ...

ocean n océan m

o'clock adv **at four o'clock** à quatre heures; **It's five o'clock.** Il est cinq heures.

October n octobre m; **in October** en octobre

octopus n pieuvre f

odd adj ❶ bizarre ▷ That's odd! C'est bizarre! ❷ impair(e) ▷ an odd number un chiffre impair

of prep

de changes to **d'** before a vowel and most words beginning with "h". **de + le** changes to **du**, and **de + les** changes to **des**. ① de, d', du, des ▷ *a boy of ten* un garçon de dix ans ▷ *a kilo of oranges* un kilo d'oranges ▷ *the end of the film* la fin du film ▷ *the end of the holidays* la fin des vacances ② (*with quantity, amount*) en ▷ *Can I have half of that?* Je peux en avoir la moitié?; **three of us** trois d'entre nous; **a friend of mine** un de mes amis; **the 14th of September** le quatorze septembre; **That's very kind of you.** C'est très gentil de votre part.; **It's made of wood.** C'est en bois.

off adv, prep, adj
For other expressions with **off**, see the verbs **get**, **take**, **turn** etc. ① (*heater, light, TV*) éteint(e) ▷ *All the lights are off.* Toutes les lumières sont éteintes. ② (*tap, gas*) fermé(e) ▷ *Are you sure the tap is off?* Tu es sûr que le robinet est fermé? ③ (*cancelled*) annulé(e) ▷ *The match is off.* Le match est annulé.; **to be off sick** être malade; **a day off** un jour de congé ▷ *to take a day off work* prendre un jour de congé; **She's off school today.** Elle n'est pas à l'école aujourd'hui.; **I must be off now.** Je dois m'en aller maintenant.; **I'm off.** Je m'en vais.

offence (*US* offense) n (*crime*) délit m

offer n proposition f ▷ *a good offer* une proposition intéressante; **"on special offer"** "en promotion"
▶ vb proposer ▷ *He offered to help me.* Il m'a proposé de m'aider.

office n bureau m (pl bureaux) ▷ *She works in an office.* Elle travaille dans un bureau.

officer n officier m

official adj officiel (f officielle)

off-licence n marchand m de vins et spiritueux

offside adj (*in football*) hors jeu

often adv souvent ▷ *It often rains.* Il pleut souvent. ▷ *How often do you go to the gym?* Tu vas souvent à la gym?

oil n ① (*for lubrication, cooking*) huile f; **an oil painting** une peinture à l'huile ② (*crude oil*) pétrole m ▷ *North Sea oil* le pétrole de la mer du Nord
▶ vb graisser

oil rig n plateforme f pétrolière ▷ *He works on an oil rig.* Il travaille sur une plateforme pétrolière.

ointment n pommade m

okay excl, adj (*agreed*) d'accord ▷ *Could you call back later?* — *Okay!* Tu peux rappeler plus tard? — D'accord! ▷ *Is that okay?* C'est d'accord?; **I'll do it tomorrow, if that's okay with you.** Je le ferai demain, si tu es d'accord.; **Are you okay?** Ça va?; **How was your holiday?** — **It was okay.** C'était comment tes vacances? — Pas mal.; **What's your teacher like?** — **He's okay.** Il est comment ton prof? — Il est sympa. (*informal*)

old *adj* ❶ vieux, vieil (*f* vieille)

> vieux changes to **vieil** before a vowel and most words beginning with "h".

▷ *an old dog* un vieux chien ▷ *an old man* un vieil homme ▷ *an old house* une vieille maison

> When talking about people it is more polite to use **âgé** instead of **vieux**.

❷ âgé(e) ▷ *old people* les personnes âgées ❸ (*former*) ancien (*f* ancienne) ▷ *my old English teacher* mon ancien professeur d'anglais; **How old are you?** Quel âge as-tu?; **He's ten years old.** Il a dix ans.; **my older brother** mon frère aîné ▷ *my older sister* ma sœur aînée; **She's two years older than me.** Elle a deux ans de plus que moi.; **I'm the oldest in the family.** Je suis l'aîné de la famille.

old age pensioner *n* retraité *m*, retraitée *f* ▷ *She's an old age pensioner.* Elle est retraitée.

old-fashioned *adj* ❶ démodé(e) ▷ *She wears old-fashioned clothes.* Elle porte des vêtements démodés. ❷ (*person*) vieux jeu *inv* ▷ *My parents are old-fashioned.* Mes parents sont vieux jeu.

olive *n* olive *f*

olive oil *n* huile *f* d'olive

Olympic *adj* olympique; **the Olympics** les Jeux olympiques

omelette *n* omelette *f*

on *prep, adv*

> There are several ways of translating **on**. Scan the examples to find one that is similar to what you want to say. For other expressions with **on**, see the verbs **go**, **put**, **turn** etc.

❶ sur ▷ *on the table* sur la table ❷ à ▷ *on the left* à gauche ▷ *on the 2nd floor* au deuxième étage ▷ *I go to school on my bike.* Je vais à l'école à vélo.; *on TV* à la télé ▷ *What's on TV?* Qu'est-ce qu'il y a à la télé?; **on the radio** à la radio ▷ *I heard it on the radio.* Je l'ai entendu à la radio.; **on the bus (1)** (*by bus*) en bus ▷ *I go into town on the bus.* Je vais en ville en bus. **(2)** (*inside*) dans le bus ▷ *There were no empty seats on the bus.* Il n'y avait pas de places libres dans le bus.; **on holiday** en vacances ▷ *They're on holiday.* Ils sont en vacances.; **on strike** en grève

> With days and dates **on** is not translated.

▷ *on Friday* vendredi ▷ *on Fridays* le vendredi ▷ *on Christmas Day* le jour de Noël ▷ *on my birthday* le jour de mon anniversaire

▶ *adj* ❶ (*heater, light, TV*) allumé(e) ▷ *I think I left the light on.* Je crois que j'ai laissé la lumière allumée. ❷ (*tap, gas*) ouvert(e) ▷ *Leave the tap on.* Laisse le robinet ouvert. ❸ (*machine*) en marche ▷ *Is the dishwasher on?* Est-ce que le lave-vaisselle est en marche?; **What's**

on at the cinema? Qu'est-ce qui passe au cinéma?

once adv une fois ▷ once a week une fois par semaine ② once more encore une fois; **Once upon a time ...** Il était une fois ...; **at once** tout de suite; **once in a while** de temps en temps

one num, pron

Use un for masculine nouns and une for feminine nouns.

① un, une ▷ one day un jour ▷ Do you need a stamp? — No thanks, I've got one. Est-ce que tu as besoin d'un timbre? — Non merci, j'en ai un. ▷ one minute une minute ▷ I've got one brother and one sister. J'ai un frère et une sœur. ② (impersonal) on ▷ One never knows. On ne sait jamais.; **this one (1)** (masculine) celui-ci ▷ Which foot is hurting? — This one. Quel pied te fait mal? — Celui-ci. **(2)** (feminine) celle-ci ▷ Which is the best photo? — This one. Quelle est la meilleure photo? — Celle-ci.; **that one (1)** (masculine) celui-là ▷ Which bag is yours? — That one. Lequel est ton sac? — Celui-là. **(2)** (feminine) celle-là ▷ Which seat do you want? — That one. Quelle place voulez-vous? — Celle-là.

oneself pron ① se ▷ to hurt oneself se faire mal ② soi-même ▷ It's quicker to do it oneself. C'est plus rapide de le faire soi-même.

one-way adj **a one-way street** une impasse

onion n oignon m ▷ onion soup la soupe à l'oignon

only adv, adj, conj ① seul(e) ▷ French is the only subject I like. Le français est la seule matière que j'aime. ② seulement ▷ How much was it? — Only 10 euros. Combien c'était? — Seulement dix euros. ③ ne ... que ▷ We only want to stay for one night. Nous ne voulons rester qu'une nuit. ④ mais ▷ I'd like the same sweater, only in black. Je voudrais le même pull, mais en noir.; **an only child** un enfant unique

onwards adv à partir de ▷ from July onwards à partir de juillet

open adj ouvert(e) ▷ The baker's is open on Sunday morning. La boulangerie est ouverte le dimanche matin.; **in the open air** en plein air

▶ vb ① ouvrir ▷ Can I open the window? Est-ce que je peux ouvrir la fenêtre? ▷ What time do the shops open? Les magasins ouvrent à quelle heure? ② s'ouvrir ▷ The door opens automatically. La porte s'ouvre automatiquement.

opening hours npl heures fpl d'ouverture

opera n opéra m

operate vb ① fonctionner ▷ I don't know how the electoral system operates in France. Je ne sais pas comment fonctionne le système électoral en France. ② faire fonctionner ▷ How do you operate the video? Comment fait-on fonctionner le magnétoscope? ③ (medically) opérer; **to operate on someone** opérer quelqu'un

a
b
c
d
e
f
g
h
i
j
k
l
m
n
o
p
q
r
s
t
u
v
w
x
y
z

operation n opération f ▷ a major
operation une grave opération; **to
have an operation** se faire opérer
▷ I have never had an operation. Je ne
me suis jamais fait opérer.

opinion n avis m ▷ in my opinion à
mon avis ▷ He asked me my opinion.
Il m'a demandé mon avis.; **What's
your opinion?** Qu'est-ce que vous
en pensez?

opinion poll n sondage m

opponent n adversaire mf

opportunity n occasion f; **to
have the opportunity to do
something** avoir l'occasion de
faire quelque chose ▷ I've never
had the opportunity to go to France.
Je n'ai jamais eu l'occasion d'aller
en France.

opposed adj I've always been
opposed to violence. J'ai toujours
été contre la violence.; **as
opposed to** par opposition à

opposite adj, adv, prep ❶ opposé(e)
▷ It's in the opposite direction. C'est
dans la direction opposée. ❷ en
face ▷ They live opposite. Ils habitent
en face. ❸ en face de ▷ the girl
sitting opposite me la fille assise en
face de moi; **the opposite sex**
l'autre sexe

opposition n opposition f

optician n opticien m, opticienne
f ▷ She's an optician. Elle est
opticienne.

optimistic adj optimiste

option n ❶ (choice) choix m ▷ I've
got no option. Je n'ai pas le choix.
❷ (optional subject) matière f à

option ▷ I'm doing geography as
my option. La géographie est ma
matière à option.

or conj ❶ ou ▷ Would you like tea or
coffee? Est-ce que tu veux du thé
ou du café?

⎪ Use **ni ... ni** in negative
⎪ sentences.

▷ I don't eat meat or fish. Je ne mange
ni viande, ni poisson. ❷ (otherwise)
sinon ▷ Hurry up or you'll miss the
bus. Dépêche-toi, sinon tu vas
rater le bus.; **Give me the money,
or else!** Donne-moi l'argent, sinon
tu vas le regretter!

oral adj oral(e) (mpl oraux); **an oral
exam** un oral

▶ n oral m (pl oraux) ▷ I've got my
French oral soon. Je vais bientôt
passer mon oral de français.

orange n orange f; **an orange
juice** un jus d'orange

▶ adj orange inv

orchard n verger m

orchestra n orchestre m ▷ I play
in the school orchestra. Je joue dans
l'orchestre de l'école.

order n ❶ (sequence) ordre m ▷ in
alphabetical order dans l'ordre
alphabétique ❷ (instruction)
commande f ▷ The waiter took
our order. Le garçon a pris notre
commande.; **in order to** pour ▷ He
does it in order to earn money. Il le fait
pour gagner de l'argent.; **"out of
order"** "en panne"

▶ vb commander ▷ Are you
ready to order? Vous êtes prêt à
commander?; **to order somebody**

about donner des ordres à quelqu'un ▷ *She was fed up with being ordered about.* Elle en avait marre qu'on lui donne des ordres en permanence.

ordinary adj ❶ ordinaire ▷ *an ordinary day* une journée ordinaire ❷ (people) comme les autres ▷ *an ordinary family* une famille comme les autres

organ n (instrument) orgue m ▷ *I play the organ.* Je joue de l'orgue.

organic adj (vegetables, fruit) biologique

organization n organisation f

organize vb organiser

original adj original(e) (mpl originaux) ▷ *It's a very original idea.* C'est une idée très originale. ▷ *Our original plan was to go camping.* À l'origine nous avions l'intention de faire du camping.

originally adv à l'origine

Orkneys npl Orcades fpl; **in the Orkneys** dans les Orcades

ornament n bibelot m

orphan n orphelin m, orpheline f

other adj, pron autre ▷ *Have you got these jeans in other colours?* Est-ce que vous avez ce jean dans d'autres couleurs? ▷ *the other day* l'autre jour; **the other one** l'autre ▷ *This one? — No, the other one.* Celui-ci? — Non, l'autre.; **the others** les autres ▷ *The others are going but I'm not.* Les autres y vont mais pas moi.

otherwise adv, conj ❶ (if not) sinon ▷ *Note down the number, otherwise you'll forget it.* Note le numéro,

sinon tu vas l'oublier. ❷ (in other ways) à part ça ▷ *I'm tired, but otherwise I'm fine.* Je suis fatigué, mais à part ça, ça va.

ought vb

> To translate **ought to** use the conditional tense of **devoir**.
>
> ▷ *I ought to phone my parents.* Je devrais appeler mes parents.

our adj notre (pl nos) ▷ *Our house is quite big.* Notre maison est plutôt grande.

ours pron le nôtre (f la nôtre, pl les nôtres) ▷ *Your garden is very big, ours is much smaller.* Votre jardin est très grand, le nôtre est beaucoup plus petit. ▷ *Your school is very different from ours.* Votre école est très différente de la nôtre. ▷ *Our teachers are strict. — Ours are too.* Nos professeurs sont sévères. — Les nôtres aussi.; **Is this ours?** C'est à nous? ▷ *This car is ours.* Cette voiture est à nous.

ourselves pron ❶ nous ▷ *We really enjoyed ourselves.* Nous nous sommes vraiment bien amusés. ❷ nous-mêmes ▷ *We built our garage ourselves.* Nous avons construit notre garage nous-mêmes.

out adv

> There are several ways of translating **out**. Scan the examples to find one that is similar to what you want to say. For other expressions with **out**, see the verbs **go**, **put**, **turn** etc.

❶ (*outside*) <u>dehors</u> ▷ *It's cold out.*
Il fait froid dehors. ❷ (*light, fire*)
<u>éteint(e)</u> ▷ *All the lights are out.*
Toutes les lumières sont éteintes.;
She's out. Elle est sortie.; **She's
out shopping.** Elle est sortie faire
des courses.; **She's out for the
afternoon.** Elle ne sera pas là
de tout l'après-midi.; **out there**
dehors ▷ *It's cold out there.* Il fait
froid dehors.; **to go out** sortir ▷ *I'm
going out tonight.* Je sors ce soir.; **to
go out with somebody** sortir avec
quelqu'un ▷ *I've been going out with
him for two months.* Je sors avec lui
depuis deux mois.; **out of** ❶ dans
▷ *to drink out of a glass* boire dans
un verre **(2)** sur ▷ *in 9 cases out of 10*
dans neuf cas sur dix **(3)** en dehors
de ▷ *He lives out of town.* Il habite
en dehors de la ville.; **3 km out of
town** à trois kilomètres de la ville;
out of curiosity par curiosité; **out
of work** sans emploi; **That is out
of the question.** C'est hors de
question.; **You're out!** (*in game*)
Tu es éliminé!; **"way out"** "sortie"

outdoor *adj* en plein air ▷ *an
outdoor swimming pool* une piscine
en plein air; **outdoor activities** les
activités de plein air

outdoors *adv* au grand air

outfit *n* tenue f ▷ *She bought a
new outfit for the wedding.* Elle a
acheté une nouvelle tenue pour
le mariage.; **a cowboy outfit** une
panoplie de cowboy

outing *n* sortie f ▷ *to go on an outing*
faire une sortie

outline *n* ❶ (*summary*) <u>grandes
lignes</u> *fpl* ▷ *This is an outline of
the plan.* Voici les grandes lignes
du projet. ❷ (*shape*) <u>contours</u>
mpl ▷ *We could see the outline of
the mountain in the mist.* Nous
distinguions les contours de la
montagne dans la brume.

outside *n* extérieur *m*
▶ *adj, adv, prep* ❶ extérieur(e) ▷ *the
outside walls* les murs extérieurs
❷ dehors ▷ *It's very cold outside.* Il
fait très froid dehors.; **en dehors
de** ▷ *outside the school* en dehors
de l'école ▷ *outside school hours* en
dehors des heures de cours

outskirts *npl* banlieue f ▷ *on
the outskirts of the town* dans les
banlieues de la ville

outstanding *adj* remarquable

oval *adj* ovale

oven *n* four *m*

over *prep, adv, adj*

> When there is movement over
> something, use **par-dessus**;
> when something is located
> above something, use **au-
> dessus de**.

❶ par-dessus ▷ *The ball went
over the wall.* Le ballon est passé
par-dessus le mur. ❷ au-dessus de
▷ *There's a mirror over the washbasin.*
Il y a une glace au-dessus du
lavabo. ❸ (*more than*) plus de ▷ *It's
over twenty kilos.* Ça pèse plus de
vingt kilos. ▷ *The temperature was
over thirty degrees.* Il faisait une
température de plus de trente
degrés. ❹ (*during*) pendant ▷ *over*

the holidays pendant les vacances
③ *(finished)* terminé(e) ▷ *I'll be
happy when the exams are over.* Je
serai content quand les examens
seront terminés.; **over here**
ici; **over there** là-bas; **all over
Scotland** dans toute l'Écosse;
The baker's is over the road. La
boulangerie est de l'autre côté de
la rue.; **I spilled coffee over my
shirt.** J'ai renversé du café sur ma
chemise.

overcast *adj* couvert(e) ▷ *The sky
was overcast.* Le ciel était couvert.

overdose *n (of drugs)* overdose *f*
▷ *to take an overdose* prendre une
overdose

overdraft *n* découvert *m*; **to have
an overdraft** être à découvert

overseas *adv* à l'étranger ▷ *I'd
like to work overseas.* J'aimerais
travailler à l'étranger.

overtake *vb* dépasser

overtime *n* heures *fpl*
supplémentaires ▷ *to work overtime*
faire des heures supplémentaires

overtook *vb see* **overtake**

overweight *adj* trop gros (*f* trop
grosse)

owe *vb* devoir; **to owe somebody
something** devoir quelque chose à
quelqu'un ▷ *I owe you 50 euros.* Je te
dois cinquante euros.

owing to *prep* en raison de
▷ *owing to bad weather* en raison du
mauvais temps

owl *n* hibou *m* (*pl* hiboux)

own *adj* propre ▷ *I've got my own
bathroom.* J'ai ma propre salle de

bain.; **I'd like a room of my own.**
J'aimerais avoir une chambre à
moi.; **on his own** tout seul ▷ **on her
own** toute seule
▶ *vb* posséder

own up *vb* avouer; **to own up to
something** admettre quelque
chose

owner *n* propriétaire *mf*

oxygen *n* oxygène *m*

oyster *n* huître *f*

ozone layer *n* couche *f* d'ozone

a
b
c
d
e
f
g
h
i
j
k
l
m
n
o
p
q
r
s
t
u
v
w
x
y
z

P

Pacific n Pacifique m

pack vb faire ses bagages ▷ I'll help you pack. Je vais t'aider à faire tes bagages.; **I've already packed my case.** J'ai déjà fait ma valise.; **Pack it in!** (stop it) Laisse tomber!
► n ❶ (packet) paquet m ▷ a pack of cigarettes un paquet de cigarettes ❷ (of yoghurts, cans) pack m ▷ a six-pack un pack de six; **a pack of cards** un jeu de cartes

package n paquet m; **a package holiday** un voyage organisé

packed adj bondé(e) ▷ The cinema was packed. Le cinéma était bondé.

packed lunch n repas m froid ▷ I take a packed lunch to school. J'apporte un repas froid à l'école.

packet n paquet m ▷ a packet of cigarettes un paquet de cigarettes

pad n (notepad) bloc-notes m (pl blocs-notes)

paddle vb ❶ (canoe) pagayer ❷ (in water) faire trempette
► n (for canoe) pagaie f; **to go for a paddle** faire trempette

padlock n cadenas m

paedophile n pédophile m

page n (of book) page f
► vb **to page somebody** faire appeler quelqu'un

pain n douleur f ▷ a terrible pain. une douleur insupportable; **I've got a pain in my stomach.** J'ai mal à l'estomac.; **to be in pain** souffrir ▷ She's in a lot of pain. Elle souffre beaucoup.; **He's a real pain.** Il est vraiment pénible.

painful adj douloureux (f douloureuse) ▷ to suffer from painful periods souffrir de règles douloureuses; **Is it painful?** Ça te fait mal?

painkiller n analgésique m

paint n peinture f
► vb peindre ▷ to paint something green peindre quelque chose en vert

paintbrush n pinceau m (pl pinceaux)

painter n peintre m

painting n ❶ peinture f ▷ My hobby is painting. Je fais de la peinture. ❷ (picture) tableau m (pl tableaux) ▷ a painting by Picasso un tableau de Picasso

pair n paire f ▷ a pair of shoes une paire de chaussures; **a pair of trousers** un pantalon; **a pair of jeans** un jean;

a pair of pants (1) (*briefs*) un slip
(2) (*boxer shorts*) un caleçon; **in
pairs** deux par deux ▷ *We work in
pairs.* On travaille deux par deux.
Pakistan *n* Pakistan *m*; **in
Pakistan** au Pakistan; **to Pakistan**
au Pakistan; **He's from Pakistan.**
Il est pakistanais.
Pakistani *n* Pakistanais *m*,
Pakistanaise *f*
▶ *adj* pakistanais(e)
palace *n* palais *m*
pale *adj* pâle ▷ *a pale blue shirt* une
chemise bleu pâle
Palestine *n* Palestine *f*; **in
Palestine** en Palestine
Palestinian *adj* palestinien
(*f* palestinienne)
▶ *n* Palestinien *m*, Palestinienne *f*
palm *n* (*of hand*) paume *f*; **a palm
tree** un palmier
pan *n* ❶ (*saucepan*) casserole *f*
❷ (*frying pan*) poêle *f*
pancake *n* crêpe *f*; **Pancake Day**
mardi gras
● **Pancake Day** is celebrated in
France as well. Children dress up
and eat pancakes (**crêpes**).
panic *n* panique *f*
▶ *vb* s'affoler ▷ *Don't panic!* Pas de
panique!
panther *n* panthère *f*
pantomime *n* spectacle *m* de Noël
pour enfants
pants *npl* ❶ (*briefs*) slip *m* ▷ *a pair of
pants* un slip ❷ (*boxer shorts*)
caleçon *m* ▷ *a pair of pants* un
caleçon ❸ (*US: trousers*) pantalon
m ▷ *a pair of pants* un pantalon

pantyhose *npl* (*US*) collant *m*
paper *n* ❶ papier *m* ▷ *a piece
of paper* un morceau de papier
▷ *a paper towel* une serviette en
papier ❷ (*newspaper*) journal *m*
(*pl* journaux) ▷ *I saw an advert in
the paper.* J'ai vu une annonce dans
le journal.; **an exam paper** une
épreuve écrite
paperback *n* livre *m* de poche
paper clip *n* trombone *m*
paper round *n* tournée *f* de
distribution de journaux
parachute *n* parachute *m*
parade *n* défilé *m*
paradise *n* paradis *m*
paragraph *n* paragraphe *m*
parallel *adj* parallèle
paralysed *adj* paralysé(e)
paramedic *n* auxiliaire *m* médical,
auxiliaire *f* médicale
parcel *n* colis *m*
pardon *n* **Pardon?** Pardon?
parent *n* ❶ (*father*) père *m*
❷ (*mother*) mère *f*; **my parents**
mes parents *mpl*
Paris *n* Paris *f*; **in Paris** à Paris; **to
Paris** à Paris; **She's from Paris.** Elle
est parisienne.
Parisian *adj* parisien (*f* parisienne)
▶ *n* Parisien *m*, Parisienne *f*
park *n* parc *m*; **a national park** un
parc national; **a theme park** un parc
à thème; **a car park** un parking
▶ *vb* ❶ garer ▷ *Where can I park my
car?* Où est-ce que je peux garer ma
voiture? ❷ se garer ▷ *We couldn't
find anywhere to park.* Nous avons
eu du mal à nous garer.

parking n stationnement m ▷ *"no parking"* "stationnement interdit"

> Be careful not to translate **parking** by the French word **parking**.

parking lot n (US) parking m
parking meter n parcmètre m
parking ticket n p.-v. m (informal)
parliament n parlement m
parole n **on parole** en liberté conditionnelle
parrot n perroquet m
parsley n persil m
part n ❶ (section) partie f ▷ *The first part of the film was boring.* La première partie du film était ennuyeuse. ❷ (component) pièce f ▷ *spare parts* les pièces de rechange ❸ (in play, film) rôle m; **to take part in something** participer à quelque chose ▷ *A lot of people took part in the demonstration.* Beaucoup de gens ont participé à la manifestation.
particular adj particulier (f particulière) ▷ *Are you looking for anything particular?* Est-ce que vous voulez quelque chose de particulier?; **nothing in particular** rien de particulier
particularly adv particulièrement
partly adv en partie
partner n ❶ (in game) partenaire mf ❷ (in business) associé m, associée f ❸ (in dance) cavalier m, cavalière f ❹ (boyfriend/girlfriend) compagnon m, compagne f
part-time adj, adv à temps partiel ▷ *a part-time job* un travail à temps partiel ▷ *She works part-time.* Elle

travaille à temps partiel.
party n ❶ fête f ▷ *a birthday party* une fête d'anniversaire ❷ (more formal) soirée f ▷ *I'm going to a party on Saturday.* Je vais à une soirée samedi. ❶ (political) parti m ▷ *the Conservative Party* le Parti conservateur ❹ (group) groupe m ▷ *a party of tourists* un groupe de touristes
pass n ❶ (in mountains) col m ▷ *The pass was blocked with snow.* Le col était enneigé. ❷ (in football) passe f; **to get a pass** (in exam) être reçu ▷ *I got six passes.* J'ai été reçu dans six matières.; **a bus pass** une carte de bus
> ▶ vb ❶ (exam) être reçu(e) ▷ *to pass an exam* être reçu à un examen ▷ *Did you pass?* Tu as été reçu? ❷ passer ▷ *Could you pass me the salt, please?* Est-ce que vous pourriez me passer le sel, s'il vous plaît? ▷ *The time has passed quickly.* Le temps a passé rapidement. ❶ passer devant ▷ *I pass his house on my way to school.* Je passe devant chez lui en allant à l'école.

> Be careful not to translate **to pass an exam** by **passer un examen**.

pass out vb (faint) s'évanouir
passage n ❶ (piece of writing) passage m ▷ *Read the passage carefully.* Lisez attentivement le passage. ❷ (corridor) couloir m
passenger n passager m, passagère f
passion n passion f

passive adj passif (f passive);
passive smoking le tabagisme
passif

Passover n Pâque f juive ▷ at
Passover à la Pâque juive

passport n passeport m ▷ passport
control le contrôle des passeports

password n mot m de passe

past adv, prep (beyond) après ▷ It's on
the right, just past the station. C'est
sur la droite, juste après la gare.;
to go past (1) passer ▷ The bus
went past without stopping. Le bus
est passé sans s'arrêter. **(2)** passer
devant ▷ The bus goes past our house.
Le bus passe devant notre maison.;
It's half past ten. Il est dix heures
et demie.; **It's quarter past nine.**
Il est neuf heures et quart.; **It's ten
past eight.** Il est huit heures dix.;
It's past midnight. Il est minuit
passé.
▶ n passé m ▷ She lives in the past.
Elle vit dans le passé.; **in the past**
(previously) autrefois ▷ This was
common in the past. C'était courant
autrefois.

pasta n pâtes fpl ▷ Pasta is easy
to cook. Les pâtes sont faciles à
préparer.

pasteurized adj pasteurisé(e)

pastry n pâte f; **pastries** les
pâtisseries fpl

patch n ❶ pièce f ▷ a patch of
material une pièce de tissu ❷ (for
flat tyre) rustine f; **He's got a bald
patch.** Il a le crâne dégarni.

path n ❶ (footpath) chemin m
❷ (in garden, park) allée f

pathetic adj lamentable ▷ Our
team was pathetic. Notre équipe a
été lamentable.

patience n ❶ patience f ▷ He
hasn't got much patience. Il n'a pas
beaucoup de patience. ❷ (card
game) réussite f ▷ to play patience
faire une réussite

patient n patient m, patiente f
▶ adj patient(e)

patio n patio m

patrol n patrouille f

patrol car n voiture f de police

pattern n motif m ▷ a geometric
pattern un motif géométrique;
a sewing pattern un patron

pause n pause f

pavement n trottoir m

paw n patte f

pay n salaire m
▶ vb ❶ payer ▷ They pay me more
on Sundays. Je suis payé davantage
le dimanche. ❷ régler ▷ to pay
by cheque régler par chèque ▷ to
pay by credit card régler par carte
de crédit; **to pay for something**
payer quelque chose ▷ I paid for
my ticket. J'ai payé mon billet.; **to
pay extra for something** payer un
supplément pour quelque chose
▷ You have to pay extra for parking.
Il faut payer un supplément pour
le parking.; **to pay attention** faire
attention ▷ Don't pay any attention
to him! Ne fais pas attention à lui!;
to pay somebody a visit rendre
visite à quelqu'un ▷ Paul paid us a
visit last night. Paul nous a rendu
visite hier soir.; **to pay somebody**

back rembourser quelqu'un
▷ *I'll pay you back tomorrow.* Je te
rembourserai demain.

payment n paiement m

payphone n téléphone m public

PC n (= personal computer) PC m ▷ *She
typed the report on her PC.* Elle a tapé
le rapport sur son PC.

PDA n (= personal digital assistant)
agenda m électronique

PE n EPS f ▷ *We do PE twice a week.*
Nous avons EPS deux fois par
semaine.

pea n petit pois m

peace n ❶ (after war) paix f
❷ (quietness) calme m

peaceful adj ❶ (calm) paisible
▷ *a peaceful afternoon* un après-
midi paisible ❷ (not violent)
pacifique ▷ *a peaceful protest* une
manifestation pacifique

peach n pêche f

peacock n paon m

peak n (of mountain) cime f; **the
peak rate** le plein tarif ▷ *You pay
the peak rate for calls at this time of
day.* On paie le plein tarif quand on
appelle à cette heure-ci.; **in peak
season** en haute saison

peanut n cacahuète f ▷ *a packet of
peanuts* un paquet de cacahuètes

peanut butter n beurre m de
cacahuètes ▷ *a peanut-butter
sandwich* un sandwich au beurre de
cacahuètes

pear n poire f

pearl n perle f

pebble n galet m ▷ *a pebble beach*
une plage de galets

peculiar adj bizarre ▷ *He's a peculiar
person.* Il est bizarre. ▷ *It tastes
peculiar.* Ça a un goût bizarre.

pedal n pédale f

pedestrian n piéton m

pedestrian crossing n passage
m pour piétons

pee n **to have a pee** faire pipi

peel n (of orange) écorce f
▶ vb ❶ éplucher ▷ *Shall I peel the
potatoes?* J'épluche les pommes de
terre? ❷ peler ▷ *My nose is peeling.*
Mon nez pèle.

peg n ❶ (for coats) portemanteau m
(pl portemanteaux) ❷ (clothes peg)
pince f à linge ❸ (tent peg) piquet m

pelvis n bassin m

pen n stylo m

penalty n ❶ (punishment) peine f;
the death penalty la peine de
mort ❷ (in football) penalty m
❸ (in rugby) pénalité f; **a penalty
shoot-out** les tirs au but

pence npl pence mpl

pencil n crayon m; **in pencil** au
crayon

pencil case n trousse f

pencil sharpener n taille-
crayon m

pendant n pendentif m

penfriend n correspondant m,
correspondante f

penguin n pingouin m

penicillin n pénicilline f

penis n pénis m

penknife n canif m

penny n penny m (pl pence)

pension n retraite f

pensioner n retraité m, retraitée f

people npl ❶ gens mpl ▷ a lot
of people beaucoup de gens
❷ (individuals) personnes fpl
▷ six people six personnes; **How
many people are there in your
family?** Vous êtes combien dans
votre famille?; **French people** les
Français; **black people** les Noirs;
People say that ... On dit que ...

pepper n ❶ (spice) poivre m ▷ Pass
the pepper, please. Passez-moi le
poivre, s'il vous plaît. ❷ (vegetable)
poivron m ▷ a green pepper un
poivron vert

peppermill n moulin m à poivre

peppermint n (sweet) pastille f
de menthe; **peppermint
chewing gum** le chewing-gum à
la menthe

per prep par ▷ per day par jour ▷ per
week par semaine; **30 miles per
hour** trente miles à l'heure

per cent adv pour cent ▷ fifty per
cent cinquante pour cent

percentage n pourcentage m

percussion n percussion f ▷ I play
percussion. Je joue des percussions.

perfect adj parfait(e) ▷ Chantal
speaks perfect English. Chantal parle
un anglais parfait.

perfectly adv parfaitement

perform vb (act, play) jouer

performance n ❶ (show)
spectacle m ▷ The performance lasts
two hours. Le spectacle dure deux
heures. ❷ (acting) interprétation
f ▷ his performance as Hamlet
son interprétation d'Hamlet
❸ (results) performance f ▷ the

team's poor performance la médiocre
performance de l'équipe

perfume n parfum m

perhaps adv peut-être ▷ Perhaps
he's ill. Il est peut-être malade.;
perhaps not peut-être pas

period n ❶ période f ▷ for a
limited period pour une période
limitée ❷ (in history) époque
f ▷ the Victorian period l'époque
victorienne ❸ (menstruation)
règles fpl ▷ I'm having my period. J'ai
mes règles. ❹ (lesson time) cours
m ▷ Each period lasts forty minutes.
Chaque cours dure quarante
minutes.

perm n permanente f ▷ She's got
a perm. Elle a une permanente.;
to have a perm se faire faire une
permanente

permanent adj permanent(e)

permission n permission f ▷ Could
I have permission to leave early?
Pourrais-je avoir la permission de
partir plus tôt?

permit n permis m ▷ a fishing permit
un permis de pêche

persecute vb persécuter

person n personne f ▷ She's a very
nice person. C'est une personne
très sympathique.; **in person** en
personne

personal adj personnel (f
personnelle); **personal column** les
annonces personnelles

personality n personnalité f

personally adv personnellement
▷ I don't know him personally. Je ne le
connais pas personnellement.

personal stereo n walkman® m

perspiration n transpiration f

persuade vb persuader; **to persuade somebody to do something** persuader quelqu'un de faire quelque chose ▷ *She persuaded me to go with her.* Elle m'a persuadé de l'accompagner.

pessimistic adj pessimiste

pest n (person) casse-pieds mf ▷ *He's a real pest!* C'est un vrai casse-pieds!

pester vb importuner

pet n animal familier ▷ *Have you got a pet?* Est-ce que tu as un animal familier?; **She's the teacher's pet.** C'est la chouchoute de la maîtresse.

petrol n essence f; **unleaded petrol** l'essence sans plomb

> Be careful not to translate **petrol** by pétrole.

petrol station n station-service f (pl stations-service)

pharmacy n pharmacie f

- Pharmacies in France are
- identified by a special green
- cross outside the shop.

pheasant n faisan m

philosophy n philosophie f

phobia n phobie f

phone n téléphone m ▷ *Where's the phone?* Où est le téléphone?; **by phone** par téléphone; **to be on the phone** être au téléphone ▷ *She's on the phone at the moment.* Elle est au téléphone en ce moment.; **Can I use the phone, please?** Est-ce que je peux téléphoner, s'il vous plaît?

▶ vb appeler ▷ *I'll phone the station.* Je vais appeler la gare.

phone bill n facture f de téléphone

phone book n annuaire m

phone box n cabine f téléphonique

phone call n appel m ▷ *There's a phone call for you.* Il y a un appel pour vous.; **to make a phone call** téléphoner ▷ *Can I make a phone call?* Est-ce que peux téléphoner?

phonecard n carte f de téléphone

phone number n numéro m de téléphone

photo n photo f; **to take a photo** prendre une photo; **to take a photo of somebody** prendre quelqu'un en photo

photocopier n photocopieuse f

photocopy n photocopie f

▶ vb photocopier

photograph n photo f; **to take a photograph** prendre une photo; **to take a photograph of somebody** prendre quelqu'un en photo

▶ vb photographier

photographer n photographe mf ▷ *She's a photographer.* Elle est photographe.

photography n photo f ▷ *My hobby is photography.* Je fais de la photo.

phrase n expression f

phrase book n guide m de conversation

physical adj physique

▶ n (US) examen m médical

physicist n physicien m,

physicienne f ▷ *He's a physicist.* Il est physicien.

physics n physique f ▷ *She teaches physics.* Elle enseigne la physique.

physiotherapist n kinésithérapeute mf

physiotherapy n kinésithérapie f

pianist n pianiste mf

piano n piano m ▷ *I play the piano.* Je joue du piano. ▷ *I have piano lessons.* Je prends des leçons de piano.

pick n Take your pick! Faites votre choix!
▷ vb ❶ (choose) choisir ▷ *I picked the biggest piece.* J'ai choisi le plus gros morceau. ❷ (for team) sélectionner ▷ *I've been picked for the team.* J'ai été sélectionné pour faire partie de l'équipe. ❸ (fruit, flowers) cueillir; **to pick on somebody** harceler quelqu'un ▷ *She's always picking on me.* Elle me harcèle constamment.; **to pick out** choisir ▷ *I like them all — it's difficult to pick one out.* Ils me plaisent tous — c'est difficile d'en choisir un.; **to pick up (1)** (collect) venir chercher ▷ *We'll come to the airport to pick you up.* Nous irons vous chercher à l'aéroport. **(2)** (from floor) ramasser ▷ *Could you help me pick up the toys?* Tu peux m'aider à ramasser les jouets? **(3)** (learn) apprendre ▷ *I picked up some Spanish during my holiday.* J'ai appris quelque mots d'espagnol pendant mes vacances.

pickpocket n pickpocket m

picnic n pique-nique m; **to have a picnic** pique-niquer ▷ *We had a picnic on the beach.* Nous avons pique-niqué sur la plage.

picture n ❶ illustration f ▷ *Children's books have lots of pictures.* Il y a beaucoup d'illustrations dans les livres pour enfants. ❷ photo f ▷ *My picture was in the paper.* Ma photo était dans le journal. ❸ (painting) tableau m (pl tableaux) ▷ *a famous picture* un tableau célèbre; **to paint a picture of something** peindre quelque chose ❹ (drawing) dessin m; **to draw a picture of something** dessiner quelque chose; **the pictures** (cinema) le cinéma ▷ *Shall we go to the pictures?* On va au cinéma?

picture messaging n envoi m de photos par MMS

pie n tourte f ▷ *an apple pie* une tourte aux pommes

piece n morceau m (pl morceaux) ▷ *A small piece, please.* Un petit morceau, s'il vous plaît.; **a piece of furniture** un meuble; **a piece of advice** un conseil

pier n jetée f

pierce vb percer ▷ *She's going to have her ears pierced.* Elle va se faire percer les oreilles.

pierced adj percé(e) ▷ *I've got pierced ears.* J'ai les oreilles percées.

piercing n piercing m ▷ *She has several piercings.* Elle a plusieurs piercings.

pig n cochon m

pigeon n pigeon m

piggy bank n tirelire f

pigtail n natte f
pile n ❶ (untidy heap) tas m ❷ (tidy stack) pile f
pill n pilule f; **to be on the pill** prendre la pilule
pillow n oreiller m
pilot n pilote m ▷ He's a pilot. Il est pilote.
pimple n bouton m
pin n épingle f; **I've got pins and needles.** J'ai des fourmis dans les jambes.
PIN n (= personal identification number) code m confidentiel
pinball n flipper m ▷ to play pinball jouer au flipper; **a pinball machine** un flipper
pinch vb ❶ pincer ▷ He pinched me! Il m'a pincé! ❷ (informal: steal) piquer ▷ Who's pinched my pen? Qui est-ce qui m'a piqué mon stylo?
pine n pin m ▷ a pine table une table en pin
pineapple n ananas m
pink adj rose
pint n pinte f
  ● In France measurements are in litres and centilitres. A pint is about 0.6 litres.
to have a pint boire une bière ▷ He's gone out for a pint. Il est parti boire une bière.; **a pint of milk** un demi-litre de lait
pipe n ❶ (for water, gas) conduite f ▷ The pipes froze. Les conduites d'eau ont gelé. ❷ (for smoking) pipe f ▷ He smokes a pipe. Il fume la pipe.; **the pipes**

(bagpipes) la cornemuse ▷ He plays the pipes. Il joue de la cornemuse.
pirate n pirate m
pirated adj pirate ▷ a pirated video une vidéo pirate
Pisces n Poissons mpl ▷ I'm Pisces. Je suis Poissons.
pistachio n pistache f
pistol n pistolet m
pitch n terrain m ▷ a football pitch un terrain de football
  ▶ vb (tent) dresser ▷ We pitched our tent near the beach. Nous avons dressé notre tente près de la plage.
pity n pitié f; **What a pity!** Quel dommage!
  ▶ vb plaindre
pizza n pizza f
place n ❶ (location) endroit m ▷ It's a quiet place. C'est un endroit tranquille. ❷ (space) place f ▷ a parking place une place de parking ▷ a university place une place à l'université; **to change places** changer de place ▷ Tamsin, change places with Delphine! Tamsin, change de place avec Delphine!; **to take place** avoir lieu; **at your place** chez toi ▷ Shall we meet at your place? On se retrouve chez toi?; **to my place** chez moi ▷ Do you want to come round to my place? Tu veux venir chez moi?
  ▶ vb ❶ poser ▷ He placed his hand on hers. Il a posé la main sur la sienne. ❷ (in competition, contest) classer
placement n stage m; **to do a work placement** faire un stage en entreprise

plain n plaine f
▶ adj, adv ❶ (not patterned) uni(e) ▷ a plain carpet un tapis uni ❷ (not fancy) simple ▷ a plain white blouse un chemisier blanc simple

plain chocolate n chocolat m à croquer

plait n natte f ▷ She wears her hair in a plait. Elle a une natte.

plan n ❶ projet m ▷ What are your plans for the holidays? Quels sont tes projets pour les vacances? ▷ to make plans faire des projets; **Everything went according to plan.** Tout s'est passé comme prévu. ❷ (map) plan m ▷ a plan of the campsite un plan du terrain de camping; **my essay plan** le plan de ma dissertation
▶ vb ❶ (make plans for) préparer ▷ We're planning a trip to France. Nous préparons un voyage en France. ❷ (make schedule for) planifier ▷ Plan your revision carefully. Planifiez vos révisions avec soin.; **to plan to do something** avoir l'intention de faire quelque chose ▷ I'm planning to get a job in the holidays. J'ai l'intention de trouver un job pour les vacances.

plane n avion m ▷ by plane en avion

planet n planète f

plant n ❶ plante f ▷ to water the plants arroser les plantes ❷ (factory) usine f
▶ vb planter

plaster n ❶ (sticking plaster) pansement m adhésif ▷ Have you got a plaster, by any chance? Vous n'auriez pas un pansement adhésif, par hasard? ❷ (for fracture) plâtre m ▷ Her leg's in plaster. Elle a la jambe dans le plâtre.

plastic n plastique m ▷ It's made of plastic. C'est en plastique.
▶ adj en plastique ▷ a plastic bag un sac en plastique

plate n (for food) assiette f

platform n ❶ (at station) quai m ▷ on platform 7 sur le quai numéro sept ❷ (for performers) estrade f

play n pièce f ▷ a play by Shakespeare une pièce de Shakespeare; **to put on a play** monter une pièce
▶ vb ❶ jouer ▷ He's playing with his friends. Il joue avec ses amis. ❷ (against person, team) jouer contre ▷ France will play Scotland next month. La France jouera contre l'Écosse le mois prochain. ❸ (sport, game) jouer à ▷ I play hockey. Je joue au hockey. ▷ Can you play pool? Tu sais jouer au billard américain? ❹ (instrument) jouer de ▷ I play the guitar. Je joue de la guitare. ❺ (record, CD, music) écouter ▷ She's always playing that CD. Elle écoute tout le temps ce CD.

player n ❶ (of sport) joueur m, joueuse f ▷ a football player un joueur de football ❷ (of instrument) musicien m, musicienne f; **a piano player** un pianiste; **a saxophone player** un saxophoniste

playground n ❶ (at school) cour f de récréation ❷ (in park) aire f de jeux

playgroup n garderie f

playing card n carte f à jouer (pl cartes à jouer)

playing field n terrain m de sport

playtime n récréation f

pleasant adj agréable

please excl ❶ (polite form) s'il vous plaît ▷ Two coffees, please. Deux cafés, s'il vous plaît. ❷ (familiar form) s'il te plaît ▷ Please write back soon. Réponds vite, s'il te plaît.

pleased adj content(e) ▷ My mother's not going to be very pleased. Ma mère ne va pas être contente du tout.; **Pleased to meet you!** Enchanté!

pleasure n plaisir m ▷ I read for pleasure. Je lis pour le plaisir.

plenty n largement assez ▷ That's plenty, thanks. Ça suffit largement, merci.; **plenty of (1)** (a lot) beaucoup de ▷ I've got plenty to do. J'ai beaucoup de choses à faire. **(2)** (enough) largement assez de ▷ I've got plenty of money. J'ai largement assez d'argent. ▷ We've got plenty of time. Nous avons largement le temps.

pliers npl pince f; **a pair of pliers** une pince

plot n ❶ (of story, play) intrigue f ❷ (against somebody) conspiration f ▷ a plot against the president une conspiration contre le président ❸ (of land) carré m ▷ a vegetable plot un carré de légumes
▶ vb comploter ▷ They were plotting to kill him. Ils complotaient de le tuer.

plough n charrue f
▶ vb labourer

plug n ❶ (electrical) prise f de courant ▷ The plug is faulty. La prise est défectueuse. ❷ (for sink) bouchon m

plug in vb brancher ▷ Is it plugged in? Est-ce que c'est branché?

plum n prune f ▷ plum jam la confiture de prunes

plumber n plombier m ▷ He's a plumber. Il est plombier.

plump adj dodu(e)

plural n pluriel m

plus prep, adj plus ▷ 4 plus 3 equals 7. Quatre plus trois égalent sept. ▷ three children plus a dog trois enfants plus un chien; **I got a B plus.** J'ai eu un Bien.

p.m. abbr **at 8 p.m.** à huit heures du soir
● In France times are often given
● using the 24-hour clock.
at 2 p.m. à quatorze heures

pneumonia n pneumonie f

poached adj poché(e) ▷ a poached egg un œuf poché

pocket n poche f; **pocket money** argent m de poche ▷ £8 a week pocket money huit livres d'argent de poche par semaine

podcast n podcast m
▶ vb podcaster

poem n poème m

poet n poète m

poetry n poésie f

point n (spot, score) point m
▷ a point on the horizon un point à l'horizon ▷ They scored 5 points.

Ils ont marqué cinq points.
❷ (comment) remarque f ▷ He made
some interesting points. Il a fait
quelque remarques intéressantes.
❸ (tip) pointe f ▷ a pencil with a
sharp point un crayon à la pointe
aiguisée ❹ (in time) moment m
▷ At that point, we decided to leave.
À ce moment-là, nous avons
décidé de partir.; **a point of view**
un point de vue; **to get the point**
comprendre ▷ Sorry, I don't get the
point. Désolé, je ne comprends
pas.; **That's a good point!** C'est
vrai!; **There's no point.** Cela ne
sert à rien. ▷ There's no point in
waiting. Cela ne sert à rien
d'attendre.; **What's the point?**
À quoi bon? ▷ What's the point of
leaving so early? À quoi bon partir si
tôt?; **Punctuality isn't my strong
point.** La ponctualité n'est pas
mon fort.; **two point five (2.5)**
deux virgule cinq (2,5)
▶ vb montrer du doigt ▷ Don't
point! Ne montre pas du doigt!;
to point at somebody montrer
quelqu'un du doigt ▷ She pointed at
Anne. Elle a montré Anne du doigt.;
to point a gun at somebody
braquer un revolver sur
quelqu'un; **to point something
out (1)** (show) montrer quelque
chose ▷ The guide pointed out
Notre-Dame to us. Le guide nous a
montré Notre-Dame. **(2)** (mention)
signaler quelque chose ▷ I should
point out that ... Je dois vous
signaler que ...

pointless adj inutile ▷ It's pointless
to argue. Il est inutile de discuter.
poison n poison m
▶ vb empoisonner
poisonous adj ❶ (snake) venimeux
(f venimeuse) ❷ (plant, mushroom)
vénéneux (f vénéneuse) ❸ (gas)
toxique
poke vb **He poked the ground
with his stick.** Il tapotait le sol
avec sa canne.; **She poked me in
the ribs.** Elle m'a enfoncé le doigt
dans les côtes.
poker n poker m ▷ I play poker. Je
joue au poker.
Poland n Pologne f; **in Poland** en
Pologne; **to Poland** en Pologne
polar bear n ours m blanc
Pole n (Polish person) Polonais m,
Polonaise f
pole n poteau m (pl poteaux)
▷ a telegraph pole un poteau
télégraphique; **a tent pole** un
montant de tente; **a ski pole** un
bâton de ski; **the North Pole**
le pôle Nord; **the South Pole** le
pôle Sud
police npl police f sg ▷ We called
the police. Nous avons appelé la
police.; **a police car** une voiture
de police; **a police station** un
commissariat de police
policeman n policier m ▷ He's a
policeman. Il est policier.
policewoman n femme f policier
▷ She's a policewoman. Elle est
femme policier.
Polish adj polonais(e)
▶ n (language) polonais m

polish n ❶ (for shoes) cirage m
❷ (for furniture) cire f
▶ vb ❶ (shoes, furniture) cirer
❷ (glass) faire briller

polite adj poli(e)

politely adv poliment

political adj politique

politician n politicien m,
politicienne f

politics npl politique f ▷ I'm not
interested in politics. La politique ne
m'intéresse pas.

pollute vb polluer

polluted adj pollué(e)

pollution n pollution f

polo-necked sweater n pull m
à col roulé

polythene bag n sac m en
plastique

pond n ❶ (big) étang m ❷ (smaller)
mare f ❸ bassin m ▷ We've got a
pond in our garden. Nous avons un
bassin dans notre jardin.

pony n poney m

ponytail n queue f de cheval ▷ He's
got a ponytail. Il a une queue de
cheval.

pony trekking n to go pony
trekking faire une randonnée à
dos de poney

poodle n caniche m

pool n ❸ (puddle) flaque f ❷ (pond)
étang m ❸ (for swimming) piscine f
❹ (game) billard m américain
▷ Shall we have a game of pool? Si on
jouait au billard américain?;
the pools (football) le loto sportif
▷ to do the pools jouer au loto
sportif

poor adj ❶ pauvre ▷ a poor family
une famille pauvre ▷ Poor David,
he's very unlucky! Le pauvre David,
il n'a vraiment pas de chance!; the
poor les pauvres ❷ (bad) médiocre
▷ a poor mark une note médiocre

pop adj pop inv ▷ pop music la
musique pop ▷ a pop star une
pop star

pop in vb passer ▷ I just popped in
to say hello. Je suis juste passé pour
bonjour.

popcorn n pop-corn m

pope n pape m

poppy n coquelicot m

popular adj populaire ▷ She's a
very popular girl. C'est une fille très
populaire.

population n population f

porch n porche m

pork n porc m ▷ a pork chop une
côtelette de porc

porridge n porridge m

port n ❶ (harbour) port m ❷ (wine)
porto m ▷ a glass of port un verre
de porto

portable adj portable ▷ a portable
TV un téléviseur portable

porter n ❶ (in hotel) portier m
❷ (at station) porteur m

portion n portion f ▷ a large portion
of chips une grosse portion de frites

portrait n portrait m

Portugal n Portugal m; in
Portugal au Portugal; We went
to Portugal. Nous sommes allés
au Portugal.

Portuguese adj portugais(e)
▶ n ❶ (person) Portugais m,

Portugaise f ② (language)
portugais m

posh adj chic inv ▷ a posh hotel un
hôtel chic

position n position f ▷ an
uncomfortable position une position
inconfortable

positive adj ① (good) positif
(f positive) ▷ a positive attitude
une attitude positive ② (sure)
certain(e) ▷ I'm positive. J'en suis
certain.

possession n Have you got all
your possessions? Est-ce que tu as
toutes tes affaires?

possibility n It's a possibility.
C'est possible.

possible adj possible ▷ as soon as
possible aussitôt que possible

possibly adv (perhaps) peut-être
▷ Are you coming to the party? —
Possibly. Est-ce que tu viens à la
soirée? — Peut-être.; ... if you
possibly can. ... si cela vous est
possible.; I can't possibly come.
Je ne peux vraiment pas venir.

post n ① (letters) courrier m ▷ Is
there any post for me? Est-ce qu'il y
a du courrier pour moi? ② (pole)
poteau m (pl poteaux) ▷ The ball
hit the post. Le ballon a heurté le
poteau.
▶ vb poster ▷ I've got some cards to
post. J'ai quelques cartes à poster.

postbox n boîte f aux lettres

postcard n carte f postale

postcode n code m postal

poster n ① poster m ▷ I've got
posters on my bedroom walls. J'ai

des posters sur les murs de ma
chambre.

In French you pronounce
poster as "post-air".

② (advertising) affiche f ▷ There
are posters all over town. Il y a des
affiches dans toute la ville.

postman n facteur m ▷ He's a
postman. Il est facteur.

post office n poste f ▷ Where's the
post office, please? Où est la poste,
s'il vous plaît?

postpone vb remettre à plus tard
▷ The match has been postponed. Le
match a été remis à plus tard.

postwoman n factrice f ▷ She's a
postwoman. Elle est factrice.

pot n ① pot m ▷ a pot of jam un pot
de confiture ② (teapot) théière f
③ (coffeepot) cafetière f
④ (marijuana) herbe f ▷ to smoke pot
fumer de l'herbe; the pots and
pans les casseroles

potato n pomme f de terre ▷ potato
salad la salade de pommes de terre;
mashed potatoes la purée;
boiled potatoes les pommes
vapeur; a baked potato une
pomme de terre en robe des
champs

pottery n poterie f

pound n (weight, money) livre f
▷ How many euros do you get for a
pound? Combien d'euros a-t-on
pour une livre?

In France measurements are
in grammes and kilogrammes.
One pound is about 450
grammes.

▷ *a pound of carrots* un demi-kilo de carottes

pour vb ❶ (liquid) verser ▷ *She poured some water into the pan.* Elle a versé de l'eau dans la casserole.; **She poured him a drink.** Elle lui a servi à boire.; **Shall I pour you a cup of tea?** Je vous sers une tasse de thé? ❷ (rain) pleuvoir à verse ▷ *It's pouring.* Il pleut à verse.; **in the pouring rain** sous une pluie torrentielle

poverty n pauvreté f

powder n poudre f

power n ❶ (electricity) courant m ▷ *The power's off.* Le courant est coupé.; **a power cut** une coupure de courant; **a power point** une prise de courant; **a power station** une centrale électrique ❷ (energy) énergie f ▷ *nuclear power* l'énergie nucléaire ❸ (authority) pouvoir m ▷ *to be in power* être au pouvoir

powerful adj puissant(e)

practical adj pratique ▷ *a practical suggestion* un conseil pratique; **She's very practical.** Elle a l'esprit pratique.

practically adv pratiquement ▷ *It's practically impossible.* C'est pratiquement impossible.

practice n (for sport) entraînement m ▷ *football practice* l'entraînement de foot; **I've got to do my piano practice.** Je dois travailler mon piano.; **It's normal practice in our school.** C'est ce qui se fait dans notre école.;

in practice en pratique; **a medical practice** un cabinet médical

practise (US **practice**) vb ❶ (music, hobby) s'exercer ▷ *I ought to practise more.* Je devrais m'exercer davantage. ❷ (instrument) travailler ▷ *I practise the flute every evening.* Je travaille ma flûte tous les soirs. ❸ (language) pratiquer ▷ *I practised my French when we were on holiday.* J'ai pratiqué mon français pendant les vacances. ❹ (sport) s'entraîner ▷ *I don't practise enough.* Je ne m'entraîne pas assez.

praise vb faire l'éloge de ▷ *The teachers praised our work.* Les professeurs ont fait l'éloge de notre travail.

pram n landau m

prawn n crevette f

pray vb prier ▷ *to pray for something* prier pour quelque chose

prayer n prière f

precious adj précieux (f précieuse)

precise adj précis(e) ▷ *at that precise moment* à cet instant précis

precisely adv précisément ▷ *Precisely!* Précisément!; **at 10 a.m. precisely** à dix heures précises

predict vb prédire

prefect n

- French schools do not have
- prefects. You could explain what
- a prefect is using the example
- given.

My sister's a prefect. Ma sœur est en dernière année et est chargée de maintenir la discipline.

prefer vb préférer ▷ Which would you prefer? Lequel préfères-tu? ▷ I prefer French to chemistry. Je préfère le français à la chimie.

pregnant adj enceinte ▷ She's six months pregnant. Elle est enceinte de six mois.

prejudice n ❶ préjugé m ▷ That's just a prejudice. C'est un préjugé. ❷ préjugés mpl ▷ There's a lot of racial prejudice. Il y a beaucoup de préjugés raciaux.

prejudiced adj to be prejudiced against somebody avoir des préjugés contre quelqu'un

premature adj prématuré(e); a premature baby un prématuré

Premier League n première division f ▷ in the Premier League en première division

premises npl locaux mpl ▷ They're moving to new premises. Ils vont occuper de nouveaux locaux.

prep n (homework) devoirs mpl ▷ history prep les devoirs d'histoire

preparation n préparation f

prepare vb préparer ▷ She has to prepare lessons in the evening. Elle doit préparer ses cours le soir.; to prepare for something se préparer pour quelque chose ▷ We're preparing for our skiing holiday. Nous nous préparons pour nos vacances à la neige.

prepared adj to be prepared to do something être prêt à faire quelque chose ▷ I'm prepared to help you. Je suis prêt à t'aider.

prep school n école f primaire privée

prescribe vb prescrire

prescription n ordonnance f ▷ You can't get it without a prescription. On ne peut pas se le procurer sans ordonnance.

present adj ❶ (in attendance) présent(e) ▷ He wasn't present at the meeting. Il n'était pas présent à la réunion. ❷ (current) actuel (f actuelle) ▷ the present situation la situation actuelle; the present tense le présent ▶ n ❶ (gift) cadeau m (pl cadeaux) ▷ I'm going to buy presents. Je vais acheter des cadeaux.; to give somebody a present offrir un cadeau à quelqu'un ▷ (present m ❷ (time) présent m ▷ up to the present jusqu'à présent; for the present pour l'instant; at present en ce moment ▶ vb to present somebody with something (prize, medal) remettre quelque chose à quelqu'un

presenter n (on TV) présentateur m, présentatrice f

president n président m, présidente f

press n presse f; a press conference une conférence de presse ▶ vb ❶ appuyer ▷ Don't press too hard! N'appuie pas trop fort! ❷ appuyer sur ▷ He pressed the accelerator. Il a appuyé sur l'accélérateur.

press-up n to do press-ups faire
des pompes ▷ I do twenty press-ups
every morning. Je fais vingt pompes
tous les matins.

pressure n pression f ▷ He's under
a lot of pressure at work. Il est sous
pression au travail.; **a pressure
group** un groupe de pression
▶ vb faire pression sur ▷ My parents
are pressuring me. Mes parents font
pression sur moi.

presume vb supposer ▷ I presume
so. Je suppose que oui.

pretend vb to pretend to do
something faire semblant de
faire quelque chose ▷ He pretended
to be asleep. Il faisait semblant de
dormir.

▌ Be careful not to translate to
pretend by prétendre.

pretty adj, adv ❶ joli(e) ▷ She's very
pretty. Elle est très jolie. ❷ (rather)
plutôt ▷ That film was pretty bad.
Ce film était plutôt mauvais.;
The weather was pretty awful.
Il faisait un temps minable.; **It's
pretty much the same.** C'est
pratiquement la même chose.

prevent vb empêcher; to
prevent somebody from doing
something empêcher quelqu'un
de faire quelque chose ▷ They try
to prevent us from smoking. Ils
essaient de nous empêcher de
fumer.

previous adj précédent(e)

previously adv auparavant

price n prix m

price list n liste f des prix

prick vb piquer ▷ I've pricked my
finger. Je me suis piqué le doigt.

pride n fierté f

priest n prêtre m ▷ He's a priest.
Il est prêtre.

primarily adv principalement

primary adj principal(e)
(mpl principaux)

primary school n école f primaire
▷ She's still at primary school. Elle est
encore à l'école primaire.

prime minister n Premier
ministre m

prince n prince m ▷ the Prince of
Wales le prince de Galles

princess n princesse f ▷ Princess
Anne la princesse Anne

principal adj principal(e) (mpl
principaux)
▶ n (of college) principal m

principle n principe m (pl
principaux); **on principle** par
principe

print n ❶ (photo) tirage m ▷ colour
prints des tirages en couleur
❷ (letters) caractères mpl ▷ in
small print en petits caractères
❸ (fingerprint) empreinte f digitale
❹ (picture) gravure f ▷ a framed print
une gravure encadrée

printer n (machine) imprimante f

printout n tirage m

priority n priorité f

prison n prison f; **in prison** en
prison

prisoner n prisonnier m,
prisonnière f

private adj privé(e) ▷ a private
school une école privée; **private**

property la propriété privée; **"private"** (on envelope) "personnel"; **a private bathroom** une salle de bain individuelle; **I have private lessons.** Je prends des cours particuliers.

prize n prix m ▷ **to win a prize** gagner un prix

prize-giving n distribution f des prix

prizewinner n gagnant m, gagnante f

pro n **the pros and cons** le pour et le contre ▷ We weighed up the pros and cons. Nous avons pesé le pour et le contre.

probability n probabilité f

probable adj probable

probably adv probablement ▷ **probably not** probablement pas

problem n problème m ▷ No problem! Pas de problème!

process n processus m ▷ the peace process le processus de paix; **to be in the process of doing something** être en train de faire quelque chose ▷ We're in the process of painting the kitchen. Nous sommes en train de peindre la cuisine.

procession n (religious) procession f

produce vb ① (manufacture) produire ② (play, show) monter

producer n (of play, show) metteur m en scène (pl metteurs en scène)

product n produit m

production n ① production f ▷ They're increasing production of

luxury models. Ils augmentent la production des modèles de luxe. ② (play, show) mise f en scène ▷ a production of "Hamlet" une mise en scène de "Hamlet"

profession n profession f

professional n professionnel m, professionnelle f
▶ adj (player) professionnel (f professionnelle) ▷ a professional musician un musicien professionnel; **a very professional piece of work** un vrai travail de professionnel

professor n professeur m d'université; **He's the French professor.** Il est titulaire de la chaire de français.

profit n bénéfice m

profitable adj rentable

program n programme m ▷ a computer program un programme informatique; **a TV program** (US) une émission de télévision
▶ vb (computer) programmer

programme n ① (on TV, radio) émission f ② (of events) programme m

programmer n programmeur m, programmeuse f ▷ She's a programmer. Elle est programmeuse.

progress n progrès m ▷ You're making progress! Vous faites des progrès!

prohibit vb interdire ▷ Smoking is prohibited. Il est interdit de fumer.

project n ① (plan) projet m ▷ a development project un projet de

développement ❷ (research)
<u>dossier</u> m ▷ *I'm doing a project on
education in France.* Je prépare un
dossier sur l'éducation en France.

projector n projecteur m

promise n promesse f ▷ *He made me
a promise.* Il m'a fait une promesse.;
That's a promise! C'est promis!
▶ vb promettre ▷ *She promised to
write.* Elle a promis d'écrire.

promote vb **to be promoted** être
promu(e) ▷ *She was promoted after
six months.* Elle a été promue au
bout de six mois.

promotion n promotion f

prompt adj, adv rapide ▷ *a prompt
reply* une réponse rapide; **at eight
o'clock prompt** à huit heures
précises

pronoun n pronom m

pronounce vb prononcer ▷ *How do
you pronounce that word?* Comment
est-ce qu'on prononce ce mot?

pronunciation n prononciation f

proof n preuve f

proper adj ❶ (genuine) vrai(e)
▷ *proper French bread* du vrai
pain français; **It's difficult to
get a proper job.** Il est difficile
de trouver un travail correct.
❷ adéquat(e) ▷ *You have to have
the proper equipment.* Il faut avoir
l'équipement adéquat. ▷ *We need
proper training.* Il nous faut une
formation adéquate.; **If you had
come at the proper time …** Si tu
étais venu à l'heure dite …

properly adv ❶ (correctly) comme
il faut ▷ *You're not doing it properly.*

Tu ne t'y prends pas comme il faut.
❷ (appropriately) convenablement
▷ *Dress properly for your interview.*
Habille-toi convenablement pour
ton entretien.

property n propriété f; **"private
property"** "propriété privée";
stolen property les objets volés

propose vb proposer ▷ *I propose
a new plan.* Je propose un
changement de programme.;
to propose to do something
avoir l'intention de faire quelque
chose ▷ *What do you propose to do?*
Qu'est-ce que tu as l'intention de
faire?; **to propose to somebody**
(for marriage) demander quelqu'un
en mariage ▷ *He proposed to her at
the restaurant.* Il l'a demandée en
mariage au restaurant.

prosecute vb poursuivre en justice
▷ *They were prosecuted for murder.*
Ils ont été poursuivis en justice
pour meurtre.; **"Trespassers will
be prosecuted"** "Défense d'entrer
sous peine de poursuites"

prostitute n prostituée f; **a male
prostitute** un prostitué

protect vb protéger

protection n protection f

protein n protéine f

protest n protestation f ▷ *He
ignored their protests.* Il a ignoré
leurs protestations.; **a protest
march** une manifestation
▶ vb protester

Protestant n protestant m,
protestante f ▷ *I'm a Protestant.*
Je suis protestant.

▶ adj protestant(e) ▷ a Protestant church une église protestante

protester n manifestant m, manifestante f

proud adj fier (f fière) ▷ Her parents are proud of her. Ses parents sont fiers d'elle.

prove vb prouver ▷ The police couldn't prove it. La police n'a pas pu le prouver.

proverb n proverbe m

provide vb fournir; **to provide somebody with something** fournir quelque chose à quelqu'un ▷ They provided us with maps. Ils nous ont fourni des cartes.

provided conj à condition que

▌ **à condition que** has to be followed by the subjunctive.
▷ He'll play in the next match provided he's fit. Il jouera dans le prochain match, à condition qu'il soit en forme.

prune n pruneau m (pl pruneaux)

PS abbr (= postscript) PS m

psychiatrist n psychiatre mf ▷ She's a psychiatrist. Elle est psychiatre.

psychological adj psychologique

psychologist n psychologue mf ▷ He's a psychologist. Il est psychologue.

psychology n psychologie f

PTO abbr (= please turn over) T.S.V.P. (tournez, s'il vous plaît)

pub n pub m

public n public m ▷ open to the public ouvert au public; **in public** en public

▶ adj public (f publique); **a public holiday** un jour férié; **public opinion** opinion f publique; **the public address system** les haut-parleurs mpl

publicity n publicité f

public school n école f privée

public transport n transports mpl en commun

publish vb publier

publisher n éditeur m

pudding n dessert m ▷ What's for pudding? Qu'est-ce qu'il y a comme dessert?; **rice pudding** le riz au lait; **black pudding** le boudin noir

puddle n flaque f

puff pastry n pâte feuilletée f

pull vb (tooth, weed) tirer ▷ Pull! Tirez!; **He pulled the trigger.** Il a appuyé sur la gâchette.; **to pull a muscle** se froisser un muscle ▷ I pulled a muscle when I was training. Je me suis froissé un muscle à l'entraînement.; **You're pulling my leg!** Tu me fais marcher!; **to pull down** démolir; **to pull out (1)** (tooth, weed) arracher **(2)** (car) déboîter ▷ The car pulled out to overtake. La voiture a déboîté pour doubler. **(3)** (withdraw) se retirer ▷ She pulled out of the tournament. Elle s'est retirée du tournoi.; **to pull through** s'en sortir ▷ They think he'll pull through. Ils pensent qu'il va s'en sortir.; **to pull up** s'arrêter ▷ A black car pulled up beside me. Une voiture noire s'est arrêtée à côté de moi.

pullover n pull-over m

pulse n pouls m ▷ The nurse felt his pulse. L'infirmière a pris son pouls.

pump n ❶ pompe f ▷ a bicycle pump une pompe à vélo ▷ a petrol pump une pompe à essence ❷ (shoe) chausson m de gym
▶ vb (tyre) pomper; **to pump up** gonfler

pumpkin n potiron m

punch n ❶ (blow) coup m de poing ▷ He gave me a punch. Il m'a donné un coup de poing. ❷ (drink) punch m
▶ vb ❶ (hit) donner un coup de poing à ▷ He punched me! Il m'a donné un coup de poing! ❷ (in ticket machine) composter ▷ Punch your ticket before you get on the train. Compostez votre billet avant de monter dans le train. ❸ (by hand) poinçonner ▷ He forgot to punch my ticket. Il a oublié de poinçonner mon billet.

punctual adj ponctuel (f ponctuelle)

punctuation n ponctuation f

puncture n crevaison f ▷ I had to mend a puncture. J'ai dû réparer une crevaison.; **to have a puncture** crever ▷ I had a puncture on the motorway. J'ai crevé sur l'autoroute.

punish vb punir; **to punish somebody for something** punir quelqu'un de quelque chose; **to punish somebody for doing something** punir quelqu'un d'avoir fait quelque chose

punishment n punition f

punk n (person) punk mf; **a punk rock band** un groupe de punk rock

pupil n élève mf

puppet n marionnette f

puppy n chiot m

purchase vb acheter

pure adj pur(e) ▷ pure orange juice du pur jus d'orange

purple adj violet (f violette)

purpose n but m ▷ What is the purpose of these changes? Quel est le but de ces changements?; **on purpose** exprès ▷ He did it on purpose. Il l'a fait exprès.

purr vb ronronner

purse n ❶ porte-monnaie m (pl porte-monnaie) ❷ (US: handbag) sac m à main (pl sacs à main)

pursue vb poursuivre

push n to give somebody a push pousser quelqu'un ▷ He gave me a push. Il m'a poussé.
▶ vb ❶ pousser ▷ Don't push! Arrêtez de pousser! ❷ (button) appuyer sur; **to push somebody to do something** pousser quelqu'un à faire quelque chose ▷ My parents are pushing me to go to university. Mes parents me poussent à entrer à l'université.; **to push drugs** revendre de la drogue; **Push off!** Dégage!

push around vb bousculer ▷ He likes pushing people around. Il aime bien bousculer les gens.

pushchair n poussette f

push-up n pompe f; **to do push-ups** faire des pompes

put vb ① (place) mettre ▷ Where shall I put my things? Où est-ce que je peux mettre mes affaires? ▷ She's putting the baby to bed. Elle met le bébé au lit. ② (write) écrire ▷ Don't forget to put your name on the paper. N'oubliez pas d'écrire votre nom sur la feuille.

put away vb ranger ▷ Can you put away the dishes, please? Tu peux ranger la vaisselle, s'il te plaît?

put back vb (replace) remettre en place ▷ Put it back when you've finished with it. Remets-le en place une fois que tu auras fini.

put down vb ① poser ▷ I'll put these bags down for a minute. Je vais poser ces sacs une minute. ② (in writing) noter ▷ I've put down a few ideas. J'ai noté quelques idées.; **to have an animal put down** faire piquer un animal ▷ We had to have our old dog put down. Nous avons dû faire piquer notre vieux chien.

put in vb (install) installer ▷ We're going to get central heating put in. Nous allons faire installer le chauffage central.; **He has put in a lot of work on this project.** Il a fourni beaucoup de travail pour ce projet.

put off vb ① (switch off) éteindre ▷ Shall I put the light off? Est-ce que j'éteins la lumière? ② (postpone) remettre à plus tard ▷ I keep putting it off. Je n'arrête pas de remettre ça à plus tard. ③ (distract) déranger ▷ Stop putting me off! Arrête de me déranger! ④ (discourage)

décourager ▷ He's not easily put off. Il ne se laisse pas facilement décourager.

put on vb ① (clothes, lipstick, record) mettre ▷ I'll put my coat on. Je vais mettre mon manteau. ② (light, heater, telly) allumer ▷ Shall I put the heater on? J'allume le chauffage? ③ (play, show) monter ▷ We're putting on "Bugsy Malone". Nous sommes en train de monter "Bugsy Malone". ④ mettre à cuire ▷ I'll put the potatoes on. Je vais mettre les pommes de terre à cuire.; **to put on weight** grossir ▷ He's put on a lot of weight. Il a beaucoup grossi.

put out vb (light, cigarette, fire) éteindre ▷ It took them five hours to put out the fire. Ils ont mis cinq heures à éteindre l'incendie.

put through vb passer ▷ Can you put me through to the manager? Est-ce que vous pouvez me passer le directeur?; **I'm putting you through.** Je vous passe la communication.

put up vb ① (pin up) mettre ▷ The poster's great. I'll put it up on my wall. Le poster est super. Je vais le mettre au mur. ② (tent) monter ▷ We put up our tent in a field. Nous avons monté la tente dans un champ. ③ (price) augmenter ▷ They've put up the price. Ils ont augmenté le prix. ④ (accommodate) héberger ▷ My friend will put me up for the night. Mon ami va m'héberger pour la nuit.; **to put one's hand up** lever la main ▷ *If you have any questions, put up your hand.* Si vous avez une question, levez la main.; **to put up with something** supporter quelque chose ▷ *I'm not going to put up with it any longer.* Je ne vais pas supporter ça plus longtemps.

puzzle n *(jigsaw)* puzzle m

puzzled adj perplexe ▷ *You look puzzled!* Tu as l'air perplexe!

pyjamas npl pyjama m ▷ *my pyjamas* mon pyjama; **a pair of pyjamas** un pyjama; **a pyjama top** un haut de pyjama

pylon n pylône m

pyramid n pyramide f

Pyrenees npl les Pyrénées fpl; **in the Pyrenees** dans les Pyrénées; **We went to the Pyrenees.** Nous sommes allés dans les Pyrénées.

q

qualification n diplôme m ▷ *to leave school without any qualifications* quitter l'école sans aucun diplôme; **vocational qualifications** des qualifications professionnelles

qualified adj ❶ *(trained)* qualifié(e) ▷ *a qualified driving instructor* un moniteur d'auto-école qualifié ❷ *(nurse, teacher)* diplômé(e) ▷ *a qualified nurse* une infirmière diplômée

qualify vb ❶ *(for job)* obtenir son diplôme ▷ *She qualified as a teacher last year.* Elle a obtenu son diplôme de professeur l'année dernière. ❷ *(in competition)* se qualifier ▷ *Our team didn't qualify.* Notre équipe ne s'est pas qualifiée.

quality n qualité f ▷ a good quality of life une bonne qualité de vie ▷ She's got lots of good qualities. Elle a beaucoup de qualités.

quantity n quantité f

quarantine n quarantaine f ▷ in quarantine en quarantaine

quarrel n dispute f
▶ vb se disputer

quarry n (for stone) carrière f

quarter n quart m; **three quarters** trois quarts; **a quarter of an hour** un quart d'heure ▷ three quarters of an hour trois quarts d'heure; **a quarter past ten** dix heures et quart; **a quarter to eleven** onze heures moins le quart

quarter final n quart m de finale

quartet n quatuor m ▷ a string quartet un quatuor à cordes

quay n quai m

queen n ❶ reine f ▷ Queen Elizabeth la reine Élisabeth ❷ (playing card) dame f ▷ the queen of hearts la dame de cœur; **the Queen Mother** la reine mère

query n question f
▶ vb mettre en question ▷ No one queried my decision. Personne n'a mis en question ma décision.

question n question f ▷ Can I ask a question? Est-ce que je peux poser une question? ▷ That's a difficult question. C'est une question difficile.; **It's out of the question.** C'est hors de question.
▶ vb interroger ▷ He was questioned by the police. Il a été interrogé par la police.

question mark n point m d'interrogation

questionnaire n questionnaire m

queue n queue f
▶ vb faire la queue; **to queue for something** faire la queue pour avoir quelque chose ▷ We had to queue for tickets. Nous avons dû faire la queue pour avoir les billets.

quick adj, adv rapide ▷ a quick lunch un déjeuner rapide ▷ It's quicker by train. C'est plus rapide en train.; **Be quick!** Dépêche-toi!; **She's a quick learner.** Elle apprend vite.; **Quick, phone the police!** Téléphonez vite à la police!

quickly adv vite ▷ It was all over very quickly. Ça s'est passé très vite.

quiet adj ❶ (not talkative or noisy) silencieux (f silencieuse) ▷ You're very quiet today. Tu es bien silencieux aujourd'hui. ▷ The engine's very quiet. Le moteur est très silencieux. ❷ (peaceful) tranquille ▷ a quiet weekend un week-end tranquille; **Be quiet!** Tais-toi!; **Quiet!** Silence!

quietly adv ❶ (speak) doucement ▷ "She's dead," he said quietly. "Elle est morte" dit-il doucement. ❷ (move) silencieusement; **He quietly opened the door.** Il a ouvert la porte sans faire de bruit.

quilt n (duvet) couette f

quit vb (place, premises, job) quitter ▷ She's decided to quit her job. Elle a décidé de quitter son emploi.; **I quit!** J'abandonne!

quite adv ❶ (rather) assez ▷ It's quite warm today. Il fait assez bon aujourd'hui. ❷ (entirely) tout à fait ▷ I'm not quite sure. Je n'en suis pas tout à fait sûr.; **quite good** pas mal; **I've been there quite a lot.** J'y suis allé pas mal de fois.; **quite a lot of money** pas mal d'argent; **It costs quite a lot to go abroad.** Ça coûte assez cher d'aller à l'étranger.; **It's quite a long way.** C'est assez loin.; **It was quite a shock.** Ça a été un sacré choc.; **There were quite a few people there.** Il y avait pas mal de gens.

quiz n jeu-concours m

quotation n citation f ▷ a quotation from Shakespeare une citation de Shakespeare

quote n citation f ▷ a Shakespeare quote une citation de Shakespeare; **quotes** (quotation marks) les guillemets ▷ in quotes entre guillemets
▶ vb citer ▷ He's always quoting Shakespeare. Il n'arrête pas de citer Shakespeare.

r

rabbi n rabbin m

rabbit n lapin m; **a rabbit hutch** un clapier

race n ❶ (sport) course f ▷ a cycle race une course cycliste ❷ (species) race f ▷ the human race la race humaine; **race relations** les relations interraciales
▶ vb ❶ courir ▷ We raced to catch the bus. Nous avons couru pour attraper le bus. ❷ (have a race) faire la course ▷ I'll race you! On fait la course!

racecourse n champ m de courses

racer n (bike) vélo m de course

racetrack n piste f

racial adj racial(e) (mpl raciaux) ▷ racial discrimination la discrimination raciale

racing car n voiture f de course

racing driver n pilote m de course

racism n racisme m

racist adj raciste
▶ n raciste mf

rack n (for luggage) porte-bagages m (pl porte-bagages)

racket n ❶ (for sport) raquette f ▷ my tennis racket ma raquette de tennis ❷ (noise) boucan m (informal) ▷ They're making a terrible racket. Ils font un boucan de tous les diables.

racquet n raquette f

radar n radar m

radiation n radiation f

radiator n radiateur m

radio n radio f; **on the radio** à la radio; **a radio station** une station de radio

radioactive adj radioactif (f radioactive)

radish n radis m

RAF n (= Royal Air Force) R.A.F. f ▷ He's in the RAF. Il est dans la R.A.F.

raffle n tombola f ▷ a raffle ticket un billet de tombola

raft n radeau m (pl radeaux)

rag n chiffon m ▷ a piece of rag un chiffon; **dressed in rags** en haillons

rage n rage f ▷ mad with rage fou de rage; **to be in a rage** être furieux ▷ She was in a rage. Elle était furieuse.; **It's all the rage.** Ça fait fureur.

rail n ❶ (on stairs) rampe f ❷ (on bridge, balcony) balustrade f ▷ Don't lean over the rail! Ne vous penchez pas sur la balustrade! ❸ (on railway line) rail m; **by rail** en train

railcard n carte f de chemin de fer ▷ a young person's railcard une carte de chemin de fer tarif jeune

railroad n (US) = **railway**

railway n chemin m de fer ▷ the privatization of the railways la privatisation des chemins de fer; **a railway line** une ligne de chemin de fer; **a railway station** une gare

rain n pluie f ▷ in the rain sous la pluie
▶ vb pleuvoir ▷ It rains a lot here. Il pleut beaucoup par ici.; **It's raining.** Il pleut.

rainbow n arc-en-ciel m (pl arcs-en-ciel)

raincoat n imperméable m

rainforest n forêt f tropicale humide

rainy adj pluvieux (f pluvieuse)

raise vb ❶ (lift) lever ▷ He raised his hand. Il a levé la main. ❷ (improve) améliorer ▷ They want to raise standards in schools. Ils veulent améliorer le niveau dans les écoles.; **to raise money** collecter des fonds ▷ The school is raising money for a new gym. L'école collecte des fonds pour un nouveau gymnase.

raisin n raisin m sec

⬛ Word for word, the French means "dried grape".

rake n râteau m (pl râteaux)

rally n ❶ (of people) rassemblement m ❷ (sport) rallye m ▷ a rally driver un pilote de rallye ❸ (in tennis) échange m

rambler n randonneur m, randonneuse f

ramp n (for wheelchairs) rampe f d'accès

ran vb see **run**

rang vb see **ring**

range n choix m ▷ a wide range of colours un grand choix de coloris; **a range of subjects** diverses matières ▷ We study a range of subjects. Nous étudions diverses matières.; **a mountain range** une chaîne de montagnes

▶ vb **to range from ... to** se situer entre ... et ▷ Temperatures in summer range from 20 to 35 degrees. Les températures estivales se situent entre vingt et trente-cinq degrés.; **Tickets range from £2 to £20.** Les billets coûtent entre deux et vingt livres.

rap n (music) rap m

rape n viol m

▶ vb violer

rapids npl rapides mpl

rare adj ① (unusual) rare ▷ a rare plant une plante rare ② (steak) saignant(e)

raspberry n framboise f ▷ raspberry jam la confiture de framboises

rat n rat m

rather adv plutôt ▷ I was rather disappointed. J'étais plutôt déçu.; **rather a lot of** pas mal de ▷ I've got rather a lot of homework to do. J'ai pas mal de devoirs à faire.; **rather than** plutôt que ▷ We decided to camp, rather than stay at a hotel. Nous avons décidé de camper plutôt que d'aller à l'hôtel.; **I'd rather ...** J'aimerais mieux ... ▷ I'd

rather stay in tonight. J'aimerais mieux rester à la maison ce soir. ▷ Would you like a sweet? — I'd rather have an apple. Tu veux un bonbon? — J'aimerais mieux une pomme.

rattlesnake n serpent m à sonnette

rave n (party) rave f

ravenous adj **to be ravenous** avoir une faim de loup ▷ I'm ravenous! J'ai une faim de loup!

raw adj (food) cru(e); **raw materials** les matières premières

razor n rasoir m ▷ some disposable razors des rasoirs jetables; **a razor blade** une lame de rasoir

RE n éducation f religieuse

reach n **out of reach** hors de portée ▷ The light switch was out of reach. L'interrupteur était hors de portée.; **within easy reach of** à proximité de ▷ The hotel is within easy reach of the town centre. L'hôtel se trouve à proximité du centre-ville.

▶ vb ① arriver à ▷ We reached the hotel at 7 p.m. Nous sommes arrivés à l'hôtel à sept heures du soir.; **We hope to reach the final.** Nous espérons aller en finale. ② (decision) parvenir à ▷ Eventually they reached a decision. Ils sont finalement parvenus à une décision.; **He reached for his gun.** Il a tendu la main pour prendre son revolver.

reaction n réaction f

reactor n réacteur m ▷ a nuclear reactor un réacteur nucléaire

read vb lire ▷ I don't read much. Je ne lis pas beaucoup. ▷ Read the text out loud. Lis le texte à haute voix.

read out vb lire ▷ He read out the article to me. Il m'a lu l'article.; **to read out the results** annoncer les résultats

reading n lecture f ▷ Reading is one of my hobbies. La lecture est l'une de mes activités favorites.

ready adj prêt(e) ▷ She's nearly ready. Elle est presque prête. ▷ He's always ready to help. Il est toujours prêt à rendre service.; **a ready meal** un plat cuisiné; **to get ready** se préparer ▷ She's getting ready to go out. Elle est en train de se préparer pour sortir.; **to get something ready** préparer quelque chose ▷ He's getting the dinner ready. Il est en train de préparer le dîner.

real adj ① vrai(e) ▷ He wasn't a real policeman. Ce n'était pas un vrai policier. ▷ Her real name is Cordelia. Son vrai nom est Cordelia. ② véritable ▷ It's real leather. C'est du cuir véritable. ▷ It was a real nightmare. C'était un véritable cauchemar.; **in real life** dans la réalité

realistic adj réaliste

reality n réalité f; **reality TV** téléréalité f

realize vb **to realize that ...** se rendre compte que ... ▷ We realized that something was wrong. Nous nous sommes rendu compte que quelque chose n'allait pas.

really adv vraiment ▷ She's really nice. Elle est vraiment sympathique. ▷ Do you want to go? — Not really. Tu veux y aller? — Pas vraiment.; **I'm learning German. — Really?** J'apprends l'allemand. — Ah bon?; **Do you really think so?** Tu es sûr?

realtor n (US) agent m immobilier

reason n raison f ▷ There's no reason to think that ... Il n'y a aucune raison de penser que ...; **for security reasons** pour des raisons de sécurité; **That was the main reason I went.** C'est surtout pour ça que j'y suis allé.

reasonable adj ① (sensible) raisonnable ▷ Be reasonable! Sois raisonnable! ② (not bad) correct ▷ He wrote a reasonable essay. Sa dissertation était correcte.

reasonably adv raisonnablement ▷ The team played reasonably well. L'équipe a joué raisonnablement bien.; **reasonably priced accommodation** un logement à un prix raisonnable

reassure vb rassurer

reassuring adj rassurant(e)

rebellious adj rebelle

receipt n reçu m

receive vb recevoir

receiver n (of phone) combiné m; **to pick up the receiver** décrocher

recent adj récent(e)

recently adv ces derniers temps ▷ I've been doing a lot of training recently. Je me suis beaucoup entraîné ces derniers temps.

reception n réception f ▷ Please leave your key at reception. Merci de laisser votre clé à la réception. ▷ The reception will be at a big hotel. La réception aura lieu dans un grand hôtel.

receptionist n réceptionniste mf

recipe n recette f

reckon vb penser ▷ What do you reckon? Qu'est-ce que tu en penses?

recognize vb reconnaître ▷ You'll recognize me by my red hair. Vous me reconnaîtrez à mes cheveux roux.

recommend vb conseiller ▷ What do you recommend? Qu'est-ce que vous me conseillez?

reconsider vb reconsidérer

record n ① (recording) disque m ▷ my favourite record mon disque préféré ② (sport) record m ▷ the world record le record du monde; **in record time** en un temps record ▷ She finished the job in record time. Elle a terminé le record en un temps record.; **a criminal record** un casier judiciaire ▷ He's got a criminal record. Il a un casier judiciaire.; **records** (of police, hospital) archives fpl ▷ I'll check in the records. Je vais vérifier dans les archives.; **There is no record of your booking.** Il n'y a aucune trace de votre réservation.

▶ vb (on film, tape) enregistrer ▷ They've just recorded their new album. Ils viennent d'enregistrer leur nouveau disque.

recorded delivery n to send something recorded delivery

envoyer quelque chose en recommandé

recorder n (instrument) flûte f à bec ▷ She plays the recorder. Elle joue de la flûte à bec.; **a cassette recorder** un magnétophone à cassettes; **a video recorder** un magnétoscope

recording n enregistrement m

record player n tourne-disque m

recover vb se remettre ▷ He's recovering from a knee injury. Il se remet d'une blessure au genou.

recovery n rétablissement m ▷ Best wishes for a speedy recovery! Meilleurs vœux de prompt rétablissement!

rectangle n rectangle m

rectangular adj rectangulaire

recycle vb recycler

recycling n recyclage m

red adj ① rouge ▷ a red rose une rose rouge ▷ red meat la viande rouge; **a red light** (traffic light) un feu rouge ▷ to go through a red light brûler un feu rouge ② (hair) roux (f rousse) ▷ Tamsin's got red hair. Tamsin a les cheveux roux.

Red Cross n Croix-Rouge f

redcurrant n groseille f

redecorate vb ① (with wallpaper) retapisser ② (with paint) refaire les peintures

redo vb refaire

reduce vb réduire ▷ at a reduced price à prix réduit; **"reduce speed now"** "ralentir"

reduction n réduction f ▷ a 5% reduction une réduction de cinq pour cent; **"huge reductions!"** "prix sacrifiés!"

redundant adj **to be made redundant** être licencié(e) ▷ *He was made redundant yesterday.* Il a été licencié hier.

refer vb **to refer to** faire allusion à ▷ *What are you referring to?* À quoi faites-vous allusion?

referee n arbitre m

reference n ❶ allusion f ▷ *He made no reference to the murder.* Il n'a fait aucune allusion au meurtre. ❷ (for job application) références fpl ▷ *Would you please give me a reference?* Pouvez-vous me fournir des références?; **a reference book** un ouvrage de référence

refill vb remplir à nouveau ▷ *He refilled my glass.* Il a rempli mon verre à nouveau.

reflect vb (light, image) refléter

reflection n (in mirror) reflet m

reflex n réflexe m

reflexive adj réfléchi(e) ▷ *a reflexive verb* un verbe réfléchi

refreshing adj rafraîchissant(e)

refreshments npl rafraîchissements mpl

refrigerator n réfrigérateur m

refuge n refuge m

refugee n réfugié m, réfugiée f

refund n remboursement m
▶ vb rembourser

refuse vb refuser
▶ n ordures fpl; **refuse collection** le ramassage des ordures

regain vb **to regain consciousness** reprendre connaissance

regard n **Give my regards to Alice.** Transmettez mon bon souvenir à Alice.; **Louis sends his regards.** Vous avez le bonjour de Louis.; **"with kind regards"** "bien cordialement"
▶ vb **to regard something as** considérer quelque chose comme; **as regards ...** concernant ...

regiment n régiment m

region n région f

regional adj régional(e) (pl régionaux)

register n (in school) registre m d'absences
▶ vb (at school, college) s'inscrire

registered adj **a registered letter** une lettre recommandée

registration n ❶ (roll call) appel m ❷ (of car) numéro m d'immatriculation

regret n regret m; **I've got no regrets.** Je ne regrette rien.
▶ vb regretter ▷ *Give me the money or you'll regret it!* Donne-moi l'argent, sinon tu vas le regretter!

regular adj ❶ régulier (f régulière) ▷ *at regular intervals* à intervalles réguliers ▷ *a regular verb* un verbe régulier; **to take regular exercise** faire régulièrement de l'exercice ❷ (average) normal (pl normaux) ▷ *a regular portion of fries* une portion de frites normale

regularly adv régulièrement

regulation n règlement m

rehearsal n répétition f

rehearse vb répéter

rein n rêne f ▷ **the reins** les rênes

reindeer n renne m

reject vb (idea, suggestion) rejeter
▷ We rejected that idea straight away.
Nous avons immédiatement
rejeté cette idée.; **I applied but
they rejected me.** J'ai posé ma
candidature mais ils l'ont rejetée.

related adj (people) apparenté(e)
▷ We're related. Nous sommes
apparentés.; **The two events
were not related.** Il n'y avait
aucun rapport entre les deux
événements.

relation n ❶ (person) parent m,
parente f ▷ He's a distant relation.
C'est un parent éloigné. ▷ my close
relations mes parents proches;
my relations ma famille; **I've
got relations in London.** J'ai de la
famille à Londres. ❷ (connection)
rapport m ▷ It has no relation to
reality. Cela n'a aucun rapport
avec la réalité.; **in relation to** par
rapport à

relationship n relations fpl ▷ We
have a good relationship. Nous avons
de bonnes relations.; **I'm not in
a relationship at the moment.**
Je ne sors avec personne en ce
moment.

relative n parent m, parente f ▷ my
close relatives mes proches parents;
all her relatives toute sa famille

relatively adv relativement

relax vb se détendre ▷ I relax
listening to music. Je me détends en
écoutant de la musique.; **Relax!
Everything's fine.** Ne t'en fais pas!
Tout va bien.

relaxation n détente f ▷ I don't have

much time for relaxation. Je n'ai pas
beaucoup de moments de détente.

relaxed adj détendu(e)

relaxing adj reposant(e); **I find
cooking relaxing.** Cela me détend
de faire la cuisine.

relay n a relay race une course
de relais

release vb ❶ (prisoner) libérer
❷ (report, news) divulguer
❸ (record, video) sortir
▶ n (from prison) libération f
▷ the release of Nelson Mandela la
libération de Nelson Mandela;
the band's latest release le
dernier disque du groupe

relevant adj (documents)
approprié(e); **That's not relevant.**
Ça n'a aucun rapport.; **to be
relevant to something** être
en rapport avec quelque chose
▷ Education should be relevant to real
life. L'enseignement devrait être en
rapport avec la réalité.

reliable adj fiable ▷ a reliable car
une voiture fiable ▷ He's not very
reliable. Il n'est pas très fiable.

relief n soulagement m ▷ That's a
relief! Quel soulagement!

relieved adj soulagé(e) ▷ I was
relieved to hear ... J'ai été soulagé
d'apprendre ...

religion n religion f ▷ What religion
are you? Quelle est votre religion?

religious adj ❶ religieux
(f religieuse) ▷ my religious beliefs
mes croyances religieuses
❷ croyant(e) ▷ I'm not religious.
Je ne suis pas croyant.

reluctant adj to be reluctant to do something être peu disposé à faire quelque chose ▷ They were reluctant to help us. Ils étaient peu disposés à nous aider.

reluctantly adv à contrecœur

rely on vb compter sur ▷ I'm relying on you. Je compte sur toi.

remain vb rester; to remain silent garder le silence

remaining adj le reste de ▷ the remaining ingredients le reste des ingrédients

remark n remarque f

remarkable adj remarquable

remarkably adv remarquablement

remember vb se souvenir de ▷ I can't remember his name. Je ne me souviens pas de son nom. ▷ I don't remember. Je ne m'en souviens pas.

> In French you often say "don't forget" instead of **remember**. ▷ Remember your passport! N'oublie pas ton passeport!

remind vb rappeler ▷ It reminds me of Scotland. Cela me rappelle l'Écosse. ▷ I'll remind you tomorrow. Je te le rappellerai demain.

remote adj isolé(e) ▷ a remote village un village isolé

remote control n télécommande f

remotely adv I'm not remotely interested. Je ne suis absolument pas intéressé.; Do you think it would be remotely possible? Pensez-vous que cela serait éventuellement possible?

remove vb ❶ enlever ▷ Please remove your bag from my seat. Est-ce que vous pouvez enlever votre sac de mon siège? ❷ (stain) faire partir ▷ Did you remove the stain? Est-ce que tu as fait partir la tache?

renew vb (passport, licence) renouveler

renewable adj (energy, resource) renouvelable

renovate vb rénover ▷ The building's been renovated. Le bâtiment a été rénové.

rent n loyer m
> ▶ vb louer ▷ We rented a car. Nous avons loué une voiture.

reorganize vb réorganiser

rep n (= representative) représentant m, représentante f

repaid vb see **repay**

repair vb réparer; to get something repaired faire réparer quelque chose ▷ I got the washing machine repaired. J'ai fait réparer la machine à laver.
> ▶ n réparation f

repay vb (money) rembourser

repeat vb répéter
> ▶ n reprise f ▷ There are too many repeats on TV. Il y a trop de reprises à la télé.

repeatedly adv à plusieurs reprises

repetitive adj (movement, work) répétitif (f répétitive)

replace vb remplacer

replay n There will be a replay on Friday. Le match sera rejoué vendredi.
> ▶ vb (match) rejouer

reply n réponse f
▶ vb répondre

report n ❶ (of event) compte m rendu (pl comptes rendus) ❷ (news report) reportage m ▷ a report in the paper un reportage dans le journal ❸ (at school) bulletin m scolaire ▷ I got a good report this term. J'ai un bon bulletin scolaire ce trimestre.
▶ vb ❶ signaler ▷ I reported the theft to the police. J'ai signalé le vol au commissariat. ❷ se présenter ▷ Report to reception when you arrive. Présentez-vous à la réception à votre arrivée.

reporter n reporter m ▷ I'd like to be a reporter. J'aimerais être reporter.

represent vb représenter

representative adj représentatif (f représentative)

reptile n reptile m

republic n république f

reputation n réputation f

request n demande f
▶ vb demander

require vb exiger ▷ The job requires a sound knowledge of classical music. Cet emploi exige une bonne connaissance de la musique classique.; **What qualifications are required?** Quelles sont les diplômes requis?

rescue vb sauver
▶ n ❶ sauvetage m ▷ a rescue operation une opération de sauvetage; **a mountain rescue team** une équipe de sauvetage en montagne ❷ secours m ▷ the rescue services les services de

secours; **to come to somebody's rescue** venir au secours de quelqu'un ▷ He came to my rescue. Il est venu à mon secours.

research n ❶ (experimental) recherche f ▷ He's doing research. Il fait de la recherche. ❷ (theoretical) recherches fpl ▷ She's doing some research in the library. Elle fait des recherches à la bibliothèque.

resemblance n ressemblance f

resemble vt ressembler à

resent vb être contrarié(e) par ▷ I really resented your criticism. J'ai été vraiment contrarié par tes critiques.

resentful adj plein(e) de ressentiment; **to feel resentful towards somebody** en vouloir à quelqu'un

reservation n ❶ (booking) réservation f ▷ I'd like to make a reservation for this evening. J'aimerais faire une réservation pour ce soir.

reserve n ❶ (place) réserve f ▷ a nature reserve une réserve naturelle ❷ (person) remplaçant m, remplaçante f ▷ I was reserve in the game last Saturday. J'étais remplaçant dans le match de samedi dernier.
▶ vb réserver ▷ I'd like to reserve a table for tomorrow evening. J'aimerais réserver une table pour demain soir.

reserved adj réservé(e) ▷ a reserved seat une place réservée ▷ He's quite reserved. Il est assez réservé.

resident n résident m, résidente f

residential adj résidentiel (f résidentielle) ▷ a residential area un quartier résidentiel

resign vb donner sa démission

resist vt résister à

resit vb repasser ▷ I'm resitting the exam in December. Je vais repasser l'examen en décembre.

resolution n résolution f; **Have you made any New Year's resolutions?** Tu as pris de bonnes résolutions pour l'année nouvelle?

resort n (at seaside) station f balnéaire ▷ It's a resort on the Costa del Sol. C'est une station balnéaire sur la Costa del Sol.; **a ski resort** une station de ski; **as a last resort** en dernier recours

resource n ressource f

respect n respect m
  ▶ vb respecter

respectable adj ❶ respectable ❷ (standard, marks) correct

responsibility n responsabilité f

responsible adj ❶ (in charge) responsable; **to be responsible for something** être responsable de quelque chose ▷ He's responsible for booking the tickets. Il est responsable de la réservation des billets.; **It's a responsible job.** C'est un poste à responsabilités. ❷ (mature) sérieux (f sérieuse) ▷ You should be more responsible. Tu devrais être un peu plus sérieux.

rest n ❶ (relaxation) repos m ▷ five minutes' rest cinq minutes de repos; **to have a rest** se reposer ▷ We stopped to have a rest. Nous nous sommes arrêtés pour nous reposer. ❷ (remainder) reste m ▷ I'll do the rest. Je ferai le reste. ▷ the rest of the money le reste de l'argent; **the rest of them** les autres ▷ The rest of them went swimming. Les autres sont allés nager.
  ▶ vb ❶ (relax) se reposer ▷ She's resting in her room. Elle se repose dans sa chambre. ❷ (not overstrain) ménager ▷ He has to rest his knee. Il doit ménager son genou. ❸ (lean) appuyer ▷ I rested my bike against the window. J'ai appuyé mon vélo contre la fenêtre.

restaurant n restaurant m ▷ We don't often go to restaurants. Nous n'allons pas souvent au restaurant.; **a restaurant car** un wagon-restaurant

restless adj agité(e)

restore vb (building, picture) restaurer

restrict vb limiter

rest room n (US) toilettes fpl

result n résultat m ▷ my exam results mes résultats d'examen
  ▶ vb **to result in** entraîner

resume vb reprendre ▷ They've resumed work. Ils ont repris le travail.

  █ Be careful not to translate **to resume** by résumer.

résumé n (US) curriculum vitae m

retire vb prendre sa retraite ▷ He retired last year. Il a pris sa retraite l'an dernier.

a b c d e f g h i j k l m n o p q r s t u v w x y z

retired adj retraité(e) ▷ *She's retired.* Elle est retraitée.; **a retired teacher** un professeur à la retraite

retirement n retraite f

return n ❶ retour m ▷ *after our return* à notre retour; **the return journey** le voyage de retour; **a return match** un match retour ❷ (ticket) aller retour m ▷ *A return to Avignon, please.* Un aller retour pour Avignon, s'il vous plaît.; **in return** en échange ▷ *... and I help her in return* ... et je l'aide en échange; **in return for** en échange de; **Many happy returns!** Bon anniversaire!
▶ vb ❶ (come back) revenir ▷ *I've just returned from holiday.* Je viens de revenir de vacances.; **to return home** rentrer à la maison ❷ (go back) retourner ▷ *He returned to France the following year.* Il est retourné en France l'année suivante. ❸ (give back) rendre ▷ *She borrows my things and doesn't return them.* Elle m'emprunte mes affaires et ne me les rend pas.

reunion n réunion f

reveal vb révéler

revenge n vengeance f ▷ *in revenge* par vengeance; **to take revenge** se venger ▷ *They planned to take revenge on him.* Ils voulaient se venger de lui.

reverse vb (car) faire marche arrière ▷ *He reversed without looking.* Il a fait marche arrière sans regarder.; **to reverse the charges** (telephone) appeler en PCV

● In France, reversing the charges
● is only possible for international
● calls.

▷ *I'd like to make a reverse charge call to Britain.* Je voudrais appeler la Grande-Bretagne en PCV.
▶ adj inverse ▷ *in reverse order* dans l'ordre inverse; **in reverse gear** en marche arrière

review n (of book, film, programme) critique f ▷ *The book had good reviews.* Ce livre a eu de bonnes critiques.
▶ adj inverse ▷ *in reverse order* dans

revise vb réviser ▷ *I haven't started revising yet.* Je n'ai pas encore commencé à réviser.; **I've revised my opinion.** J'ai changé d'opinion.

revision n révisions fpl ▷ *Have you done a lot of revision?* Est-ce que tu as fait beaucoup de révisions?

revolting adj dégoûtant(e)

revolution n révolution f; **the French Revolution** la Révolution française

reward n récompense f

rewarding adj gratifiant(e) ▷ *a rewarding job* un travail gratifiant

rewind vb rembobiner ▷ *to rewind a cassette* rembobiner une cassette

Rhine n Rhin m

rhinoceros n rhinocéros m

Rhone n Rhône m

rhubarb n rhubarbe f ▷ *a rhubarb tart* une tarte à la rhubarbe

rhythm n rythme m

rib n côte f

ribbon n ruban m

rice n riz m; **rice pudding** le riz au lait

rich adj riche; **the rich** les riches

rid vb **to get rid of** se débarrasser de ▷ I want to get rid of some old clothes. Je veux me débarrasser de vieux vêtements.

ridden vb see **ride**

ride n **to go for a ride (1)** (on horse) monter à cheval **(2)** (on bike) faire un tour en vélo ▷ We went for a bike ride. Nous sommes allés faire un tour en vélo.; **It's a short bus ride to the town centre.** Ce n'est pas loin du centre-ville en bus.
▶ vb (on horse) monter à cheval ▷ I'm learning to ride. J'apprends à monter à cheval.; **to ride a bike** faire du vélo ▷ Can you ride a bike? Tu sais faire du vélo?

rider n **①** (on horse) cavalier m, cavalière f ▷ She's a good rider. C'est une bonne cavalière. **②** (on bike) cycliste mf

ridiculous adj ridicule ▷ Don't be ridiculous! Ne sois pas ridicule!

riding n équitation f; **to go riding** faire de l'équitation; **a riding school** une école d'équitation

rifle n fusil m ▷ a hunting rifle un fusil de chasse

right adj, adv
| There are several ways of translating **right**. Scan the examples to find one that is similar to what you want to say.

① (factually correct, suitable) bon (f bonne) ▷ the right answer la bonne réponse ▷ Is it the right size. Ce n'est pas la bonne taille. ▷ We're on the right train. Nous

sommes dans le bon train.; **Is this the right road for Arles?** Est-ce que c'est bien la route pour aller à Arles? **②** (correctly) correctement ▷ Am I pronouncing it right? Est-ce que je prononce ça correctement?; **to be right (1)** (person) avoir raison ▷ You were right! Tu avais raison! **(2)** (statement, opinion) être vrai(e) ▷ That's right! C'est vrai **③** (accurate) juste ▷ Do you have the right time? Est-ce que vous avez l'heure juste? **④** (morally correct) bien ▷ It's not right to behave like that. Ce n'est pas bien d'agir comme ça.; **I think you did the right thing.** Je pense que tu as bien fait. **⑤** (not left) droit(e) ▷ my right hand ma main droite **⑥** (turn, look) à droite ▷ Turn right at the traffic lights. Tournez à droite aux prochains feux.; **Right! Let's get started.** Bon! On commence.; **right away** tout de suite ▷ I'll do it right away. Je vais le faire tout de suite.
▶ n **①** droit m ▷ You've got no right to do that. Vous n'avez pas le droit de faire ça. **②** (not left) droite f; **on the right** à droite ▷ Remember to drive on the right. N'oubliez pas de conduire à droite.; **right of way** la priorité ▷ It was our right of way. Nous avions la priorité.

right-hand adj **the right-hand side** la droite ▷ It's on the right-hand side. C'est à droite.

right-handed adj droitier (f droitière)

rightly adv avec raison ▷ *She rightly decided not to go.* Elle a décidé, avec raison, de ne pas y aller.; **if I remember rightly** si je me souviens bien

ring n ❶ anneau m (pl anneaux) ▷ *a gold ring* un anneau en or ❷ (with stones) bague f ▷ *a diamond ring* une bague de diamants; **a wedding ring** une alliance ❸ (circle) cercle m ▷ *to stand in a ring* se mettre en cercle ❹ (of bell) coup m de sonnette ▷ *I was woken by a ring at the door.* J'ai été réveillé par un coup de sonnette.; **to give somebody a ring** appeler quelqu'un ▷ *I'll give you a ring this evening.* Je t'appellerai ce soir.

▷ vb ❶ téléphoner ▷ *Your mother rang this morning.* Ta mère a téléphoné ce matin.; **to ring somebody** appeler quelqu'un ▷ *I'll ring you tomorrow morning.* Je t'appellerai demain matin.; **to ring somebody up** donner un coup de fil à quelqu'un ❷ sonner ▷ *The phone's ringing.* Le téléphone sonne.; **to ring the bell** (doorbell) sonner à la porte ▷ *I rang the bell three times.* J'ai sonné trois fois à la porte.; **to ring back** rappeler ▷ *I'll ring back later.* Je rappellerai plus tard.

ring binder n classeur m

rinse vb rincer

riot n émeute f
▷ vb faire une émeute

rip vb ❶ déchirer ▷ *I've ripped my jeans.* J'ai déchiré mon jean. ❷ se

déchirer ▷ *My skirt's ripped.* Ma jupe s'est déchirée.

rip off vb arnaquer ▷ *The hotel ripped us off.* L'hôtel nous a arnaqués.

rip up vb déchirer ▷ *He read the note and then ripped it up.* Il a lu le mot, puis l'a déchiré.

ripe adj mûr(e)

rip-off n (informal); **It's a rip-off!** C'est de l'arnaque!

rise n ❶ (in prices, temperature) hausse f ▷ *a sudden rise in temperature* une hausse subite de température ❷ (pay rise) augmentation f
▷ vb ❶ (increase) augmenter ▷ *Prices are rising.* Les prix augmentent. ❷ se lever ▷ *The sun rises early in June.* Le soleil se lève tôt en juin.

risk n risque m; **to take risks** prendre des risques; **It's at your own risk.** C'est à vos risques et périls.
▷ vb risquer ▷ *You risk getting a fine.* Vous risquez de recevoir une amende.; **I wouldn't risk it if I were you.** À votre place, je ne prendrais pas ce risque.

rival n rival m, rivale f (pl rivaux)
▷ adj ❶ rival(e) (pl rivaux) ▷ *a rival gang* une bande rivale ❷ concurrent(e) ▷ *a rival company* une société concurrente

river n rivière f ▷ *The river runs alongside the canal.* La rivière longe le canal. ❷ (major) fleuve m ▷ *the rivers of France* les fleuves de France; **the river Seine** la Seine

road n ❶ route f ▷ *There's a lot of traffic on the roads.* Il y a beaucoup de circulation sur les routes. ❷ (street) rue f ▷ *They live across the road.* Ils habitent de l'autre côté de la rue.

road map n carte f routière

road rage n agressivité f au volant

road sign n panneau m de signalisation (pl panneaux de signalisation)

roadworks npl travaux mpl

roast adj rôti(e) ▷ *roast chicken* le poulet rôti; **roast pork** le rôti de porc; **roast beef** le rôti de bœuf

rob vb **to rob somebody** voler quelqu'un ▷ *I've been robbed.* On m'a volé.; **to rob somebody of something** voler quelque chose à quelqu'un ▷ *He was robbed of his wallet.* On lui a volé son portefeuille.; **to rob a bank** dévaliser une banque

robber n voleur m; **a bank-robber** un cambrioleur de banques

robbery n vol m; **a bank robbery** un hold-up; **armed robbery** le vol à main armée

robin n rouge-gorge m

robot n robot m

rock n ❶ (substance) roche f ▷ *They tunnelled through the rock.* Ils ont creusé un tunnel dans la roche. ❷ (boulder) rocher m ▷ *I sat on a rock.* Je me suis assis sur un rocher. ❸ (music) rock m ▷ *a rock concert* un concert de rock

▶ vb ébranler ▷ *The explosion rocked the building.* L'explosion a ébranlé le bâtiment.

rocket n (firework, spacecraft) fusée f

rocking horse n cheval m à bascule

rod n (for fishing) canne f à pêche

rode vb see **ride**

role n rôle m

role play n jeu m de rôle (pl jeux de rôles) ▷ **to do a role play** faire un jeu de rôle

roll n ❶ rouleau m (pl rouleaux) ▷ *a roll of tape* un rouleau de ruban adhésif ▷ *a toilet roll* un rouleau de papier hygiénique ❷ (bread) petit pain m

▶ vb rouler; **to roll out the pastry** étaler la pâte

Rollerblade® n roller m ▷ *a pair of Rollerblades* une paire de rollers

rollercoaster n montagnes fpl russes

roller skates npl patins mpl à roulettes

roller-skating n patin m à roulettes; **to go roller-skating** faire du patin à roulettes

Roman adj, n (ancient) romain(e) ▷ *a Roman villa* une villa romaine ▷ *the Roman empire* l'empire romain

Roman Catholic n catholique mf ▷ *He's a Roman Catholic.* Il est catholique.

romance n ❶ (novels) romans mpl d'amour ▷ *I read a lot of romance.* Je lis beaucoup de romans d'amour. ❷ (glamour) charme m ▷ *the romance of Paris* le charme de Paris;

a holiday romance une idylle de vacances

Romania n Roumanie f; **in Romania** en Roumanie

Romanian adj roumain(e)

romantic adj romantique

roof n toit m

roof rack n galerie f

room n ❶ (space) pièce f ▷ the biggest room in the house la plus grande pièce de la maison ❷ (bedroom) chambre f ▷ She's in her room. Elle est dans sa chambre.; **a single room** une chambre pour une personne; **a double room** une chambre pour deux personnes ❸ (in school) salle f ▷ the music room la salle de musique ❹ (space) place f ▷ There's no room for that box. Il n'y a pas de place pour cette boîte.

root n racine f

root around vb fouiller ▷ She started rooting around in her handbag. Elle a commencé à fouiller dans son sac à main.

root out vb traquer ▷ They are determined to root out corruption. Ils sont déterminés à traquer la corruption.

rope n corde f

rope in vb enrôler ▷ I was roped in to help with the refreshments. J'ai été enrôlé pour servir les rafraîchissements.

rose n (flower) rose f

▶ vb see **rise**

rot n pourrir

rotten adj (decayed) pourri(e) ▷ a rotten apple une pomme pourrie;

rotten weather un temps pourri; **That's a rotten thing to do.** Ce n'est vraiment pas gentil.; **to feel rotten** être mal fichu (informal)

rough adj ❶ (surface) rêche ▷ My hands are rough. J'ai les mains rêches. ❷ (game) violent ▷ Rugby's a rough sport. Le rugby est un sport violent. ❸ (place) difficile ▷ It's a rough area. C'est un quartier difficile. ❹ (water) houleux (f houleuse) ▷ The sea was rough. La mer était houleuse. ❺ approximatif (f approximative) ▷ I've got a rough idea. J'en ai une idée approximative.; **to feel rough** ne pas être dans son assiette ▷ I feel rough. Je ne suis pas dans mon assiette.

roughly adv à peu près ▷ It weighs roughly 20 kilos. Ça pèse à peu près vingt kilos.

round adj, adv, prep ❶ rond(e) ▷ a round table une table ronde ❷ (around) autour de ▷ We were sitting round the table. Nous étions assis autour de la table.; **It's just round the corner.** (very near) C'est tout près.; **to go round to somebody's house** aller chez quelqu'un ▷ I went round to my friend's house. Je suis allé chez mon ami.; **to have a look round** faire un tour ▷ We're going to have a look round. Nous allons faire un tour.; **to go round a museum** visiter un musée; **round here** près d'ici ▷ Is there a chemist's round here? Est-ce qu'il y a une pharmacie près d'ici?;

He lives round here. Il habite dans les parages.; **all round** partout ▷ *There were vineyards all round.* Il y avait des vignobles partout.; **all year round** toute l'année; **round about** (*roughly*) environ ▷ *It costs round about £100.* Cela coûte environ cent livres. ▷ *round about 8 o'clock* à huit heures environ
▶ *n* ❶ (*of tournament*) manche *f* ❷ (*of boxing match*) round *m*; **a round of golf** une partie de golf; **a round of drinks** une tournée ▷ *He bought a round of drinks.* Il a offert une tournée.

round off *vb* terminer ▷ *They rounded off the meal with liqueurs.* Ils ont terminé le repas par des liqueurs.

round up *vb* ❶ (*sheep, cattle, suspects*) rassembler ❷ (*figure*) arrondir

roundabout *n* ❶ (*at junction*) rond-point *m* (*pl* ronds-points) ❷ (*at funfair*) manège *m*

rounders *n*
- Rounders is not played in France. People play baseball instead.

round trip *n* (*US*) aller et retour *m*

route *n* ❶ itinéraire *m* ▷ *We're planning our route.* Nous établissons notre itinéraire. ❷ (*of bus*) parcours *m*

routine *n* **my daily routine** mes occupations quotidiennes

row *n*
> This word has two pronunciations. Make sure you choose the right translation.

❶ rangée *f* ▷ *a row of houses* une rangée de maisons ❷ (*of seats*) rang *m* ▷ *Our seats are in the front row.* Nos places se trouvent au premier rang.; **five times in a row** cinq fois d'affilée ❸ (*noise*) vacarme *m* ▷ *What's that terrible row?* qu'est-ce que c'est que ce vacarme? ❹ (*quarrel*) dispute *f*; **to have a row** se disputer ▷ *They've had a row.* Ils se sont disputés.
▶ *vb* ❶ ramer ▷ *We took turns to row.* Nous avons ramé à tour de rôle. ❷ (*as sport*) faire de l'aviron

rowboat *n* (*US*) bateau *m* à rames

rowing *n* (*sport*) aviron *m* ▷ *My hobby is rowing.* Je fais de l'aviron.; **a rowing boat** un bateau à rames

royal *adj* royal(e) (*mpl* royaux); **the royal family** la famille royale

rub *vb* ❶ (*stain*) frotter ❷ (*part of body*) se frotter ▷ *Don't rub your eyes!* Ne te frotte pas les yeux!; **to rub something out** effacer quelque chose

rubber *n* ❶ caoutchouc *m* ▷ *rubber soles* des semelles en caoutchouc ❷ (*eraser*) gomme *f* ▷ *Can I borrow your rubber?* Je peux emprunter ta gomme?; **a rubber band** un élastique

rubbish *n* ❶ (*refuse*) ordures *fpl* ▷ *When do they collect the rubbish?* Quand est-ce qu'ils ramassent les ordures? ❷ (*junk*) camelote *f* ▷ *They sell a lot of rubbish at the market.* Ils vendent beaucoup de camelote au marché. ❸ (*nonsense*) bêtises *fpl* ▷ *Don't talk rubbish!* Ne dis pas de bêtises!; **That's a load of rubbish!** C'est vraiment n'importe quoi! (informal); **a rubbish bin** une poubelle; **a rubbish dump** une décharge

▸ adj nul (f nulle) ▷ They're a rubbish team! Cette équipe est nulle!

rucksack n sac m à dos

rude adj ❶ (impolite) impoli(e) ▷ It's rude to interrupt. C'est impoli de couper la parole aux gens. ❷ (offensive) grossier (f grossière) ▷ He was very rude to me. Il a été très grossier avec moi.; **a rude word** un gros mot

rug n ❶ tapis m ▷ a Persian rug un tapis persan ❷ (blanket) couverture f ▷ a tartan rug une couverture écossaise

rugby n rugby m ▷ I play rugby. Je joue au rugby.

ruin n ruine f ▷ the ruins of the castle les ruines du château; **in ruins** en ruine

▸ vb ❶ abîmer ▷ You'll ruin your shoes. Tu vas abîmer tes chaussures. ❷ gâcher ▷ It ruined our holiday. Ça a gâché nos vacances. ❸ (financially) ruiner

rule n ❶ règle f ▷ the rules of grammar les règles de grammaire; **as a rule** en règle générale ❷ (regulation) règlement m ▷ It's against the rules. C'est contre le règlement.

ruler n règle f ▷ Can I borrow your ruler? Je peux emprunter ta règle?

rum n rhum m

rumour (US rumor) n rumeur f

▸ It's just a rumour. Ce n'est qu'une rumeur.

run n (in cricket) point m ▷ to score a run marquer un point; **to go for a run** courir ▷ I go for a run every morning. Je cours tous les matins.; **I did a ten-kilometre run.** J'ai couru dix kilomètres.; **on the run** en fuite ▷ The criminals are still on the run. Les criminels sont toujours en fuite.; **in the long run** à long terme

▸ vb ❶ courir ▷ I ran five kilometres. J'ai couru cinq kilomètres.; **to run a marathon** participer à un marathon ❷ (manage) diriger ▷ He runs a large company. Il dirige une grosse société. ❸ (organize) organiser ▷ They run music courses in the holidays. Ils organisent des cours de musique pendant les vacances. ❹ (water) couler ▷ Don't leave the tap running. Ne laisse pas couler le robinet.; **to run a bath** faire couler un bain ❺ (by car) conduire ▷ I can run you to the station. Je peux te conduire à la gare.; **to run away** s'enfuir ▷ They ran away before the police came. Ils se sont enfuis avant l'arrivée de la police.; **Time is running out.** Il ne reste plus beaucoup de temps.; **to run out of something** se trouver à court de quelque chose ▷ We ran out of money. Nous nous sommes trouvés à court d'argent.; **to run somebody over** écraser quelqu'un; **to get run over** se faire écraser ▷ Be careful, or you'll get run over! Fais attention, sinon tu vas te faire écraser!

rung vb see **ring**

runner n coureur m, coureuse f

runner-up n second m, seconde f

running n course f ▷ Running is my favourite sport. La course est mon sport préféré.

run-up n **in the run-up to Christmas** pendant la période de préparation de Noël

runway n piste f

rush n hâte f; **in a rush**. à la hâte
▶ vb ❶ (run) se précipiter
▷ Everyone rushed outside. Tout le monde s'est précipité dehors.
❷ (hurry) se dépêcher ▷ There's no need to rush. Ce n'est pas la peine de se dépêcher.

rush hour n heures fpl de pointe
▷ in the rush hour aux heures de pointe

Russia n Russie f; **in Russia** en Russie; **to Russia** en Russie

Russian adj russe
▶ n ❶ (person) Russe mf
❷ (language) russe m

rust n rouille f

rusty adj rouillé(e) ▷ a rusty bike un vélo rouillé ▷ My French is very rusty. Mon français est très rouillé.

rye n seigle m; **rye bread** le pain de seigle

S

Sabbath n ❶ (Christian) dimanche m ❷ (Jewish) sabbat m

sack n sac m; **to get the sack** être mis à la porte
▶ vb **to sack somebody** mettre quelqu'un à la porte ▷ He was sacked. On l'a mis à la porte.

sacred adj sacré(e)

sacrifice n sacrifice m

sad adj triste

saddle n selle f

saddlebag n sacoche f

safe n coffre-fort m (pl coffres-forts) ▷ She put the money in the safe. Elle a mis l'argent dans le coffre-fort.
▶ adj ❶ sans danger ▷ Don't worry, it's perfectly safe. Ne vous inquiétez pas, c'est absolument sans danger.; **Is it safe?** Ça n'est

pas dangereux? ❷ (machine, ladder) sûr(e) ▷ This car isn't safe. Cette voiture n'est pas sûre. ❸ (out of danger) hors de danger ▷ You're safe now. Vous êtes hors de danger maintenant.; **to feel safe** se sentir en sécurité; **safe sex** le sexe sans risques

safety n sécurité f; **a safety belt** une ceinture de sécurité; **a safety pin** une épingle de nourrice

Sagittarius n Sagittaire mf ▷ I'm Sagittarius. Je suis Sagittaire.

said vb see **say**

sail n voile f
▶ vb ❶ (travel) naviguer ❷ (set off) prendre la mer ▷ The boat sails at eight o'clock. Le bateau prend la mer à huit heures.

sailing n voile f ▷ His hobby is sailing. Son passe-temps, c'est la voile.; **to go sailing** faire de la voile; **a sailing boat** un voilier; **a sailing ship** un grand voilier

sailor n marin m ▷ He's a sailor. Il est marin.

saint n saint m, sainte f

sake n **for the sake of** dans l'intérêt de

salad n salade f; **salad dressing** la vinaigrette

salami n salami m

salary n salaire m

sale n (reductions) soldes mpl ▷ There's a sale on at Harrods. Ce sont les soldes chez Harrods.; **on sale** en vente; **The factory's for sale.** L'usine est en vente.; "**for sale**" "à vendre"

sales assistant n vendeur m, vendeuse f ▷ She's a sales assistant. Elle est vendeuse.

salesman n ❶ (sales rep) représentant m ▷ He's a salesman. Il est représentant.; **a double-glazing salesman** un représentant en doubles vitrages ❷ (sales assistant) vendeur m

saleswoman n ❶ (sales rep) représentante f ▷ She's a saleswoman. Elle est représentante. ❷ (sales assistant) vendeuse f

salmon n saumon m

salon n salon m ▷ a hair salon un salon de coiffure

salt n sel m

salty adj salé(e)

Salvation Army n armée f du Salut

same adj même ▷ at the same time en même temps; **They're exactly the same.** Ils sont exactement pareils.; **It's not the same.** Ça n'est pas pareil.

sample n échantillon m

sand n sable m

sandal n sandale f ▷ a pair of sandals une paire de sandales

sand castle n château m de sable (pl châteaux de sable)

sandwich n sandwich m ▷ a cheese sandwich un sandwich au fromage

sang vb see **sing**

sanitary towel n serviette f hygiénique

sank vb see **sink**

Santa Claus n père m Noël

sarcastic adj sarcastique

sardine n sardine f

SARS abbr (= Severe Acute Respiratory Syndrome) pneumonie f atypique

sat vb see **sit**

satchel n cartable m

satellite n satellite m ▷ satellite television la télévision par satellite; **a satellite dish** une antenne parabolique

satisfactory adj satisfaisant(e)

satisfied adj satisfait(e)

Saturday n samedi m ▷ on Saturday samedi ▷ on Saturdays le samedi ▷ every Saturday tous les samedis ▷ last Saturday samedi dernier ▷ next Saturday samedi prochain; **I've got a Saturday job.** Je travaille le samedi.

sauce n sauce f

saucepan n casserole f

saucer n soucoupe f

Saudi Arabia n Arabie f Saoudite; **in Saudi Arabia** en Arabie Saoudite

sausage n ❶ saucisse f ❷ (salami) saucisson m; **a sausage roll** un friand à la saucisse

save vb ❶ (save up money) mettre de côté ▷ I've saved £50 already. J'ai déjà mis cinquante livres de côté. ❷ (spend less) économiser ▷ I saved £20 by waiting for the sales. J'ai économisé vingt livres en attendant les soldes.; **to save time** gagner du temps ▷ It saved us time. Ça nous a fait gagner du temps. ❸ (rescue) sauver ▷ Luckily, all the passengers were saved. Heureusement, tous les passagers

ont été sauvés. ❹ (on computer) sauvegarder ▷ I saved the file onto a diskette. J'ai sauvegardé le fichier sur disquette.; **to save up** mettre de l'argent de côté ▷ I'm saving up for a new bike. Je mets de l'argent de côté pour un nouveau vélo.

savings npl économies fpl ▷ She spent all her savings on a computer. Elle a dépensé toutes ses économies en achetant un ordinateur.

savoury adj salé(e) ▷ Is it sweet or savoury? C'est sucré ou salé?

saw n scie f
▶ vb see **see**

saxophone n saxophone m ▷ I play the saxophone. Je joue du saxophone.

say vb dire ▷ What did he say? Qu'est-ce qu'il a dit? ▷ Did you hear what she said? Tu as entendu ce qu'elle a dit?; **Could you say that again?** Pourriez-vous répéter s'il vous plaît?; **That goes without saying.** Cela va sans dire.

saying n dicton m ▷ It's just a saying. C'est juste un dicton.

scale n ❶ (of map) échelle f ▷ a large-scale map une carte à grande échelle ❷ (size, extent) ampleur f ▷ a disaster on a massive scale un désastre d'une ampleur incroyable ❸ (in music) gamme f

scales npl (in kitchen, shop) balance f; **bathroom scales** pèse-personne m

scampi npl scampi mpl

scandal n ❶ (outrage) scandale m
▷ It caused a scandal. Ça a fait
scandale. ❷ (gossip) ragots mpl
▷ It's just scandal. Ce ne sont que
des ragots.

Scandinavia n Scandinavie f;
in Scandinavia en Scandinavie

Scandinavian adj scandinave

scanner n scanner m

scar n cicatrice f

scarce adj limité(e) ▷ scarce
resources des ressources limitées;
Jobs are scarce these days. Il y a
peu de travail ces temps-ci.

scarcely adv à peine ▷ I scarcely
knew him. Je le connaissais à peine.

scare n panique f; **a bomb scare**
une alerte à la bombe
▶ vb **to scare somebody** faire peur
à quelqu'un ▷ He scares me. Il me
fait peur.

scarecrow n épouvantail m

scared adj **to be scared** avoir
peur ▷ I was scared stiff. J'avais
terriblement peur.; **to be scared
of** avoir peur de ▷ Are you scared of
him? Est-ce que tu as peur de lui?

scarf n ❶ (long) écharpe f
❷ (square) foulard m

scary adj effrayant(e) ▷ It was really
scary. C'était vraiment effrayant.

scene n ❶ (place) lieux mpl ▷ the
scene of the crime les lieux du crime
❷ (event, sight) spectacle m ▷ It
was an amazing scene. C'était un
spectacle étonnant.; **to make a
scene** faire une scène

scenery n (landscape) paysage m

schedule n programme m ▷ a busy

schedule un programme chargé;
on schedule comme prévu; **to be
behind schedule** avoir du retard

scheduled flight n vol m régulier

scheme n ❶ (idea) truc m ▷ a crazy
scheme he dreamed up un truc farfelu
qu'il a inventé ❷ (project) projet m
▷ a council road-widening scheme un
projet municipal d'élargissement
des routes

scholarship n bourse f

school n école f; **to go to school**
aller à l'école

schoolbag n cartable m

schoolbook n livre m scolaire

schoolboy n écolier m

schoolchildren npl écoliers mpl

schoolgirl n écolière f

science n science f

science fiction n science-fiction f

scientific adj scientifique

scientist n chercheur m,
chercheuse f; **He trained as a
scientist.** Il a une formation
scientifique.

scissors npl ciseaux mpl ▷ a pair of
scissors une paire de ciseaux

scooter n ❶ scooter m ❷ (child's
toy) trottinette f

score n score m ▷ The score was three
nil. Le score était trois à zéro.
▶ vb ❶ (goal, point) marquer ▷ to
score a goal marquer un but; **to
score 6 out of 10** obtenir un
score de six sur dix ❷ (keep score)
compter les points ▷ Who's going to
score? Qui va compter les points?

Scorpio n Scorpion m ▷ I'm Scorpio.
Je suis Scorpion.

Scot n Écossais m, Écossaise f

Scotch tape® n (US) scotch m

Scotland n Écosse f; **in Scotland** en Écosse; **to Scotland** en Écosse; **I'm from Scotland.** Je suis écossais.

Scots adj écossais(e) ▷ a Scots accent un accent écossais

Scotsman n Écossais m

Scotswoman n Écossaise f

Scottish adj écossais(e) ▷ a Scottish accent un accent écossais

scout n scout m ▷ I'm in the Scouts. Je suis scout.

scrambled eggs npl œufs mpl brouillés

scrap n bout m ▷ a scrap of paper un bout de papier
▶ vb (plan) abandonner ▷ The idea was scrapped. L'idée a été abandonnée.

scrapbook n album m

scratch vb se gratter ▷ Stop scratching! Arrête de te gratter!
▶ n (on skin) égratignure f;
to start from scratch partir de zéro

scream n hurlement m
▶ vb hurler

screen n écran m

screen-saver n économiseur m d'écran

screw n vis f

screwdriver n tournevis m

scribble vb griffonner

scrub vb récurer ▷ to scrub a pan récurer une casserole

sculpture n sculpture f

sea n mer f

seafood n fruits mpl de mer
▷ I don't like seafood. Je n'aime pas les fruits de mer.

seagull n mouette f

seal n ❶ (animal) phoque m
❷ (on letter) cachet m
▶ vb ❶ (document) sceller ❷ (letter) coller

seaman n marin m

search vb fouiller ▷ They searched the woods for her. Ils ont fouillé les bois pour la trouver.; **to search for something** chercher quelque chose ▷ He searched for evidence. Il cherchait des preuves.
▶ n fouille f

search party n expédition f de secours

seashore n bord m de la mer ▷ on the seashore au bord de la mer

seasick adj **to be seasick** avoir le mal de mer

seaside n bord m de la mer ▷ at the seaside au bord de la mer

season n saison f ▷ What's your favourite season? Quelle est ta saison préférée?; **out of season** hors saison ▷ It's cheaper to go there out of season. C'est moins cher d'y aller hors saison.; **during the holiday season** en période de vacances; **a season ticket** une carte d'abonnement

seat n siège m

seat belt n ceinture f de sécurité

seaweed n algues f pl

second adj deuxième ▷ on the second page à la deuxième page;
to come second (in race) arriver

deuxième; **to travel second class** voyager en seconde; **the second of March** le deux mars
▶ *n* seconde *f* ▷ *It'll only take a second.* Ça va prendre juste une seconde.

secondary school *n* ❶ collège *m* ❷ lycée *m*
○ In France pupils go to a **collège** between the ages of 11 and 15, and then to a **lycée** until the age of 18.

second-class *adj, adv* ❶ (ticket, compartment) de seconde classe; **to travel second-class** voyager en seconde ❷ (stamp, letter) à tarif réduit ▷ *to send something second-class* envoyer quelque chose à tarif réduit

secondhand *adj* d'occasion
▷ *a secondhand car* une voiture d'occasion

secondly *adv* deuxièmement; **firstly ... secondly ...** d'abord ... ensuite ... ▷ *Firstly, it's too expensive. Secondly, it wouldn't work anyway.* D'abord, c'est trop cher. Ensuite, ça ne marcherait quand même pas.

secret *adj* secret (*f* secrète) ▷ *a secret mission* une mission secrète
▶ *n* secret *m* ▷ *It's a secret.* C'est un secret. ▷ *Can you keep a secret?* Tu sais garder un secret?; **in secret** en secret

secretary *n* secrétaire *mf* ▷ *She's a secretary.* Elle est secrétaire.

secretly *adv* secrètement

section *n* section *f*

security *n* ❶ (on guard) sécurité *f* ▷ *a feeling of security* un sentiment de sécurité ▷ *a campaign to improve airport security* une campagne visant à améliorer la sécurité dans les aéroports; **job security** la sécurité de l'emploi; **a security guard** un garde chargé de la sécurité ❷ (transporting money) un convoyeur de fonds

security guard *n* vigile *m* ▷ *She's a security guard.* Elle est vigile.

see *vb* voir ▷ *I can't see.* Je n'y vois rien. ▷ *I saw him yesterday.* Je l'ai vu hier. ▷ *Have you seen him?* Est-ce que tu l'as vu?; **See you!** Salut!; **See you soon!** À bientôt!; **to see to something** s'occuper de quelque chose ▷ *The window's stuck again. Can you see to it please?* La fenêtre est encore coincée. Tu peux t'en occuper s'il te plaît?

seed *n* graine *f* ▷ *sunflower seeds* des graines de tournesol

seek *vb* chercher; **to seek help** chercher de l'aide

seem *vb* avoir l'air ▷ *She seems tired.* Elle a l'air fatiguée. ▷ *The shop seemed to be closed.* Le magasin avait l'air d'être fermé.; **That seems like a good idea.** Ce n'est pas une mauvaise idée.; **It seems that ...** Il paraît que ... ▷ *It seems she's getting married.* Il paraît qu'elle va se marier.; **There seems to be a problem.** Il semble y avoir un problème.

seen *vb see* see

seesaw *n* tapecul *m*

seldom adv rarement

select vb sélectionner

selection n sélection f

self-catering adj **a self-catering apartment** un appartement de vacances

self-confidence n confiance f en soi ▷ He hasn't got much self-confidence. Il n'a pas très confiance en lui.

self-conscious adj **to be self-conscious** (1) (embarrassed) être mal à l'aise ▷ She was self-conscious at first. Elle était mal à l'aise au début. (2) (shy) manquer d'assurance ▷ He's always been rather self-conscious. Il a toujours manqué un peu d'assurance.

self-defence (US **self-defense**) n autodéfense f ▷ self-defence classes les cours d'autodéfense; **She killed him in self-defence.** Elle l'a tué en légitime défense.

self-employed adj **to be self-employed** travailler à son compte ▷ He's self-employed. Il travaille à son compte.; **the self-employed** les travailleurs indépendants

selfish adj égoïste ▷ Don't be so selfish. Ne sois pas si égoïste.

self-service adj **It's self-service.** (café, shop) C'est un self-service.; **a self-service restaurant** un restaurant self-service

sell vb vendre ▷ He sold it to me. Il me l'a vendu.; **to sell off** liquider

sell out vb se vendre ▷ The tickets sold out in three hours. Les billets se sont tous vendus en trois heures.

▷ The show didn't quite sell out. Ce spectacle ne s'est pas très bien vendu.; **The tickets are all sold out.** Il ne reste plus de billets.

sell-by date n date f limite de vente

Sellotape® n scotch® m

semi n maison f jumelée ▷ We live in a semi. Nous habitons dans une maison jumelée.

semicircle n demi-cercle m

semicolon n point-virgule m

semi-detached house n maison f jumelée ▷ We live in a semi-detached house. Nous habitons dans une maison jumelée.

semi-final n demi-finale f

semi-skimmed milk n lait m demi-écrémé

send vb envoyer ▷ She sent me a birthday card. Elle m'a envoyé une carte d'anniversaire.; **to send back** renvoyer; **to send off** (1) (goods, letter) envoyer (2) (in sports match) renvoyer du terrain ▷ He was sent off. On l'a renvoyé du terrain.; **to send off for something** (1) (free) se faire envoyer quelque chose ▷ I've sent off for a brochure. Je me suis fait envoyer une brochure. (2) (paid for) commander quelque chose par correspondance ▷ She sent off for a book. Elle a commandé un livre par correspondance.; **to send out** envoyer; **to send out for** commander par téléphone ▷ Shall we send out for a pizza? Et si on commandait une pizza par téléphone?

senior adj haut placé(e); **senior management** les cadres supérieurs; **senior school** lycée m; **senior pupils** les grandes classes

senior citizen n personne f du troisième âge (pl personnes du troisième âge)

sensational adj sensationnel (f sensationnelle)

sense n ❶ (wisdom) bon sens m ▷ Use your common sense! Un peu de bon sens, voyons!; **It makes sense.** C'est logique.; **It doesn't make sense.** Ça n'a pas de sens. ❷ (faculty) sens m ▷ the five senses les cinq sens; **the sense of touch** le toucher; **the sense of smell** l'odorat m; **the sixth sense** le sixième sens; **sense of humour** le sens de l'humour ▷ He's got no sense of humour. Il n'a aucun sens de l'humour.

sensible adj raisonnable ▷ Be sensible! Sois raisonnable!

> Be careful not to translate **sensible** by the French word **sensible**.

sensitive adj sensible ▷ She's very sensitive. Elle est très sensible.

sent vb see **send**

sentence n ❶ phrase f ▷ What does this sentence mean? Que veut dire cette phrase? ❷ (judgment) condamnation f ❸ (punishment) peine f ▷ the death sentence la peine de mort; **He got a life sentence.** Il a été condamné à la réclusion à perpétuité.

▶ vb **to sentence somebody to life imprisonment** condamner quelqu'un à la réclusion à perpétuité; **to sentence somebody to death** condamner quelqu'un à mort

sentimental adj sentimental(e) (mpl sentimentaux)

separate adj séparé(e) ▷ I wrote it on a separate sheet. Je l'ai écrit sur une feuille séparée.; **The children have separate rooms.** Les enfants ont chacun leur chambre.; **on separate occasions** à différentes reprises

▶ vb ❶ séparer ❷ (married couple) se séparer

separately adv séparément

separation n séparation f

September n septembre m; **in September** en septembre

sequel n (book, film) suite f

sergeant n ❶ (army) sergent m ❷ (police) brigadier m

serial n feuilleton m

series n ❶ série f ▷ a TV series une série télévisée ❷ (of numbers) suite f

serious adj ❶ sérieux (f sérieuse) ▷ You look very serious. Tu as l'air sérieux.; **Are you serious?** Sérieusement? ❷ (illness, mistake) grave

seriously adv sérieusement ▷ No, but seriously ... Non, mais sérieusement ...; **to take somebody seriously** prendre quelqu'un au sérieux; **seriously injured** gravement blessé; **Seriously?** Vraiment?

servant n domestique mf

serve vb ❶ servir ▷ Dinner is served. Le dîner est servi. ▷ It's Federer's turn to serve. C'est à Federer de servir. ❷ (prison sentence) purger; **to serve time** être en prison; **It serves you right.** C'est bien fait pour toi.
▶ n (tennis) service m; **It's your serve.** C'est à toi de servir.

service vb (car, washing machine) réviser
▶ n ❶ service m ▷ Service is included. Le service est compris. ❷ (of car) révision f ❸ (church service) office m; **the Fire Service** les sapeurs-pompiers; **the armed services** les forces armées

service charge n service m
▷ There's no service charge. Le service est compris.

service station n station-service f (pl stations-service)

serviette n serviette f

session n séance f

set n ❶ jeu m (pl jeux) ▷ a set of keys un jeu de clés ▷ a chess set un jeu d'échecs; **a train set** un train électrique ❷ (in tennis) set m
▶ vb ❶ (alarm clock) mettre à sonner ▷ I set the alarm for 7 o'clock. J'ai mis le réveil à sept heures. ❷ (record) établir ▷ The world record was set last year. Le record du monde a été établi l'année dernière. ❸ (sun) se coucher ▷ The sun was setting. Le soleil se couchait.; **The film is set in Morocco.** L'action du film se

déroule au Maroc.; **to set off** partir ▷ We set off for London at 9 o'clock. Nous sommes partis pour Londres à neuf heures.; **to set out** partir ▷ We set out for London at 9 o'clock. Nous sommes partis pour Londres à neuf heures.; **to set sail** prendre la mer; **to set the table** mettre le couvert

settee n canapé m

settle vb ❶ (problem) résoudre ❷ (argument, account) régler; **to settle down** (calm down) se calmer; **Settle down!** Du calme!; **to settle in** s'installer; **to settle on something** opter pour quelque chose

seven num sept ▷ She's seven. Elle a sept ans.

seventeen num dix-sept ▷ He's seventeen. Il a dix-sept ans.

seventeenth adj dix-septième ▷ her seventeenth birthday son dix-septième anniversaire ▷ the seventeenth floor le dix-septième étage; **the seventeenth of August** le dix-sept août

seventh adj septième ▷ the seventh floor le septième étage; **the seventh of August** le sept août

seventy num soixante-dix

several adj, pron plusieurs ▷ several schools plusieurs écoles; **several of them** plusieurs ▷ I've seen several of them. J'en ai vu plusieurs.

sew vb coudre; **to sew up** (tear) recoudre

sewing n couture f ▷ I like sewing. J'aime faire de la couture.;

a sewing machine une machine à coudre

sewn vb see sew

sex n sexe m; to have sex with somebody coucher avec quelqu'un; sex education éducation f sexuelle

sexism n sexisme m

sexist adj sexiste

sexual adj sexuel (f sexuelle) ▷ sexual discrimination la discrimination sexuelle ▷ sexual harassment le harcèlement sexuel

sexuality n sexualité f

sexy adj sexy inv

shabby adj miteux (f miteuse)

shade n ❶ ombre f; in the shade à l'ombre ▷ It was 35 degrees in the shade. Il faisait trente-cinq à l'ombre. ❷ (colour) nuance f ▷ a shade of blue une nuance de bleu

shadow n ombre f

shake vb ❶ secouer ▷ She shook the rug. Elle a secoué le tapis. ❷ (tremble) trembler ▷ He was shaking with cold. Il tremblait de froid.; to shake one's head (in refusal) faire non de la tête; to shake hands with somebody serrer la main à quelqu'un ▷ They shook hands. Ils se sont serré la main.

shaken adj secoué(e) ▷ I was feeling a bit shaken. J'étais un peu secoué.

shall vb Shall I shut the window? Vous voulez que je ferme la fenêtre?; Shall we ask him to come with us? Si on lui demandait de venir avec nous?

shallow adj (water, pool) peu profond(e)

shambles n pagaille f ▷ It's a complete shambles. C'est la pagaille complète.

shame n honte f ▷ The shame of it! Quelle honte!; What a shame! Quel dommage!; It's a shame that … c'est dommage que …

> **c'est dommage que** has to be followed by a verb in the subjunctive.

▷ It's a shame he isn't here. C'est dommage qu'il ne soit pas ici.

shampoo n shampooing m ▷ a bottle of shampoo une bouteille de shampooing

shandy n panaché m

shape n forme f

share n ❶ (in company) action f ▷ They've got shares in British Gas. Ils ont des actions de British Gas. ❷ part f ▷ Everybody pays their share. Tout le monde paie sa part. ▶ vb partager ▷ to share a room with somebody partager une chambre avec quelqu'un; to share out distribuer ▷ They shared the sweets out among the children. Ils ont distribué les bonbons aux enfants.

shark n requin m

sharp adj ❶ (razor, knife) tranchant(e) ❷ (spike, point) pointu(e) ❸ (clever) intelligent(e) ▷ She's very sharp. Elle est très intelligente.; at two o'clock sharp à deux heures pile

sharpener n taille-crayon m

shave vb (have a shave) se raser;

to shave one's legs se raser les jambes

shaver n **an electric shaver** un rasoir électrique

shaving cream n crème f à raser

shaving foam n mousse f à raser

she pron elle ▷ She's very nice. Elle est très gentille.

shed n remise f

she'd = she had; she would

sheep n mouton m

sheepdog n chien m de berger (pl chiens de berger)

sheer adj pur(e) ▷ It's sheer greed. C'est de l'avidité pure.

sheet n (on bed) drap m; **a sheet of paper** une feuille de papier

shelf n ❶ (in house) étagère f ❷ (in shop) rayon m

shell n ❶ (on beach) coquillage m ❷ (of egg, nut) coquille f ❸ (explosive) obus m

she'll = she will

shellfish n fruits mpl de mer

shelter n **to take shelter** se mettre à l'abri; **a bus shelter** un arrêt d'autobus

shelves npl see **shelf**

shepherd n berger m

sherry n xérès m

she's = she is; she has

Shetland Islands npl îles fpl Shetland

shift n service m ▷ His shift starts at 8 o'clock. Il prend son service à huit heures. ▷ the night shift le service de nuit; **to do shift work** faire les trois-huit

▶ vb (move) déplacer ▷ I couldn't

shift the wardrobe on my own. Je n'ai pas pu déplacer l'armoire tout seul.; **Shift yourself!** (informal) Pousse-toi de là!

shin n tibia m

shine vb briller ▷ The sun was shining. Le soleil brillait.

shiny adj brillant(e)

ship n ❶ bateau m (pl bateaux) ❷ (warship) navire m

shirt n ❶ (man's) chemise f ❷ (woman's) chemisier m

shiver vb frissonner

shock n choc m; **to get a shock** (1) (surprise) avoir un choc (2) (electric) recevoir une décharge; **an electric shock** une décharge

▶ vb ❶ (upset) bouleverser ▷ They were shocked by the tragedy. Ils ont été bouleversés par la tragédie. ❷ (scandalize) choquer ▷ I was rather shocked by her attitude. J'ai été assez choqué par son attitude.

shocked adj choqué(e) ▷ He'll be shocked if you say that. Tu vas le choquer si tu dis ça.

shocking adj choquant(e) ▷ It's shocking! C'est choquant!; **a shocking waste** un gaspillage épouvantable

shoe n chaussure f

shoelace n lacet m

shoe polish n cirage m

shoe shop n magasin m de chaussures

shone vb see **shine**

shook vb see **shake**

shoot vb ❶ (kill) abattre ▷ He was shot by a sniper. Il a été abattu

a
b
c
d
e
f
g
h
i
j
k
l
m
n
o
p
q
r
s
t
u
v
w
x
y
z

par un franc-tireur. ❷ (execute) fusiller ▷ He was shot at dawn. Il a été fusillé à l'aube. ❸ (gun) tirer ▷ Don't shoot! Ne tirez pas!; **to shoot at somebody** tirer sur quelqu'un; **He shot himself with a revolver.** (dead) Il s'est suicidé d'un coup de revolver.; **He was shot in the leg.** (wounded) Il a reçu une balle dans la jambe.; **to shoot an arrow** envoyer une flèche ❹ (film) tourner ▷ The film was shot in Prague. Le film a été tourné à Prague. ❺ (in football) shooter

shooting n ❶ coups mpl de feu ▷ They heard shooting. Ils ont entendu des coups de feu.; **a shooting** une fusillade ❷ (hunting) chasse f ▷ to go shooting aller à la chasse

shop n magasin m ▷ a sports shop un magasin de sports

shop assistant n vendeur m, vendeuse f ▷ She's a shop assistant. Elle est vendeuse.

shopkeeper n commerçant m, commerçante f ▷ He's a shopkeeper. Il est commerçant.

shoplifting n vol m à l'étalage

shopping n (purchases) courses fpl ▷ Can you get the shopping from the car? Tu peux aller chercher les courses dans la voiture?; **I love shopping.** J'adore faire du shopping.; **to go shopping** (1) (for food) faire des courses (2) (for pleasure) faire du shopping; **a shopping bag** un sac à provisions; **a shopping centre** un centre commercial

shop window n vitrine f

shore n rivage m; **on shore** à terre

short adj ❶ court(e) ▷ a short skirt une jupe courte ▷ short hair les cheveux courts; **too short** trop court ▷ It was a great holiday, but too short. C'étaient des vacances super, mais trop courtes. ❷ (person, period of time) petit(e) ▷ She's quite short. Elle est assez petite. ▷ a short break une petite pause ▷ a short walk une petite promenade; **to be short of something** être à court de quelque chose ▷ I'm short of money. Je suis à court d'argent.; **at short notice** au dernier moment; **In short, the answer's no.** Bref, la réponse est non.

shortage n pénurie f ▷ a water shortage une pénurie d'eau

short cut n raccourci m ▷ I took a short cut. J'ai pris un raccourci.

shortly adv bientôt

shorts npl short m; **a pair of shorts** un short

short-sighted adj myope

shot n ❶ (gunshot) coup m de feu (pl coups de feu) ❷ (photo) photo f ▷ a shot of Edinburgh Castle une photo du château d'Édimbourg ❸ (vaccination) vaccin m

▶ vb see **shoot**

shotgun n fusil m de chasse (pl fusils de chasse)

should vb

▌ When **should** means "ought to", use **devoir**.

devoir ▷ You should take more exercise. Vous devriez faire plus d'exercice. ▷ *That shouldn't be too hard.* Ça ne devrait pas être trop difficile.; **should have** avoir dû ▷ *I should have told you before.* J'aurais dû te le dire avant.

When **should** means "would", use the conditional tense.

I should go if I were you. Si j'étais vous, j'irais.; **I should be so lucky!** Ça serait trop beau!

shoulder n épaule f; **a shoulder bag** un sac à bandoulière

shouldn't = **should not**

shout vb crier ▷ *Don't shout!* Ne criez pas! ▷ *"Go away!" he shouted.* "Allez-vous-en!" a-t-il crié.
▶ n cri m

shovel n pelle f

show n ❶ (*performance*) spectacle m ❷ (*programme*) émission f ❸ (*exhibition*) salon m
▶ vb ❶ montrer; **to show somebody something** montrer quelque chose à quelqu'un ▷ *Have I shown you my new trainers?* Je t'ai montré mes nouvelles baskets? ❷ faire preuve de ▷ *She showed great courage.* Elle a fait preuve de beaucoup de courage.; **It shows.** Ça se voit. ▷ *I've never been riding before. — It shows.* Je n'ai jamais fait de cheval. — Ça se voit.; **to show off** frimer (*informal*); **to show up** (*turn up*) se pointer ▷ *He showed up late as usual.* Il s'est pointé en retard comme d'habitude.

shower n ❶ douche f; **to have a shower** prendre une douche ❷ (*of rain*) averse f

shown vb see **show**

show-off n frimeur m, frimeuse f

shrank vb see **shrink**

shriek vb hurler

shrimps npl crevettes fpl

shrink vb (*clothes, fabric*) rétrécir

Shrove Tuesday n mardi m gras

shrug vb **to shrug one's shoulders** hausser les épaules

shrunk vb see **shrink**

shuffle vb **to shuffle the cards** battre les cartes

shut vb fermer ▷ *What time do you shut?* À quelle heure est-ce que vous fermez? ▷ *What time do the shops shut?* À quelle heure est-ce que les magasins ferment?; **to shut down** fermer ▷ *The cinema shut down last year.* Le cinéma a fermé l'année dernière.; **to shut up** (1) (*close*) fermer (2) (*be quiet*) se taire ▷ *Shut up!* Tais-toi!

shuttle n navette f

shuttlecock n (*badminton*) volant m

shy adj timide

Sicily n Sicile f; **in Sicily** en Sicile; **to Sicily** en Sicile

sick adj ❶ (*ill*) malade ▷ *He was sick for four days.* Il a été malade pendant quatre jours. ❷ (*joke, humour*) de mauvais goût ▷ *That's really sick!* C'est vraiment de mauvais goût!; **to be sick** (*vomit*) vomir ▷ *I feel sick.* J'ai envie de vomir.; **to be sick of something** en avoir assez de quelque chose ▷ *I'm sick of your jokes.* J'en ai assez de tes plaisanteries.

sickness n maladie f

side n ❶ (of object, building, car) côté m ▷ He was driving on the wrong side of the road. Il roulait du mauvais côté de la route. ❷ (of pool, river, road) bord m ▷ by the side of the lake au bord du lac ❸ (of hill) flanc m ❹ (team) équipe f; He's on my side. (2) (supporting me) Il est de mon côté.; side by side côte à côte; the side entrance l'entrée latérale; to take sides prendre parti ▷ She always takes his side. Elle prend toujours son parti.

sideboard n buffet m

side-effect n effet m secondaire

sidewalk n (US) trottoir m

sideways adv ❶ (look, be facing) de côté ❷ (move) de travers; sideways on de profil

sieve n passoire f

sigh n soupir m

▶ vb soupirer

sight n ❶ vue f ▷ to have poor sight avoir une mauvaise vue; to know somebody by sight connaître quelqu'un de vue ▷ It was an amazing sight. C'était un spectacle étonnant.; in sight visible; out of sight hors de vue; the sights (tourist spots) les attractions touristiques; to see the sights of London visiter Londres

sightseeing n tourisme m; to go sightseeing faire du tourisme

sign n ❶ (notice) panneau m (pl panneaux) ▷ There was a big sign saying "private". Il y avait un grand panneau indiquant "privé".; a road sign un panneau ❷ (gesture, indication) signe m ▷ There's no sign of improvement. Il n'y a aucun signe d'amélioration.; What sign are you? (star sign) Tu es de quel signe?

▶ vb signer; to sign on (1) (as unemployed) s'inscrire au chômage (2) (for course) s'inscrire

signal n signal m (pl signaux)

▶ vb to signal to somebody faire un signe à quelqu'un

signature n signature f

significance n importance f

significant adj important(e)

sign language n langage m des signes

signpost n poteau m indicateur

silence n silence m

silent adj silencieux (f silencieuse)

silk n soie f

▶ adj en soie ▷ a silk scarf un foulard en soie

silky adj soyeux (f soyeuse)

silly adj bête

silver n argent m ▷ a silver medal une médaille d'argent

SIM card n carte f SIM

similar adj semblable; similar to semblable à

simple adj ❶ simple ▷ It's very simple. C'est très simple. ❷ (simple-minded) simplet (f simplette) ▷ He's a bit simple. Il est un peu simplet.

simply adv simplement ▷ It's simply not possible. Ça n'est tout simplement pas possible.

sin n péché m

since prep, adv, conj ❶ depuis
▷ since Christmas depuis Noël
▷ since then depuis ce moment-là
▷ I haven't seen him since. Je ne l'ai
pas vu depuis.; **ever since** depuis
ce moment-là ❷ depuis que
▷ I haven't seen her since she left.
Je ne l'ai pas vue depuis qu'elle
est partie. ❶ (because) puisque
▷ Since you're tired, let's stay at home.
Puisque tu es fatigué, restons à
la maison.

sincere adj sincère

sincerely adv **Yours sincerely ...**
(1) (in business letter) Veuillez agréer
l'expression de mes sentiments les
meilleurs ... **(2)** (in personal letter)
Cordialement ...

sing vb chanter ▷ He sang out of
tune. Il chantait faux.

singer n chanteur m, chanteuse f

singing n chant m

single adj (unmarried) célibataire;
a single room une chambre pour
une personne; **not a single thing**
rien du tout
▶ n ❶ (ticket) aller m simple ▷ A
single to Toulouse, please. Un aller
simple pour Toulouse, s'il vous
plaît. ❷ (record) 45 tours m; **a CD
single** un CD single

single parent n **She's a single
parent.** Elle élève ses enfants
toute seule.; **a single parent
family** une famille monoparentale

singular n singulier m ▷ in the
singular au singulier

sink n évier m
▶ vb couler

sir n monsieur m; **Yes sir.** Oui,
Monsieur.

siren n sirène f

sister n ❶ sœur f ▷ my little
sister ma petite sœur ❷ (nurse)
infirmière f en chef

sister-in-law n belle-sœur f
(pl belles-sœurs)

sit vb s'asseoir; **to sit on
something** s'asseoir sur quelque
chose ▷ She sat on the chair. Elle
s'est assise sur la chaise.; **to sit
down** s'asseoir; **to be sitting** être
assis(e); **to sit an exam** passer
un examen

site n ❶ site m ▷ an archaeological
site un site archéologique; **the
site of the accident** le lieu de
l'accident ❷ (campsite) camping m;
a building site un chantier

sitting room n salon m

situation n situation f

six num six ▷ He's six. Il a six ans.

sixteen num seize ▷ He's sixteen.
Il a seize ans.

sixteenth adj seizième ▷ the
sixteenth floor le seizième étage;
the sixteenth of August le seize
août

sixth adj sixième ▷ the sixth floor
le sixième étage; **the sixth of
August** le six août

sixty num soixante

size n
● France uses the European
● system to show clothing and
● shoe sizes.
❶ (of object, clothing) taille f ▷ What
size do you take? Quelle taille est-ce

que vous faites?; **I'm a size ten.**
Je fais du trente-huit. ❷ (of shoes)
pointure f; **I take size six.** Je fais du
trente-neuf.

skate vb ❶ (ice-skate) faire du patin
à glace ❷ (roller-skate) faire du
patin à roulettes

skateboard n skateboard m

skateboarding n skateboard
m ▷ **to go skateboarding** faire du
skateboard

skates n patins mpl

skating n patin m à glace ▷ **to go
skating** faire du patin à glace;
a skating rink une patinoire

skeleton n squelette m

sketch n (drawing) croquis m
▶ vb **to sketch something** faire un
croquis de quelque chose

ski n ski m; **ski boots** les chaussures
de ski; **a ski lift** un remonte-pente;
ski pants fuseau m; **a ski pole** un
bâton de ski; **a ski slope** une piste
de ski; **a ski suit** une combinaison
de ski
▶ vb skier ▷ **Can you ski?** Tu sais
skier?

skid vb déraper

skier n skieur m, skieuse f

skiing n ski m ▷ **to go skiing** faire du
ski; **to go on a skiing holiday** aller
aux sports d'hiver

skilful adj adroit(e)

skill n talent m ▷ **He played with
great skill.** Il a joué avec beaucoup
de talent.

skilled adj **a skilled worker** un
ouvrier spécialisé

skimmed milk n lait m écrémé

skin n peau f (pl peaux); **skin
cancer** le cancer de la peau

skinhead n skinhead mf

skinny adj maigre

skip n (container) benne f
▶ vb sauter ▷ **to skip a meal** sauter
un repas; **to skip a lesson** sécher
un cours

skirt n jupe f

skive vb (be lazy) tirer au flanc;
to skive off (informal) sécher ▷ **to
skive off school** sécher les cours

skull n crâne m

sky n ciel m

skyscraper n gratte-ciel m (pl
gratte-ciel)

slam vb claquer ▷ **The door slammed.**
La porte a claqué. ▷ **She slammed
the door.** Elle a claqué la porte.

slang n argot m

slap n claque f
▶ vb **to slap somebody** donner
une claque à quelqu'un

slate n ardoise f

slave n esclave mf

sledge n luge f

sledging n **to go sledging** faire
de la luge

sleep n sommeil m; **I need some
sleep.** J'ai besoin de dormir.; **to go
to sleep** s'endormir
▶ vb dormir ▷ **I couldn't sleep
last night.** J'ai mal dormi la
nuit dernière.; **to sleep with
somebody** coucher avec
quelqu'un; **to sleep together**
coucher ensemble

sleep in vb ❶ (accidentally) ne pas
se réveiller ▷ **I'm sorry I'm late, I slept**

in. Désolé d'être en retard: je ne me
suis pas réveillé. ❸ *(on purpose)*
faire la grasse matinée

sleeping bag n sac m de couchage
(pl sacs de couchage)

sleeping pill n somnifère m

sleepy adj **to feel sleepy** avoir
sommeil ▷ *I was feeling sleepy.*
J'avais sommeil.; **a sleepy little
village** un petit village tranquille

sleet n neige f fondue
▷ vb **It's sleeting.** Il tombe de la
neige fondue.

sleeve n ❶ manche f ▷ *long sleeves*
les manches longues ❷ *(record
sleeve)* pochette f

slept vb *see* **sleep**

slice n tranche f
▷ vb couper en tranches

slide n ❶ *(in playground)* toboggan
m ❷ *(photo)* diapositive f ❸ *(hair
slide)* barrette f
▷ vb glisser

slight adj léger (f légère) ▷ *a slight
problem* un léger problème ▷ *a
slight improvement* une légère
amélioration

slightly adv légèrement

slim adj mince
▷ vb *(be on a diet)* faire un régime
▷ *I'm slimming.* Je fais un régime.

sling n écharpe f ▷ *She had her arm in
a sling.* Elle avait le bras en écharpe.

slip n ❶ *(mistake)* erreur f
❷ *(underskirt)* jupon m ❸ *(full-
length underskirt)* combinaison f;
a slip of paper un bout de papier;
a slip of the tongue un lapsus
▷ vb glisser ▷ *He slipped on the ice.*

Il a glissé sur le verglas.; **to slip up**
(make a mistake) faire une erreur

slipper n chausson m; **a pair of
slippers** des chaussons

slippery adj glissant(e)

slip-up n erreur f

slope n pente f

slot n fente f

slot machine n ❶ *(for gambling)*
machine f à sous ❷ *(vending
machine)* distributeur m
automatique

slow adj, adv ❶ lent(e) ▷ *He's
a bit slow.* Il est un peu lent.
❷ lentement ▷ *to go slow (person,
car)* aller lentement ▷ *Drive slower!*
Conduisez plus lentement!; **My
watch is slow.** Ma montre retarde.

slow down vb ralentir

slowly adv lentement

slug n limace f

slum n ❶ *(area)* quartier m
insalubre ❷ *(house)* taudis m

smack n tape f
▷ vb **to smack somebody** donner
une tape à quelqu'un

small adj petit(e); **small change** la
petite monnaie

smart adj ❶ *(elegant)* chic inv
❷ *(clever)* intelligent(e); **a smart
idea** une idée astucieuse

smashing adj formidable ▷ *I
think he's smashing.* Je le trouve
formidable.

smell n odeur f; **the sense of smell**
l'odorat m
▷ vb ❶ sentir mauvais ▷ *That old
dog really smells!* Qu'est-ce qu'il sent
mauvais, ce vieux chien!; **to smell**

of something sentir quelque chose ▷ It smells of petrol. Ça sent l'essence. ❷ (detect) sentir ▷ I can't smell anything. Je ne sens rien.

smelly adj qui sent mauvais ▷ He's got smelly feet. Il a les pieds qui sentent mauvais.

smelt vb see **smell**

smile n sourire m
▶ vb sourire

smiley n émoticon m

smoke n fumée f
▶ vb fumer ▷ I don't smoke. Je ne fume pas.

smoker n fumeur m, fumeuse f

smoking n to give up smoking arrêter de fumer; **Smoking is bad for you.** Le tabac est mauvais pour la santé.; **"no smoking"** "défense de fumer"

smooth adj ❶ (surface) lisse ❷ (person) mielleux (f mielleuse)

SMS n (= short message service) SMS m ▷ an SMS message un message SMS

smudge n bavure f

smuggle vb ❶ (goods) passer en fraude ▷ to smuggle cigarettes into a country faire passer des cigarettes en fraude dans un pays ❷ (people) faire passer clandestinement; **They managed to smuggle him out of prison.** Ils ont réussi à le faire sortir de prison clandestinement.

smuggler n contrebandier m, contrebandière f

smuggling n contrebande f

snack n en-cas m (pl en-cas); to have a snack prendre un en-cas

snack bar n snack-bar m

snail n escargot m

snake n serpent m

snap vb (break) casser net ▷ The branch snapped. La branche a cassé net.; **to snap one's fingers** faire claquer ses doigts

snatch vb to snatch something from somebody arracher quelque chose à quelqu'un ▷ He snatched the keys from my hand. Il m'a arraché les clés des mains.; **My bag was snatched.** On m'a arraché mon sac.

sneak vb to sneak in entrer furtivement; **to sneak out** sortir furtivement; **to sneak up on somebody** s'approcher de quelqu'un sans faire de bruit

sneeze vb éternuer

sniff vb ❶ renifler ▷ Stop sniffing! Arrête de renifler! ❷ flairer ▷ The dog sniffed my hand. Le chien m'a flairé la main.; **to sniff glue** sniffer de la colle

snob n snob mf

snooker n billard m ▷ to play snooker jouer au billard

snooze n petit somme m ▷ to have a snooze faire un petit somme

snore vb ronfler

snow n neige f
▶ vb neiger ▷ It's snowing. Il neige.

snowball n boule f de neige (pl boules de neige)

snowflake n flocon m de neige (pl flocons de neige)

snowman n bonhomme m de neige (pl bonshommes de neige)

▷ **to build a snowman** faire un bonhomme de neige

so conj, adv ❶ alors ▷ The shop was closed, so I went home. Le magasin était fermé, alors je suis rentré chez moi. ▷ So, have you always lived in London? Alors, vous avez toujours vécu à Londres?; **So what?** Et alors? ❷ (so that) donc ▷ It rained, so I got wet. Il pleuvait, donc j'ai été mouillé. ❸ (very) tellement ▷ It was so heavy! C'était tellement lourd!; **It's not so heavy!** Ça n'est pas si lourd que ça!; **How's your father? — Not so good.** Comment va ton père? — Pas très bien.; **so much** (a lot) tellement ▷ I love you so much. Je t'aime tellement.; **so much ..., so many ...** tellement de ... ▷ I've got so much work. J'ai tellement de travail. ❹ (in comparisons) aussi ▷ He's like his sister but not so clever. Il est comme sa sœur mais pas aussi intelligent.; **so do I** moi aussi ▷ I love horses. — So do I. J'aime les chevaux. — Moi aussi.; **so have we** nous aussi ▷ I've been to France twice. — So have we. Je suis allé en France deux fois. — Nous aussi.; **I think so.** Je crois.; **I hope so.** J'espère bien.; **That's not so.** Ça n'est pas le cas.; **so far** jusqu'à présent ▷ It's been easy so far. Ça a été facile jusqu'à présent.; **so far so good** jusqu'ici ça va; **ten or so people** environ dix personnes; **at five o'clock or so** à environ cinq heures

soak vb tremper

soaking adj trempé(e) ▷ By the time we got back we were soaking. Nous sommes rentrés trempés.; **soaking wet** trempé(e) ▷ Your shoes are soaking wet. Tes chaussures sont trempées.

soap n savon m

soap opera n feuilleton m à l'eau de rose (pl feuilletons à l'eau de rose)

soap powder n lessive f

sob vb sangloter ▷ She was sobbing. Elle sanglotait.

sober adj sobre

sober up vb dessoûler

soccer n football m ▷ to play soccer jouer au football; **a soccer player** un joueur de football

social adj social(e) (mpl sociaux) ▷ a social class une classe sociale; **I have a good social life.** Je vois beaucoup de monde.

socialism n socialisme m

socialist adj socialiste
▶ n socialiste mf

social security n ❶ (money) aide f sociale; **to be on social security** recevoir de l'aide sociale ❷ (organization) sécurité f sociale

social worker n ❶ (woman) assistante f sociale ▷ She's a social worker. Elle est assistante sociale. ❷ (man) travailleur m social (pl travailleurs sociaux) ▷ He's a social worker. Il est travailleur social.

society n ❶ société f ▷ We live in a multi-cultural society. Nous vivons dans une société multiculturelle. ❷ club m ▷ a drama society un club de théâtre

sociology n sociologie f
sock n chaussette f
socket n prise f de courant
(pl prises de courant)
sofa n canapé m
soft adj ❶ (fabric, texture) doux
(f douce) ❷ (pillow, bed) mou
(f molle); **soft cheeses** les
fromages à pâte molle ❸ (hair)
fin(e); **to be soft on somebody**
(be kind to) être indulgent(e) avec
quelqu'un; **a soft drink** une
boisson non alcoolisée; **soft
drugs** les drogues douces; **a
soft option** une solution de
facilité
software n logiciel m
soil n terre f
solar adj solaire; **solar panel** le
panneau solaire
solar power n énergie f solaire
sold vb see **sell**
soldier n soldat m ▷ He's a soldier. Il
est soldat.
solicitor n ❶ (for lawsuits)
avocat m, avocate f ▷ He's a solicitor.
Il est avocat. ❷ (for wills, property)
notaire m ▷ She's a solicitor. Elle est
notaire.
solid adj ❶ (not hollow) massif
(f massive) ▷ solid gold l'or massif
❷ solide ▷ a solid wall un mur
solide; **for three hours solid**
pendant trois heures entières
solo n solo m ▷ a guitar solo un solo
de guitare
solution n solution f
solve vb résoudre
some adj, pron

When **some** means "a certain
amount of", use **du**, **de la** or
des according to the gender of
the French noun that follows
it. **du** and **de la** become **de l'**
when they are followed by a
noun starting with a vowel.

❶ du, de la, de l' (pl des) ▷ Would
you like some bread? Voulez-vous
du pain? ▷ Would you like some
beer? Voulez-vous de la bière?
▷ Have you got some mineral water?
Avez-vous de l'eau minérale? ▷ I've
got some Madonna CDs. J'ai des CDs
de Madonna.; **Some people say
that ...** Il y a des gens qui disent
que ...; **some day** un de ces jours;
some day next week un jour la
semaine prochaine ❷ (some but
not all) certains (f certaines) ▷ Are
these mushrooms poisonous? — Only
some. Est-ce que ces champignons
sont vénéneux? — Certains le
sont.; **some of them** quelques-
uns ▷ I only sold some of them. J'en ai
seulement vendu quelques-uns.;
I only took some of it. J'en ai
seulement pris un peu.; **I'm going
to buy some stamps. Do you
want some too?** Je vais acheter
des timbres. Tu en veux aussi?;
**Would you like some coffee? —
No thanks, I've got some.** Tu veux
du café? — Non merci, j'en ai déjà.
somebody pron quelqu'un
▷ Somebody stole my bag. Quelqu'un
a volé mon sac.
somehow adv **I'll do it somehow.**
Je trouverai le moyen de le faire.

Somehow I don't think he believed me. Quelque chose me dit qu'il ne m'a pas cru.

someone pron = **somebody**

someplace adv (US) = **somewhere**

something pron quelque chose ▷ something special quelque chose de spécial ▷ That's really something! C'est vraiment quelque chose! ▷ It cost £100, or something like that. Ça a coûté cent livres, ou quelque chose comme ça.; **His name is Pierre or something.** Il s'appelle Pierre, ou quelque chose comme ça.

sometime adv un de ces jours ▷ You must come and see us sometime. Passez donc nous voir un de ces jours.; **sometime last month** dans le courant du mois dernier

sometimes adv quelquefois ▷ Sometimes I think she hates me. Quelquefois j'ai l'impression qu'elle me déteste.

somewhere adv quelque part ▷ I left my keys somewhere. J'ai laissé mes clés quelque part.

son n fils m

song n chanson f

son-in-law n gendre m

soon adv bientôt ▷ very soon très bientôt; **soon afterwards** peu après; **as soon as possible** aussitôt que possible

sooner adv plus tôt ▷ Can't you come a bit sooner? Tu ne peux pas venir un peu plus tôt?; **sooner or later** tôt ou tard

soprano n (singer) soprano mf

sorcerer n sorcier m

sore adj **My feet are sore.** J'ai mal aux pieds.; **It's sore.** Ça fait mal.; **That's a sore point.** C'est un point sensible.
▶ n plaie f

sorry adj désolé(e) ▷ I'm really sorry. Je suis vraiment désolé. ▷ I'm sorry I'm late. Je suis désolé d'être en retard.; **sorry!** pardon!; **sorry?** pardon?; **I'm sorry about the noise.** Je m'excuse pour le bruit.; **You'll be sorry!** Tu le regretteras!; **to feel sorry for somebody** plaindre quelqu'un

sort n sorte f ▷ What sort of bike have you got? Quelle sorte de vélo as-tu?

sort out vb ❶ (objects) ranger ❷ (problems) résoudre

sought vb see **to seek**

soul n ❶ (spirit) âme f ❷ (music) soul f

sound n ❶ (noise) bruit m ▷ Don't make a sound! Pas un bruit! ▷ the sound of footsteps des bruits de pas ❷ son m ▷ Can I turn the sound down? Je peux baisser le son?
▶ vb **That sounds interesting.** Ça a l'air intéressant.; **It sounds as if she's doing well at school.** Elle a l'air de bien travailler à l'école.; **That sounds like a good idea.** C'est une bonne idée.
▶ adj, adv bon (f bonne) ▷ That's sound advice. C'est un bon conseil.; **sound asleep** profondément endormi(e)

soundtrack n bande f sonore

soup n soupe f ▷ vegetable soup la soupe aux légumes

sour adj aigre

south adj, adv ❶ sud inv ▷ the south coast la côte sud; **south of** au sud de ▷ It's south of London. C'est au sud de Londres. ❸ vers le sud ▷ We were travelling south. Nous allions vers le sud.
  ▶ n sud m ▷ in the south dans le sud ▷ the South of France le sud de la France

South Africa n Afrique f du Sud; **in South Africa** en Afrique du Sud; **to South Africa** en Afrique du Sud

South America n Amérique f du Sud; **in South America** en Amérique du Sud; **to South America** en Amérique du Sud

South American adj sud-américain(e)
  ▶ n Sud-Américain m, Sud-Américaine f

southeast n sud-est m ▷ southeast England le sud-est de l'Angleterre

southern adj **the southern part of the island** la partie sud de l'île; **Southern England** le sud de l'Angleterre

South Pole n pôle m Sud

southwest n sud-ouest m
  ▷ southwest France le sud-ouest de la France

souvenir n souvenir m; **a souvenir shop** une boutique de souvenirs

Soviet adj **the former Soviet Union** l'ex-Union f Soviétique

soya n soja m

soy sauce n sauce f de soja

space n ❶ place f ▷ There isn't enough space. Il n'y a pas

suffisamment de place.; **a parking space** une place de parking
❷ (universe, gap) espace m ▷ Leave a space after your answer. Laissez un espace après votre réponse.

spacecraft n engin m spatial

spade n pelle f; **spades** (in cards) le pique ▷ the ace of spades l'as de pique

spaghetti n spaghetti mpl

Spain n Espagne f; **in Spain** en Espagne; **to Spain** en Espagne

spam n (email) spam m

Spaniard n Espagnol m, Espagnole f

spaniel n épagneul m

Spanish adj espagnol(e) ▷ She's Spanish. Elle est espagnole.
  ▶ n (language) espagnol m; **the Spanish** les Espagnols

spanner n clé f anglaise

spare adj de rechange ▷ spare batteries des piles de rechange ▷ a spare part une pièce de rechange; **a spare room** une chambre d'amis; **spare time** le temps libre ▷ What do you do in your spare time? Qu'est-ce que tu fais pendant ton temps libre?; **spare wheel** une roue de secours
  ▶ vb **Can you spare a moment?** Vous pouvez m'accorder un instant?; **I can't spare the time.** Je n'ai pas le temps.; **There's no room to spare.** Il n'y a plus de place.; **We arrived with time to spare.** Nous sommes arrivés en avance.
  ▶ n **a spare** un autre ▷ I've lost my

key. — Have you got a spare? J'ai perdu ma clé. — Tu en as une autre?

sparkling adj (water) pétillant(e); **sparkling wine** mousseux m

sparrow n moineau m (pl moineaux)

spat vb see **spit**

speak vb parler ▷ Do you speak English? Est-ce que vous parlez anglais?; **to speak to somebody** parler à quelqu'un ▷ Have you spoken to him? Tu lui as parlé? ▷ She spoke to him about it. Elle lui en a parlé.; **spoken French** le français parlé

speaker n ❶ (loudspeaker) enceinte f ❷ (in debate) intervenant m

special adj spécial(e) (mpl spéciaux)

specialist n spécialiste mf

speciality n spécialité f

specialize vb se spécialiser ▷ We specialize in skiing equipment. Nous nous spécialisons dans les articles de ski.

specially adv ❶ spécialement ▷ It's specially designed for teenagers. C'est spécialement conçu pour les adolescents.; **not specially** pas spécialement ▷ Do you like opera? — Not specially. Tu aimes l'opéra? — Pas spécialement. ❷ surtout ▷ It can be very cold here, specially in winter. Il peut faire très froid ici, surtout en hiver.

species n espèce f

specific adj ❶ (particular) particulier (f particulière) ▷ certain specific issues certains problèmes particuliers ❷ (precise) précis(e) ▷ Could you be more specific? Est-ce que vous pourriez être plus précis?

specs, spectacles npl lunettes fpl

spectacular adj spectaculaire

spectator n spectateur m, spectatrice f

speech n discours m ▷ to make a speech faire un discours

speechless adj muet (f muette) ▷ speechless with admiration muet d'admiration; **I was speechless.** Je suis resté sans voix.

speed n vitesse f ▷ a three-speed bike un vélo à trois vitesses ▷ at top speed à toute vitesse

speed up vb accélérer

speedboat n vedette f

speeding n excès m de vitesse ▷ He was fined for speeding. Il a reçu une contravention pour excès de vitesse.

speed limit n limitation f de vitesse; **to break the speed limit** faire un excès de vitesse

spell vb ❶ (in writing) écrire ▷ How do you spell that? Comment est-ce que ça s'écrit? ❷ (out loud) épeler ▷ Can you spell that please? Est-ce que vous pouvez épeler, s'il vous plaît?; **I can't spell.** Je fais des fautes d'orthographe.

▶ n **to cast a spell on somebody** jeter un sort à quelqu'un; **to be under somebody's spell** être sous le charme de quelqu'un

spelling n orthographe f ▷ My spelling is terrible. Je fais beaucoup

de fautes d'orthographe.;
a spelling mistake une faute
d'orthographe

spelt vb see **spell**

spend vb ❶ (money) dépenser
❷ (time) passer ▷ He spent a month
in France. Il a passé un mois en
France.

spice n épice f

spicy adj épicé(e)

spider n araignée f

spill vb ❶ (tip over) renverser ▷ He
spilled his coffee over his trousers.
Il a renversé son café sur son
pantalon. ❷ (get spilt) se répandre
▷ The soup spilled all over the table.
La soupe s'est répandue sur la
table.

spinach n épinards mpl

spine n colonne f vertébrale

spire n flèche f

spirit n ❶ (courage) courage m; **to
be in good spirits** être de bonne
humeur ❷ (energy) énergie f

spirits npl alcools mpl forts ▷ I don't
drink spirits. Je ne bois pas d'alcools
forts.

spiritual adj religieux (f religieuse)
▷ the spiritual leader of Tibet le chef
religieux du Tibet

spit vb cracher; **to spit something
out** cracher quelque chose

spite n **in spite of** malgré

spiteful adj ❶ (action) méchant(e)
❷ (person) rancunier (f rancunière)

splash vb éclabousser ▷ Careful!
Don't splash me! Attention! Ne
m'éclabousse pas!
▶ n plouf m ▷ I heard a splash. J'ai

entendu un plouf.; **a splash of
colour** une touche de couleur

splendid adj splendide

splinter n écharde f

split vb ❶ (break apart) fendre
▷ He split the wood with an axe. Il
a fendu le bois avec une hache.
❷ se fendre ▷ The ship hit a rock and
split in two. Le bateau a percuté
un rocher et s'est fendu en deux.
❸ (divide up) partager ▷ They
decided to split the profits. Ils ont
décidé de partager les bénéfices.;
to split up (1) (couple) rompre
(2) (group) se disperser

spoil vb ❶ (object) abîmer
❷ (occasion) gâcher ❸ (child) gâter

spoiled adj gâté(e) ▷ a spoiled child
un enfant gâté

spoilsport n trouble-fête mf

spoilt adj gâté(e) ▷ a spoilt child un
enfant gâté
▶ vb see **spoil**

spoken vb see **speak**

spokesman n porte-parole m (pl
porte-parole)

spokeswoman n porte-parole m
(pl porte-parole)

sponge n éponge f; **a sponge bag**
une trousse de toilette; **a sponge
cake** un biscuit de Savoie

sponsor n donateur m, donatrice f
▶ vb parrainer ▷ The festival was
sponsored by … Le festival a été
parrainé par …

spontaneous adj spontané(e)

spooky adj ❶ (eerie) sinistre; **a
spooky story** une histoire qui
fait froid dans le dos ❷ (strange)

étrange ▷ *a spooky coincidence* une étrange coïncidence

spoon n cuiller f; **a spoonful** une cuillerée

sport n sport m ▷ *What's your favourite sport?* Quel est ton sport préféré?; **a sports bag** un sac de sport; **a sports car** une voiture de sport; **a sports jacket** une veste de sport; **Go on, be a sport!** Allez, sois sympa!

sportsman n sportif m

sportswear n vêtements mpl de sport

sportswoman n sportive f

sporty adj sportif (f sportive) ▷ *I'm not very sporty.* Je ne suis pas très sportif.

spot n ❶ (mark) tache f ▷ *There's a spot on your shirt.* Il y a une tache sur ta chemise. ❷ (in pattern) pois m ▷ *a red dress with white spots* une robe rouge à pois blancs ❸ (pimple) bouton m ▷ *He's covered in spots.* Il est couvert de boutons. ❹ (place) coin m ▷ *It's a lovely spot for a picnic.* C'est un coin agréable pour un pique-nique.; **on the spot** (1) (immediately) sur-le-champ m ▷ *They gave her the job on the spot.* Ils lui ont offert le poste sur-le-champ. (2) (at the same place) sur place ▷ *Luckily they were able to mend the car on the spot.* Heureusement ils ont pu réparer la voiture sur place.

▶ vb repérer ▷ *I spotted a mistake.* J'ai repéré une faute.

spotless adj immaculé(e)

spotlight n projecteur m; **The universities have been in the spotlight recently.** Les universités ont été sous le feu des projecteurs ces derniers temps.

spotty adj (pimply) boutonneux (f boutonneuse)

sprain vb **to sprain one's ankle** se faire une entorse à la cheville
▶ n entorse f ▷ *It's just a sprain.* C'est juste une entorse.

spray n (spray can) bombe f
▶ vb ❶ vaporiser ▷ *to spray perfume on one's hand* se vaporiser du parfum sur la main ❷ (crops) traiter ❸ (graffiti) peindre avec une bombe ▷ *Somebody had sprayed graffiti on the wall.* Quelqu'un avait peint des graffiti avec une bombe sur le mur.

spread vb ❶ étaler ▷ *to spread butter on a slice of bread* étaler du beurre sur une tranche de pain ❷ (disease, news) se propager ▷ *The news spread rapidly.* La nouvelle s'est propagée rapidement.

spreadsheet n (computer program) tableur m

spring n ❶ (season) printemps m; **in spring** au printemps ❷ (metal coil) ressort m ❸ (water hole) source f

springtime n printemps m; **in springtime** au printemps

sprint n sprint m
▶ vb courir à toute vitesse ▷ *She sprinted for the bus.* Elle a couru à toute vitesse pour attraper le bus.

sprouts npl Brussels sprouts les choux de Bruxelles

spy n espion m, espionne f
▸ vb to spy on somebody espionner quelqu'un

spying n espionnage m

square n ❶ carré m ▷ a square and a triangle un carré et un triangle ❷ place f ▷ the town square la place de l'hôtel de ville
▸ adj carré(e) ▷ two square metres deux mètres carrés; It's 2 metres square. Ça fait deux mètres sur deux.

squash n (sport) squash m ▷ I play squash. Je joue au squash.; a squash court un court de squash; a squash racket une raquette de squash; orange squash orangeade f; lemon squash citronnade f
▸ vb écraser ▷ You're squashing me. Tu m'écrases.

squeak vb ❶ (mouse, child) pousser un petit cri ❷ (creak) grincer

squeeze vb ❶ (fruit, toothpaste) presser ❷ (hand, arm) serrer; to squeeze into some tight jeans rentrer tout juste dans un jean serré

squirrel n écureuil m

stab vb poignarder

stable n écurie f
▸ adj stable ▷ a stable relationship une relation stable

stack n pile f ▷ a stack of books une pile de livres

stadium n stade m

staff n ❶ (in company) personnel m

❷ (in school) professeurs mpl

staffroom n salle f des professeurs

stage n ❶ (in plays) scène f ❷ (for speeches, lectures) estrade f; at this stage (1) à ce stade ▷ at this stage in the negotiations à ce stade des négociations (2) pour l'instant ▷ At this stage, it's too early to comment. Pour l'instant, il est trop tôt pour se prononcer.; to do something in stages faire quelque chose étape par étape

> Be careful not to translate stage by the French word stage.

stain n tache f
▸ vb tacher

stainless steel n inox m

stair n (step) marche f

staircase n escalier m

stairs npl escalier m

stale adj (bread) rassis(e)

stalemate n (in chess) pat m

stall n stand m ▷ He's got a market stall. Il a un stand au marché.; the stalls (in cinema, theatre) l'orchestre m

stammer n bégaiement m; He's got a stammer. Il bégaie.

stamp vb (letter) affranchir; to stamp one's foot taper du pied
▸ n ❶ timbre m ▷ My hobby is stamp collecting. Je collectionne les timbres.; a stamp album un album de timbres; a stamp collection une collection de timbres ❷ (rubber stamp) tampon m

stand vb ❶ (be standing) être debout ▷ He was standing by the

door. Il était debout à la porte.
❷ (*stand up*) se lever ❸ (*tolerate, withstand*) supporter ▷ *I can't stand all this noise.* Je ne supporte pas tout ce bruit.; **to stand for (1)** (*be short for*) être l'abréviation de ▷ *"BT" stands for "British Telecom".* "BT" est l'abréviation de "British Telecom". **(2)** (*tolerate*) supporter ▷ *I won't stand for it!* Je ne supporterai pas ça!; **to stand in for somebody** remplacer quelqu'un; **to stand out** se distinguer ▷ *All the contestants were good, but none of them stood out.* Tous les concurrents étaient bons, mais aucun ne se distinguait.; **She really stands out in that orange coat.** Tout le monde la remarque avec ce manteau orange.; **to stand up** (*get up*) se lever; **to stand up for** défendre ▷ *Stand up for your rights!* Défendez vos droits!

standard adj ❶ courant(e)
▷ *standard French* le français courant ❷ (*equipment*) ordinaire;
the standard procedure la procédure normale
▶ *n* niveau *m* (pl niveaux) ▷ *The standard is very high.* Le niveau est très haut.; **the standard of living** le niveau de vie; **She's got high standards.** Elle est très exigeante.

Standard Grades npl (*in Scottish schools*) brevet *m* des collèges

stands npl (*at sports ground*) tribune *f* sg

stank vb see **stink**

staple *n* agrafe *f*
▶ *vb* agrafer

stapler *n* agrafeuse *f*

star *n* ❶ (*in sky*) étoile *f* ❷ (*celebrity*) vedette *f* ▷ *He's a TV star.* C'est une vedette de la télé.; **the stars** (*horoscope*) l'horoscope *m*
▶ *vb* être la vedette ▷ *to star in a film* être la vedette d'un film; **The film stars Glenda Jackson.** Le film a pour vedette Glenda Jackson.;
... starring Johnny Depp ... avec Johnny Depp

stare vb **to stare at something** fixer quelque chose

star sign *n* signe *m* du zodiaque

start *n* ❶ début *m* ▷ *It's not much, but it's a start.* Ce n'est pas grand chose, mais c'est un début.; **Shall we make a start on the washing-up?** On commence à faire la vaisselle? ❷ (*of race*) départ *m*
▶ *vb* ❶ commencer ▷ *What time does it start?* À quelle heure est-ce que ça commence?; **to start doing something** commencer à faire quelque chose ▷ *I started learning French three years ago.* J'ai commencé à apprendre le français il y a trois ans. ❷ (*organization*) créer ▷ *He wants to start his own business.* Il veut créer sa propre entreprise. ❸ (*campaign*) organiser ▷ *She started a campaign against drugs.* Elle a organisé une campagne contre la drogue.
❹ (*car*) démarrer ▷ *He couldn't start the car.* Il n'a pas réussi à démarrer la voiture. ▷ *The car*

wouldn't start. La voiture ne voulait pas démarrer.; **to start off** (leave) partir ▷ *We started off first thing in the morning.* Nous sommes partis en début de matinée.

starter n (first course) entrée f

starve vb mourir de faim ▷ *People were literally starving.* Les gens mouraient littéralement de faim.; **I'm starving!** Je meurs de faim!

state n état m; **he was in a real state** il était dans tous ses états; **the state** (government) l'État; **the States** (USA) les États-Unis
▶ vb ① (say) déclarer ▷ *He stated his intention to resign.* Il a déclaré son intention de démissionner. ② (give) donner ▷ *Please state your name and address.* Veuillez donner vos nom et adresse.

statement n déclaration f

station n (railway) gare f; **the bus station** la gare routière; **a police station** un poste de police; **a radio station** une station de radio

stationary adj à l'arrêt

stationer's n papeterie f

stationery n petit matériel m de bureau

statue n statue f

stay vb ① (remain) rester ▷ *Stay here!* Reste ici!; **to stay in** (not go out) rester à la maison; **to stay up** rester debout ▷ *We stayed up till midnight.* Nous sommes restés debout jusqu'à minuit. ② (spend the night) loger ▷ *to stay with friends* loger chez des amis; **to stay the night** passer la nuit; **We stayed in**

Belgium for a few days. Nous avons passé quelques jours en Belgique.
▶ n séjour m ▷ *my stay in France* mon séjour en France

steady adj ① régulier (f régulière) ▷ *steady progress* des progrès réguliers ② stable ▷ *a steady job* un emploi stable ③ (voice, hand) ferme ④ (person) calme; **a steady boyfriend** un copain; **a steady girlfriend** une copine; **Steady on!** Doucement!

steak n (beef) steak m ▷ *steak and chips* un steak frites

steal vb voler

steam n vapeur f ▷ *a steam engine* une locomotive à vapeur

steel n acier m ▷ *a steel door* une porte en acier

steep adj (slope) raide

steeple n clocher m

steering wheel n volant m

step n ① (pace) pas m ▷ *He took a step forward.* Il a fait un pas en avant. ② (stair) marche f ▷ *She tripped over the step.* Elle a trébuché sur la marche.
▶ vb **to step aside** faire un pas de côté; **to step back** faire un pas en arrière

stepbrother n demi-frère m

stepdaughter n belle-fille f (pl belles-filles)

stepfather n beau-père m (pl beaux-pères)

stepladder n escabeau m (pl escabeaux)

stepmother n belle-mère f (pl belles-mères)

stepsister n demi-sœur f

stepson n beau-fils m (pl beaux-fils)

stereo n chaîne f stéréo (pl chaînes stéréo)

sterling adj £5 sterling cinq livres sterling

stew n ragoût m

steward n steward m

stewardess n hôtesse f de l'air

stick n ❶ bâton m ❷ (walking stick) canne f
▶ vb (with adhesive) coller ▷ Stick the stamps on the envelope. Collez les timbres sur l'enveloppe.

stick out vb (project) sortir ▷ A pen was sticking out of his pocket. Un stylo sortait de sa poche.; **Stick your tongue out and say "ah".** Tirez la langue et dites "ah".

sticker n autocollant m

stick insect n phasme m

sticky adj ❶ poisseux (f poisseuse) ▷ to have sticky hands avoir les mains poisseuses ❷ adhésif (f adhésive) ▷ a sticky label une étiquette adhésive

stiff adj, adv (rigid) rigide; **to have a stiff back** avoir mal au dos; **to feel stiff** avoir des courbatures; **to be bored stiff** s'ennuyer à mourir; **to be frozen stiff** être mort de froid; **to be scared stiff** être mort de peur

still adv ❶ encore ▷ I still haven't finished. Je n'ai pas encore fini. ▷ Are you still in bed? Tu es encore au lit?; **better still** encore mieux ❷ (even so) quand même ▷ She knows I don't like it, but she still does it. Elle

sait que je n'aime pas ça, mais elle le fait quand même. ❸ (after all) enfin ▷ Still, it's the thought that counts. Enfin, c'est l'intention qui compte.
▶ adj **Keep still!** Ne bouge pas!; **Sit still!** Reste tranquille!

sting n piqûre f ▷ a bee sting une piqûre d'abeille
▶ vb piquer ▷ I've been stung. J'ai été piqué.

stink vb puer ▷ It stinks! Ça pue!
▶ n puanteur f

stir vb remuer

stitch vb (cloth) coudre
▶ n ❶ (in sewing) point m ❷ (in wound) point m de suture ▷ I had five stitches. J'ai eu cinq points de suture.

stock n ❶ (supply) réserve f ❷ (in shop) stock m ▷ in stock en stock; **out of stock** épuisé(e) ❸ bouillon m ▷ chicken stock du bouillon de volaille
▶ vb (have in stock) avoir ▷ Do you stock camping stoves? Vous avez des camping-gaz?; **to stock up** s'approvisionner ▷ to stock up with something s'approvisionner en quelque chose

stock cube n cube m de bouillon

stocking n bas m

stole, stolen vb see **steal**

stomach n estomac m

stomachache n **to have a stomachache** avoir mal au ventre

stone n ❶ (rock) pierre f ▷ a stone wall un mur en pierre ❷ (in fruit) noyau m (pl noyaux) ▷ a peach stone

un noyau de pêche
- In France, weight is expressed in kilos. A stone is about 6.3 kg.
I weigh eight stone. Je pèse cinquante kilos.

stood vb see **stand**

stool n tabouret m

stop vb ❶ arrêter ▷ a campaign to stop whaling une campagne pour arrêter la chasse à la baleine ❷ s'arrêter ▷ The bus doesn't stop there. Le bus ne s'arrête pas là. ▷ I think the train's going to stop. Je pense qu'il va s'arrêter de pleuvoir.; **to stop doing something** arrêter de faire quelque chose ▷ to stop smoking arrêter de fumer; **to stop somebody doing something** empêcher quelqu'un de faire quelque chose; **Stop!** Stop!
▶ n arrêt m ▷ a bus stop un arrêt de bus; **This is my stop.** Je descends ici.

stopwatch n chronomètre m

store n ❶ (shop) magasin m ▷ a furniture store un magasin de meubles ❷ (stock, storeroom) réserve f
▶ vb ❶ garder ▷ They store potatoes in the cellar. Ils gardent des pommes de terre dans la cave. ❷ (information) enregistrer

storey n étage m ▷ a three-storey building un immeuble à trois étages

storm n ❶ (gale) tempête f ❷ (thunderstorm) orage m

stormy adj orageux (f orageuse)

story n histoire f

stove n ❶ (in kitchen) cuisinière f ❷ (camping stove) réchaud m

straight adj ❶ droit(e) ▷ a straight line une ligne droite ❷ raide ▷ straight hair les cheveux raides ❸ (heterosexual) hétéro; **straight away** tout de suite; **straight on** tout droit

straightforward adj simple

strain n stress m; **It was a strain.** C'était éprouvant.
▶ vb se faire mal à ▷ I strained my back. Je me suis fait mal au dos.; **to strain a muscle** se froisser un muscle

strange adj bizarre ▷ That's strange! C'est bizarre!

stranger n inconnu m, inconnue f ▷ Don't talk to strangers. Ne parle pas aux inconnus.; **I'm a stranger here.** Je ne suis pas d'ici.

strangle vb étrangler

strap n ❶ (of bag, camera, suitcase) courroie f ❷ (of bra, dress) bretelle f ❸ (on shoe) lanière f ❹ (of watch) bracelet m

straw n paille f; **That's the last straw!** Ça, c'est le comble!

strawberry n fraise f ▷ strawberry jam la confiture de fraises

stray n a stray cat un chat perdu

stream n ruisseau m (pl ruisseaux)

street n rue f ▷ in the street dans la rue

streetlamp n réverbère m

street map n plan m de la ville

streetwise adj dégourdi(e)

strength n force f

stress vb souligner ▷ I would like to stress that ... J'aimerais souligner que ...
▶ n stress m

stretch vb ❶ (person, animal) s'étirer ▷ The dog woke up and stretched. Le chien s'est réveillé et s'est étiré. ❷ (get bigger) se détendre ▷ My sweater stretched when I washed it. Mon pull s'est détendu au lavage. ❸ (stretch out) tendre ▷ They stretched a rope between two trees. Ils ont tendu une corde entre deux arbres.; **to stretch out one's arms** tendre les bras

stretcher n brancard m

stretchy adj élastique

strict adj strict(e)

strike n grève f; **to be on strike** être en grève; **to go on strike** faire grève
▶ vb ❶ (clock) sonner ▷ The clock struck three. L'horloge a sonné trois heures. ❷ (go on strike) faire grève ❸ (hit) frapper; **to strike a match** frotter une allumette

striker n ❶ (person on strike) gréviste mf ❷ (footballer) buteur m

string n ❶ ficelle f ▷ a piece of string un bout de ficelle ❷ (of violin, guitar) corde f

strip vb (get undressed) se déshabiller
▶ n bande f; **a strip cartoon** une bande dessinée

stripe n rayure f

striped adj à rayures ▷ a striped skirt une jupe à rayures

stroke vb caresser
▶ n attaque f ▷ to have a stroke avoir une attaque

stroll n to go for a stroll aller faire une petite promenade

stroller n (US) landau m

strong adj ❶ fort(e) ▷ She's very strong. Elle est très forte. ❷ (material) résistant(e)

strongly adv fortement ▷ We recommend strongly that ... Nous recommandons fortement que ...; **He smelt strongly of tobacco.** Il sentait fort le tabac.; **strongly built** solidement bâti; **I don't feel strongly about it.** Ça m'est égal.

struck vb see **strike**

struggle vb ❶ (physically) se débattre ▷ He struggled, but he couldn't escape. Il s'est débattu, mais il n'a pas pu s'échapper.; **to struggle to do something** (1) (fight) se battre pour faire quelque chose ▷ He struggled to get custody of his daughter. Il s'est battu pour obtenir la garde de sa fille. (2) (have difficulty) avoir du mal à faire quelque chose
▶ n (for independence, equality) lutte f; **It was a struggle.** Ça a été laborieux.

stubborn adj têtu(e)

stuck adj (jammed) coincé(e) ▷ It's stuck. C'est coincé.; **to get stuck** rester coincé ▷ We got stuck in a traffic jam. Nous sommes restés coincés dans un embouteillage.
▶ vb see **stick**

stuck-up adj (informal) coincé(e)

stud n ❶ (earring) boucle f d'oreille ❷ (on football boots) clou m

student n étudiant m, étudiante f

studio n studio m ▷ a TV studio un studio de télévision; **a studio flat** un studio

study vb ❶ (at university) faire des études ▷ I plan to study biology. J'ai l'intention de faire des études de biologie. ❷ (do homework) travailler ▷ I've got to study tonight. Je dois travailler ce soir.

stuff n ❶ (substance) truc m ▷ I need some stuff for my hay fever. J'ai besoin d'un truc contre le rhume des foins. ❷ (things) trucs mpl ▷ There's some stuff on the table for you. Il y a des trucs sur la table pour toi. ❸ (possessions) affaires fpl ▷ Have you got all your stuff? Est-ce que tu as toutes tes affaires?

stuffy adj (room) mal aéré(e); **It's really stuffy in here.** On étouffe ici.

stumble vb trébucher

stung vb see **sting**

stunk vb see **stink**

stunned adj (amazed) sidéré(e) ▷ I was stunned. J'étais sidéré.

stunning adj superbe

stunt n (in film) cascade f

stuntman n cascadeur m

stuntwoman n cascadeuse f

stupid adj stupide ▷ a stupid joke une plaisanterie stupide; **Me, go jogging? Don't be stupid!** Moi, faire du footing? Ne dis pas de bêtises!

stutter vb bégayer
  ▶ n He's got a stutter. Il bégaie.

style n style m ▷ That's not his style. Ça n'est pas son style.

subject n ❶ sujet m ▷ The subject of my project was the internet. Le sujet de mon projet était l'Internet. ❷ (at school) matière f ▷ What's your favourite subject? Quelle est ta matière préférée?

subjunctive n subjonctif m

submarine n sous-marin m

subscription n (to paper, magazine) abonnement m; **to take out a subscription to** s'abonner à

subsidy n subvention f

substance n substance f

substitute n (person) remplaçant m, remplaçante f
  ▶ vb substituer ▷ to substitute A for B substituer A à B

subtitled adj sous-titré(e)

subtitles npl sous-titres mpl ▷ a French film with English subtitles un film français avec des sous-titres en anglais

subtle adj subtil(e)

subtract vb retrancher ▷ to subtract 3 from 5 retrancher trois de cinq

suburb n banlieue f ▷ a suburb of Paris une banlieue de Paris ▷ They live in the suburbs. Ils habitent en banlieue.

subway n (underpass) passage m souterrain

succeed vb réussir ▷ to succeed in doing something réussir à faire quelque chose

success n succès m ▷ The play was a great success. La pièce a eu beaucoup de succès.

successful adj réussi(e) ▷ a successful attempt une tentative réussie; **to be successful in doing something** réussir à faire quelque chose; **He's a successful businessman.** Ses affaires marchent bien.

successfully adv avec succès

such adj, adv si ▷ such nice people des gens si gentils; **such a lot of** tellement de ▷ such a lot of work tellement de travail; **such as** (like) comme ▷ hot countries, such as India les pays chauds, comme l'Inde; **not as such** pas exactement ▷ He's not an expert as such, but ... Ce n'est pas exactement un expert, mais ...; **There's no such thing.** Ça n'existe pas. ▷ There's no such thing as the yeti. Le yéti n'existe pas.

such-and-such adj tel ou tel (f telle ou telle) ▷ such-and-such a place tel ou tel endroit

suck vb sucer ▷ to suck one's thumb sucer son pouce

sudden adj soudain(e) ▷ a sudden change un changement soudain; **all of a sudden** tout à coup

suddenly adv ① (stop, leave, change) brusquement ② (die) subitement ③ (at beginning of sentence) soudain ▷ Suddenly, the door opened. Soudain, la porte s'est ouverte.

suede n daim m ▷ a suede jacket une veste en daim

suffer vb souffrir ▷ She was really suffering. Elle souffrait beaucoup.; **to suffer from a disease** avoir une

maladie ▷ I suffer from hay fever. J'ai le rhume des foins.

suffocate vb suffoquer

sugar n sucre m ▷ Do you take sugar? Est-ce que vous prenez du sucre?

suggest vb suggérer ▷ I suggested they set off early. Je leur ai suggéré de partir de bonne heure.

suggestion n suggestion f ▷ to make a suggestion faire une suggestion

suicide n suicide m; **to commit suicide** se suicider

suit n ① (man's) costume m ② (woman's) tailleur m ▷ vb ① (be convenient for) convenir à ▷ What time would suit you? Quelle heure vous conviendrait?; **That suits me fine.** Ça m'arrange.; **Suit yourself!** Comme tu veux! ② (look good on) aller bien à ▷ That dress really suits you. Cette robe te va vraiment bien.

suitable adj ① convenable ▷ a suitable time une heure convenable ② (clothes) approprié(e) ▷ suitable clothing des vêtements appropriés

suitcase n valise f

suite n (of rooms) suite f; **a bedroom suite** une chambre à coucher

sulk vb bouder

sultana n raisin m sec (pl raisins secs)

sum n ① (calculation) calcul m ▷ She's good at sums. Elle est bonne en calcul. ② (amount) somme f ▷ a sum of money une somme d'argent

sum up vb résumer

summarize vb résumer
summary n résumé m
summer n été m; **in summer**
en été; **summer clothes** les
vêtements d'été; **the summer
holidays** les vacances d'été; **a
summer camp** (US) une colonie
de vacances
summertime n été m; **in
summertime** en été
summit n sommet m
sun n soleil m ▷ **in the sun** au soleil
sunbathe vb se bronzer
sunblock n écran m total
sunburn n coup m de soleil
sunburnt adj **I got sunburnt.** J'ai
attrapé un coup de soleil.
Sunday n dimanche m ▷ **on
Sunday** dimanche ▷ **on Sundays** le
dimanche ▷ **every Sunday** tous les
dimanches ▷ **last Sunday** dimanche
dernier ▷ **next Sunday** dimanche
prochain
Sunday school n catéchisme m
● **le catéchisme**, the French
● equivalent of **Sunday school**,
● takes place during the week
● after school rather than on a
● Sunday.
sunflower n tournesol m
sung vb see **sing**
sunglasses npl lunettes fpl de
soleil
sunk vb see **sink**
sunlight n soleil m
sunny adj ensoleillé(e) ▷ **a sunny
morning** une matinée ensoleillée;
It's sunny. Il fait du soleil.; **a sunny
day** une belle journée

sunrise n lever m du soleil
sunroof n toit m ouvrant
sunscreen n crème f solaire
sunset n coucher m du soleil
sunshine n soleil m
sunstroke n insolation f ▷ **to get
sunstroke** attraper une insolation
suntan n bronzage m; **suntan
lotion** lait m solaire; **suntan oil**
huile f solaire
super adj formidable
supermarket n supermarché m
supernatural adj surnaturel
(f surnaturelle)
superstitious adj superstitieux
(f superstitieuse)
supervise vb surveiller
supervisor n ❶ (in factory)
surveillant m, surveillante f
❷ (in department store) chef m
de rayon
supper n dîner m
supplement n supplément m
supplies npl (food) vivres mpl
supply vb (provide) fournir;
**to supply somebody with
something** fournir quelque chose
à quelqu'un ▷ **The centre supplied
us with all the equipment.** Le centre
nous a fourni tout l'équipement.
▶ n provision f ▷ **a supply of
paper** une provision de papier;
the water supply (to town)
l'approvisionnement m en eau
supply teacher n suppléant m,
suppléante f
support n (backing) soutien m
▶ vb ❶ soutenir ▷ **My mum has
always supported me.** Ma mère

m'a toujours soutenu. ❸ **être supporter de** ▷ *What team do you support?* Tu es supporter de quelle équipe? ❸ *(financially)* **subvenir aux besoins de** ▷ *She had to support five children on her own.* Elle a dû subvenir toute seule aux besoins de cinq enfants.

> Be careful not to translate **to support** by supporter.

supporter n ❶ **supporter** m ▷ *a Liverpool supporter* un supporter de Liverpool ❷ **sympathisant** m, **sympathisante** f ▷ *a supporter of the Labour Party* un sympathisant du parti travailliste

suppose vb **imaginer** ▷ *I suppose he's late.* J'imagine qu'il en est retard.; **I suppose so.** J'imagine.; **to be supposed to do something** être censé faire quelque chose ▷ *You're supposed to show your passport.* On est censé montrer son passeport.

supposing conj **si** ▷ *Supposing you won the lottery* ... Si tu gagnais à la loterie ...

sure adj **sûr(e)** ▷ *Are you sure?* Tu es sûr?; **Sure!** Bien sûr!; **to make sure that** ... vérifier que ... ▷ *I'm going to make sure the door's locked.* Je vais vérifier que la porte est fermée à clé.

surely adv **Surely you've been to London?** J'imagine que tu es allé à Londres, non?; **The shops are closed on Sundays, surely?** J'imagine que les magasins sont fermés le dimanche, non?

surf n **ressac** m
▶ vb **surfer**; **to go surfing** faire du surf; **to surf the Net** surfer sur le Net

surface n **surface** f

surfboard n **planche** f **de surf** (pl planches de surf)

surfing n **surf** m ▷ *to go surfing* faire du surf

surgeon n **chirurgien** m ▷ *She's a surgeon.* Elle est chirurgien.

surgery n *(doctor's surgery)* **cabinet** m **médical**; **surgery hours** les heures de consultation

surname n **nom** m **de famille** (pl noms de famille)

surprise n **surprise** f

surprised adj **surpris(e)** ▷ *I was surprised to see him.* J'ai été surpris de le voir.

surprising adj **surprenant(e)**

surrender vb **capituler**

surrogate mother n **mère** f **porteuse**

surround vb **encercler** ▷ *The police surrounded the house.* La police a encerclé la maison.; **surrounded by** entouré de ▷ *The house is surrounded by trees.* La maison est entourée d'arbres.

surroundings npl **cadre** m ▷ *a hotel in beautiful surroundings* un hôtel situé dans un beau cadre

survey n *(research)* **enquête** f

survivor n **survivant** m, **survivante** f ▷ *There were no survivors.* Il n'y a pas eu de survivants.

suspect vb **soupçonner**
▶ n **suspect** m, **suspecte** f

suspend vb ❶ (from school, team) exclure ▷ He's been suspended. Il s'est fait exclure. ❷ (from job) suspendre

suspense n ❶ (waiting) attente f ▷ The suspense was terrible. L'attente a été terrible. ❷ (in story) suspense m ▷ a film with lots of suspense un film avec beaucoup de suspense

suspicious adj ❶ méfiant(e) ▷ He was suspicious at first. Il était méfiant au début. ❷ (suspicious-looking) louche ▷ a suspicious person un individu louche

swallow vb avaler

swam vb see **swim**

swan n cygne m

swap vb échanger ▷ to swap A for B échanger A contre B

swear vb (make an oath, curse) jurer

swearword n gros mot m

sweat n transpiration f
▶ vb transpirer

sweater n pull m

sweatshirt n sweat m

Swede n (person) Suédois m, Suédoise f

Sweden n Suède f; **in Sweden** en Suède; **to Sweden** en Suède

Swedish adj suédois(e) ▷ She's Swedish. Elle est suédoise.
▶ n (language) suédois m

sweep vb balayer; **to sweep the floor** balayer

sweet n ❶ (candy) bonbon m ▷ a bag of sweets un paquet de bonbons ❷ (pudding) dessert m ▷ What sweet did you have? Qu'est-ce que vous avez mangé comme dessert?

▶ adj ❶ (not savoury) sucré(e) ❷ (kind) gentil (f gentille) ▷ That was really sweet of you. C'était vraiment gentil de ta part. ❸ (cute) mignon (f mignonne) ▷ Isn't she sweet? Comme elle est mignonne!; **sweet and sour pork** le porc à la sauce aigre-douce

sweetcorn n maïs m doux

swept vb see **sweep**

swerve vb faire une embardée ▷ He swerved to avoid the cyclist. Il a fait une embardée pour éviter le cycliste.

swim n **to go for a swim** aller se baigner
▶ vb nager ▷ Can you swim? Tu sais nager?; **She swam across the river.** Elle a traversé la rivière à la nage.

swimmer n nageur m, nageuse f ▷ She's a good swimmer. C'est une bonne nageuse.

swimming n natation f ▷ Do you like swimming? Tu aimes la natation?; **to go swimming** (in a pool) aller à la piscine; **a swimming cap** un bonnet de bain; **a swimming costume** un maillot de bain; **a swimming pool** une piscine; **swimming trunks** maillot m de bain

swimsuit n maillot m de bain

swing n (in playground, garden) balançoire f
▶ vb ❶ se balancer ▷ A bunch of keys swung from his belt. Un trousseau de clés se balançait à sa ceinture.; **Sam was swinging an**

umbrella as he walked. Sam balançait son parapluie en marchant. ❷ <u>virer</u> ▷ *The canoe swung round sharply.* Le canoë a viré brusquement.

Swiss *adj* <u>suisse</u> ▷ *Sabine's Swiss.* Sabine est suisse.
　▶ *n* (person) <u>Suisse</u> *mf*; **the Swiss** les Suisses

switch *n* (for light, radio etc) <u>bouton</u> *m*
　▶ *vb* <u>changer de</u> ▷ *We switched partners.* Nous avons changé de partenaire.

switch off *vb* ❶ (electrical appliance) <u>éteindre</u> ❷ (engine, machine) <u>arrêter</u>

switch on *vb* ❶ (electrical appliance) <u>allumer</u> ❷ (engine, machine) <u>mettre en marche</u>

Switzerland *n* <u>Suisse</u> *f*; **in Switzerland** en Suisse

swollen *adj* (arm, leg) <u>enflé(e)</u>

swop *vb* <u>échanger</u> ▷ *to swop A for B* échanger A contre B

sword *n* <u>épée</u> *f*

swore, sworn *vb see* **swear**

swot *n* <u>bûcheur</u> *m*, <u>bûcheuse</u> *f*
　▶ *vb* <u>bosser dur</u> ▷ *I'll have to swot for my maths exam.* Je vais devoir bosser dur pour mon examen de maths.

swum *vb see* **swim**

swung *vb see* **swing**

syllabus *n* <u>programme</u> *m* ▷ *on the syllabus* au programme

symbol *n* <u>symbole</u> *m*

sympathetic *adj* <u>compréhensif</u> (*f* compréhensive)

Be careful not to translate **sympathetic** by **sympathique**.

sympathize *vb* **to sympathize with somebody** comprendre quelqu'un

sympathy *n* <u>compassion</u> *f*

symptom *n* <u>symptôme</u> *m*

synagogue *n* <u>synagogue</u> *f*

syringe *n* <u>seringue</u> *f*

system *n* <u>système</u> *m*

a
b
c
d
e
f
g
h
i
j
k
l
m
n
o
p
q
r
s
t
u
v
w
x
y
z

t

table n table f ▷ *to lay the table* mettre la table

tablecloth n nappe f

tablespoon n grande cuillère f; **a tablespoonful of sugar** une cuillerée à soupe de sucre

tablet n comprimé m

table tennis n ping-pong m ▷ *to play table tennis* jouer au ping-pong

tact n tact m

tactful adj plein(e) de tact

tactics npl tactique f

tadpole n têtard m

tag n (label) étiquette f

tail n queue f; **Heads or tails?** Pile ou face?

tailor n tailleur m

take vb ❶ prendre ▷ *He took a plate from the cupboard.* Il a pris une assiette dans le placard. ▷ *It takes*
about an hour. Ça prend environ une heure. ❷ (person) emmener ▷ *He goes to London every week, but he never takes me.* Il va à Londres toutes les semaines, mais il ne m'emmène jamais.; **to take something somewhere** emporter quelque chose quelque part ▷ *Don't take anything valuable with you.* N'emportez pas d'objets de valeur.; **I'm going to take my coat to the cleaner's.** Je vais donner mon manteau à nettoyer. ❸ (effort, skill) demander ▷ *that takes a lot of courage* cela demande beaucoup de courage; **It takes a lot of money to do that.** Il faut beaucoup d'argent pour faire ça. ❹ (tolerate) supporter ▷ *He can't take being criticized.* Il ne supporte pas d'être critiqué. ❺ (exam, test) passer ▷ *Have you taken your driving test yet?* Est-ce que tu as déjà passé ton permis de conduire? ❻ (subject) faire ▷ *I decided to take French instead of German.* J'ai décidé de faire du français au lieu de l'allemand.

take apart vb **to take something apart** démonter quelque chose

take away vb ❶ (object) emporter ❷ (person) emmener; **to take something away** (confiscate) confisquer quelque chose; **hot meals to take away** des plats chauds à emporter

take back vb rapporter ▷ *I took it back to the shop.* Je l'ai rapporté au magasin.; **I take it all back!** Je n'ai rien dit!

take off vb ① (plane) décoller
▷ *The plane took off twenty minutes late.* L'avion a décollé avec vingt minutes de retard. ② (clothes) enlever ▷ *Take your coat off.* Enlevez votre manteau.

take out vb (from container, pocket) sortir; **He took her out to the theatre.** Il l'a emmenée au théâtre.

take over vb prendre la relève ▷ *I'll take over now.* Je vais prendre la relève.; **to take over from somebody** remplacer quelqu'un

takeaway n ① (meal) plat m à emporter ② (shop) restaurant m qui vend des plats à emporter ▷ *a Chinese takeaway* un restaurant chinois qui vend des plats à emporter

taken vb see **take**

takeoff n (of plane) décollage m

tale n (story) conte f

talent n talent m ▷ *She's got lots of talent.* Elle a beaucoup de talent.; **to have a talent for something** être doué pour quelque chose ▷ *He's got a real talent for languages.* Il est vraiment doué pour les langues.

talented adj **She's a talented pianist.** C'est une pianiste de talent.

talk n ① (speech) exposé m ▷ *She gave a talk on rock climbing.* Elle a fait un exposé sur la varappe. ② (conversation) conversation f ▷ *I had a talk with my Mum about it.* J'ai eu une petite conversation avec ma mère à ce sujet. ③ (gossip)

racontars mpl ▷ *It's just talk.* Ce sont des racontars.
▶ vb parler ▷ *to talk about something* parler de quelque chose; **to talk something over with somebody** discuter de quelque chose avec quelqu'un

talkative adj bavard(e)

tall adj ① (person, tree) grand(e); **to be 2 metres tall** mesurer deux mètres ② (building) haut(e)

tame adj (animal) apprivoisé(e) ▷ *They've got a tame hedgehog.* Ils ont un hérisson apprivoisé.

tampon n tampon m

tan n bronzage m ▷ *She's got an amazing tan.* Elle a un bronzage superbe.

tangerine n mandarine f

tangle n ① (ropes, cables) enchevêtrement m ② (hair) nœud m; **to be in a tangle (1)** (ropes, cables) être enchevêtré(e) **(2)** (hair) être emmêlé(e)

tank n ① (for water, petrol) réservoir m ② (military) char m d'assaut; **a fish tank** un aquarium

tanker n ① (ship) pétrolier m; **an oil tanker** un pétrolier m; **an truck** camion-citerne m; **a petrol tanker** un camion-citerne

tap n ① (water tap) robinet m ② (gentle blow) petite tape f

tap-dancing n claquettes fpl ▷ *I do tap-dancing.* Je fais des claquettes.

tape vb (record) enregistrer ▷ *Did you tape that film last night?* As-tu enregistré le film hier soir?
▶ n ① cassette f ▷ *a tape of*

Sinead O'Connor une cassette de Sinead O'Connor ❷ *(sticky tape)* scotch® m

tape measure n mètre m à ruban

tape recorder n magnétophone m

tar n goudron m

target n cible f

tart n tarte f ▷ *an apple tart* une tarte aux pommes

tartan adj écossais(e) ▷ *a tartan scarf* une écharpe écossaise

task n tâche f

taste n goût m ▷ *It's got a really strange taste.* Ça a un goût vraiment bizarre. ▷ *a joke in bad taste* une plaisanterie de mauvais goût; **Would you like a taste?** Tu veux goûter?
▶ vb goûter ▷ *Would you like to taste it?* Vous voulez y goûter?; **to taste of something** avoir un goût de quelque chose ▷ *It tastes of fish.* Ça a un goût de poisson.; **You can taste the garlic in it.** Ça a bien le goût d'ail.

tasty adj savoureux (f savoureuse)

tattoo n tatouage m

taught vb see **teach**

Taurus n Taureau m ▷ *I'm Taurus.* Je suis Taureau.

tax n ❶ *(on income)* impôts mpl ❷ *(on goods, alcohol)* taxe f

taxi n taxi m; **a taxi driver** un chauffeur de taxi

taxi rank n station f de taxis

TB n tuberculose f

tea n ❶ thé m ▷ *a cup of tea* une tasse de thé; **a tea bag** un sachet de thé ❷ *(evening meal)* dîner m; **We were having tea.** Nous étions en train de dîner.

teach vb ❶ apprendre ▷ *My sister taught me to swim.* Ma sœur m'a appris à nager. ❷ *(in school)* enseigner ▷ *She teaches physics.* Elle enseigne la physique.

teacher n ❶ *(in secondary school)* professeur m ▷ *a maths teacher* un professeur de maths ▷ *She's a teacher.* Elle est professeur.
❷ *(in primary school)* instituteur m, institutrice f ▷ *He's a primary school teacher.* Il est instituteur.

teaching n enseignement m

team n équipe f ▷ *a football team* une équipe de football

teapot n théière f

tear n larme f ▷ *She was in tears.* Elle était en larmes.
▶ vb ❶ déchirer ▷ *Be careful or you'll tear the page.* Fais attention, tu vas déchirer la page. ❷ se déchirer ▷ *It won't tear, it's very strong.* Ça ne se déchire pas, c'est très solide.; **to tear up** déchirer ▷ *He tore up the letter.* Il a déchiré la lettre.

tease vb ❶ *(unkindly)* tourmenter ▷ *Stop teasing that poor animal!* Arrête de tourmenter cette pauvre bête! ❷ *(jokingly)* taquiner ▷ *He's teasing you.* Il te taquine.; **I was only teasing.** Je plaisantais.

teaspoon n petite cuillère f; **a teaspoonful of sugar** une cuillerée à café de sucre

teatime n *(in evening)* heure f du dîner ▷ *It was nearly teatime.*

C'était presque l'heure du dîner.; **Teatime!** À table!

tea towel n torchon m

technical adj technique; **a technical college** un lycée technique

technician n technicien m, technicienne f

technological adj technologique

technology n technologie f

teddy bear n nounours m

teenage adj ❶ pour les jeunes ▷ *a teenage magazine* un magazine pour les jeunes ❷ (boys, girls) adolescent ▷ *She has two teenage daughters.* Elle a deux filles adolescentes.

teenager n adolescent m, adolescente f

teens npl **She's in her teens.** C'est une adolescente.

tee-shirt n tee-shirt m

teeth npl dents fpl

telephone n téléphone m ▷ *on the telephone* au téléphone; **a telephone box** une cabine téléphonique; **a telephone call** un coup de téléphone; **the telephone directory** l'annuaire m; **a telephone number** un numéro de téléphone

telescope n télescope m

television n télévision f; **on television** à la télévision; **a television licence** une redevance de télévision; **a television programme** une émission de télévision

tell vb dire; **to tell somebody something** dire quelque chose à quelqu'un ▷ *Did you tell your mother?* Tu l'as dit à ta mère? ▷ *I told him that I was going on holiday.* Je lui ai dit que je partais en vacances.; **to tell somebody to do something** dire à quelqu'un de faire quelque chose ▷ *He told me to wait a moment.* Il m'a dit d'attendre un moment.; **to tell lies** dire des mensonges; **to tell a story** raconter une histoire; **I can't tell the difference between them.** Je n'arrive pas à les distinguer.

tell off vb gronder

telly n télé f ▷ *to watch telly* regarder la télé; **on telly** à la télé

temper n caractère m ▷ *He's got a terrible temper.* Il a un sale caractère.; **to be in a temper** être en colère; **to lose one's temper** se mettre en colère ▷ *I lost my temper.* Je me suis mis en colère.

temperature n (of oven, water, person) température f; **The temperature was 30 degrees.** Il faisait trente degrés.; **to have a temperature** avoir de la fièvre

temple n temple m

temporary adj temporaire

temptation n tentation f

tempting adj tentant(e)

ten num dix ▷ *She's ten.* Elle a dix ans.

tend vb **to tend to do something** avoir tendance à faire quelque chose ▷ *He tends to arrive late.* Il a tendance à arriver en retard.

a b c d e f g h i j k l m n o p q r s t u v w x y z

tennis n tennis m ▷ Do you play tennis? Vous jouez au tennis?;
a tennis ball une balle de tennis;
a tennis court un court de tennis;
a tennis racket une raquette de tennis

tennis player n joueur m de tennis, joueuse f de tennis ▷ He's a tennis player. Il est joueur de tennis.

tenor n ténor m

tenpin bowling n bowling m ▷ to go tenpin bowling jouer au bowling

tense adj tendu(e)
▶ n the present tense le présent; **the future tense** le futur

tension n tension f

tent n tente f; **a tent peg** un piquet de tente; **a tent pole** un montant de tente

tenth adj dixième ▷ the tenth floor le dixième étage; **the tenth of August** le dix août

term n ① (at school) trimestre m ② terme m ▷ a short-term solution une solution à court terme; **to come to terms with something** accepter quelque chose

terminal adj (illness, patient) incurable
▶ n (of computer) un terminal; **an oil terminal** un terminal pétrolier; **an air terminal** une aérogare

terminally adv **to be terminally ill** être condamné

terrace n ① (patio) terrasse f ② (row of houses) rangée f de maisons; **the terraces** (at stadium) les gradins mpl

terraced adj **a terraced house** une maison mitoyenne

terrible adj épouvantable ▷ My French is terrible. Mon français est épouvantable.

terribly adv ① terriblement ▷ He suffered terribly. Il souffre terriblement. ② vraiment ▷ I'm terribly sorry. Je suis vraiment désolé.

terrific adj (wonderful) super inv ▷ That's terrific! C'est super!; **You look terrific!** Tu es superbe!

terrified adj terrifié(e) ▷ I was terrified! J'étais terrifié!

terrorism n terrorisme m

terrorist n terroriste mf; **a terrorist attack** un attentat terroriste

test n ① (at school) interrogation f ▷ I've got a test tomorrow. J'ai une interrogation demain. ② (trial, check) essai m ▷ nuclear tests les essais nucléaires ③ (medical) analyse f ▷ a blood test une analyse de sang ▷ They're going to do some more tests. Ils vont faire d'autres analyses.; **driving test** l'examen du permis de conduire; **He's got his driving test tomorrow.** Il passe son permis de conduire demain.
▶ vb ① essayer ▷ to test something out essayer quelque chose
② (class) interroger ▷ He tested us on the vocabulary. Il nous a interrogés sur le vocabulaire.; **She was tested for drugs.** On lui a fait subir un contrôle antidopage.

test tube n éprouvette f

text n ❶ texte m ❷ (on mobile phone) SMS m
▸ vb **to text someone** envoyer un SMS à quelqu'un

textbook n manuel m ▷ A French textbook un manuel de français

text message n SMS m

Thames n Tamise f

than conj que ▷ She's taller than me. Elle est plus grande que moi.; **more than ten years** plus de dix ans; **more than once** plus d'une fois

thank vb remercier ▷ Don't forget to write and thank them. N'oublie pas de leur écrire pour les remercier.; **thank you** merci; **thank you very much** merci beaucoup

thanks excl merci!; **thanks to** grâce à ▷ Thanks to him, everything went OK. Grâce à lui, tout s'est bien passé.

that adj, pron, conj

> Use **ce** when **that** is followed by a masculine noun, and **cette** when **that** is followed by a feminine noun. **ce** changes to **cet** before a vowel and before most words beginning with "h".

❶ ce, cet (f cette) ▷ that book ce livre ▷ that man cet homme ▷ that woman cette femme; that road cette route; **THAT road** cette route-là; **that one** celui-là (f celle-là) ▷ This man? — No, that one. Cet homme-ci? — Non, celui-là. ▷ Do you like this photo? — No, I prefer that one. Tu aimes

cette photo? — Non, je préfère celle-là. ❷ ça ▷ You see that? Tu vois ça?; **What's that?** Qu'est-ce que c'est?; **Who's that?** Qui est-ce?; **Is that you?** C'est toi?; **That's ...** C'est ... ▷ That's my teacher. C'est mon prof. ▷ That's what he said. C'est ce qu'il a dit.

> In relative phrases use **qui** when **that** refers to the subject of the sentence, and **que** when it refers to the object.

❸ qui ▷ the man that saw us l'homme qui nous a vus ❹ que ▷ the man that we saw l'homme que nous avons vu

> **que** changes to **qu'** before a vowel and before most words beginning with "h".

▷ the dog that she bought le chien qu'elle a acheté ▷ He thought that Henri was ill. Il pensait qu'Henri était malade.; **It was that big.** Il était grand comme ça.; **It's about that high.** C'est à peu près haut comme ça.; **It's not that difficult.** Ça n'est pas si difficile que ça.

the def art

> Use **le** with a masculine noun, and **la** with a feminine noun. Use **l'** before a vowel and most words beginning with "h". For plural nouns always use **les**.

le, la, l' (pl les) ▷ the boy le garçon ▷ the girl la fille ▷ the man l'homme m ▷ the air l'air m ▷ the habit l'habitude f ▷ the children les enfants mpl

theatre(US **theater**) n théâtre m
theft n vol m
their adj leur (pl leurs) ▷ their house
leur maison ▷ their parents leurs
parents
theirs pron le leur (f la leur, pl les
leurs) ▷ It's not our garage, it's theirs.
Ce n'est pas notre garage, c'est
le leur. ▷ It's not our car, it's theirs.
Ce n'est pas notre voiture, c'est la
leur. ▷ They're not our ideas, they're
theirs. Ce ne sont pas nos idées,
ce sont les leurs. ▷ **Is this theirs?**
(1) (masculine owners) C'est à eux?
(2) (feminine owners) C'est à elles?
▷ This car is theirs. Cette voiture
est à eux.
them pron ❶ les ▷ I didn't see them.
Je ne les ai pas vus.

Use **leur** when **them** means
to them.

❷ leur ▷ I told them the truth. Je leur
ai dit la vérité.

Use **eux** or **elles** after a
preposition.

❸ eux m (f elles) ▷ It's for them. C'est
pour eux.
theme park n parc m d'attractions
themselves pron ❶ se ▷ Did they
hurt themselves? Est-ce qu'ils se sont
fait mal? ❷ eux-mêmes (f elles-
mêmes) ▷ They did it themselves. Ils
l'ont fait eux-mêmes.
then adv, conj ❶ (next) ensuite ▷ I
get dressed. Then I have breakfast.
Je m'habille. Ensuite je prends
mon petit déjeuner. ❷ (in that
case) alors ▷ My pen's run out. — Use
a pencil then! Il n'y a plus d'encre

dans mon stylo. — Alors utilise un
crayon! ❸ (at that time) à l'époque
▷ There was no electricity then. Il n'y
avait pas d'électricité à l'époque.;
now and then de temps en temps
▷ Do you play chess? — Now and
then. Vous jouez aux échecs? — De
temps en temps.; **By then it was
too late.** Il était déjà trop tard.
there adv ❶ là ▷ Put it there, on the
table. Mets-le là, sur la table.; **over
there** là-bas; **in there** là; **on there**
là; **up there** là-haut; **down there**
là-bas; **There he is!** Le voilà! ❷ y
▷ He went there on Friday. Il y est
allé vendredi.; **There is ...** Il y a ...
▷ There's a factory near my house. Il
y a une usine près de chez moi.;
There are ... Il y a ... ▷ There are
five people in my family. Il y a cinq
personnes dans ma famille.; **There
has been an accident.** Il y a eu un
accident.
therefore adv donc
there's = there is; there has
thermometer n thermomètre m
these adj, pron ❶ ces ▷ these shoes
ces chaussures; **THESE shoes** ces
chaussures-là ❷ ceux-ci (f celles-
ci) ▷ I want these! Je veux ceux-ci!
▷ I'm looking for some sandals. Can I
try these? Je cherche des sandales.
Je peux essayer celles-ci?
they pron

Check if **they** stands for a
masculine or feminine noun.

ils (fpl elles) ▷ Are there any tickets
left? — No, they're all sold. Est-ce qu'il
reste des billets? — Non, ils sont

tous vendus.; **They say that ...** On dit que ...

they'd = they had; they would

they'll = they will

they're = they are

they've = they have

thick adj ❶ (not thin) épais (f épaisse); **The walls are one metre thick.** Les murs font un mètre d'épaisseur. ❷ (stupid) bête

thief n voleur m, voleuse f; **Stop thief!** Au voleur!

thigh n cuisse f

thin adj ❶ (person, slice) mince ❷ (skinny) maigre

thing n ❶ chose f ▷ beautiful things de belles choses ❷ (thingy) truc m ▷ What's that thing called? Comment s'appelle ce truc?; **my things** (belongings) mes affaires; **You poor thing!** Mon pauvre!

think vb ❶ (believe) penser ▷ I think you're wrong. Je pense que vous avez tort. ▷ What do you think about the war? Que pensez-vous de la guerre? ❷ (spend time thinking) réfléchir ▷ Think carefully before you reply. Réfléchis bien avant de répondre. ▷ I'll think about it. Je vais y réfléchir.; **What are you thinking about?** À quoi tu penses? ❸ (imagine) imaginer ▷ Think what life would be like without cars. Imaginez la vie sans voitures.; **I think so.** Oui, je crois.; **I don't think so.** Je ne crois pas.; **I'll think it over.** Je vais y réfléchir.

third adj troisième ▷ the third day le troisième jour ▷ the third time

la troisième fois ▷ I came third. Je suis arrivé troisième.; **the third of March** le trois mars

▶ n tiers m ▷ a third of the population un tiers de la population

thirdly adv troisièmement

Third World n tiers monde m

thirst n soif f

thirsty adj **to be thirsty** avoir soif

thirteen num treize ▷ I'm thirteen. J'ai treize ans.

thirteenth adj treizième ▷ her thirteenth birthday son treizième anniversaire ▷ the thirteenth floor le treizième étage; **the thirteenth of August** le treize août

thirty num trente

this adj, pron

> Use **ce** when **this** is followed by a masculine noun, and **cette** when **this** is followed by a feminine noun. **ce** changes to **cet** before a vowel and before most words beginning with "h".

❶ ce, cet (f cette) ▷ this book ce livre ▷ this man cet homme ▷ this woman cette femme; **this road** cette route; **THIS road** cette route-ci; **this one** celui-ci (f celle-ci) ▷ Pass me that pen. — This one? Passe-moi ce stylo. — Celui-ci? ❷ ça ▷ You see this? Tu vois ça?; **What's this?** Qu'est-ce c'est?; **This is my mother.** (introduction) Je te présente ma mère.; **This is Gavin speaking.** (on the phone) C'est Gavin à l'appareil.

thistle n chardon m

thorough adj minutieux
(fminutieuse) ▷ She's very thorough.
Elle est très minutieuse.

those adj, pron ❶ ces ▷ those shoes
ces chaussures; **THOSE** shoes ces
chaussures-là ❷ ceux-là (fcelles-
là) ▷ I want those! Je veux ceux-là!
▷ I'm looking for some sandals. Can I
try those? Je cherche des sandales.
Je peux essayer celles-là?

though conj, adv bien que

bien que has to be followed by
a verb in the subjunctive.
▷ Though it's raining … Bien qu'il
pleuve …; **He's a nice person,
though he's not very clever.** Il est
sympa, mais pas très malin.

thought n (idea) idée f ▷ I've just had
a thought. Je viens d'avoir une idée.;
It was a nice thought, thank you.
C'est gentil de ta part, merci.
▶ vb see **think**

thoughtful adj ❶ (deep in
thought) pensif (fpensive) ▷ You
look thoughtful. Tu as l'air pensif.
❷ (considerate) prévenant(e)
▷ She's very thoughtful. Elle est très
prévenante.

thoughtless adj He's completely
thoughtless. Il ne pense
absolument pas aux autres.

thousand num a thousand
mille ▷ a thousand euros mille
euros; **£2000** deux mille livres;
thousands of people des milliers
de personnes

thousandth adj, n millième m

thread n fil m

threat n menace f

threaten vb menacer ▷ to threaten
to do something menacer de faire
quelque chose

three num trois ▷ She's three. Elle
a trois ans.

three-quarters npl trois-quarts mpl

threw vb see **throw**

thrilled adj I was thrilled. (pleased)
J'étais absolument ravi(e).

thriller n thriller m

thrilling adj palpitant(e)

throat n gorge f ▷ to have a sore
throat avoir mal à la gorge

through prep, adj, adv ❶ par
▷ through the window par la fenêtre;
to go through a tunnel traverser
un tunnel ❷ à travers ▷ through the
crowd à travers la foule; **a through
train** un train direct; **"no through
road"** "impasse"

throughout prep throughout
Britain dans toute la Grande-
Bretagne; **throughout the year**
pendant toute l'année

throw vb lancer ▷ He threw the
ball to me. Il m'a lancé le ballon.;
to throw a party organiser une
soirée; **That really threw him.**
Ça l'a déconcerté.; **to throw
away** (1) (rubbish) jeter (2) (chance)
perdre; **to throw out** (1) (throw
away) jeter (2) (person) mettre à la
porte ▷ I threw him out. Je l'ai mis à
la porte.; **to throw up** vomir

thumb n pouce m

thumb tack n (US) punaise f

thump vb to thump somebody
donner un coup de poing à
quelqu'un

thunder n tonnerre m

thunderstorm n orage m

Thursday n jeudi m ▷ on Thursday jeudi ▷ on Thursdays le jeudi ▷ every Thursday tous les jeudis ▷ last Thursday jeudi dernier ▷ next Thursday jeudi prochain

tick n ❶ (mark) coche f ❷ (of clock) tic-tac m; **I'll be back in a tick.** J'en ai pour une seconde.
▶ vb ❶ cocher ▷ Tick the appropriate box. Cochez la case correspondante. ❷ (clock) faire tic-tac

tick off vb ❶ (check) cocher ▷ He ticked off our names on the list. Il a coché nos noms sur la liste. ❷ (tell off) passer un savon à ▷ She ticked me off for being late. Elle m'a passé un savon à cause de mon retard.

ticket n

Be careful to choose correctly between **le ticket** and **le billet**.

❶ (for bus, tube, cinema, museum) ticket m ▷ an underground ticket un ticket de métro ❷ (for plane, train, theatre, concert) billet m; **a parking ticket** un p.-v.

ticket inspector n contrôleur m, contrôleuse f

ticket office n guichet m

tickle vb chatouiller

tide n marée f; **high tide** la marée haute; **low tide** la marée basse

tidy adj ❶ (room) bien rangé(e) ▷ Your room's very tidy. Ta chambre est bien rangée. ❷ (person) ordonné(e) ▷ She's very tidy. Elle est très ordonnée.

▶ vb ranger ▷ Go and tidy your room. Va ranger ta chambre.; **to tidy up** ranger ▷ Don't forget to tidy up afterwards. N'oubliez pas de ranger après.

tie n (necktie) cravate f; **It was a tie.** (in sport) Ils ont fait match nul.
▶ vb ❶ (ribbon, shoelaces) nouer; **to tie a knot in something** faire un nœud à quelque chose ❷ (in sport) faire match nul ▷ They tied three all. Ils ont fait match nul, trois à trois.; **to tie up (1)** (parcel) ficeler **(2)** (dog, boat) attacher **(3)** (prisoner) ligoter

tiger n tigre m

tight adj ❶ (tight-fitting) moulant(e) ▷ tight clothes les vêtements moulants ❷ (too tight) juste ▷ This dress is a bit tight. Cette robe est un peu juste.

tighten vb ❶ (rope) tendre ❷ (screw) resserrer

tightly adv (hold) fort

tights npl collant m

tile n ❶ (on roof) tuile f ❷ (on wall, floor) carreau m (pl carreaux)

till n caisse f
▶ prep, conj ❶ jusqu'à ▷ I waited till ten o'clock. J'ai attendu jusqu'à dix heures.; **till now** jusqu'à présent; **till then** jusque-là

Use **avant** if the sentence you want to translate contains a negative, such as "not" or "never".

❷ avant ▷ It won't be ready till next week. Ça ne sera pas prêt avant la semaine prochaine.

time n ❶ (on clock) heure f
▷ What time is it? Quelle heure
est-il? ▷ What time do you get up?
À quelle heure tu te lèves?; **on
time** à l'heure ▷ He never arrives on
time. Il n'arrive jamais à l'heure.
❷ (amount of time) temps m ▷ I'm
sorry, I haven't got time. Je suis
désolé, je n'ai pas le temps.; **from
time to time** de temps en temps;
in time à temps ▷ We arrived in time
for lunch. Nous sommes arrivés à
temps pour le déjeuner.; **just in
time** juste à temps; **in no time**
en un rien de temps ▷ It was ready
in no time. Ça a été prêt en un rien
de temps.; **It's time to go.** Il est
temps de partir. ❸ (moment)
moment m ▷ This isn't a good time to
ask him. Ce n'est pas le moment de
lui demander.; **for the time being**
pour le moment ❹ (occasion) fois
f ▷ this time cette fois-ci ▷ next time
la prochaine fois ▷ two at a time
deux à la fois; **How many times?**
Combien de fois?; **at times** parfois
; **a long time** longtemps ▷ Have
you lived here for a long time? Vous
habitez ici depuis longtemps?; **in
a week's time** dans une semaine
▷ I'll come back in a month's time. Je
reviendrai dans un mois.; **Come
and see us any time.** Venez nous
voir quand vous voulez.; **to have
a good time** bien s'amuser ▷ Did
you have a good time? Vous vous êtes
bien amusés?; **2 times 2 is 4** deux
fois deux égalent quatre

time off n temps m libre

timetable n ❶ (for train, bus)
horaire m ❷ (at school) emploi m
du temps

tin n ❶ boîte f ▷ a tin of soup une
boîte de soupe ▷ a biscuit tin une
boîte à biscuits ❷ boîte f de
conserve ▷ The bin was full of tins. La
poubelle était pleine de boîtes de
conserve. ❸ (type of metal) étain m

tin opener n ouvre-boîte m

tiny adj minuscule

tip n ❶ (money) pourboire m ▷ Shall
I give him a tip? Je lui donne un
pourboire? ❷ (advice) tuyau m
(informal) (pl tuyaux) ▷ a useful tip
un bon tuyau ❸ (end) bout m ▷ It's
on the tip of my tongue. Je l'ai sur
le bout de la langue.; **a rubbish
tip** une décharge; **This place is a
complete tip!** Quel fouillis!
▷ vb donner un pourboire à ▷ Don't
forget to tip the taxi driver. N'oubliez
pas de donner un pourboire au
chauffeur de taxi.

tipsy adj pompette

tiptoe n **on tiptoe** sur la pointe
des pieds

tired adj fatigué(e) ▷ I'm tired. Je suis
fatigué.; **to be tired of something**
en avoir assez de quelque chose

tiring adj fatigant(e)

tissue n kleenex® m ▷ Have you got
a tissue? Tu as un kleenex?

title n titre m

to prep

　　à + **le** changes to **au**. à + **les**
　　changes to **aux**.

❶ à, au (pl aux) ▷ to go to Paris aller
à Paris ▷ to go to school aller à l'école

▷ *a letter to his mother* une lettre à sa mère ▷ *the answer to the question* la réponse à la question ▷ *to go to the theatre* aller au théâtre ▷ *We said goodbye to the neighbours.* Nous avons dit au revoir aux voisins.; **ready to go** prêt à partir; **ready to eat** prêt à manger; **It's easy to do.** C'est facile à faire.; **something to drink** quelque chose à boire; **I've got things to do.** J'ai des choses à faire.; **from ... to ...** de ... à ... ▷ *from nine o'clock to half past three* de neuf heures à trois heures et demie **➋** *de* ▷ *the train to London* le train de Londres ▷ *the road to Edinburgh* la route d'Édimbourg ▷ *the key to the front door* la clé de la porte d'entrée; **It's difficult to say.** C'est difficile à dire.; **It's easy to criticize.** C'est facile de critiquer.

> When referring to someone's house, shop or office, use **chez**.

➊ *chez* ▷ *to go to the doctor's* aller chez le docteur ▷ *to go to the butcher's* aller chez le boucher ▷ *Let's go to Anne's house.* Si on allait chez Anne?

> When **to** refers to a country which is feminine, use **en**; when the country is masculine, use **au**.

➍ *en, au* ▷ *to go to France* aller en France ▷ *to go to Portugal* aller au Portugal **➎** (*up to*) *jusqu'à* ▷ *to count to ten* compter jusqu'à dix **➏** (*in order to*) *pour* ▷ *I did it to help you.* Je l'ai fait pour vous aider.

▷ *She's too young to go to school.* Elle est trop jeune pour aller à l'école.

toad *n* crapaud *m*

toast *n* **➊** pain *m* grillé ▷ *a piece of toast* une tranche de pain grillé **➋** (*speech*) toast *m* ▷ *to drink a toast to somebody* porter un toast à quelqu'un

toaster *n* grille-pain *m* (*pl* grille-pain)

toastie *n* sandwich *m* chaud; **a cheese and ham toastie** un croque-monsieur

tobacco *n* tabac *m*

tobacconist's *n* bureau *m* de tabac (*pl* bureaux de tabac)

today *adv* aujourd'hui ▷ *What did you do today?* Qu'est-ce que tu as fait aujourd'hui?

toddler *n* bambin *m*

toe *n* doigt *m* de pied

> Word for word, the French means "foot finger".

toffee *n* caramel *m*

together *adv* **➊** ensemble ▷ *Are they still together?* Ils sont toujours ensemble? **➋** (*at the same time*) en même temps ▷ *Don't all speak together!* Ne parlez pas tous en même temps!; **together with** (*with person*) avec

toilet *n* toilettes *fpl*

toilet paper *n* papier *m* hygiénique

toiletries *npl* articles *mpl* de toilette

toilet roll *n* rouleau *m* de papier hygiénique (*pl* rouleaux de papier hygiénique)

told vb see **tell**

toll n (on bridge, motorway) péage m

tomato n tomate f ▷ tomato sauce la sauce tomate ▷ tomato soup de la soupe à la tomate

tomorrow adv demain ▷ tomorrow morning demain matin ▷ tomorrow night demain soir; **the day after tomorrow** après-demain

ton n tonne f ▷ That old bike weighs a ton. Ce vieux vélo pèse une tonne.
  ● In France measurements are
  ● in metric tonnes rather than
  ● tons. A ton is slightly more than
  ● a tonne.

tongue n langue f; **to say something tongue in cheek** dire quelque chose en plaisantant

tonic n (tonic water) Schweppes® m; **a gin and tonic** un gin tonic

tonight adv ● (this evening) ce soir ▷ Are you going out tonight? Tu sors ce soir? ● (during the night) cette nuit ▷ I'll sleep well tonight. Je dormirai bien cette nuit.

tonsillitis n angine f

tonsils npl amygdales fpl

too adv, adj ● (as well) aussi ▷ My sister came too. Ma sœur est venue aussi. ● (excessively) trop ▷ The water's too hot. L'eau est trop chaude. ▷ We arrived too late. Nous sommes arrivés trop tard.; **too much (1)** (with noun) trop de ▷ too much noise trop de bruit **(2)** (with verb) trop ▷ At Christmas we always eat too much. À Noël nous mangeons toujours trop. **(3)** (too expensive) trop cher ▷ Fifty euros?

That's too much. Cinquante euros? C'est trop cher.; **too many** trop de ▷ too many hamburgers trop de hamburgers; **too bad!** tant pis!

took vb see **take**

tool n outil m; **a tool box** une boîte à outils

tooth n dent f

toothache n mal m de dents ▷ to have toothache avoir mal aux dents

toothbrush n brosse f à dents

toothpaste n dentifrice m

top n ● (of page, ladder, garment) haut m ▷ at the top of the page en haut de la page; **a bikini top** un haut de bikini ● (of mountain) sommet m ● (of table) dessus m; **on top of** (on) sur m ▷ on top of the fridge sur le frigo; **There's a surcharge on top of that.** Il a un supplément en plus.; **from top to bottom** de fond en comble ▷ I searched the house from top to bottom. J'ai fouillé la maison de fond en comble. ● (of box, jar) couvercle m ● (of bottle) bouchon m
▶ adj (first-class) grand(e) ▷ a top surgeon un grand chirurgien; **a top model** un top model; **He always gets top marks in French.** Il a toujours d'excellentes notes en français.; **the top floor** le dernier étage ▷ on the top floor au dernier étage

topic n sujet m ▷ The essay can be on any topic. Cette dissertation peut être sur n'importe quel sujet.

torch n lampe f de poche

tore, torn vb see **tear**

tortoise n tortue f

torture n torture f ⊳ It was pure torture. C'était une vraie torture.
▶ vb torturer ⊳ Stop torturing that poor animal! Arrête de torturer cette pauvre bête!

total adj total(e) (mpl totaux); **the total amount** le total
▶ n total m (pl totaux); **the grand total** le total

totally adv complètement ⊳ He's totally useless. Il est complètement nul.

touch vb **to get in touch with somebody** prendre contact avec quelqu'un; **to keep in touch with somebody** ne pas perdre contact avec quelqu'un; **Keep in touch!** Donne-moi de tes nouvelles!; **to lose touch** se perdre de vue; **to lose touch with somebody** perdre quelqu'un de vue
▶ vb toucher; **Don't touch that!** N'y touche pas!

touchpad n pavé m tactile

tough adj ❶ dur(e) ⊳ It was tough, but I managed OK. C'était dur, mais je m'en suis tiré. ⊳ It's a tough job. C'est dur.; ⊳ The meat's tough. La viande est coriace. ❷ (strong) solide ⊳ She's tough. She can take it. Elle est solide. Elle tiendra le coup. ❸ (rough, violent) dangereux (f dangereuse); **He thinks he's a tough guy.** Il se prend pour un gros dur.; **Tough luck!** C'est comme ça!

tour n ❶ (of town, museum) visite f ⊳ We went on a tour of the city. Nous avons visité la ville.; **a package tour** un voyage organisé ❷ (by singer, group) tournée f ⊳ on tour en tournée; **to go on tour** faire une tournée
▶ vb **Paul Weller's touring Europe.** (singer, artiste) Paul Weller est en tournée en Europe.

tourism n tourisme m

tourist n touriste mf; **tourist information office** office m du tourisme

tow vb remorquer

towards prep ❶ (in the direction of) vers ⊳ He came towards me. Il est venu vers moi. ❷ (of attitude) envers ⊳ my feelings towards him mes sentiments envers lui

towel n serviette f

tower n tour f; **a tower block** une tour

town n ville f ⊳ a town plan un plan de ville; **the town centre** le centre-ville; **the town hall** la mairie

tow truck n (US) dépanneuse f

toy n jouet m ⊳ a toy shop un magasin de jouets; **a toy car** une petite voiture

trace n trace f ⊳ There was no trace of the robbers. Il n'y avait pas de trace des voleurs.
▶ vb (draw) décalquer

tracing paper n papier m calque

track n ❶ (dirt road) chemin m ❷ (railway line) voie f ferrée ❸ (in sport) piste f ⊳ two laps of the track deux tours de piste ❹ (song) chanson f ⊳ This is my favourite

track. C'est ma chanson préférée.
❺ (trail) traces fpl ▷ They followed
the tracks for miles. Ils ont suivi les
traces pendant des kilomètres.

track down vb to track
somebody down retrouver
quelqu'un ▷ The police never tracked
down the killer. La police n'a jamais
retrouvé l'assassin.

tracksuit n jogging m

tractor n tracteur m

trade n (skill, job) métier m ▷ to learn
a trade apprendre un métier

trademark n marque f de fabrique

trade union n syndicat m

tradition n tradition f

traditional adj traditionnel (f
traditionnelle)

traffic n circulation f ▷ The
traffic was terrible. Il y avait une
circulation épouvantable.

traffic circle n (US) rond-point m
(pl ronds-points)

traffic jam n embouteillage m

traffic lights npl feux mpl

traffic warden n contractuel m,
contractuelle f

tragedy n tragédie f

tragic adj tragique

trailer n ❶ (vehicle) remorque f
❷ (film advert) bande-annonce f

train n ❶ train m ❷ (on
underground) rame f
▶ vb (sport) s'entraîner ▷ to train for
a race s'entraîner pour une course;
to train as a teacher suivre une
formation d'enseignant; to train
an animal to do something dresser
un animal à faire quelque chose

trained adj She's a trained nurse.
Elle est infirmière diplômée.

trainee n ❶ (in profession) stagiaire
mf ▷ She's a trainee. Elle est
stagiaire. ❷ (apprentice) apprenti
m, apprentie f ▷ a trainee plumber un
apprenti plombier

trainer n ❶ (sports coach)
entraîneur m ❷ (of animals)
dompteur m, dompteuse f

trainers npl baskets fpl ▷ a pair of
trainers une paire de baskets

training n ❶ formation f ▷ a
training course un stage de
formation ❷ (sport) entraînement
m

tram n tramway m

tramp n clochard m, clocharde f

trampoline n trampoline m

transfer n (sticker) décalcomanie f

transit n transit m ▷ in transit en
transit

transit lounge n salle f de transit

translate vb traduire ▷ to translate
something into English traduire
quelque chose en anglais

translation n traduction f

translator n traducteur m,
traductrice f ▷ Anita's a translator.
Anita est traductrice.

transparent adj transparent(e)

transplant n greffe f ▷ a heart
transplant une greffe du cœur

transport n transport m ▷ public
transport les transports en
commun

trap n piège m

trash n (US) ordures fpl; the trash
can la poubelle

travel n voyages mpl
▶ vb voyager ▷ I prefer to travel by train. Je préfère voyager en train.; **I'd like to travel round the world.** J'aimerais faire le tour du monde.; **We travelled over 800 kilometres.** Nous avons fait plus de huit cents kilomètres.; **News travels fast!** Les nouvelles circulent vite!

travel agency n agence f de voyages

travel agent n She's a travel agent. Elle travaille dans une agence de voyages.

traveller (US **traveler**) n ❶ (on bus, train, plane) voyageur m, voyageuse f ❷ (gypsy) nomade mf

traveller's cheque (US **traveler's check**) n chèque m de voyage

travelling (US **traveling**) n I love travelling. J'adore les voyages.

travel sickness n mal m des transports

tray n plateau m (pl plateaux)

tread vb marcher ▷ to tread on something marcher sur quelque chose

treasure n trésor m

treat n ❶ (present) petit cadeau m ❷ (food) gâterie f; **to give somebody a treat** faire plaisir à quelqu'un
▶ vb (well, badly) traiter; **to treat somebody to something** offrir quelque chose à quelqu'un ▷ He treated us to an ice cream. Il nous a offert une glace.

treatment n traitement m

treble vb tripler ▷ The cost of living there has trebled. Le coût de la vie y a triplé.

tree n arbre m

tremble vb trembler

tremendous adj énorme ▷ a tremendous success un succès énorme

trend n (fashion) mode f

trendy adj branché(e)

trial n (in court) procès m

triangle n triangle m

tribe n tribu f

trick n ❶ tour m ▷ to play a trick on somebody jouer un tour à quelqu'un ❷ (knack) truc m ▷ It's not easy: there's a trick to it. Ce n'est pas facile: il y a un truc.
▶ vb to trick somebody rouler quelqu'un

tricky adj délicat(e)

tricycle n tricycle m

trip n voyage m ▷ to go on a trip faire un voyage; **a day trip** une excursion d'une journée
▶ vb (stumble) trébucher

triple adj triple

triplets npl triplés mpl (fpl triplées)

triumph n triomphe f

trivial adj insignifiant(e)

trod, trodden vb see tread

trolley n chariot m

trombone n trombone m ▷ I play the trombone. Je joue du trombone.

troops npl troupes fpl ▷ British troops les troupes britanniques

trophy n trophée m ▷ to win a trophy gagner un trophée

tropical adj tropical(e)
(pl tropicaux) ▷ The weather was
tropical. Il faisait une chaleur
tropicale.

trouble n problème m ▷ The trouble
is, it's too expensive. Le problème,
c'est que c'est trop cher.; **to be
in trouble** avoir des ennuis;
What's the trouble? Qu'est-ce
qui ne va pas?; **stomach trouble**
troubles gastriques; **to take a
lot of trouble over something**
se donner beaucoup de mal pour
quelque chose; **Don't worry, it's
no trouble.** Mais non, ça ne me
dérange pas du tout.

troublemaker n élément m
perturbateur

trousers npl pantalon m

trout n truite f

truant n **to play truant** faire l'école
buissonnière

truck n camion m; **a truck driver**
un camionneur ▷ He's a truck driver.
Il est camionneur.

true adj vrai(e); **That's true.**
C'est vrai.; **to come true** se réaliser
▷ I hope my dream will come true.
J'espère que mon rêve se
réalisera.; **true love** le grand
amour

truly adv vraiment ▷ It was a truly
remarkable victory. C'était vraiment
une victoire remarquable.; **Yours
truly.** Je vous prie d'agréer mes
salutations distinguées.

trumpet n trompette f ▷ She
plays the trumpet. Elle joue de la
trompette.

trunk n ❶ (of tree) tronc m
❷ (of elephant) trompe f
❸ (luggage) malle f ❹ (US: of car)
coffre m

trunks npl swimming trunks le
maillot de bain

trust n confiance f ▷ to have trust
in somebody avoir confiance en
quelqu'un
▶ vb **to trust somebody** faire
confiance à quelqu'un ▷ Don't
you trust me? Tu ne me fais pas
confiance?

truth n vérité f

try n essai m ▷ his third try son
troisième essai; **to have a
try** essayer; **It's worth a try.** Ça
vaut la peine d'essayer.; **to give
something a try** essayer quelque
chose
▶ vb ❶ (attempt) essayer ▷ to try
to do something essayer de faire
quelque chose; **to try again**
refaire un essai ❷ (taste) goûter
▷ Would you like to try some? Voulez-
vous goûter?; **to try on** (clothes)
essayer; **to try something out**
essayer quelque chose

T-shirt n tee-shirt m

tube n tube m; **the Tube**
(underground) le métro

tuberculosis n tuberculose f

Tuesday n mardi m ▷ on Tuesday
mardi ▷ on Tuesdays le mardi
▷ every Tuesday tous les mardis
▷ last Tuesday mardi dernier ▷ next
Tuesday mardi prochain; **Shrove
Tuesday, Pancake Tuesday** le
mardi gras

tuition n cours mpl; **private tuition** les cours particuliers

tulip n tulipe f

tumble dryer n sèche-linge m (pl sèche-linge)

tummy n ventre m

tuna n thon m

tune n (melody) air m; **to play in tune** jouer juste; **to sing out of tune** chanter faux

Tunisia n Tunisie f; **in Tunisia** en Tunisie; **to Tunisia** en Tunisie

tunnel n tunnel m; **the Channel Tunnel** le tunnel sous la Manche

Turk n Turc m, Turque f

Turkey n Turquie f; **in Turkey** en Turquie; **to Turkey** en Turquie

turkey n ① (meat) dinde f ② (live bird) dindon m

Turkish adj turc (f turque)
▶ n (language) turc m

turn n ① (bend in road) tournant m; **"no left turn"** "défense de tourner à gauche" ② (go) tour m ▷ It's my turn! C'est mon tour!
▶ vb ① tourner ▷ Turn right at the lights. Tournez à droite aux feux. ② (become) devenir ▷ to turn red devenir rouge; **to turn into something** se transformer en quelque chose ▷ The frog turned into a prince. La grenouille s'est transformée en prince.

turn back vb faire demi-tour
▷ We turned back. Nous avons fait demi-tour.

turn down vb ① (offer) refuser ② (radio, TV, heating) baisser
▷ Shall I turn the heating down? Je baisse le chauffage?

turn off vb ① (light, radio) éteindre ② (tap) fermer ③ (engine) arrêter

turn on vb ① (light, radio) allumer ② (tap) ouvrir ③ (engine) mettre en marche

turn out vb It turned out to be a mistake. Il s'est avéré que c'était une erreur.; **It turned out that she was right.** Il s'est avéré qu'elle avait raison.

turn round vb ① (car) faire demi-tour ② (person) se retourner

turn up vb ① (arrive) arriver ② (heater) monter; **Could you turn up the radio?** Tu peux monter le son de la radio?

turning n It's the third turning on the left. C'est la troisième à gauche.; **We took the wrong turning.** Nous n'avons pas tourné au bon endroit.

turnip n navet m

turquoise adj (colour) turquoise inv

turtle n tortue f

tutor n (private teacher) professeur m particulier

TV n télé f

tweezers npl pince f à épiler

twelfth adj douzième ▷ the twelfth floor le douzième étage; **the twelfth of August** le douze août

twelve num douze ▷ She's twelve. Elle a douze ans.; **twelve o'clock (1)** (midday) midi **(2)** (midnight) minuit

twentieth adj vingtième ▷ the twentieth time la vingtième fois; **the twentieth of May** le vingt mai

twenty num vingt ▷ He's twenty.
Il a vingt ans.

twice adv deux fois; **twice as
much** deux fois plus ▷ He gets twice
as much pocket money as me. Il a
deux fois plus d'argent de poche
que moi.

twin n jumeau m, jumelle f (pl
jumeaux); **my twin brother** mon
frère jumeau; **her twin sister** sa
sœur jumelle; **identical twins** les
vrais jumeaux; **a twin room** une
chambre à deux lits

twinned adj jumelé(e) ▷ Stroud is
twinned with Châteaubriant. Stroud
est jumelée avec Châteaubriant.

twist vb ❶ (bend) tordre ❷ (distort)
déformer ▷ You're twisting my words.
Tu déformes ce que j'ai dit.

two num deux ▷ She's two. Elle a
deux ans.

type n type m ▷ What type of camera
have you got? Quel type d'appareil
photo as-tu?
  ▶ vb taper à la machine ▷ Can you
type? Tu sais taper à la machine?;
to type a letter taper une lettre

typewriter n machine f à écrire

typical adj typique ▷ That's just
typical! C'est typique!

tyre n pneu m; **the tyre pressure**
la pression des pneus

u

UFO n OVNI m (objet volant non
identifié)

ugly adj laid(e)

UK n (= United Kingdom)
Royaume-Uni m; **from the UK**
du Royaume-Uni; **in the UK** au
Royaume-Uni; **to the UK** au
Royaume-Uni

ulcer n ulcère m; **a mouth ulcer**
un aphte

Ulster n Irlande f du Nord; **in
Ulster** en Irlande du Nord

umbrella n ❶ parapluie m
❷ (for sun) parasol m

umpire n ❶ (in cricket) arbitre m
❷ (in tennis) juge m de chaise

UN n ONU f (Organisation des
Nations Unies)

unable adj **to be unable to do
something** ne pas pouvoir faire

quelque chose ▷ *I was unable to come*. Je n'ai pas pu venir.

unanimous *adj* unanime ▷ *a unanimous decision* une décision unanime

unavoidable *adj* inévitable

unbearable *adj* insupportable

unbelievable *adj* incroyable

unbreakable *adj* incassable

uncertain *adj* incertain(e) ▷ *The future is uncertain*. L'avenir est incertain.; **to be uncertain about something** ne pas être sûr de quelque chose

uncle *n* oncle *m* ▷ *my uncle* mon oncle

uncomfortable *adj* pas confortable ▷ *The seats are rather uncomfortable*. Les sièges ne sont pas très confortables.

unconscious *adj* sans connaissance

uncontrollable *adj* incontrôlable

under *prep* **①** sous ▷ *The cat's under the table*. Le chat est sous la table. ▷ *The tunnel goes under the Channel*. Le tunnel passe sous la Manche.; **under there** là-dessous ▷ *What's under there?* Qu'est-ce qu'il y a là-dessous? **②** (*less than*) moins de ▷ *under 20 people* moins de vingt personnes ▷ *children under 10* les enfants de moins de dix ans

underage *adj* **He's underage**. Il n'a pas l'âge réglementaire.

underground *adj, adv* **①** souterrain(e) ▷ *an underground car park* un parking souterrain **②** sous terre ▷ *Moles live*

underground. Les taupes vivent sous terre.

▶ *n* métro *m* ▷ *Is there an underground in Lille?* Est-ce qu'il y a un métro à Lille?

underline *vb* souligner

underneath *prep, adv* **①** sous ▷ *underneath the carpet* sous la moquette **②** dessous ▷ *I got out of the car and looked underneath*. Je suis descendu de la voiture et j'ai regardé dessous.

underpants *npl* slip *m*

underpass *n* **①** (*for people*) passage *m* souterrain **②** (*for cars*) passage *m* inférieur

undershirt *n* (*US*) maillot *m* de corps

understand *vb* comprendre ▷ *Do you understand?* Vous comprenez? ▷ *I don't understand this word*. Je ne comprends pas ce mot. ▷ *Is that understood?* C'est compris?

understanding *adj* compréhensif (*f* compréhensive) ▷ *She's very understanding*. Elle est très compréhensive.

understood *vb see* **understand**

undertaker *n* entrepreneur *m* des pompes funèbres

underwater *adj, adv* sous l'eau ▷ *This sequence was filmed underwater*. Cette séquence a été filmée sous l'eau.; **an underwater camera** un appareil photo de plongée; **underwater photography** la photographie subaquatique

underwear *n* sous-vêtements *mpl*

undo vb ❶ (buttons, knot) défaire
❷ (parcel) déballer

undress vb (get undressed) se
déshabiller ▷ The doctor told me to
undress. Le médecin m'a dit de me
déshabiller.

unemployed adj au chômage
▷ He's unemployed. Il est au
chômage.; **the unemployed** les
chômeurs mpl

unemployment n chômage m

unexpected adj inattendu(e)
▷ an unexpected visitor un visiteur
inattendu

unexpectedly adv à l'improviste
▷ They arrived unexpectedly. Ils sont
arrivés à l'improviste.

unfair adj injuste ▷ It's unfair to
girls. C'est injuste pour les filles.

unfamiliar adj **I heard an
unfamiliar voice.** J'ai entendu une
voix que je ne connaissais pas.

unfashionable adj démodé(e)

unfit adj **I'm rather unfit at the
moment.** Je ne suis pas en très
bonne condition physique en ce
moment.

unfold vb déplier ▷ She unfolded the
map. Elle a déplié la carte.

unforgettable adj inoubliable

unfortunately adv
malheureusement ▷ Unfortunately,
I arrived late. Malheureusement, je
suis arrivé en retard.

unfriendly adj pas aimable ▷ The
waiters are a bit unfriendly. Les
serveurs ne sont pas très
aimables.

ungrateful adj ingrat(e)

unhappy adj malheureux
(f malheureuse) ▷ He was very
unhappy as a child. Il était très
malheureux quand il était petit.;
to look unhappy avoir l'air triste

unhealthy adj ❶ (person) maladif
(f maladive) ❷ (place, habit)
malsain(e) ❸ (food) pas sain(e)

uni n (university) fac f ▷ to go to uni
aller à la fac

uniform n uniforme m ▷ the school
uniform l'uniforme scolaire

uninhabited adj inhabité(e)

union n (trade union) syndicat m

Union Jack n drapeau m du
Royaume-Uni

unique adj unique

unit n ❶ unité f ▷ a unit of
measurement une unité de mesure
❷ (piece of furniture) élément m ▷ a
kitchen unit un élément de cuisine

United Kingdom n Royaume-
Uni m

United Nations n ONU f
(Organisation des Nations Unies)

United States n États-Unis mpl;
in the United States aux États-
Unis; **to the United States** aux
États-Unis

universe n univers m

university n université f ▷ She's at
university. Elle va à l'université.
▷ Do you want to go to university?
Tu veux aller à l'université?

unleaded petrol n essence f
sans plomb

unless conj unless he leaves
à moins qu'il ne parte ▷ I won't
come unless you phone me. Je ne

viendrai pas à moins que tu ne me téléphones.

> à moins que has to be followed by a verb in the subjunctive.

unlikely adj peu probable ▷ It's possible, but unlikely. C'est possible, mais peu probable.

unload vb décharger ▷ We unloaded the car. Nous avons déchargé la voiture. ▷ The lorries go there to unload. Les camions y vont pour être déchargés.

unlock vb ouvrir ▷ He unlocked the door of the car. Il a ouvert la portière de la voiture.

unlucky adj to be unlucky **(1)** (number, object) porter malheur ▷ They say thirteen is an unlucky number. On dit que le nombre treize porte malheur. **(2)** (person) ne pas avoir de chance ▷ Did you win? — No, I was unlucky. Vous avez gagné? — Non, je n'ai pas eu de chance.

unmarried adj (person) célibataire ▷ an unmarried mother une mère célibataire; an unmarried couple un couple non marié

unnatural adj pas naturel (f pas naturelle)

unnecessary adj inutile

unpack vb ❶ défaire ▷ I unpacked my suitcase. J'ai défait ma valise. ❷ déballer ses affaires ▷ I went to my room to unpack. Je suis allé dans ma chambre pour déballer mes affaires. ▷ I haven't unpacked my clothes yet. Je n'ai pas encore déballé mes affaires.

unpleasant adj désagréable

unplug vb débrancher

unpopular adj impopulaire

unrealistic adj peu réaliste

unreasonable adj pas raisonnable ▷ Her attitude was completely unreasonable. Son attitude n'était pas du tout raisonnable.

unreliable adj (car, machine) pas fiable ▷ It's a nice car, but a bit unreliable. C'est une belle voiture, mais elle n'est pas très fiable.; He's completely unreliable. On ne peut pas du tout compter sur lui.

unroll vb dérouler

unscrew vb dévisser ▷ She unscrewed the top of the bottle. Elle a dévissé le bouchon de la bouteille.

unsuccessful adj (attempt) vain(e); to be unsuccessful in doing something ne pas réussir à faire quelque chose ▷ an unsuccessful artist un artiste qui n'a pas réussi

unsuitable adj (clothes, equipment) inapproprié(e)

untidy adj ❶ en désordre ▷ My bedroom's always untidy. Ma chambre est toujours en désordre. ❷ (appearance, person) débraillé(e) ▷ He's always untidy. Il est toujours débraillé. ❸ (in character) désordonné(e) ▷ He's a very untidy person. Il est très désordonné.

untie vb ❶ (knot, parcel) défaire ❷ (animal) détacher

until prep, conj ❶ jusqu'à ▷ I waited until ten o'clock. J'ai attendu jusqu'à dix heures.; **until now** jusqu'à présent ▷ *It's never been a problem until now.* Ça n'a jamais été un problème jusqu'à présent.; **until then** jusque-là ▷ *Until then I'd never been to France.* Jusque-là je n'étais jamais allé en France.

> Use **avant** if the sentence you want to translate contains a negative, such as "not" or "never".

❷ avant ▷ *It won't be ready until next week.* Ça ne sera pas prêt avant la semaine prochaine.

unusual *adj* ❶ insolite ▷ *an unusual shape* une forme insolite ❷ rare ▷ *It's unusual to get snow at this time of year.* Il est rare qu'il neige à cette époque de l'année.

unwilling *adj* **to be unwilling to do something** ne pas être disposé à faire quelque chose ▷ *He was unwilling to help me.* Il n'était pas disposé à m'aider.

unwrap *vb* déballer ▷ *After the meal we unwrapped the presents.* Après le repas nous avons déballé les cadeaux.

up *prep, adv*

> For other expressions with **up**, see the verbs **go**, **come**, **put**, **turn** etc.

en haut ▷ *up on the hill* en haut de la colline; **up here** ici; **up there** là-haut; **up north** dans le nord; **to be up** (out of bed) être levé ▷ *We were up at 6.* Nous étions levés à six heures. ▷ *He's not up yet.* Il n'est pas encore levé.; **What's up?** Qu'est-ce qu'il

y a? ▷ *What's up with her?* Qu'est-ce qu'elle a?; **to get up** (in the morning) se lever ▷ *What time do you get up?* À quelle heure est-ce que tu te lèves?; **to go up** monter ▷ *The bus went up the hill.* Le bus a monté la colline.; **to go up to somebody** s'approcher de quelqu'un ▷ *She came up to me.* Elle s'est approchée de moi.; **up to** (as far as) jusqu'à ▷ *to count up to fifty* compter jusqu'à cinquante ▷ *up to now* jusqu'à présent; **It's up to you.** C'est à vous de décider.

update *vb* mettre à jour

uphill *adv* **to go uphill** monter

upper *adj* supérieur(e) ▷ *on the upper floor* à l'étage supérieur

upper sixth *n* **the upper sixth** la terminale ▷ *She's in the upper sixth.* Elle est en terminale.

upright *adj* **to stand upright** se tenir droit

upset *n* **a stomach upset** une indigestion

> *adj* contrarié(e) ▷ *She's still a bit upset.* Elle est encore un peu contrariée. ▷ **I had an upset stomach.** J'avais l'estomac dérangé.

> *vb* **to upset somebody** contrarier quelqu'un

upside down *adv* à l'envers ▷ *That painting is upside down.* Ce tableau est à l'envers.

upstairs *adv* en haut ▷ *Where's your coat? — It's upstairs.* Où est ton manteau? — Il est en haut.; **to go upstairs** monter

up-to-date adj ❶ (car, stereo) moderne ❷ (information) à jour ▷ an up-to-date timetable un horaire à jour; **to bring something up to date** moderniser quelque chose

upwards adv vers le haut ▷ to look upwards regarder vers le haut

urgent adj urgent(e) ▷ Is it urgent? C'est urgent?

US n USA mpl

us pron nous ▷ They helped us. Ils nous ont aidés.

USA n USA mpl

use n **It's no use.** Ça ne sert à rien. ▷ It's no use shouting, she's deaf. Ça ne sert à rien de crier, elle est sourde.; **It's no use, I can't do it.** Il n'y a rien à faire, je n'y arrive pas.; **to make use of something** utiliser quelque chose
▸ vb utiliser ▷ Can we use a dictionary in the exam? Est-ce qu'on peut utiliser un dictionnaire pendant l'examen?; **Can I use your phone?** Je peux téléphoner?; **to use the toilet** aller aux W.C.; **to use up** (1) finir ▷ We've used up all the paint. Nous avons fini la peinture. (2) (money) dépenser; **I used to live in London.** J'habitais à Londres autrefois.; **I used not to like maths, but now ...** Avant, je n'aimais pas les maths, mais maintenant ...; **to be used to something** avoir l'habitude de quelque chose ▷ Don't worry, I'm used to it. Ne t'inquiète pas, j'ai l'habitude.; **a used car** une voiture d'occasion

useful adj utile

useless adj nul (f nulle) ▷ This map is just useless. Cette carte est vraiment nulle. ▷ You're useless! Tu es null; **It's useless!** Ça ne sert à rien!

user n utilisateur m, utilisatrice f

user-friendly adj facile à utiliser

username n identifiant m

usual adj habituel (f habituelle); **as usual** comme d'habitude

usually adv ❶ (generally) en général ▷ I usually get to school at about half past eight. En général, j'arrive à l'école vers huit heures et demie. ❷ (when making a contrast) d'habitude ▷ Usually I don't wear make-up, but today is a special occasion. D'habitude je ne me maquille pas, mais aujourd'hui c'est différent.

V

vacancy n ❶ (job) poste m vacant
❷ (room in hotel) chambre f
disponible; **"no vacancies"**
(on sign) "complet"

vacant adj libre

vacation n (US) vacances fpl ▷ to be
on vacation être en vacances ▷ to take
a vacation prendre des vacances

vaccinate vb vacciner

vacuum vb passer l'aspirateur ▷ to
vacuum the hall passer l'aspirateur
dans le couloir

vacuum cleaner n aspirateur m

vagina n vagin m

vague adj vague

vain adj vaniteux (f vaniteuse)
▷ He's so vain! Qu'est-ce qu'il est
vaniteux!; **in vain** en vain

Valentine card n carte f de la
Saint-Valentin

Valentine's Day n Saint-
Valentin f

valid adj valable ▷ This ticket is
valid for three months. Ce billet est
valable trois mois.

valley n vallée f

valuable adj ❶ de valeur ▷ a
valuable picture un tableau de
valeur ❷ précieux (f précieuse)
▷ valuable help une aide précieuse

value n valeur f

van n camionnette f

vandal n vandale mf

vandalism n vandalisme m

vandalize vb saccager

vanilla n vanille f; **vanilla ice
cream** glace f à la vanille

vanish vb disparaître

variety n variété f

various adj plusieurs ▷ We visited
various villages in the area. Nous
avons visité plusieurs villages dans
la région.

vary vb varier

vase n vase m

VAT n (= value added tax) TVA f (taxe
sur la valeur ajoutée)

VCR n (= video cassette recorder)
magnétoscope m

VDU n (= visual display unit)
console f

veal n veau m

vegan n végétalien m,
végétalienne f ▷ I'm a vegan. Je suis
végétalien.

vegetable n légume m ▷ vegetable
soup la soupe aux légumes

vegetarian adj végétarien
(f végétarienne) ▷ I'm vegetarian.

Je suis végétarien. ▷ *vegetarian lasagne* les lasagnes végétariennes
▶ n végétarien m, végétarienne f ▷ *I'm a vegetarian.* Je suis végétarien.

vehicle n véhicule m

vein n veine f

velvet n velours m

vending machine n distributeur m automatique

verb n verbe m

verdict n verdict m

vertical adj vertical(e) (mpl verticaux)

vertigo n vertige m ▷ *I get vertigo.* J'ai le vertige.

very adv très ▷ *very tall* très grand ▷ *not very interesting* pas très intéressant; **very much** beaucoup

vest n ❶ (underclothing) maillot m de corps ❷ (US: waistcoat) gilet m

vet n vétérinaire mf ▷ *She's a vet.* Elle est vétérinaire.

via prep en passant par ▷ *We went to Paris via Boulogne.* Nous sommes allés à Paris en passant par Boulogne.

vicar n pasteur m ▷ *He's a vicar.* Il est pasteur.

vicious adj ❶ brutal(e) (mpl brutaux) ▷ *a vicious attack* une agression brutale ❷ (dog, person) méchant(e); **a vicious circle** un cercle vicieux

victim n victime f ▷ *He was the victim of a mugging.* Il a été victime d'une agression.

victory n victoire f

video vb ❶ (from TV) enregistrer

❷ (with video camera) filmer
▶ n ❶ (film) vidéo f ▷ *to watch a video* regarder une vidéo ▷ *It's out on video.* C'est sorti en vidéo. ❷ (video cassette) cassette f vidéo ▷ *She lent me a video.* Elle m'a prêté une cassette vidéo. ❸ (video recorder) magnétoscope m ▷ *Have you got a video?* Tu as un magnétoscope?; **a video camera** une caméra vidéo; **a video cassette** une cassette vidéo; **a video game** un jeu vidéo ▷ *He likes playing video games.* Il aime les jeux vidéo.; **a video recorder** un magnétoscope; **a video shop** un vidéoclub

Vietnam n Viêt-Nam m; **in Vietnam** au Viêt-Nam

Vietnamese adj vietnamien (f vietnamienne)

view n ❶ vue f ▷ *There's an amazing view.* Il y a une vue extraordinaire. ❷ (opinion) avis m ▷ *in my view* à mon avis

viewer n téléspectateur m, téléspectatrice f

viewpoint n point m de vue

vile adj (smell, food) dégoûtant(e)

villa n villa f

village n village m

vine n vigne f

vinegar n vinaigre m

vineyard n vignoble m

viola n alto m ▷ *I play the viola.* Je joue de l'alto.

violence n violence f

violent adj violent(e)

violin n violon m ▷ *I play the violin.* Je joue du violon.

violinist n violoniste mf
virgin n vierge f ▷ to be a virgin
être vierge
Virgo n Vierge f ▷ I'm Virgo. Je suis
Vierge.
virtual reality n réalité f virtuelle
virus n (also computing) virus m
visa n visa m
visible adj visible
visit n ❶ (to museum) visite f
❷ (to country) séjour m ▷ Did you
enjoy your visit to France? Ton séjour
en France s'est bien passé?; **my
last visit to my grandmother** la
dernière fois que je suis allé voir ma
grand-mère
▶ vb ❶ (person) rendre visite à
▷ to visit somebody rendre visite
à quelqu'un ❷ (place) visiter
▷ We'd like to visit the castle. Nous
voudrions visiter le château.
visitor n ❶ (tourist) visiteur m,
visiteuse f ❷ (guest) invité m,
invitée f; **to have a visitor** avoir
de la visite
visual adj visuel (f visuelle)
vital adj vital(e) (mpl vitaux)
vitamin n vitamine f
vivid adj (colour) vif (f vive); **to have
a vivid imagination** avoir une
imagination débordante
vocabulary n vocabulaire m
vocational adj professionnel
(f professionnelle); **a vocational
course** un stage de formation
professionnelle
vodka n vodka f
voice n voix f (pl voix)
voicemail n messagerie f vocale

volcano n volcan m
volleyball n volley-ball m ▷ to play
volleyball jouer au volley-ball
volume n volume m
voluntary adj (contribution,
statement) volontaire; **to do
voluntary work** travailler
bénévolement
volunteer n volontaire mf
▶ vb **to volunteer to do
something** se proposer pour faire
quelque chose
vomit vb vomir
vote vb voter
voucher n bon m ▷ a gift voucher un
bon d'achat
vowel n voyelle f
vulgar adj vulgaire

W

wage n salaire m ▷ He collected his wages. Il a retiré son salaire.

waist n taille f

waistcoat n gilet m

wait vb attendre; **to wait for something** attendre quelque chose; **to wait for somebody** attendre quelqu'un ▷ I'll wait for you. Je t'attendrai.; **Wait for me!** Attends-moi!; **Wait a minute!** Attends!; **to keep somebody waiting** faire attendre quelqu'un ▷ They kept us waiting for hours. Ils nous ont fait attendre pendant des heures.; **I can't wait for the holidays.** J'ai hâte d'être en vacances.; **I can't wait to see him again.** J'ai hâte de le revoir.

waiter n serveur m; **Waiter!** Garçon!

waiting list n liste f d'attente

waiting room n salle f d'attente

waitress n serveuse f

wake up vb se réveiller ▷ I woke up at six o'clock. Je me suis réveillé à six heures.; **to wake somebody up** réveiller quelqu'un ▷ Please would you wake me up at seven o'clock? Pourriez-vous me réveiller à sept heures?

Wales n pays m de Galles; **in Wales** au pays de Galles; **to Wales** au pays de Galles; **I'm from Wales.** Je suis gallois.; **the Prince of Wales** le prince de Galles

walk vb ❶ marcher ▷ He walks fast. Il marche vite. ❷ (go on foot) aller à pied ▷ We walked 10 kilometres. Nous avons fait dix kilomètres à pied.; **to walk the dog** promener le chien ▶ n promenade f ▷ to go for a walk faire une promenade; **It's 10 minutes' walk from here.** C'est à dix minutes d'ici à pied.

walking n randonnée f ▷ I did some walking in the Alps last summer. J'ai fait de la randonnée dans les Alpes l'été dernier.

walking stick n canne f

Walkman® n baladeur m

wall n mur m

wallet n portefeuille m

wallpaper n papier m peint

walnut n noix f (pl noix)

wander vb **to wander around** flâner ▷ I just wandered around for a while. J'ai flâné un peu.

want vb vouloir ▷ Do you want some cake? Tu veux du gâteau?; **to want**

to do something vouloir faire quelque chose ▷ *I want to go to the cinema.* Je veux aller au cinéma.

war n guerre f

ward n (*room in hospital*) salle f

wardrobe n (*piece of furniture*) armoire f

warehouse n entrepôt m

warm adj ❶ chaud(e) ▷ *warm water* l'eau chaude; **It's warm in here.** Il fait chaud ici.; **to be warm** (*person*) avoir chaud ▷ *I'm too warm.* J'ai trop chaud. ❷ chaleureux (f chaleureuse) ▷ *a warm welcome* un accueil chaleureux; **to warm up (1)** (*for sport*) s'échauffer **(2)** (*food*) réchauffer ▷ *I'll warm up some lasagne for you.* Je vais te réchauffer des lasagnes.

warn vb prévenir ▷ *Well, I warned you!* Je t'avais prévenu!; **to warn somebody to do something** conseiller à quelqu'un de faire quelque chose

warning n avertissement m

wart n verrue f

was vb see **be**

wash n **to have a wash** se laver ▷ *I had a wash.* Je me suis lavé.; **to give something a wash** laver quelque chose ▷ *He gave the car a wash.* Il a lavé la voiture.
▷ vb ❶ laver ▷ *to wash something* laver quelque chose ❷ (*have a wash*) se laver ▷ *Every morning I get up, wash and get dressed.* Tous les matins je me lève, je me lave et je m'habille.; **to wash one's hands** se laver les mains; **to wash one's**

hair se laver les cheveux; **to wash up** faire la vaisselle

washbasin n lavabo m

washcloth n (*US*) gant m de toilette

washing n linge m ▷ *dirty washing* du linge sale; **Have you got any washing?** Tu as du linge à laver?; **to do the washing** faire la lessive

washing machine n machine f à laver

washing powder n lessive f

washing-up n **to do the washing-up** faire la vaisselle

washing-up liquid n produit m à vaisselle

wasn't = **was not**

wasp n guêpe f

waste n ❶ gaspillage m ▷ *It's such a waste!* C'est vraiment du gaspillage!; **It's a waste of time.** C'est une perte de temps. ❷ (*rubbish*) déchets mpl ▷ *nuclear waste* les déchets nucléaires
▷ vb gaspiller ▷ *I don't like wasting money.* Je n'aime pas gaspiller de l'argent.; **to waste time** perdre du temps ▷ *There's no time to waste.* Il n'y a pas de temps à perdre.

wastepaper basket n corbeille f à papier

watch n montre f
▷ vb ❶ regarder ▷ *to watch television* regarder la télévision ❷ (*keep a watch on*) surveiller ▷ *The police were watching the house.* La police surveillait la maison.; **to watch out** faire attention; **Watch out!** Attention!

water n eau f
▶ vb arroser ▷ He was watering his tulips. Il arrosait ses tulipes.

waterfall n cascade f

watering can n arrosoir m

watermelon n pastèque f

waterproof adj imperméable ▷ Is this jacket waterproof? Ce blouson est-il imperméable?; **a waterproof watch** une montre étanche

water-skiing n ski m nautique ▷ to go water-skiing faire du ski nautique

wave n ❶ (in water) vague f
❷ (of hand) signe m ▷ We gave him a wave. Nous lui avons fait signe.
▶ vb faire un signe de la main ▷ to wave at somebody faire un signe de la main à quelqu'un; **to wave goodbye** faire au revoir de la main ▷ I waved her goodbye. Je lui ai fait au revoir de la main.

wax n cire f

way n ❶ (manner) façon f ▷ She looked at me in a strange way. Elle m'a regardé d'une façon étrange.; **This book tells you the right way to do it.** Ce livre explique comment il faut faire.; **You're doing it the wrong way.** Ce n'est pas comme ça qu'il faut faire.; **in a way ...** dans un sens ...; **a way of life** un mode de vie ❷ (route) chemin m ▷ I don't know the way. Je ne connais pas le chemin.; **on the way** en chemin ▷ We stopped on the way. Nous nous sommes arrêtés en chemin.; **It's a long way.** C'est loin. ▷ Paris is a long way from London. Paris est loin de Londres.; **Which way is it?** C'est

par où?; **The supermarket is this way.** Le supermarché est par ici.; **Do you know the way to the station?** Vous savez comment aller à la gare?; **He's on his way.** Il arrive.; **"way in"** "entrée"; **"way out"** "sortie"; **by the way ...** au fil ...

we pron ❶ nous ▷ We're staying here for a week. Nous restons une semaine ici. ❷ on ▷ Shall we start? On commence?

> There are two ways of saying "we". In spoken French **on** is used more often than **nous**.

weak adj faible

wealthy adj riche

weapon n arme f

wear vb (clothes) porter ▷ She was wearing a hat. Elle portait un chapeau.; **She was wearing black.** Elle était en noir.

weather n temps m ▷ What was the weather like? Quel temps a-t-il fait? ▷ The weather was lovely. Il a fait un temps magnifique.

weather forecast n météo f

web n web m

web address n adresse f Web

web browser n navigateur m

webcam n webcam f

website n site m web

we'd = we had; we would

wedding n mariage m; **wedding anniversary** anniversaire m de mariage; **wedding dress** robe f de mariée

Wednesday n mercredi m ▷ on Wednesday mercredi ▷ on

a b c d e f g h i j k l m n o p q r s t u v w x y z

Wednesdays le mercredi ▷ *every Wednesday* tous les mercredis ▷ *last Wednesday* mercredi dernier ▷ *next Wednesday* mercredi prochain

weed n mauvaise herbe f ▷ *The garden's full of weeds.* Le jardin est plein de mauvaises herbes.

week n semaine f ▷ *last week* la semaine dernière ▷ *every week* toutes les semaines ▷ *next week* la semaine prochaine ▷ *in a week's time* dans une semaine; **a week on Friday** vendredi en huit

weekday n *on weekdays* en semaine

weekend n week-end m ▷ *at weekends* le week-end ▷ *last weekend* le week-end dernier ▷ *next weekend* le week-end prochain

weigh vb peser ▷ *How much do you weigh?* Combien est-ce que tu pèses?; **to weigh oneself** se peser

weight n poids m; **to lose weight** maigrir; **to put on weight** grossir

weightlifting n haltérophilie f

weird adj bizarre

welcome n accueil m ▷ *They gave her a warm welcome.* Ils lui ont fait un accueil chaleureux.; **Welcome!** Bienvenue! ▷ *Welcome to France!* Bienvenue en France!

▶ vb **to welcome somebody** accueillir quelqu'un; **Thank you! — You're welcome!** Merci — De rien!

well adj, adv ❶ bien ▷ *You did that really well.* Tu as très bien fait ça.; **to do well** réussir bien ▷ *She's doing really well at school.* Elle réussit vraiment bien à l'école.; **to be**

well (*in good health*) aller bien ▷ *I'm not very well at the moment.* Je ne vais pas très bien en ce moment.; **get well soon!** remets-toi vite!; **well done!** bravo! ❸ enfin ▷ *It's enormous! Well, quite big anyway.* C'est énorme! Enfin, c'est assez grand.; **as well** aussi ▷ *We worked hard, but we had some fun as well.* Nous avons travaillé dur, mais nous nous sommes bien amusés aussi. ▷ *We went to Chartres as well as Paris.* Nous sommes allés à Paris et à Chartres aussi.

▶ n puits m (pl puits)

we'll = we will

well-behaved adj sage

wellingtons npl bottes fpl en caoutchouc

well-known adj célèbre ▷ *a well-known film star* une vedette de cinéma célèbre

well-off adj aisé(e)

Welsh adj gallois(e) ▷ *She's Welsh.* Elle est galloise.; **Welsh people** les Gallois

▶ n (*language*) gallois m

Welshman n Gallois m

Welshwoman n Galloise f

went vb see **go**

were vb see **be**

we're = we are

weren't = were not

west adj, adv ❶ ouest inv ▷ *the west coast* la côte ouest; **west of** à l'ouest de ▷ *Stroud is west of Oxford.* Stroud est à l'ouest d'Oxford.; **the West Country** le sud-ouest de l'Angleterre ❷ vers l'ouest ▷ *We* *were travelling west.* Nous allions vers l'ouest.

▶ *n* ouest *m* ▷ *in the west* dans l'ouest

westbound *adj* **The truck was westbound on the M5.** Le camion roulait sur la M5 en direction de l'ouest.; **Westbound traffic is moving very slowly.** La circulation en direction de l'ouest est très ralentie.

western *n* (film) western *m*

▶ *adj* **the western part of the island** la partie ouest de l'île; **Western Europe** l'Europe de l'Ouest

West Indian *adj* antillais(e) ▷ *She's West Indian.* Elle est antillaise.

▶ *n* (person) Antillais *m*, Antillaise *f*

West Indies *npl* Antilles *fpl*; **in the West Indies** aux Antilles

wet *adj* mouillé(e) ▷ *wet clothes* les vêtements mouillés; **to get wet** se faire mouiller; **dripping wet** trempé(e); **wet weather** le temps pluvieux; **It was wet all week.** Il a plu toute la semaine.

wetsuit *n* combinaison *f* de plongée (*pl* combinaisons de plongée)

we've = **we have**

whale *n* baleine *f*

what *adj, pron* ❶ (which) quel (*f* quelle) ▷ *What colour is it?* C'est de quelle couleur? ▷ *What's the capital of Finland?* Quelle est la capitale de la Finlande? ▷ *What a mess!* Quel fouillis! ❷ qu'est-ce que ▷ *What are you doing?* Qu'est-ce que vous

faites? ▷ *What did you say?* Qu'est-ce que vous avez dit? ▷ *What is it?* Qu'est-ce que c'est? ▷ *What's the matter?* Qu'est-ce qu'il y a? ❸ qu'est-ce qui ▷ *What happened?* Qu'est-ce qui s'est passé?

> In relative phrases use **ce qui** or **ce que** depending on whether **what** refers to the subject or the object of the sentence.

❶ (subject) ce qui ▷ *I saw what happened.* J'ai vu ce qui est arrivé. ❷ (object) ce que ▷ *Tell me what you did.* Dites-moi ce que vous avez fait.; **What?** (what did you say) Comment?; **What!** (shocked) Quoi!

wheat *n* blé *m*

wheel *n* roue *f*; **the steering wheel** le volant

wheelbarrow *n* brouette *f*

wheelchair *n* fauteuil *m* roulant

when *adv, conj* quand ▷ *When did he go?* Quand est-ce qu'il est parti? ▷ *She was reading when I came in.* Elle lisait quand je suis entré.

where *adv, conj* où ▷ *Where's Emma today?* Où est Emma aujourd'hui? ▷ *Where do you live?* Où habites-tu?

whether *conj* si ▷ *I don't know whether to go or not.* Je ne sais pas si y aller ou non.

which *adj, pron* ❶ quel (*f* quelle) ▷ *Which flavour do you want?* Quel parfum est-ce que tu veux?

> When asking **which one** use **lequel** or **laquelle**, depending on whether the noun is masculine or feminine.

I know his brother. — Which one?
Je connais son frère. — Lequel?;
I know his sister. — Which one?
Je connais sa sœur. — Laquelle?;
Which would you like? Lequel
est-ce que vous voulez?; **Which
of these are yours?** Lesquels sont
à vous?

> In relative phrases use **qui** or
> **que** depending on whether
> **which** refers to the subject or
> the object of the sentence.

❷ (subject) qui ▷ the CD which
is playing now le CD qui passe
maintenant ❷ (object) que ▷ the
CD which I bought today le CD que
j'ai acheté hier

while conj ❶ pendant que ▷ You
hold the torch while I look inside.
Tiens la lampe électrique pendant
que je regarde à l'intérieur. ❷ alors
que ▷ Isobel is very dynamic, while
Kay is more laid-back. Isobel est
très dynamique, alors que Kay est
plus relax.
▶ n moment m ▷ after a while au
bout d'un moment; **a while ago** il
y a un moment ▷ He was here a while
ago. Il était là il y a un moment.; **for
a while** pendant quelque temps
▷ I lived in London for a while. J'ai
vécu à Londres pendant quelque
temps.; **quite a while** longtemps
▷ quite a while ago il y a longtemps

whip n fouet m
▶ vb ❶ (person, animal) fouetter
❷ (eggs) battre

whipped cream n crème f
fouettée

whiskers npl moustaches fpl
whisky n whisky m (pl whiskies)
whisper vb chuchoter
whistle n sifflet m; **The referee
blew his whistle.** L'arbitre a sifflé.
▶ vb siffler
white adj blanc (f blanche) ▷ He's
got white hair. Il a les cheveux
blancs.; **white wine** vin m blanc;
white bread pain m blanc; **white
coffee** café m au lait; **a white man**
un Blanc; **a white woman** une
Blanche; **white people** les Blancs
Whitsun n Pentecôte f
who pron ❶ qui ▷ Who said that?
Qui a dit ça?

> In relative phrases use **qui** or
> **que** depending on whether
> **who** refers to the subject or
> the object of the verb.

❷ (subject) qui ▷ the man who saw us
l'homme qui nous a vus ❸ (object)
que ▷ the man who we saw l'homme
que nous avons vu
whole adj tout(e) ▷ the whole class
toute la classe ▷ the whole afternoon
tout l'après-midi; **a whole box
of chocolates** toute une boîte de
chocolats; **the whole world** le
monde entier
▶ n The whole of Wales was
affected. Le pays de Galles tout
entier a été touché.; **on the whole**
dans l'ensemble
wholemeal adj complet
(f complète); **wholemeal bread**
pain m complet
wholewheat adj (US)
= **wholemeal**

whom pron qui ▷ Whom did you see? Qui avez-vous vu? ▷ the man to whom I spoke l'homme à qui j'ai parlé

whose pron, adj ① à qui ▷ Whose is this? À qui est-ce? ▷ I know whose it is. Je sais à qui c'est. ② (after noun) dont ▷ the girl whose picture was in the paper la jeune fille dont la photo était dans le journal

why adv pourquoi ▷ Why did you do that? Pourquoi avez-vous fait ça? ▷ That's why he did it. Voilà pourquoi il a fait ça. ▷ Tell me why. Dis-moi pourquoi.; I've never been to France. — Why not? Je ne suis jamais allé en France. — Pourquoi?; All right, why not? D'accord, pourquoi pas?

wicked adj ① (evil) méchant(e) ② (really great) génial(e) (mpl géniaux)

wide adj, adv large ▷ a wide road une route large; wide open grand(e) ouvert(e) ▷ The door was wide open. La porte était grande ouverte.; wide awake complètement réveillé(e)

widow n veuve f ▷ She's a widow. Elle est veuve.

widower n veuf m ▷ He's a widower. Il est veuf.

width n largeur f

wife n femme f ▷ She's his wife. C'est sa femme.

Wi-fi n wifi m

wig n perruque f

wild adj ① (not tame) sauvage ▷ a wild animal un animal sauvage

② (crazy) fou (f folle) ▷ She's a bit wild. Elle est un peu folle.

wildlife n nature f ▷ I'm interested in wildlife. Je m'intéresse à la nature.

will n testament m ▷ He left me some money in his will. Il m'a laissé de l'argent dans son testament.
▶ vb I'll show you your room. Je vais te montrer ta chambre.; I'll give you a hand. Je vais t'aider.

> Use the French future tense when referring to the more distant future.

I will finish it tomorrow. Je le finirai demain.; It won't take long. Ça ne prendra pas longtemps.; Will you wash up? — No, I won't. Est-ce que tu peux faire la vaisselle? — Non.; Will you help me? Est-ce que tu peux m'aider?; Will you be quiet! Voulez-vous bien vous taire!; That will be the postman. Ça doit être le facteur.

willing adj to be willing to do something être prêt à faire quelque chose

win vb gagner ▷ Did you win? Est-ce que tu as gagné?; to win a prize remporter un prix
▶ n victoire f

wind vb ① (rope, wool, wire) enrouler ② (river, path) serpenter ▷ The road winds through the valley. La route serpente à travers la vallée.
▶ n vent m ▷ There was a strong wind. Il y avait beaucoup de vent.; a wind instrument un instrument

à vent; **wind power** énergie f
éolienne

window n ❶ (of building) fenêtre
f ❷ (in car, train) vitre f; **a shop
window** une vitrine ❸ (window
pane) carreau m (pl carreaux) ▷ **to
break a window** casser un carreau
▷ **a broken window** un carreau cassé

windscreen n pare-brise m (pl
pare-brise)

windscreen wiper n essuie-glace
m (pl essuie-glace)

windshield n (US) = **windscreen**

windshield wiper n (US)
= **windscreen wiper**

windsurfing n planche f à voile

windy adj (place) venteux (f
venteuse); **It's windy.** Il y a du
vent.

wine n vin m ▷ **a bottle of wine** une
bouteille de vin ▷ **a glass of wine**
un verre de vin; **white wine** vin
m blanc; **red wine** vin m rouge;
a wine bar un bar à vin; **a wine
glass** un verre à vin; **the wine list**
la carte des vins

wing n aile f

wink vb **to wink at somebody**
faire un clin d'œil à quelqu'un
▷ **He winked at me.** Il m'a fait un clin
d'œil.

winner n gagnant m, gagnante f

winning adj **the winning team**
l'équipe gagnante; **the winning
goal** le but décisif

winter n hiver m; **in winter** en
hiver

wipe vb essuyer; **to wipe one's
feet** s'essuyer les pieds ▷ **Wipe your**
feet! Essuie-toi les pieds!; **to wipe
up** essuyer

wire n fil m de fer

wisdom tooth n dent f de sagesse
(pl dents de sagesse)

wise adj sage

wish vb **to wish for something**
souhaiter quelque chose ▷ **What
more could you wish for?** Que
pourrais-tu souhaiter de plus?; **to
wish to do something** désirer
faire quelque chose ▷ **I wish to make
a complaint.** Je désire porter
plainte.; **I wish you were here!** Si
seulement tu étais ici!; **I wish
you'd told me!** Si seulement tu
m'en avais parlé!

▶ n vœu m (pl vœux) ▷ **to make a
wish** faire un vœu; **"best wishes"**
(on greetings card) "meilleurs vœux";
"with best wishes, Kathy" "bien
amicalement, Kathy"

wit n (humour) esprit m

witch n sorcière f

with prep ❶ avec ▷ **Come with me.**
Venez avec moi. ▷ **He walks with a
stick.** Il marche avec une canne.;
a woman with blue eyes une
femme aux yeux bleus ❷ (at the
home of) chez ▷ **We stayed with
friends.** Nous avons logé chez des
amis. ❸ de ▷ **green with envy** vert
de jalousie ▷ **to shake with fear**
trembler de peur ▷ **Fill the jug with
water.** Remplis la carafe d'eau.

without prep sans ▷ **without a coat**
sans manteau ▷ **without speaking**
sans parler

witness n témoin m ▷ There were no

witnesses. Il n'a pas eu de témoins.
witty adj spirituel (f spirituelle)
wives npl see **wife**
wizard n magicien m
woke up, woken up vb see **wake up**
wolf n loup m
woman n femme f ▷ a woman doctor une femme médecin
won vb see **win**
wonder vb se demander ▷ I wonder why she said that. Je me demande pourquoi elle a dit ça. ▷ I wonder what that means. Je me demande ce que ça veut dire. ▷ I wonder where Caroline is. Je me demande où est Caroline.
wonderful adj formidable
won't = **will not**
wood n (timber, forest) bois m ▷ It's made of wood. C'est en bois. ▷ We went for a walk in the wood. Nous sommes allés nous promener dans le bois.
wooden adj en bois ▷ a wooden chair une chaise en bois
woodwork n menuiserie f ▷ My hobby is woodwork. Je fais de la menuiserie.
wool n laine f ▷ It's made of wool. C'est en laine.
word n mot m ▷ a difficult word un mot difficile; **What's the word for "shop" in German?** Comment dit-on "magasin" en allemand?; **in other words** en d'autres termes; **to have a word with somebody** parler avec quelqu'un; **the words** (lyrics) les paroles mpl ▷ I really like

the words of this song. J'adore les paroles de cette chanson.
word processing n traitement m de texte
word processor n machine f de traitement de texte
wore vb see **wear**
work n travail m (pl travaux) ▷ She's looking for work. Elle cherche du travail. ▷ He's at work at the moment. Il est au travail en ce moment.; **It's hard work.** C'est dur.; **to be off work** (sick) être malade ▷ He's been off work for a week. Il est malade depuis une semaine.; **He's out of work.** Il est sans emploi.
▶ vb ❶ (person) travailler ▷ to work hard travailler dur ❷ (machine, plan) marcher ▷ The heating isn't working. Le chauffage ne marche pas.; **to work out** (1) (exercise) faire de l'exercice ▷ I work out twice a week. Je fais de l'exercice deux fois par semaine. (2) (turn out) marcher ▷ In the end it worked out really well. Au bout du compte, ça a très bien marché. (3) (figure out) arriver à comprendre ▷ I just couldn't work it out. Je n'arrivais pas du tout à comprendre.; **It works out at £10 each.** Ça fait dix livres chacun.
worker n (in factory) ouvrier m, ouvrière f; **He's a factory worker.** Il est ouvrier.; **She's a good worker.** Elle travaille bien.
work experience n stage m ▷ I'm going to do work experience in a factory. Je vais faire un stage dans une usine.

a b c d e f g h i j k l m n o p q r s t u v **w** x y z

working-class adj ouvrier
(f ouvrière) ▷ *a working-class family*
une famille ouvrière
workman n ouvrier m
worksheet n feuille f d'exercices
workshop n atelier m ▷ *a drama
workshop* un atelier de théâtre
workspace n (computing) espace
m de travail
workstation n poste m de travail
(pl postes de travail)
world n monde m; *He's the world
champion.* Il est champion du
monde.
worm n ver m
worn adj usé(e) ▷ *The carpet is a
bit worn.* La moquette est un peu
usée.; **worn out** (tired) épuisé(e)
▶ vb see **wear**
worried adj inquiet (f inquiète)
▷ *She's very worried.* Elle est très
inquiète.; **to be worried about
something** s'inquiéter pour
quelque chose ▷ *I'm worried about
the exams.* Je m'inquiète pour les
examens.; **to look worried** avoir
l'air inquiet ▷ *She looks a bit worried.*
Elle a l'air un peu inquiète.
worry vb s'inquiéter; **Don't worry!**
Ne t'inquiète pas!
worse adj, adv ❶ pire ▷ *It was even
worse than that.* C'était encore pire
que ça. ❷ plus mal ▷ *I'm feeling
worse.* Je me sens plus mal.
worst adj **the worst** le plus
mauvais (f la plus mauvaise) ▷ *He
got the worst mark in the whole class.*
Il a eu la plus mauvaise note de
toute la classe.; **my worst enemy**

mon pire ennemi; **Maths is my
worst subject.** Je suis vraiment nul
en maths.
▶ n pire m ▷ *The worst of it is that ...*
Le pire c'est que ...; **at worst** au
pire; **if the worst comes to the
worst** au pire
worth adj **to be worth** valoir
▷ *It's worth a lot of money.* Ça vaut
très cher. ▷ *How much is it worth?*
Ça vaut combien?; **It's worth it.**
Ça vaut la peine. ▷ *Is it worth it?*
Est-ce que ça vaut la peine?
▷ *It's not worth it.* Ça ne vaut pas
la peine.
would vb **Would you like a biscuit?**
Vous voulez un biscuit?; **Would
you like to go and see a film?** Est-
ce que tu veux aller voir un film?;
Would you close the door please?
Vous pouvez fermer la porte, s'il
vous plaît?; **I'd like ...** J'aimerais ...
▷ *I'd like to go to America.* J'aimerais
aller en Amérique.; **I said I would
do it.** J'ai dit que je le ferais.; **If you
asked him he'd do it.** Si vous le lui
demandiez, il le ferait.; **If you had
asked him he would have done
it.** Si vous le lui aviez demandé, il
l'aurait fait.
wouldn't = **would not**
wound n blessure f
▶ vb blesser ▷ *He was wounded in the
leg.* Il a été blessé à la jambe.
wrap vb emballer ▷ *She's wrapping
her Christmas presents.* Elle est en
train d'emballer ses cadeaux de
Noël.; **Can you wrap it for me
please?** (in shop) Vous pouvez me

faire un papier cadeau, s'il vous plaît?; **to wrap up** emballer

wrapping paper n papier m cadeau

wreck n ❶ (vehicle, machine) tas m de ferraille ▷ That car is a wreck! Cette voiture est un tas de ferraille! ❷ (person) loque f ▷ After the exams I was a complete wreck. Après les examens j'étais une véritable loque.

▶ vb ❶ (building, vehicle) démolir ▷ The explosion wrecked the whole house. L'explosion a démoli toute la maison. ❷ (plan, holiday) ruiner ▷ The trip was wrecked by bad weather. Le voyage a été ruiné par le mauvais temps.

wrestler n lutteur m, lutteuse f

wrestling n lutte f

wrinkled adj ridé(e)

wrist n poignet m

write vb écrire ▷ to write a letter écrire une lettre; **to write to somebody** écrire à quelqu'un ▷ I'm going to write to her in French. Je vais lui écrire en français.; **to write down** noter ▷ I wrote down the address. J'ai noté l'adresse.; **Can you write it down for me, please?** Vous pouvez me l'écrire, s'il vous plaît?

writer n écrivain m ▷ She's a writer. Elle est écrivain.

writing n écriture f ▷ I can't read your writing. Je n'arrive pas à lire ton écriture.; **in writing** par écrit

written vb see **write**

wrong adj, adv ❶ (incorrect) faux (f fausse) ▷ The information they gave us was wrong. Les renseignements qu'ils nous ont donnés étaient faux.; **the wrong answer** la mauvaise réponse; **You've got the wrong number.** Vous vous êtes trompé de numéro. ❷ (morally bad) mal ▷ I think hunting is wrong. Je trouve que c'est mal de chasser.; **to be wrong** (mistaken) se tromper ▷ You're wrong about that. Tu te trompes.; **to do something wrong** se tromper ▷ You've done it wrong. Tu t'es trompé.; **to go wrong** (plan) mal tourner ▷ The robbery went wrong and they got caught. Le cambriolage a mal tourné et ils ont été pris.; **What's wrong?** Qu'est-ce qu'il y a?; **What's wrong with her?** Qu'est-ce qu'elle a?

wrote vb see **write**

WWW n (= WorldWideWeb) Web m

a
b
c
d
e
f
g
h
i
j
k
l
m
n
o
p
q
r
s
t
u
v
w
x
y
z

X

Xerox® *n* photocopie *f*
  ▶ *vb* photocopier
Xmas *n* (= Christmas) Noël
X-ray *vb* **to X-ray something** faire
  une radio de quelque chose ▷ *They
  X-rayed my arm.* Ils ont fait une
  radio de mon bras.
  ▶ *n* radio *f* ▷ *to have an X-ray* passer
  une radio

yacht *n* ❶ (*sailing boat*) voilier *m*
  ❷ (*luxury motorboat*) yacht *m*
yawn *vb* bâiller
year *n* an *m* ▷ *last year* l'an dernier
  ▷ *next year* l'an prochain; **to be 15
  years old** avoir quinze ans; **an
  eight-year-old child** un enfant
  de huit ans
  ● In French secondary schools,
  ● years are counted from the
  ● **sixième** (youngest) to **première**
  ● and **terminale** (oldest).
  ▷ *year 7* la sixième ▷ *year 8* la
  cinquième ▷ *year 9* la quatrième
  ▷ *year 10* la troisième ▷ *year 11* la
  seconde; **She's in year 11.** Elle est
  en seconde.; **He's a first-year.**
  Il est en sixième.
yell *vb* hurler
yellow *adj* jaune

yes adv ① oui ▷ *Do you like it? — Yes. Tu aimes ça? — Oui.*; **Would you like a cup of tea? — Yes please.** *Voulez-vous une tasse de thé? — Je veux bien.*

> Use **si** when answering negative questions.

② si ▷ *Don't you like it? — Yes! Tu n'aimes pas ça? — Si!*

yesterday adv hier ▷ *yesterday morning* hier matin ▷ *yesterday afternoon* hier après-midi ▷ *yesterday evening* hier soir ▷ *all day yesterday* toute la journée d'hier

yet adv encore; **not yet** pas encore ▷ *It's not finished yet.* Ce n'est pas encore fini.; **not as yet** pas encore ▷ *There's no news as yet.* Nous n'avons pas encore de nouvelles.; **Have you finished yet?** Vous avez fini?

yoghurt n yaourt m

yolk n jaune m d'œuf (pl jaunes d'œuf)

you pron

> Only use **tu** when speaking to one person of your own age or younger. If in doubt use **vous**.

① (polite form or plural) vous ▷ *Do you like football?* Est-ce que vous aimez le football? ▷ *Can I help you?* Est-ce que je peux vous aider? ② (familiar singular) tu ▷ *Do you like football?* Tu aimes le football?

> **vous** never changes, but **tu** has different forms. When you is the object of the sentence use **te** not **tu**. **te** becomes **t'** before a vowel sound.

▷ te, t' ▷ *I know you.* Je te connais. ▷ *I saw you.* Je t'ai vu.

> **toi** is used instead of **tu** after a preposition and in comparisons.

② toi ▷ *It's for you.* C'est pour toi. ▷ *She's younger than you.* Elle est plus jeune que toi.

young adj jeune; **young people** les jeunes

younger adj plus jeune ▷ *He's younger than me.* Il est plus jeune que moi.; **my younger brother** mon frère cadet; **my younger sister** ma sœur cadette

youngest adj le plus jeune (fla plus jeune) ▷ *my youngest brother* mon plus jeune frère ▷ *She's the youngest.* C'est la plus jeune.

your adj

> Only use **ton/ta/tes** when speaking to one person of your own age or younger. If in doubt use **votre/vos**.

① (polite form or plural) votre (pl vos) ▷ *your house* votre maison ▷ *your seats* vos places ② (familiar singular) ton (f ta, pl tes) ▷ *your brother* ton frère ▷ *your sister* ta sœur ▷ *your parents* tes parents

> **ta** becomes **ton** before a vowel sound.

your friend (1) (male) ton ami **(2)** (female) ton amie

> Do not use **votre/vos** or **ton/ta/tes** with parts of the body.

▷ *Would you like to wash your hands?* Est-ce que vous voulez vous laver les mains?

yours pron

Only use **le tien/la tienne/les tiens/les tiennes** when talking to one person of your own age or younger. If in doubt use **le vôtre/la vôtre/les vôtres**. The same applies to **à toi** and **à vous.**

❶ le vôtre (f la vôtre) ▷ *I like that car. Is it yours?* J'aime cette voiture-là. C'est le vôtre? ▷ *my parents and yours* mes parents et les vôtres; **Is this yours?** C'est à vous? ▷ *This book is yours.* Ce livre est à vous. ▷ *Whose is this? — It's yours.* C'est à qui? — À vous.; **Yours sincerely ...** Veuillez agréer l'expression de mes sentiments les meilleurs ... ❷ le tien (f la tienne) ▷ *I like that car. Is it yours?* J'aime cette voiture-là. C'est la tienne? ▷ *my parents and yours* mes parents et les tiens; **Is this yours?** C'est à toi? ▷ *This book is yours.* Ce livre est à toi. ▷ *Whose is this? — It's yours.* C'est à qui? — À toi.

yourself pron

Only use **te** when talking to one person of your own age or younger; use **vous** to everyone else. If in doubt use **vous.**

❶ (polite form) vous ▷ *Have you hurt yourself?* Est-ce que vous vous êtes fait mal? ▷ *Tell me about yourself!* Parlez-moi de vous! ❷ (familiar form) te ▷ *Have you hurt yourself?* Est-ce que tu t'es fait mal?

After a preposition, use **toi** instead of **te.**

❸ (familiar form) toi ❹ toi-même

▷ *Do it yourself!* Fais-le toi-même! ❺ vous-même ▷ *Do it yourself!* Faites-le vous-même!

yourselves pron ❶ vous ▷ *Did you enjoy yourselves?* Vous vous êtes bien amusés? ❷ vous-mêmes ▷ *Did you make it yourselves?* Vous l'avez fait vous-mêmes?

youth club n centre m de jeunes
youth hostel n auberge f de jeunesse (pl auberges de jeunesse)
Yugoslavia n Yougoslavie f; **in the former Yugoslavia** en ex-Yougoslavie

Z

zany *adj* loufoque
zebra *n* zèbre *m*
zebra crossing *n* passage *m* clouté
zero *n* zéro *m*
zigzag *n* zigzag *m*
zip *n* fermeture *f* éclair® (*pl* fermetures éclair)
zip code *n* (US) code *m* postal
zipper *n* (US) = **zip**
zodiac *n* zodiaque *m* ▷ *the signs of the zodiac* les signes du zodiaque
zone *n* zone *f*
zoo *n* zoo *m*
zoom lens *n* zoom *m*
zucchini *n* (US) courgette *f*

VERB TABLES

Introduction

The verb tables in the following section contain 93 tables of French verbs (some regular and some irregular) in alphabetical order. Each table shows you the following form:

Present	*eg* je fais = **I do** *or* **I'm doing**
Present Subjunctive	*eg* je fasse = **I do**
Perfect	*eg* j'ai fait = **I did** *or* **I have done**
Imperfect	*eg* je faisais = **I was doing** *or* **I did**
Future	*eg* je ferai = **I will do**
Conditional	*eg* je ferais = **I would do**
Imperative	*eg* fais = **do**
Past Participle	*eg* fait = **done**
Present Participle	*eg* faisant = **doing**

On the French-English side of the dictionary, all the French verbs are followed by a number (eg: **donner** [**29**] *vb* to give). This number corresponds to a page number in the Verb Tables. All the French verbs in this dictionary follow the pattern of one of these 93 verbs (eg: 'aimer [**29**] vb **to love**' follows the same pattern as **donner**, shown on page **29**).

In order to help you use the verbs shown in the Verb Tables correctly, there are also a number of example phrases at the bottom of each page to show the verb as it is used in context.

Remember:

je/j'	=	I
tu	=	you (*to one person you know well*)
il	=	he/it
elle	=	she/it
on	=	we/one
nous	=	we
vous	=	you (*polite form or plural*)
ils/elles	=	they

Table
2

acheter *to buy*

PRESENT		PRESENT SUBJUNCTIVE	
j'	achète	j'	achète
tu	achètes	tu	achètes
il/elle/on	achète	il/elle/on	achète
nous	achetons	nous	achetions
vous	achetez	vous	achetiez
ils/elles	achètent	ils/elles	achètent

PERFECT		IMPERFECT	
j'	ai acheté	j'	achetais
tu	as acheté	tu	achetais
il/elle/on	a acheté	il/elle/on	achetait
nous	avons acheté	nous	achetions
vous	avez acheté	vous	achetiez
ils/elles	ont acheté	ils/elles	achetaient

FUTURE		CONDITIONAL	
j'	achèterai	j'	achetais
tu	achèteras	tu	achetais
il/elle/on	achètera	il/elle/on	achetait
nous	achèterons	nous	achetions
vous	achèterez	vous	achetiez
ils/elles	achèteront	ils/elles	achetaient

IMPERATIVE
achète / achetons / achetez

PAST PARTICIPLE
acheté

PRESENT PARTICIPLE
achetant

EXAMPLE PHRASES

J'ai acheté des gâteaux à la pâtisserie.

I bought some cakes at the cake shop.

Qu'est-ce que tu lui **as acheté** pour son anniversaire?

What did you buy him for his birthday?

Je **n'achète** jamais de chips.

I never buy crisps.

Table
3

to acquire **acquérir**

PRESENT

j'	acquiers
tu	acquiers
il/elle/on	acquiert
nous	acquérons
vous	acquérez
ils/elles	acquièrent

PRESENT SUBJUNCTIVE

j'	acquière
tu	acquières
il/elle/on	acquière
nous	acquérions
vous	acquériez
ils/elles	acquièrent

PERFECT

j'	ai acquis
tu	as acquis
il/elle/on	a acquis
nous	avons acquis
vous	avez acquis
ils/elles	ont acquis

IMPERFECT

j'	acquérais
tu	acquérais
il/elle/on	acquérait
nous	acquérions
vous	acquériez
ils/elles	acquéraient

FUTURE

j'	acquerrai
tu	acquerras
il/elle/on	acquerra
nous	acquerrons
vous	acquerrez
ils/elles	acquerront

CONDITIONAL

j'	acquerrais
tu	acquerrais
il/elle/on	acquerrait
nous	acquerrions
vous	acquerriez
ils/elles	acquerraient

IMPERATIVE
acquiers / acquérons / acquérez

PAST PARTICIPLE
acquis

PRESENT PARTICIPLE
acquérant

--- EXAMPLE PHRASES ---

Elle **a acquis** la nationalité française en 2003.

She acquired French nationality in 2003.

Table
4

aller *to go*

PRESENT

je	vais
tu	vas
il/elle/on	va
nous	allons
vous	allez
ils/elles	vont

PRESENT SUBJUNCTIVE

j'	aille
tu	ailles
il/elle/on	aille
nous	allions
vous	alliez
ils/elles	aillent

PERFECT

je	suis allé(e)
tu	es allé(e)
il/elle/on	est allé(e)
nous	sommes allé(e)s
vous	êtes allé(e)(s)
ils/elles	sont allé(e)s

IMPERFECT

j'	allais
tu	allais
il/elle/on	allait
nous	allions
vous	alliez
ils/elles	allaient

FUTURE

j'	irai
tu	iras
il/elle/on	ira
nous	irons
vous	irez
ils/elles	iront

CONDITIONAL

j'	irais
tu	irais
il/elle/on	irait
nous	irions
vous	iriez
ils/elles	iraient

IMPERATIVE

va / allons / allez

PAST PARTICIPLE

allé

PRESENT PARTICIPLE

allant

——————— EXAMPLE PHRASES ———————

Vous **allez** au cinéma?
Je **suis allé** à Londres.
Est-ce que tu **es** déjà **allé** en Allemagne?

Are you going to the cinema?
I went to London.
Have you ever been to Germany?

PRESENT

j'	appelle
tu	appelles
il/elle/on	appelle
nous	appelons
vous	appelez
ils/elles	appellent

PRESENT SUBJUNCTIVE

j'	appelle
tu	appelles
il/elle/on	appelle
nous	appelions
vous	appeliez
ils/elles	appellent

PERFECT

j'	ai appelé
tu	as appelé
il/elle/on	a appelé
nous	avons appelé
vous	avez appelé
ils/elles	ont appelé

IMPERFECT

j'	appelais
tu	appelais
il/elle/on	appelait
nous	appelions
vous	appeliez
ils/elles	appelaient

FUTURE

j'	appellerai
tu	appelleras
il/elle/on	appellera
nous	appellerons
vous	appellerez
ils/elles	appelleront

CONDITIONAL

j'	appellerais
tu	appellerais
il/elle/on	appellerait
nous	appellerions
vous	appelleriez
ils/elles	appelleraient

IMPERATIVE
appelle / appelons / appelez

PAST PARTICIPLE
appelé

PRESENT PARTICIPLE
appelant

——————————— EXAMPLE PHRASES ———————————

Elle **a appelé** le médecin.
J'**ai appelé** Richard à Londres.
Comment tu **t'appelles**?

She called the doctor.
I called Richard in London.
What's your name?

- Note that *s'appeler* follows the same pattern, but takes **être** in the perfect tense.
  For an example of a reflexive verb in full, see verb table **7 s'asseoir**.

Table
6

arriver *to arrive*

PRESENT		PRESENT SUBJUNCTIVE	
j'	arrive	j'	arrive
tu	arrives	tu	arrives
il/elle/on	arrive	il/elle/on	arrive
nous	arrivons	nous	arrivions
vous	arrivez	vous	arriviez
ils/elles	arrivent	ils/elles	arrivent

PERFECT		IMPERFECT	
je	suis arrivé(e)	j'	arrivais
tu	es arrivé(e)	tu	arrivais
il/elle/on	est arrivé(e)	il/elle/on	arrivait
nous	sommes arrivé(e)s	nous	arrivions
vous	êtes arrivé(e)(s)	vous	arriviez
ils/elles	sont arrivé(e)s	ils/elles	arrivaient

FUTURE		CONDITIONAL	
j'	arriverai	j'	arriverais
tu	arriveras	tu	arriverais
il/elle/on	arrivera	il/elle/on	arriverait
nous	arriverons	nous	arriverions
vous	arriverez	vous	arriveriez
ils/elles	arriveront	ils/elles	arriveraient

IMPERATIVE

arrive / arrivons / arrivez

PAST PARTICIPLE

arrivé

PRESENT PARTICIPLE

arrivant

———————— EXAMPLE PHRASES ————————

J'**arrive** à l'école à huit heures.   *I arrive at school at 8 o'clock.*
Le prof n'**est** pas encore **arrivé**.   *The teacher hasn't arrived yet.*
Qu'est-ce qui **est arrivé** à Aurélie?   *What happened to Aurélie?*

PRESENT

je	m'assieds/m'assois
tu	t'assieds/t'assois
il/elle/on	s'assied/s'assoit
nous	nous asseyons/nous assoyons
vous	vous asseyez/vous assoyez
ils/elles	s'asseyent/s'assoient

PRESENT SUBJUNCTIVE

je	m'asseye
tu	t'asseyes
il/elle/on	s'asseye
nous	nous asseyions
vous	vous asseyiez
ils/elles	s'asseyent

PERFECT

je	me suis assis(e)
tu	t'es assis(e)
il/elle/on	s'est assis(e)
nous	nous sommes assis(es)
vous	vous êtes assis(e(s))
ils/elles	se sont assis(es)

IMPERFECT

je	m'asseyais
tu	t'asseyais
il/elle/on	s'asseyait
nous	nous asseyions
vous	vous asseyiez
ils/elles	s'asseyaient

FUTURE

je	m'assiérai
tu	t'assiéras
il/elle/on	s'assiéra
nous	nous assiérons
vous	vous assiérez
ils/elles	s'assiéront

CONDITIONAL

je	m'assiérais
tu	t'assiérais
il/elle/on	s'assiérait
nous	nous assiérions
vous	vous assiériez
ils/elles	s'assiéraient

IMPERATIVE

assieds-toi / asseyons-nous / asseyez-vous

PAST PARTICIPLE

assis

PRESENT PARTICIPLE

s'asseyant

— EXAMPLE PHRASES —

Assieds-toi, Nicole.	*Sit down Nicole.*
Asseyez-vous, les enfants.	*Sit down children.*
Je peux **m'assoir**?	*May I sit down?*
Je **me suis assise** sur un chewing-gum!	*I've sat on some chewing gum!*

Table
8

attendre *to wait*

PRESENT		PRESENT SUBJUNCTIVE	
j'	attends	j'	attende
tu	attends	tu	attendes
il/elle/on	attend	il/elle/on	attende
nous	attendons	nous	attendions
vous	attendez	vous	attendiez
ils/elles	attendent	ils/elles	attendent

PERFECT		IMPERFECT	
j'	ai attendu	j'	attendais
tu	as attendu	tu	attendais
il/elle/on	a attendu	il/elle/on	attendait
nous	avons attendu	nous	attendions
vous	avez attendu	vous	attendiez
ils/elles	ont attendu	ils/elles	attendaient

FUTURE		CONDITIONAL	
j'	attendrai	j'	attendrais
tu	attendras	tu	attendrais
il/elle/on	attendra	il/elle/on	attendrait
nous	attendrons	nous	attendrions
vous	attendrez	vous	attendriez
ils/elles	attendront	ils/elles	attendraient

IMPERATIVE
attends / attendons / attendez

PAST PARTICIPLE
attendu

PRESENT PARTICIPLE
attendant

--- EXAMPLE PHRASES ---

Attends-moi!
Tu **attends** depuis longtemps?
Je l'**ai attendu** à la poste.
Je **m'attends** à ce qu'il soit en
retard.

Wait for me!
Have you been waiting long?
I waited for him at the post office.
I expect he'll be late.

• Note that s'attendre follows the same pattern, but take **être** in the perfect tense.
For an example of a reflexive verb in full, see verb table **7** s'asseoir.

PRESENT

j'	ai
tu	as
il/elle/on	a
nous	avons
vous	avez
ils/elles	ont

PRESENT SUBJUNCTIVE

j'	aie
tu	aies
il/elle/on	ait
nous	ayons
vous	ayez
ils/elles	aient

PERFECT

j'	ai eu
tu	as eu
il/elle/on	a eu
nous	avons eu
vous	avez eu
ils/elles	ont eu

IMPERFECT

j'	avais
tu	avais
il/elle/on	avait
nous	avions
vous	aviez
ils/elles	avaient

FUTURE

j'	aurai
tu	auras
il/elle/on	aura
nous	aurons
vous	aurez
ils/elles	auront

CONDITIONAL

j'	aurais
tu	aurais
il/elle/on	aurait
nous	aurions
vous	auriez
ils/elles	auraient

IMPERATIVE

aie / ayons / ayez

PAST PARTICIPLE

eu

PRESENT PARTICIPLE

ayant

——————— EXAMPLE PHRASES ———————

Il **a** les yeux bleus.	*He's got blue eyes.*
Quel âge **as**-tu?	*How old are you?*
Il **a eu** un accident.	*He's had an accident.*
J'**avais** faim.	*I was hungry.*
Il y **a** beaucoup de monde.	*There are lots of people.*

Table
10

battre *to beat*

PRESENT		PRESENT SUBJUNCTIVE	
je	bats	je	batte
tu	bats	tu	battes
il/elle/on	bat	il/elle/on	batte
nous	battons	nous	battions
vous	battez	vous	battiez
ils/elles	battent	ils/elles	battent

PERFECT		IMPERFECT	
j'	ai battu	je	battais
tu	as battu	tu	battais
il/elle/on	a battu	il/elle/on	battait
nous	avons battu	nous	battions
vous	avez battu	vous	battiez
ils/elles	ont battu	ils/elles	battaient

FUTURE		CONDITIONAL	
je	battrai	je	battrais
tu	battras	tu	battrais
il/elle/on	battra	il/elle/on	battrait
nous	battrons	nous	battrions
vous	battrez	vous	battriez
ils/elles	battront	ils/elles	battraient

IMPERATIVE

bats / battons / battez

PAST PARTICIPLE

battu

PRESENT PARTICIPLE

battant

--- EXAMPLE PHRASES ---

On les **a battus** deux à un. — *We beat them 2-1.*
J'ai le cœur qui **bat**! — *My heart's beating (fast)!*
Arrêtez de **vous battre**! — *Stop fighting!*

- Note that **se battre** follows the same pattern, but takes **être** in the perfect tense.
  For an example of a reflexive verb in full, see verb table **83 se taire**.

PRESENT

je	bois
tu	bois
il/elle/on	boit
nous	buvons
vous	buvez
ils/elles	boivent

PRESENT SUBJUNCTIVE

je	boive
tu	boives
il/elle/on	boive
nous	buvions
vous	buviez
ils/elles	boivent

PERFECT

j'	ai bu
tu	as bu
il/elle/on	a bu
nous	avons bu
vous	avez bu
ils/elles	ont bu

IMPERFECT

je	buvais
tu	buvais
il/elle/on	buvait
nous	buvions
vous	buviez
ils/elles	buvaient

FUTURE

je	boirai
tu	boiras
il/elle/on	boira
nous	boirons
vous	boirez
ils/elles	boiront

CONDITIONAL

je	boirais
tu	boirais
il/elle/on	boirait
nous	boirions
vous	boiriez
ils/elles	boiraient

IMPERATIVE

bois / buvons / buvez

PAST PARTICIPLE

bu

PRESENT PARTICIPLE

buvant

— EXAMPLE PHRASES —

Qu'est-ce que tu veux **boire**?	What would you like to drink?
Il ne **boit** jamais d'alcool.	He never drinks alcohol.
J'**ai bu** un litre d'eau.	I drank a litre of water.

Table
12

bouillir *to boil*

PRESENT

je	bous
tu	bous
il/elle/on	bout
nous	bouillons
vous	bouillez
ils/elles	bouillent

PRESENT SUBJUNCTIVE

je	bouille
tu	bouilles
il/elle/on	bouille
nous	bouillions
vous	bouilliez
ils/elles	bouillent

PERFECT

j'	ai bouilli
tu	as bouilli
il/elle/on	a bouilli
nous	avons bouilli
vous	avez bouilli
ils/elles	ont bouilli

IMPERFECT

je	bouillais
tu	bouillais
il/elle/on	bouillait
nous	bouillions
vous	bouilliez
ils/elles	bouillaient

FUTURE

je	bouillirai
tu	bouilliras
il/elle/on	bouillira
nous	bouillirons
vous	bouillirez
ils/elles	bouilliront

CONDITIONAL

je	bouillirais
tu	bouillirais
il/elle/on	bouillirait
nous	bouillirions
vous	bouilliriez
ils/elles	bouilliraient

IMPERATIVE
bous / bouillons / bouillez

PAST PARTICIPLE
bouilli

PRESENT PARTICIPLE
bouillant

——————————— EXAMPLE PHRASES ———————————

L'eau **bout**.	*The water's boiling.*
Tu peux mettre de l'eau à **bouillir**?	*Can you boil some water?*

Table
13

to begin **commencer**

PRESENT		PRESENT SUBJUNCTIVE	
je	commence	je	commence
tu	commences	tu	commences
il/elle/on	commence	il/elle/on	commence
nous	commençons	nous	commencions
vous	commencez	vous	commenciez
ils/elles	commencent	ils/elles	commencent

PERFECT		IMPERFECT	
j'	ai commencé	je	commençais
tu	as commencé	tu	commençais
il/elle/on	a commencé	il/elle/on	commençait
nous	avons commencé	nous	commencions
vous	avez commencé	vous	commenciez
ils/elles	ont commencé	ils/elles	commençaient

FUTURE		CONDITIONAL	
je	commencerai	je	commencerais
tu	commenceras	tu	commencerais
il/elle/on	commencera	il/elle/on	commencerait
nous	commencerons	nous	commencerions
vous	commencerez	vous	commenceriez
ils/elles	commenceront	ils/elles	commenceraient

IMPERATIVE
commence / commençons / commencez

PAST PARTICIPLE
commencé

PRESENT PARTICIPLE
commençant

——————— EXAMPLE PHRASES ———————

Il **a commencé** à pleuvoir.	*It started to rain.*
Les cours **commencent** à neuf heures.	*Lessons start at 9 o'clock.*
Tu **as** déjà **commencé** de réviser pour les examens?	*Have you started revising for the exams?*

Table
14

conclure *to conclude*

PRESENT

je	conclus
tu	conclus
il/elle/on	conclut
nous	concluons
vous	concluez
ils/elles	concluent

PRESENT SUBJUNCTIVE

je	conclue
tu	conclues
il/elle/on	conclue
nous	concluions
vous	concluiez
ils/elles	concluent

PERFECT

j'	ai conclu
tu	as conclu
il/elle/on	a conclu
nous	avons conclu
vous	avez conclu
ils/elles	ont conclu

IMPERFECT

je	concluais
tu	concluais
il/elle/on	concluait
nous	concluions
vous	concluiez
ils/elles	concluaient

FUTURE

je	conclurai
tu	concluras
il/elle/on	conclura
nous	conclurons
vous	conclurez
ils/elles	concluront

CONDITIONAL

je	conclurais
tu	conclurais
il/elle/on	conclurait
nous	conclurions
vous	concluriez
ils/elles	concluraient

IMPERATIVE

conclus / concluons / concluez

PAST PARTICIPLE

conclu

PRESENT PARTICIPLE

concluant

———————— EXAMPLE PHRASES ————————

Ils **ont conclu** un marché.	*They concluded a deal.*
J'en **ai conclu** qu'il était parti.	*I concluded that he had gone.*
Je **conclurai** par ces mots…	*I will conclude with these words…*

Table
15

to know **connaître**

PRESENT

je	connais
tu	connais
il/elle/on	connaît
nous	connaissons
vous	connaissez
ils/elles	connaissent

PRESENT SUBJUNCTIVE

je	connaisse
tu	connaisses
il/elle/on	connaisse
nous	connaissions
vous	connaissiez
ils/elles	connaissent

PERFECT

j'	ai connu
tu	as connu
il/elle/on	a connu
nous	avons connu
vous	avez connu
ils/elles	ont connu

IMPERFECT

je	connaissais
tu	connaissais
il/elle/on	connaissait
nous	connaissions
vous	connaissiez
ils/elles	connaissaient

FUTURE

je	connaîtrai
tu	connaîtras
il/elle/on	connaîtra
nous	connaîtrons
vous	connaîtrez
ils/elles	connaîtront

CONDITIONAL

je	connaîtrais
tu	connaîtrais
il/elle/on	connaîtrait
nous	connaîtrions
vous	connaîtriez
ils/elles	connaîtraient

IMPERATIVE

connais / connaissons / connaissez

PRESENT PARTICIPLE

connaissant

PAST PARTICIPLE

connu

=== EXAMPLE PHRASES ===

Je ne **connais** pas du tout cette région.	I don't know the area at all.
Vous **connaissez** M Amiot?	Do you know Mr Amiot?
Il n'a pas **connu** son grand-père.	He never knew his grandad.
Ils **se sont connus** à Rouen.	They first met in Rouen.

- Note that **se connaître** follows the same pattern, but takes **être** in the perfect tense. For an example of a reflexive verb in full, see verb table **83 se taire**.

Table
16

coudre *to sew*

PRESENT		PRESENT SUBJUNCTIVE	
je	couds	je	couse
tu	couds	tu	couses
il/elle/on	coud	il/elle/on	couse
nous	cousons	nous	cousions
vous	cousez	vous	cousiez
ils/elles	cousent	ils/elles	cousent

PERFECT		IMPERFECT	
j'	ai cousu	je	cousais
tu	as cousu	tu	cousais
il/elle/on	a cousu	il/elle/on	cousait
nous	avons cousu	nous	cousions
vous	avez cousu	vous	cousiez
ils/elles	ont cousu	ils/elles	cousaient

FUTURE		CONDITIONAL	
je	coudrai	je	coudrais
tu	coudras	tu	coudrais
il/elle/on	coudra	il/elle/on	coudrait
nous	coudrons	nous	coudrions
vous	coudrez	vous	coudriez
ils/elles	coudront	ils/elles	coudraient

IMPERATIVE
couds / cousons / cousez

PAST PARTICIPLE
cousu

PRESENT PARTICIPLE
cousant

--- EXAMPLE PHRASES ---

Tu sais **coudre**?
Elle **a cousu** elle-même son costume.

Can you sew?
She made her costume herself.

PRESENT

je	cours
tu	cours
il/elle/on	court
nous	courons
vous	courez
ils/elles	courent

PRESENT SUBJUNCTIVE

je	coure
tu	coures
il/elle/on	coure
nous	courions
vous	couriez
ils/elles	courent

PERFECT

j'	ai couru
tu	as couru
il/elle/on	a couru
nous	avons couru
vous	avez couru
ils/elles	ont couru

IMPERFECT

je	courais
tu	courais
il/elle/on	courait
nous	courions
vous	couriez
ils/elles	couraient

FUTURE

je	courrai
tu	courras
il/elle/on	courra
nous	courrons
vous	courrez
ils/elles	courront

CONDITIONAL

je	courrais
tu	courrais
il/elle/on	courrait
nous	courrions
vous	courriez
ils/elles	courraient

IMPERATIVE

cours / courons / courez

PAST PARTICIPLE

couru

PRESENT PARTICIPLE

courant

––––––––– EXAMPLE PHRASES –––––––––

Je ne **cours** pas très vite.
Elle est sortie en **courant**.
Ne **courez** pas dans le couloir.
J'**ai couru** jusqu'à l'école.

I can't run very fast.
She ran out.
Don't run in the corridor.
I ran all the way to school.

Table
18

craindre *to fear*

PRESENT		PRESENT SUBJUNCTIVE	
je	crains	je	craigne
tu	crains	tu	craignes
il/elle/on	craint	il/elle/on	craigne
nous	craignons	nous	craignions
vous	craignez	vous	craigniez
ils/elles	craignent	ils/elles	craignent

PERFECT		IMPERFECT	
j'	ai craint	je	craignais
tu	as craint	tu	craignais
il/elle/on	a craint	il/elle/on	craignait
nous	avons craint	nous	craignions
vous	avez craint	vous	craigniez
ils/elles	ont craint	ils/elles	craignaient

FUTURE		CONDITIONAL	
je	craindrai	je	craindrais
tu	craindras	tu	craindrais
il/elle/on	craindra	il/elle/on	craindrait
nous	craindrons	nous	craindrions
vous	craindrez	vous	craindriez
ils/elles	craindront	ils/elles	craindraient

IMPERATIVE

crains / craignons / craignez

PAST PARTICIPLE

craint

PRESENT PARTICIPLE

craignant

——————————— EXAMPLE PHRASES ———————————

Tu n'as rien à **craindre**.
Je **crains** le pire.

You've got nothing to fear.
I fear the worst.

PRESENT

je	crée
tu	crées
il/elle/on	crée
nous	créons
vous	créez
ils/elles	créent

PRESENT SUBJUNCTIVE

je	crée
tu	crées
il/elle/on	crée
nous	créions
vous	créiez
ils/elles	créent

PERFECT

j'	ai créé
tu	as créé
il/elle/on	a créé
nous	avons créé
vous	avez créé
ils/elles	ont créé

IMPERFECT

je	créais
tu	créais
il/elle/on	créait
nous	créions
vous	créiez
ils/elles	créaient

FUTURE

je	créerai
tu	créeras
il/elle/on	créera
nous	créerons
vous	créerez
ils/elles	créeront

CONDITIONAL

je	créerais
tu	créerais
il/elle/on	créerait
nous	créerions
vous	créeriez
ils/elles	créeraient

IMPERATIVE
crée / créons / créez

PAST PARTICIPLE
créé

PRESENT PARTICIPLE
créant

———————— EXAMPLE PHRASES ————————

Il **a créé** une nouvelle invention.
He's created a new invention.

Ce virus **crée** des difficultés dans le monde entier.
This virus is creating difficulties all over the world.

Le gouvernement **créera** deux mille emplois supplémentaires.
The government will create an extra 2000 jobs.

Table
20

crier to shout

PRESENT

je	crie
tu	cries
il/elle/on	crie
nous	crions
vous	criez
ils/elles	crient

PRESENT SUBJUNCTIVE

je	crie
tu	cries
il/elle/on	crie
nous	criions
vous	criiez
ils/elles	crient

PERFECT

j'	ai crié
tu	as crié
il/elle/on	a crié
nous	avons crié
vous	avez crié
ils/elles	ont crié

IMPERFECT

je	criais
tu	criais
il/elle/on	criait
nous	criions
vous	criiez
ils/elles	criaient

FUTURE

je	crierai
tu	crieras
il/elle/on	criera
nous	crierons
vous	crierez
ils/elles	crieront

CONDITIONAL

je	crierais
tu	crierais
il/elle/on	crierait
nous	crierions
vous	crieriez
ils/elles	crieraient

IMPERATIVE

crie / crions / criez

PAST PARTICIPLE

crié

PRESENT PARTICIPLE

criant

─────────────── EXAMPLE PHRASES ───────────────

Ne **crie** pas comme ça!
Elle **a crié** au secours.
"Attention!", **cria**-t-il.

Don't shout!
She cried for help.
"Watch out!" he shouted.

PRESENT

je	crois
tu	crois
il/elle/on	croit
nous	croyons
vous	croyez
ils/elles	croient

PRESENT SUBJUNCTIVE

je	croie
tu	croies
il/elle/on	croie
nous	croyions
vous	croyiez
ils/elles	croient

PERFECT

j'	ai cru
tu	as cru
il/elle/on	a cru
nous	avons cru
vous	avez cru
ils/elles	ont cru

IMPERFECT

je	croyais
tu	croyais
il/elle/on	croyait
nous	croyions
vous	croyiez
ils/elles	croyaient

FUTURE

je	croirai
tu	croiras
il/elle/on	croira
nous	croirons
vous	croirez
ils/elles	croiront

CONDITIONAL

je	croirais
tu	croirais
il/elle/on	croirait
nous	croirions
vous	croiriez
ils/elles	croiraient

IMPERATIVE

crois / croyons / croyez

PAST PARTICIPLE

cru

PRESENT PARTICIPLE

croyant

——————— EXAMPLE PHRASES ———————

Je ne te **crois** pas.	I don't believe you.
J'**ai cru** que tu n'allais pas venir.	I thought you weren't going to come.
Elle **croyait** encore au père Noël.	She still believed in Santa.

Table
22

croître *to grow*

PRESENT

je	croîs
tu	croîs
il/elle/on	croît
nous	croissons
vous	croissez
ils/elles	croissent

PRESENT SUBJUNCTIVE

je	croisse
tu	croisses
il/elle/on	croisse
nous	croissions
vous	croissiez
ils/elles	croissent

PERFECT

j'	ai crû
tu	as crû
il/elle/on	a crû
nous	avons crû
vous	avez crû
ils/elles	ont crû

IMPERFECT

je	croissais
tu	croissais
il/elle/on	croissait
nous	croissions
vous	croissiez
ils/elles	croissaient

FUTURE

je	croîtrai
tu	croîtras
il/elle/on	croîtra
nous	croîtrons
vous	croîtrez
ils/elles	croîtront

CONDITIONAL

je	croîtrais
tu	croîtrais
il/elle/on	croîtrait
nous	croîtrions
vous	croîtriez
ils/elles	croîtraient

IMPERATIVE

croîs / croissons / croissez

PAST PARTICIPLE

crû (NB: crue, crus, crues)

PRESENT PARTICIPLE

croissant

--- EXAMPLE PHRASES ---

Les ventes **croissent** de 6% par an.
C'est une plante qui **croît** dans les pays chauds.

Sales are growing by 6% per year.
This plant grows in hot countries.

PRESENT

je	cueille
tu	cueilles
il/elle/on	cueille
nous	cueillons
vous	cueillez
ils/elles	cueillent

PRESENT SUBJUNCTIVE

je	cueille
tu	cueilles
il/elle/on	cueille
nous	cueillions
vous	cueilliez
ils/elles	cueillent

PERFECT

j'	ai cueilli
tu	as cueilli
il/elle/on	a cueilli
nous	avons cueilli
vous	avez cueilli
ils/elles	ont cueilli

IMPERFECT

je	cueillais
tu	cueillais
il/elle/on	cueillait
nous	cueillions
vous	cueilliez
ils/elles	cueillaient

FUTURE

je	cueillerai
tu	cueilleras
il/elle/on	cueillera
nous	cueillerons
vous	cueillerez
ils/elles	cueilleront

CONDITIONAL

je	cueillerais
tu	cueillerais
il/elle/on	cueillerait
nous	cueillerions
vous	cueilleriez
ils/elles	cueilleraient

IMPERATIVE
cueille / cueillons / cueillez

PAST PARTICIPLE
cueilli

PRESENT PARTICIPLE
cueillant

──────── EXAMPLE PHRASES ────────

J'**ai cueilli** quelques fraises dans le jardin.

Il est interdit de **cueillir** des fleurs sauvages dans la montagne. .

I've picked a few strawberries in the garden.

It's forbidden to pick wild flowers in the mountains.

Table
24

cuire *to cook*

PRESENT

je	cuis
tu	cuis
il/elle/on	cuit
nous	cuisons
vous	cuisez
ils/elles	cuisent

PRESENT SUBJUNCTIVE

je	cuise
tu	cuises
il/elle/on	cuise
nous	cuisions
vous	cuisiez
ils/elles	cuisent

PERFECT

j'	ai cuit
tu	as cuit
il/elle/on	a cuit
nous	avons cuit
vous	avez cuit
ils/elles	ont cuit

IMPERFECT

je	cuisais
tu	cuisais
il/elle/on	cuisait
nous	cuisions
vous	cuisiez
ils/elles	cuisaient

FUTURE

je	cuirai
tu	cuiras
il/elle/on	cuira
nous	cuirons
vous	cuirez
ils/elles	cuiront

CONDITIONAL

je	cuirais
tu	cuirais
il/elle/on	cuirait
nous	cuirions
vous	cuiriez
ils/elles	cuiraient

IMPERATIVE

cuis / cuisons / cuisez

PAST PARTICIPLE

cuit

PRESENT PARTICIPLE

cuisant

─────────── EXAMPLE PHRASES ───────────

Je les **ai cuits** au beurre.	*I cooked them in butter.*
En général, je **cuis** les légumes à la vapeur.	*I usually steam vegetables.*
Ce gâteau prend environ une heure à **cuire**.	*This cake takes about an hour to bake.*

Table
25

to go down **descendre**

PRESENT		PRESENT SUBJUNCTIVE	
je	descends	je	descende
tu	descends	tu	descendes
il/elle/on	descend	il/elle/on	descende
nous	descendons	nous	descendions
vous	descendez	vous	descendiez
ils/elles	descendent	ils/elles	descendent

PERFECT		IMPERFECT	
je	suis descendu(e)	je	descendais
tu	es descendu(e)	tu	descendais
il/elle/on	est descendu(e)	il/elle/on	descendait
nous	sommes descendu(e)(s)	nous	descendions
vous	êtes descendu(e)(s)	vous	descendiez
ils/elles	sont descendu(e)s	ils/elles	descendaient

FUTURE		CONDITIONAL	
je	descendrai	je	descendrais
tu	descendras	tu	descendrais
il/elle/on	descendra	il/elle/on	descendrait
nous	descendrons	nous	descendrions
vous	descendrez	vous	descendriez
ils/elles	descendront	ils/elles	descendraient

IMPERATIVE

descends / descendons / descendez

PAST PARTICIPLE

descendu

PRESENT PARTICIPLE

descendant

--------- EXAMPLE PHRASES ---------

Descendez la rue jusqu'au rond-point.

Go down the street to the roundabout.

Reste en bas: je **descends**!

Stay downstairs – I'm coming down!

Nous **sommes descendus** à la station Trocadéro.

We got off at the Trocadéro station.

Vous pouvez **descendre** ma valise, s'il vous plaît?

Can you get my suitcase down, please?

- Note that **descendre** takes *avoir* in the perfect tense when it is used with a direct object.

Table
26

devenir *to become*

PRESENT

je	deviens
tu	deviens
il/elle/on	devient
nous	devenons
vous	devenez
ils/elles	deviennent

PRESENT SUBJUNCTIVE

je	devienne
tu	deviennes
il/elle/on	devienne
nous	devenions
vous	deveniez
ils/elles	deviennent

PERFECT

je	suis devenu(e)
tu	es devenu(e)
il/elle/on	est devenu(e)
nous	sommes devenu(e)s
vous	êtes devenu(e)(s)
ils/elles	sont devenu(e)s

IMPERFECT

je	devenais
tu	devenais
il/elle/on	devenait
nous	devenions
vous	deveniez
ils/elles	devenaient

FUTURE

je	deviendrai
tu	deviendras
il/elle/on	deviendra
nous	deviendrons
vous	deviendrez
ils/elles	deviendront

CONDITIONAL

je	deviendrais
tu	deviendrais
il/elle/on	deviendrait
nous	deviendrions
vous	deviendriez
ils/elles	deviendraient

IMPERATIVE

deviens / devenons / devenez

PAST PARTICIPLE

devenu

PRESENT PARTICIPLE

devenant

─────────── EXAMPLE PHRASES ───────────

Il **est devenu** médecin.	He became a doctor.
Ça **devient** de plus en plus difficile.	It's becoming more and more difficult.
Qu'est-ce qu'elle **est devenue**?	What has become of her?

PRESENT

je	dois
tu	dois
il/elle/on	doit
nous	devons
vous	devez
ils/elles	doivent

PRESENT SUBJUNCTIVE

je	doive
tu	doives
il/elle/on	doive
nous	devions
vous	deviez
ils/elles	doivent

PERFECT

j'	ai dû
tu	as dû
il/elle/on	a dû
nous	avons dû
vous	avez dû
ils/elles	ont dû

IMPERFECT

je	devais
tu	devais
il/elle/on	devait
nous	devions
vous	deviez
ils/elles	devaient

FUTURE

je	devrai
tu	devras
il/elle/on	devra
nous	devrons
vous	devrez
ils/elles	devront

CONDITIONAL

je	devrais
tu	devrais
il/elle/on	devrait
nous	devrions
vous	devriez
ils/elles	devraient

IMPERATIVE

dois / devons / devez

PAST PARTICIPLE

dû (NB: due, dus, dues)

PRESENT PARTICIPLE

devant

─────── EXAMPLE PHRASES ───────

Je **dois** aller faire les courses ce matin.	I have to do the shopping this morning.
À quelle heure est-ce que tu **dois** partir?	What time do you have to leave?
Il **a dû** faire ses devoirs hier soir.	He had to do his homework last night.
Il **devait** prendre le train pour aller travailler.	He had to go to work by train.

Table
28

dire *to say*

PRESENT		PRESENT SUBJUNCTIVE	
je	dis	je	dise
tu	dis	tu	dises
il/elle/on	dit	il/elle/on	dise
nous	disons	nous	disions
vous	dites	vous	disiez
ils/elles	disent	ils/elles	disent

PERFECT		IMPERFECT	
j'	ai dit	je	disais
tu	as dit	tu	disais
il/elle/on	a dit	il/elle/on	disait
nous	avons dit	nous	disions
vous	avez dit	vous	disiez
ils/elles	ont dit	ils/elles	disaient

FUTURE		CONDITIONAL	
je	dirai	je	dirais
tu	diras	tu	dirais
il/elle/on	dira	il/elle/on	dirait
nous	dirons	nous	dirions
vous	direz	vous	diriez
ils/elles	diront	ils/elles	diraient

IMPERATIVE

dis / disons / dites

PAST PARTICIPLE

dit

PRESENT PARTICIPLE

disant

──────── EXAMPLE PHRASES ────────

Qu'est-ce qu'elle **dit**?	What is she saying?
"Bonjour!", a-t-il **dit**.	"Hello!" he said.
Ils m'**ont dit** que le film était nul.	They told me that the film was rubbish.
Comment ça **se dit** en anglais?	How do you say that in English?

• Note that *se dire* follows the same pattern, but takes *être* in the perfect tense.
For an example of a reflexive verb in full, see verb table *83 se taire*.

PRESENT

je	donne
tu	donnes
il/elle/on	donne
nous	donnons
vous	donnez
ils/elles	donnent

PRESENT SUBJUNCTIVE

je	donne
tu	donnes
il/elle/on	donne
nous	donnions
vous	donniez
ils/elles	donnent

PERFECT

j'	ai donné
tu	as donné
il/elle/on	a donné
nous	avons donné
vous	avez donné
ils/elles	ont donné

IMPERFECT

je	donnais
tu	donnais
il/elle/on	donnait
nous	donnions
vous	donniez
ils/elles	donnaient

FUTURE

je	donnerai
tu	donneras
il/elle/on	donnera
nous	donnerons
vous	donnerez
ils/elles	donneront

CONDITIONAL

je	donnerais
tu	donnerais
il/elle/on	donnerait
nous	donnerions
vous	donneriez
ils/elles	donneraient

IMPERATIVE

donne / donnons / donnez

PAST PARTICIPLE

donné

PRESENT PARTICIPLE

donnant

——————— EXAMPLE PHRASES ———————

Donne-moi la main.	*Give me your hand.*
Est-ce que je t'**ai donné** mon adresse?	*Did I give you my address?*
L'appartement **donne** sur la place.	*The flat overlooks the square.*

Table
30

dormir *to sleep*

PRESENT		PRESENT SUBJUNCTIVE	
je	dors	je	dorme
tu	dors	tu	dormes
il/elle/on	dort	il/elle/on	dorme
nous	dormons	nous	dormions
vous	dormez	vous	dormiez
ils/elles	dorment	ils/elles	dorment

PERFECT		IMPERFECT	
j'	ai dormi	je	dormais
tu	as dormi	tu	dormais
il/elle/on	a dormi	il/elle/on	dormait
nous	avons dormi	nous	dormions
vous	avez dormi	vous	dormiez
ils/elles	ont dormi	ils/elles	dormaient

FUTURE		CONDITIONAL	
je	dormirai	je	dormirais
tu	dormiras	tu	dormirais
il/elle/on	dormira	il/elle/on	dormirait
nous	dormirons	nous	dormirions
vous	dormirez	vous	dormiriez
ils/elles	dormiront	ils/elles	dormiraient

IMPERATIVE
dors / dormons / dormez

PAST PARTICIPLE
dormi

PRESENT PARTICIPLE
dormant

--- EXAMPLE PHRASES ---

Tu **as** bien **dormi**?	*Did you sleep well?*
Nous **dormons** dans la même chambre.	*We sleep in the same bedroom.*
À 9 heures, il **dormait** déjà.	*He was already asleep by nine.*

PRESENT

j'	écris
tu	écris
il/elle/on	écrit
nous	écrivons
vous	écrivez
ils/elles	écrivent

PRESENT SUBJUNCTIVE

j'	écrive
tu	écrives
il/elle/on	écrive
nous	écrivions
vous	écriviez
ils/elles	écrivent

PERFECT

j'	ai écrit
tu	as écrit
il/elle/on	a écrit
nous	avons écrit
vous	avez écrit
ils/elles	ont écrit

IMPERFECT

j'	écrivais
tu	écrivais
il/elle/on	écrivait
nous	écrivions
vous	écriviez
ils/elles	écrivaient

FUTURE

j'	écrirai
tu	écriras
il/elle/on	écrira
nous	écrirons
vous	écrirez
ils/elles	écriront

CONDITIONAL

j'	écrirais
tu	écrirais
il/elle/on	écrirait
nous	écririons
vous	écririez
ils/elles	écriraient

IMPERATIVE

écris / écrivons / écrivez

PAST PARTICIPLE

écrit

PRESENT PARTICIPLE

écrivant

--- EXAMPLE PHRASES ---

Tu **as écrit** à ta correspondante récemment?
Elle **écrit** des romans.
Comment ça **s'écrit**, "brouillard"?

Have you written to your penfriend lately?
She writes novels.
How do you spell "brouillard"?

- Note that **s'écrire** follows the same pattern, but take **être** in the perfect tense. For an example of a reflexive verb in full, see verb table **7 s'asseoir**.

Table
32

émouvoir *to move*

PRESENT			PRESENT SUBJUNCTIVE	
j'	émeus		j'	émeuve
tu	émeus		tu	émeuves
il/elle/on	émeut		il/elle/on	émeuve
nous	émouvons		nous	émouvions
vous	émouvez		vous	émouviez
ils/elles	émeuvent		ils/elles	émeuvent

PERFECT			IMPERFECT	
j'	ai ému		j'	émouvais
tu	as ému		tu	émouvais
il/elle/on	a ému		il/elle/on	émouvait
nous	avons ému		nous	émouvions
vous	avez ému		vous	émouviez
ils/elles	ont ému		ils/elles	émouvaient

FUTURE			CONDITIONAL	
j'	émouvrai		j'	émouvrais
tu	émouvras		tu	émouvrais
il/elle/on	émouvra		il/elle/on	émouvrait
nous	émouvrons		nous	émouvrions
vous	émouvrez		vous	émouvriez
ils/elles	émouvront		ils/elles	émouvraient

IMPERATIVE
émeus / émouvons / émouvez

PAST PARTICIPLE
ému

PRESENT PARTICIPLE
émouvant

——————— EXAMPLE PHRASES ———————

Ce film nous **a ému**.
Cette histoire m'**émeut** toujours
beaucoup.

This film moved us.
This story always moves me to
tears.

PRESENT

j'	entre
tu	entres
il/elle/on	entre
nous	entrons
vous	entrez
ils/elles	entrent

PRESENT SUBJUNCTIVE

j'	entre
tu	entres
il/elle/on	entre
nous	entrions
vous	entriez
ils/elles	entrent

PERFECT

je	suis entré(e)
tu	es entré(e)
il/elle/on	est entré(e)
nous	sommes entré(e)s
vous	êtes entré(e)(s)
ils/elles	sont entré(e)s

IMPERFECT

j'	entrais
tu	entrais
il/elle/on	entrait
nous	entrions
vous	entriez
ils/elles	entraient

FUTURE

j'	entrerai
tu	entreras
il/elle/on	entrera
nous	entrerons
vous	entrerez
ils/elles	entreront

CONDITIONAL

j'	entrerais
tu	entrerais
il/elle/on	entrerait
nous	entrerions
vous	entreriez
ils/elles	entreraient

IMPERATIVE

entre / entrons / entrez

PAST PARTICIPLE

entré

PRESENT PARTICIPLE

entrant

--- EXAMPLE PHRASES ---

Je peux **entrer**?
Essuie-toi les pieds en **entrant**.
Ils **sont** tous **entrés** dans la maison.

Can I come in?
Wipe your feet as you come in.
They all went into the house.

Table
34

envoyer *to send*

PRESENT		PRESENT SUBJUNCTIVE	
j'	envoie	j'	envoie
tu	envoies	tu	envoies
il/elle/on	envoie	il/elle/on	envoie
nous	envoyons	nous	envoyions
vous	envoyez	vous	envoyiez
ils/elles	envoient	ils/elles	envoient

PERFECT		IMPERFECT	
j'	ai envoyé	j'	envoyais
tu	as envoyé	tu	envoyais
il/elle/on	a envoyé	il/elle/on	envoyait
nous	avons envoyé	nous	envoyions
vous	avez envoyé	vous	envoyiez
ils/elles	ont envoyé	ils/elles	envoyaient

FUTURE		CONDITIONAL	
j'	enverrai	j'	enverrais
tu	enverras	tu	enverrais
il/elle/on	enverra	il/elle/on	enverrait
nous	enverrons	nous	enverrions
vous	enverrez	vous	enverriez
ils/elles	enverront	ils/elles	enverraient

IMPERATIVE
envoie / envoyons / envoyez

PAST PARTICIPLE
envoyé

PRESENT PARTICIPLE
envoyant

=========== EXAMPLE PHRASES ===========

J'**ai envoyé** une carte postale à ma tante.

I sent my aunt a postcard.

Envoie-moi un e-mail.

Send me an email.

Je t'**enverrai** ton cadeau par la poste.

I'll send you your present by post.

PRESENT

j'	espère
tu	espères
il/elle/on	espère
nous	espérons
vous	espérez
ils/elles	espèrent

PRESENT SUBJUNCTIVE

j'	espère
tu	espères
il/elle/on	espère
nous	espérions
vous	espériez
ils/elles	espèrent

PERFECT

j'	ai espéré
tu	as espéré
il/elle/on	a espéré
nous	avons espéré
vous	avez espéré
ils/elles	ont espéré

IMPERFECT

j'	espérais
tu	espérais
il/elle/on	espérait
nous	espérions
vous	espériez
ils/elles	espéraient

FUTURE

j'	espérerai
tu	espéreras
il/elle/on	espérera
nous	espérerons
vous	espérerez
ils/elles	espéreront

CONDITIONAL

j'	espérerais
tu	espérerais
il/elle/on	espérerait
nous	espérerions
vous	espéreriez
ils/elles	espéreraient

IMPERATIVE
espère / espérons / espérez

PAST PARTICIPLE
espéré

PRESENT PARTICIPLE
espérant

———————————— EXAMPLE PHRASES ————————————

J'**espère** que tu vas bien.
Il **espérait** pouvoir venir.
Tu penses réussir tes examens? –
J'**espère** bien!

I hope you're well.
He was hoping he'd be able to come.
Do you think you'll pass your exams?
– I hope so!

Table
36

être *to be*

PRESENT

je	suis
tu	es
il/elle/on	est
nous	sommes
vous	êtes
ils/elles	sont

PRESENT SUBJUNCTIVE

je	sois
tu	sois
il/elle/on	soit
nous	soyons
vous	soyez
ils/elles	soient

PERFECT

j'	ai été
tu	as été
il/elle/on	a été
nous	avons été
vous	avez été
ils/elles	ont été

IMPERFECT

j'	étais
tu	étais
il/elle/on	était
nous	étions
vous	étiez
ils/elles	étaient

FUTURE

je	serai
tu	seras
il/elle/on	sera
nous	serons
vous	serez
ils/elles	seront

CONDITIONAL

je	serais
tu	serais
il/elle/on	serait
nous	serions
vous	seriez
ils/elles	seraient

IMPERATIVE

sois / soyons / soyez

PAST PARTICIPLE

été

PRESENT PARTICIPLE

étant

--- EXAMPLE PHRASES ---

Mon père **est** professeur.
Quelle heure **est**-il? – Il **est** dix heures.
Ils ne **sont** pas encore arrivés.

My father's a teacher.
What time is it? – It's 10 o'clock.
They haven't arrived yet.

Table
37

to do; to make **faire**

PRESENT

je	fais
tu	fais
il/elle/on	fait
nous	faisons
vous	faites
ils/elles	font

PRESENT SUBJUNCTIVE

je	fasse
tu	fasses
il/elle/on	fasse
nous	fassions
vous	fassiez
ils/elles	fassent

PERFECT

j'	ai fait
tu	as fait
il/elle/on	a fait
nous	avons fait
vous	avez fait
ils/elles	ont fait

IMPERFECT

je	faisais
tu	faisais
il/elle/on	faisait
nous	faisions
vous	faisiez
ils/elles	faisaient

FUTURE

je	ferai
tu	feras
il/elle/on	fera
nous	ferons
vous	ferez
ils/elles	feront

CONDITIONAL

je	ferais
tu	ferais
il/elle/on	ferait
nous	ferions
vous	feriez
ils/elles	feraient

IMPERATIVE
fais / faisons / faites

PAST PARTICIPLE
fait

PRESENT PARTICIPLE
faisant

—————— EXAMPLE PHRASES ——————

Qu'est-ce que tu **fais**?	*What are you doing?*
Qu'est-ce qu'il **a fait**?	*What has he done?* or *What did he do?*
J'**ai fait** un gâteau.	*I've made a cake.* or *I made a cake.*
Il **s'est fait** couper les cheveux.	*He's had his hair cut.*

- Note that **se faire** follows the same pattern, but takes **être** in the perfect tense. For an example of a reflexive verb in full, see verb table **83 se taire**.

Table
38

falloir *to be necessary*

PRESENT	**PRESENT SUBJUNCTIVE**
il faut	il faille

PERFECT	**IMPERFECT**
il a fallu	il fallait

FUTURE	**CONDITIONAL**
il faudra	il faudrait

IMPERATIVE	**PAST PARTICIPLE**
not used	fallu

PRESENT PARTICIPLE
not used

─────────── EXAMPLE PHRASES ───────────

Il **faut** se dépêcher!   *We have to hurry up!*
Il me **fallait** de l'argent.   *I needed money.*
Il **faudra** que tu sois là à 8 heures.   *You'll have to be there at 8.*

PRESENT

je	finis
tu	finis
il/elle/on	finit
nous	finissons
vous	finissez
ils/elles	finissent

PRESENT SUBJUNCTIVE

je	finisse
tu	finisses
il/elle/on	finisse
nous	finissions
vous	finissiez
ils/elles	finissent

PERFECT

j'	ai fini
tu	as fini
il/elle/on	a fini
nous	avons fini
vous	avez fini
ils/elles	ont fini

IMPERFECT

je	finissais
tu	finissais
il/elle/on	finissait
nous	finissions
vous	finissiez
ils/elles	finissaient

FUTURE

je	finirai
tu	finiras
il/elle/on	finira
nous	finirons
vous	finirez
ils/elles	finiront

CONDITIONAL

je	finirais
tu	finirais
il/elle/on	finirait
nous	finirions
vous	finiriez
ils/elles	finiraient

IMPERATIVE
finis / finissons / finissez

PAST PARTICIPLE
fini

PRESENT PARTICIPLE
finissant

— EXAMPLE PHRASES —

Finis ta soupe!
J'ai **fini**!
Je **finirai** mes devoirs demain.

Finish your soup!
I've finished!
I'll finish my homework tomorrow.

Table
40

fuir *to flee*

PRESENT		PRESENT SUBJUNCTIVE	
je	fuis	je	fuie
tu	fuis	tu	fuies
il/elle/on	fuit	il/elle/on	fuie
nous	fuyons	nous	fuyions
vous	fuyez	vous	fuyiez
ils/elles	fuient	ils/elles	fuient

PERFECT		IMPERFECT	
j'	ai fui	je	fuyais
tu	as fui	tu	fuyais
il/elle/on	a fui	il/elle/on	fuyait
nous	avons fui	nous	fuyions
vous	avez fui	vous	fuyiez
ils/elles	ont fui	ils/elles	fuyaient

FUTURE		CONDITIONAL	
je	fuirai	je	fuirais
tu	fuiras	tu	fuirais
il/elle/on	fuira	il/elle/on	fuirait
nous	fuirons	nous	fuirions
vous	fuirez	vous	fuiriez
ils/elles	fuiront	ils/elles	fuiraient

IMPERATIVE	PAST PARTICIPLE
fuis / fuyons / fuyez	fui

PRESENT PARTICIPLE
fuyant

——————————— EXAMPLE PHRASES ———————————

Ils **ont fui** leur pays.	*They fled their country.*
Le robinet **fuit**.	*The tap is dripping.*

PRESENT

je	hais
tu	hais
il/elle/on	hait
nous	haïssons
vous	haïssez
ils/elles	haïssent

PRESENT SUBJUNCTIVE

je	haïsse
tu	haïsses
il/elle/on	haïsse
nous	haïssions
vous	haïssiez
ils/elles	haïssent

PERFECT

j'	ai haï
tu	as haï
il/elle/on	a haï
nous	avons haï
vous	avez haï
ils/elles	ont haï

IMPERFECT

je	haïssais
tu	haïssais
il/elle/on	haïssait
nous	haïssions
vous	haïssiez
ils/elles	haïssaient

FUTURE

je	haïrai
tu	haïras
il/elle/on	haïra
nous	haïrons
vous	haïrez
ils/elles	haïront

CONDITIONAL

je	haïrais
tu	haïrais
il/elle/on	haïrait
nous	haïrions
vous	haïriez
ils/elles	haïraient

IMPERATIVE

hais / haïssons / haïssez

PAST PARTICIPLE

haï

PRESENT PARTICIPLE

haïssant

— EXAMPLE PHRASES —

Je te **hais**!
Elle **haïssait** tout le monde.
Ils **se haïssent**.

I hate you!
She hated everyone.
They hate each other.

• Note that *se haïr* follows the same pattern, but takes *être* in the perfect tense. For an example of a reflexive verb in full, see verb table **83 se taire**.

Table
42

jeter *to throw*

PRESENT	
je	jette
tu	jettes
il/elle/on	jette
nous	jetons
vous	jetez
ils/elles	jettent

PRESENT SUBJUNCTIVE	
je	jette
tu	jettes
il/elle/on	jette
nous	jetions
vous	jetiez
ils/elles	jettent

PERFECT	
j'	ai jeté
tu	as jeté
il/elle/on	a jeté
nous	avons jeté
vous	avez jeté
ils/elles	ont jeté

IMPERFECT	
je	jetais
tu	jetais
il/elle/on	jetait
nous	jetions
vous	jetiez
ils/elles	jetaient

FUTURE	
je	jetterai
tu	jetteras
il/elle/on	jettera
nous	jetterons
vous	jetterez
ils/elles	jetteront

CONDITIONAL	
je	jetterais
tu	jetterais
il/elle/on	jetterait
nous	jetterions
vous	jetteriez
ils/elles	jetteraient

IMPERATIVE
jette / jetons / jetez

PRESENT PARTICIPLE
jetant

PAST PARTICIPLE
jeté

--- EXAMPLE PHRASES ---

Ne **jette** pas tes vêtements par terre.
Don't throw your clothes on the floor.

Elle **a jeté** son chewing-gum par la fenêtre.
She threw her chewing gum out of the window.

Ils ne **jettent** jamais rien.
They never throw anything away.

PRESENT

je	joins
tu	joins
il/elle/on	joint
nous	joignons
vous	joignez
ils/elles	joignent

PRESENT SUBJUNCTIVE

je	joigne
tu	joignes
il/elle/on	joigne
nous	joignions
vous	joigniez
ils/elles	joignent

PERFECT

j'	ai joint
tu	as joint
il/elle/on	a joint
nous	avons joint
vous	avez joint
ils/elles	ont joint

IMPERFECT

je	joignais
tu	joignais
il/elle/on	joignait
nous	joignions
vous	joigniez
ils/elles	joignaient

FUTURE

je	joindrai
tu	joindras
il/elle/on	joindra
nous	joindrons
vous	joindrez
ils/elles	joindront

CONDITIONAL

je	joindrais
tu	joindrais
il/elle/on	joindrait
nous	joindrions
vous	joindriez
ils/elles	joindraient

IMPERATIVE
joins / joignons / joignez

PAST PARTICIPLE
joint

PRESENT PARTICIPLE
joignant

--- EXAMPLE PHRASES ---

Où est-ce qu'on peut te **joindre** ce week-end?
On **a joint** les deux tables.

Where can we contact you this weekend?
We put the two tables together.

Table
44

lever *to lift*

PRESENT

je	lève
tu	lèves
il/elle/on	lève
nous	levons
vous	levez
ils/elles	lèvent

PRESENT SUBJUNCTIVE

je	lève
tu	lèves
il/elle/on	lève
nous	levions
vous	leviez
ils/elles	lèvent

PERFECT

j'	ai levé
tu	as levé
il/elle/on	a levé
nous	avons levé
vous	avez levé
ils/elles	ont levé

IMPERFECT

je	levais
tu	levais
il/elle/on	levait
nous	levions
vous	leviez
ils/elles	levaient

FUTURE

je	lèverai
tu	lèveras
il/elle/on	lèvera
nous	lèverons
vous	lèverez
ils/elles	lèveront

CONDITIONAL

je	lèverais
tu	lèverais
il/elle/on	lèverait
nous	lèverions
vous	lèveriez
ils/elles	lèveraient

IMPERATIVE

lève / levons / levez

PAST PARTICIPLE

levé

PRESENT PARTICIPLE

levant

—————————— EXAMPLE PHRASES ——————————

Lève la tête. — Lift your head up.
Levez la main! — Put your hand up!
Je **me lève** tous les jours à sept heures. — I get up at 7 every day.

- Note that *se lever* follows the same pattern, but takes **être** in the perfect tense. For an example of a reflexive verb in full, see verb table **83 se taire**.

PRESENT

je	lis
tu	lis
il/elle/on	lit
nous	lisons
vous	lisez
ils/elles	lisent

PRESENT SUBJUNCTIVE

je	lise
tu	lises
il/elle/on	lise
nous	lisions
vous	lisiez
ils/elles	lisent

PERFECT

j'	ai lu
tu	as lu
il/elle/on	a lu
nous	avons lu
vous	avez lu
ils/elles	ont lu

IMPERFECT

je	lisais
tu	lisais
il/elle/on	lisait
nous	lisions
vous	lisiez
ils/elles	lisaient

FUTURE

je	lirai
tu	liras
il/elle/on	lira
nous	lirons
vous	lirez
ils/elles	liront

CONDITIONAL

je	lirais
tu	lirais
il/elle/on	lirait
nous	lirions
vous	liriez
ils/elles	liraient

IMPERATIVE
lis / lisons / lisez

PAST PARTICIPLE
lu

PRESENT PARTICIPLE
lisant

--- EXAMPLE PHRASES ---

Vous **avez lu** "Madame Bovary"?
Je le **lirai** dans l'avion.
Elle lui **lisait** une histoire.

Have you read "Madame Bovary"?
I'll read it on the plane.
She was reading him a story.

Table
46

manger *to eat*

PRESENT

je	mange
tu	manges
il/elle/on	mange
nous	mangeons
vous	mangez
ils/elles	mangent

PRESENT SUBJUNCTIVE

je	mange
tu	manges
il/elle/on	mange
nous	mangions
vous	mangiez
ils/elles	mangent

PERFECT

j'	ai mangé
tu	as mangé
il/elle/on	a mangé
nous	avons mangé
vous	avez mangé
ils/elles	ont mangé

IMPERFECT

je	mangeais
tu	mangeais
il/elle/on	mangeait
nous	mangions
vous	mangiez
ils/elles	mangeaient

FUTURE

je	mangerai
tu	mangeras
il/elle/on	mangera
nous	mangerons
vous	mangerez
ils/elles	mangeront

CONDITIONAL

je	mangerais
tu	mangerais
il/elle/on	mangerait
nous	mangerions
vous	mangeriez
ils/elles	mangeraient

IMPERATIVE

mange / mangeons / mangez

PAST PARTICIPLE

mangé

PRESENT PARTICIPLE

mangeant

--- EXAMPLE PHRASES ---

Nous ne **mangeons** pas souvent ensemble.
Tu **as** assez **mangé**?
Je **mangerai** plus tard.

We don't often eat together.
Have you had enough to eat?
I'll eat later on.

PRESENT

je	maudis
tu	maudis
il/elle/on	maudit
nous	maudissons
vous	maudissez
ils/elles	maudissent

PRESENT SUBJUNCTIVE

je	maudisse
tu	maudisses
il/elle/on	maudisse
nous	maudissions
vous	maudissiez
ils/elles	maudissent

PERFECT

j'	ai maudit
tu	as maudit
il/elle/on	a maudit
nous	avons maudit
vous	avez maudit
ils/elles	ont maudit

IMPERFECT

je	maudissais
tu	maudissais
il/elle/on	maudissait
nous	maudissions
vous	maudissiez
ils/elles	maudissaient

FUTURE

je	maudirai
tu	maudiras
il/elle/on	maudira
nous	maudirons
vous	maudirez
ils/elles	maudiront

CONDITIONAL

je	maudirais
tu	maudirais
il/elle/on	maudirait
nous	maudirions
vous	maudiriez
ils/elles	maudiraient

IMPERATIVE

maudis / maudissons / maudissez

PAST PARTICIPLE

maudit

PRESENT PARTICIPLE

maudissant

--------- EXAMPLE PHRASES ---------

Ils **maudissent** leurs ennemis.   _They curse their enemies._
Ce **maudit** stylo ne marche pas!   _This blasted pen doesn't work!_

Table
48

mettre *to put*

PRESENT		PRESENT SUBJUNCTIVE	
je	mets	je	mette
tu	mets	tu	mettes
il/elle/on	met	il/elle/on	mette
nous	mettons	nous	mettions
vous	mettez	vous	mettiez
ils/elles	mettent	ils/elles	mettent

PERFECT		IMPERFECT	
j'	ai mis	je	mettais
tu	as mis	tu	mettais
il/elle/on	a mis	il/elle/on	mettait
nous	avons mis	nous	mettions
vous	avez mis	vous	mettiez
ils/elles	ont mis	ils/elles	mettaient

FUTURE		CONDITIONAL	
je	mettrai	je	mettrais
tu	mettras	tu	mettrais
il/elle/on	mettra	il/elle/on	mettrait
nous	mettrons	nous	mettrions
vous	mettrez	vous	mettriez
ils/elles	mettront	ils/elles	mettraient

IMPERATIVE
mets / mettons / mettez

PAST PARTICIPLE
mis

PRESENT PARTICIPLE
mettant

─────── EXAMPLE PHRASES ───────

Mets ton manteau!   *Put your coat on!*
Où est-ce que tu **as mis** les clés?   *Where have you put the keys?*
J'**ai mis** le livre sur la table.   *I put the book on the table.*
Elle **s'est mise** à pleurer.   *She started crying.*

• Note that *se mettre* follows the same pattern, but takes **être** in the perfect tense. For an example of a reflexive verb in full, see verb table **83 se taire**.

PRESENT

je	monte
tu	montes
il/elle/on	monte
nous	montons
vous	montez
ils/elles	montent

PRESENT SUBJUNCTIVE

je	monte
tu	montes
il/elle/on	monte
nous	montions
vous	montiez
ils/elles	montent

PERFECT

je	suis monté(e)
tu	es monté(e)
il/elle/on	est monté(e)
nous	sommes monté(e)s
vous	êtes monté(e)(s)
ils/elles	sont monté(e)s

IMPERFECT

je	montais
tu	montais
il/elle/on	montait
nous	montions
vous	montiez
ils/elles	montaient

FUTURE

je	monterai
tu	monteras
il/elle/on	montera
nous	monterons
vous	monterez
ils/elles	monteront

CONDITIONAL

je	monterais
tu	monterais
il/elle/on	monterait
nous	monterions
vous	monteriez
ils/elles	monteraient

IMPERATIVE

monte / montons / montez

PAST PARTICIPLE

monté

PRESENT PARTICIPLE

montant

EXAMPLE PHRASES

Je **suis montée** tout en haut de la tour.

I went all the way up the tower.

Monte dans la voiture, je t'emmène.

Get into the car, I'll take you there.

Il s'est tordu la cheville en **montant** à une échelle.

He twisted his ankle going up a ladder.

- Note that **monter** takes **avoir** in the perfect tense when it is used with a direct object.
- The verb **surmonter** follows the same pattern as **monter**, but takes **avoir** in the perfect tense.

Table
50

mordre *to bite*

PRESENT

je	mords
tu	mords
il/elle/on	mord
nous	mordons
vous	mordez
ils/elles	mordent

PRESENT SUBJUNCTIVE

je	morde
tu	mordes
il/elle/on	morde
nous	mordions
vous	mordiez
ils/elles	mordent

PERFECT

j'	ai mordu
tu	as mordu
il/elle/on	a mordu
nous	avons mordu
vous	avez mordu
ils/elles	ont mordu

IMPERFECT

je	mordais
tu	mordais
il/elle/on	mordait
nous	mordions
vous	mordiez
ils/elles	mordaient

FUTURE

je	mordrai
tu	mordras
il/elle/on	mordra
nous	mordrons
vous	mordrez
ils/elles	mordront

CONDITIONAL

je	mordrais
tu	mordrais
il/elle/on	mordrait
nous	mordrions
vous	mordriez
ils/elles	mordraient

IMPERATIVE
mords / mordons / mordez

PAST PARTICIPLE
mordu

PRESENT PARTICIPLE
mordant

=========== EXAMPLE PHRASES ===========

Le chien m'a **mordue**.
Il ne va pas te **mordre**!

The dog bit me.
He won't bite!

PRESENT

je	mouds
tu	mouds
il/elle/on	moud
nous	moulons
vous	moulez
ils/elles	moulent

PRESENT SUBJUNCTIVE

je	moule
tu	moules
il/elle/on	moule
nous	moulions
vous	mouliez
ils/elles	moulent

PERFECT

j'	ai moulu
tu	as moulu
il/elle/on	a moulu
nous	avons moulu
vous	avez moulu
ils/elles	ont moulu

IMPERFECT

je	moulais
tu	moulais
il/elle/on	moulait
nous	moulions
vous	mouliez
ils/elles	moulaient

FUTURE

je	moudrai
tu	moudras
il/elle/on	moudra
nous	moudrons
vous	moudrez
ils/elles	moudront

CONDITIONAL

je	moudrais
tu	moudrais
il/elle/on	moudrait
nous	moudrions
vous	moudriez
ils/elles	moudraient

IMPERATIVE
mouds / moulons / moulez

PAST PARTICIPLE
moulu

PRESENT PARTICIPLE
moulant

──────── EXAMPLE PHRASES ────────

J'**ai moulu** du café pour demain matin.

I've ground some coffee for tomorrow morning.

Table
52

mourir *to die*

PRESENT

je	meurs
tu	meurs
il/elle/on	meurt
nous	mourons
vous	mourez
ils/elles	meurent

PRESENT SUBJUNCTIVE

je	meure
tu	meures
il/elle/on	meure
nous	mourions
vous	mouriez
ils/elles	meurent

PERFECT

je	suis mort(e)
tu	es mort(e)
il/elle/on	est mort(e)
nous	sommes mort(e)s
vous	êtes mort(e)(s)
ils/elles	sont mort(e)s

IMPERFECT

je	mourais
tu	mourais
il/elle/on	mourait
nous	mourions
vous	mouriez
ils/elles	mouraient

FUTURE

je	mourrai
tu	mourras
il/elle/on	mourra
nous	mourrons
vous	mourrez
ils/elles	mourront

CONDITIONAL

je	mourrais
tu	mourrais
il/elle/on	mourrait
nous	mourrions
vous	mourriez
ils/elles	mourraient

IMPERATIVE

meurs / mourons / mourez

PAST PARTICIPLE

mort

PRESENT PARTICIPLE

mourant

EXAMPLE PHRASES

Elle **est morte** en 1998. *She died in 1998.*
Ils **sont morts**. *They're dead.*
On **meurt** de froid ici! *We're freezing to death in here!*

PRESENT

je	nais
tu	nais
il/elle/on	naît
nous	naissons
vous	naissez
ils/elles	naissent

PRESENT SUBJUNCTIVE

je	naisse
tu	naisses
il/elle/on	naisse
nous	naissions
vous	naissiez
ils/elles	naissent

PERFECT

je	suis né(e)
tu	es né(e)
il/elle/on	est né(e)
nous	sommes né(e)s
vous	êtes né(e)(s)
ils/elles	sont né(e)s

IMPERFECT

je	naissais
tu	naissais
il/elle/on	naissait
nous	naissions
vous	naissiez
ils/elles	naissaient

FUTURE

je	naîtrai
tu	naîtras
il/elle/on	naîtra
nous	naîtrons
vous	naîtrez
ils/elles	naîtront

CONDITIONAL

je	naîtrais
tu	naîtrais
il/elle/on	naîtrait
nous	naîtrions
vous	naîtriez
ils/elles	naîtraient

IMPERATIVE

nais / naissons / naissez

PAST PARTICIPLE

né

PRESENT PARTICIPLE

naissant

--- EXAMPLE PHRASES ---

Je **suis née** le 12 février.	I was born on 12 February.
Le bébé de Delphine **naîtra** en mars.	Delphine is going to have a baby in March.
Quand est-ce que tu **es né**?	When were you born?

Table
54

nettoyer *to clean*

PRESENT

je	nettoie
tu	nettoies
il/elle/on	nettoie
nous	nettoyons
vous	nettoyez
ils/elles	nettoient

PRESENT SUBJUNCTIVE

je	nettoie
tu	nettoies
il/elle/on	nettoie
nous	nettoyions
vous	nettoyiez
ils/elles	nettoient

PERFECT

j'	ai nettoyé
tu	as nettoyé
il/elle/on	a nettoyé
nous	avons nettoyé
vous	avez nettoyé
ils/elles	ont nettoyé

IMPERFECT

je	nettoyais
tu	nettoyais
il/elle/on	nettoyait
nous	nettoyions
vous	nettoyiez
ils/elles	nettoyaient

FUTURE

je	nettoierai
tu	nettoieras
il/elle/on	nettoiera
nous	nettoierons
vous	nettoierez
ils/elles	nettoieront

CONDITIONAL

je	nettoierais
tu	nettoierais
il/elle/on	nettoierait
nous	nettoierions
vous	nettoieriez
ils/elles	nettoieraient

IMPERATIVE

nettoie / nettoyons / nettoyez

PAST PARTICIPLE

nettoyé

PRESENT PARTICIPLE

nettoyant

─────────────── EXAMPLE PHRASES ───────────────

Richard **a nettoyé** tout l'appartement.

Richard has cleaned the whole flat.

Elle **nettoyait** le sol en écoutant la radio.

She was cleaning the floor while listening to the radio.

Je ne **nettoie** pas souvent mes lunettes.

I don't clean my glasses very often.

Table
55

to offer **offrir**

PRESENT

j'	offre
tu	offres
il/elle/on	offre
nous	offrons
vous	offrez
ils/elles	offrent

PRESENT SUBJUNCTIVE

j'	offre
tu	offres
il/elle/on	offre
nous	offrions
vous	offriez
ils/elles	offrent

PERFECT

j'	ai offert
tu	as offert
il/elle/on	a offert
nous	avons offert
vous	avez offert
ils/elles	ont offert

IMPERFECT

j'	offrais
tu	offrais
il/elle/on	offrait
nous	offrions
vous	offriez
ils/elles	offraient

FUTURE

j'	offrirai
tu	offriras
il/elle/on	offrira
nous	offrirons
vous	offrirez
ils/elles	offriront

CONDITIONAL

j'	offrirais
tu	offrirais
il/elle/on	offrirait
nous	offririons
vous	offririez
ils/elles	offriraient

IMPERATIVE
offre / offrons / offrez

PAST PARTICIPLE
offert

PRESENT PARTICIPLE
offrant

--- EXAMPLE PHRASES ---

On lui **a offert** un poste de secrétaire.
Offre-lui des fleurs.
Viens, je t'**offre** à boire.
Je **me suis offert** un nouveau stylo.

They offered her a secreterial post.

Give her some flowers.
Come on, I'll buy you a drink.
I treated myself to a new pen.

• Note that s'**offrir** follows the same pattern, but takes *être* in the perfect tense. For an example of a reflexive verb in full, see verb table **7** *s'asseoir*.

Table
56

ouvrir *to open*

PRESENT		PRESENT SUBJUNCTIVE	
j'	ouvre	j'	ouvre
tu	ouvres	tu	ouvres
il/elle/on	ouvre	il/elle/on	ouvre
nous	ouvrons	nous	ouvrions
vous	ouvrez	vous	ouvriez
ils/elles	ouvrent	ils/elles	ouvrent

PERFECT		IMPERFECT	
j'	ai ouvert	j'	ouvrais
tu	as ouvert	tu	ouvrais
il/elle/on	a ouvert	il/elle/on	ouvrait
nous	avons ouvert	nous	ouvrions
vous	avez ouvert	vous	ouvriez
ils/elles	ont ouvert	ils/elles	ouvraient

FUTURE		CONDITIONAL	
j'	ouvrirai	j'	ouvrirais
tu	ouvriras	tu	ouvrirais
il/elle/on	ouvrira	il/elle/on	ouvrirait
nous	ouvrirons	nous	ouvririons
vous	ouvrirez	vous	ouvririez
ils/elles	ouvriront	ils/elles	ouvriraient

IMPERATIVE
ouvre / ouvrons / ouvrez

PAST PARTICIPLE
ouvert

PRESENT PARTICIPLE
ouvrant

--- EXAMPLE PHRASES ---

Elle **a ouvert** la porte.	*She opened the door.*
Est-ce que tu pourrais **ouvrir** la fenêtre?	*Could you open the window?*
Je me suis coupé en **ouvrant** une boîte de conserve.	*I cut myself opening a tin.*
La porte **s'est ouverte**.	*The door opened.*

- Note that *s'ouvrir* follows the same pattern, but takes *être* in the perfect tense. For an example of a reflexive verb in full, see verb table **7** *s'asseoir*.

PRESENT

je	parais
tu	parais
il/elle/on	paraît
nous	paraissons
vous	paraissez
ils/elles	paraissent

PRESENT SUBJUNCTIVE

je	paraisse
tu	paraisses
il/elle/on	paraisse
nous	paraissions
vous	paraissiez
ils/elles	paraissent

PERFECT

j'	ai paru
tu	as paru
il/elle/on	a paru
nous	avons paru
vous	avez paru
ils/elles	ont paru

IMPERFECT

je	paraissais
tu	paraissais
il/elle/on	paraissait
nous	paraissions
vous	paraissiez
ils/elles	paraissaient

FUTURE

je	paraîtrai
tu	paraîtras
il/elle/on	paraîtra
nous	paraîtrons
vous	paraîtrez
ils/elles	paraîtront

CONDITIONAL

je	paraîtrais
tu	paraîtrais
il/elle/on	paraîtrait
nous	paraîtrions
vous	paraîtriez
ils/elles	paraîtraient

IMPERATIVE
parais / paraissons / paraissez

PAST PARTICIPLE
paru

PRESENT PARTICIPLE
paraissant

--- EXAMPLE PHRASES ---

Elle **paraissait** fatiguée.	She seemed tired.
Gisèle **paraît** plus jeune que son âge.	Gisèle doesn't look her age.
Il **paraît** qu'il fait chaud toute l'année là-bas.	Apparently it's hot all year round over there.

- Note that the verb **apparaître** follows the same pattern as **paraître**, but takes **être** in the perfect tense.

Table
58

partir *to go; to leave*

PRESENT		PRESENT SUBJUNCTIVE	
je	pars	je	parte
tu	pars	tu	partes
il/elle/on	part	il/elle/on	parte
nous	partons	nous	partions
vous	partez	vous	partiez
ils/elles	partent	ils/elles	partent

PERFECT		IMPERFECT	
je	suis parti(e)	je	partais
tu	es parti(e)	tu	partais
il/elle/on	est parti(e)	il/elle/on	partait
nous	sommes parti(e)s	nous	partions
vous	êtes parti(e)(s)	vous	partiez
ils/elles	sont parti(e)s	ils/elles	partaient

FUTURE		CONDITIONAL	
je	partirai	je	partirais
tu	partiras	tu	partirais
il/elle/on	partira	il/elle/on	partirait
nous	partirons	nous	partirions
vous	partirez	vous	partiriez
ils/elles	partiront	ils/elles	partiraient

IMPERATIVE
pars / partons / partez

PAST PARTICIPLE
parti

PRESENT PARTICIPLE
partant

— EXAMPLE PHRASES —

On **part** en vacances le 15 août.
Ne **partez** pas sans moi!
Elle **est partie** tôt ce matin.

We're going on holiday on 15 August.
Don't leave without me!
She left early this morning.

Table
59

to pass **passer**

PRESENT		PRESENT SUBJUNCTIVE	
je	passe	je	passe
tu	passes	tu	passes
il/elle/on	passe	il/elle/on	passe
nous	passons	nous	passions
vous	passez	vous	passiez
ils/elles	passent	ils/elles	passent

PERFECT		IMPERFECT	
j'	ai passé	je	passais
tu	as passé	tu	passais
il/elle/on	a passé	il/elle/on	passait
nous	avons passé	nous	passions
vous	avez passé	vous	passiez
ils/elles	ont passé	ils/elles	passaient

FUTURE		CONDITIONAL	
je	passerai	je	passerais
tu	passeras	tu	passerais
il/elle/on	passera	il/elle/on	passerait
nous	passerons	nous	passerions
vous	passerez	vous	passeriez
ils/elles	passeront	ils/elles	passeraient

IMPERATIVE
passe / passons / passez

PAST PARTICIPLE
passé

PRESENT PARTICIPLE
passant

―――――― EXAMPLE PHRASES ――――――

Les mois **ont passé**.	Months passed.
Il **a passé** son examen en juin.	He took his exam in June.
Elle y **a passé** deux mois.	She spent two months there.
Elle **est passée** me dire bonjour.	She came by to say hello.
L'histoire **se passe** au Mexique.	The story takes place in Mexico.

- Note that *passer* can also take **être** in the perfect tense when it means "to call in" or "to go through".
- Note that *se passer* follows the same pattern, but takes **être** in the perfect tense. For an example of a reflexive verb in full, see verb table **7** *s'asseoir*.

Table
60

payer *to pay*

PRESENT

je	paye
tu	payes
il/elle/on	paye
nous	payons
vous	payez
ils/elles	payent

PRESENT SUBJUNCTIVE

je	paye
tu	payes
il/elle/on	paye
nous	payions
vous	payiez
ils/elles	payent

PERFECT

j'	ai payé
tu	as payé
il/elle/on	a payé
nous	avons payé
vous	avez payé
ils/elles	ont payé

IMPERFECT

je	payais
tu	payais
il/elle/on	payait
nous	payions
vous	payiez
ils/elles	payaient

FUTURE

je	payerai
tu	payeras
il/elle/on	payera
nous	payerons
vous	payerez
ils/elles	payeront

CONDITIONAL

je	payerais
tu	payerais
il/elle/on	payerait
nous	payerions
vous	payeriez
ils/elles	payeraient

IMPERATIVE
paye / payons / payez

PAST PARTICIPLE
payé

PRESENT PARTICIPLE
payant

---------------- EXAMPLE PHRASES ----------------

Tu l'**as payé** combien? — *How much did you pay for it?*
Ma patronne me **paiera** demain. — *My boss will pay me tomorrow.*
Les étudiants **payent** moitié prix. — *Students pay half price.*

Table
61

to paint **peindre**

PRESENT

je	peins
tu	peins
il/elle/on	peint
nous	peignons
vous	peignez
ils/elles	peignent

PRESENT SUBJUNCTIVE

je	peigne
tu	peignes
il/elle/on	peigne
nous	peignions
vous	peigniez
ils/elles	peignent

PERFECT

j'	ai peint
tu	as peint
il/elle/on	a peint
nous	avons peint
vous	avez peint
ils/elles	ont peint

IMPERFECT

je	peignais
tu	peignais
il/elle/on	peignait
nous	peignions
vous	peigniez
ils/elles	peignaient

FUTURE

je	peindrai
tu	peindras
il/elle/on	peindra
nous	peindrons
vous	peindrez
ils/elles	peindront

CONDITIONAL

je	peindrais
tu	peindrais
il/elle/on	peindrait
nous	peindrions
vous	peindriez
ils/elles	peindraient

IMPERATIVE

peins / peignons / peignez

PAST PARTICIPLE

peint

PRESENT PARTICIPLE

peignant

——————— EXAMPLE PHRASES ———————

On **a peint** l'entrée en bleu clair.
Ce tableau **a été peint** en 1913.

We painted the hall light blue.
This picture was painted in 1913.

Table
62

perdre *to lose*

PRESENT

je	perds
tu	perds
il/elle/on	perd
nous	perdons
vous	perdez
ils/elles	perdent

PRESENT SUBJUNCTIVE

je	perde
tu	perdes
il/elle/on	perde
nous	perdions
vous	perdiez
ils/elles	perdent

PERFECT

j'	ai perdu
tu	as perdu
il/elle/on	a perdu
nous	avons perdu
vous	avez perdu
ils/elles	ont perdu

IMPERFECT

je	perdais
tu	perdais
il/elle/on	perdait
nous	perdions
vous	perdiez
ils/elles	perdaient

FUTURE

je	perdrai
tu	perdras
il/elle/on	perdra
nous	perdrons
vous	perdrez
ils/elles	perdront

CONDITIONAL

je	perdrais
tu	perdrais
il/elle/on	perdrait
nous	perdrions
vous	perdriez
ils/elles	perdraient

IMPERATIVE
perds / perdons / perdez

PAST PARTICIPLE
perdu

PRESENT PARTICIPLE
perdant

=========== EXAMPLE PHRASES ===========

J'**ai perdu** mon porte-monnaie dans le métro.
I lost my purse on the underground.

L'Italie **a perdu** un à zéro.
Italy lost one-nil.

Si tu **te perds**, appelle-moi.
Call me if you get lost.

• Note that *se perdre* follows the same pattern, but takes *être* in the perfect tense.
For an example of a reflexive verb in full, see verb table **83 se taire**.

PRESENT

je	plais
tu	plais
il/elle/on	plaît
nous	plaisons
vous	plaisez
ils/elles	plaisent

PRESENT SUBJUNCTIVE

je	plaise
tu	plaises
il/elle/on	plaise
nous	plaisions
vous	plaisiez
ils/elles	plaisent

PERFECT

j'	ai plu
tu	as plu
il/elle/on	a plu
nous	avons plu
vous	avez plu
ils/elles	ont plu

IMPERFECT

je	plaisais
tu	plaisais
il/elle/on	plaisait
nous	plaisions
vous	plaisiez
ils/elles	plaisaient

FUTURE

je	plairai
tu	plairas
il/elle/on	plaira
nous	plairons
vous	plairez
ils/elles	plairont

CONDITIONAL

je	plairais
tu	plairais
il/elle/on	plairait
nous	plairions
vous	plairiez
ils/elles	plairaient

IMPERATIVE

plais / plaisons / plaisez

PAST PARTICIPLE

plu

PRESENT PARTICIPLE

plaisant

——————— EXAMPLE PHRASES ———————

Le menu ne me **plaît** pas.	I don't like the menu.
Ça te **plairait** d'aller à la mer?	Would you like to go to the seaside?
Ça t'**a plu**, le film?	Did you like the film?
s'il te **plaît**	please
s'il vous **plaît**	please

Table
64

pleuvoir *to rain*

PRESENT	PRESENT SUBJUNCTIVE
il pleut	il pleuve

PERFECT	IMPERFECT
il a plu	il pleuvait

FUTURE	CONDITIONAL
il pleuvra	il pleuvrait

IMPERATIVE	PAST PARTICIPLE
not used	plu

PRESENT PARTICIPLE
not used

—————— EXAMPLE PHRASES ——————

Il **a plu** toute la journée.	*It rained all day long.*
Il **pleut** beaucoup à Glasgow.	*It rains a lot in Glasgow.*
J'espère qu'il ne **pleuvra** pas demain.	*I hope it won't be raining tomorrow.*

PRESENT

je	peux
tu	peux
il/elle/on	peut
nous	pouvons
vous	pouvez
ils/elles	peuvent

PRESENT SUBJUNCTIVE

je	puisse
tu	puisses
il/elle/on	puisse
nous	puissions
vous	puissiez
ils/elles	puissent

PERFECT

j'	ai pu
tu	as pu
il/elle/on	a pu
nous	avons pu
vous	avez pu
ils/elles	ont pu

IMPERFECT

je	pouvais
tu	pouvais
il/elle/on	pouvait
nous	pouvions
vous	pouviez
ils/elles	pouvaient

FUTURE

je	pourrai
tu	pourras
il/elle/on	pourra
nous	pourrons
vous	pourrez
ils/elles	pourront

CONDITIONAL

je	pourrais
tu	pourrais
il/elle/on	pourrait
nous	pourrions
vous	pourriez
ils/elles	pourraient

IMPERATIVE

not used

PAST PARTICIPLE

pu

PRESENT PARTICIPLE

pouvant

——————— EXAMPLE PHRASES ———————

Je **peux** t'aider, si tu veux.	I can help you if you like.
J'ai fait tout ce que j'**ai pu**.	I did all I could.
Je ne **pourrai** pas venir samedi.	I won't be able to come on Saturday.

Table
66

prendre *to take*

PRESENT

je	prends
tu	prends
il/elle/on	prend
nous	prenons
vous	prenez
ils/elles	prennent

PRESENT SUBJUNCTIVE

je	prenne
tu	prennes
il/elle/on	prenne
nous	prenions
vous	preniez
ils/elles	prennent

PERFECT

j'	ai pris
tu	as pris
il/elle/on	a pris
nous	avons pris
vous	avez pris
ils/elles	ont pris

IMPERFECT

je	prenais
tu	prenais
il/elle/on	prenait
nous	prenions
vous	preniez
ils/elles	prenaient

FUTURE

je	prendrai
tu	prendras
il/elle/on	prendra
nous	prendrons
vous	prendrez
ils/elles	prendront

CONDITIONAL

je	prendrais
tu	prendrais
il/elle/on	prendrait
nous	prendrions
vous	prendriez
ils/elles	prendraient

IMPERATIVE
prends / prenons / prenez

PAST PARTICIPLE
pris

PRESENT PARTICIPLE
prenant

──────────── EXAMPLE PHRASES ────────────

J'**ai pris** plein de photos.	I took lots of pictures.
N'oublie pas de **prendre** ton passeport.	Don't forget to take your passport.
Il **prendra** le train de 8h20.	He'll take the 8.20 train.
Pour qui est-ce qu'il **se prend**?	Who does he think he is?

- Note that **se prendre** follows the same pattern, but takes **être** in the perfect tense. For an example of a reflexive verb in full, see verb table **83 se taire**.

PRESENT

je	protège
tu	protèges
il/elle/on	protège
nous	protégeons
vous	protégez
ils/elles	protègent

PRESENT SUBJUNCTIVE

je	protège
tu	protèges
il/elle/on	protège
nous	protégions
vous	protégiez
ils/elles	protègent

PERFECT

j'	ai protégé
tu	as protégé
il/elle/on	a protégé
nous	avons protégé
vous	avez protégé
ils/elles	ont protégé

IMPERFECT

je	protégeais
tu	protégeais
il/elle/on	protégeait
nous	protégions
vous	protégiez
ils/elles	protégeaient

FUTURE

je	protégerai
tu	protégeras
il/elle/on	protégera
nous	protégerons
vous	protégerez
ils/elles	protégeront

CONDITIONAL

je	protégerais
tu	protégerais
il/elle/on	protégerait
nous	protégerions
vous	protégeriez
ils/elles	protégeraient

IMPERATIVE

protège / protégeons / protégez

PAST PARTICIPLE

protégé

PRESENT PARTICIPLE

protégeant

--- EXAMPLE PHRASES ---

Il **protège** sa petite sœur à l'école.

Protège ton livre de la pluie.
Le champ **est protégé** du vent
par la colline.

He protects his little sister at
school.
Protect your book from the rain.
The field is sheltered from the wind
by the hill.

Table
68

recevoir *to receive*

PRESENT		**PRESENT SUBJUNCTIVE**	
je	reçois	je	reçoive
tu	reçois	tu	reçoives
il/elle/on	reçoit	il/elle/on	reçoive
nous	recevons	nous	recevions
vous	recevez	vous	receviez
ils/elles	reçoivent	ils/elles	reçoivent

PERFECT		**IMPERFECT**	
j'	ai reçu	je	recevais
tu	as reçu	tu	recevais
il/elle/on	a reçu	il/elle/on	recevait
nous	avons reçu	nous	recevions
vous	avez reçu	vous	receviez
ils/elles	ont reçu	ils/elles	recevaient

FUTURE		**CONDITIONAL**	
je	recevrai	je	recevrais
tu	recevras	tu	recevrais
il/elle/on	recevra	il/elle/on	recevrait
nous	recevrons	nous	recevrions
vous	recevrez	vous	recevriez
ils/elles	recevront	ils/elles	recevraient

IMPERATIVE
reçois / recevons / recevez

PAST PARTICIPLE
reçu

PRESENT PARTICIPLE
recevant

━━━━━━━━━━━ EXAMPLE PHRASES ━━━━━━━━━━━

Elle **a reçu** une lettre de
Charlotte.
Je ne **reçois** jamais de courrier.
Elle **recevra** une réponse la
semaine prochaine.

She received a letter from Charlotte.

I never get any mail.
She'll get an answer next week.

Table
69

to go back; to go in **rentrer**

PRESENT

je	rentre
tu	rentres
il/elle/on	rentre
nous	rentrons
vous	rentrez
ils/elles	rentrent

PRESENT SUBJUNCTIVE

je	rentre
tu	rentres
il/elle/on	rentre
nous	rentrions
vous	rentriez
ils/elles	rentrent

PERFECT

je	suis rentré(e)
tu	es rentré(e)
il/elle/on	est rentré(e)
nous	sommes rentré(e)s
vous	êtes rentré(e)(s)
ils/elles	sont rentré(e)s

IMPERFECT

je	rentrais
tu	rentrais
il/elle/on	rentrait
nous	rentrions
vous	rentriez
ils/elles	rentraient

FUTURE

je	rentrerai
tu	rentreras
il/elle/on	rentrera
nous	rentrerons
vous	rentrerez
ils/elles	rentreront

CONDITIONAL

je	rentrerais
tu	rentrerais
il/elle/on	rentrerait
nous	rentrerions
vous	rentreriez
ils/elles	rentreraient

IMPERATIVE

rentre / rentrons / rentrez

PAST PARTICIPLE

rentré

PRESENT PARTICIPLE

rentrant

EXAMPLE PHRASES

Ne **rentre** pas trop tard.
Ils **sont rentrés** dans le magasin.
À quelle heure est-ce qu'elle **est
rentrée**?
Je **rentre** déjeuner à midi.
Il **a** déjà **rentré** la voiture dans le
garage.

Don't come home too late.
They went into the shop.
What time did she get in?

I go home for lunch.
*He's already brought the car into the
garage.*

• Note that **rentrer** takes **avoir** in the perfect tense when it is used with a direct
object.

Table
70

répondre *to answer*

PRESENT		PRESENT SUBJUNCTIVE	
je	réponds	je	réponde
tu	réponds	tu	répondes
il/elle/on	répond	il/elle/on	réponde
nous	répondons	nous	répondions
vous	répondez	vous	répondiez
ils/elles	répondent	ils/elles	répondent

PERFECT		IMPERFECT	
j'	ai répondu	je	répondais
tu	as répondu	tu	répondais
il/elle/on	a répondu	il/elle/on	répondait
nous	avons répondu	nous	répondions
vous	avez répondu	vous	répondiez
ils/elles	ont répondu	ils/elles	répondaient

FUTURE		CONDITIONAL	
je	répondrai	je	répondrais
tu	répondras	tu	répondrais
il/elle/on	répondra	il/elle/on	répondrait
nous	répondrons	nous	répondrions
vous	répondrez	vous	répondriez
ils/elles	répondront	ils/elles	répondraient

IMPERATIVE
réponds / répondons / répondez

PAST PARTICIPLE
répondu

PRESENT PARTICIPLE
répondant

─────── EXAMPLE PHRASES ───────

Lisez le texte et **répondez** aux questions.
Read the text and answer the questions.

C'est elle qui **a répondu** au téléphone.
She answered the phone.

Ça ne **répond** pas.
There's no reply.

PRESENT

je	résous
tu	résous
il/elle/on	résout
nous	résolvons
vous	résolvez
ils/elles	résolvent

PRESENT SUBJUNCTIVE

je	résolve
tu	résolves
il/elle/on	résolve
nous	résolvions
vous	résolviez
ils/elles	résolvent

PERFECT

j'	ai résolu
tu	as résolu
il/elle/on	a résolu
nous	avons résolu
vous	avez résolu
ils/elles	ont résolu

IMPERFECT

je	résolvais
tu	résolvais
il/elle/on	résolvait
nous	résolvions
vous	résolviez
ils/elles	résolvaient

FUTURE

je	résoudrai
tu	résoudras
il/elle/on	résoudra
nous	résoudrons
vous	résoudrez
ils/elles	résoudront

CONDITIONAL

je	résoudrais
tu	résoudrais
il/elle/on	résoudrait
nous	résoudrions
vous	résoudriez
ils/elles	résoudraient

IMPERATIVE
résous / résolvons / résolvez

PAST PARTICIPLE
résolu

PRESENT PARTICIPLE
résolvant

––––––––– EXAMPLE PHRASES –––––––––

J'**ai résolu** le problème.
La violence ne **résout** rien.

I've solved the problem.
Violence doesn't solve anything.

- Note that the verb **dissoudre** follows the same pattern as **résoudre**, except for its past participle which is **dissous** (m), **dissoute** (f).

Table
72

rester *to remain*

PRESENT		PRESENT SUBJUNCTIVE	
je	reste	je	reste
tu	restes	tu	restes
il/elle/on	reste	il/elle/on	reste
nous	restons	nous	restions
vous	restez	vous	restiez
ils/elles	restent	ils/elles	restent

PERFECT		IMPERFECT	
je	suis resté(e)	je	restais
tu	es resté(e)	tu	restais
il/elle/on	est resté(e)	il/elle/on	restait
nous	sommes resté(e)s	nous	restions
vous	êtes resté(e)(s)	vous	restiez
ils/elles	sont resté(e)s	ils/elles	restaient

FUTURE		CONDITIONAL	
je	resterai	je	resterais
tu	resteras	tu	resterais
il/elle/on	restera	il/elle/on	resterait
nous	resterons	nous	resterions
vous	resterez	vous	resteriez
ils/elles	resteront	ils/elles	resteraient

IMPERATIVE
reste / restons / restez

PAST PARTICIPLE
resté

PRESENT PARTICIPLE
restant

─────────── EXAMPLE PHRASES ───────────

Cet été, je **reste** en Écosse.
I'm staying in Scotland this summer.
Ils ne **sont** pas **restés** très longtemps.
They didn't stay very long.
Il leur **restait** encore un peu d'argent.
They still had some money left.

PRESENT

je	retourne
tu	retournes
il/elle/on	retourne
nous	retournons
vous	retournez
ils/elles	retournent

PRESENT SUBJUNCTIVE

je	retourne
tu	retournes
il/elle/on	retourne
nous	retournions
vous	retourniez
ils/elles	retournent

PERFECT

je	suis retourné(e)
tu	es retourné(e)
il/elle/on	est retourné(e)
nous	sommes retourné(e)s
vous	êtes retourné(e)(s)
ils/elles	sont retourné(e)s

IMPERFECT

je	retournais
tu	retournais
il/elle/on	retournait
nous	retournions
vous	retourniez
ils/elles	retournaient

FUTURE

je	retournerai
tu	retourneras
il/elle/on	retournera
nous	retournerons
vous	retournerez
ils/elles	retourneront

CONDITIONAL

je	retournerais
tu	retournerais
il/elle/on	retournerait
nous	retournerions
vous	retourneriez
ils/elles	retourneraient

IMPERATIVE

retourne / retournons / retournez

PAST PARTICIPLE

retourné

PRESENT PARTICIPLE

retournant

—— EXAMPLE PHRASES ——

Tu **es retournée** à Londres?
J'aimerais bien **retourner** en Italie un jour.
Elle **a retourné** la carte pour vérifier.
Zoë, **retourne-toi**!

Have you been back to London?
I'd like to go back to Italy one day.

She turned the card over to check.
Turn around Zoë!

- Note that *retourner* takes *avoir* in the perfect tense when it is used with a direct object.
- Note that *se retourner* follows the same pattern, and takes *être* in the perfect tense. For an example of a reflexive verb in full, see verb table **83 se taire**.

Table
74

revenir *to come back*

PRESENT

je	reviens
tu	reviens
il/elle/on	revient
nous	revenons
vous	revenez
ils/elles	reviennent

PRESENT SUBJUNCTIVE

je	revienne
tu	reviennes
il/elle/on	revienne
nous	revenions
vous	reveniez
ils/elles	reviennent

PERFECT

je	suis revenu(e)
tu	es revenu(e)
il/elle/on	est revenu(e)
nous	sommes revenu(e)s
vous	êtes revenu(e)(s)
ils/elles	sont revenu(e)s

IMPERFECT

je	revenais
tu	revenais
il/elle/on	revenait
nous	revenions
vous	reveniez
ils/elles	revenaient

FUTURE

je	reviendrai
tu	reviendras
il/elle/on	reviendra
nous	reviendrons
vous	reviendrez
ils/elles	reviendront

CONDITIONAL

je	reviendrais
tu	reviendrais
il/elle/on	reviendrait
nous	reviendrions
vous	reviendriez
ils/elles	reviendraient

IMPERATIVE

reviens / revenons / revenez

PAST PARTICIPLE

revenu

PRESENT PARTICIPLE

revenant

——————————— EXAMPLE PHRASES ———————————

Mon chat n'**est** toujours pas **revenu**.

My cat still hasn't come back.

Je **reviens** dans cinq minutes!

I'll be back in five minutes!

Ça me **revient**!

It's coming back to me now!

PRESENT

je	ris
tu	ris
il/elle/on	rit
nous	rions
vous	riez
ils/elles	rient

PRESENT SUBJUNCTIVE

je	rie
tu	ries
il/elle/on	rie
nous	riions
vous	riiez
ils/elles	rient

PERFECT

j'	ai ri
tu	as ri
il/elle/on	a ri
nous	avons ri
vous	avez ri
ils/elles	ont ri

IMPERFECT

je	riais
tu	riais
il/elle/on	riait
nous	riions
vous	riiez
ils/elles	riaient

FUTURE

je	rirai
tu	riras
il/elle/on	rira
nous	rirons
vous	rirez
ils/elles	riront

CONDITIONAL

je	rirais
tu	rirais
il/elle/on	rirait
nous	ririons
vous	ririez
ils/elles	riraient

IMPERATIVE

ris / rions / riez

PAST PARTICIPLE

ri

PRESENT PARTICIPLE

riant

—— EXAMPLE PHRASES ——

On **a** bien **ri**.
Ne **ris** pas, ce n'est pas drôle!
C'était juste pour **rire**.

We had a good laugh.
Don't laugh, it's not funny!
It was only for a laugh.

Table
76

rompre *to break*

PRESENT

je	romps
tu	romps
il/elle/on	rompt
nous	rompons
vous	rompez
ils/elles	rompent

PRESENT SUBJUNCTIVE

je	rompe
tu	rompes
il/elle/on	rompe
nous	rompions
vous	rompiez
ils/elles	rompent

PERFECT

j'	ai rompu
tu	as rompu
il/elle/on	a rompu
nous	avons rompu
vous	avez rompu
ils/elles	ont rompu

IMPERFECT

je	rompais
tu	rompais
il/elle/on	rompait
nous	rompions
vous	rompiez
ils/elles	rompaient

FUTURE

je	romprai
tu	rompras
il/elle/on	rompra
nous	romprons
vous	romprez
ils/elles	rompront

CONDITIONAL

je	romprais
tu	romprais
il/elle/on	romprait
nous	romprions
vous	rompriez
ils/elles	rompraient

IMPERATIVE

romps / rompons / rompez

PAST PARTICIPLE

rompu

PRESENT PARTICIPLE

rompant

--- EXAMPLE PHRASES ---

Elle **a rompu** le silence.
Paul et Jo **ont rompu**.

She broke the silence.
Paul and Jo have split up.

PRESENT

je	sais
tu	sais
il/elle/on	sait
nous	savons
vous	savez
ils/elles	savent

PRESENT SUBJUNCTIVE

je	sache
tu	saches
il/elle/on	sache
nous	sachions
vous	sachiez
ils/elles	sachent

PERFECT

j'	ai su
tu	as su
il/elle/on	a su
nous	avons su
vous	avez su
ils/elles	ont su

IMPERFECT

je	savais
tu	savais
il/elle/on	savait
nous	savions
vous	saviez
ils/elles	savaient

FUTURE

je	saurai
tu	sauras
il/elle/on	saura
nous	saurons
vous	saurez
ils/elles	sauront

CONDITIONAL

je	saurais
tu	saurais
il/elle/on	saurait
nous	saurions
vous	sauriez
ils/elles	sauraient

IMPERATIVE

sache / sachons / sachez

PAST PARTICIPLE

su

PRESENT PARTICIPLE

sachant

—————————— EXAMPLE PHRASES ——————————

Tu **sais** ce que tu vas faire l'année prochaine?	Do you know what you're doing next year?
Je ne **sais** pas.	I don't know.
Elle ne **sait** pas nager.	She can't swim.
Tu **savais** que son père était pakistanais?	Did you know her father was Pakistani?

Table
78

sentir *to smell; to feel*

PRESENT		PRESENT SUBJUNCTIVE	
je	sens	je	sente
tu	sens	tu	sentes
il/elle/on	sent	il/elle/on	sente
nous	sentons	nous	sentions
vous	sentez	vous	sentiez
ils/elles	sentent	ils/elles	sentent

PERFECT		IMPERFECT	
j'	ai senti	je	sentais
tu	as senti	tu	sentais
il/elle/on	a senti	il/elle/on	sentait
nous	avons senti	nous	sentions
vous	avez senti	vous	sentiez
ils/elles	ont senti	ils/elles	sentaient

FUTURE		CONDITIONAL	
je	sentirai	je	sentirais
tu	sentiras	tu	sentirais
il/elle/on	sentira	il/elle/on	sentirait
nous	sentirons	nous	sentirions
vous	sentirez	vous	sentiriez
ils/elles	sentiront	ils/elles	sentiraient

IMPERATIVE

sens / sentons / sentez

PAST PARTICIPLE

senti

PRESENT PARTICIPLE

sentant

─────── EXAMPLE PHRASES ───────

Ça **sentait** mauvais.	*It smelt bad.*
Je n'**ai** rien **senti**.	*I didn't feel a thing.*
Elle ne **se sent** pas bien.	*She's not feeling well.*

- Note that *se sentir* follows the same pattern, but takes **être** in the perfect tense. For an example of a reflexive verb in full, see verb table **83 se taire**.

Table
79

to serve **servir**

PRESENT		PRESENT SUBJUNCTIVE	
je	sers	je	serve
tu	sers	tu	serves
il/elle/on	sert	il/elle/on	serve
nous	servons	nous	servions
vous	servez	vous	serviez
ils/elles	servent	ils/elles	servent

PERFECT		IMPERFECT	
j'	ai servi	je	servais
tu	as servi	tu	servais
il/elle/on	a servi	il/elle/on	servait
nous	avons servi	nous	servions
vous	avez servi	vous	serviez
ils/elles	ont servi	ils/elles	servaient

FUTURE		CONDITIONAL	
je	servirai	je	servirais
tu	serviras	tu	servirais
il/elle/on	servira	il/elle/on	servirait
nous	servirons	nous	servirions
vous	servirez	vous	serviriez
ils/elles	serviront	ils/elles	serviraient

IMPERATIVE
sers / servons / servez

PAST PARTICIPLE
servi

PRESENT PARTICIPLE
servant

─────────── EXAMPLE PHRASES ───────────

On vous **sert**?
Are you being served?
Ça **sert** à quoi ce bouton?
What is this button for?
Servez-vous en viande.
Help yourself to meat.

- Note that *se servir* follows the same pattern, but takes *être* in the perfect tense. For an example of a reflexive verb in full, see verb table *83 se taire*.

Table
80

sortir *to go out*

PRESENT

je	sors
tu	sors
il/elle/on	sort
nous	sortons
vous	sortez
ils/elles	sortent

PRESENT SUBJUNCTIVE

je	sorte
tu	sortes
il/elle/on	sorte
nous	sortions
vous	sortiez
ils/elles	sortent

PERFECT

je	suis sorti(e)
tu	es sorti(e)
il/elle/on	est sorti(e)
nous	sommes sorti(e)s
vous	êtes sorti(e)(s)
ils/elles	sont sorti(e)s

IMPERFECT

je	sortais
tu	sortais
il/elle/on	sortait
nous	sortions
vous	sortiez
ils/elles	sortaient

FUTURE

je	sortirai
tu	sortiras
il/elle/on	sortira
nous	sortirons
vous	sortirez
ils/elles	sortiront

CONDITIONAL

je	sortirais
tu	sortirais
il/elle/on	sortirait
nous	sortirions
vous	sortiriez
ils/elles	sortiraient

IMPERATIVE
sors / sortons / sortez

PRESENT PARTICIPLE
sortant

PAST PARTICIPLE
sorti

--- EXAMPLE PHRASES ---

Je ne **suis** pas **sortie** ce week-end.
Aurélie **sort** avec Bruno.
Elle **est sortie** de l'hôpital hier.
Je n'**ai** pas **sorti** le chien parce qu'il pleuvait.

I didn't go out this weekend.
Aurélie is going out with Bruno.
She came out of hospital yesterday.
I didn't take the dog out for a walk because it was raining.

- Note that **sortir** takes **avoir** in the perfect tense when it is used with a direct object.

PRESENT

je	suffis
tu	suffis
il/elle/on	suffit
nous	suffisons
vous	suffisez
ils/elles	suffisent

PRESENT SUBJUNCTIVE

je	suffise
tu	suffises
il/elle/on	suffise
nous	suffisions
vous	suffisiez
ils/elles	suffisent

PERFECT

j'	ai suffi
tu	as suffi
il/elle/on	a suffi
nous	avons suffi
vous	avez suffi
ils/elles	ont suffi

IMPERFECT

je	suffisais
tu	suffisais
il/elle/on	suffisait
nous	suffisions
vous	suffisiez
ils/elles	suffisaient

FUTURE

je	suffirai
tu	suffiras
il/elle/on	suffira
nous	suffirons
vous	suffirez
ils/elles	suffiront

CONDITIONAL

je	suffirais
tu	suffirais
il/elle/on	suffirait
nous	suffirions
vous	suffiriez
ils/elles	suffiraient

IMPERATIVE

suffis / suffisons / suffisez

PAST PARTICIPLE

suffi

PRESENT PARTICIPLE

suffisant

——————— EXAMPLE PHRASES ———————

Ça te **suffira**, 10 euros?	Will 10 euros be enough?
Ça **suffit**!	That's enough!
Il **suffisait** de me le demander.	You only had to ask.

- Note that the verb **frire** follows the same pattern as **suffire**, but that it is used mainly in the present singular and in compound tenses such as the perfect tense. Its past participle is **frit**.

Table
82

suivre *to follow*

PRESENT

je	suis
tu	suis
il/elle/on	suit
nous	suivons
vous	suivez
ils/elles	suivent

PRESENT SUBJUNCTIVE

je	suive
tu	suives
il/elle/on	suive
nous	suivions
vous	suiviez
ils/elles	suivent

PERFECT

j'	ai suivi
tu	as suivi
il/elle/on	a suivi
nous	avons suivi
vous	avez suivi
ils/elles	ont suivi

IMPERFECT

je	suivais
tu	suivais
il/elle/on	suivait
nous	suivions
vous	suiviez
ils/elles	suivaient

FUTURE

je	suivrai
tu	suivras
il/elle/on	suivra
nous	suivrons
vous	suivrez
ils/elles	suivront

CONDITIONAL

je	suivrais
tu	suivrais
il/elle/on	suivrait
nous	suivrions
vous	suivriez
ils/elles	suivraient

IMPERATIVE

suis / suivons / suivez

PAST PARTICIPLE

suivi

PRESENT PARTICIPLE

suivant

--- EXAMPLE PHRASES ---

Mon chat me **suit** partout dans la maison.

My cat follows me everywhere around the house.

Il **a suivi** un cours d'allemand pendant six mois.

He did a German course for 6 months.

Elles n'arrivent pas à **suivre** en maths.

They can't keep up in maths.

PRESENT

je	me tais
tu	te tais
il/elle/on	se tait
nous	nous taisons
vous	vous taisez
ils/elles	se taisent

PRESENT SUBJUNCTIVE

je	me taise
tu	te taises
il/elle/on	se taise
nous	nous taisions
vous	vous taisiez
ils/elles	se taisent

PERFECT

je	me suis tu(e)
tu	t'es tu(e)
il/elle/on	s'est tu(e)
nous	nous sommes tu(e)s
vous	vous êtes tu(e)(s)
ils/elles	se sont tu(e)s

IMPERFECT

je	me taisais
tu	te taisais
il/elle/on	se taisait
nous	nous taisions
vous	vous taisiez
ils/elles	se taisaient

FUTURE

je	me tairai
tu	te tairas
il/elle/on	se taira
nous	nous tairons
vous	vous tairez
ils/elles	se tairont

CONDITIONAL

je	me tairais
tu	te tairais
il/elle/on	se tairait
nous	nous tairions
vous	vous tairiez
ils/elles	se tairaient

IMPERATIVE

tais-toi / taisons-nous / taisez-vous

PAST PARTICIPLE

tu

PRESENT PARTICIPLE

se taisant

─────────── EXAMPLE PHRASES ───────────

Il **s'est tu**.	*He stopped talking.*
Taisez-vous!	*Be quiet!*
Sophie, **tais-toi**!	*Be quiet Sophie!*

Table
84

tenir *to hold*

PRESENT

je	tiens
tu	tiens
il/elle/on	tient
nous	tenons
vous	tenez
ils/elles	tiennent

PRESENT SUBJUNCTIVE

je	tienne
tu	tiennes
il/elle/on	tienne
nous	tenions
vous	teniez
ils/elles	tiennent

PERFECT

j'	ai tenu
tu	as tenu
il/elle/on	a tenu
nous	avons tenu
vous	avez tenu
ils/elles	ont tenu

IMPERFECT

je	tenais
tu	tenais
il/elle/on	tenait
nous	tenions
vous	teniez
ils/elles	tenaient

FUTURE

je	tiendrai
tu	tiendras
il/elle/on	tiendra
nous	tiendrons
vous	tiendrez
ils/elles	tiendront

CONDITIONAL

je	tiendrais
tu	tiendrais
il/elle/on	tiendrait
nous	tiendrions
vous	tiendriez
ils/elles	tiendraient

IMPERATIVE

tiens / tenons / tenez

PAST PARTICIPLE

tenu

PRESENT PARTICIPLE

tenant

— EXAMPLE PHRASES —

Tiens-moi la main. — *Hold my hand.*
Elle **tenait** beaucoup à son chat. — *She was really attached to her cat.*
Tiens, prends mon stylo. — *Here, have my pen.*
Tiens-toi droit! — *Sit up straight!*

- Note that *se tenir* follows the same pattern, but takes **être** in the perfect tense. For an example of a reflexive verb in full, see verb table 83 *se taire*.

PRESENT

je	tombe
tu	tombes
il/elle/on	tombe
nous	tombons
vous	tombez
ils/elles	tombent

PRESENT SUBJUNCTIVE

je	tombe
tu	tombes
il/elle/on	tombe
nous	tombions
vous	tombiez
ils/elles	tombent

PERFECT

je	suis tombé(e)
tu	es tombé(e)
il/elle/on	est tombé(e)
nous	sommes tombé(e)s
vous	êtes tombé(e)(s)
ils/elles	sont tombé(e)s

IMPERFECT

je	tombais
tu	tombais
il/elle/on	tombait
nous	tombions
vous	tombiez
ils/elles	tombaient

FUTURE

je	tomberai
tu	tomberas
il/elle/on	tombera
nous	tomberons
vous	tomberez
ils/elles	tomberont

CONDITIONAL

je	tomberais
tu	tomberais
il/elle/on	tomberait
nous	tomberions
vous	tomberiez
ils/elles	tomberaient

IMPERATIVE

tombe / tombons / tombez

PAST PARTICIPLE

tombé

PRESENT PARTICIPLE

tombant

———————————— EXAMPLE PHRASES ————————————

Attention, tu vas **tomber**!
Nicole **est tombée** de cheval.
Elle s'est fait mal en **tombant**
dans l'escalier.

Be careful, you'll fall!
Nicole fell off her horse.
She hurt herself falling down the
stairs.

Table
86

traire *to milk*

PRESENT

je	trais
tu	trais
il/elle/on	trait
nous	trayons
vous	trayez
ils/elles	traient

PRESENT SUBJUNCTIVE

je	traie
tu	traies
il/elle/on	traie
nous	trayions
vous	trayiez
ils/elles	traient

PERFECT

j'	ai trait
tu	as trait
il/elle/on	a trait
nous	avons trait
vous	avez trait
ils/elles	ont trait

IMPERFECT

je	trayais
tu	trayais
il/elle/on	trayait
nous	trayions
vous	trayiez
ils/elles	trayaient

FUTURE

je	trairai
tu	trairas
il/elle/on	traira
nous	trairons
vous	trairez
ils/elles	trairont

CONDITIONAL

je	trairais
tu	trairais
il/elle/on	trairait
nous	trairions
vous	trairiez
ils/elles	trairaient

IMPERATIVE

trais / trayons / trayez

PAST PARTICIPLE

trait

PRESENT PARTICIPLE

trayant

––––––––––– EXAMPLE PHRASES –––––––––––

À la ferme, on a appris à **traire** les vaches.

We learnt to milk cows on the farm.

Elle **trait** les vaches à six heures du matin.

She milks the cows at 6 am.

PRESENT

je	vaincs
tu	vaincs
il/elle/on	vainc
nous	vainquons
vous	vainquez
ils/elles	vainquent

PRESENT SUBJUNCTIVE

je	vainque
tu	vainques
il/elle/on	vainque
nous	vainquions
vous	vainquiez
ils/elles	vainquent

PERFECT

j'	ai vaincu
tu	as vaincu
il/elle/on	a vaincu
nous	avons vaincu
vous	avez vaincu
ils/elles	ont vaincu

IMPERFECT

je	vainquais
tu	vainquais
il/elle/on	vainquait
nous	vainquions
vous	vainquiez
ils/elles	vainquaient

FUTURE

je	vaincrai
tu	vaincras
il/elle/on	vaincra
nous	vaincrons
vous	vaincrez
ils/elles	vaincront

CONDITIONAL

je	vaincrais
tu	vaincrais
il/elle/on	vaincrait
nous	vaincrions
vous	vaincriez
ils/elles	vaincraient

IMPERATIVE

vaincs / vainquons / vainquez

PAST PARTICIPLE

vaincu

PRESENT PARTICIPLE

vainquant

─────────── EXAMPLE PHRASES ───────────

L'armée **a été vaincue**.
La France **a vaincu** la Corée trois buts à deux.

The army was defeated.
France beat Korea 3 goals to 2.

Table
88

valoir *to be worth*

PRESENT		PRESENT SUBJUNCTIVE	
je	vaux	je	vaille
tu	vaux	tu	vailles
il/elle/on	vaut	il/elle/on	vaille
nous	valons	nous	valions
vous	valez	vous	valiez
ils/elles	valent	ils/elles	vaillent

PERFECT		IMPERFECT	
j'	ai valu	je	valais
tu	as valu	tu	valais
il/elle/on	a valu	il/elle/on	valait
nous	avons valu	nous	valions
vous	avez valu	vous	valiez
ils/elles	ont valu	ils/elles	valaient

FUTURE		CONDITIONAL	
je	vaudrai	je	vaudrais
tu	vaudras	tu	vaudrais
il/elle/on	vaudra	il/elle/on	vaudrait
nous	vaudrons	nous	vaudrions
vous	vaudrez	vous	vaudriez
ils/elles	vaudront	ils/elles	vaudraient

IMPERATIVE
vaux / valons / valez

PAST PARTICIPLE
valu

PRESENT PARTICIPLE
valant

--- EXAMPLE PHRASES ---

Ça **vaut** combien?	How much is it worth?
Ça **vaudrait** la peine d'essayer.	It would be worth a try.
Il **vaut** mieux ne pas y penser.	It's best not to think about it.

PRESENT

je	vends
tu	vends
il/elle/on	vend
nous	vendons
vous	vendez
ils/elles	vendent

PRESENT SUBJUNCTIVE

je	vende
tu	vendes
il/elle/on	vende
nous	vendions
vous	vendiez
ils/elles	vendent

PERFECT

j'	ai vendu
tu	as vendu
il/elle/on	a vendu
nous	avons vendu
vous	avez vendu
ils/elles	ont vendu

IMPERFECT

je	vendais
tu	vendais
il/elle/on	vendait
nous	vendions
vous	vendiez
ils/elles	vendaient

FUTURE

je	vendrai
tu	vendras
il/elle/on	vendra
nous	vendrons
vous	vendrez
ils/elles	vendront

CONDITIONAL

je	vendrais
tu	vendrais
il/elle/on	vendrait
nous	vendrions
vous	vendriez
ils/elles	vendraient

IMPERATIVE

vends / vendons / vendez

PAST PARTICIPLE

vendu

PRESENT PARTICIPLE

vendant

––––––––––– EXAMPLE PHRASES –––––––––––

Il m'a **vendu** son vélo pour 50 euros.	He sold me his bike for 50 euros.
Est-ce que vous **vendez** des piles?	Do you sell batteries?
Elle voudrait **vendre** sa voiture.	She would like to sell her car.

Table
90

venir *to come*

PRESENT		PRESENT SUBJUNCTIVE	
je	viens	je	vienne
tu	viens	tu	viennes
il/elle/on	vient	il/elle/on	vienne
nous	venons	nous	venions
vous	venez	vous	veniez
ils/elles	viennent	ils/elles	viennent

PERFECT		IMPERFECT	
je	suis venu(e)	je	venais
tu	es venu(e)	tu	venais
il/elle/on	est venu(e)	il/elle/on	venait
nous	sommes venu(e)s	nous	venions
vous	êtes venu(e)(s)	vous	veniez
ils/elles	sont venu(e)s	ils/elles	venaient

FUTURE		CONDITIONAL	
je	viendrai	je	viendrais
tu	viendras	tu	viendrais
il/elle/on	viendra	il/elle/on	viendrait
nous	viendrons	nous	viendrions
vous	viendrez	vous	viendriez
ils/elles	viendront	ils/elles	viendraient

IMPERATIVE

viens / venons / venez

PAST PARTICIPLE

venu

PRESENT PARTICIPLE

venant

--- EXAMPLE PHRASES ---

Elle ne **viendra** pas cette année.	She won't be coming this year.
Fatou et Malik **viennent** du Sénégal.	Fatou and Malik come from Senegal.
Je **viens** de manger.	I've just eaten.

- Note that the verbs **convenir** and **prévenir** follow the same pattern as **venir**, but take **avoir** in the perfect tense.

PRESENT

je	vêts
tu	vêts
il/elle/on	vêt
nous	vêtons
vous	vêtez
ils/elles	vêtent

PRESENT SUBJUNCTIVE

je	vête
tu	vêtes
il/elle/on	vête
nous	vêtions
vous	vêtiez
ils/elles	vêtent

PERFECT

j'	ai vêtu
tu	as vêtu
il/elle/on	a vêtu
nous	avons vêtu
vous	avez vêtu
ils/elles	ont vêtu

IMPERFECT

je	vêtais
tu	vêtais
il/elle/on	vêtait
nous	vêtions
vous	vêtiez
ils/elles	vêtaient

FUTURE

je	vêtirai
tu	vêtiras
il/elle/on	vêtira
nous	vêtirons
vous	vêtirez
ils/elles	vêtiront

CONDITIONAL

je	vêtirais
tu	vêtirais
il/elle/on	vêtirait
nous	vêtirions
vous	vêtiriez
ils/elles	vêtiraient

IMPERATIVE

vêts / vêtons / vêtez

PRESENT PARTICIPLE

vêtant

PAST PARTICIPLE

vêtu

EXAMPLE PHRASES

Il **était vêtu** d'un pantalon et d'un pull.

He was wearing trousers and a jumper.

Il faut se lever, se laver et **se vêtir** en 10 minutes.

You have to get up, get washed and get dressed in 10 minutes.

- Note that **se vêtir** follows the same pattern, but takes **être** in the perfect tense. For an example of a reflexive verb in full, see verb table **83 se taire**.

Table
92

vivre *to live*

PRESENT

je	vis
tu	vis
il/elle/on	vit
nous	vivons
vous	vivez
ils/elles	vivent

PRESENT SUBJUNCTIVE

je	vive
tu	vives
il/elle/on	vive
nous	vivions
vous	viviez
ils/elles	vivent

PERFECT

j'	ai vécu
tu	as vécu
il/elle/on	a vécu
nous	avons vécu
vous	avez vécu
ils/elles	ont vécu

IMPERFECT

je	vivais
tu	vivais
il/elle/on	vivait
nous	vivions
vous	viviez
ils/elles	vivaient

FUTURE

je	vivrai
tu	vivras
il/elle/on	vivra
nous	vivrons
vous	vivrez
ils/elles	vivront

CONDITIONAL

je	vivrais
tu	vivrais
il/elle/on	vivrait
nous	vivrions
vous	vivriez
ils/elles	vivraient

IMPERATIVE

vis / vivons / vivez

PAST PARTICIPLE

vécu

PRESENT PARTICIPLE

vivant

--- EXAMPLE PHRASES ---

Ma sœur **vit** en Espagne.
Il **a vécu** dix ans à Lyon.
Les gorilles **vivent** surtout dans la forêt.

My sister lives in Spain.
He lived in Lyons for 10 years.
Gorillas mostly live in the forest.

PRESENT

je	vois
tu	vois
il/elle/on	voit
nous	voyons
vous	voyez
ils/elles	voient

PRESENT SUBJUNCTIVE

je	voie
tu	voies
il/elle/on	voie
nous	voyions
vous	voyiez
ils/elles	voient

PERFECT

j'	ai vu
tu	as vu
il/elle/on	a vu
nous	avons vu
vous	avez vu
ils/elles	ont vu

IMPERFECT

je	voyais
tu	voyais
il/elle/on	voyait
nous	voyions
vous	voyiez
ils/elles	voyaient

FUTURE

je	verrai
tu	verras
il/elle/on	verra
nous	verrons
vous	verrez
ils/elles	verront

CONDITIONAL

je	verrais
tu	verrais
il/elle/on	verrait
nous	verrions
vous	verriez
ils/elles	verraient

IMPERATIVE

vois / voyons / voyez

PAST PARTICIPLE

vu

PRESENT PARTICIPLE

voyant

— EXAMPLE PHRASES —

Venez me **voir** demain.	Come and see me tomorrow.
Je ne **vois** rien sans mes lunettes.	I can't see anything without my glasses.
Est-ce que tu **l'as vu**?	Did you see him? or Have you seen him?
Est-ce que cette tache **se voit**?	Does that stain show?

- Note that **se voir** follows the same pattern, but takes **être** in the perfect tense. For an example of a reflexive verb in full, see verb table **83 se taire**.
- The verb **prévoir** follows the same pattern as **voir**, except for the future tense (**je prévoirai**, etc) and the conditional (**je prévoirais**, etc).

Table
94

vouloir *to want*

PRESENT

je	veux
tu	veux
il/elle/on	veut
nous	voulons
vous	voulez
ils/elles	veulent

PRESENT SUBJUNCTIVE

je	veuille
tu	veuilles
il/elle/on	veuille
nous	voulions
vous	vouliez
ils/elles	veuillent

PERFECT

j'	ai voulu
tu	as voulu
il/elle/on	a voulu
nous	avons voulu
vous	avez voulu
ils/elles	ont voulu

IMPERFECT

je	voulais
tu	voulais
il/elle/on	voulait
nous	voulions
vous	vouliez
ils/elles	voulaient

FUTURE

je	voudrai
tu	voudras
il/elle/on	voudra
nous	voudrons
vous	voudrez
ils/elles	voudront

CONDITIONAL

je	voudrais
tu	voudrais
il/elle/on	voudrait
nous	voudrions
vous	voudriez
ils/elles	voudraient

IMPERATIVE

veuille / veuillons / veuillez

PAST PARTICIPLE

voulu

PRESENT PARTICIPLE

voulant

--- EXAMPLE PHRASES ---

Elle **veut** un vélo pour Noël.
Ils **voulaient** aller au cinéma.
Tu **voudrais** une tasse de thé?

She wants a bike for Christmas.
They wanted to go to the cinema.
Would you like a cup of tea?